THE UNIVERSITY OF CALIFORNIA

CREATING, NURTURING, AND MAINTAINING
ACADEMIC QUALITY IN A PUBLIC UNIVERSITY SETTING

C. JUDSON KING

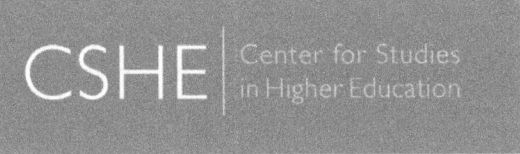

Berkeley

© 2018 C. Judson King
All rights reserved.

Second Printing: October, 2018

ISBN: **0999498002**
ISBN 13: **978-0-9994980-0-2**
Library of Congress Control Number: **2017918127**
LCCN Imprint Name: **Center for Studies in Higher Education, University of California, Berkeley CA**

CONTENTS

Figures and Tables   vii

Preface   xi

PART I. INTRODUCTION

1. The University of California: A Remarkable Success Story   1
Measures of Success · How Did This Happen? · An Emphasis on Science

2. The History of the University of California as It Affects Structure, Governance, and Academics   11
The Early Years · The Later 1800s · The Wheeler Era · The Berkeley Revolution · Robert Gordon Sproul · Clark Kerr's Presidency · Transitions ·The Hitch and Saxon Eras · The Gardner Era · The Turn of the Millennium · The Decline of State Funding and Adjustments to It · Troubled Times, 2005–08 · Two Presidents from Outside UC, 2008 to Date

3. The Kerr Legacy   81
Kerr's Thinking and Values · The Structure of the University · Governance and Decision-Making · Building Academic Strength

PART II. STRUCTURE AND GOVERNANCE

4. Interactions with State Government: Constitutional Status and Oversight   95
Constitutional and/or Charter Status · Composition of Governing Boards · State-Level Coordination and Oversight · Accountability

5. The California Master Plan   123
Development of the Master Plan · Elements of the Master Plan · Recognition · Benefits of the Master Plan · Current Issues Associated with the Master Plan · Objectives for Modification · Summary and Conclusions

6. Structure, Organization, and Internal Budgeting of UC: One University, with Campuses Empowered   165
One University · Decentralization · Distribution of Functions between University-Wide and Campus Levels · The Optimal Degree of Decentralization

7. Shared Governance   207
Shared Governance at the University of California · Shared Governance in Research Universities · Summary and Conclusions

8. Operational Governance of the Multicampus University   235
Governance Mechanisms · Parochialism, Understanding, and Respect · What Can Go Wrong

PART III. CREATING, SPREADING, AND SUSTAINING EXCELLENCE

9. Creating Research Excellence: The Physical Sciences at Berkeley   245
Astronomy, the Lick Observatory, and Armin Leuschner · The Board of Research · The College of Chemistry and Gilbert Newton Lewis · Physics, Raymond Birge, Ernest Lawrence, and the Lawrence Berkeley Laboratory · Mathematics and Griffith Evans · Geology and Geophysics · Summary Observations

*

10. Spreading Excellence: Developing New Campuses   **293**
UC Los Angeles (UCLA) · UC Davis · UC Santa Barbara · UC Riverside · UC San Francisco · UC San Diego · UC Irvine · UC Santa Cruz · UC Merced · Summary Comparative Analyses

11. Sustaining Excellence: Faculty Appointments and Advancement   **417**
Maintaining the Culture · Principles Used in the University of California · Budget Committee/Committee on Academic Personnel · Methodology · Criteria · Quality versus Quantity · Resolving Disagreements · Comparison with Other Universities · What Is Gained by the UC Methodology · Challenging Aspects · Comment · Other Facets

12. Sustaining Excellence: Program Review, Planning, and Change   **443**
Change · Program Reviews · Academic Planning Processes · Four Cases of Change in Academic Programs at Berkeley · Adaptations of Research Universities to Major Forces of Change

PART IV. FOSTERING RESEARCH AND TEACHING

13. National Laboratories   **483**
World War II, the Berkeley Radiation Laboratory, and New Mexico · After World War II · Transformations for the Laboratories · Synergies between the Lawrence Berkeley National Laboratory and the Berkeley Campus · The Relationships with Los Alamos and Livermore

14. Promoting and Enabling Multidisciplinary Research and Teaching   **511**
Roles of Disciplines and Academic Departments · Multidisciplinary Needs and Opportunities · Facilitation of Multidisciplinary Research · Institutes of Science and Innovation · Undergraduate Education · Avoiding Departmental Structures

PART V. INTERACTIONS WITH THE PUBLIC, THE STATE, AND INDUSTRY

15. Providing Access: Eligibility and Admissions   533
Goals · Selective Admissions · The Development of Admissions Policies · The Effects of the 1960 Master Plan · Balance of Enrollment among Campuses · Attentiveness to Race · Surge of Application Pressure and Backlash · UC Regents' Resolution SP-1 and Statewide Proposition 209 · Rethinking Admissions · Whither the Bubbling Cauldron? · Admissions to Graduate and Professional Programs

16. Serving the State of California and the Public   563
Agriculture · The California Digital Library · Education Partnerships and Outreach · California Council on Science and Technology · Identification and Documentation of Economic Impact

17. Support from the State   585
Self-Governance · High Priority for Resources and Investment · Maintaining the Caliber of the Best Universities, Private or Public · Differentiation of Missions · Creating Multiple Campuses and Capping Their Enrollments · An Enabling State Science and Technology Policy · Retention of a Substantial Portion of Indirect Costs from Contacts and Grants

18. Relations with Industry, Technology Transfer, and Economic Development   603
The Challenges of Technology Transfer for Universities · What It Takes to "Transfer" Technology · Industrial Relations and Technology Transfer at the University of California · Industry-University Cooperative Research · Regional Influences: Technological Innovation and Economic Development · Biotechnology · University of California Policies and Administrative Structures Pertaining to Relations with Industry · Mechanisms for Assisting Commercialization of Research and Corporate Start-ups

19. Location   661
The Early Days · Large and Continual Growth · The Lure of California Life and Climate · The Sierra Nevada Mountains and Conservation · The Pacific Rim · Mexico · Earthquake Country · Varied Climate and Topography

PART VI. SYNOPSIS AND LOOKING FORWARD

20. Retrospective   673
The Importance of Research Universities · Academic Excellence and Rankings · The Rationale for Research Universities: Synergy · Features of Successful, High-Impact Research Universities · The Attributes Most Important for the University of California

21. The Future for the University of California and Public Research Universities   691
Challenges · Prospects for Improvement · Predictions and Advice from Many Quarters · Two Fundamental Uncertainties · Paths Forward · Governance Changes for Changing Times

Appendix

National and International Reputations, Ratings, and Rankings of Universities   753
Measures and Surrogates of Standing and Accomplishment · General Issues · Rankings of Research Universities · General Comment

Index   765

Figures and Tables

Figures:

2-1. Lick Observatory, 1900   21

2-2. Increase of University of California funding during the Wheeler era (1899–1919)   23

2-3. Phoebe Hearst, circa 1890   25

2-4. Newly emeritus UC president Benjamin Ide Wheeler on stage at the Greek Theater with former Princeton University president Woodrow Wilson, then president of the United States, 1919   27

2-5. The alpha calutron "racetrack" at the Y-12 plant, Oak Ridge, Tennessee, 1944   33

2-6. Faculty press conference on the loyalty oath controversy, March 1, 1950   38

2-7. The twin Keck telescopes atop Mauna Kea, Hawaii   52

2-8. State general fund appropriations per enrolled student over time, inflation adjusted   67

3-1. Clark Kerr (1911–2003), first chancellor of the Berkeley campus (1952–58) and twelfth president of the University of California (1958–67)   84

3-2. Total University of California enrollment (general campus plus health sciences) versus year   88

5-1. The Master Plan Survey Team, 1959   129

6-1. Robert Gordon Sproul and Clark Kerr at the Inauguration of Kerr as UC President, Septermber 29, 1958   176

6-2. The Kaiser Center, Oakland, California   189

6-3. The University of California Washington Center   191

7-1. The newly empowered Academic Senate meets in the Faculty Club, 1920   211

8-1. Academic governance structure of the University of California **237**

9-1. Armin O. Leuschner **250**

9-2. An 1899 photo of the Old Chemistry Building at Berkeley, built in 1897 **255**

9-3. Gilbert Newton Lewis, 1925 **259**

9-4. Joel H. Hildebrand, 1924 **262**

9-5. Raymond T. Birge at his desk, circa 1920 **271**

9-6. Sketch of the operating principle of the cyclotron, from the original patent application **275**

9-7. Oppenheimer, Seaborg, and Lawrence examine controls associated with a cyclotron **280**

9-8. A 1963 photo of seven Berkeley/LBL Nobelists **282**

9-9. Evans Hall, named for Griffith Evans, frames the Berkeley campus campanile in this photograph **286**

9-10. The California Geological Survey, 1863 **288**

9-11. Joseph LeConte, 1875 **289**

10-1. Aerial View of the UCLA Westwood Campus Site, shortly before the opening of the campus, 1929 **295**

10-2. Anderson School of Management, UCLA **300**

10-3. The University Farm at Davis **309**

10-4. The Robert and Margrit Mondavi Center for the Performing Arts, University of California, Davis **314**

10-5. Kohn Hall, Home of the Kavli institute for Theoretical Physics, UCSB **323**

10-6. Marine Biotechnology Laboratory, opened 1964, UCSB **324**

10-7. Citrus Experiment Station in 1930, Riverside, California, below Mount Rubidoux **328**

10-8. Center for Environmental Research and Technology (CE-CERT, UC Riverside 336

10-9. Aerial view of UCSF Parnassus Heights campus, below Mount Sutro 351

10-10. The initial UCSF building at Mission Bay (Genentech Hall) under construction, 2002 352

10-11. Roger Revelle at the Scripps Institute of Oceanography pier 354

10-12. Jacobs School of Engineering, UC San Diego 366

10-13. (a) Original 1962 plan for the Irvine campus; (b) aerial view of the Irvine campus, circa 2006 371

10-14. President Lyndon B. Johnson at the site dedication for the Irvine campus, June 20, 1964 373

10-15. Aerial view of Crown and Merrill Colleges, the third and the fourth of the UC Santa Cruz colleges 385

10-16. College Eight, UC Santa Cruz 386

10-17. A vernal pool in Merced Vernal Pools and Grassland Reserve 400

10-18. First Lady Michelle Obama speaks at the first commencement of the Merced campus, May 16, 2009 404

12-1. The Valley Life Sciences Building, with Life Sciences Annex in the shadow to the right 464

12-2. South Hall, one of the two original buildings of the Berkeley campus and now the home of the School of Information 470

13-1. A meeting in Berkeley regarding the 184-inch Cyclotron Project. 485

13-2. General Leslie Groves presenting the Army-Navy "E" Award flag to Robert Oppenheimer and UC president Robert Gordon Sproul in October, 1945, in front of the Los Alamos Ranch School building. 489

13-3. Ernest Lawrence and Edward Teller, founders of the Livermore Laboratory, along with Herbert York, the first director, 1952 494

15-1. Percent of underrepresented minority students in the freshman class compared to California high school graduates, fall 1989 to 2008 **554**

17-1. Average professorial series faculty salaries (assistant, associate, full), general campus only, University of California and comparison eight universities **595**

18-1. Aerial view of University of California, San Diego, campus, with Geisel Library in the upper-left quadrant and buildings of Salk Institute and Scripps Research Institute at the top across Torrey Pines Road **632**

21-1. Resident, US Nonresident, and International Undergraduate Enrollments at UC and Comparison US Public Universities, Fall 2016 **727**

Tables:

1-1. Primary factors important to the success of the University of California **9**

3-1. Total enrollments of University of California campuses, fall 2016 **89**

4-1. Subjects in 2011 University of California Accountability Report **120**

5-1. CSU joint doctorates as of 2015 **144**

6-1. Funding per undergraduate-equivalent student in 2009, before rebenching **182**

7-1. Committees of the Academic Council, 2015 **215**

7-2. Committees of the Berkeley Division of the Academic Senate, 2015 **216**

15-1. Criteria that may be used by campuses in comprehensive review of applications by UC-eligible students for freshman admission **552**

18-1. University of California top-earning inventions, fiscal year 2015 **651**

19-1. Historical population of California **665**

Preface

At 150 years following its founding in 1868, the University of California is regarded by many as the most successful and highly respected public research university in the world. Particularly impressive are the very high standings of its campuses in national and international rankings, the size of the ten-campus university, the high quality of the education it provides, the access and the route of upward mobility that it affords for students in the state, the success that it has had in developing new campuses that have achieved strong reputations in surprisingly short times, the attractiveness of the university to students and their families, and the substantial role that the university has played in the unparalleled technological innovation climate of California.

During my years in academic administration at the University of California and its Berkeley campus, I have encountered many visitors from other countries and from other states of the United States who have inquired about the University of California, how it works, and how it has become so successful and highly regarded. The purpose of this book is to explore the essential factors that answer those questions.

Any large institution has experienced problems and failures along with successes and has dealt with mixed situations where the balance between benefits and losses is difficult to determine. The University of California is no exception. This book therefore also includes mixed or lessons-learned types of experiences, along with the analysis of those positive factors that led to success overall.

The book is not a history of the University of California, per se. Several of those already exist, covering various periods during the development of the university. Instead, it is an analysis of the structural, policy, operational, and environmental matters that have contributed to the success of the University of California and a discussion of what makes UC tick and the approaches that have made it tick best. In that sense it is a selective, topical history and analysis for those subjects. Given my own background as an academic chemical engineer, it is essentially akin to an engineering analysis. The format is such that the book can serve as a reference work, and for that reason many cross-references among chapters have been included, along with a substantial index and many citations in footnotes.[1] Most chapters have summary conclusions, distilling the most important points.

The book is written from the point of view of one who has been concerned for many years with making the university work well academically, through successive positions as department chair, dean, and then provost for the professional schools and colleges on the Berkeley campus, and then vice provost for research for a year, followed by nine years as provost and senior vice president, academic affairs at the university-wide level. A subsequent decade directing the Center for Studies in Higher Education on the Berkeley campus gave me perspective and the opportunity to think about this subject broadly. Although many books have been written by ex-presidents of universities, many fewer have been written by ex-provosts. Yet because of the large extramural roles of presidents, it is probably the provosts who best know the inner academic operations of modern American universities, as they are totally immersed in them.

The book does not trace back to primary sources, nor is it based substantially on subject-specific interviews. It makes use of others' collections of information along with my own varied experiences for analyses and judgments. I am therefore both grateful for and reliant upon the work of many other people.

The intended audience for this book is the global higher-education community, as well as others interested in the University of California and the development and functioning of universities, and particularly public universities, in the United States. The book should be useful to those in governments who are concerned with public universities, as well as those in other states and other countries who would like to understand the University of California and assess what about it could

---

[1] Several points about the references deserve mention. First, numbering of footnotes begins anew at the start of each chapter. Second, the full reference is given the first time a particular reference appears in any chapter but then subsequently in that chapter it is cited as simply author, year, *loc. cit.* (for references to the same page or location) and as author, year, *op. cit.*, page number (for references to the same work, different page). Third, many references are to Internet sites. Since URL citations change continually and can be eliminated as well, I include the date of access along with URL citations, with the intent that the reader can use the Internet Archive (https://archive.org/index.php) to find references for which the cited URL no longer works. In some cases the site is already archived. *[See, however Preface to the Second Printing, infra.]*

*

be useful in connection with the development of their own systems and institutions of higher education.

I am grateful for the help of colleagues who have reviewed and provided me with insightful comments on drafts of the entire book or individual chapters. They include Patricia Pelfrey, Steven Brint, Ami Zusman, Saul Geiser, John Douglass, Paula Fass, Ellen Switkes, Paul Gray, Stephen Handel, Keith Alexander, and Stephen Arditti. Their thoughts have helped the book immensely, but of course I assume responsibility myself for the veracity of what is in the book. Rachael Samberg, Scholarly Communications Officer of the Berkeley campus library, was very helpful in steering me in the right directions for open access publishing.

I owe a particular debt of gratitude to the institution about which I am writing. It has afforded me a rewarding career of fifty-five years and counting as well as opportunities that are unsurpassed. Thanks are in order to many other people as well—first of all, to many Berkeley and University of California colleagues, notably to Doris Calloway, Mike Heyman, Rod Park, Jack Peltason, Walter Massey and Dick Atkinson, all of whom selected me for administrative positions and with whom I enjoyed working; to Neil Smelser, Karl Pister, John Douglass, Patricia Pelfrey, John Prausnitz, Marian Gade, and colleagues in Berkeley's Wellman Group, with all of whom I have spent many hours discussing the University of California and higher education; to Ruth Fix, Gary Matteson, Jane Scheiber, Norma Esherick, Barbara Gerber, and Mark Sessler, who provided high-caliber administrative support throughout my career; and to Jenny Hanson, Carletta Starks, and Diana Gee, who provided noble assistance during my own campus-wide and university-wide administrative years. My grandson, Christopher Hickey, capably joined me on the cover design.

But above all, my thanks go to my dear wife, Jeanne, who has been right there with me in all ways and totally supportive for what is now over sixty years.

C. Judson King
Berkeley, California
January 2018

PREFACE TO THE SECOND PRINTING

In the Second Printing I have corrected errata from the original printing and have also endeavoured to deal in a better way with the problem of "link rot" – changes in urls for web pages, continual modifications of web pages, and disappearance of web pages. My main approach has been to create permanent links (Perma Links) to cited versions of web pages by using the services of use Perma.cc. These links serve to preserve web pages as I consulted them during the preparation of the book. Perma Links do not have operative secondary links. Where the original url still exists, it can be reached by means of the "view the live page" feature of Perma.cc. If the original url does not still exist or has been modified, searches on the content of the cited Perma Link and/or use of the Wayback Machine of the Internet Archive can be useful. In a number of cases where Perma Links for some reason cannot be created and/or secondary links are important I have instead used citations to the Internet Archive itself or to other archiving sites. I have changed some online references that were available to University of California readers through license but are not open access. In general, page contents remain the same as in the original printing.

    I am very grateful to my Berkeley colleague, Xia Teng, for carrying out conversions to Perma Link citations in the first half of the book, and also for her help in discovering typographical and formatting errors.

C. Judson King
Berkeley CA
September 2018

*

1.

The University of California: A Remarkable Success Story

In the past 60 years, California has...led the world in policy and provision of higher education and university-based science, while at the same time leading the evolution of ideas about university education. California is unmatched in its concentration of high-quality public campuses (for example, University of California, Berkeley; University of California, Los Angeles; University of California, San Diego)...Only the Boston corridor, where private education plays a greater role, is in the same league as universities in California, and Boston lags behind
   —*Simon Marginson*[1]

No aspect of our revised class of Research 1 universities is more arresting than the inclusion of all eight general campuses of the University of California. The eye-catching additions...are the UC campuses at Santa Barbara, Riverside, and Santa Cruz. The speed with which these institutions rose from modest beginnings is astonishing.
   —*Hugh Davis Graham and Nancy Diamond*[2]

This university is truly the crown jewel of public higher education—not just in California—but in the country. If the great research universities deserve our support for what they do now and what they could do if given more support, then UC Berkeley is a special case in that we are not only supporting great work, we are supporting an important social concept—the importance of public education and universal access for our best and brightest students, irrespective of their ability to pay.
   —*Walter Hewlett*[3]

---

[1] Simon Marginson, "California and the Future of Public Higher Education," *International Higher Education*, no. 82 (Fall 2015), https://ejournals.bc.edu/ojs/index.php/ihe/article/view/8872/7943.
[2] Hugh D. Graham and Nancy Diamond, *The Rise of American Research Universities: Elites and Challengers in the Postwar Era* (Baltimore, MD: Johns Hopkins University Press, 1997), p. 149.
[3] "9.10.2007—Walter Hewlett on the Hewlett Challenge," University of California, Berkeley,

The University of California is struggling with budget woes that have deeply affected campus life. Yet the system's nine colleges still lead the nation in providing top-flight college education to the masses.
—David Leonhardt[4]

The University of California has been a major success when viewed from any of a number of different viewpoints.

MEASURES OF SUCCESS

Institutional Stature within the Academic World. University of California campuses constitute fully 10 percent (six out of sixty) of the US member institutions of the Association of American Universities (AAU).[5] Quantitative ranking systems for universities, which have appeared profusely as the twenty-first century has begun, generally place the University of California, Berkeley, as the number-one public research university campus in the world, and the University of California, Los Angeles, often vies with the University of Michigan for the second spot among US public universities. These ranking systems and the factors considered in them are described and discussed in the appendix.

---

https://perma.cc/EU9R-N32U.
[4] David Leonhardt, "California's Upward Mobility Machine," *New York Times,* September 16, 2015.
[5] "Membership in AAU is by invitation and is based on the high quality of programs of academic research and scholarship and undergraduate, graduate, and professional education in a number of fields, as well as general recognition that a university is outstanding by reason of the excellence of its research and education programs." From Association of American Universities, "AAU Membership," https://perma.cc/MG2T-2ZT2.

Rapid Development of New Campuses to Eminence. Graham and Diamond[6] have remarked upon, and have essentially built a book around, the extremely rapid development of the newer University of California campuses to eminence in the decades following World War II. UC San Diego, which first admitted graduate students in 1960, achieved AAU membership in 1982, only twenty-two years later. UC Santa Barbara and UC Davis both were elected to AAU membership thirty-seven years after being designated general campuses in 1958 and 1959, respectively. UC Irvine achieved AAU membership thirty-one years after opening in 1965. UCLA was elected to the AAU in 1974, thirty-six years after giving its first PhD and only sixteen years after being accorded "equal opportunity" with Berkeley by President Clark Kerr and the UC Regents in 1958 (see chapter 2).

Research Quality and Impact. The University of California, through well-established peer-review processes, receives between 9 and 10 percent of the research support awarded by the US federal government for university research.[7] The university is generally regarded as a major driver of the California economy, with many successful start-up companies utilizing University of California research and/or stemming from University of California faculty members. Particular examples, amplified in chapters 16 and 18, are the California agriculture and wine industries, the growth of Silicon Valley after its start from Stanford, and the San Francisco and San Diego clusters of the biotechnology industry.

Individual Faculty Accomplishment. A total of sixty-one faculty members associated with the University of California for part or all of their careers have so far won Nobel Prizes.[8] Twenty-two Berkeley faculty members have been Nobel Laureates, as well as twenty-five Berkeley alumni, eighteen of them with PhD degrees from UC Berkeley, and eleven of those eighteen from chemistry alone.[9]

---

[6] Hugh Davis Graham and Nancy Diamond, 1997, *op. cit.*
[7] University of California, *Accountability Report 2015*, section 9.3, "Research Activities," https://perma.cc/2DZY-5XW3.
[8] University of California, "Nobel Laureates," https://perma.cc/7LA2-ENUZ.
[9] University of California, Berkeley, "Nobel Prize Winners associated with UC Berkeley," http://perma.cc/WG9A-H7AU.

As of 2015-16, University of California faculty had won 67 US National Medals of Science, and UC had 370 members of the National Academy of Sciences,[10] over 500 members of the American Academy of Arts and Sciences,[11] 168 members of the National Academy of Engineering,[12] and over 200 members of the National Academy of Medicine (formerly Institute of Medicine).[13] UC faculty members constitute 16.4 percent of the National Academy of Sciences, 8.4 percent of the National Academy of Engineering (only about half of the membership of which is from universities), and about 10 percent of the National Academy of Medicine.

Breadth of Accomplishment and Distinction. Although the figures in the previous section pertain to science, medicine, and engineering only, the distinction extends across the board. For example, 29 out of 213 (14 percent) of new members of the American Academy of Arts and Sciences in 2016 were from the University of California.[14] Faculty members from the university are solidly represented among winners of the National Humanities Medal, the Forbes 30 under 30 list, Guggenheim Fellowships, the Thomson-Reuters list of highly cited researchers, and other such measures of academic distinction, over a wide spread of disciplines. The surveys of the American Council on Education/National Research Council discussed in the appendix have consistently placed the Berkeley campus as having high distinction over a range of disciplines.

---

[10] Search for "University of California" on "Member Profile Search," National Academy of Sciences, https://perma.cc/NVL6-EZWV, April 18, 2016.
[11] *University of California Accountability Report*, 2015, chapter 5, "Faculty and Other Academic Employees," https://perma.cc/PL4L-RVZH.
[12] National Academy of Engineering, *Directory of Members and Foreign Members*, Washington, DC, 2015.
[13] University of California, "Six Members Elected to Institute of Medicine," October 20, 2014, https://perma.cc/2YYL-S85V.
[14] "Twenty-Nine UC Scholars Elected to the American Academy of Arts and Sciences," University of California Newsroom, April 20, 2016, https://perma.cc/M9Y5-JU8D.

Student Demand. Application pressure to the University of California is very high. The Los Angeles and Berkeley campuses received 92,722 [15] and 78,918 [16] applications, respectively, for 2015 fall admission. UCLA receives the greatest number of applications for admission of all universities in the United States. Both these campuses could admit only 17 percent of applicants. By the California Master Plan for Higher Education, eligibility for the University of California is restricted to the top 12.5 percent of graduates of public high schools and those with equivalent records from private high schools. None of the eight undergraduate campuses—except the new campus at Merced—have the capacity that would enable them to admit all UC-eligible applicants to the campus.

Access and the Mission to Make Higher Education Available to All Members of Society. Pell Grants, given by the US federal government, are generally available to all families making $50,000 or less per year, with most of the funding going to students from families making $30,000 or less per year. [17] In fall 2013, 42 percent of UC undergraduates were Pell Grant recipients, 42 percent were first-generation college students, and 26 percent were from underrepresented minority groups. Pell Grant recipients for 2012–13 ranged from 36 percent at the Berkeley and Los Angeles campuses to 60 percent at the new Merced campus. These percentages are much higher than for comparable private and public institutions; in fact, each of five UC campuses individually admits more Pell Grant recipients than does the entire Ivy League.[18] David Leonhardt of the *New York Times* has carried out analyses and rankings of US universities on a measure of public access that combines the fraction of the undergraduate student body with Pell Grants and the percentage of Pell Grant

---

[15] University of California, Los Angeles, "UCLA Offers Admission to More Than 16,000 Talented Students for Fall 2015," https://perma.cc/F57D-R53U.
[16] University of California, Berkeley, "In a Competitive Year, Berkeley Admits 13,321 Prospective Freshmen," https://perma.cc/UBB8-SQZK.
[17] "Federal Pell Grant Qualifications," *College Loan Consultant*, https://perma.cc/8SML-C2XJ.
[18] University of California, "The University of California Delivers on Its Commitment to Promote Social Mobility," https://web.archive.org/web/20161006142643/http://www.ucop.edu/institutional-research-academic-planning/_files/social_mobility_2-20-15.pdf.

recipients who graduate with the average actual price (tuition and fees minus financial aid) paid by enrolled students (an inverse measure). Six of the top seven universities in the 2016 analysis were University of California campuses.[19]

It is striking in view of these figures on student access that graduation rates at the bachelor's level for UC are also high in comparison with other public universities—a six-year graduation rate of 85 percent for the 2011 entering freshman cohort. This increases to 88 percent when students who transfer to non-UC institutions and still graduate within a total six years are taken into account. Freshman entrants take an average of 4.1 years to graduate. The 2011 entering group of transfer students had a four-year graduation rate of 88 percent.[20] Longer times to degree can often be rationalized in terms of students who need to have simultaneous employment.

Service to the State and Nation. The University of California has had a tradition of service to the state of California and the US government. Service to the state, treated in more detail in chapter 16, includes the extensive Cooperative Extension system for agriculture, the university as a whole functioning as the acknowledged research arm of the state government, and participation of UC faculty in many state panels and commissions.

Considering service to the nation by faculty from the Berkeley campus alone, Ernest Lawrence, Robert Oppenheimer, and many other faculty members were heavily involved during World War II in the Manhattan Project, resulting in the first three atomic bombs. Since 1943 the US government has entrusted the university with management[21] of three of its most vital national laboratories. Berkeley chemist Kenneth Pitzer served as director of research for the Atomic Energy Commission from 1949 to 1951, its critical early years. Berkeley chemist and Nobelist Glenn Seaborg served as chairman of the Atomic

---

[19] David Leonhardt, *op. cit.*; also "College Access Index, 2015: The Details," and "Top Colleges Doing the Most for Low Income Students," *New York Times*, September 16, 2015.
[20] University of California, *Accountability Report 2016*, chapter 3, "Undergraduate Student Success," https://perma.cc/2E3Y-YNWB.
[21] Now shared for two of the laboratories with various industrial companies.

Energy Commission under three US presidents from 1961 to 1971. Berkeley economists Laura Tyson (1993–95), Janet Yellen (1997–99), and Christine Romer (2009–10) have all served as chair of the Council of Economic Advisors to the US president. From 2014 to 2018 Janet Yellen was chair of the US Federal Reserve Board of Governors, the most visible financial position in the country and perhaps the world.

HOW DID THIS HAPPEN?

What enabled the University of California to achieve this standing? It was surely not a foreordained or automatic outcome, considering the beginnings of the state.

The University of California was founded in 1868, just nineteen years after the California gold rush of 1849 brought an eclectic crowd of gold seekers, and a very rough and relatively lawless group at that, into the state. The start of the university was also just six years after the Morrill Act of 1862, which established the land-grant mechanism for the individual states of the United States to establish and fund public universities. Yet the University of California, then only at Berkeley, was highly respected by the early 1900s and was widely admired as of and after World War II, just eighty years after its founding. Even more impressive in some ways is the fact that newer campuses of the University of California have risen to the top tier of respect in even shorter periods of time, as already noted.

How did this happen, and what are the essential and perhaps unusual factors that led to this success? To explore that territory is the purpose of this book. The book is not intended to be a history. It is instead selective and analytical. It seeks to identify and distill out those factors that have been most important to the success that the University of California as a whole and its various campuses individually have achieved and to explore in depth the ways in which those factors have been important. I deal more with values, structures, policies, approaches, and environmental factors than with individual people. The people are largely reflected in their lasting values and approaches.

What Has Been Most Important for the Success of the University of California?

It should be helpful to the reader to have a broad list of the factors that have been most important to the development of the University of California and hence to its resultant stature. In that way the reader can be on the lookout for these factors as they come into the discussion, can follow the ways in which they developed and have been influential, and can continually come back to a single list.

I am not the first to seek to identify the most essential factors for the success of the University of California. Such efforts have been made to various degrees by former UC president David Gardner,[22, 23] by Patricia Pelfrey in her short book on the history of UC,[24] and by George Breslauer[25] for the Berkeley campus. Clark Kerr underscored constitutional autonomy and the unprecedented authority that was given to the Academic Senate.[26] In table 1-1, I present my own list, keyed to chapters in this book. The order of items in the list is not a priority ranking.

---

[22] David P. Gardner, *Earning My Degree: Memoirs of an American University President* (Berkeley: University of California Press, 2005), pp. 164–167.

[23] David P. Gardner, "The California System: Governing and Management Principles and Their Link to Academic Excellence," 25th David Dodd Henry Lecture, University of Illinois at Chicago, Chicago IL, 2005, http://web.archive.org/web/20130606071116/http://www.uic.edu/depts/oaa/ddh/25th_DDH.pdf.

[24] Patricia A. Pelfrey, *A Brief History of the University of California*, 2nd ed. (Berkeley: University of California, 2004; distributed by University of California Press), pp. 1–3.

[25] George W. Breslauer, "What Made Berkeley Great? The Sources of Berkeley's Sustained Academic Excellence," Research and Occasional Papers Series no. 3.11 (January 2011), Center for Studies in Higher Education, Berkeley, CA, https://perma.cc/5D2P-NAQG.

[26] Clark Kerr, foreword, in Angus E. Taylor, *The Academic Senate of the University of California* (Berkeley: Institute of Governmental Studies Press, University of California, 1998), p. xi, https://perma.cc/S6CL-UJ7P.

TABLE 1-1. Primary factors important to the success of the University of California

- Hiring the best and the brightest faculty members and then empowering them to do creative research and teaching limited only by their own time and abilities (chapters 9 and 10)
- A structure as a single university with multiple campuses, all having the same undifferentiated mission (chapter 6)[G]
- The nature and effectiveness of the structured shared-governance roles of the Academic Senate (chapter 7)[K, P, G]
- Career-long reviews of faculty members, evaluating and rewarding academic accomplishment, performance, and quality (chapter 11)
- Building from within (chapters 6 and 10)
- Historically high levels of support by the people and government of California (chapters 2 and 17)[G, P, B]
- Constitutional autonomy (chapter 4)[K, P, G]
- The 1960 California Master Plan for Higher Education (chapter 5)[P]
- Location: geographic, intellectual, and economic (chapter 19)
- Encouragement and facilitation of multidisciplinary research; Lawrence Berkeley National Laboratory (chapters 13 and 14)
- Integration of the professional fields fully into the academic mission and governance (chapters 7, 8, 11, 12, and 14)

Superscripts:
B—Also identified by Breslauer
G—Also identified by Gardner
K—Also one of Kerr's "two greatest gifts"
P—Also identified by Pelfrey

Most of the book explores these and other factors. I then try to generalize and address the needs for creation or development of a premier research university (chapter 20), after which I consider what are likely to be future models for the University of California itself as well as for other leading public research universities (chapter 21).

The inclusion of the list in table 1-1 and, indeed, the entire subject matter of this book do not constitute a prescription for what will work best or well for other universities in other countries, or even other states within the United States. The factors that led to the success of the University of California are embedded in the history, culture, and other institutions of California and in the particular eras when they took place. These approaches may not work as well in another era, another locale, or another culture. But they can certainly serve as starting points for serious consideration.

AN EMPHASIS ON SCIENCE

Primary attention is given to science disciplines throughout this book. There are several reasons for that approach. Most reputational surveys and research-university ranking systems (see appendix) are tilted toward science. It was through science that a preeminent reputation for academic quality first developed in the University of California, and it is largely science that propelled several of the newer campuses—most notably San Diego, Santa Barbara, and San Francisco—rapidly to the forefront. Much of the interest in other countries in building and improving universities is for science and engineering and their commercial applications. Finally, my own disciplinary background is chemical engineering.

I do not want to convey an impression that I believe that disciplines other than science and engineering are somehow less important for a university. I firmly believe in the essentiality of comprehensive coverage of disciplines within universities and the resultant opportunities for liberal education and multidisciplinary interactions in research and teaching, including the need to combine areas other than science and engineering with sciences and engineering in both education and research. This is supplemented in a more specific area by my belief that breadth in the education of engineers is essential.[27]

---

[27] C. Judson King, "Let Engineers Go to College," *Issues in Science and Technology* 22, no. 4 (Summer 2006), https://perma.cc/4MNC-ZWZN.

2.
The History of the University of California as It Affects Structure, Governance, and Academics

Westward the Course of Empire takes its Way;
The first four Acts already past.
A fifth shall close the Drama with the Day;
Time's noblest Offspring is the last.
   —George Berkeley, Bishop of Cloyne[1]

It is a "University," and not a high-school, nor a college, nor an academy of sciences, nor an industrial-school, which we are charged to build. Some of these features may, indeed, be included in or developed with the University; but the University means more than any or all of them. The University is the most comprehensive term which can be employed to indicate a foundation for the promotion [and] diffusion of knowledge—a group of agencies organized to advance the arts and sciences of every sort, and to train young men as scholars for all the intellectual callings of life.
   —Daniel Coit Gilman[2]

It was a stunning run. When [Pat] Brown was elected, the University of California had two major branches, plus a couple of satellites and two medical schools...When he left, there were eight campuses, five medical schools, and scores of other operations, a "multiversity," in President Clark Kerr's newly minted word, that, in its graduate faculties and programs, quickly became the equal of any research university on

---

[1] George Berkeley, *Verses on the Prospect of Planting Arts and Learning in America* (1728), https://perma.cc/A6DV-8SUA. "Westward the Course of Empire Takes Its Way" is also the title of a noted painting by Emanuel Leutze currently displayed behind the western staircase of the House of Representatives chamber in the US Capitol Building.
[2] Daniel C. Gilman, "The Building of the University," Inaugural Address as President of the University of California, November 7, 1872, https://perma.cc/FPH3-BM3G.

earth, an enterprise so vast, ambitious, and all-encompassing that it awed even those who created it.
   —Peter Schrag[3]

The purpose of this chapter is a selective, rather than comprehensive, examination of historical aspects of the University of California. The goal is to identify those aspects of the history that have had greater effects, directly or indirectly, on the development, enhancement, and preservation of the academic quality and reputation of the university. What follows in the subsequent chapters is an exploration of particular subject areas that relate closely to academic quality. They constitute topical histories, supplemented by analysis. For a comprehensive history of the first one hundred years of the University of California, see Stadtman.[4] For a general collection of historical material, see many individual items on Calisphere[5] and the Online Archive of California,[6] as well as the University of California History Digital Archives.[7] For an engaging short history, see Pelfrey.[8] Kerr[9] and Gardner[10] cover many historical aspects of their times as University of California president and, in the case of Kerr, chancellor of the Berkeley campus as well. Pelfrey covers the period of Richard Atkinson's presidency, 1995–2003.[11]

---

[3] Peter Schrag, *Paradise Lost: California's Experience, America's Future* (Berkeley: University of California Press, 1998), p. 36.
[4] Verne A. Stadtman, *The University of California, 1868–1968* (New York: McGraw-Hill, 1970).
[5] Calisphere, California Digital Library, University of California, https://calisphere.org/.
[6] Online Archive of California (OAC), California Digital Library, University of California, http://www.oac.cdlib.org/.
[7] University of California History Digital Archives, https://web.archive.org/web/20170709235449/http://www.lib.berkeley.edu/uchistory/. (This is a static website, no longer being updated.)
[8] Patricia A. Pelfrey, *A Brief History of the University of California* (Regents of the University of California; distributed by University of California Press, 2004).
[9] Clark Kerr, *The Gold and the Blue: A Personal Memoir of the University of California, 1949–1967*, vol. 1, *Academic Triumphs*, and vol. 2, *Political Turmoil* (Berkeley: University of California Press, 2001, 2003).
[10] David P. Gardner, *Earning My Degree: Memoirs of an American University President* (Berkeley: University of California Press, 2005).
[11] Patricia A. Pelfrey, *Entrepreneurial President: Richard Atkinson and the University of California, 1995–2003* (Berkeley: University of California Press, 2013).

THE EARLY YEARS[12]

The University of California grew out of a small private institution in Oakland known as the College of California and founded in 1853 by Henry Durant. It is striking how close that founding year of 1853 and indeed the founding date of 1868 for the University of California itself were to the major gold rush year of 1849, when California first received substantial immigration through the rapid influx of a large and unruly population of gold seekers. Before the Bear Flag Revolution of 1846, California had been a sparsely populated northern portion of Mexico.

Seeking larger facilities, Durant and the College of California acquired, between 1857 and 1861, 124 acres of land along Strawberry Creek four miles north of Oakland, directly across San Francisco Bay from the Golden Gate. At a meeting of the trustees of the College of California in May 1866, at what is now known as Founder's Rock on the new land, it was proposed that the new site of the college and the surrounding area be called Berkeley, in commemoration of the author of the lines cited at the beginning of this chapter. Durant and several other founders were graduates of Yale University, to which Bishop George Berkeley[13] had been a generous donor. One of the residential colleges at Yale, Berkeley College, has since been given his name as well. The close ties of the early founders with Yale also led to the selection of the school colors in 1868: Yale blue and California gold.[14]

The landmark Morrill Act,[15] signed by President Abraham Lincoln in 1862 and named for Vermont senator Justin Morrill, who had introduced the bill, provided federal government funding in the form of title to what had been federal government land ("land grants"). The proceeds from the sale of this land could be used toward the creation of public universities that would include the agricultural and

---

[12] More specifics on these early years are given by Stadtman, 1970, *op. cit.*, from whom this description is largely summarized.
[13] The actual pronunciation of Berkeley's name was, by English custom, "bark-ley." The name, both in California and at Yale, has been given the American pronunciation, "burk-ley."
[14] "California Golden Bears—Traditions," *Calbears.com*, https://perma.cc/3GR3-BEN9.
[15] "Our Documents—Transcript of Morrill Act (1862)," https://perma.cc/VM2D-Y437.

mechanical (A&M) arts.[16] Through an organic act of 1866, the state of California originally pursued the development of a college of agricultural, mining, and mechanical arts that would utilize the Morrill Act funds for the state. However, in 1867 Benjamin Silliman,[17] the noted professor of chemistry at Yale, delivered the commencement address at the College of California, a ceremony in which California's governor, Frederick Low, also participated. Silliman urged that, instead of a college of agricultural, mining, and mechanical arts, the state should establish a full university, including the subjects specified in the Morrill Act but more in the intellectually broad model of the fine private universities in the eastern United States. Such a structure would still satisfy the requirements of the Morrill Act.

Governor Low was convinced, reversed course, and arranged with the state government to accept an earlier offer from Henry Durant and the College of California to participate in a merger, wherein the formerly private College of California would become the public university of the state and contribute its Berkeley land. A second organic act,[18] introduced by Assemblyman John Dwinelle, was signed into law by Governor Henry Haight on March 23, 1868, thereby establishing the University of California.

The initial faculty of the university numbered ten people. Most prominent among them were John and Joseph LeConte, who had been respected faculty members in physics (John) and geology, botany, and natural history (Joseph) in Georgia and South Carolina. Both those states had been in the Confederate States of America during the Civil War, and both LeContes had served in military operations. California was one of the few places in the United States where Confederate veterans could gain employment as faculty members in substantial universities. The two LeContes were endorsed to the university by Benjamin Silliman, Joseph Henry of the Smithsonian Institution, and

---

[16] Interestingly, the substance of the Morrill Act had been proposed in previous years, but it was only after the secession of the southern states at the start of the US Civil War that the proportion of favorable votes in the US Congress was high enough for its passage.
[17] Arthur W. Wright, "Benjamin Silliman, 1816–1885," Biographical Memoirs, National Academy of Sciences, Washington, DC, 1911, https://perma.cc/R4U9-CLGU.
[18] "The Organic Act—Chapter 244 of the Statutes of 1867–1868," https://perma.cc/J4TN-Q2CX.

Louis Agassiz of Harvard, three of the most prominent science academics of their day. John LeConte was the first (acting) president of the university, serving until a permanent president could be found and brought on board.

Following a somewhat bizarre initial offer to former US general and unsuccessful 1864 US presidential candidate George McClellan, and another offer, also unsuccessful, to Daniel Coit Gilman,[19] secretary of the Sheffield Scientific School at Yale, the regents in 1870 selected Henry Durant as the initial president, no longer with the adjective "acting." Durant served for two years until he reached age seventy. Following his retirement the regents tried again, and this time succeeded in bringing Gilman in 1872 from Yale to Berkeley as president of the University of California.

Gilman vigorously and capably undertook development of the university, stressing academic components. He obtained a number of substantial private donations, including a gift from eccentric philanthropist James Lick[20] for what would be the largest telescope in the world. He also arranged with surgeon-physician Hugh Toland[21] for affiliation of Toland's preexisting medical college in San Francisco with the university. However, two disruptive episodes arose after Gilman's first year. Corruption charges surrounded the construction of the university's first building, North Hall. These involved a regent and not Gilman, but they nonetheless weakened the university. The second matter involved Ezra Carr, the initial professor of agriculture, who surreptitiously and energetically worked to better the interests of agriculture as he saw them. Carr stimulated and engaged the support of the state grange,[22] joining with UC literature professor William Swinton to seek to return the primary focus of the university to agriculture, whereupon there would be substantially increased

---

[19] Fabian Franklin, *The Life of Daniel Coit Gilman* (New York, 1910), https://archive.org/details/lifeofdanielcoit00fran.

[20] "The Lick Observatory Collections Project: The Life of James Lick," https://perma.cc/BV29-P9C5.

[21] "Hugh Huger Toland—Biography—A History of UCSF," https://perma.cc/LCW3-PBDH.

[22] State granges were fraternal organizations devoted to improving the life and circumstances of farmers. The movement had started only a few years before the Gilman-Carr episode.

resources for that area. As well, they wanted to modify the structure of the university by expanding the Board of Regents through the addition of members elected by popular vote from each congressional district. Carr and the grange also claimed mismanagement of the university, charging it with operating counter to the specifications of the Morrill Act. This effort revived the original question of whether the university should focus entirely, or nearly entirely, on agriculture and mechanical arts. It also led to an investigation of the university by a joint senate-assembly committee of the state legislature. The issues were hotly contested, but the finding was for Gilman and the university.[23]

Confronted with Carr's activities and his insubordination, Gilman requested that Carr resign, which Carr refused to do. The regents then dismissed Carr, who, however, continued to have substantial support from those who believed that a highly practical education was what was needed in such a new state. Carr, in fact, ran for and was elected state superintendent of public Instruction on the statewide ballot in 1875, after his dismissal from the University of California. In that post he was ex officio a regent of the university from 1875 to 1880.[24] Carr continued to work toward his desired ends. Those efforts again did not succeed.

Discouraged by these episodes and the infighting, in April 1874 Gilman tendered his resignation with these words: "For University fighting I have no training; in University work I delight."[25] The regents persuaded Gilman to withdraw his resignation, but shortly thereafter he was offered the opportunity to be the initial president of the new Johns Hopkins University in Baltimore, which he accepted. Gilman is generally credited with having used the launch of Johns Hopkins to bring the German style of research-based education to the United States. That concept that has flourished over time and forms the basis for present US research universities.

---

[23] John Aubrey Douglass, "How and Why the University of California Got Its Autonomy," Research and Occasional Papers, no. 4-15 (April 2015), https://perma.cc/8KP4-3NLE.
[24] Regents of the University of California, p. 2, University of California, https://perma.cc/J37G-W9RZ.
[25] Douglass, 2015, *loc. cit.*

For unrelated reasons, the state of California called a constitutional convention in 1878, resulting in a new state constitution being adopted in 1879. As part of the development of that constitution, the nature and structure of the University of California were again argued, and by a narrow margin, the existing definition and structure were retained. As well a condition was added that has proven over subsequent years to be vitally important. That condition is constitutional autonomy, considered further in chapter 4.

The early years of the University of California were turbulent, but brought about two decisions that have been vital to the future of the university. One of these was the decision to build a full university rather than one limited to agriculture and the mechanical arts, and the other was the establishment of constitutional autonomy for the university.

THE LATER 1800S

A period of relatively weak and uninvolved presidents ensued for most of the rest of the nineteenth century along with state-funded budgets that were barely adequate, if that. The regents actively exercised control much deeper into the university than is the case today. One reason for that was, of course, the much smaller size.[26] The university had not yet grown much toward the degree of intellectual stature that it has today. There were, however, some significant events.

Eugene Hilgard. The person hired to replace Carr as professor of agriculture proved to be an outstanding choice. He was Eugene Woldemar Hilgard, a native Bavarian who had been a faculty member at the University of Mississippi during the Civil War and then at the University of Michigan. Hilgard came to California after the transfer of Michigan's agricultural activities from the University of Michigan to Michigan State University. Overcoming the displeasure among California farmers with Carr's dismissal, Hilgard developed good relations with them and started field stations around the state,

---

[26] In 1888 the student enrollment was still only 477 (Stadtman, 1970, *op. cit.*, p. 115).

including in Davis and at what became the Kearney Field Station near Fresno. He promoted a scientific, rather than practical, approach to agriculture with well-recognized results. Hilgard became interested in the potential of viticulture (grape growing) and the making of superior wines for California. He carried out studies on control of the grape-vine pest *phylloxera*, and was influential in bringing about as of 1880 an annual appropriation to the university from the California legislature for research that could foster a California wine industry.[27] Hilgard is also generally recognized as a key founder of the field of soil science.[28]

San Francisco Affiliates. Another important development was the establishment of institutions affiliated with the university. At the time of the 1868 Organic Act, the legislature also authorized the regents to enter into affiliation with "any incorporated College of Medicine or Law, or any other special course of instruction now existing, or which may hereafter be created, upon such compliance as to the respective corporations may be deemed expedient."[29] This language was probably spurred by the known desire of Dr. Hugh Toland to affiliate his existing Toland Medical College with the university. The affiliations had the essential purpose of providing professional education, with degrees given and certified by the University of California, but at no expense to the state (i.e., on fully self-supporting bases).

Several affiliations were formed, all with institutions in San Francisco. After substantial political maneuvering, the Toland offer was accepted by President Gilman in 1873. As described in chapter 10, this affiliated institution was eventually taken fully into the university and became the heart of the UC San Francisco (UCSF) campus.[30] Another affiliation entered into by President Gilman was with the California College of Pharmacy in 1872 and is now reflected in the School of Pharmacy with UCSF. A dental school was formed and affiliated as the Department of Dentistry in 1881. This too is now a school within UCSF.

---

[27] Maynard A. Amerine, "Hilgard and California Viticulture," *Hilgardia* 33, no. 1 (July 1962), https://perma.cc/ZFD4-3HJD. These efforts have now led to a major industry for the state.
[28] Hans Jenny, *E. W. Hilgard and the Birth of Modern Soil Science* (Pisa: Agrochimica, Instituto di Chimica Agraria dell'Università Pisa, 1961).
[29] Stadtman, 1970, *op. cit.*, p. 125.
[30] "UCSF History," UC San Francisco, https://perma.cc/ZPH9-3KKB.

The final health-related affiliation was with the California Veterinary College in 1894, lasting until 1901. The university's one School of Veterinary Medicine is now a stalwart of the Davis campus.

Another interesting and complex story of affiliation is in the field of law. In 1878 Serranus Hastings, a highly successful lawyer, banker, and businessman and an early chief justice and attorney general of California, obtained legislation whereby in return for his contribution of $100,000[31] to the state treasury, the "law department of the University of California" would be created in his name. This legislation was effectively an amendment to the Organic Act of 1868, and by incorporation of the Organic Act into the California Constitution of 1879 became constitutionally protected. Such an act of the legislature defining the structure of the university was no longer possible after the implementation of the 1879 constitution, because of the concept of constitutional autonomy (chapter 4).

The affiliation of the Hastings College of the Law with the University of California remains a legal curiosity. Although it identifies itself as "UC Hastings College of the Law,"[32] the school has its own state-appointed board [33] and operates in San Francisco fully independently of UC. It does, however, share in the various University of California benefit programs and generally follows the *Academic Personnel Manual* of the University of California (chapter 11). The first law school fully within the University of California was established by the regents at Berkeley in 1912, through a gift of $100,000 from Elizabeth Joselyn Boalt, who followed up with $365,000 for endowed professorships. The Berkeley Law School was known until recently as Boalt Hall. The university now has five law schools, including ones at Los Angeles, Davis, and Irvine, in addition to Berkeley and Hastings.

Land at Parnassus Heights below Mount Sutro in San Francisco was donated to the university in 1895 by San Francisco mayor Adolph Sutro. A legislative appropriation was obtained in the same year to erect buildings on the site for the medical affiliates and the Hastings College of the Law. However, in the earlier years, only one of the

---

[31] Recognize that there has been substantial inflation since 1878.
[32] "UC Hastings College of the Law," https://perma.cc/B8QX-V72Z.
[33] Appointment of directors is by the governor, with confirmation by the state senate required within a year, and twelve-year terms, as is the case for the University of California Regents.

affiliates, the California College of Pharmacy, actually moved to the site, leaving space available for other purposes, which included housing the extensive and valuable archeological and anthropological collections given to the university by Regent Phoebe Apperson Hearst (see below). The Parnassus site thereby became the UC home of Ishi, the last of the California Yahi tribe, whose life was famously studied by UC anthropologist Alfred Kroeber.[34] These collections later moved to what is now the Phoebe Apperson Hearst Museum of Anthropology on the Berkeley campus.

Yet another affiliate was and is the San Francisco Art Institute, with which the regents affiliated in 1893, when the mansion of railroad magnate Mark Hopkins atop Nob Hill was left to the regents "for the exclusive uses and purposes of instruction in and illustrations of the Fine Arts, Music and Literature...including the maintenance of galleries, reading rooms, and other suitable means of such instruction and illustration."[35] The mansion was subsequently torn down to enable construction of the Mark Hopkins Hotel, and the institute was moved to another site in San Francisco, but the affiliation with UC remains.

Lick Observatory. As already mentioned, another gift secured by Gilman during his short presidency was the commitment from James Lick, an eccentric and successful San Francisco businessman, for what was at the time to be the world's largest telescope. The telescope was built between 1876 and 1888 on Mount Hamilton above San Jose, California, and was turned over to the regents upon completion (see figure 2-1). It served to launch the university toward forefront prominence in astronomy (chapter 9) and served as the lure to attract a president of UC, Edward S. Holden, who simultaneously became the first director of the Lick Observatory.

THE WHEELER ERA

In 1899 the regents made only their third successful venture outside the university and the state of California for a president, the

---

[34] Theodora Kroeber, *Ishi in Two Worlds: A Biography of the Last Wild Indian in North America* (Berkeley: University of California Press, 1961).
[35] Stadtman, 1970, *op. cit.*, p. 138.

previous ones having been Gilman and Holden. As had been done for Gilman, they went to a distinguished private university of the eastern United States. The target was Benjamin Ide Wheeler, professor of Greek and comparative philology at Cornell.

Figure 2-1. The Lick Observatory, 1900[36]

Wheeler was aware of the history of relatively weak presidents and close regental control. He presented four conditions to the regents for his acceptance,[37] as follows:
1. That the president should be in *fact*, as in theory, the sole organ of communication between the faculty and regents
2. That the president shall have sole initiative in appointments and removals of professors and other teachers and in matters affecting salary

---

[36] "Lick Observatory," *Wikipedia*, https://perma.cc/YZA8-HJ8G.
[37] Stadtman, 1970, *op. cit.*, p. 181.

3. That the Board, however divided in opinion during discussion, should in all things the president is called upon to do regarding the faculty, support him as a unit
4. That the president shall be charged with the direction, subject to the board, of all officers and employees of the university

The regents accepted these conditions, and Wheeler thereby became president for a period of twenty years (1899–1919), over twice as long as the service of any of his predecessors. During his time as president, Wheeler brought the university to distinction and stability on a variety of fronts. His accomplishments included building and establishing the role and power of the president; overseeing a major expansion of enrollment and faculty; enhancing and improving relations with the regents, the state government, and the public; achieving large increases in both state funding and private philanthropy for core needs and initiatives of the university; launching and nurturing the way forward to preeminent research; and improving student behavior and decorum while also building and supporting student government.

The Progressives and Public Funding.[38] During Wheeler's time, the Progressive movement came into being in California, having started as a resistance to the Southern Pacific Railroad and other monopolizing practices. The Progressives were essentially a reformist movement, but they recognized the value of public higher education as an avenue to reform. Wheeler worked with the Progressives and the state government to obtain major increases in state funding for the university and obtained recognition of the principle that increased enrollment should bring increased state funding, replacing a previous procedure whereby the university had, since 1886, been budgeted annually one cent (later raised to two, and then three cents) for every hundred dollars of taxable property in the state.[39] That previous formula had borne no relationship to enrollment or development of the university. The dramatic rise in state funding during Wheeler's time is shown graphically in figure 2-2. It was only then that state funding rose far above private funding.

---

[38] John A. Douglass, *The California Idea and American Higher Education: 1850 to the 1960 Master Plan* (Stanford University Press, 2000), pp. 105–113.
[39] Stadtman, 1970, *op. cit.*, pp. 114, 120, 123–124, 189–191.

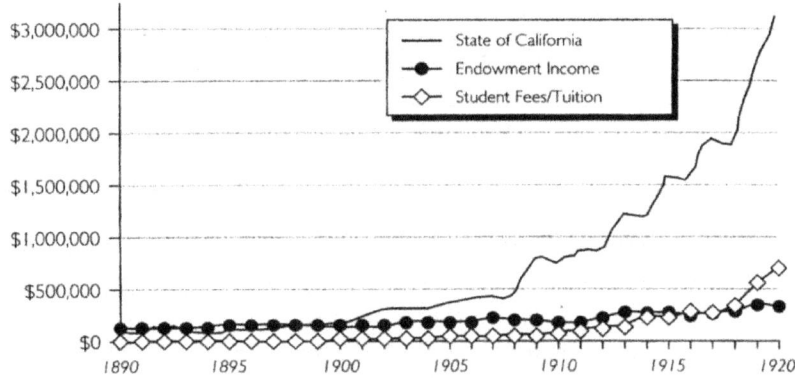

Figure 2-2. Increase of University of California funding during the Wheeler era (1899–1919) [40]

Tripartite Public Higher Education. As Douglass[41] describes, it was also during Wheeler's time that the California model of tripartite higher education took form. The concept of junior colleges, which later became the community colleges, arose from and was promoted by Professor Alexis Lange of UC and David Starr Jordan, president of Stanford University. That movement, plus the establishment of roles for the state teacher's colleges (later the California State Colleges and then the California State University) served to accommodate enrollment that otherwise would have logically needed to be subsumed by the University of California and thereby enabled UC to concentrate more on building academic quality. As later fleshed out through the Master Plan of 1960 (chapter 5) the tripartite structure also provided economic efficiency for the state and made California a large-scale pioneer in transfer education.

---

[40] Douglass, 2000, *op. cit.*, p. 110, figure 2. Original source is "Financial Affairs," *Centennial Record of the University of California* (University of California Printing Dept., 1967), pp. 295–296, https://perma.cc/7CFM-TVNX.
[41] Douglass, 2000, *op. cit.*, pp. 118–130.

Geographical and Programmatic Expansion; Building Research. Although Wheeler emphasized cohesion and the core community of the university, there were also efforts during his time to bring the university into new geographical areas within the state. In fact, some of these initiatives formed the roots from which new campuses eventually sprang. Several of them were enabled by generous philanthropy.

- In 1915, at the request of Wheeler, the regents created the Board of Research (chapter 9) equipped with $2000, which increased by another $1000 each of the next two years to cover the incidental costs of research, such as travel. This was the first explicit funding of research with university funds.
- Among the off-site agricultural research locations were the University Farm at Davis and the Citrus Experiment Station at Riverside, both founded in 1905.
- The development of scholarship and research in the humanities and social sciences was substantially enhanced through growth of the library collection and the completion of the Doe Library in 1911, made possible by a gift from Charles Franklin Doe that provided over half the construction cost.
- The Bancroft Library, a landmark collection on the history of the western United States, was purchased from Hubert H. Bancroft by the university in 1905.
- Phoebe Apperson Hearst[42] (figure 2-3), who was a regent for twenty-two years, from 1897 until her death in 1919, provided the funds for an architectural and planning competition for the Berkeley campus, completed in 1899. She also supplied generous funding for the construction of the Hearst Memorial Mining Building[43] (1907) on the Berkeley campus. But, perhaps most significant of all, she sponsored and financed numerous archaeological expeditions that acquired artifacts relating to ancient mankind. She funded the university to receive and curate these materials, which now form the basis for the Phoebe

---

[42] "Phoebe Hearst," *Wikipedia*, https://perma.cc/V2UR-NGT9.
[43] Harvey Helfand, *University of California, Berkeley: An Architectural Tour and Photographs* (New York: Princeton Architectural Press, 2002), pp. 100—07.

Apperson Hearst Museum of Anthropology,[44] a massive research collection. Mrs. Hearst was the wife of miner and US senator George Hearst, for whom the building was named, and the mother of the publisher William Randolph Hearst.

Figure 2-3. Phoebe Apperson Hearst, circa 1890, California Museum (*Wikipedia Commons*), https://perma.cc/2SKN-PF5N

- During the period 1903 through 1912, a private organization funded generously by the Scripps family (newspaper publishing) developed a marine-biology research facility in La Jolla, just north of San Diego, for the use of University of California researchers. When it was completed, ownership of this facility was transferred to the Regents of the University of California. Over the years this institution reached great distinction.
- Since the days of Toland, the Medical Department of the university had been located in what had been the affiliated Toland College of Medicine in San Francisco, and instruction had been given by practicing physicians and surgeons. A new plan for medical education was created in 1902. By that plan, two-year, premedical education was given at Berkeley, and academic departments of

---

[44] "Welcome to the Hearst Museum: Phoebe A. Hearst Museum of Anthropology," https://perma.cc/29UE-7LAZ.

physiology, anatomy, and pathology were created at Berkeley as parts of that program. Private funding was secured for buildings, equipment, and some endowment. This plan was important in three ways: (1) as a transformation of medical education into a form based upon fundamental sciences; (2) as a precursor to the Joint (Berkeley-San Francisco) Medical Program, which was formally created in 1971 and exists to this day;[45] and (3) as the rationale for the establishment of three of the multitude of biology departments that were transformed organizationally in the reorganization of biosciences at Berkeley in the early 1980s (see chapter 12). It should be noted that the University of California plan of 1902 preceded the Flexner Report[46] of 1910 on medical education, which revolutionized medical education in the United States into its present form.

These various programs and facilities that came into existence during Wheeler's time served as vehicles for building the roles and stature of the university in academic research. It was also during Wheeler's time that the university undertook major faculty recruitments with the specific aim of building topflight involvement and stature in research. In the physical sciences, that started with the 1912 recruitment of Gilbert Newton Lewis from MIT (chapter 9).

Philanthropy. An important point is that the University of California received a very substantial portion of its total revenue from private philanthropy in its early years, as is shown in figure 2-2. The percentage of private support within total revenue decreased as the state budget for the university grew during most of the rest of the twentieth century. But as of about the early 1980s, major efforts were made at the more established campuses to generate increased private support, and enhanced private support has now become a necessity, as state support for public universities in California and most other states has become constrained—less in per-student, and, in many cases, absolute terms. In a very real sense, the University of California has

---

[45] "Welcome to the UC Berkeley-UCSF Joint Medical Program," *UC Berkeley School of Public Health*, https://perma.cc/5UHC-HH43 .
[46] Abraham Flexner, *Medical Education in the United States and Canada: A Report to the Carnegie Foundation for the Advancement of Teaching*, 1910, https://perma.cc/B4DV-ASTM.

now returned to the days of high dependence upon private support that existed at the start of the twentieth century, a point developed further in chapter 21.

Figure 2-4. Newly emeritus UC president Benjamin Ide Wheeler on stage at the Greek Theater with former Princeton University president Woodrow Wilson, then president of the United States, 1919[47]

It is interesting to explore and compare the apparent motivations of several of the early philanthropists who supported the University of California as it grew. James Lick was primarily devoted to the concept of building the world's largest telescope. Even though the university had not yet achieved distinction, the University of California was a convenient home for it. Hugh Toland was driven by the opportunity to achieve prominence and sustained distinction for his preexisting medical college. The affiliation with UC satisfied both of those aims. Phoebe Apperson Hearst, a great philanthropist, was driven by a desire to build the stature and capabilities of the university of her home state. The Scripps family was driven by both interest in marine research and the desire to develop the San Diego area. It was natural, then, that lead

---

[47] University of California, Berkeley, https://perma.cc/R9SY-GCU6.

researchers for the Scripps project would come from the University of California, so as to be followed by a research-driven affiliation with UC.

The Southland. When the university was chartered in 1868, only about 8 percent of California's population lived south of the Tehachapi Mountains (i.e., in what are now the greater Los Angeles and San Diego areas). By 1910, the population of the Los Angeles area exceeded that of the San Francisco area, and that difference widened in subsequent years. Because of these trends, pressures that there should be a state university in the Los Angeles area increased during Wheeler's presidency. The effort initially took the form of a proposed bill in the legislature in 1911 to convert the Throop Polytechnic Institute in Pasadena into a state university, to be called the California Institute of Technology, with an independent board of trustees. The University of California opposed that effort, not wanting to split authority, budget, and efforts between two institutions, and the relevant bill was defeated in the legislature.[48] The Southern California initiative then evolved toward one of having the University of California develop core educational activities in the Los Angeles area. In response, UC gave extension courses and summer offerings and explored how it might incorporate the Los Angeles State Normal School, which was the most prominent public institution in the area at the time, into the University of California as the Southern Branch of the university. That transfer occurred in 1919, at the end of Wheeler's presidency.

From 1919 through 1923 the Southern Branch expanded from giving only the first two years to giving all four years of baccalaureate education. This entire process of developing the southern campus was one of initiatives and pushing from the south, coupled with reluctance, resignation, and then acceptance by the university in the north. The Southern Branch became the University of California at Los Angeles (UCLA) in 1927.

The Southern Branch episode, although hardly planned, amounted to tacit adoption of the concept that the single University of California would serve the entire state of California and would do that by having more than one campus.

---

[48] In 1921 the Throop Polytechnic Institute did become the California Institute of Technology (Caltech), but in a very different form, as a small and elite private university.

Monroe Deutsch, later longtime provost of the university (1931–47) edited a book of Wheeler's papers and speeches pertaining to his administration as president.[49] Henry May, longtime professor of history at Berkeley, wrote concerning the various approaches and philosophies toward education during Wheeler's presidency.[50]

THE BERKELEY REVOLUTION

The conditions sought and obtained by Benjamin Ide Wheeler as he accepted the presidency were needed and effective for bringing the university community together and focusing leadership for all the development and building that took place during his presidency. However, toward the end of his term, Wheeler had come to be seen by many on the faculty as being overly autocratic. Although the Academic Senate had existed formally since the beginning of the university, Wheeler circumvented the senate and dealt directly with deans and department chairs on matters such as the hiring and promotion of faculty, appointments of deans and chairs, allocation of the budget, and even selection of members of Academic Senate committees. He presided over senate meetings. Wheeler could take these two latter roles because the bylaws of the Academic Senate then and now state, "The President of the University is *ex officio* President of the Academic Senate."[51]

The situation was further complicated by the fact that Wheeler had come under attack for his seeming German sympathies during World War I and had begun to show signs of senility.[52] Wheeler was

---

[49] Benjamin Ide Wheeler, *The Abundant Life*, Monroe E. Deutsch, ed. (UC Press, 1926), http://www.oac.cdlib.org/ark:/13030/hb8489p1d9/?brand=oac4.
[50] Henry F. May, *Three Faces of Berkeley: Competing Ideologies in the Wheeler Era, 1899–1919*, Center for Studies in Higher Education (Berkeley: University of California, 1993), https://perma.cc/8ZTW-UTX3 .
[51] Bylaws of the Academic Senate, University of California, part 1, title I, no. 10, https://perma.cc/69JU-2CSM.
[52] Joel H. Hildebrand, interview by Edna Tartaul Daniel, *Joel H. Hildebrand, Chemistry, Education, and the University of California* (Berkeley: Regional Oral History Office, University of California, 1962), p. 130, https://perma.cc/J6RL-M3VX.

persuaded to end his presidency in 1919. With the departure of Wheeler as president, the regents decided to delay the selection of a new president for about six months (from July to December, 1919) and instead invested presidential authority in a three-man administrative board, something that did not work well in practice.

During the period of the troika, the Academic Senate moved to deal directly with the regents to enhance the role of the senate. That process is described in chapter 7 and resulted in establishing that the president should consult with the Academic Senate on appointments, promotions, and dismissal of faculty members and on recommendations to the regents of appointments of deans and directors. As well, it was agreed that the president should give reports to the senate on matters of educational policy. The regents gave several roles directly to the faculty, including the rights for the Academic Senate to determine its own membership, select its own chair, appoint its own committees, determine the conditions for admission and degrees, supervise all courses of instruction, recommend candidates for degrees, and advise the president on budget matters.[53]

David Barrows, a former dean of the faculties, was selected to become president in December 1919. The negotiations between the regents and the senate were not complete at that point, and Barrows did not participate in those negotiations going forward. Barrows was generally accepting of the results, although there remained some contention on the senate role during the remainder of Barrow's three-year presidency and into the subsequent presidency (1923–30) of William Wallace Campbell, who had been director of the Lick Observatory and continued to be so during his presidency.[54, 55]

---

[53] Angus E. Taylor, *The Academic Senate of the University of California* (Berkeley: Institute of Governmental Studies Press, University of California, 1998), pp. 3–6, https://perma.cc/9UMD-UX3A.

[54] Taylor, 1998, *op. cit.*, pp. 1–8.

[55] Stadtman, V. A., *The University of California, 1868–1968* (New York: McGraw-Hill, 1970), pp. 239–257.

ROBERT GORDON SPROUL

Following Campbell, Robert Gordon Sproul became University of California president for a remarkable tenure of twenty-eight years, from 1930 until 1958. Sproul was a legendary figure with two impressive personal attributes—a booming voice and an amazing memory for names and facts. He was also not from the faculty. His background was in civil engineering, in which he had a 1913 bachelor's degree from the university, and in finance. Before becoming president at age thirty-eight, he had been simultaneously vice president for business and financial affairs, comptroller, secretary of the regents, and land agent for the university. The appointment of Sproul effectively resolved the issues of the functions of the Academic Senate, since it was natural for the senate to have its roles and influences with the president having no faculty background.

An early issue for Sproul was to deal with the effects of the Great Depression on the university. When it became necessary to cut state funding by 25 percent, the regents asked the president to consider salary cuts for faculty and pruning of the academic program. The president turned to the senate for assistance through the appointment of a Special Committee on Educational Policy, chaired by respected chemistry professor Joel Hildebrand (chapter 9), to consider the issues and provide advice. This committee recommended a formulaic means of applying salary cuts across the scale of faculty salaries, ranging from 2 percent for the lowest-paid faculty members to 7.6 percent for those at the top of the scale and on up to 10 percent for those with salaries above the scale and senior administrators.[56,57,58] The fact that the particular scheme for salary reductions had been devised by the faculty themselves greatly defused the intensity of the issue within the university. The senate valued the committee so greatly that they made it a standing committee, which it has been ever since, now both university-wide and on each campus.

---

[56] Taylor, 1998, *op. cit.*, pp. 8–15.
[57] Hildebrand, 1962, *op. cit.*, pp. 171–172.
[58] John A. Douglass, "Shared Governance at the University of California: An Historical Overview," Research and Occasional Papers Series, no. 1-98, Center for Studies in Higher Education, University of California, Berkeley, CA, March 1998, https://perma.cc/SMS7-B8PN.

Sproul was known throughout the state and was highly effective both in dealing with the state government in Sacramento and in building and sustaining public support for the university, even during the difficult years of the Depression. He was continually confronted with desires in various quarters of the state to create four-year state-supported institutions by means such as converting teachers' colleges, upgrading community colleges, or creating non-UC campuses de novo. There was also the matter of the status of, and prospects for, UCLA. Sproul's consistent approach was to keep the University of California as one university with one administration and to discourage as much as possible efforts to create new campuses outside the University of California. He initiated independent, external studies of higher education in California at various times.

Despite his different background, Sproul did as much as any UC president, except Clark Kerr, to build the university academically. He promoted the growth of research at Berkeley and more hesitantly at UCLA, including the remarkable development of the physical sciences at Berkeley described in chapter 9. He was key in keeping Ernest Lawrence well supported and encouraging his move to big science and what ultimately became the Lawrence Berkeley National Laboratory on the hill east of the campus in Berkeley (chapters 9 and 13).

World War II. Several developments associated with World War II and its aftermath created major and permanent changes for the university. As described in chapter 13, both Ernest Lawrence as an individual and his laboratory as an institution became vital cogs in national science policy and in the Manhattan Project, which produced the atomic bomb. Calutrons (California University tron) offered the first large-scale separation method for enriching uranium-235 at the Y-12 plant in Oak Ridge, Tennessee. These devices worked on the principle of the mass spectrometer, akin to Lawrence's cyclotron. The calutrons (figure 2-5) reflected Lawrence's own design, salesmanship, and doggedness in bringing them to sufficiently reliable working status.

Lawrence was also instrumental in the selection of Robert Oppenheimer, his theoretical-physicist Berkeley faculty colleague, to be the scientific director for the atomic bomb project at Los Alamos in New Mexico. As a result of Lawrence's efforts and World War II, the University of California came to manage three national laboratories:

Los Alamos, Livermore, and the Lawrence Berkeley National Laboratory. The wartime efforts of Lawrence and his associates placed the university in a favorable position for acquiring government grants for research as the number of these grants grew markedly after World War II, launched multidisciplinary research within the university (chapter 14), and gave faculty members who were also scientists in the Lawrence laboratory additional avenues toward support of research.

Figure 2-5. The alpha calutron "racetrack" at the Y-12 Plant, Oak Ridge, Tennessee, 1944. These devices prepared the initial enriched uranium-238 for the atomic bomb. ("Calutron," *Wikipedia*, https://web.archive.org/web/20160615091629/https://en.wikipedia.org/wiki/Calutron

On the economic front, the financial stringencies of the Depression of the 1930s finally ended, and the state developed a booming economy driven by defense industries, a budgetary surplus that was to benefit the university greatly in the years after the war, and a massive surge of population brought on by the first two factors.

Another event of the World War II era was the transfer of the Santa Barbara State College to the University of California in 1944, as described more fully in chapter 10. That transfer ultimately gave the university the challenge of upgrading what had been a normal school into a campus of a research university. With that transfer, the university had eight locations: the two general campuses at Berkeley and UCLA; the medical, dental, and nursing programs in San Francisco; the University Farm at Davis; the Scripps Institution of Oceanography at La Jolla; the Citrus Experiment Station at Riverside; the Lick Observatory near San Jose; and the newly acquired Santa Barbara campus—as well as two affiliates, which were at that point Hastings and the San Francisco Art Institute.

Post–World War II. The postwar period brought major growth for the University of California, with a great surge of returning veterans as students funded under the GI Bill [59] as well as large general demographic growth because of the attractiveness of the climate, geography, and living conditions of the state of California and the economic opportunities that it provided. Primarily because of the GI Bill, the enrollment of the University of California (all locations) swelled 65 percent from what had been a high of 29,767 in 1939–40 before and during the war to 49,122 in 1948–49, which was the high point of the postwar surge.[60] This enrollment was accommodated primarily at Berkeley (53 percent) and UCLA (34 percent), with the remaining 13 percent scattered among the other locations.

Sproul was a strong believer in maintaining the structure as one university and doing so through a single central administration to an extent that was viewed by many as extreme. His approach was to administer the Berkeley campus himself and then to have provosts at UCLA, Riverside, and Santa Barbara; however, relatively little was delegated to those provosts. Over time, the seemingly picayune nature of many of the matters that had to be sent to Berkeley for decision or approval by Sproul became legendary.

Shortly after World War II, in 1947, the University of California Regents commissioned a study to make "recommendations to the Regents for a properly balanced, coordinated administration." To carry this out, they chose the Public Administration Service, a nonprofit consulting firm serving public agencies. The report, submitted in 1948, recommended a decentralized structure very similar to the chancellorial structure now used.[61] However, Sproul effectively buried

---

[59] Glenn Altshuler and Stuart Blumin, *The GI Bill: The New Deal for Veterans* (Oxford University Press, 2009).
[60] "Enrollment," in Verne Stadtman, ed., *The Centennial Record of the University of California* (University of California Printing Department, Regents of the University of California, 1967), https://perma.cc/M8UT-8VV9.
[61] Eugene C. Lee, *The Origins of the Chancellorship: The Buried Report of 1948* (Center for Studies in Higher Education and Institute of Governmental Studies, University of California, Berkeley, 1996), https://perma.cc/3P29-H447.

this report, and it was not until 1952, under further pressures from the regents and the campuses, that he reluctantly formed separate chancellor positions for Berkeley and UCLA and created provost positions for Davis, Santa Barbara, and San Francisco, along with the one at Riverside. He did not define those positions well and did not pass along any substantial responsibilities to the two chancellors. Clark Kerr, who was appointed as the initial Berkeley chancellor, describes[62] the situation that he encountered, along with the ways in which he identified and built up desirable functions, notably in planning.

Another very positive and important development following World War II was the transformative decision by the US government to build its support of university-based research. This decision was based heavily upon a well-known 1945 report[63] from Vannevar Bush,[64] the head of the wartime Office of Scientific Research and Development. The formation of the National Science Foundation in 1950 and the building of the research-grant functions of today's National Institutes of Health; Environmental Protection Agency; and Departments of Energy, Defense, Interior, Agriculture, and so forth, are the result. As already noted, the University of California had an advantage in securing support from this infusion of federal funding, through the existence and distinction of Lawrence's laboratory and everything that had gone into it, as well as the distinguished research that had come from Berkeley sciences (chapter 9). Lawrence's Laboratory further blossomed and branched out into other areas in the postwar period, most notably through creation and identification of no fewer than ten transuranium elements (plutonium, americium, curium, berkelium, californium, einsteinium, fermium, mendelevium, nobelium, and element 106, now known as seaborgium) by Glenn Seaborg and his associates, all but the first in the period from 1946 to 1968.[65]

---

[62] Kerr, 2001, *op. cit.*, pp. 23–55.
[63] Vannevar Bush, *Science: The Endless Frontier*, Report to the President (Washington, DC: U S Government Printing Office, 1945), https://web.archive.org/web/20170612201238/https://www.nsf.gov/about/history/nsf50/vbush1945.jsp.
[64] G. Pascal Zachary, *Endless Frontier: Vannevar Bush, Engineer of the American Century* (New York: Free Press, 1997).
[65] Darleane C. Hoffman, "Glenn Theodore Seaborg, 1912–1999," Biographical Memoirs, National Academy of Sciences, 2000, https://perma.cc/9C5C-6MUF

The Loyalty Oath Controversy. Another major, yet negative, event for the university in the postwar period was what became known as the loyalty oath controversy and is described comprehensively by David Gardner,[66] Bob Blauner,[67] and, from the view of a faculty member and Academic Senate leader, Angus Taylor.[68] This was the first of three events over a fifty-year period from 1946 through 1995 when the regents involved themselves and the university politically in very visible and ultimately academically damaging ways. After World War II, there was considerable concern within the United States about subversion of the government by communists. This concern became manifest in many different ways, including through Senator Jack Tenney's Un-American Activities Committee within the California legislature and then later the well-known activities of Senator Joseph McCarthy on the national level.[69] Prompted by the activities of the Tenney committee in California, University of California Regents John Francis Neylan and Farnham Griffiths spurred the board to require all employees of the university to sign an oath of allegiance to the Constitution of the United States, specifically acknowledging that they were not members of the Communist Party or any other organization advocating overthrow of the US government. This was viewed by many as an attempt to use such a requirement to deflect accusations coming from various directions that the university was harboring subversives within its ranks.

An insightful summary analysis of the give-and-take surrounding the consideration of the loyalty oath issue is given by Stadtman.[70] With advice from the leadership of the Academic Senate, but also without an appreciation of the full spread of faculty opinions and the strengths with which they were held, President Sproul worked with the regents and accepted a resolution worded as follows:

---

[66] David P. Gardner, *The California Oath Controversy* (University of California Press, 1967).
[67] Bob Blauner, *Resisting McCarthyism: To Sign or Not to Sign California's Loyalty Oath* (Palo Alto, CA: Stanford University Press, 2009).
[68] Angus E. Taylor, *Speaking Freely: A Scholar's Memoir of Experience in the University of California, 1938–1967* (Berkeley: Institute for Governmental Studies Press, University of California, 2000), pp. 57–76.
[69] See, e. g., David M. Oshinsky, *A Conspiracy So Immense: The World of Joe McCarthy* (Oxford: Oxford University Press, 2005).
[70] Stadtman, 1970, *op. cit.*, pp. 319–329.

> The following oath [shall] be subscribed to by all members of the faculty, employees and administration of the University: "I do solemnly swear (or affirm) that I will support the Constitution of the United States and the Constitution of California, and that I will faithfully discharge the duties of my office according to the best of my ability; that I am not a member of the Communist Party or under any oath, or party to any agreement, or under any commitment that is in conflict with my obligation under oath."

This motion was adopted by the regents unanimously at their June 1949 meeting.

However, when the time came for the oaths to be signed in September of the same year, a large portion of the faculty chose not to do so; only 50 percent and 40 percent of faculty members at Berkeley and Los Angeles, respectively, had returned signed oaths.[71] Substantial arguments were made in various venues by faculty members in favor of academic freedom and against coercion and excessive intrusion. Sproul endeavored to moderate the situation, but the stances of the regents and many on the faculty hardened. In February 1950, the regents adopted by a 12–6 vote a resolution indicating that any faculty members who had not signed and returned oaths by April 30 of that year should be considered to have severed their relationships with the university as of June 30.[72] On March 1, Governor Earl Warren was quoted as criticizing the oath requirement as being one "that any communist would take...and laugh," and three days later, President Sproul publicly objected to the enforcement of the oath requirement. Yet the regents held firm (barely) with a 10–10 vote on a motion to rescind, which thereby failed because of the tie.[73] Ultimately, after review and consideration of individual cases, thirty-one faculty members were dismissed by the regents on August 25, 1950, by a 12–..10 vote. Among those faculty members were noted psychologist Edward Tolman and physicist and later UC president David Saxon.

---

[71] Stadtman, 1970, op. cit., p. 329.
[72] Taylor, 2000, op. cit., p. 66.
[73] Stadtman, 1970, op. cit., p. 331.

Figure 2-6. Faculty press conference on the loyalty oath controversy, March 1, 1950. Joel Hildebrand is fourth from the left.[74]

The nonsigners then brought suit against the regents, and the case was ultimately decided by the California Supreme Court in October 1952 in favor of the nonsigners, invoking an interpretation of state law that no state institution could separately require loyalty oaths or declarations other than those prescribed for all state employees. The regents chose not to appeal, and the faculty members were offered reinstatement, restoration of sabbatical-leave and pension benefits, and financial settlements equal to lost compensation above what they had received through any interim employment elsewhere.

The loyalty oath controversy received much coverage at the time and was a blot on the image of the university. Kerr,[75] Stadtman,[76] and

---

[74] Online Archive of California, California Digital Library, University of California, https://perma.cc/PMG5-BQGU.
[75] Kerr, 2001, *op. cit.*, pp. 27–28.
[76] Stadtman, 1970, *op. cit.*, p. 238.

Geiger[77] all note an incident at a board meeting of the Center for Advanced Study in the Behavioral Sciences at Stanford where, spurred by the loyalty oath controversy, Provost Paul Buck of Harvard initiated discussion on "Who Will Take Berkeley's Place in the Big Six?"—the Big Six being Harvard, Yale, Columbia, Chicago, Michigan, and Berkeley. Ultimately, Clark Kerr's answer, "no one," proved to be correct.

Research Recognition. One of the main reasons that Kerr's "no one" proved to be the right answer was the extremely strong recognition being given to Berkeley's research accomplishments at the time of the loyalty oath matter and in the years following it. No fewer than eleven Nobel Prize recipients of that period were or had been Berkeley faculty members in physics and chemistry whose recognized work had been done at Berkeley. Starting with Ernest Lawrence in 1939, the Nobelists included William Giauque (1949), Glenn Seaborg and Edwin McMillan (1951), Emilio Segré and Owen Chamberlain (1959), Willard Libby (1960), Donald Glaser (1960), Melvin Calvin (1961), and Luis Alvarez (1968). Eight of these ten were associated with the Lawrence Laboratory, bearing out emphatically the wisdom of Sproul's massive efforts to support and retain Lawrence (chapters 9 and 13). Although it was the Nobel Prizes in chemistry and physics that captured public attention, research distinction was also growing immensely in other disciplines at Berkeley and at the newer campuses.

CLARK KERR'S PRESIDENCY

Clark Kerr faced a number of fundamental planning and organizational issues when he became president of the University of California in 1958 following the twenty-eight-year tenure of Sproul. One of these involved the roles and relationships of the three different sectors of public higher education in California. Another centered on the statuses, natures of, and relations among the different UC campus locations around the state. A third was planning for a predicted

---

[77] Roger L. Geiger, *Research and Relevant Knowledge: American Research Universities since World War II*, (Oxford: Oxford University Press, 1993), p. 73.

forthcoming massive surge in college-age population. He attacked these issues simultaneously in a highly coordinated way.

Demographics. Underlying everything was the matter of projected demographics. It was estimated that the annual number of graduates from California high schools would increase by a striking 175 percent, from 123,800 to 341,400, between 1957–58 and 1974–75.[78] This prediction took into account births in California that had already occurred (a 210 percent rise from 1940 to 1959) along with an estimate of net migration into the state over the years to come and the increase in eighteen-year-olds associated with that net migration. For this purpose it was assumed that the rates of 1945–60 would continue. Another unknown factor would be the change in college-going rates of high school graduates, and, relating to it, changes in the California economy and the needs of the job market.

The California Master Plan of 1960. Handling such a surge of enrollment in higher education required greater agreement on the relative roles of the three sectors of higher education in California and the enrollments anticipated for each of them. The California State Colleges came under the State Board of Education, as did the K–12 school system of the state. The state colleges had for the most part started as teachers' colleges and had spread toward more general higher-education roles after 1935. They were jockeying in a relatively uncoordinated fashion to add master's and doctoral degree programs and to strengthen their positions relative to the University of California. Some community colleges sought wider roles and the ability to give the full bachelor's degree. There was much sporadic involvement from members of the legislature.

Clark Kerr, as the new University of California president, worked together with state assembly member Dorothy Donohue to arrange for a 1959 legislative resolution asking the Liaison Committee, the relatively ineffective body that was charged at the time with coordinating higher education in California, to produce a plan for California higher education. Importantly, the resolution also declared a two-year moratorium on legislative actions pertaining to higher

---

[78] Peter Hall, "Two Near-Disasters: California's New Campuses and Britain's National Library," in *Great Planning Disasters* (Berkeley: University of California Press, 1982), pp. 152–170.

education while this process took place. In effect, the legislature said that we'll give you two years to fix it yourselves, and then if you haven't done it, we will do so.

Although Kerr was not actually on the special committee that was formed, he was the principal figure in the negotiations that took place. The result was the 1960 Master Plan for Higher Education in California, which looks to many like a beautifully designed de novo plan, but was actually the result of multifaceted negotiations and compromise. The Master Plan served to fix the complementary roles of the sectors of higher education, establish the standards for eligibility of students and the criteria for transfer education, and methods of coordination, among other aspects. The path to the Master Plan, the reasoning behind it, and the effects of it are discussed in more detail in chapter 5.

The Campuses and the Structure of the University. For several cogent reasons, Kerr took several major and difficult steps that had the effect of creating the multicampus, single-university system of equal-opportunity campuses that the university has today. One driver, of course, was the fact that the size and geographical spread of the university were such that Sproul's structure of a single administration in Berkeley simply could not work well. A second large driver was the enormity of the demographic projections mentioned above. And a third driver was the discontent, especially at UCLA, about the lack of local autonomy and recognition.

The earliest step taken by Kerr was to affirm equal opportunity for UCLA—that is, that UCLA would given the same status as the Berkeley campus and would be able to develop to high distinction. This did away with the single-flagship-campus concept that has been part of university planning in other states and some countries.

In the late Sproul years, it had already been acknowledged that there would be enhanced undergraduate roles for Davis, Riverside, and Santa Barbara. Davis had been the University Farm for agricultural research and had already taken on undergraduate students. Riverside had "Watkins College" (chapter 10), which had been opened in 1954. Santa Barbara had been brought into UC in 1944 but had not yet been brought up to the nature or standards of UC. The late Sproul years had also seen the initial planning that led to choices of the general geographic areas for three entirely new campuses. In Kerr's early years, the specific sites for all three were chosen—La Jolla, the Irvine Ranch in Orange County, and the Cowell Ranch above Santa Cruz.

Upon his arrival as president, Kerr worked with the regents to establish that all six of these other campuses—the three new ones, along with Davis, Riverside, and Santa Barbara—would be general campuses, in that they would offer a wide spectrum of educational opportunities and would emphasize research and graduate education along with undergraduate education. They too would have the equal opportunity that UCLA was to have. Thus the multicampus university composed of campuses all with equal opportunity was fully established. Kerr and the regents believed that this large amount of expansion, made in recognition of a 27,500 per-campus cap on student enrollments on any one campus, was what was needed to accommodate the demographic surge projected for the years ahead.

Another major change made by Kerr was marked decentralization of governance of the university. The two chancellors of 1952 became chancellors for all six campuses in 1958 and for the three new campuses as they were formed. Academic governance and many administrative support functions were devolved to campuses, as is described in chapters 6 and 8.

Kerr took another important and vital step for the San Francisco campus when he acceded to the arguments of faculty leaders at that campus that the first chancellor, John Saunders, should be replaced. This enabled the launch of the singular and vital process that led in a remarkably short time to the rise of UC San Francisco to the very top levels of research (chapter 10).

Campus Unrest and the Dismissal of a President. In fall of 1963, Kerr delivered three Godkin Lectures at Harvard University. These lectures became the book *The Uses of the University* and included a passage[79] that was later cited in retrospect by Angus Taylor:[80]

> The undergraduate students are coming to look on themselves more as a "class"; some may even feel like a "lumpen proletariat." A few of the "non-conformists" have another kind of revolt in mind. They seek, instead to turn the

---

[79] Clark Kerr, *The Uses of the University*, 5th ed. (Cambridge, MA: Harvard University Press, 2001), p. 78.
[80] Angus E. Taylor, 2000, *op. cit.*, p. 145.

university, on the Latin American or Japanese models, into a fortress from which they can safely sally forth with impunity to make their attacks on society.

This is indeed what turned out to happen in a series of events starting in the fall of 1964 with the Free Speech Movement (FSM) at Berkeley. Student activism continued through the concern with People's Park in 1967 and several waves of other issues, many of which involved the Vietnam War. The surge of activism did not end until after the large student movement objecting to the invasion of Cambodia in 1970 and the shootings at Kent State University in Ohio that same year. Demonstrations and actions spread to university campuses throughout the United States, and indeed the world, but FSM at Berkeley was clearly the first.

The story of what happened at Berkeley is told in a book edited by Cohen and Zelnik,[81] in a documentary video,[82] by Kerr from his own viewpoint in the second volume of his memoirs,[83] by Taylor[84] from his vantage point as chair of both the Academic Council and Assembly of the Academic Senate at the time, and by Smelser[85] from the standpoint of a young faculty member brought into service in the Berkeley chancellor's office because of his expertise on crowd dynamics. Student unrest spread to other University of California campuses as well. The situation for the San Diego campus has been described by McGill.[86]

Kerr's approach was one of mediation and seeking compromise, befitting his Quaker upbringing and his experience as a labor negotiator. But the activists wanted attention and media coverage, not compromise, and they succeeded greatly in getting public attention. The resultant prominence made the unrest and the nature of the

---

[81] Robert Cohen and Reginald E. Zelnick, eds., *The Free Speech Movement: Reflections on Berkeley in the 1960s* (Berkeley: University of California Press, 2002).

[82] *Berkeley in the Sixties*, documentary video, directed by Mark Kitchell, 1990, https://perma.cc/EKS2-MR5X.

[83] Clark Kerr, *The Gold and the Blue: A Personal Memoir of the University of California, 1949–1967*; vol. 2, *Political Turmoil* (Berkeley: University of California Press, 2003).

[84] Taylor, 2000, *op. cit.*, pp. 145–219. See also, Taylor, 1998, *op. cit.*, pp. 69–73.

[85] Neil J. Smelser, *Reflections on the University of California: From the Free Speech Movement to the Global University*, chapter 1, "Spring 1965: An Analytic and Autobiographical Account" (Berkeley: University of California Press, 2010), pp. 9–55.

[86] William J. McGill, *The Year of the Monkey: Revolt on Campus, 1968–69* (New York: McGraw-Hill, 1982).

student demands a major political issue with much backlash. Former movie actor Ronald Reagan ran for governor of California in 1966 with "cleaning up the mess at Berkeley" as one of his main campaign issues. After he won election and became governor in 1967, the second large intrusion of state politics into the University of California of the second half of the twentieth century occurred. In January 1967 at the first regents meeting following Reagan's inauguration, Kerr was dismissed as president by the regents at Reagan's instigation by a vote of 14 to 8. Thus the academically most transformative president since Gilman was summarily removed over a political issue.

This action threw the university into an uncertain state, which calmed somewhat as the well-liked vice president, Harry Wellman, agreed to serve as acting president during a search for a new president.

TRANSITIONS

The dismissal of Clark Kerr by the UC Regents was a major point of transition for the University of California. It coincided with a change from a time of relative affluence in the state budget and in funding of the university by the state to a period of budget difficulties and uncertainty. It also is the point in time at which the academic structure, modus operandi, and quality-supporting aspects of the university had effectively become established. Interestingly, it was also (almost) the centennial of the university as well as two-thirds of the time from founding to the present day. Following Kerr's presidency, several challenges to academic quality arose, financial and otherwise. The main focus of building academic quality now changed to maintaining academic quality in the face of various stresses.

This is also the point at which the historical narratives and reflections of Stadtman's book and Kerr's memoirs leave off. The historical surveys available for the ensuing years are more fragmented. The approach of this chapter beyond this point will be to identify the challenges intermixed with further development and maintenance of academic quality, more or less chronologically and issue by issue. Many of these matters are developed further in the remainder of this book.

THE HITCH AND SAXON ERAS

Charles J. Hitch, the vice president for administration of the university, was appointed to succeed Kerr as president in 1968. Hitch was also a noted scholar of economics and had been one of the "best and the brightest" brought into the administration of President John F. Kennedy, where he had served as assistant secretary and controller in the Department of Defense. Previously he had been with the RAND Corporation. Hitch was succeeded in 1975 by David Saxon, a professor of physics from UCLA, who had been UCLA's executive vice chancellor and who had also been one of the faculty members dismissed and then reinstated during the loyalty oath period. Saxon served until 1983.

The terms of both these presidents were difficult times. Hitch was faced with dealing with continuing student activism and the resultant punitive desires of government officials. He did so effectively and without generating rancor himself. A tribute from three of the University of California's best who worked closely with him at the time noted that "Charlie was superb. He had the determination, the endurance, the integrity. His great victory was in preserving one of the best of all universities during one of the worst of all possible times."[87] David Saxon was described by himself and others as "a university president who is still a member of the faculty and is accepted as such, not as a foreigner but as a native of academe," as well as someone who had an immense understanding of the workings of universities.[88] Both were very well suited to their times.

Tightening of the California State Budget. Both Hitch and Saxon were faced with state budget difficulties. The budgetary stringency resulted from several sources. One was a general downward adjustment of state revenue following the postwar boom. Another was the negative view of the university in legislative and gubernatorial circles stemming from student activism. A third was the tax revolt that

---

[87] Frederick E. Balderston, Clark Kerr, and Angus E. Taylor, "Charles Johnston Hitch, Economics: Berkeley," In Memoriam, University of California, 1995, https://perma.cc/XEQ3-CGF3.
[88] Richard C. Atkinson, "David Stephen Saxon, President Emeritus," In Memoriam, University of California, 2005, https://perma.cc/5CLH-ZTAG.

led in 1978 to Proposition 13,[89, 90] the ballot measure that sharply reduced property-tax revenues to the communities of the state, thereby necessitating allocations of state funds to keep the public school system in operation. Yet a fourth cause was the unusual and inherently volatile nature of the revenue side of the state budget, described in the next section.

Keeping the university going through this fifteen-year period with no loss in quality was a large challenge, but that is essentially what happened through the perseverance of these two presidents.

The Volatility of California State Revenues and Budget. Since the 1978 passage of Proposition 13, along with subsequent ballot initiatives, California's state revenues have become both highly constrained and highly volatile. This situation strongly affects state funding of the University of California.

State revenues change substantially from year to year in ways that can be large and difficult to predict. Since there are also now limits on deficit spending,[91] this means that state expenditures must drop sharply downward in some years, unless voters approve bond issues. An increase in state spending during a time of boom revenue, followed by a downturn in revenue and resultant stringencies, led to the recall of Governor Gray Davis in 2003 through a vote of the electorate.

An unusually high percentage, 60 percent, of the revenue of the state of California now comes from income tax. The other major sources are sales tax and corporation tax. About 55 percent of income tax revenue comes from people with annual incomes of $500,000 or greater; that is, about half of income tax revenue comes from the top 1 percent of income earners.[92] This is the result of a wide distribution of incomes within the state and a highly progressive income tax structure. However, the highest wage earners have more opportunities to shelter

---

[89] "What is Proposition 13?," California Property Tax Data, https://perma.cc/4E55-HACC.
[90] Arthur O'Sullivan, Terri A. Sexton, and Steven M. Sheffrin, *Property Taxes and Tax Revolts: The Legacy of Proposition 13* (Cambridge University Press, 2007).
[91] "Proposition 58: The California Balanced Budget Act", https://perma.cc/MUD8-S583.
[92] "California's Major Revenue Sources and Tax Agencies," Legislative Analyst's Office, State of California, February 23, 2015, https://perma.cc/5ZPF-HRCB.

income from taxation, and they take advantage of them. Income tax on capital gains constitutes a large portion of tax liability of the highest earners and hence a large portion of total income tax revenue to the state. Capital-gains-tax revenues vary sharply from year to year depending upon the economy and incentives for sales of stocks and other properties. This is a prime factor making for the large year-to-year volatility in state revenue.

Further complicating the situation, only about 10 percent of California state expenditures are discretionary to the legislature, and higher education appears in that discretionary portion of the budget along with prisons and other needs. The remaining 90 percent of the budget is mandated in various ways and is thereby not subject to legislative control. One cause of the high percentage of mandated expenditures was the 1988 passage by the voters of Proposition 98,[93] which specified the portion of the state budget that must go to school expenditures, including both K–12 public schools and community colleges. Although Proposition 98 provides schools and community colleges a specified 40 percent of the state budget,[94] other aspects of the nondiscretionary budget require specified absolute payments. Hence the variability of the discretionary portion of the budget from year to year becomes, as a percentage, even greater than that of the state budget as a whole. The developments that led to these budgetary restrictions in California stemmed largely from voter-initiated ballot measures, as described in more detail by others.[95, 96] Some of the initiatives have mandated expenditures without supplying the necessary corresponding revenue source.

Finally, as for most states in the United States, retiree benefits are a growing portion of the state budget, both because of the burden of longer lives on defined-benefit plans and because contract settlements with public-employee unions have at times mortgaged the future by

---

[93] "Proposition 98 Primer," Legislative Analyst's Office, State of California, February 2005, https://perma.cc/XP6M-S9A8.
[94] Or an increase equivalent to the percentage increase in the product of enrollment and cost of living, if that is greater.
[95] Peter Schrag, 1998, op. cit.
[96] Joe Mathews and Mark Paul, *California Crackup: How Reform Broke the Golden State and How We Can Fix It* (Berkeley: University of California Press, 2010).

increasing retirement benefits as an alternative to increasing current wages.

The history and causes of fluctuations and restrictions in state funding for the University of California from the end of the Kerr era to the present have been well summarized and depicted by Wellman.[97]

The fluctuations and constraints associated with state revenue have had continual effects upon the University of California, as is described in succeeding sections. Multiyear budgeting would be one way of smoothing out the booms and busts. The present governor of California, Jerry Brown, has encouraged the buildup of a "rainy day" fund that can be carried over from year to year; however, it is difficult to keep such funds from being spent without some sort of constitutional protection. Greater diversification of types of taxation revenue would be another avenue toward reducing the volatility. However, given the current antipathy of the public and hence politicians to increased taxation, that route too is difficult and might necessitate a constitutional convention in order to be accomplished.

Development Operations. Looking to the future, Saxon strongly encouraged the campuses to grow their development, or private fund-raising, activities.[98] Although private funds had provided half or more of the financial support of the one-campus university in the early years, public funds had been dominant since the increases of the Wheeler era. Furthermore, there had been, in effect, a tacit arrangement between the University of California and the private universities, notably Stanford, that organized private fund-raising was an arena left for the private universities with the understanding that the private universities would support the budget requests of the University of 33California to the state. UCLA and UCSF changed that course and built up fund-raising first, as did some professional schools (Business, Engineering, and Law) at Berkeley. Only in 1983 did Berkeley add its first true vice chancellor for development, who promptly went to work

---

[97] Jane Wellman, "Historic Dynamics Shaping the Higher Education Budget in California," commissioned background research for "Securing the Public Trust: Practical Steps toward Higher Education Finance Reform in California," College Futures Foundation, 2016, https://perma.cc/V4U3-ZTPL.
[98] Patricia A. Pelfrey, 2004, *op. cit.*

on the matter of private funds to lever with state funding for the biosciences reorganization project that is described in chapter 12.

Admissions Issues. It was also in the Hitch and Saxon eras that affirmative action for admissions crystallized as an issue. This is a complex and sensitive matter examined in chapters 15 and 16.

As background, California has acquired and is still developing a population that is extremely diverse ethnically. As of 2014 it is the second state of the United States (after New Mexico) where the Latino[99] population has exceeded the white or Caucasian population.[100] For 2014, California's population (all ages) was 38.6 percent Hispanic or Latino, 38.5 percent non-Hispanic white, 14.5 percent Asian, 6.5 percent black or African American, 1.7 percent American Indian, 0.5 percent Native Hawaiian or other Pacific Islander, and 3.7 percent two or more (i.e., mixed) races.[101]

The percentages of high school graduates from these ethnic groups achieving eligibility for the University of California differ greatly. The last eligibility survey[102] done by the California Postsecondary Commission before it was defunded in 2011 examined eligibility data for students graduating from high school in 2007. It found that 29.4 percent of Asians, 14.6 percent of whites, 6.9 percent of Latinos, and 6.3 percent of blacks were eligible for the University of California, for an overall eligibility rate of 13.4 percent. The large differences among ethnicities reflect culture and traditions, income differences, and the considerable differences in quality of the public school systems around the state. The eligibility percentages for blacks and Latinos had been even lower in earlier eligibility studies, in the range of 3–5 percent.

---

[99] Analyses of race and ethnic background are complicated by several factors. Terms such as *Latino* and *Asian* are each inclusive of a number of ethically quite different populations, as is the term *Caucasian*. There is also a significant and sharply growing mixed-race population.
[100] Mark Hugo Lopez, "In 2014, Latinos Will Surpass Whites as Largest Racial/ethnic Group in California," *Pew Research Center*, January 24, 2014, https://perma.cc/UHC7-5QS4.
[101] "Population Estimates, July 1, 2015", https://web.archive.org/web/20161110234841/http://www.census.gov/quickfacts/. These figures add up to a bit over 100 percent since nonwhite Hispanics (Latinos) are counted twice.
[102] California Postsecondary Education Commission, "University Eligibility Study for the Class of 2007," Report no. 8-20 (December 2008), https://perma.cc/9KY5-ZJGE.

Such disparities have major import for public universities, since they by definition emphasize access and are both seen and intended as routes of upward mobility in society. In addition to simply being matters of fairness, the differences are also politically important in dealings with the state government.

More or less simultaneously with the arrival of national affirmative action policies in the 1960s, the University of California undertook efforts of various sorts to increase attendance by students from the underrepresented groups at the university. Since eligibility requirements were fixed and depended upon grade point averages in college-going courses and standardized test scores, efforts were directed in two directions: (1) outreach to underrepresented communities to increase the achievement of eligibility by students from those groups and (2) special considerations for underrepresented groups in admissions decisions by oversubscribed campuses as they chose among eligible students. These activities are considered in more detail in chapters 15 and 16.

Using underrepresented-minority status as a criterion for admissions in public universities was, is, and will continue to be a highly charged political issue. In 1974 a lawsuit arose over what was then the practice of the UC Davis Medical School to put aside 16 percent of the slots in its entering class for underrepresented minorities. A denied applicant, Allan Bakke, contended that he had qualifications that were superior to those of some of the minority-group applicants who were admitted, and that therefore he should have been admitted. The case went ultimately to the Supreme Court of the United States, which in a complex, multiopinion decision declared that the quantitative quota was not constitutional but that it was permissible for under-represented-minority status to be taken into account as one among many factors in making university admissions decisions. The Bakke decision then governed admissions policies at US universities, including the University of California, until the adoption of the UC Regents' resolutions in 1995 (see below and chapter 15).[103]

---

[103] Howard Ball, *The Bakke Case: Race, Education, and Affirmative Action* (Lawrence, KS: University Press of Kansas, 2000).

THE GARDNER ERA

David Gardner became president of the University of California in 1983. In his student days at Berkeley, he had been driver for Clark Kerr and had written a definitive book on the loyalty oath controversy as his doctoral dissertation project. He had been vice president of UC for extended academic and public service programs and then president of the University of Utah before returning to the University of California as president.

A Surge in the State Budget for UC. Gardner arrived almost simultaneously with a new governor, George Deukmejian. The two bonded well, and together they were able to propose and work with the legislature toward approval of a state budget for 1984–85 that increased the state operating funds for the University of California by a remarkable 30 percent, the largest percentage increase in the history of the university. The strong budgets continued throughout most of Gardner's presidency and Deukmejian's eight-year governorship, although budget difficulties did develop again in the last two years of the Gardner presidency at the start of the 1990s. The 1984–85 increase enabled the university to recover within a single year from the stringencies of the previous sixteen years. State capital budgets for the university also increased greatly, by a factor of nearly fifteen(!), from $16.5 million in 1983 to $240 million in 1993.[104] In his memoirs[105] and an oral history,[106] Gardner has provided his own analysis of the ways in which his relationship with Deukmejian developed and the arguments to the governor that were persuasive.

The enhanced budget enabled the return of faculty salaries to the levels corresponding to the Comparison-8 methodology (chapter 17), facilitated numerous academic initiatives in both education and research, and considerably upgraded faculty morale, which had lagged during the sixteen years of stringent state funding.

---

[104] Pelfrey, 2004, *op. cit.*, pp. 62–64.
[105] David P. Gardner, *Earning My Degree: Memoirs of an American University President* (Berkeley: University of California Press, 2005), pp. 199–208.
[106] David P. Gardner, interview by Ann Lage, *A Life in Higher Education: Fifteenth President of the University of California at Berkeley, 1983–1992* (Berkeley: Oral History Office, University of California, 1995–96), pp. 244–252, https://archive.org/details/highereducation00gardrich.

Ten-Meter Telescopes.[107] One venture that had begun during David Saxon's presidency and reached fruition during David Gardner's presidency was the project, joint with Caltech, for construction of two matched and interacting ten-meter telescopes (figure 2-7) atop Mauna Kea on the Big Island of Hawaii. These telescopes, still the largest in the world, are known as the Keck telescopes, named after the person who endowed the donor foundation. These telescopes have enabled the UC campuses and Caltech to have state-of-the-art observing facilities and have had much to do with the stature and accomplishments in astronomy at Caltech and on several of the UC campuses. The telescopes use an innovative adaptive segmented-mirror design, conceived by Jerry Nelson of the University of California.[108] The first Keck telescope had first light in 1993, and the second in 1996. The National Aeronautics and Space Administration (NASA) became an additional partner in 1996.

Figure 2-7. The Twin Keck telescopes atop Mauna Kea, Hawaii ("W. M. Keck Observatory," *Wikipedia*, https://perma.cc/K7ZH-AGPR)

---

[107] The author, as university-wide provost of UC, had the privilege of chairing the board of the California Association for Research in Astronomy, which oversees the Keck Telescopes, 2003–2006, preceded by being vice chair, 2000–2003.

[108] Lynn Yarris, "Keck Revolution in Telescope Design Pioneered at Lawrence Berkeley Lab,", *Science Beat*, Lawrence Berkeleley Nationak Laboratory, Winter 1992, https://perma.cc/3US8-YFCX.

The Keck telescopes have an interesting story behind their funding. First, a naming gift[109] for the original telescope was pledged to David Gardner by a wealthy widow who died unexpectedly the next day without the papers yet having been signed. Second, it was decided to build a second telescope to take advantage of capabilities created by the use of interferometry joining the two telescopes, which also enabled the gift from the Keck Foundation. Third, the Keck Foundation decided to fund both telescopes once the second telescope was put forward. Fourth, the Keck Foundation decided that it would fund the private university (Caltech) but not the public one (UC).[110] UC then shared costs by providing operating funds for the first twenty-five years.

A subsequent project for a still larger thirty-meter telescope, also using the segmented-mirror design and again the largest in the world, is currently (2017) being carried out by a partnership consisting of Caltech, the University of California, and governmental organizations of Canada, China, India, and Japan. The Gordon and Betty Moore Foundation is funding both UC and Caltech for this purpose.[111] The estimated cost as of 2010 was about $1.5 billion. The telescope is intended for another site atop Mauna Kea but has been caught up in political and legal proceedings relating to siting and permitting. The University of Hawaii is landlord for the mountaintop, which is also considered to be sacred ground by native Hawaiian people.

Initiative for a New Campus. Projections of enrollment made during the 1980s recognized that rates of net in-migration to the state were once again increasing and that there was a steady increase in the "take" rate, the percentage of UC-eligible students who actually enrolled. Also the "echo" of the post–World War II baby boom (the children of the "boomers") would begin increasing student demand around 1995. From the data, it was apparent that in the early 2000s the university would run out of capacity to accommodate all eligible students.[112] Recognizing these facts and the lead time required for

---

[109] A naming gift places the donr's name on the facility.
[110] Gardner, 2005, *op. cit.*, pp. 212–219.
[111] Thirty Meter Telescope, https://perma.cc/7QA6-WS4Z.
[112] See, e.g., figure 1.1, p. 5, of Karen Merritt, "Why a New Research University at Merced?," in Karen Merritt and Jane F. Lawrence, eds., *From Rangeland to Research University: The Birth of*

creating new campuses, President Gardner devoted a meeting of the regents in 1988 to long-range-enrollment planning, making a case for up to three additional campuses to open in the early 2000s as the way to accommodate growth under the Master Plan while not overtaxing the carrying capacities of the existing campuses.[113, 114] After ensuing explorations with the legislature and others, Gardner limited the initiative to one new campus, to be opened around the year 2000.

The processes of site selection and planning for the new campus were started soon thereafter, proceeding forward in stages. By virtue of constitutional autonomy, this process was carried out within the university under the auspices of the UC Regents, not within the state government. The first step was to examine three geographical bands—northern, central, and southern—across the state to determine by needs analysis and other means which general area was most appropriate for the new campus. The central band, specifically the San Joaquin Valley, was determined as the most suitable general area, since the Valley was the largest unserved population area of the state and had a participation rate at the University of California only half the statewide average. In 1989, the regents established a Site Selection Task Force composed of regents and UC administrators to analyze and make recommendations for a San Joaquin Valley site.[115]

The process slowed down through the early 1990s as the university went through the period of financial stringency described below. But in July 1995, the process had been brought to the point where there were three finalists from among which a site near the city of Merced was chosen. The other two finalist sites were closer to the city of Fresno, which has over six times the population of Merced. Reasons for the selection of the Merced site included the donation of a single large plot of land, secure water rights, and a well-organized and effective citizens' group supporting the campus.

Voluntary Early Retirement Incentive Programs. In the early 1990s, California's economy and revenues took major downswings.

University of California, Merced (San Francisco: New Directions for Higher Education, Jossey-Bass, 2007).
[113] Gardner, 2005, *op. cit.*, pp. 240–245
[114] Gardner, 1995–96, *op. cit.*, pp. 447–459.
[115] Merritt, 2007, *op. cit.*, p. 5.

Starting with the 1991–92 budget, state funding for the University of California fell below what a continuation of prior practices would have provided by hundreds of millions of dollars per year, with the shortfall growing continually over three years. In all, from 1990 to 1996, state appropriations to UC dropped by 20 percent. By contrast, the University of California Retirement System [116] was considered overfunded and had even been providing a "holiday" from both employer and employee contributions starting in 1990 and ultimately lasting until 2010. The overfunding and the lack of need for contributions reflected what had been very successful investment of funds already in the plan.

The decision was made in the final year of the Gardner presidency to institute a Voluntary Early Retirement Incentive Program (VERIP).[117] When the state financial situation deteriorated further the next year, a second such program was offered, and when state finances worsened further in the third year, yet another such program was offered. The three programs had the effect of transferring massive amounts of salary expenditures from the state budget to the retirement system.[118] All told, nearly two thousand faculty members and over ten thousand staff members accepted retirement. The most generous of these programs, the third, added five years of service credit and three years of age in the retirement formula.[119]

Since slightly over 20 percent of UC's regular faculty members elected retirement under the VERIPs, there could have been very large, negative effects on academic standing if the university had lost its most recognized people in academic fields or if big names had retired from UC and transferred to other, competing universities. As well,

---

[116] The University of California has its own retirement system (UCRP), independent of the Public Employees Retirement System (PERS), which covers other public employees within the state.
[117] Ellen S. Switkes, "The University of California Voluntary Early Retirement Incentive Program," in Robert Clark and P. Brett Hammond, eds., *To Retire or Not? Retirement Policy and Practice in Higher Education* (Philadelphia: University of Pennsylvania Press, 2001). See also the summary of this article, "Looking Back on the VERIPs: Who Took Them, and What Effects Did They Have?" *Notice* 25, no. 1 (October 2001), Academic Senate, University of California, https://perma.cc/EL8X-CRL8.
[118] Gardner, 2005, *op. cit.*, pp. 326–332.
[119] For employees hired prior to July 1, 2016, the retirement system has been a defined benefit plan, based upon the products of three factors: the HAPC (highest average plan compensation—the average of the highest three years of covered salary), an age factor, and years of service.

enrollments did not decline, and thus the burdens on the remaining faculty members could be expected to increase. The potential effects of those concerns were largely offset in several ways. Taking the Berkeley campus as an example, there was provision for continued office and laboratory space for VERIP faculty retirees, including the creation of a new title, professor of the graduate school,[120] which would enable retired faculty members to continue research and supervise students. Second, if they wished, those newly retired faculty members could be recalled to do teaching at a much lower cost per course, and many did so. The third remedy, enabled by the fact that the "take" rate on the third VERIP was greater than anticipated, was a substantial rate of hiring of new faculty members, who were at earlier points in their careers and thereby drew lower salaries than the VERIP retirees had. Since this was a time of relatively low faculty hiring by universities across the United States, UC found itself in the pleasant situation of a buyer's market for new faculty. The loss of support staff members was more of a problem and caused difficulties until time and readjustments improved the situation.

The University of California VERIPs of the early 1990s have now formed a large database for retrospection and through which possible effects of such programs for other institutions can be judged (see, e.g., Switkes[121] and Pencavel[122, 123]).

The VERIPs were a clear success at the time as a way out of a very difficult budget situation. However, they did have two problematic longer-term effects. The first was the shock to the retirement system, which became significantly less overfunded and then dropped to being somewhat underfunded as the years went on (see below). The second effect is that the success of the VERIPs in absorbing state budget cuts may have created an unrealistic assumption at the state level that it

---

[120] The title was initially professor *in* the graduate school, but then the resultant acronym was recognized.
[121] Switkes, 2001, *loc. cit.*
[122] John Pencavel, "The Response of Employees to Severance Incentives: The University of California's Faculty, 1991–94," *The Journal of Human Resources* 36, no. 1 (2001), pp. 58–84.
[123] John Pencavel, "Faculty Retirement Incentives by Colleges and Universities," pres. at TIAA-CREF Institute Conference, *Recruitment, Retention, and Retirement: The Three R's of Higher Education In the 21st Century*, New York, NY, April, 2004, https://perma.cc/49LC-PZMJ.

was not so difficult for the University of California to take budget cuts after all. Yet the VERIPs were a one-time possibility, relating to the overly comfortable funding of the retirement system at the time.

THE TURN OF THE MILLENNIUM[124]

Jack Peltason, chancellor of the Irvine campus, became University of California president in 1992 upon the departure of David Gardner. He was followed as president by Richard Atkinson, who served as president from 1995 until 2003.

Affirmative Action, Redux. In 1995, after twelve years of Republican governors, the Regents of the University of California were very largely Republican appointees, yet in a state where the legislature had been heavily Democratic for years. The tensions surrounding affirmative action for admissions and employment were stoked up again that year during the short-lived campaign of the California governor, Pete Wilson, for the Republican nomination for the presidency of the United States. That time coincided with the strong interest of several regents in doing away with preferences of any sort in UC admissions and employment. In connection with the presidential campaign, affirmative action was seen as a "wedge" issue[125] that would divide and/or draw supporters of other candidates. Thus came about the third large intrusion of politics into University of California affairs in the second half of the twentieth century.

In July of 1995, the UC Regents adopted, by substantially split votes, two resolutions calling for an end to any kinds of preferences, including by race or ethnicity, in admissions and employment. They did so less than sixteen months before the passage of a statewide referendum, Proposition 209, which would, and did, accomplish the same end. The regents adopted these resolutions even though Proposition 209 was already under development for the ballot at the

---

[124] These are the years (1994–2004) when the author was part of the university-wide administration, first as vice provost for research for a year, and then as provost and senior vice president for academic affairs for the remainder of the time. For most of this period (1995–2003), Richard Atkinson was president.
[125] USLegal.com, "Wedge Issue Law and Legal Definition," https://perma.cc/N2TV-5UKR.

time. Thus the university was placed in a singular position rather than being left to conform to state law however the ballot proposition turned out. The episode has been detailed and analyzed by both Douglass[126] and Pusser,[127] and is also explored at greater length in chapter 15.

Another result of the passage of these two resolutions of the UC Regents was a sharp split between the UC Regents and the Democratic legislative leadership, and in particular the Latino Caucus within the legislature. That split brought about political complications for the university on budget and other state-government matters.

Admissions Readjustment. As is described in more detail in chapter 15, the UC Regents' resolutions and the adoption of Proposition 209 into the California Constitution led, over several years, to fundamental reexaminations by the University of California of its eligibility and admissions requirements. The significant changes made were (1) addition of the top percentage of each school as eligible; (2) institution of a comprehensive review policy consisting of fourteen allowable criteria for selection among eligible students applying to oversubscribed campuses; and (3) a change in national testing policies for the SAT, spurred by President Atkinson, a well-recognized scholar himself in psychology.

Educational Outreach and School Partnerships. Part of the 1995 resolution on admissions called for a large effort to design programs that could increase the eligibility rates of underrepresented classes of students. The university convened an Outreach Task Force, described in chapter 16, to define appropriate programs and the associated costs. The 1997 report of the task force defined two primary approaches— expanding work with individual motivated but at-risk students and building partnerships with schools. Both avenues for outreach were funded by the legislature in the next state budget, and in 2000 total funding for school and student outreach programs through the University of California rose to $328 million per year. Of that, $184 million came from the state, with the remainder from the federal

---

[126] John A. Douglass, *The Conditions for Admission* (Stanford, CA: Stanford University Press, 2007), pp. 151–183.
[127] Brian Pusser, *Burning Down the House*: Politics, Governance, and Affirmative Action at the University of California (Albany, NY: SUNY Press, 2004).

government, private foundations, and individuals.[128] The expectations associated with this funding required an enormous gearing up of programs carried out largely through campuses and coordinated university-wide at the Office of the President. Unfortunately these activities were cut back substantially after the peak year of 2000, in the face of new financial stringencies facing the state.

The California Digital Library and Online Research. The rapid growth of information-technology capabilities has unleashed new, more powerful, and faster avenues for doing research, bringing substantial changes and new capabilities to scholarship in many different disciplines.[129] A major research university must therefore give high priority to enabling its faculty members and students to take full advantage of evolving research methodologies. The University of California has endeavored to be at the forefront of supporting faculty in those ways, in line with the goal of sustaining and enhancing academic quality.

As well, during the last decades of the twentieth century, the cost of acquisitions of books and journals for university libraries grew sharply. This was the result of two major factors: (1) the continued exponential growth of knowledge, scholarly publications, and scholarly journals, and (2) control of much of the scholarly publishing industry by a few large conglomerate companies. In addition, storage needs for accumulated books and journals increased so much that in 1982 the University of California had to create two large regional storage facilities, one in the north at the Richmond Field Station near Berkeley and one in the south at UCLA. These facilities receive overflow books and journals from the libraries of northern and southern campuses, respectively, and are coupled with a system for rapid delivery of materials from them to users upon request, which in turn couples with a system for moving library books efficiently among campuses.

---

[128] Patricia A. Pelfrey, 2012, *op. cit.*, pp. 82–84.
[129] A study of seven academic disciplines demonstrates the importance to academic research of new capabilities based on information technology and shows how different the effects are from discipline to discipline: Diane Harley, Sophia K. Acord, Sarah Earl-Novell, Shannon Lawrence, and C. Judson King, "Assessing the Future Landscape of Scholarly Communication: An Exploration of Faculty Values and Needs in Seven Disciplines," Center for Studies in Higher Education, University of California, Berkeley, January 2010, https://escholarship.org/uc/item/15x7385g.

The University of California was then a leader in creating a digital library and associated capabilities that would provide a diverse digital collection and various means of utilizing modern information technology for research. It did so in the form of the California Digital Library,[130] which was launched as a project in 1997 and brought online in January 1999.[131] This online library provides access for UC users to a large collection of electronic books, journals, databases, and many other items and provides tools for working with them. It is one of the largest such libraries in the world in terms of accessible materials. Pursuing the digital library made enormous sense for UC for several reasons.

First of all, there was a need to enable faculty members to have full access to ways of doing research more effectively and efficiently and to do it from their desktop or laptop computers. As well, anything available electronically could offset the need for up to ten print copies in the individual campus libraries. The digital holdings would provide an instant library for the new Merced campus and indeed for any new and/or remote location. Furthermore the purchasing and negotiation power of the University as a whole could be brought to bear upon licensing arrangements for content of the digital library.

In line with UC's role of service to the state of California, the digital library was designed for as much use by the public as would be consistent with licensing limitations and was therefore named the California Digital Library rather than simply the University of California Digital Library. Public-access components of the California Digital Library are described in chapter 16.

The services restricted to University of California users, remotely as well as all UC locations, as of March 2016 were the following:
- Over fifty thousand licensed electronic journals and thirty thousand open-access electronic journals
- Digitized books, licensed from vendors (e.g., Springer), owned, or open-access

---

[130] "California Digital Library," https://perma.cc/AC58-CAUW.
[131] "With No Walls to Confine It, the California Digital Library Is Moving in Many Directions," *Notice* 25, no. 1, Academic Senate, University of California, October 2001, https://perma.cc/E5BC-FBVV.

- The UC Curation Center (UC3),[132] which provides ways for researchers, museums, libraries, and the like to manage digital data and information. Within it, the Merritt Repository Service[133] provides an interface and storage capacity for depositing, sharing, managing, and preserving data long-term, including providing control over access and permanent identifiers (persistent URLs).
- The UC Shared Images project,[134] providing a repository of shared images (art, maps, architecture, and so forth) that can be used interchangeably for instruction in University of California courses.

Open-Access, Electronic, and Multimedia Publishing. In response to soaring library costs, monopolization practices within the publishing industry, and desires to maximize both rapid dissemination and the reach of faculty publications, the University of California as of the late 1990s began an initiative to develop alternative publication methods that could break the cycle whereby the university's researchers supply their papers to private journals, who then use university researchers as (usually unpaid) reviewers and then sell the journals containing the universities' own research product back to the universities. This initiative has coincided with the worldwide open-access movement.

In 1991 Paul Ginsparg at the Los Alamos National Laboratory had started arXiv[135] as an open-access repository for physics preprints. Now hosted at Cornell University, arXiv has expanded to a number of other fields and as of March 2016 had received and posted over 1.1 million e-prints. Following this example, in 2000 the University of California launched eScholarship,[136] an open-access electronic repository for publications by University of California authors. Placement of materials with eScholarship is at the author's option and is subject to prior copyright considerations, although UC/eScholarship does not take copyright ownership itself. The Academic Senate of the University of

---

[132] "UC3: University of California Curation Center," https://perma.cc/28V2-ZGBP.
[133] "Merritt," https://perma.cc/H55S-RR9U.
[134] "UC Shared Images: California Digital Library," https://perma.cc/B3UR-ZCU2.
[135] "arXiv.org E-Print Archive," https://perma.cc/KZK3-PYCH.
[136] "eScholarship," University of California, http://escholarship.org/.

California adopted a resolution[137] in 2013 asking faculty members to grant to the university a nonexclusive, irrevocable, worldwide license to their research publications so that the papers may be placed into eScholarship for open access. This does not preclude subsequent publication in journals, which, however, should be compatible with the nonexclusive license to UC. This policy was extended and became UC presidential policy[138] in 2015.

eScholarship contains research papers, working papers, books, journals, conference proceedings, and previously published works for which the authors have secured, reclaimed, or retained copyright. As of March 2016, it had over one hundred thousand publications. Component units of the University of California serve as individual publishers, as the Berkeley Center for Studies in Higher Education is doing for this book, and design their own editorial policies. Open access is often equated with a lack of peer review, but open access and peer review are two independent issues, and open access does not equate to a lack of peer review. The publishing units can exercise whatever peer-review policies they choose. Units of the university can also publish e-books and print-on-demand (POD) hard-copy books through any of the many self-publishing services and then make them available through various marketing services.

Development and Opening of the Merced Campus. As noted previously, Merced had been chosen by the UC Regents in July 1995 as the site for the tenth campus. As Richard Atkinson became University of California president in October of the same year, the question became when and how to move forward on the Merced campus, and to what degree. This was primarily a matter of forecasting state funding, since it would be important to move along steadily once the project was launched to bring the campus into being. State budget projections were complicated by the year-to-year volatility of the state budget and slow recovery from the state financial stringencies of the earlier 1990s. There was also the question of when the campus would

---

[137] UC Systemwide Academic Senate Open Access Policy, Academic Senate, University of California, July 24, 2013, https://perma.cc/3Y4P-KR8T.
[138] UC Presidential Open Access Policy, University of California, October 23, 2015, https://perma.cc/8Y83-4CHU.

be needed to absorb capacity and how long a time it would take to develop the campus after its opening so that it could absorb the needed capacity. Finally, there was the universal problem associated with new campuses—the fact that it was seen by the nine existing campuses as competition for precious state resources.

As the budget decline leveled off in the mid-1990s and the VERIP programs absorbed much of the budget cuts, the decision was made to put the Merced campus in motion. A new position, vice provost for academic initiatives, was created in the Office of the President in 1997, with the Merced campus being primary among the initiatives for that vice provost. An agreement was reached with the state government to treat funding for the Merced campus as a separate line item in the state budget. This had the beneficial effect of visibly reducing competition between the Merced project and the budget for the nine existing campuses, but it also subjected the funding for the Merced campus to more political exposure and risk, and there were indeed powerful people within the state government who saw Merced as a low-priority use of the state budget.[139, 140]

The university undertook a search for a Merced chancellor and in 1999 appointed Carol Tomlinson-Keasey, who had been vice provost for academic initiatives. The project continued its turbulent course, complicated by permitting issues built around the presence of fairy shrimp, an endangered species, in vernal pools on the site. That matter provided an avenue for environmental lawsuits from those in the area who objected to the creation of the campus. There was then a decision to move the site to an adjoining golf course that had already received permits, followed by a need to finance the acquisition of the golf course, which was done with a grant from the Packard Foundation. This sequence of events was further complicated by ups and downs in the state budget and continual political dealings back and forth with the state government.[141, 142, 143] The new campus finally opened in fall 2005.

---

[139] Carol Tomlinson-Keasey, "A Delicate Dance," in Karen Merritt and Jane F. Lawrence, eds., *From Rangeland to Research University: The Birth of University of California, Merced*, New Directions for Higher Education, no. 139 (San Francisco: Jossey-Bass, 2007).
[140] Lindsay A. Desrochers, "A Fragile Birth," in Karen Merritt and Jane F. Lawrence, eds., 2007, *op. cit.*
[141] Tomlinson-Keasey, 2007, *op. cit.*
[142] Desrochers, 2007, *loc. cit.*

The academic organization, approach, and subsequent growth are described in chapter 10. This history contrasts sharply with the dynamic process through which the three new campuses of the 1960s were created.

Budget Partnerships and Compacts. A review of the University of California budget, budgeting procedures, and dealings with the state government on budget from the 1990s to date has been given in recent annual budget documents of the university.[144] After the budgetary stringencies of the early 1990s, the approach taken by the university with the executive arm of the state government was to establish a series of partnerships and compacts, which lasted through a succession of three governors. An effort to stabilize funding from year to year, these arrangements established an expected level of state funding for the university that was based upon enrollment and expected costs per student and/or student/faculty ratio. New initiatives could also be proposed and would be considered to the extent that additional funding could be made available. This approach did indeed provide stability for a number of years until 2008 and thereby facilitated planning.

Two problems developed with this approach. One was that the state legislature was not a party to the agreements and thus would make its own changes. If those changes were reductions from the governor's proposed budget, the governor could not add them back. The other problem was that in years of severe reduction in state income, often accentuated by the volatility of the state budget, both the Governor and the legislature would take whatever steps were needed to balance the budget regardless of the agreements. Following several years that were already quite stringent, the Great Recession of 2008–09 occurred and precluded funding for the compact then in place with Governor Arnold Schwarzenegger. The approaches to state budgeting since then through 2017 have been much more *ad hoc*.

---

[143] William Trombley and Carl Irving, "The Turbulent History of UC Merced," *National CrossTalk* 9, no. 1 (Winter 2001), https://perma.cc/RJ3B-XPGU.

[144] See, e.g., "Historical Perspective," pp. 195–210, in Budget for Current Operations, 2015–16, University of California, updated December 2014, https://perma.cc/4UCN-VPR8.

Research Initiatives. Another emphasis during the Atkinson administration was building appreciation of University of California research, and thereby building support for it at the state level. The Industry-University Cooperative Research Program (IUCRP) (chapter 18) was established in 1996 and then built up through a succession of add-on budget initiatives, reaching peak funding of $40 million annually from state, industrial, and UC sources.

Another state initiative during the Atkinson years stemmed from the interests of Governor Gray Davis, who through his previous service as a regent as lieutenant governor had come to appreciate the contributions of University of California research to the California economy. In 2000 he secured appropriation of capital funds ultimately in the amount of $400 million to establish what are now the four Governor Gray Davis Institutes of Science and Innovation (chapter 14). The state funding drew more than the required 2:1 match from nonstate sources, obtained mostly from industry. The four institutes deal with subjects that are considered important to the future economy of California—telecommunications and information technology, quantitative biotechnology, nanoscale systems, and information technology research in the interest of society.

The four institutes have served as spin-off points for new corporations based upon technology from the institutes. As well, at Berkeley the Institute for Quantitative Biotechnology served as a springboard for two other large, extramurally funded research institutes—the Energy Biosciences Institute)[145] ($500 million from BP over ten years, see chapter 18) and the Joint BioEnergy Institute[146] of the U. S. Department of Energy, funded at $25 million per year and operated by a consortium of four national laboratories (including Lawrence Berkeley and Lawrence Livermore) and three academic institutions, including the Berkeley and Davis campuses of UC.

National Laboratories. Historically, since World War II, the University of California has, by contract with the US government, provided management of three national laboratories—the Lawrence

---

[145] "Energy Biosciences Institute," https://perma.cc/7SN2-QCQ2.
[146] "JBEI Overview: From Biomass to Biofuels," Joint Bioenergy Institute, https://perma.cc/CX3D-EH6R.

Berkeley National Laboratory, the Los Alamos National Laboratory, and, once it was formed in 1952, the Lawrence Livermore National Laboratory. Because the latter two laboratories carry out nuclear weapons research and development and because of laws establishing openness of information, the two weapons laboratories are objects of particular attention from the media. During the Atkinson era, two quite public issues arose in connection with the Los Alamos laboratory (chapter 13). The first of these dealt with accusations that a laboratory scientist had removed classified material from the laboratory and possibly delivered it outside the country. The second involved the temporary disappearance of two classified portable computer hard drives within the laboratory for six weeks.

Ultimately, in a 2004–05 competition for contract renewal, the university changed its management roles at Los Alamos and Livermore so as to focus on scientific management, joining with industrial firms to create two limited-liability corporations, each to manage one of the weapons laboratories (chapter 13). These arrangements bring in more industrial and business expertise but can also dilute university oversight of, and involvement with, the scientific program. This, in turn, can lessen the value of university management.

THE DECLINE OF STATE FUNDING AND ADJUSTMENTS TO IT

The Decline of State Funding. The most marked event for the University of California in the early years of the new millennium was a sharp reduction in state funding for the university. This decline was part of a general national trend, but the severity of this drop for the University of California was accentuated by the volatility of state revenues, the small portion of the state budget that remained discretionary, and competition from other state budgeting needs.

The extreme severity of the reduction is shown in figure 2-8, where results for the California State University are also shown for comparison. Inflation-adjusted state funding per student for UC fell from about $25,000 in 2000–01 to about $10,000 in 2011–12. What was about 23 percent of university operations funding coming from the state at the start of this period became about 12 percent after the drop. Yet another measure of the impact of reduced state funding is the student-faculty ratio, which increased from 17.6 in 1989–90 to 21.1 in 2010–11.[147] More detail on the nature of the budget changes in these years is given in the annual University of California budget documents.[148]

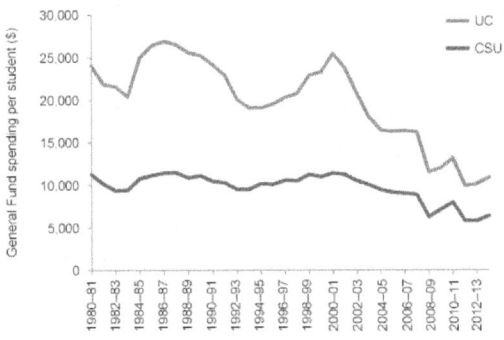

Figure 2-8. State General Fund Appropriations per Enrolled Student over Time, Inflation-Adjusted.[149]
[UC and CSU are top and bottom curves, respectively.]

Adjusting to the Situation. Accommodating to this large drop in state funding has been a considerable challenge, and of course there has been a larger issue of maintaining the academic quality and stature of the university through such a precipitous drop in its core budget. In addition to seeking and gaining operating efficiencies and reducing

---

[147] Nathan Brostrom and Patrick J. Lenz, "Revised Long-Term Budget Model," September 13, 2013 (PowerPoint), Display 11, https://perma.cc/AXB4-B89H.
[148] See, e.g., "Historical Perspective," pp. 195–210 in University of California, Budget for Current Operations, Summary and Detail, 2015–16, updated December 2014, https://perma.cc/F3FR-448Y.
[149] California Budget Project, "From State to Student: How State Disinvestment Has Shifted Higher Education Costs to Students and Families", May 6, 2014, https://perma.cc/7RX4-Z4EK. Hans Johnson, Kevin Cook, Patrick Murphy, and Margaret Weston, "Higher Education in California: Institutional Costs", Public Policy Institute of California, San Francisco CA, November 2014, https://perma.cc/2L2L-BRA5.

services, the university has increased student fees (now finally formally called *tuition*), selectively increased tuition further for specialized programs, admitted a greater number of nonresident students, and raised money from other sources. The resources were no longer present in the retirement fund to enable further incentive-retirement programs. One-third of all fee increases for undergraduates has been designated for need-based financial aid, now limited to California residents, so as to preserve access to the university.

Over the decade between 2002 and 2012, undergraduate tuition for California residents more than tripled, from $3,834 in 2002 to $12,192 in 2012.[150] Separate, much higher fees were instituted for a number of graduate professional programs.[151] In addition, fully self-supporting graduate professional-degree programs with still larger tuition charges have been created.[152] The tuition for nonresident students also increased greatly, with the annual supplement over resident tuition roughly doubling from $12,000 in 2002 to $23,000 in 2012. On the other hand, the steady dedication of one-third of fee increases to need-based financial aid for undergraduates has kept the University of California campuses at the very top among US universities in the percentages of their students who are from low-income families, as measured through Pell Grant data cited and analyzed in chapter 5 and in annual surveys presented by David Leonhardt.[153]

Historically, the University of California had been quite low in percentage of nonresident undergraduate students in comparison with other major research public universities. This reflected a view within the state government that UC is a prized taxpayer-supported resource,

---

[150] Johnson et al., 2014, *loc. cit.*
[151] "2014–15 Total Charges for Professional Degree Students by Program and Campus," appendix display 15, p. 225, in University of California, Budget for Current Operations, Summary and Detail, 2015–16, updated December 2014, https://perma.cc/4SU7-YQ69.
[152] "2015–16 Self-Supporting Graduate Professional Degree Programs," University of California, https://perma.cc/Z4C2-KZYE.
[153] David Leonhardt, "The Assault on Colleges—and the American Dream," and "Top Colleges Doing the Most for the American Dream," *New York Times*, May 25, 2017. See also appendix.

and as such should be primarily available to California residents. As a means of coping with the reduced state appropriations, the university undertook to increase the number of full-fee-paying nonresident undergraduate students, both from other states and from other countries, to bring in additional funds that could help support the education of in-state students. As of 2015 percentages of incoming freshman students who were not California residents had risen to 30-31 percent at Berkeley, UCLA, and San Diego, and 23 percent for the university overall. In 2017, the UC Regents limited the percentage to the values existing at Berkeley, San Diego, UCLA, and Irvine for the 2017–18 academic year, and 18 percent for the other undergraduate campuses.[154] This issue is discussed further in chapter 15.

An example of successful generation of funding from other sources to support the instructional program is a $113 million Hewlett Foundation gift[155] made to the Berkeley campus in 2007. This gift supported half of each of one hundred endowed chairs, for which $220 million of matching funds were raised in return for naming the chairs. After $25,000 scholarly allowance for the chair holder, one-third of the annual proceeds from the chairs are used for graduate student support, and two-thirds are used for the faculty salary pool, thereby defraying state funds that had been used for that purpose.[156] Beyond the graduate student support, a 4.5 percent annual yield results in a permanent annual offset for over $8 million for faculty salaries.

The Retirement System. Funding of the University of California retirement system interplays strongly with UC's other budget issues because of the large size of the retirement system and the particular history of funding for it. In 1990, at the start of the twenty-year period during which employees and the employer (i.e., the state of California)

---

[154] "Establishment of Policy on Non-Resident Student Enrollment," Regents of the University of California, adopted May 18, 2017, https://perma.cc/HCZ6-T3X3. Larry Gordon, "UC Adopts Limits on Undergraduates from Outside State, but Allows Some Growth," Edsource, May 18, 2017, https://perma.cc/X6BD-PGGR.

[155] José Rodríguez et al., "Campus Completes Landmark Hewlett Challenge—More Than Two Years ahead of Schedule," *Berkeley News*, November 5, 2012, https://perma.cc/YVP7-7685.

[156] Guidelines for Payout from Endowed Chairs and Professorships, rev. February 2013, University of California, Berkeley, https://perma.cc/ZY6H-CT2D.

did not pay into the UC Retirement Plan, the plan was funded at 137 percent of obligations. By 2010, through the payment holiday, less successful investment, and the use of the assets of the plan for the Voluntary Early Retirement Incentive Programs (VERIPs) of the early 1990s, the assets of the plan had dropped to 75 percent of obligations. Employee contributions were therefore resumed. However, the state did not resume annual coverage of employer contributions in the UC budget and left them as a major unfunded liability for the university, even though the state had continually funded employer contributions for the California State University and the community colleges. This placed a major additional financial burden on the university.

In 2016 an entirely new and financially more sustainable pension plan[157] was adopted for new employees starting July 2016. The change in the retirement system was necessary in order to maintain financial viability, since the structure of the pre-2016 defined-benefit plan was based on shorter anticipated lifetimes after retirement than now occur. However, the change also converted much of the coverage from defined benefit to defined contribution, thereby lessening what has been a considerable inducement for University of California faculty members to stay with the university throughout their careers.[158]

TROUBLED TIMES, 2005–08

Executive Compensation. In addition to facing the decline of state funding for the university and the issues associated with it, the University of California underwent a crisis of public image over executive compensation practices and charges of an endemic culture of secrecy relating to these matters. The issue actually began in 1992–93

---

[157] Recommendation for New University of California Retirement Program, Item F-1, Meeting of University of California Regents, March 23, 2016, https://perma.cc/MKN5-E7DV.

[158] A mid- or late-career University of California faculty member would have to weigh against a competing offer the fact that staying at UC would substantially increase the benefits available upon retirement. The changes are analyzed by J. Daniel Hare and James A. Chalfant, "A Guide to Reviewing the Recommendations of the Retirement Options Task Force," January 15, 2016, https://perma.cc/2P43-J7PX.

with outcries over the retirement arrangements made for departing UC president David Gardner, as described by Pelfrey,[159] articles from the press at the time,[160] and Gardner from his own viewpoint.[161] The essential issue was that the UC Regents had established enhanced retirement packages for the president and certain other senior executives with a requirement of a minimum duration of service for them to be eligible to receive it. The regents' procedures had enabled this arrangement to be set up by a subcommittee of the board without approval by the full board or release at the time as public information. When Gardner actually left the presidency, he was close to, but had not completed, that period of service. Because of the tragic and unexpected death of his wife, the regents approved granting the retirement package despite that fact. The objections to this arrangement that arose both in the media and the legislature related to the size of the packages, the less-than-public way in which it had been set up, and the ultimate exception to the original terms.

In 1992, in response to this episode, the UC Regents established principles for review of executive compensation.[162] These principles included approval of all aspects of compensation in open session of the regents and an annual summary report on executive compensation from the president to the regents.

In 2006 a major media conflagration erupted once again over processes, secrecy, and specific practices for executive compensation at the University of California.[163] This situation has been analyzed in

---

[159] Patricia A. Pelfrey, "Origins of the Principles for Review of Executive Compensation 1992-93", Research and Occasional Papers Series No. 6, 2008, Center for Studies in Higher Education, University of California, Berkeley, https://perma.cc/EUK8-XZTZ.

[160] See, e.g., Jack McCurdy, "University President's Retirement Package Criticized," *The Chronicle of Higher Education*, April 15, 1992.

[161] David P. Gardner, 2005, *op. cit.*, pp. 341–351.

[162] "Regents Policy 7201: Principles for Review of Executive Compensation,"Board of Regents, https://perma.cc/922L-ECCA.

[163] See, e.g., Todd Wallack, Tanya Schevitz, and Chronicle Staff Writers, "CALIFORNIA / UC Admits Regents Should Have OKd Extra Pay / Review Indicates Compensation Policies Violated," *SFGate*, https://perma.cc/C5VJ-H85F.
Paul Fain, "California Regents Meet with System President as Inquiry Into Pay Practices Continues," *The Chronicle of Higher Education*, May 26, 2006.

depth by Pelfrey.[164] One factor involved was that efforts were made to augment compensation in new ways beyond base pay so UC would remain competitive in an intense market. A second factor was reliance upon the annual report of executive compensation to describe full compensation rather than putting all aspects of compensation into the UC Regents' items for individual appointments. A third factor was the failure to submit the required annual reports for 2004 and 2005, apparently due to bureaucratic oversight. The university clearly made mistakes here, but, as Pelfrey shows in her referenced paper, both the media coverage and an external audit commissioned by the Office of the President made the departures from policy and process look much more widespread and secretive than they had actually been. The university could have defended itself more than it actually did but apparently made the choice not to do so and to take a mea culpa approach to the state government and the public instead.

The executive compensation crisis of 2006 placed the university in a bad public light with unfortunate fallouts of several sorts. There was a tragic suicide by a chancellor.[165] The issues concerning executive compensation clashed in the public eye with the severe financial situation of the state and the university. After a crisis of confidence in UC president Robert Dynes, the regents chose to elevate the university-wide provost to a position of chief operating officer for the university for a year, taking on many of the president's duties while a search was carried out for a new president.[166]

---

[164] Patricia A. Pelfrey, "Executive Compensation at the University of California: An Alternative View", Research and Occasional Papers Series no. 8, 2008, Center for Studies in Higher Education, University of California, Berkeley, May 2008, https://perma.cc/AQ93-HMML.
[165] Paul Fain, "Chancellor's Suicide Came after Months of Politicized Controversy and Angst over Her Compensation," *The Chronicle of Higher Education*, June 27, 2006.
[166] Richard C. Paddock, "UC President Announces He'll Step Down from His Post by June," *Los Angeles Times*, August 14, 2007, https://perma.cc/26K6-T6XJ.

TWO PRESIDENTS FROM OUTSIDE UC, 2008 TO DATE

As a result of the events of 2006 and 2007, the leadership of the regents concluded that a new look from outside would be valuable, and that the roles of the president's office should be revisited and probably downsized and refocused. The UC Regents engaged Mark Yudof, chancellor of the University of Texas System and former president of the University of Minnesota. He became the first president without previous University of California experience since Benjamin Ide Wheeler. About a month and a half before the announcement of his appointment Yudof had written a commentary[167] in the *Chronicle of Higher Education* on the subject of public-university systems, contrasting the limited and focused functions of the chancellor's office in the University of Texas system with those of the president's office of the University of California. This may have contributed or been related to his selection as UC president.

Soon after his arrival, Yudof and Russell Gould, chair of the Board of Regents, established the Commission on the Future of the University of California, which carried out an extensive set of deliberations, culminating in a 2010 report[168] that provided guidance for improving the match of program and resources in the years ahead. The report cannot be regarded as a plan in the classic sense, since it was primarily advisory to the other established forms of governance that are described in chapters 6, 7, and 8. Interestingly, Fethke and Policano in their book on the new financial situation for public research universities label this report as recommending the easy and obvious steps without delving into the changes in "governance structures, budgetary process, or reward and incentive structure that...are critical as universities become more self-reliant."[169] Chapter 21 explores in more detail the extents to which such changes are needed and feasible.

---

[167] Mark G. Yudof, "Are University Systems a Good Idea?," *Chronicle of Higher Education* 54, no. 23 (February 15, 2008): p. A37.
[168] University of California Commission on the Future, *Final Report*, November 2010, https://perma.cc/4KGK-5ULG.
[169] Gary C. Fethke and Andrew J. Policano, *Public No More: A New Path to Excellence for America's Public Universities* (Palo Alto, CA: Stanford Business Books, 2012), p. 19.

Restructuring of the Office of the President. Yudof did reduce the size and budget of the Office of the President markedly, through both shifting of reporting lines of programs to campuses[170] and eliminating functions and thereby positions. During his tenure (2008–13) and the subsequent administration of President Janet Napolitano (2013–present), people with more diverse experience and professional backgrounds were brought into high-level positions. One result was that the number of executive and senior vice presidents grew from three to six, while the number of career academics in positions of associate vice president or vice provost and higher was reduced from what had been five to three.[171] These changes may have accentuated the view from the campuses that the Office of the President is nonacademic or "corporate," a point further explored in chapter 6.

Innovations. Two effective innovations during Yudof's time were annual accountability reports and the creation of an understandable financial pledge to low-income students. The accountability reports,[172] the first of which was for the year 2009, provide essential public information on the University of California and its accomplishments and were designed to take the initiative in meeting growing accountability interests in the United States. These reports and the surrounding circumstances are described further in chapter 4. The financial pledge, known as the Blue and Gold Opportunity Plan,[173] ensures that a California-resident undergraduate student whose total family income is less than $80,000 a year will receive full coverage of tuition and fees. The Berkeley campus has taken that a step further with its Middle Class Access Plan (MCAP)[174] for students who are California residents and whose family income ranges from $80,000 to

---

[170] As examples, Continuing Education of the Bar (a large program of updating publications and continuing education for the legal profession) was shifted to oversight by UCLA, even though it geographically remained in Oakland, and the Sacramento Center was shifted to oversight by UC Davis.

[171] Or from six to four, if the health sciences position is included.

[172] University of California Accountability Report, 2015, https://perma.cc/K3VA-JNGH. See also the archive and subsequent reports.

[173] "Blue and Gold Opportunity Plan," UC Admissions, https://perma.cc/59JS-G8GS.

[174] "Middle Class Access Plan," Financial Aid and Scholarships, UC Berkeley, https://perma.cc/KWU3-WTW8.

$150,000 annually with typical family assets. For these students, MCAP assures that the contribution that parents make toward the annual cost of a UC Berkeley education (tuition, fees, and living expenses) is capped at 15 percent of their total income. Middle-income access has become an issue because of the increases in tuition, which are not offset by Pell Grants, Cal Grants, and other like programs.

Statewide Coordination. A key element of the Master Plan was a mechanism for statewide coordination of higher education, advisory to the governor and the legislature. This function was first carried out by the Coordinating Council for Higher Education and then the California Postsecondary Education Commission (CPEC). CPEC was totally defunded by Governor Jerry Brown as of 2011 (see chapter 4), reflecting his view that it was not needed. This has left California without a mechanism of coordination. That lack is almost surely unstable. If the situation is left as it is, one or more major issues will arise to which the answer is that there should have been better coordination among the sectors of California higher education. That, in turn, could lead to a rush toward establishing a more draconian mechanism of coordination with line authority—a structure which has worked poorly in most states that have it because of the direct impact of politics and political pressures on the coordination body. It would be much better, and a guard against such overreaction, to keep the sort of advisory body that CPEC has been and restore state funding to it.

A President with a Different Background. In appointing the president to succeed Mark Yudof in 2013, the UC Regents went in a different direction, selecting and securing Janet Napolitano, the secretary of Homeland Security in the federal government. Before that, she had been governor of Arizona, and she had not previously held a position in the university world. She is also the first woman to be president of the University of California.

There have been precedents for the appointment of research university presidents from other walks of life, usually from government but sometimes also from the military and industry. That approach has been analyzed by Beardsley.[175] Some other recent examples are the

---

[175] Scott C. Beardsley, *Higher Calling: The Rise of Nontraditional Leaders in Academia* (Charlottesville VA: University of Virginia Press, 2017).

appointments of former Indiana governor Mitch Daniels as president of Purdue (2013), former secretary of education Margaret Spellings as president of the University of North Carolina System (2016), and retired four-star admiral William McRaven as chancellor of the University of Texas System (2015). Some previous instances of this sort have, at least in part, brought unhappiness for the institutions and individuals involved (e.g., Robert King, legislator and budget director of the state of New York, who became chancellor of the SUNY system, 2000–05[176]; Tim Wolfe, former CEO of Novell Americas, who was president of the University of Missouri system, 2011–15;[177] and even to a degree Dwight Eisenhower as president of Columbia University, 1948–53[178]). Other cases have been more successful, notably former Oklahoma governor and US senator David Boren, who was president of the University of Oklahoma for twenty-four years from 1994 to 2018, and Robert Gates, who, following a career in the Central Intelligence Agency (CIA) that culminated in his being CIA Director, became president of Texas A&M University (2002–06). Gates then went on to serve as secretary of defense under a Republican and then a Democratic president (2006–11). Subsequent to that (2012 to date), he has been chancellor of the College of William and Mary, a largely ceremonial post in the British tradition.

A rationale for the appointment of university presidents or chancellors with high-level experience in government is that they will have the ability and insights to work effectively with the leaders of the state government to the benefit of the university. A former governor, cabinet secretary, military leader, or industrial executive will also have experience leading and managing a large and complex organization. However, research universities are different in that they are, for

---

[176] Karen W. Arenson, "State University Chancellor, a Pataki Friend, to Leave Post," *The New York Times*, April 5, 2005.

[177] Douglas Belkin and Melissa Korn, "University of Missouri System President Tim Wolfe Resigns," *Wall Street Journal*, November 10, 2015.

[178] Douglas E. Clark, *Eisenhower in Command at Columbia* (Lanham, MD: Lexington Books, Rowman & Littlefield, 2013); Stephen E. Ambrose, *Eisenhower: Soldier and President* (New York: Simon & Schuster, 1991), pp. 238–68.

reasons described throughout this book, institutions oriented toward faculty enablement and consultative governance. This structure is often difficult and unnatural for those who come into top university leadership from other walks of life. There is a large adjustment to be made to the expectations of shared governance, for example.

An interesting additional consideration for a person who comes from a successful political career to a university presidency is that he or she can be considered as a logical contender for statewide or national office. The relations of the university with the state government and the media can thereby become complicated by politics associated with that possibility.

With a nonacademic as president of the University of California, there are also implications for the continuing evolution of the respective roles of the university-wide and campus administrations (chapter 6). President Napolitano has strong background to carry out the responsibilities of the Office of the President in dealing with the state government and being the focal point for the determination and negotiation of the state budget for the university. However, another natural result is for the determination of the academic vectors of the university to remain all the more with the campuses, and in that sense the Office of the President can evolve more toward being driven by political and business needs, rather than academic needs. This can accentuate campus perceptions of a gulf of understanding between the Office of the President and the campuses. It is important to have respected long-time academics sufficiently represented in senior positions at the Office of the President so that their experiences are reflected in the decisions that are made at that level.

Summary Conclusion
The historical events that have been most important for the development of the academic quality and stature of the University of California include the following:
- the resolution of the Gilman-Carr disputes of the 1870s to have a university in the model of the great eastern US universities;
- the provision of constitutional autonomy in the California Constitution of 1879 (see also chapter 4);

- the development of early research facilities such as the Lick Observatory and the Scripps Institution of Oceanography and the demonstration by Hilgard and others of the utility of research to the state and to agriculture;
- the leadership of President Benjamin Ide Wheeler in emphasizing academic quality and securing improved funding by working with the Progressive movement in California state government;
- the leadership of Armin Leuschner, Edmund O'Neill, and Wheeler in recruiting Gilbert Newton Lewis in 1912, leading to the rise of physical sciences at Berkeley to the very top (see also chapter 9);
- the Berkeley Revolution of 1919, whereby the modern role of the Academic Senate was established and the nature of shared governance became codified (see also chapter 7);
- Ernest Lawrence and his laboratory, which developed many Nobelists and set Berkeley on a path of fostering multidisciplinary research (see also chapters 9 and 13);
- the development of the tripartite system of public higher education in California in the early twentieth century, which lessened undergraduate enrollment needs for the University of California and enabled it to focus on research and doctoral education;
- the subsequent codification of the tripartite system so effectively into the Master Plan for Higher Education of 1960 (chapter 5);
- the decisions over the years and particularly in the Kerr era (see also chapter 3) leading to the structure of multiple campuses all with the same research mission and opportunities;
- the state budgetary surplus that stemmed from World War II, and the high priority given by Governors Earl Warren and Pat Brown to using those funds to develop public higher education in general, and the University of California in particular;
- the work of Clark Kerr during his presidency to promote academic quality, decentralize, and institute a highly consultative governance structure (chapter 3);
- furtherance of multidisciplinary research, notably through the Governor Gray Davis Institutes for Science and Innovation (see also chapter 14);

- diversification of the student body economically and racially through emphasis on access as a high priority over the last five decades;
- enablement of forefront approaches to research and scholarship as the information age has developed, through means such as the California Digital Library and open-access publishing and research opportunities;
- sustaining the public and research missions and quality despite three large political intrusions into the university over the past seventy years; and
- managing through a major loss of state funding over the past several decades so as to sustain academic quality and diversify funding sources as best possible.

3.
The Kerr Legacy

Clark Kerr...created the blueprint for public higher education in the United States while president of the University of California system in the 1950s and '60s..."Clark Kerr did for higher education what Henry Ford did for the automobile," said Arthur Levine, president of Teachers College, Columbia University. "He mass produced low-cost quality education and research potential for a nation that hungered deeply for both."
—New York Times *Obituary*[1]

[Clark Kerr's] years at the helm—from 1952 to 1958 as chancellor of the Berkeley campus and from 1958 to 1967 as the university's president—were the golden years. Berkeley rose to the peak of scientific and scholarly stature during this period, and the contours for the rise of the University of California system to its preeminent place were laid with the invention and the consolidation of the 1960 Master Plan for Higher Education. As the university's visionary, architect, leader, entrepreneur, fighter, and implementer for those years, Kerr established his deserved reputation as one of the century's great figures in higher education.
—Neil J. Smelser[2]

The basic reality for the university is the widespread recognition that new knowledge is the most important factor in economic and social growth. We are just now perceiving that the university's invisible product, knowledge, may be the most powerful single element in our culture, affecting the rise and fall of professions, and even of social classes, or regions, and even nations.
—Clark Kerr, in 1963[3]

---

[1] Grace Hechinger, "Clark Kerr, Leading Public Educator and Former Head of California's Universities, Dies at 92," *New York Times*, December 2, 2003.
[2] Neil J. Smelser, Foreword to Clark Kerr, *The Gold and the Blue: A Personal Memoir of the University of California, 1949–1967* (Berkeley: University of California Press, 2001).
[3] Clark Kerr, *The Uses of the University*, 5th ed., Preface, 1963 (Cambridge, MA: Harvard University Press, 2001), p. xii.

The fact was that I had left the presidency of the university as I had entered it: "fired with enthusiasm..."
—Clark Kerr[4]

It is striking to recognize how much of the University of California as we see it today stems directly from Clark Kerr. Kerr was, after all, chancellor of Berkeley for only six years (1952–58) and president for nine years (1958–67), not unusually long times. Part of the reason for Kerr's importance is timing. He was chancellor at Berkeley as the chancellorship began, and he was president during a period of massive growth and restructuring of the university. But more of the reason was the nature of Kerr himself.

It was during Kerr's time as chancellor and president that
- the Berkeley campus completed its climb to top overall distinction,
- the decision was made to have a university composed of multiple campuses, all of whom would have the same mission and the same opportunities for development,
- the decision was made to proceed with the conversion of three existing sites (Davis, Riverside, and Santa Barbara) and three new sites (San Diego, Irvine, and Santa Cruz) into general campuses to accommodate much increased enrollment,
- the roles of the one president and now ten chancellors were defined in view of that model, and
- the current modes of consultative leadership and continual substantive review for advancement of faculty members came into being in their present forms.

Also, beyond the University of California, Kerr was the main intellectual force behind the 1960 California Master Plan for Higher Education and was, subsequent to his UC presidency, the leader of the Carnegie

---

[4] Clark Kerr, *The Gold and the Blue: A Personal Memoir of the University of California, 1948–1967, vol. 2: Political Turmoil* (2003), p. 309.

Commission on Higher Education and then the Carnegie Council on Policy Studies in Higher Education,[5] which produced an array of insightful and influential studies that has not subsequently been matched. Such a broad swath of accomplishment and initiative by any one person is effectively unparalleled in the definition and leadership of higher education in the United States. Although we will meet these accomplishments again at various points throughout this book, it is worth reiterating and summarizing them here.

KERR'S THINKING AND VALUES

In his Godkin Lectures, presented at Harvard in 1963 and written up in a book[6] that went through five editions with added chapters and prefaces in each new edition, Clark Kerr presented a highly insightful and prescient view of the ongoing development of the modern American research university. Among his themes were (1) the growing economic and social values of knowledge generated and codified by universities,[7] (2) the strong influences of two great forces—the land-grant (i.e., public-university) movement and the massive growth in support of research by the federal government after World War II, and (3) the consequent development of what he called the "multiversity," a complex university of many different purposes and functions, reflecting the societal value of knowledge, growth of multifaceted research, service roles, and synergies among those missions.

Kerr recognized three successive crucial struggles and resultant models that the University of California had gone through during its history.[8] The first was the contention in the 1870s that resulted in establishing that the university would be comprehensive, constitutionally autonomous, and based on the model of the great

---

[5] Arthur Levine, "Clark Kerr and the Carnegie Commission and Council," chapter 2 in Sheldon Rothblatt, ed., *Clark Kerr's World of Higher Education Reaches the Twenty-First Century* (New York: Springer, 2012).
[6] Clark Kerr, *The Uses of the University* (Cambridge, MA: Harvard University Press, 1963, 1972, 1982, 1995, 2001).
[7] See the quote at the beginning of this chapter.
[8] Clark Kerr, *The Gold and the Blue: A Personal Memoir of the University of California, 1949–1967*. vol. 1., Academic Triumphs (Berkeley: University of California Press, 2001, pp. 143–50.

private universities in the eastern United States. He denotes this as the Yale-Gilman model. The second struggle was during the remainder of the 1800s, resulting in the appointment of Benjamin Ide Wheeler as president in 1899 with a large transfer to the new president of responsibilities and functions that had previously belonged to the UC Regents. This strong-president model, labeled by Kerr as the Wheeler-Sproul-Academic Senate Model, continued through the first half of the twentieth century and the presidency of Robert Gordon Sproul. That model was substantially enhanced by the buildup of research eminence in the physical sciences (chapter 9) and other disciplines and by the roles given to the Academic Senate in the Berkeley Revolution of 1919–20. The final stage Kerr calls the Twenty-First-Century Federal Model, marked by a more federated rather than unitary structure of the campuses of the university, the growth of government support of academic research, and an effective national policy of universal access to public higher education.

Figure 3-1. Clark Kerr (1911–2003), first chancellor of the Berkeley Campus, 1952–58, and twelfth president of the University of California, 1958–67.
https://perma.cc/9FX6-B7ST

Kerr's thinking, his manner, and his styles of leadership have been examined by numerous subsequent writers, among them the varied authors of chapters in the book[9] edited by Rothblatt, authors of books

---

[9] Sheldon Rothblatt, ed., *Clark Kerr's World of Higher Education Reaches the Twenty-First Century* (New York: Springer, 2012).

stemming from the UC Center for Studies in Higher Education's Clark Kerr Lecture series on the Role of Higher Education in Society,[10, 11, 12, 13, 14] and the analysis carried out by Gonzalez.[15]

THE STRUCTURE OF THE UNIVERSITY

Multiple Campuses with a Common Mission and Equal Opportunities for Development. When he became the first Berkeley chancellor in 1952 and especially when he became president of the University of California in 1958 Kerr molded the university in ways that set the form that it takes today.

The UC Board of Regents had already, by degrees over time, established that the university would have multiple campuses. That understanding came into being with the establishment of the Los Angeles campus in 1919, the acceptance of the Santa Barbara State College in 1944, the opening of a College of Letters and Science at the site of the Citrus Experiment Station in Riverside in 1954, and the general recognition that activities at Davis should be expanded. But it was Kerr, upon his arrival as president in 1958, who decided that these other campuses should become full general campuses of the university and persuaded the UC Regents to adopt that goal.

As is described in chapter 5, it was also Kerr, as the principal motivating force behind the 1960 Master Plan, who secured the position of the University of California as the one and only public research university of the state and who established that the full

---

[10] Harold Shapiro, *A Larger Sense of Purpose: Higher Education and Society* (Princeton, NJ: Princeton University Press, 2005).
[11] Charles M. Vest, *The American Research University from World War II to World Wide Web: Governments, the Private Sector, and the Emerging Meta-University* (Berkeley: University of California Press, 2007).
[12] Hanna H. Gray, *Searching for Utopia: Universities and Their Histories* (Berkeley: University of California Press, 2011).
[13] Neil J. Smelser, *Dynamics of the Contemporary University: Growth, Accretion, and Conflict* (Berkeley: University of California Press, 2013).
[14] Simon Marginson, *Clark Kerr, the Global Impact of the California Idea of Public Higher Education, and Its Growing Crisis at Home* (Berkeley: University of California Press, 2016).
[15] Cristina Gonzalez, *Clark Kerr's University of California: Leadership, Diversity, and Planning in Higher Education* (New Brunswick, NJ: Transaction Publishers, 2011).

research mission (i.e., "equal opportunity") would be available to all UC campuses. Assigning the public-university research mission to UC guarded against dilution through funding for that mission being spread to other public institutions. It also left to UC the important determination of how many research-university campuses there would be, their sizes, and where they would be located. Furthermore, the formal differentiation of mission among the three public sectors of higher education and the codification of the transfer function, both accomplished by the Master Plan, assured that the California State University and the California Community Colleges would both carry out substantial amounts of public undergraduate education. This enabled the University of California to give the attention to graduate education that would mesh with and build its research mission.

Controlling Campus Size. Another result of planning initiated by Kerr while he was chancellor of the Berkeley campus was to identify 27,500 as the enrollment cap for the campus.[16] This cap was then extended to the other campuses. The cap was set by combining considerations of the physical capacity of the campus with attention to the quality and individuality of education. When the cap was extended to UCLA and other campuses, it provided a backdrop for manageable rates of growth on individual campuses within the university, even in a period of large overall growth. The 27,500 enrollment cap developed in the 1950s crept upward over the years to become about 30,000 by the end of the twentieth century) and in 2017 about 40,000. But, even though California is by far the largest state in population, the individual University California campuses are still smaller than those of a number of other large public research universities, such as Ohio State at 65,000, Minnesota at 51,000, and Arizona State at 83,000, all 2014–15 figures.

Capacity and Quality of New Campuses

Planning: Near-Disaster or Triumph? Peter Hall[17] in his 1982 book, *Great Planning Disasters*, calls the expansion of UC's campuses in the 1960s a "near disaster" and says that when he initially planned the book it was "on the disaster list." To understand this surprising

---

[16] Kerr, 2001, *op. cit.*, pp. 71–82.
[17] Peter Hall, chapter 7, "Two Near-Disasters: California's New Campuses and Britain's National Library," in *Great Planning Disasters* (Berkeley: University of California Press, 1982), pp. 152–170.

comment, it is important to recognize that Hall's book was published in 1982. What happened was that population growth was not as great as in the demographic projections that had guided planning, and state funding for higher education in California ran into difficulties. As Hall relates, the birth rate in California declined in the 1960s and 1970s, and net migration into California in the early 1970s became one tenth the rate of the 1960s. Total growth in University of California enrollment for the five-year period between 1974 and 1978 was a mere 4.25 percent, and enrollment actually fell from 1976 to 1977. In the late 1970s, it looked like enrollment might actually drop in the 1980s after the wave from the post–World War II baby boom had gone through. In addition, general fiscal stringency augmented by the reactions of government leaders to the student activism of the 1960s led the state of California to tighten allocations to the university. At the time some concluded that it had been a mistake to launch all three new campuses and that the needed growth could have been accommodated to a greater extent on existing campuses (see, e.g., Sinsheimer[18]).

The actual enrollments over time, summed for all campuses, are shown in figure 3-2. Note the sharp rise in the 1960s, the leveling off in the 1970s, a rise in the late 1980s associated with the children of the postwar baby boom, a dip in the mid-1990s as that echo ended, and finally another rise as the new millennium started, reflecting in part the grandchildren of the baby boomers.

Hall's conclusion of disaster or near-disaster was from viewpoints twenty or twenty-five years beyond the 1960 Master Plan. We now have the advantage of looking back nearly sixty years after that plan. As is shown in table 3-1, the new campuses of the 1960s and the conversions to general campuses that shortly preceded them have now almost fully served their purposes in terms of accommodating enrollment, especially when it is recognized that enrollments at Santa Barbara and Santa Cruz are constrained by agreements with those two communities. The Master Plan, originally targeted for fifteen years, has served now for well over fifty years. Only recently has the state approached the point of being unable to sustain California public

---

[18] Robert Sinsheimer, *The Strands of a Life* (Berkeley: University of California Press, 1994), pp. 163–164.

higher education. The new campuses were fully needed in the last part of the twentieth century and into the twenty-first. Fortunately, they were launched when it was feasible from a financial viewpoint. It would not have been financially possible to have such a massive physical development effort at any later time. It was indeed foresighted and opportune that the University of California, through Kerr, chose to undertake the massive development efforts that he did in the 1960s. In that sense the new campuses of the 1960s are an unmitigated planning triumph. The triumph is also attested to from an academic standpoint, borne out by the very rapid rises of the new campuses to academic distinction (chapter 10).[19]

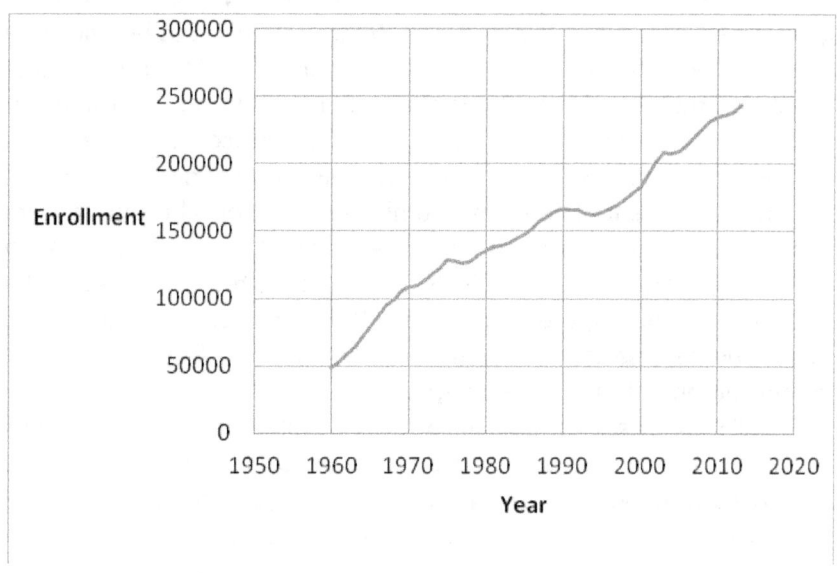

Figure 3-2. Total University of California fall enrollment (general campus plus health sciences) versus year (data from Kerr[20] and "Fall Enrollment at a Glance"[21])

---

[19] Hugh D. Graham and Nancy Diamond, *The Rise of American Research Universities: Elites and Challengers in the Postwar Era* (Baltimore: Johns Hopkins University Press, 1997), pp. 149–150, 195–196.
[20] Kerr, 2001, *op. cit.*, appendix 3, pp. 470–471.
[21] "Fall Enrollment at a Glance," InfoCenter, University of California, https://www.universityofcalifornia.edu/infocenter/fall-enrollment-glance.

TABLE 3-1. Total enrollments of University of California campuses, fall 2016[22]

Berkeley	40,173	Riverside	22,990
Davis	37,397	San Diego	35,816
Irvine	33,467	San Francisco	4,857
Los Angeles	44,947	Santa Barbara	24,346
Merced	7,336	Santa Cruz	18,783
		TOTAL	270,112

GOVERNANCE AND DECISION-MAKING

As is amplified in chapter 6, when he became president, Kerr decentralized many governance responsibilities to campuses, giving them essentially full academic responsibility for their futures and devolving support services as well. Although decentralization did go further in subsequent years, it was Kerr's steps that set the pattern.

Kerr replaced the more autocratic governance style of Sproul and his predecessors with a highly consultative approach that he denoted "pluralistic decision making."[23] The Academic Senate had achieved its roles in principle in 1919–20 but had not been fully integrated into decision-making processes. Kerr recognized the capabilities and institutional supportiveness of many faculty members and built many mechanisms of consultation. The Academic Senate chose to reorganize itself from what had been separate Northern and Southern Divisions into its present structure, consisting of a university-wide organization (to advise the presidents and vice presidents) and a division of the senate on each campus (to advise the chancellor and vice chancellors). He also set up several other consultative mechanisms, as follows.[24]

- The chancellors met with the president before Regents meetings. This meeting evolved over time to include the senior and then

---

[22] "Fall Enrollment at a Glance," InfoCenter, University of California, https://www.universityofcalifornia.edu/infocenter/fall-enrollment-glance.
[23] Kerr, 2001, *op. cit.*, pp. 191–205.
[24] Kerr, 2001, *op. cit.*, pp. 201–202.

executive vice presidents. A dinner meeting before regents meetings continues, and supplements monthly, day-long Council of Chancellors meetings with the president, provost, and the more senior vice presidents on the first Wednesday of each month.
- A president's cabinet met similarly, attended by the president, the vice presidents, and the three officers of the regents—the secretary, the treasurer, and the general counsel. This group still meets, now with some additional attendees.
- A Council of ASUC (Associated Students of the University of California) met quarterly with the president. These meetings still occur intermittently.
- There were periodic meetings of those with like functions from the different campuses (e.g., deans of students, deans of letters and science, deans of graduate divisions, librarians, etc.). These meetings still occur (chapter 8).

Another innovation by Kerr as UC president was to arrange with the UC Regents for the chair and vice chair of the Academic Council to sit at the table with the regents during their meetings with full opportunity for participating in the discussion. This status had been sought by the senate since the 1919 Berkeley Revolution, but had not theretofore been arranged.[25] It still exists.

Yet another innovation brought by Kerr to the Berkeley campus during his chancellorship was the Buildings and Campus Development Committee (BCDC), made up of twenty-seven faculty members from a wide range of disciplines, to advise the chancellor and administration on physical planning of the campus. BCDC had numerous subcommittees, and Kerr indicates[26] that in his time 15 percent of the members of the faculty were engaged in the physical planning process in this way. That produced a sense of faculty ownership and pride in the grounds and buildings of the campus. The committee still exists.

Himself a hobbyist gardener, Kerr took pride in beautification of the campus, originating the concept of "the campus in the park,"[27] which persists to this day. Strawberry Creek, running through the campus, was cleared and landscaped. Buildings are built in clusters,

---

[25] Kerr, 2001, *op. cit.*, p. 199.
[26] Kerr, 2001, *op. cit.*, p. 117.
[27] Kerr, 2001, *op. cit.*, pp. 122–123.

with open space in between, with judicious use of California redwoods and other trees to create a sense of location and privacy for the buildings themselves. Not all was perfect. Kerr himself[28] notes the harsh impact of several of the massive, brutalistic concrete buildings of the 1960s on the campus. Those buildings had the added disadvantage of ultimately being found to be seismically deficient, as building codes for earthquake-prone zones advanced over the years on the basis of knowledge gained from earthquakes around the world.

Over the years BCDC gained the substantial additional role of allocating building space among units on the Berkeley campus. It was cochaired by the author during his years (1987–94) as provost for professional schools and colleges at Berkeley. While effective for gaining participation in the process and acceptance of decisions, BCDC did prove at times to be a cumbersome mechanism for dealing with transfers of relatively small amounts of space.

The creation of equal-opportunity situations among campuses and devolution of much of administrative governance to the campuses reflected both Kerr's concept of a federated university and his own experiences as Berkeley chancellor. He was careful to make a distinction between a federation and a confederation as that issue arose in the aftermath of the Byrne report (chapter 6) and was pushed by UCLA's chancellor Franklin Murphy and others.[29]

BUILDING ACADEMIC STRENGTH

Kerr's contribution to the academic development of the University of California was large and should not be lost among his major changes in structure, governance, and decision-making processes.

---

[28] Kerr, 2001, *op. cit.*, pp. 123–125.
[29] Kerr, 2001, *op. cit.*, pp. 209–214. The distinction between federation and confederation carries particular significance in United States history. The government of the United States itself is a federation; the government of the seceding southern states during the US Civil War (1861–65) was a confederation. The Articles of Confederation were the governing document of the United States before the federated form of government was adopted in the Constitution of 1789. A confederation is effectively an alliance of independent states. Federal government retains substantially more centralized power but does divide government roles between centralized power and the constituent states.

As he determined what to try to do in his newly created and ill-defined (or really nondefined) job as Berkeley chancellor, Kerr concentrated upon academic planning, both because it had not been an area of emphasis and because the Berkeley campus was entering a decade where both growth and faculty retirements would be substantial. There were over a thousand new appointments or promotions to tenure between 1952–52 and 1962–63.[30] Kerr created and chaired an academic advisory committee[31] composed of deans and Academic Senate leaders, an approach that has been repeated in various forms from time to time over the years at Berkeley. Working with this committee, he undertook a process of selective academic building.[32] Geiger[33] describes a detailed example for sociology, for which Berkeley had had no department at all before 1946. A strong leader (Herbert Blumer) was brought in from the University of Chicago in 1952 and made a number of distinguished appointments, resulting in the department being top ranked in the 1964 survey. These selective developments were the result of well-chosen and focused releases of faculty positions by Kerr to the departments, as well as judicious replacement, selection, and recruiting of department chairs.[34]

Kerr also paid particular attention to the review process for appointment, promotion, and advancement of faculty members, which is described in chapter 11. He strengthened the criteria for that process by scrutinizing the recommendations that came to him from the Budget Committee, the Academic Senate's reviewing body. Although he indicates that he never appointed, promoted, or advanced anyone against the advice of the Budget Committee, he did decide negatively on a number of cases in which the Budget Committee had recommended positively. He indicates that he never had a protest from the Budget Committee concerning these actions.[35] Geiger[36] states that, "for a time, 20% of the recommendations that had passed all other

---

[30] Kerr, 2001, *op. cit.*, p. 62.
[31] Kerr, 2001, *op. cit.*, p. 28.
[32] Kerr, 2001, *op. cit.*, pp. 83–89.
[33] Roger I. Geiger, *Research and Relevant Knowledge: American Research Universities since World War II* (Oxford: Oxford University Press, 1993), pp. 80–81.
[34] Kerr, 2001, *op. cit.*, pp. 64–65.
[35] Kerr, 2001, *op. cit.*, p. 63.
[36] Geiger, 1993, *op. cit.*, p. 93.

hurdles were refused" by Kerr. In this way Kerr established substantially higher standards for review of faculty advancement cases.

As president, starting in 1958, Kerr did much for academic development of campuses throughout the university. Following the usual search process, he selected as his successor chancellor at Berkeley Glenn Seaborg, the Nobel Prize–winning chemistry professor and co-discoverer of plutonium, which meant that high academic standards comparable to Kerr's own would continue to be applied to faculty personnel decisions. In similar fashion his selection for chancellor at Santa Barbara, where academic upgrading was a major issue, was Vernon Cheadle, who would similarly delve into personnel cases and exercise high standards of his own beyond the selectivity exerted by the Santa Barbara Committee on Academic Personnel (chapter 10). For the three new campuses—San Diego, Irvine, and Santa Cruz—Kerr worked with the Academic Senate to create the three faculty committees that served as the first Academic Senates for those campuses. That approach was repeated for the subsequent Merced campus. He was generally accepting and supportive of the ambitious Revelle plan for the San Diego campus, described in chapter 10, over the objections of chancellors and some regents who thought the approach to be too elitist and expensive. That plan led to the spectacular academic development of the San Diego campus. Seeking a superior education for undergraduates within a large public research university, he worked with Dean McHenry to create, launch, and cultivate the unique experiment of the Santa Cruz campus, which is also described in chapter 10. And, finally, he carried out the difficult removal of Chancellor John Saunders at UCSF when convinced of the academic need by a senior faculty group (again, chapter 10).

In the 1963 Godkin Lectures at Harvard, Kerr displayed a deep recognition of the influences that would come from massive support of university research by the federal government. In his structuring of university governance and administration, he factored research in with other academic endeavors, keeping as much integration of research with the rest of the academic world as possible. In line with what happened at other leading research universities, it was not until the 1980s that the position vice chancellor for research was established at Berkeley, and not until 1994 that the position vice provost, later vice president, for research (and, later, research and graduate studies) was established university-wide.[37]

SUMMARY CONCLUSIONS

Clark Kerr defined and put into place what is essentially the modern version of the University of California and built the wherewithal for developing and sustaining academic quality, including
- the structure of multiple campuses all with the same research mission and equal opportunity;
- ambitious conversion of three specialized sites and three entirely new campuses, all to become general campuses, thereby providing enrollment capacity for sixty years ahead;
- decentralized governance with the natures and scopes of academic programs defined by campuses individually, subject to presidential and regental approval of new colleges, schools, and programmatic initiatives with substantial budgetary impact;
- highly consultative methods of decision-making;
- substantial emphasis on building academic quality, including high standards and active involvement with and strengthening of the Academic Senate's roles in the academic appointment, promotion, and advancement processes; and
- strong involvement of the Academic Senate in the initial development of the three new campuses—San Diego, Irvine, and Santa Cruz—thereby helping to assume high academic quality from the start.

---

[37] The author was the initial occupant of the university-wide vice provost for research position, 1994–95.

4.
Interactions with State Government: Constitutional Status and Oversight

It will be a dangerous, a most dangerous experiment to hold these institutions subject to the rise and fall of popular parties, and the fluctuation of political opinions...Benefactors will have no certainty of effecting the object of their bounty; and learned men will be deterred from devoting themselves to the service of such institutions, from the precarious titles of their officers. Colleges and halls will be deserted by all better spirits, and become a theater for the contention of politics. Party and faction will be cherished in the places consecrated to piety and learning.
—*Daniel Webster*[1]

The two greatest gifts to the University of California have been the institutional autonomy given to its Board of Regents in the Constitution of 1878 and the unprecedented grant of authority the board assigned to the Academic Senate in 1920. These two gifts constitute the institutional foundation for the growth in distinction of the University of California.
—*Clark Kerr*[2]

[The University of California is a] constituent corporation...equal and coordinate with the legislature, the judiciary and the executive.
—*Edmund G. (Pat) Brown, while Attorney General of California*[3]

---

[1] Daniel Webster, "The Dartmouth College Case," argument before the Supreme Court of the United States, March 10, 1818, in Edwin P. Whipple, *Great Speeches and Orations of Daniel Webster* (Boston: Little, Brown & Co.), https://archive.org/stream/greatspeechesorat00webs#page/22/mode/2up.
[2] Clark Kerr, foreword, in Angus E. Taylor, *The Academic Senate of the University of California: Its Role in Shared Governance and Operation of the University of California* (Berkeley: Institute of Governmental Studies Press, University of California, 1998), https://perma.cc/W237-XW76.
[3] Edmund G. Brown, Opinion no. 57-179, October 1, 1957. Subject: Pacific Coast Intercollegiate Athletic Conference, in W. L. Hanna, ed., *Opinions of the Attorney General of California*, vol. 30 (1957), p. 166. Cited in Renée B. Flower and Brent M. Haddad, *Reawakening the Public Research*

We should be accountable to the Legislature, the parents, the taxpayers, the students. If someone says, did you have a good year at UC Santa Barbara, or did the Office of the President have a good year, or how is a particular research program doing, we ought not get away with, "We're doing great, we had a good year, and if you just sent more money we'd be in fabulous shape." People deserve an honest answer to the question of how you're doing, and it needs to be backed up by statistical data.
—Mark Yudof, president of the University of California, July 2008[4]

The public universities of the United States are creatures of the individual states rather than the federal (national) government. They are chartered by the states, making use of the provisions of the Morrill Act of 1862.[5] They are overseen by the states under conditions defined by the individual states. The roles of the national government are largely limited to three areas—provision of financial aid to needy students through Pell grants and other means; sponsorship and funding of university research by specific government agencies; and regulation in areas such as safety, employee rights, and environmental laws.

The relationship of public universities to the state governments is largely defined in four different ways: (1) the constitutional or charter status of the public university, (2) the composition and means of appointment to the governing board, (3) the mechanism of ongoing coordination and oversight, and (4) accountability measures that may be used in budgeting or in other ways. We shall consider each of the four areas in this chapter, with particular attention to the situation for the University of California, along with benefits and problems.

University, p. 487, footnote 16, eScholarship, University of California, 2014, https://escholarship.org/uc/item/8xk9n9wx.
[4] Brad Hayward, "Yudof Makes Accountability a Top Priority," *93106* 19, no. 2 (September 22, 2008), University of California, Santa Barbara, https://perma.cc/K42U-AHE3.
[5] "Transcript of Morrill Act (1862)," www.ourdocuments.gov, https://perma.cc/8NTC-QKC3.

The structures for public higher education within the individual states of the United States differ greatly and do change from time to time. The Education Commission of the States (ECS) maintains an up-to-date database of the structures and the oversight and coordination mechanisms for the fifty individual states of the United States.[6] A survey report on the subject has been produced by the Midwestern Higher Education Compact, focused upon those states that compose the compact.[7] A book[8] edited by Tierney explores the complexities and variability of state governance of higher education in the United States.

CONSTITUTIONAL AND/OR CHARTER STATUS

Constitutional Autonomy

The University of California is one of the few public universities in the United States or indeed the world to have a full form of constitutional autonomy. Only the fifteen public universities in Michigan[9] and the University of Minnesota have comparable status within the United States.[10]

The Genesis of Constitutional Autonomy for the University of California. The contentions involving Daniel Coit Gilman, the State Grange, Ezra Carr, and others described in chapter 2 were still fresh in the minds of those involved in setting the second constitution for the state of California, which was developed through a constitutional convention in 1878–79. As a result, there was a considerable awareness of the issues surrounding the new university as well as a

---

[6] Education Commission of the States, "Postsecondary Governance Structures: State Profiles," https://www.ecs.org/postsecondary-governance-structures-state-profiles/.
[7] Midwestern Higher Education Compact, *State Constitutional Provisions and Higher Education Governance: Policy Report*, May 2013, https://perma.cc/CM5D-P48V.
[8] William G. Tierney, ed., *Governance and the Public Good* (Albany, NY: State University of New York Press, 2006).
[9] "Public Colleges and Universities in Michigan: MEDC," https://perma.cc/6FZ5-3QCT.
[10] N. H. Hutchens, "Preserving the Independence of Public Higher Education: An Examination of State Constitutional Autonomy Provisions for Public Colleges and Universities," *Journal of College & University Law* 35, no. 2 (2009): pp. 271–322, https://perma.cc/M3EU-NLQL.

strong desire by some of the people involved to protect the university from further political influence or domination.

Douglass [11] describes how constitutional autonomy for the University of California came about during this constitutional convention. The 152 participants were divided among several political categories—fifty-one from the new Workingmen's Party, eleven Republicans, ten Democrats, and two Independents, along with seventy-eight delegates who were formally nonpartisan and for the most part farmers and lawyers. The farmers were largely supporters of the State Grange of California. Continuing the stresses from the Carr-Gilman contentions, the Grange and the Workingmen's Party both wanted to constrain the university to be a vocationally oriented institution with no research mission and little or no liberal arts or graduate programs. The original higher-education draft for the new constitution called for that status. However, there was an education committee designated for the convention, and it was chaired by Joseph Winans, a nonpartisan lawyer from San Francisco, who chaired that city's board of education and was also a regent of the University of California. Winans and a young UC graduate named Jacob Freud, who was a Workingmen's Party delegate but broke with the party on this issue, argued forcefully for a Gilman-like position where the university would instead be "a public trust" and would thereby have the freedom to become like the great eastern universities. A key argument was that the University of Michigan had in 1849 been given constitutional status as a "coordinate branch of state government" and had become the most successful and effective of the state universities. Much jockeying back and forth occurred as the constitutional fate of the university swung between these two extremes. Ultimately, Winans, the guiding strategist, took advantage of the absence of key opposition leaders in the final days of the convention to steer the public-trust language to adoption.

---

[11] John A. Douglass, "How and Why the University of California Got Its Autonomy," Center for Studies in Higher Education, Research & Occasional Papers, no. 4.15 (April 2015), Center for Studies in Higher Education, University of California, Berkeley, CA, https://perma.cc/V99U-QMS2. See also, John A. Douglass, *The California Idea and American Higher Education* (Stanford University Press, 2000), pp. 61–69.

What is striking about this history is that, without Winans, the issues almost certainly would have worked out the opposite way, toward a vocationally oriented institution with much control by the state government. Joseph Winans is a largely unrecognized hero of the University of California.

The Substance of Constitutional Autonomy for the University of California. Article IX of the California Constitution is devoted to education, and Section 9 of Article IX to the University of California. The pertinent original (1879) language of Article IX, Section 9, with the key language for our purposes in bold, was as follows:

> The University of California shall constitute **a public trust**, and its organization and government shall be perpetually continued in the form and character prescribed by the Organic Act creating the same, passed March twenty-third, eighteen hundred and sixty-eight (and the several Acts amendatory thereof), **subject only to such legislative control as may be necessary to insure compliance with the terms of its endowment, and the proper investment and security of its funds. It shall be entirely independent of all political or sectarian influence, and kept free therefrom in the appointment of its Regents, and in the administration of its affairs;** *provided,* that all the moneys derived from the sale of the public lands donated to this State by Act of Congress, approved July second, eighteen hundred and sixty-two (and the several Acts amendatory thereof), shall be invested as provided by said Acts of Congress, and the interest of said moneys shall be inviolably appropriated to the endowment, support, and maintenance of at least one College of Agriculture, where the leading objects shall be (without excluding other scientific and classical studies, and including military tactics) to teach such branches of learning as are related to scientific and practical agriculture and the mechanic arts, in accordance with the requirements and conditions of said Acts of Congress; and the Legislature shall provide that if, through neglect, misappropriation, or any other contingency, any portion of the funds so set apart shall be diminished or lost, the State shall replace such portion so

lost or misappropriated, so that the principal thereof shall remain forever undiminished. No person shall be debarred admission to any of the collegiate departments of the University on account of sex. [12]

The last sentence was remarkably forward-looking for the time. The Organic Act of 1968[13] referenced in this section served to create and organize the University of California (see chapter 2). The referenced act of Congress was the Morrill Act of 1862.

In 1918, during the time of Benjamin Ide Wheeler's presidency, Article IX, Section 9, was strengthened by adding language further restricting legislative control; was changed to omit mention of the Organic Act, thereby removing that act from constitutional status; and added the president of the alumni association to the Board of Regents.[14] Through this and other amendments over the years,[15] the current comparable language of Article IX, Section 9, has become the following,[16] again with the key language in bold:

> The University of California shall constitute a **public trust, to be administered by the existing corporation known as "The Regents of the University of California,"** with full powers of organization and government, subject only to such legislative control as may be necessary to insure the security of its funds and compliance with the terms of the endowments of the university and such competitive bidding procedures as may be made applicable to the university by statute for the letting of construction contracts, sales of real property, and purchasing of materials, goods, and services.

---

[12] Article IX, Education, 1879 California State Constitution, https://perma.cc/2Y9E-WSDG.
[13] "Organic Act—Chapter 244 of the Statutes of 1867–1868," State of California, https://perma.cc/BX57-G7XJ.
[14] Verne Stadtman, *The University of California, 1868–1968* (New York: McGraw-Hill, 1970), pp. 199–200.
[15] Amendments to Article IX, 1879–present, https://perma.cc/2Y9E-WSDG.
[16] Article IX, Education, California Constitution, https://perma.cc/94UY-9PS2.

Adherence to state competitive bidding procedures was added by amendment in 1976.

The Importance of Constitutional Autonomy for the University. Its standing as a public trust "with full powers of organization and government" and with the stated limitations on legislative influences has been crucial for the development of the university. It gives the Regents of the University of California a status and role that is unique within the state government and rare within the sphere of public higher education, empowering them to develop and operate the university as they see fit. Put another way, except for the specific exceptions stated in the constitution, legislation cannot be enacted that requires the University of California to do something. That can be done for the California State University and the California Community Colleges, which are chartered through statute, but legislation of that sort can only ask the Regents of the University of California to consider doing it.

Aside from the public universities in Michigan and the University of Minnesota, universities in other states have substantially lesser degrees of constitutional autonomy, ambiguous situations surrounding constitutional autonomy, or no constitutional autonomy at all. Reviews, surveys, and legal analyses of constitutional autonomy for public universities in the United States have been written by Hutchens,[17] Beckham,[18] and Glenny and Dalglish.[19] The latter authors also note ways in which constitutional autonomy can be and has been eroded over time, primarily through budget-related actions.

Constitutional autonomy protects the academic enterprise in many ways. Some of the critical areas where legislative influence has been exerted in other states or for the California State University and

---

[17] N. H. Hutchens, 2009, *op. cit.*, pp. 271–322.
[18] Joseph Beckham, "Reasonable Independence for Public Higher Education: Legal Implications of Constitutionally Autonomous Status," *Journal of Law & Education* 7, no. 2 (1978): pp. 177–192.
[19] L. A. Glenny and T. K. Dalglish, "Public Universities, State Agencies, and the Law: Constitutional Autonomy in Decline," Center for Research and Development in Higher Education, University of California, Berkeley, 1973, https://files.eric.ed.gov/fulltext/ED084984.pdf.

California Community Colleges but that are protected for the University of California are
- what may and may not be taught,
- flexibility in use of budget,
- whether, when, and where to establish new campuses,
- the right to all planning,
- autonomy for determining academic appointments, promotions, and advancement,
- determination of salaries and salary scales, and
- the establishment of tuition and fees, although the levels of these are often postulated within state budget language.

The regents have often, but by no means always, chosen to conform to legislation that has been passed for the other public sectors of higher education and which they have been asked to consider. But, crucially, they do make individual deliberations and explicit decisions on all such issues.

The list of specific instances in which constitutional autonomy has been important and even crucial for the University of California would be long. Four examples from recent decades display the value.

- During the period 1989–2005, the University of California determined the need for at least one additional campus, conducted a detailed site-selection process, and determined the start-up schedule and methodology for the new campus, which ended up opening in 2005 in Merced. There are many ways in which constitutional autonomy protected that process. It enabled the regents to determine the need for the campus through academic and fiscal criteria rather than allowing the legislature to determine the need through political criteria. It enabled the site to be selected by an internal process and the regents, without undue influence from legislators who would seek a campus in their own district. It allowed the university to determine when there was sufficient prospective budget to enable a start on the project. And it enabled the university to determine what subjects would be offered, when each would be started, and the order in which faculty would be hired.
- In the period 1988–94, the Berkeley campus carried out an extensive series of academic reviews of the School of Library

and Information Studies (see chapter 12). These eventually resulted in the closure of the school and the creation of a new School of Information Management and Systems (now School of Information), which has addressed the growing field of information organization and use. As the continuation of the old school was threatened, there was a very large letter-writing campaign organized by librarians and their supporters throughout the state aimed at government officials as well as UC administrators. In the absence of constitutional autonomy, there would almost certainly have been legislative action on behalf of these constituents to fend off the closure and/or substantial alteration of the then-existing school. The ability of the university to define, control, and modify its own programs has kept the Berkeley campus at the forefront of one of today's fastest growing fields.

- In July 1995 the regents adopted two resolutions that banned consideration of race, ethnicity, and other demographic factors in employment and admissions at the University of California (see chapter 15). At the same time, the regents chartered programs of outreach that would be designed to improve the opportunities and abilities of students from all backgrounds in the state to attend UC (see chapter 16). There are a number of ways in which the state government and politics would probably have entered the situation in the absence of constitutional autonomy. For one, given that the Democratic Party had large majorities in both houses of the legislature, there would probably have been a strong legislative activity seeking to overturn the regents' resolutions. Secondly, there would likely have been various resolutions seeking to define or limit UC's new admissions policies. And third, disagreements between Republicans and Democrats over the relative merits of outreach to schools as opposed to outreach directly to students and families would surely have resulted in legislative actions seeking to define and limit the initiatives.
- In 2009, in the aftermath of concern in the media about the size of salaries that had recently been approved by the regents for two UC chancellors, several members of the California

Legislature proposed a constitutional amendment that would remove the constitutional autonomy of the university. There was clear political motivation for this action, both because of the linkage to the very specific issue of the two salaries and because of the strong support of several labor unions for the proposal.[20] If constitutional autonomy were removed, the unions could exert much more direct pressure in labor negotiations with the university by working through the legislature, where unions are major financial supporters of Democrats and therefore have strong influence with them. Amending the state constitution through the legislature requires two-thirds votes of both houses of the legislature, followed by passage by a majority on the general ballot, and the proposal did not progress beyond the initial stage. Thus the existence of constitutional autonomy served to protect against an essentially political action that would have removed constitutional autonomy and at the same time would have placed the university in a much more vulnerable position in labor negotiations.

Political Influences, Nonetheless. Constitutional autonomy is not all-protective. First of all, there is the annual state budget process, and the legislature and governor can and often do endeavor to influence the university through that funding process. Indeed, the annual budget hearings for the university before the legislature most often equate to a series of hearings on various specific topics of interest to individual legislators and other government officials rather than covering the entire budget, per se. But, except for relatively few line items, the actual uses of the budget remain in the regents' control.

A second way in which political influences can enter is through influence of the governor on the regents, in particular those regents who were appointed by that governor. Notable examples during the past fifty years already mentioned in chapter 2 include the dismissal of Clark Kerr as president in 1967 by the regents soon after Ronald

---

[20] "UC Would No Longer Be 'Above the Law' under Proposed Constitutional Change," *California Progress Report,* May 28, 2009, https://perma.cc/R2A8-NHG6.

Reagan was elected governor and the introduction and passage of regents' resolutions SP-1 and SP-2 in 1995. When these resolutions were symbolically[21] repealed in 2001,[22] the composition of the board had changed because a Democrat, Gray Davis, had become governor in January 1999. Less direct, but still appreciable, influence on the regents from state-government officials, with the notable exception of Governor Earl Warren, came in the loyalty oath controversy of 1949, also discussed in chapter 2.

Viewed through these examples, constitutional autonomy becomes a way of putting a valuable additional layer of insulation—the Board of Regents—between the university and the state political process.

Finally, constitutional autonomy is a benefit that can be taken away through whatever methods a state uses to amend its constitution. Thus, again from a political standpoint, a university should be wary of independent actions that would inflame public opinion to the point where such an action might occur. In California, the constitution may be amended in either of two ways—by two-thirds of the votes in each house of the legislative and then a majority vote on a general-election ballot, or by gaining signatures of 8 percent of those voting in the previous general election, again followed by a majority vote on a general-election ballot. (Low turnouts in an election lead to a profusion of signature-gathering efforts for the next election.)

COMPOSITION OF GOVERNING BOARDS

Public universities typically have governing boards with members appointed by the governor of the state, often with confirmation by a legislative body being required. There are almost always also ex officio members who hold particular positions in the state government. The president of the university is usually a member. Sometimes there are members who represent the alumni of the university, and there are often one or two student members. Student members most often hold their board membership ex officio through their positions in student

---

[21] Only symbolic because of the continued existence of state law with the same requirements.
[22] Patricia A. Pelfrey, *Entrepreneurial President: Richard Atkinson and the University of California, 1995–2003* (Berkeley: University of California Press, 2012), pp. 86–91.

government. There are, however, many variations reflected in board compositions among the fifty states of the United States. Some of the most common variants are described in the following sections.

Elected Boards

In four of the fifty states of the United States, the boards of public universities are elected directly by the people. This occurs for three universities in Michigan (the University of Michigan, Michigan State University, and Wayne State University) and for the Universities of Colorado, Nebraska, and Nevada. In these cases candidates run for board positions, raising issues that have political appeal. Board members accordingly have interests that relate directly to those issues. Thus, the political process enters into the governance of these universities in yet another way. This practice, although well ingrained where it takes place, has not spread more widely because of concerns about political influences on public universities.

Tiered Boards

Five state multicampus universities or university systems—the University of North Carolina, the State University System of Florida, the State System of Higher Education in Utah, the Higher Education Coordinating Commission of Oregon, and the State University of New York—have boards at both the all-university or system level and individual campus levels, with specific divisions of duties among them. An available document specifies the delegations from the main board of the University of North Carolina to the individual campus boards of trustees.[23] For the State University of New York, there are college councils for each of the sixty-four campuses. Some of the duties delegated to the college councils are identified by Hyatt.[24]

Ohio has another variant of a tiered structure in which the central board, known as the Board of Regents, is appointed by the governor of

---

[23] The UNC Policy Manual, "Delegations of Duty and Authority to Boards of Trustees," https://perma.cc/VH3B-JY99.
[24] James A. Hyatt, "Restructuring Public Higher Education Governance to Succeed in a Highly Competitive Environment," Research and Occasional Papers Series, no. 6.15, Center for Studies in Higher Education, University of California, Berkeley, CA, June 2015, https://perma.cc/2HYG-FF3L.

Ohio and is advisory (only) to the state chancellor, who has duties and powers similar to those of the heads of state coordinating bodies.

Mixed Public-Private Boards

A few public universities have governing boards that are composed of both publicly appointed members and "private" members who are appointed either by all other board members or by the subset of the board composed of private members, rather than by a state-government process.

- Indiana University alumni elect three of the nine trustees, and Indiana's governor appoints the other six, including one student.[25]
- Clemson University, a public university in South Carolina, has a thirteen-member board, of which six are political appointees and seven are self-perpetuating, a situation that carries out the explicit language in the will[26] of Thomas Clemson, who left the money that founded the university in his name. In accepting the funds, the state of South Carolina accepted the governance specifications embedded in the will.
- The University of Vermont Board[27] has a mixture of governmentally appointed and self-perpetuating trustees, reflecting the fact that the university was created by a merger of the University of Vermont, which was at the time a private institution, with the relatively new Vermont Agricultural College, which had been formed under the Morrill Act.
- Twenty of the thirty-two members of the University of Delaware board are appointed by a vote of the majority of the full board, the remainder being publicly appointed or ex officio.[28] This composition reflects the origins of the university as Newark Academy, which was private, along with still a relatively low proportion of state funding.[29]

---

[25] "Meet Our Trustees, President, Vice Presidents, and Chancellors," Indiana University, https://perma.cc/8AES-97DP.
[26] "The Will of Thomas Green Clemson," Clemson University, https://perma.cc/BGE4-4R9Z.
[27] "Board of Trustees: University of Vermont," https://perma.cc/RZ5A-WF6S.
[28] "University of Delaware Charter," *UD Faculty Handbook*, https://perma.cc/7VNP-S5YZ.
[29] John A. Munroe, *The University of Delaware: A History*, chapter 2, "The Founding of Newark College" (Newark, DE: University of Delaware, 1986),

- In a different approach, six of the thirty-eight trustees of the Pennsylvania State University are elected by the full board to represent areas of business and industry that will be useful to board deliberations.[30]

Statutory Colleges and Schools

The state of New York has long had statutory colleges and schools, which are publicly funded portions of private universities. They can also be viewed as subject-specific public colleges and schools placed under the aegis of a private university (i.e., outsourced public colleges and schools). Cornell has four statutory colleges (Agriculture and Life Sciences, Human Ecology, Industrial and Labor Relations, and Veterinary Medicine) and one statutory school (Hotel Management). Alfred University has one statutory college (Ceramics). These units receive their funding through the state budget of the State University of New York (SUNY). Cornell has the unusual status of being a private, land-grant (Morrill Act) institution, as does MIT in Massachusetts. The membership of the Cornell Board of Trustees is heavily slanted toward successor (private) trustees. There are only six public members on its sixty-four-member board.[31]

The University of California

The University of California has twenty-six regents, of whom eighteen are appointed by the governor and must be confirmed by the state senate within a year after appointment in order to keep serving beyond that point. The terms are relatively long—originally sixteen years, but reduced to twelve years in 1976 through amendment of

---

http://web.archive.org/web/20160429132719/http://www.udel.edu/aboutus/munroe/chapter2.html.
[30] "Penn State University—Board of Trustees," https://perma.cc/HRA7-WFLJ.
[31] Bylaws of Cornell University, effective January 30, 2015, Article 2, "Board of Trustees," https://perma.cc/TCL5-X9VK.

Article IX, Section 9, of the California Constitution. The long terms are designed to enable regents to develop in-depth knowledge of the university and the issues that surround it and to enable them to move beyond feelings of political commitment to the governor who appointed them. Terms and appointments for these eighteen regents are scheduled such that two regents are appointed in each of the last three years of a governor's four-year term.

Regents are considered to be representatives of the California public overseeing the university, although they are of course de facto representatives of the university as well. The criteria expressed in the California State Constitution for regents are quite broad:[32]

> Regents shall be able persons broadly reflective of the economic, cultural, and social diversity of the State, including ethnic minorities and women. However, it is not intended that formulas or specific ratios be applied in the selection of regents.

In practice regents seem to have been selected through a wide variety of rationales, including prominence in the state; having been benefactors to the governor or the governor's political party through campaign contributions or other means; geographical, occupational, and ethnic distribution; and knowledge of the university and/or higher education in general. Becoming a regent, even though the position is unsalaried, is considered by many people to be very desirable, and thus there is no shortage of interested persons.

Through amendment in 1974, the constitution specifies a committee that should work with the Governor:[33]

> In the selection of the Regents, the Governor shall consult an advisory committee composed as follows: The Speaker of the Assembly and two public members appointed by the Speaker, the President Pro Tempore of the Senate and two public members appointed by the Rules Committee of the Senate,

---

[32] Article IX, Section 9(d), California Constitution, https://perma.cc/LJC5-9CK3.
[33] Article IX, Section 9(e), California Constitution, https://perma.cc/C4TP-SMPD.

two public members appointed by the Governor, the chairman of the regents of the university, an alumnus of the university chosen by the alumni association of the university, a student of the university chosen by the Council of Student Body Presidents, and a member of the faculty of the university chosen by the academic senate of the university. Public members shall serve for four years, except that one each of the initially appointed members selected by the Speaker of the Assembly, the President Pro Tempore of the Senate, and the Governor shall be appointed to serve for two years; student, alumni, and faculty members shall serve for one year and may not be regents of the university at the time of their service on the advisory committee.

In practice this requirement has not had much effect. The committee has sometimes met in advance of the selection of regents by the governor, but often it has met pro forma after the announcement of nominations, if at all. The requirement was well intended, and it would do the state well to follow it more closely. However, both the fact that this committee exists and the need for senate confirmation do place some restraints on appointments.

It is unusual for appointed regents not to be confirmed by the state senate, but it does happen occasionally. A common situation has been when an appointment has been made during the last year of a governor's term in office and confirmation has not occurred before the inauguration of a new governor from the other political party. Perhaps the best-known early example was the case of Leland Stanford, a former governor of California and one of the big four who oversaw the construction of the western portion of the first US transcontinental railroad. Stanford was appointed in 1882 by a Republican governor, but his nomination was withdrawn by the Democratic successor.[34] Stanford and his wife then went on to found Stanford University in honor of their deceased son. One can speculate on how history might have changed had the withdrawal of Stanford's nomination not happened!

---

[34] University of California History Digital Archives, "Regents of the University: Historical Overview," https://perma.cc/8YPS-6G6F.

Seven other regents serve ex officio. Four of these are elected state officials—the governor, the lieutenant governor, the speaker of the state assembly, and the state superintendent of public instruction (K–12). The governor attends regents' meetings only rarely, although particular issues can draw more involvement from the governor. Their positions as regents provide the lieutenant governor and the superintendent of public instruction with one of the few public platforms that are useful to them as they pursue particular issues; therefore they almost always attend. The speaker of the assembly is partway between these extremes—busy but usually an attendee and involved participant.

The other three ex officio members are the president of the university and the president and vice president of the alumni associations of the University of California, both of whom hold two-year terms as regents while they move from vice president to president.

The final regent is the student regent, who is appointed to a one-year term by the regents themselves upon the recommendation of a special committee of the regents. That special committee receives three nominations from the board of directors of the University of California Student Association, selected from ten students nominated to them by northern and southern student nominating commissions who screen applicants and nominees from the campuses. The full procedure is available.[35]

The chair and vice chair of the Academic Council, the university-wide body of the Academic Senate, sit and participate with the regents in a nonvoting capacity and have the right to be recognized and speak at any time.

The regents select a chair and a vice chair annually. The governor is president of the regents, but because the governor is rarely present, the chair presides at meetings.

---

[35] "Regents Policy 1202: Policy on Appointment of Student Regent," Board of Regents, University of California, https://perma.cc/4LUA-9BSQ .

STATE-LEVEL COORDINATION AND OVERSIGHT

State-level coordination of higher education should be differentiated from board governance. The former coordinates among institutions and works with the legislature and the governor. The latter actually governs the institution.

As is described by McGuinness[36] and can be gleaned from the aforementioned ECS database, [37] coordination of public higher education takes very different forms in the various states within the United States. McGuinness categorizes the different approaches as follows.

- Twenty-three states organize all of public higher education under one or two state boards, which have both governing and coordination functions. Utah, mentioned above, is an example.
- Twenty-four states have coordinating boards. Of these, all but two have regulatory roles—twenty-two for approval of academic programs, fifteen with significant budget authority, and six with limited budget authority. An example of a state where the coordinating board has relatively large authority is Texas, for which the charter for the Texas Higher Education Coordinating Board is available.[38] California has been one of the two states with a board but no regulatory roles for it.
- The remaining three states (Michigan, Delaware, and Pennsylvania) have planning or service agencies but no boards with roles between the governing boards of state universities and the state government.

California

The 1960 California Master Plan for Higher Education placed the coordinating role with the Coordinating Council for Higher Education, which was strengthened and succeeded in 1974 by the California

---

[36] Aims C. McGuinness Jr., "The States and Higher Education," in Philip G. Altbach, Patricia J. Gumport, and Robert O. Berdahl, eds., *American Higher Education in the Twenty-first Century*, 3rd ed. (Baltimore, MD: Johns Hopkins University Press, 2011), pp. 139–169.
[37] Education Commission of the States, *loc. cit.*
[38] Texas Charter for Public Higher Education, 1987, https://perma.cc/96KQ-UKD2.

Postsecondary Education Commission (CPEC). A description of the roles of CPEC is available from the ECS database.[39]

> The commission is not a regulatory agency or governing board. Rather, it is an advisory group to the legislature, governor and postsecondary institutions regarding major education policies. It is required to establish a statewide database containing extensive information gathered from all institutions, public and private. The commission has statutory authority to review institutional budgets, to advise on the need for and location of new campuses, and to review all proposals for new academic programs in the public sector. The commission's primary purpose is to prevent unnecessary duplication and to coordinate efforts among the education segments. The commission's efforts are directed by its work plan, which sets out education goals and statewide issues, particularly those that concern large numbers of colleges, universities and proprietary schools.

As is described in chapters 5 and 15, CPEC also had the role of compiling data for eligibility studies, which determine whether access to the University of California and the California State University stand at, above, or below the 12.5 percent and 33 percent levels prescribed in the 1960 California Master Plan for Higher Education. It was also the primary guardian of the California Master Plan for Higher Education (chapter 5). CPEC was generally effective over the years, and the "soft" (i.e., advisory) level of coordination was about right for the state. The strength of the relationship with the state government ebbed and flowed depending upon the particular people who were in leadership roles within the commission and the state government.

As the state of California experienced budgetary woes, Governor Jerry Brown decided to withdraw all funding for CPEC, and it thereby ceased functioning as of November 2011. As of 2017 California has for six years had no statewide coordinating mechanism, a situation that leaves the University of California, California State University, and California Community Colleges to follow their own conclusions as to what will be best. Since CPEC still has statutory status, it remains to be

---

[39] Education Commission of the States, *loc. cit.*

seen whether a new governor will restart the funding for it, or whether a new coordinating commission will arise in some altered form. In any event, it seems unlikely that the current situation of no coordinating mechanism can be ongoing, since some issue will surely rise in public attention and underscore the need for coordination.

ACCOUNTABILITY

Accountability has considerably increased as an issue over the past three decades for universities and colleges in the United States, particularly those in the public sector. The issue is to assure that higher education makes effective and efficient use of the government monies that are supplied to it. Whereas in earlier days it may have been possible to describe the situation as state officials being "content to 'leave the money on the stump' with few questions asked,"[40] more and more states have sought and even demanded demonstrations of accountability from universities to confirm that funds are being spent in the best ways. The same is true for funding of research and need-based financial aid by the federal government. The driving forces bringing states to pursue accountability are tighter and much more internally competitive state budgets, large tuition increases for public universities due to the reductions in state funding, rising student debt, and the need to assure access for deserving students. Federal funding of research has been caught up in questioning of specific research areas and projects, particularly those that are close to current political issues. Issues stemming from tuition concerns are graduation rates, employability, and unmanageable student debt.

One difficulty is that accountability examinations by government can be another way in which political purposes are brought to bear on public universities. Often all of higher education has been lumped together for concerns that are expressed politically. Restrictions have been urged on tuition increases and the tax status of large

---

[40] Martin Trow, "Federalism in American Higher Education," in Arthur Levine, ed., *Higher Learning in America, 1980–2000* (Baltimore: Johns Hopkins University Press, 1993), pp. 39–66; cited by William Zumeta, "Public University Accountability to the State in the Late Twentieth Century: Time for a Rethinking?," *Review of Policy Research* 15, no. 4 (1998): pp. 5–22.

endowments at major nonprofit private universities,[41] with the concerns sometimes flowing over to public universities. Concerns for the for-profit private universities are large accumulated student debt, low degree-completion rates, and less employability of graduates. These concerns, too, can carry over to nonprofit privates and the publics.

Developments to Date in the United States

The general issues of accountability are explored by Schmidtlein and Berdahl.[42] Zumeta[43] analyzes the development of the accountability movement within the United States and considers in particular four states—Tennessee, Missouri, South Carolina, and Washington. In a subsequent publication, Zumeta and Kinne[44] update accountability developments and focus on three additional states—Ohio, Indiana, and Virginia—as well as considering Tennessee again along with several other states. Dougherty et al.[45] draw upon interviews with both government and university officials, concentrating upon Indiana, Ohio, and Tennessee to analyze incentives, obstacles, and unintended impacts of performance-based funding. Tennessee has substantially linked funding of higher education with accountability. Wellman and Harvey[46] have also surveyed accountability efforts in the

---

[41] See, e.g., Victor Fleischer, "Stop Universities from Hoarding Money," *New York Times*, August 19, 2015.

[42] Frank A. Schmidtlein and Robert O. Berdahl, "Autonomy and Accountability: Who Controls Academe?," in Philip G. Altbach, Patricia J. Gumport, and Robert O. Berdahl, eds., *American Higher Education in the Twenty-First Century: Social, Political, and Economic Challenges*, 3rd ed. (Baltimore, MD: Johns Hopkins University Press, 2011).

[43] William Zumeta, "Public Policy and Accountability in Higher Education: Lessons from the Past and Present for the New Millennium," chapter 7 in D. E. Heller, ed., *The States and Public Higher Education Policy: Affordability, Access, and Accountability* (Baltimore, MD: Johns Hopkins University Press, 2001), pp. 155–197.

[44] William Zumeta and Alicia Kinne, "Accountability Policies: Directions Old and New," chapter 8 in D. E. Heller, ed., *The States and Public Higher Education Policy: Affordability, Access, and Accountability*, 2nd ed. (Baltimore, MD: Johns Hopkins University Press, 2011), pp. 173–189; Lara Pheatt and Vikash Reddy, *Performance Funding for Higher Education* (Baltimore: Johns Hopkins University Press, 2016).

[45] Kevin J. Dougherty et al., *Performance Funding for Higher Education* (Baltimore: Johns Hopkins University Press, 2016).

[46] Jane Wellman and Darcie Harvey, "Recent Statewide Reforms in Higher Education Financing and Accountability: Emerging Lessons from the States," commissioned background research for "Securing the Public Trust: Practical Steps toward Higher Education Finance Reform in California," College Futures Foundation, 2016, https://perma.cc/R428-E3G2.

different states, comparing and contrasting the extent to which they are incorporated into state budgeting or other considerations. In a series of three detailed reports, David Leveille[47, 48, 49] has explored the dimensions of accountability and has reviewed those actions that have occurred in the various states so far.

On a national scale, the Commission on the Future of Higher Education, also known as the Spellings Commission, after Margaret Spellings, the US Secretary of Education who chartered it, made accountability a prime component of its 2006 report[50] in ways that were contentious within the commission. Secretary of Education Arne Duncan within the administration of President Barack Obama undertook an initiative to rate US colleges and universities quantitatively.[51] Although there have been many rating and ranking systems undertaken by the media and other private organizations, as reported in the appendix, this was the first undertaken by the national government in the United States. The matter thereby took on elements of accountability measurement and generated questions regarding the appropriateness of this function for the federal government, as well as all the issues reflected below with regard to methodology and measurements.[52] The initiative, which had started with much fanfare, was abandoned and turned into a project for a general information website after many complications became apparent.[53]

---

[47] David E. Leveille, "An Emerging View on Accountability in American Higher Education," Research and Occasional Papers Series, no. 8-05, Center for Studies in Higher Education, University of California, Berkeley, CA, May 2006, https://perma.cc/Z9UG-Q3HM.
[48] David E. Leveille, "Accountability in Higher Education: A Public Agenda for Trust and Cultural Change," Report no. 20.06, Center for Studies in Higher Education, University of California, Berkeley, CA, December 2006, https://perma.cc/UT57-Z344.
[49] David E. Leveille, "Accountability in Postsecondary Education Revisited," Research and Occasional Papers Series, no. 9-13, Center for Studies in Higher Education, University of California, Berkeley, CA, June 2013, https://perma.cc/URU3-99F2.
[50] "A National Dialogue: The Secretary of Education's Commission on the Future of Higher Education," US Department of Education, September 2006, https://perma.cc/6R4Y-NZ6X.
[51] Tamar Levin, "Obama's Plan Aims to Lower Cost of College," *New York Times*, August 22, 2013.
[52] Michael D. Shear, "Colleges Rattled as Obama Seeks Rating System," *New York Times*, May 25, 2014.
[53] Michael D. Shear, "With Website to Research Colleges, Obama Abandons Ranking System," *New York Times*, September 12, 2015.

Issues Surrounding Accountability

Of course institutions of higher education should be accountable to governments and the public for their expenditures of public money. But the great difficulty lies in establishing how, through what means and measures, and with what results accountability should be accomplished.

First of all, should accountability be a matter of certain quantitative measures, and if so, should there be direct results on funding of an institution by the state—that is, should there be performance-based budgeting? If there are certain quantitative measures, the institutions will naturally point toward those particular measures, especially if the outcomes on those measures determine state funding. But strong performance on a certain set of measures can result in poorer performance in other areas that are also important. The desired functions of universities cannot readily be reduced to a manageable set of individual measurements, nor do various particular measures have the same importance for different types of universities.

Public research universities have very different missions from private liberal arts colleges, and those in turn have very different missions from community colleges. Yet the diversity of the United States' higher-education system has been one of its major strengths. If graduation rate is to be an accountability measure, as is frequently proposed, then universities and colleges will not take risks in admissions, and access for at-risk students will suffer. If employment of graduates is a measure, institutions will focus on majors that serve the immediate job market, to the detriment of the balance among disciplines and liberal education. Liberal education has been the hallmark of United States' higher education, yet it does not lend itself readily to accountability measures. If the average salary of graduates is a measure, then universities will emphasize high-paying professions to the detriment of public service. The development of specific accountability measures and ways of using them is, as the Obama administration found out, a hornets' nest.

The University of California and Accountability

Partnerships and Compacts. As already noted in chapter 2, in the mid-1980s and from 1995 until 2010, the University of California approach toward state funding was a "partnership" or "compact" model in which a governor agreed to seek a certain level of enrollment-based funding in return for assurances of certain performance measures being met by the university. Additional budget for specific initiatives could also be sought. Taking as an example the budget for fiscal year 2002–03,[54] the accountability measures were the following:

- admitting all eligible students who wished to attend,
- increasing graduate enrollment,
- implementing the Eligibility in the Local Context program (see chapter 15),
- increasing the number of in transfer students by 6 percent,
- keeping average time to degree reasonable (thirteen quarters for students entering in 1994),
- building state-supported summer instruction,
- increasing engineering and computer science enrollments by one thousand per year,
- building enrollment for the teaching credential,
- not increasing university-wide student fees,
- maintaining financial aid,
- sustaining planning for on-time opening of the Merced campus,
- building teacher professional development, a teacher-scholar program, and a Principal's Leadership Institute, all for K–12 education,
- building the Institutes for Science and Innovation (see chapter 14),
- sustaining and building federal research funding, and
- building further private support.

---

[54] "Progress on Accountability Measures, 2002–03, display 7, p. 23 in *2003-04 Budget for Current Operations*, Office of the President, University of California, November 2002, https://perma.cc/YS94-Z6PE.

These measures were, in effect, the existing academic plan of the university. Except for the three initiatives directed toward K–12 education, they did not require efforts beyond what the university intended to do anyhow, but they did constitute a pledge of deliverables to the state.

The reasoning behind the partnership approach is described in a published interview with Lawrence Hershman, who was at the time the principal budget officer of the university.[55]

> An agreement of this sort does several things. First, it gets the governor to buy in. Second, it sets the stage for developing a budget—you have a basic agreement with the DOF [state Department of Finance] that is a starting point for a budget, and the overall hassle is cut way down, including developing the Regents budget.[56] And last, it allows you to plan. I would be the first to admit that things are never going to work out exactly. But if you look at the history of these agreements, we have, as a matter of fact, usually gotten more, not less. George Deukmejian (1980s) did way better for UC than the original agreement over a period of years. Pete Wilson (1990s) also did better than the Compact, and Gray Davis (1999–2003) at first did a lot better than what we thought was already a good agreement.

Accountability Reports. When Mark Yudof became president of the University of California in 2008, he took the initiative to start annual accountability reports for the University of California. The idea was to demonstrate the recognition by the university that it should be

---

[55] Brenda Foust, "Taking the Long View: A Talk with UC's Vice President of Budget, Lawrence Hershman," *The Senate Source*, April 2005, https://perma.cc/7E6L-LKRC.
[56] The Board of Regents' budget is the request approved by the regents each November and transmitted to the governor and Department of Finance to be considered for the governor's proposed budget, which is announced by the governor in January for consideration by the legislature during the next five months. The budget, once approved by the legislature and with any deletions ("blue penciling") the governor then wishes to make, becomes the California state budget for the fiscal year beginning July 1st.

accountable to the public and to the state government. The university could make and state its own case through a responsible selection of the measures and issues that would be put into the reports. The reports might satisfy accountability interests within the state, and/or they would provide a solid starting point for any future accountability program. There was considerable value to getting out in front on the matter.

The most recent accountability report is available, along with an archive of past reports.[57] The subjects covered in the 2011 report, taken as an example, are given in table 4-1.

TABLE 4-1. Subjects in 2011 University of California accountability report

1. Size and Shape of the University
2. Undergraduate Students—Admissions and Enrollment
3. Undergraduate Students—Affordability
4. Undergraduate Student Success
5. Graduate Academic and Professional Degree Students
6. Faculty and Other Academic Employees
7. Staff
8. Diversity
9. Teaching and Learning
10. Research
11. Health Sciences and Services
12. University Budgets and Private Giving

One could view the accountability reports as a form of annual report for the university. The difference is that the accountability report concentrates upon what the university concludes are the most critical measures of success in its mission. An annual report is usually more comprehensive and less quantitative.

---

[57] Accountability Report 2015, University of California, https://perma.cc/3YKH-4DXS.

With the transition in the presidency in 2013, the reports took on more varied content within categories and added some special topics such as Capital Program and Sustainability, University Finances and Private Giving, and Public Service.

The reports are a useful source of university data for researchers, authors, the media, the public, and legislative staff. While they have not received great attention in the media or in the political world, they do effectively serve the purposes of evidencing university transparency and enabling questions to be answered by referring to the accountability reports. They also serve to stave off interest in what might be more draconian measures undertaken in the name of accountability.

It is important that the reports be candid sources of data. A danger is that the reports could be seen more as the university selecting favorable material that it wants to get out to the public as opposed to objective measures that include the not-so-good along with the good. It could be even more effective to define the content jointly with one or more state agencies or seek requests from agencies and the legislature for specific content.

Summary Conclusions

The relationship of the University of California to the government of the state of California has been established in ways that are conducive to academic strength and less susceptible to political influence than occurs in many other states and countries. Key factors are

- constitutional autonomy, which was established skillfully by Joseph Winans under difficult circumstances in the formulation of the state Constitution of 1879;
- comparatively long terms for members of the Board of Regents—originally sixteen years and now twelve years—with possibilities of reappointment;
- for fifty-one years after the Master Plan of 1960, the use of a statewide coordinating body that was advisory to the state government but did not have line roles in state governance decisions; and

- a recognition by recent UC presidents that it is important to get out in front of issues of accountability and provide access to both a large, open database and full public information on the university and its status.

5. The California Master Plan

The vision of higher education he [Clark Kerr] negotiated into the 1960 California Master Plan not only places him firmly in the pantheon of "shapers of higher education." The particular model his vision contained combined universal access to post-school learning at the base of a coordinate system, which included the highest level of public research universities at its summit. It remains a yardstick against which the initiatives and progress of other nations may be compared.
 —Guy Neave[1]

The particular Californian genius is that of combining public policy with private enterprise, of devising constructive competition and co-operation between and among both public and private institutions. Each of the Californian segments of higher education is aware that it cannot fulfill its own distinctive mission without the existence of and support from the others.
 —OECD Report[2]

What we were really engaged in was negotiating a treaty among the constituent parts of higher education in California that would, at the same time, be acceptable to the Governor and Legislature of the State...We did, at that moment, seize upon history and shape it rather than being overrun by it. At the time, it felt like the Perils of Pauline. In retrospect, it looks more like the triumph of good judgment.
 —Clark Kerr[3]

---

[1] Guy Neave, "Contrary Imaginations: France, Reform and the Master Plan," chapter 6, in Sheldon Rothblatt, ed., *"Clark Kerr's World of Higher Education Reaches the 21st Century"* (New York: Springer, 2012), p. 129.

[2] Organisation for Economic Co-operation and Development (OECD), *Higher Education in California* (Paris: OECD, Paris, 1990), p. 122.

[3] Clark Kerr, "The California Master Plan of 1960 for Higher Education: An *Ex Ante* View," chapter 3, in Sheldon Rothblatt, ed., *The OECD, the Master Plan and the California Dream: A Berkeley Conversation* (Berkeley: Center for Studies in Higher Education, University of California, 1992), pp. 47, 60.

Public higher education in California falls under the Master Plan for Higher Education, which was created in 1960. The Master Plan was a clear success, setting a viable and financially achievable path for the major growth in higher education and access to it that occurred in the decades following the adoption of the plan. Much has been written about the Master Plan, including histories of its development[4,5,6,7] and speculations, pro and con, on its extensibility to other states of the United States and other countries.[8,9,10,11] Two websites[12,13] provide extensive collections of information on the Master Plan.

DEVELOPMENT OF THE MASTER PLAN

Background

Although the Master Plan gives the impression of being a grand design put together starting afresh, it was in fact the result of complex negotiations in a contentious and politicized environment. The state colleges, which had for the most part originated as teacher-training institutions and later became the California State University, were not

---

[4] Neil J. Smelser, "Growth, Structural Change, and Conflict in California Public Higher Education, 1950–1970," in Neil J. Smelser and Gabriel Almond, eds., *Public Higher Education in California* (Berkeley: University of California Press, 1974), pp. 9–142.
[5] John A. Douglass, *The California Idea and American Higher Education: 1850 to the 1960 Master Plan* (Stanford, CA: Stanford University Press, 2000).
[6] Patrick M. Callan, "The Perils of Success: Clark Kerr and the Master Plan for Higher Education," chapter 3, pp. 61–84 in Rothblatt, ed., 2012, *op. cit.* See also Patrick M. Callan, *California Higher Education, the Master Plan, and the Erosion of College Opportunity* (San Jose, CA: National Center for Public Policy and Higher Education, 2009), https://perma.cc/QPL7-2XYT.
[7] Clark Kerr, 1992, *loc. cit.*
[8] Organisation for Economic Co-operation and Development (OECD), 1990, *loc. cit.*
[9] David W. Breneman and Paul E. Lingenfelter, "The California Master Plan: Influential beyond State Borders?," pp. 85–106 in Rothblatt, ed., *op. cit.*, 2012.
[10] Michael Shattock, "Parallel Worlds: The California Master Plan and the Development of British Higher Education," pp. 107–128 in Rothblatt, ed., *op. cit.*, 2012.
[11] Guy Neave, "Contrary Imaginations: France, Reform and the California Master Plan," pp. 129–162, in Sheldon Rothblatt, ed., *op. cit.*, 2012.
[12] Office of the President, University of California, "Master Plan for Higher Education in California," https://web.archive.org/web/20180502035510/https://www.ucop.edu/acadinit/mastplan/mp.htm.
[13] University of California History: Digital Archives, "Contents of the California Master Plan for Higher Education Studies and Report Collection," https://perma.cc/JZ2B-LZFR.

part of a coordinated system. New state colleges and community colleges were created through the political process by legislators.[14] Matters affecting higher education were addressed by the legislature through processes that were essentially ad hoc to the issue. There was no agreement on mission differentiation among institutions, and it was apparent that resources were not being used in an organized and efficient way. The University of California had its own Board of Regents, but the other portions of public higher education reported directly to the state board of education, which also oversaw K–12 education. That reporting line was a sore point for the state colleges. Since 1945 there had been a Liaison Committee, composed of the state superintendent of public instruction,[15] the president of the University of California, three members of the California State Board of Education, and three UC Regents, but it was not effective. The issues and problems of this era have been analyzed by Smelser,[16] Douglass,[17] and Callan.[18]

Engineering. In the late 1950s, presidents of five principal state colleges initiated a three-pronged effort to enhance the roles and status of the state colleges.[19] The three initiatives were (1) transfer of the state colleges from the jurisdiction of the State Board of Education to a new, separate board for the state colleges; (2) authorization for the state colleges to provide professional degree programs in engineering as well as the doctorate of education (EdD); and (3) state funding for research in the state colleges. The situation with regard to engineering was especially controversial and contested. As described by Akera[20] and Adams,[21] ambitions on the part of presidents at San

---

[14] This could not be done for the University of California because of its constitutionally autonomous state.
[15] This is an elected position, with responsibilities relating to K–12 education.
[16] Smelser, 1974, *loc. cit.*
[17] Douglass, 2000, *loc. cit.*
[18] Callan, 2012, *loc. cit.*
[19] Douglass, 2000, *op. cit.*, pp. 252–255.
[20] Atsushi Akera, "Engineering 'Manpower' Shortages, Regional Economic Development, and the 1960 California Master Plan for Higher Education," Paper no. AC 2010-724, in session on Historical Perspectives for Engineering Education, Annual Conference, American Society for Engineering Education, 2010, https://perma.cc/N8ES-C4Z7.
[21] Stephen B. Adams, "Their Minds Will Follow: Big Business and California Higher Education, 1954–1960," *Business and Economic History On-Line* 9 (2011), https://perma.cc/LU36-7CTC.

Diego and San Jose State Colleges and elsewhere led to desires for some state colleges to provide engineering curricula and degrees. These interests were reinforced by the engineering manpower needs perceived by corporations—primarily in the South Bay area that would become Silicon Valley, but which in the 1950s was populated mostly by branch operations of major national companies. One of the arguments made was that the large bulk of engineers did not need degrees from a research university, since their employment would not deal with research, development, or even design. The Engineers' Council on Professional Development, the engineering accrediting body that was the predecessor to today's ABET, was still in its early years, and there were issues as to whether there could or should be multiple types of undergraduate engineering degrees within an engineering discipline.

Given the pressures from the state colleges and areas of industry, the Liaison Committee commissioned two studies in the early 1950s. One of these, sparked by the University of California, was by a committee headed by Purdue University dean of engineering A. J. Potter. This study concluded that California needed no engineering colleges beyond those accredited by the ECPD and that, as the state's land-grant university, the University of California had the right and obligation to be the state's principal source of professional engineers.[22] The other study, sparked by the state colleges, was led by Stanford dean of engineering Fred Terman.[23] Terman's group saw a need of industry for engineers who were not necessarily prepared for graduate school and therefore supported the development of engineering programs in the state colleges. Terman was also concerned that

---

[22] Yet, then and now California has consistently underproduced engineers in comparison with employment needs in the state, sometimes by as much as 50 percent. This situation has led to a net flow of engineers from other parts of the United States and other parts of the world to California, and led UC president Richard Atkinson in 1998 to establish a UC budgetary initiative with the goal of a 50 percent increase in engineering and computer science majors over seven years. [Patricia A. Pelfrey, *Entrepreneurial President: Richard Atkinson and the University of California, 1995–2003* Berkeley: University of California Press, 2012), pp. 108, 179.]

[23] This was the first of two studies of engineering education needs in California led or made by Terman. The second, done as a one-person study for the Coordinating Council for Higher Education in 1968, led to the discontinuation of new engineering programs at the University of California, Riverside and Santa Cruz, campuses (chapter 10).

Stanford should not bear the burden of producing engineers of all sorts in the quantities needed by industry in the environs of Stanford. Both reports materialized in 1952.

There followed a series of efforts and countereffforts. San Jose State College, in particular, continued to develop its engineering program. Dean O'Brien at Berkeley, working closely with Dean Boelter of UCLA's still-new program (chapter 10), continued to oppose the state-college efforts and the eligibility of state colleges for engineering accreditation. He also promised, but continually stalled on, development of a University of California master's program in engineering given in the San Jose/South Bay area. This politically difficult Catch-22 situation in the face of continual statements of engineering demand from industry and the aspirations of the state colleges was reported as a primary factor in Clark Kerr's decision to replace O'Brien as Berkeley engineering dean when Kerr assumed the presidency of the University of California in 1958.[24]

Moving Toward the Master Plan

Driven by this history, Clark Kerr, then still a relatively new UC president, worked together with Assemblywoman Dorothy Donohue, who chaired the state assembly's Committee on Education. Together, they secured passage in 1959 of a legislative resolution that called upon the Liaison Committee to prepare a master plan for higher education in California and present it to the legislature at the start of the 1960 session. The resolution also specified a two-year moratorium on legislation dealing with higher education, including the commissioning of new campuses for the state and community colleges. The Liaison Committee (i.e., higher education itself) was thereby given a specified period of time to present a solution. The implication was that, if the committee did not succeed, the legislature itself would then undertake the task.

A Master Plan Survey Team (figure 5-1) was set up through the Liaison Committee to oversee the effort. The team included representatives of the private colleges and universities along with the University of California, the state colleges, and the community colleges.

---

[24] Adams, 2011, *loc. cit.*

The chairman was Arthur Coons, the president of Occidental College, a private institution. Discussions were heated and involved considerable maneuvering. [25] But eventually, and with a final compromise establishing the joint doctorate, the product was adopted and became the California Master Plan for Higher Education of 1960, with the legislature having approved salient parts.[26] Callan[27] points out that convergence was achieved by enabling all institutions to move forward toward their own aspirations in the context of the common policy goal of providing access to every high school graduate who could benefit from higher education.

ELEMENTS OF THE MASTER PLAN

The plan was a coordinated package with a number of elements,[28] as discussed below.

Systems and Boards
The state colleges became a single system, with a separate board and system-wide chancellor.[29] The community colleges also became a looser system and received their own system-wide board in 1967, although much of the governance and fiscal responsibility remained and still remains with the individual Community College Districts around the state.

---

[25] Douglass, 2000, *op. cit.*, pp. 275–297.
[26] See "The History and Future of the California Master Plan for Higher Education: Statutory Laws and Amendments," https://perma.cc/U3K9-ANYX, for an index of the various ways in which elements of the Master Plan were codified.
[27] Callan, 2012, *op. cit.*, p. 64.
[28] "Major Features of the California Master Plan for Higher Education," Office of the President, University of California, January 2007, https://perma.cc/VS5B-6L88.
[29] The titles President and Chancellor are interchanged for the University of California and the California State University. There is one President for the University of California and a Chancellor as CEO of each campus, reflecting its history as a single university with most campuses formed from within. A Chancellor heads the California State University with a President for each campus, reflecting its origins as separate state colleges.

Figure 5-1. The Master Plan Survey Team, 1959. *Front row, left to right*: Keith Sexton (aide to Assemblywoman Donahoe), Howard Campion (retired superintendent of the Los Angeles Public Schools), Arthur Coons (chair), Glenn S. Dumke (CSU), and Thomas C. Holy (UC staff). *Back row, left to right*: Dean McHenry (UC), Arthur Browne (State Board of Education staff), Henry Tyler (community colleges), and Robert Wert (Stanford U., independent colleges and universities).[30] Affiliations from Douglass.[31])

Missions

The missions of the three different systems, or sectors, of public higher education were clarified and made distinct from one another.

The University of California was confirmed to be the public research university of the state of California, with near-exclusive rights to give the doctorate. UC de facto became the designated research arm of the state. UC also had the sole right to give professional degrees in

---

[30] "The History of the California Master Plan," Center for Studies in Higher Education, University of California, Berkeley, courtesy CSU Systemwide Archives, CSU Dominguez Hills Archives and Special Collections, https://perma.cc/38YC-KVBP.
[31] Douglass, 2000, *op. cit.*, p. 272.

medicine, law, dentistry, veterinary medicine, and architecture. The restriction for architecture has since been removed.

The California State Colleges, which subsequently became the California State University, were to be dedicated to undergraduate education and graduate education through the master's degree, including other professional education. CSU thereby gained the right to give professional degrees in engineering. Faculty research is authorized for CSU consistent with the primary mission of instruction; however, state funding has not recognized research as substituting for some of the instructional mission. The CSU was chartered to give the doctorate only jointly with a UC campus or another independent doctoral-granting institution. By subsequent actions of the legislature, the California State University was given the right to give the doctorate of education (EdD) on its own in 2005, and the rights to give the doctorate of physical therapy and the doctorate of nursing practice as of 2010.[32] These are professional degrees without the research component associated with the doctor of philosophy degree.

The California Community Colleges have the mission of providing both academic and vocational instruction for students of all ages through the first two years (lower division) of undergraduate education. They can give the associate degree. More recently (2014) up to fifteen community college districts have been authorized on a trial basis to establish and offer one bachelor's degree per district in fields in which degrees are not provided by CSU and UC.[33] The community colleges are also authorized to provide remedial instruction, ESL (English as a Second Language) courses, adult instruction not for credit, and workforce training and community-service courses.

Eligibility and Guaranteed Access

The concept of eligibility was established and defined in terms of percentages of public high school graduates, ranked by statewide

---

[32] Legislative Analyst's Office, California State University, and Department of Finance, State of California, "An Evaluation of CSU Doctor of Physical Therapy Programs," January 2015, https://perma.cc/LG3P-DFPK.

[33] "Senate Bill No. 850," California State Legislature, approved by Governor September 28, 2014, https://perma.cc/4AC6-RGYW.

criteria. The upper 12.5 percent would be eligible for admission to UC; the upper 33 percent would be eligible for admission to CSU, and the California Community Colleges would admit all students "capable of benefitting from instruction."

The criteria for ranking to establish eligibility are established by UC and CSU themselves. Historically, the criteria have involved grade point averages in specified high school, college-going courses (the A-G courses[34]) and standardized-test scores (SAT, ACT) on a sliding scale. Equivalent standards are applied for graduates of private high schools. Subsequent UC and CSU practice and eventually Master Plan policy evolved to provide that all eligible California residents who apply on time are offered a place somewhere in the particular university, although not necessarily at the campus or in the major of first choice.[35] Then, to take effect in 2012, the University of California created a category denoted "eligible to review" (ETR) consisting of students whose applications would be reviewed, but who are not guaranteed admission. The compatibility of that change with the Master Plan was not independently assessed because of the defunding of the statewide coordinating body in 2011 (see below). Because actual eligibility rates became too high, the ETR category was deactivated as of 2016.

Eligibility studies are made at intervals to determine whether the eligibility criteria set by CSU and UC do indeed result in the specified 33 percent and 12.5 percent eligibility rates. Until the most recent (2016) study, these have been carried out under the aegis of the statewide coordinating body. After an eligibility study, adjustments are made by the universities to their eligibility criteria, designed to return to 12.5 and 33 percent eligibility for UC and CSU, respectively.

Eligibility does not guarantee admission to a particular campus. In fact most University of California campuses and some California State University campuses receive substantially more applications from eligible students than they can accommodate. At the extreme, Berkeley and UCLA currently (2014–15) receive about six times as many applications from eligible students as can be accommodated in the

---

[34] See "A-G Courses," University of California Admissions, https://perma.cc/YCM3-RDBV.
[35] "Access Provisions of the California Master Plan for Higher Education," University of California, https://perma.cc/K236-8N4S.

freshman class. Consequently, these oversubscribed campuses have separate admissions procedures for selecting among eligible applicants, using criteria that are chosen from an established, university-wide list. For UC these processes presently involve up to fourteen specified criteria implemented though a comprehensive review process.[36] Eligibility is discussed in more detail in chapter 15.

Transfer

An important part of the Master Plan is transfer, wherein students take the first two years of undergraduate instruction (the lower division) at a community college and then complete the remainder (upper division) of a bachelor's degree at either the University of California or the California State University.

The Master Plan specifies that the ratio of upper division to lower division enrollments for both public universities should be at least 60:40. The California State University makes this requirement with considerable room to spare. The University of California usually does meet the requirement university-wide[37] but by much less of a margin. Given the array of residence times of students in both community colleges and UC, a typical percentage of bachelor's graduates from UC who have come by the transfer route is 28 percent. For CSU that percentage is substantially greater, having dropped from a high in the range of 65 percent in 1993 to close to 50 percent at present.[38]

There are also eligibility crteria[39] for transfer, analogous to those for freshman eligibility.

Tuition and Fees

The original Master Plan reaffirmed the goal of tuition-free public education for residents of California, although it did allow for auxiliary

---

[36] "How Applications Are Reviewed," University of California Admissions, https://perma.cc/2YLG-NJ6X.
[37] But not on all campuses individually.
[38] Hans Johnson, "Higher Education: New Goals for the Master Plan," figure 5, p. 11, Public Policy Institute of California, April 2010, https://perma.cc/Z7ES-5269.
[39] "Transfer: Basic Requirements," University of California, https://perma.cc/LGT8-W3XT.

fees for purposes such as recreational facilities and parking. Over the years, the state has not been able to keep this guarantee, with the result that an educational fee was instituted and has grown substantially over the years. It is now being called resident or nonresident tuition. Tuition and fees are set by the Regents of the University of California and by the Board of Trustees of the California State University. Community college fees are set by the credit hour and remain among the lowest in the United States.

Cal Grants

A program of need-based student financial aid, now known as Cal Grants,[40] was included so as to assure that family or personal finances would not preclude a California-resident student from participating in higher education. Greater amounts are available for students attending private colleges and universities with higher levels of tuition, enabling the private colleges and universities of the state to alleviate some of the pressure for enrollment at the public institutions. The inclusion of this provision in the Master Plan drew the support of the private colleges and universities for the plan.

Statewide Coordinating Entity

The Master Plan established by statute a statewide coordinating body for higher education. This was originally the Coordinating Council for Higher Education, which in 1973 was replaced by the California Postsecondary Education Commission (CPEC). State funding for CPEC was ended as of 2011, and CPEC is thereby no longer operative. These bodies were advisory to the governor and legislature. Functions included collecting and serving as a repository for data; being the custodian and chief advocate for the Master Plan; performing analyses of state need, including advice on proposals for new campuses, schools, and the like from the individual sectors; reviewing proposed new degree programs throughout the state; and conducting the aforementioned periodic surveys of eligibility for UC and CSU.

---

[40] "Cal Grant Programs," California Student Aid Commission, https://perma.cc/U6DA-HAN7.

RECOGNITION

The Master Plan drew considerable national attention as it was created and adopted, including a cover story in the weekly news magazine, *Time*.[41] OECD, the international Organisation for Economic Co-operation and Development, carried out a Study of the Master Plan.[42] Delegations frequently came from other countries and states to California, the University of California, and other universities within California to inquire about the Master Plan. They still do so.

BENEFITS OF THE MASTER PLAN

The Master Plan provides an internally consistent basis and mutual understanding for the roles, structure, and goals of the components of public higher education in California. Potential changes can be conceived and judged in light of the plan, rather than occurring in haphazard and potentially contradictory ways. At the time of the creation of the California Master Plan, the principal benefits seen were a path-breaking commitment to opportunities for participation in public higher education; definition of the roles, sizes, and scales of the systems of higher education; and a framework to expand capacity and manage growth. The 1960 Master Plan was among the pioneering efforts in creating university systems and statewide coordination for public higher education in the United States.

Mission Definition and Control

The Master Plan defines and controls the mission of each of the three sectors of higher education such that the entire spectrum of needs is met, and the individual missions of the three sectors are both different and complementary. The differentiation enables the institutions of higher education to concentrate on their own missions and carry them out as best they can. One can denote the organizations of the three systems of public higher education in California as

---

[41] "Clark Kerr," *Time*, Oct. 17, 1960.
[42] OECD, *loc. cit.*, 1990.

"horizontal," reflecting the fact that all the constituent institutions in a given system have the same mission. In other states it is more common for university systems to be "vertical," in the sense that a single system is composed of institutions of very different sorts (i.e., research universities, comprehensive universities, two-year colleges, and specialized institutions), as is done in both New York and Texas, for example.

Cost Control

Since all universities are not trying to be all things, state financial resources are used efficiently. Also, since students can take the lower division at a community college close to home or even while living at home, the large element of transfer education in the plan means that there are large cost-of-living savings for students and/or the families of students, as well as for the state's Cal Grants financial aid program.

Planning and Appetite Control

The governance system delineated by the Master Plan places the creation of new campuses and definition of programs with the university systems themselves, as was already the case for the University of California through constitutional autonomy. Planning occurs within each system, subject to governmental approval and funding of new initiatives. This considerably reduces the influence of state-level politics on the planning process.

Potentially Efficient Transfer for Baccalaureate Education

California has a higher proportion (74 percent in 2006–2007) of higher-education enrollments in community colleges than any other state of the United States.[43] The state relies heavily upon the transfer route to the bachelor's degree and probably uses planned transfer to a greater extent than any other state. The explicit definition of transfer routes, the 60-40 specification of the Master Plan, the eligibility basis

---

[43] Saul Geiser and Richard C. Atkinson, "Beyond the Master Plan: The Case for Restructuring Baccalaureate Education in California," fig. 3, *California Journal of Politics & Policy* 4, no. 1 (2013): pp. 67–123, https://perma.cc/3BKH-MTYH.

for transfer, and now the establishment of associate degrees for transfer between community colleges and the California State University (see "Articulation for Transfer," below) all help the process. However, as is described below, there is a low completion of transfer by community college students initially interested in transfer, which is a substantial inefficiency.

Ease of Students Starting College

If the transfer system works well, it is easier for students to start college or even try it out experimentally. Students can remain near or at home with much lower tuition, and their expenses for the lower-division years are therefore lower. This feature can be as important in promoting college access as is actual financial aid. Transfer also provides a vital and much used second-chance route to a bachelor's degree for those students who were not eligible for UC or CSU as freshmen.

The Bright Line of Eligibility

The use of the same specified A-G courses in the determination of eligibility for both UC and CSU has defined the college-going curriculum for high schools throughout the state, with the result that the A-G courses are uniformly available. When changes have been made to the A-G course requirements by UC and CSU, those changes are rapidly taken up by the high schools. Furthermore, the simplicity of making the eligibility calculation from known grades and test scores means that students, families, and schools can readily determine whether or not a student is eligible for either UC or CSU. Before the addition of the ETR category in 2012, if a student was eligible, he or she was guaranteed admission, although not necessarily at the campus of choice.

Feeding California's High-Tech Economy through Research

The University of California is positioned by the Master Plan to carry out research of the highest order. That research is fostered by the ability of UC to govern itself, in addition to the facts that research is an explicit component of the mission and is funded significantly by the state. Over the fifty-seven-plus years that the Master Plan has been in existence, UC research has spurred the California economy through continual technological innovation that has spawned, enabled, and fed the agriculture, wine, computer, electronics, and biotech industries, among others (see chapter 18). The existence and strength of the California State University has been vital to that result, since CSU has capably provided a large portion of baccalaureate education that UC would have otherwise had to supply, and which in turn would have considerably diluted UC's research mission.

Potential for Continual Adjustment
The Master Plan has been continually reviewed with occasional updates. The balances among research-based and non-research-based undergraduate education and between two- and four-year undergraduate education can, in principle, be altered by changing the 12.5 percent and 33 percent eligibility rates, although that has not yet been done in practice.

CURRENT ISSUES ASSOCIATED WITH THE MASTER PLAN

No approach or plan for something as complex as public higher education can be perfect, if only because there are conflicting needs. Some problematic issues have been associated with the California Higher Education Master Plan from the start, and others have developed as societal and economic changes have occurred over time.

Community College and Transfer Issues
Imbalance of Enrollments and Degrees among the Sectors of Public Higher Education. At the time of the Master Plan and shortly thereafter, the distribution of enrollments among California's three sectors of public higher education was balanced and comparable to those of other states of the United States. In 1960, of the total number of college students in California enrolled in public higher education, 48 percent were in the community colleges, 30 percent at CSU, and 22 percent at UC. Over the years since then, the portion of high school graduates going on to higher education has increased markedly, yet the 12.5 percent and 33 percent eligibility criteria for the University of California and the California State University have not increased. The

result is that there is now a considerable imbalance in undergraduate enrollments among California's three sectors: 66.3 percent of FTE[44] enrollments in the community colleges, 20.4 percent in the California State University, and 13.3 percent in the University of California in 2010, reflecting growths by factors of 11.9, 5.8, and 5.3, respectively, for the three sectors, or a factor of 8.6 overall in public higher education over the fifty years from 1960 to 2010.[45] Head-count (per student, even if part-time) enrollment counts would be even more imbalanced.[46] Put another way, while California stands second among the fifty states in higher education enrollment per one thousand population in the eighteen-to-twenty-nine age range, it stands dead last among the states in the proportion of those higher-education students (only 26 percent) being enrolled in four-year institutions. As well, California stands forty-third among the fifty states in bachelor's degrees awarded to eighteen-to-twenty-nine-year olds, with only 23.8 per 1000.[47]

The need to grow the number of four-year degrees conflicts with the inability of the state to increase public spending for higher education. The Public Policy Institute of California forecasts that in 2030, 38 percent of California's jobs will require at least a four-year bachelor's degree, whereas only 33 percent of workers will have such a degree, leading to a 1.1 million shortfall in workers with a bachelor's degree.[48] The predicted need for workers with bachelor's degrees corresponds to the relatively large presence of high-tech businesses in the state. These results extend and update earlier studies, reflect the non-growth of the static 12.5 and 33 percent eligibility rates of UC and CSU,[49] and have resulted in proposals from the Public Policy Institute of

---

[44] FTE denotes full-time equivalent.
[45] Callan, 2012, *loc. cit.*, Table 3.2.
[46] The figure of 74% of public higher education enrollment in California in 2006–07 cited above from Geiser and Atkinson, 2013, stems from IPEDS data collected by the US National Center for Education Statistics. The difference between it and the 66.3% figure cited here for a later year (2010) probably results from the difference between FTE and headcount tallies.
[47] Geiser and Atkinson, 2013, *loc. cit.*, fig. 1 (2006–07 data).
[48] Hans Johnson, Marisol Cueller Meija, and Sarah Bohn, "Will California Run Out of College Graduates?," Public Policy Institute of California, San Francisco, CA, October 2015, https://perma.cc/56XS-7BSC.
[49] Sean Randolph and Hans Johnson, "Reforming California Public Higher Education for the 21st Century," Bay Area Council Economic Institute, December 2014, https://perma.cc/82V3-UL2B.

California and the Bay Area Council Economic Institute that the eligibility rates for UC and CSU be increased, over time, to 15 and 40 percent, respectively.[50, 51]

Growing Imbalance between the Two Essential Missions of the Community Colleges. As a result of the large growth in the portion of high school graduates enrolling in the community colleges without concomitant growth in transfers to UC and CSU, the enrollment in community colleges for vocational programs and for associate degrees as ends unto themselves has become much larger than the pretransfer enrollment. In the period from 1972 to 1987, transfers from the community colleges to CSU and UC were 32 to 35 percent of the total number of high school graduates entering community colleges two years earlier.[52] Today that percentage is substantially less, with the result that a much smaller proportion of students within community colleges carry through on a transfer track. For the cohort of students entering in 2003, 15 percent transferred to a four-year institution within seven years.[53]

Large Differences among Community Colleges in Producing Transfer Students. The 109 community colleges of California vary widely in production of transfer students. Data[54] for the 15,650 transfer students arriving at the University of California in fall 2014, typical of other years, show that 27 percent came from just six (Santa Monica, Diablo Valley, DeAnza, Santa Barbara, Pasadena, Foothill) of the 113 community colleges and that 45 percent of the transfers to UC came from just fourteen (13 percent) of the community colleges. Conversely, seventeen of the community colleges transferred 25 or fewer students per college to UC, for a total of 224 students, or 1.5 percent coming from 15 percent of the community colleges.

---

[50] Johnson, 2010, *loc. cit.*
[51] Randolph and Johnson, 2014, *loc. cit.*
[52] OECD, 1990, *op. cit.*, table 8.1, p. 73. Of course, only a fraction of students entering community colleges have transfer in mind.
[53] Ria Sengupta and Christopher Jepsen, "California's Community College Students," in Hans P. Johnson, ed., *California Counts* 8, no. 2 (November 2006), Public Policy Institute of California, https://perma.cc/FWJ2-QR2K.
[54] "Admissions by Source School," *University of California*, https://www.universityofcalifornia.edu/infocenter/admissions-source-school.

The large variation among community colleges in transfer effectiveness can be understood in several ways. The community colleges strong in transfer to UC all lie near UC campuses in relatively affluent areas, while those with very low transfer rates tend to be rural or inner-city, where the college-going tradition is much less. Proximity to a UC campus breeds familiarity and interest on the parts of students and their families. Community colleges with relatively few transfer students understandably tend to divert their resources more toward vocational programs, and potential transfer students are less able to locate suitable courses and to find and support one another on such campuses. Both those factors serve to compound the problem.

Articulation for Transfer. As was already noted, many other states place institutions of differing sorts (research/nonresearch; two-year/four-year; etcetera) together within systems. There are more direct administrative opportunities to coordinate transfer when both the source and receiving institutions involved in transfer education are within the same system. Articulation of courses for transfer has been a more complex issue for California.

For general education there is an established and accepted Intersegmental General Education Transfer Curriculum (IGETC).[55, 56] Historically, to determine whether a course at a particular community college fulfilled requirements for a particular major at a particular University of California or California State University campus, a student has had to utilize a large online database known as ASSIST.[57] Not all courses of the same title or number have been accepted by individual majors, especially at UC, because of faculty concerns about sufficiency and quality of content. This has led to situations where a student does not check into the situation soon enough and finds out after taking a course at a community college that it does not carry credit for the major at the UC or CSU campus concerned. In principle, these situations could be lessened by effective counseling and student use of

---

[55] "IGETC – Intersegmental General Education Transfer Curriculum," ASSIST, https://web.archive.org/web/20160405225727/http://www.assist.org/web-assist/help/help-igetc.html.
[56] University of California, Admissions, "IGETC," https://perma.cc/LSE4-EL7G.
[57] "Welcome to ASSIST," https://web.archive.org/web/20170603163257/http://www.assist.org/web-assist/welcome.htm.

that counseling; however, budget stringency and the imbalance among the two missions (vocational and transfer) of the community colleges have reduced counseling for transfer at many community colleges.

More recently, steps have been taken to alleviate these difficulties. In 2010 the California State University and the community colleges, working together with legislators toward an act of the legislature, established associate degrees for transfer, which bring preferred status for admission to CSU in a major that is similar to the area of the associate degree, as determined by CSU. The student is given junior-year standing upon transfer and needs to complete sixty additional prescribed units to qualify for the baccalaureate degree. The transfer student is not guaranteed admission to a specified major or CSU campus.[58] The University of California has not adopted such a blanket path for transfer, but six University of California campuses (Davis, Irvine, Merced, Riverside, Santa Barbara, and Santa Cruz) have specific and more limited transfer agreements with community colleges,[59] and blanket transfer agreements have been established for what in 2016 are twenty-one of the most popular UC majors.[60, 61, 62] These pathways provide students with a single set of course expectations that, if fulfilled, make them reliably competitive for transfer admission.

Attrition of Potential Transfer Students. As has already been noted, many more students enter community colleges with transfer as a goal than actually transfer. There are also uncertainties regarding whether a student does or does not start off on a transfer track. Sengupta and Jepsen[63] conclude that only about one-quarter of

---

[58] California State University, "The Student Transfer Achievement Reform Act." https://perma.cc/2MN9-XW2C.

[59] University of California, "Transfer Admission Guarantee," https://perma.cc/H9F2-9YK7.

[60] "University of California Streamlines Paths for Community College Transfer Students," 2015, https://perma.cc/2Y5J-4D36.

[61] "Transfer: Major Preparation," University of California Admissions, https://perma.cc/28RS-M7PV.

[62] Stephen J. Handel, "Transfer Students Deserve Better Road Maps," *Chronicle of Higher Education*, January 1, 2017.

[63] Sengupta and Jepsen, 2006, *loc. cit.*

students who are initially "transfer-focused" upon entering community college actually do transfer. Shulock and Moore[64] reported that about one-quarter of students who enter community colleges as "degree seekers" complete their degrees, either through transfer (18 percent) or through the associate degree (6 percent). Horn and Lew[65, 66] (2007a, b) examined three annual cohorts (1993–94, 1998–99, 2000–01) of entering California community college students. They found that about one-third of entering students hoped to transfer and another 10 percent hoped to obtain an associate degree or a vocational credential. They found that about 72 percent completed some transferable credits, about 40 percent completed at least twelve transfer and/or degree credits, about 27 percent completed thirty degree and/or transfer credits (half of what is needed for transfer), about 15 percent completed a transfer math course, and about 5 percent became fully transfer ready, meeting the minimum transfer requirements of UC and CSU. Two striking results were that fully one-third of students who became fully transfer eligible had not transferred within six years of their first entry, and that the majority of the students who did transfer (77 percent) were not fully transfer eligible and had to complete some requirements after entry to CSU or UC. Seventeen percent of students entering community college in 2000–01 had transferred to UC or CSU as of fall 2006.

In addition to changing career plans and indecision, the heavy attrition reflects the lack of peer support from other would-be transfer students at many community colleges because of there being relatively few transfer students there, lack of available counseling, lack of use of

---

[64] Nancy Shulock and Colleen Moore, "Rules of the Game: How State Policy Creates Barriers to Degree Completion and Impedes Student Success in the California Community Colleges," Inst. Higher Ed. Leadership & Policy, California State University, Sacramento, February 2007, https://perma.cc/CTF9-ZAWH.
[65] Laura Horn and Stephen Low, "California Community College Transfer Rates: Who is Counted Makes a Difference," MPR Research, 2007a, https://perma.cc/68WP-W2YH.
[66] Laura Horn and Stephen Low, "Unexpected Pathways: Transfer Patterns of California Community College Students," MPR Research, 2007b, https://perma.cc/G2K9-FUCU.

the counseling that is available, and the complexities of transfer requirements for specific majors, as well as financial, career-motivation, and geographical factors. This large loss of students initially interested in the transfer route is a major loss to the state, its economy, and the students involved. It also costs ethnic diversity within UC and to a lesser extent CSU, since community college students as a whole are much more diverse than are UC and CSU students.

CSU Issues

Joint Doctorate. Allowing CSU to give joint doctoral programs with University of California campuses and other PhD-granting institutions was to be the way for CSU faculty to have opportunities to participate in doctoral-level education. The twenty-six joint doctorates in existence as of 2015 are shown in table 5-1,[67] where it can be seen that, for UC, the largest number (thirteen, or half) involve the San Diego campus. UCSD chose academic areas selectively and has used the joint doctorate to obtain a broader coverage of fields. Five more of the joint doctorates are outside UC with the Claremont Graduate University, a private university. The largest CSU user of the joint doctorate is San Diego State University, the most research-intensive CSU campus, with fully nineteen of the twenty-six.

The reasons for the relatively small number of joint doctorates involving other UC and CSU campuses include the lack of incentives for UC departments to participate and the fact that most CSU faculty members have not been able to develop reputations in research of the distinction that would make them attractive to UC faculty for joint activities. The primary field for joint doctorates has been education, although the amount of joint activity in that area has lessened since 2005, when CSU was given, through legislative action, the authority to offer the doctorate of education (EdD) on its own. Just before that time, all nine UC general campuses had joint EdD degrees with one or more CSU campuses, covering nearly all CSU campuses.

---

[67] Legislative Analyst's Office, California State University, and Department of Finance, State of California, "An Evaluation of CSU Doctor of Physical Therapy Programs," p. 6, January 2015, https://perma.c3c/HT4S-P9N7.

TABLE 5-1. CSU joint doctorates as of 2015

CSU Campus	Partner	Degree	Discipline
Long Beach	Claremont	PhD	Engineering & Ind. Appl. Math
Los Angeles	UCLA	PhD	Special Education
Sacramento	UCSB	PhD	Public History
San Diego	UCSD	PhD	Math & Science Education
San Diego	UCSD	PhD	Cell & Molecular Biology
San Diego	UCSD	PhD	Chemistry
San Diego	UCSD	PhD	Clinical Psychology
San Diego	UCD	PhD	Ecology
San Diego	UCSD	PhD	Bioengineering
San Diego	UCSD	PhD	Electrical & Computer Engg.
San Diego	UCSD	PhD	Mech. & Aerospace Engg.
San Diego	UCSD	PhD	Structural Engineering
San Diego	UCB	PhD	Evolutionary Biology
San Diego	UCSB	PhD	Geography
San Diego	UCSD	PhD	Geophysics
San Diego	UCSD	PhD	Lang. & Comm. Disorders
San Diego	UCSD	PhD	Public Health
San Diego	Claremont	PhD	Information Systems
San Diego	Claremont	PhD	Education
San Diego	Claremont	PhD	Computational Sc./Statistics
San Diego	Claremont	PhD	Computational Science
San Francisco	UCB	PhD	Special Education
San Marcos	UCSD	EdD	Education Leadership
Sonoma	UCD	EdD	Education Leadership
San Francisco	UCSF	DPT	Physical Therapy
San Diego	UCSD	AuD	Audiology

Applied or Professional Doctorates. Professional doctorates are well established as the basis for practice in medicine, law, dentistry, and veterinary medicine, and for higher positions in K–12 and community college education through the EdD (doctor of education) degree. A number of other professional fields have turned recently to the doctorate as the expected professional degree. Examples include physical therapy, audiology, and nursing practice.[68, 69] Two of these, physical therapy and nursing practice, are the previously mentioned fields for which CSU was authorized as of 2010 to give professional doctorates.[70] These trends have created new issues for the mission-differentiation aspects of the Master Plan. The professional doctorate degrees are not research based. As they proliferate, questions arise as to whether the University of California can or should develop corresponding programs, and, if not, whether further roles should then be chartered for the California State University.

Further muddying the water is the fact there is no national mechanism for determining what degree contents or fields warrant the title "Doctor." The movements toward the doctorate as the professional degree have come largely from within the professions themselves. The title has been long been established for medical doctors, and leads to the colloquial term "doctor" for physicians. As the professional doctorate becomes extended to other fields, questions arise as to whether the content merits the title and the extent to which the movement reflects a quest for status and salary as opposed to there being sufficiently demanding and complex qualifications for the profession. Since most of the new professional doctorates relate to health-related services, these issues also interact with the whole matter of changes in the structure of health care delivery. Finally, the changes in degree requirements and qualifications do have impacts on the costs of education for service providers and hence on the supply of qualified professionals. To the extent that providers of higher education do not provide degree programs with enough capacity, the role may be filled by other institutions, notably for-profit universities, for which tuitions will be high and degree-completion rates may be low. However, so far for-profit institutions have not entered the

---

[68] Ami Zusman, "Degrees of Change: How New Kinds of Professional Doctorates Are Changing Higher Education," Research and Occasional Papers Series, no. 8–13, Center for Studies in Higher Education, University of California, Berkeley, June 2013, https://perma.cc/3G7K-9ZBK.
[69] Ami Zusman, "Changing Degrees: Creation and Growth of New Kinds of Professional Doctorates," *Journal of Higher Education* 88, no. 1 (2017): pp. 33–51.
[70] The approval the doctorate in nursing practice was on a pilot basis for three campuses through July 2018, subject to an evaluation review.

professional doctorate arena disproportionately, perhaps because of the higher costs associated with providing clinical education.[71]

Dissatisfaction of CSU Faculty with the CSU Mission. CSU seeks faculty members who hold the PhD as a standard of academic qualification, and most CSU faculty members do hold the doctorate. Since they participated in research as they achieved the doctorate, they tend to enjoy research and see it as a high calling. Therefore, there has always been pressure from the CSU faculty to expand their roles in doctorate education and research. This is one of the factors associated with the interest of some CSU campuses in the newer professional doctorates, even though they are not research degrees.

Statewide Coordination

Johnstone[72] and McGuiness[73] have summarized a number of the issues involved in coordination.

Coordination can, in principle, be accomplished in any one or more of three general ways—(1) through a body such as a state board of education with a line-management role, (2) through a body that is advisory to the state government, or (3) by coordination carried out directly among the systems or universities themselves. The line-management approach can lead to political influences and frequent changes responding to shifting political dynamics. Coordination among the systems and/or universities themselves tends to be limited by self-interest. The advisory role was specified in the California Master Plan and is what was used for forty-one years until the California Postsecondary Education Commission was defunded in 2011.

The cessation of funding for the coordinating body in California reflected several factors. These include difficult working relationships among the commission and some members of government, a

---

[71] Ami Zusman, personal communication, August 2016.
[72] D. Bruce Johnstone, "Higher Education Autonomy and the Apportionment of Authority among State Governments, Public Multi-Campus Systems, and Member Colleges and Universities," chapter 4 in Jason E. Lane and D. Bruce Johnstone, eds., *Higher Education Systems 3.0: Harnessing Systemness, Delivering Performance* (Albany, NY: SUNY Press, 2013).
[73] Aims McGuinness, "State Coordination of Higher Education: Nationwide Trends in State Coordination State Council," of Higher Education for Virginia, May 21, 2013 (PowerPoint), https://web.archive.org/web/20160408205422/http://www.schev.edu/council/presentations/NationwideTrendsinStateCoordMcGuinness.pdf.

penultimate director of CPEC who took an unusually aggressive approach toward the sectors of higher education, beliefs stemming at least in part from these causes that the commission was ineffective, loss of ability to fulfill its functions well because of a downward spiraling budget associated with numerous reductions over time, a lack of consensus on CPEC itself as to its mission, and ultimately a governor who did not see value in such coordination. Subsequent interviews of California legislators reported by Lambert[74] confirmed an image that CPEC "had become ineffective." Effective advisory statewide coordination requires that the coordinating agency be respected and allowed to have influence by the governor, the legislature, and the various sectors of higher education within the state.

The removal of funding from CPEC left California with no coordinating body. Yet coordination needs persist.

The Link of Research to the Top Tier of Students

The Master Plan gives the most accomplished students access to a major research university for undergraduate education. This is the usual situation for public higher education in the United States. However, different sorts of undergraduate education are best for different students, a fact that has underlain the development of many different sorts of institutions of higher education in the US. Many liberal arts colleges without a substantial component of research do a fine job of preparing undergraduate students for whatever they want to do afterward, including graduate school and research. An issue raised by Shulock et al.[75] and others is whether there should be a one-to-one match between top students and research universities. Students in the top 12.5 percent may attend CSU instead of UC, and many do so. Some CSU campuses—for example, Sonoma State University[76]—endeavor to reproduce important aspects of education at

---

[74] Matthew T. Lambert, *Privatization and the Public Good: Public Universities in the Balance* (Cambridge, MA: Harvard Education Press, 2014), pp. 210–211.
[75] Nancy Shulock, Colleen Moore, and Connie Tan, "A New Vision for California Higher Education: A Model Public Agenda," Institute for Higher Education Leadership & Policy, Sacramento State University, 2014, https://perma.cc/77KB-4TDU.
[76] Sonoma State University, "Sonoma State University Mission," https://perma.cc/JFE5-PSNJ.

liberal arts colleges. Within UC, as is described in chapter 10, there were short-lived attempts in the early days of both the Santa Barbara and Riverside campuses to create nonresearch liberal arts programs, as well as an effort on a much grander scale to reproduce the liberal arts–college experience within the research university in the original design of the UC Santa Cruz campus. None of these took root well, in part because of the lack of fit to the value systems and culture of the research university.

However, a more viable liberal arts undergraduate sector within California public higher education could be a per capita less expensive path to an education that still serves some strong students well.

The Ability of the State of California to Finance the Master Plan

The Master Plan was defined at a time of relatively strong finances for the state of California. Over the intervening more than five decades, the ability of the state to fund the Master Plan has diminished greatly, so that California residents now pay substantial tuition as opposed to what had been no tuition. The percentage of the state budget devoted to higher education has dropped from 18 percent in 1976–77 to 11.6 percent in 2014–15.[77] Callan[78] (briefly) and Schrag[79] (in substantially more detail) provide analyses of the causes of California's financial stringency over the four decades since 1970. These include a series of ballot initiatives that have been financially restrictive and have also mandated major expenses without new income, as well as general growth in costs for areas such as public pensions, health care, and prisons, coupled with a reluctance to institute new taxes.

Fees for California-resident students, now called tuition, have grown substantially from effectively zero in 1960 to about $13,000 and $6500 at UC and CSU respectively in 2014–15. At the University of California, need-based financial aid has been generated by devoting one-third of tuition and fee increases to that purpose. There are similar policies for CSU. Thus, UC and CSU maintain access essentially by charging substantial tuition for those who can pay and drawing from

---

[77] Randolph and Johnson, 2014, *loc. cit.*
[78] Callan, 2012, *loc. cit.*
[79] Peter Schrag, *Paradise Lost: California's Experience, America's Future* (Berkeley: University of California Press, 1998).

those funds to provide scholarship assistance for those of the lowest income. One measure of the success of enabling access in this way is the percentage of undergraduate students who are recipients of Pell Grants from the federal government. For the University of California as a whole, 42 percent of undergraduate students received Pell Grants[80] in 2011–12, ranging from a high of 58 percent (Merced) to a low of 33 percent (Berkeley).[81] These percentages placed UC at the top of major research universities in the proportion of recipients receiving Pell Grant aid. In 2011–12, students were eligible for Pell grants if family income was less than about $50,000.

The shift from enabling access through charging no tuition to enabling access by returning large portions of tuition and fee increases to financial aid can be regarded as necessary to compensate for the state's inability to support the Master Plan financially. It does not negate the other values of the Master Plan. From the Pell Grant data, it is evident that access of students from low-income families to the University of California has been maintained remarkably well despite the increase in tuition since the Master Plan was instituted. A recent report has compared enrollments of Pell Grant recipients among universities in the United States and confirms that the University of California stands remarkably high among selective universities in the percentage of undergraduate student enrollees who have Pell Grants.[82] The same conclusion comes from the annual ranking called the College Access Index published by David Leonhardt of the *New York Times* (chapters 1 and 2).

Student debt is another growing issue for the United States as public investment in higher education becomes less and tuitions rise. About 55 percent of the 2012–13 University of California graduating class had debt, in the average amount of $20,500. These figures compare with average debts of $25,700 for public four-year, $30,700

---

[80] "Federal Pell Grant Program," US Department of Education, https://perma.cc/V42A-XHMZ.
[81] "UC enrolls a higher percentage of Pell Grant recipients than any other top research university in the country," Indicator 3.2.1, 2014 Accountability Report, University of California https://perma.cc/JC9X-MFP8.
[82] Anthony P. Carnevale and Martin Van Der Werf, "The 20% Solution: Selective Colleges Can Afford to Admit More Pell Grant Recipients," 2017, https://perma.cc/X7FF-X53D.

for private nonprofit four-year, and $37,800 for for-profit institutions in the US the same year.[83] This subject is explored in more depth in chapter 21.

There have been extremely low fees at the California Community Colleges from the start. Although they have been increased in recent years, those fees remain among the lowest in the United States. Most of the community colleges in California are severely underfunded because of the very low fees, the funding structure for the community colleges within Proposition 98[84] (passed in 1988), and great variability in auxiliary financing obtained through local community college districts. Since community colleges do not have the same opportunities that four-year institutions and research universities have for private fund-raising, they are more constrained financially. Higher fees are needed, but the political will has not been there.

Demography, Access, and Participation

On the surface, the design of the California Master Plan to accommodate all eligible students and the high percentages of Pell Grant recipients at both UC (42 percent, as mentioned above) and CSU (53 percent in 2013–14[85]) indicate that access and economic diversity of students are being maintained. As well, both systems have taken what steps they can to sustain ethnic diversity in enrollments subject to the limitations provided by the 1996 amendment[86] to the state constitution that barred preferences in admissions and financial aid on the basis of ethnicity and a number of other factors. But deeper and more nuanced analysis reveals shortcomings.

First of all, as discussed previously, the eligibility rates of 12.5 percent and 33 percent for UC and CSU, respectively, are too low for present-day needs and the nature of the California job market. Secondly, for reasons associated with diminished state funding,

---

[83] "Undergraduate Students—Affordability," chapter 3 in Accountability Report, 2014, University of California, https://perma.cc/3QGX-VRNY.
[84] "Proposition 98—How Does It Work?," Community College of San Francisco, https://web.archive.org/web/20151123040932/http://www.ccsf.edu/dam/Organizational_Assets/About_CCSF/Admin/Governmental_Relations/Proposition98_TheTests.pdf.
[85] California State University, "Measuring the Value of the CSU," https://perma.cc/L3WY-87VP.
[86] Secretary of State, State of California, "Proposition 209: Text of Proposed Law," https://perma.cc/2XQT-3JKA.

The California Master Plan

participation of eligible students at both CSU and UC has slipped in recent years. For CSU as of 2016, seventeen of the twenty-three campuses are selective for freshman and/or transfer admission[87]; that is, they do not have the capacity to admit all eligible students who apply. Some eligible applicants are interested in only certain campuses, and the CSU system and individual campuses have taken various measures in recent years that effectively limit enrollment. As a result, CSU enrollment was essentially flat from 2008 to 2012[88] and since then still has not risen to the extent that the number of eligible students has increased.[89]

For the University of California, all undergraduate campuses except Merced are now selective. Berkeley, UCLA, and San Diego are the most selective; then Davis, Irvine, and Santa Barbara; and then Riverside and Santa Cruz. Students can and do apply to multiple campuses (an average of 3.7 campuses per freshman applicant in 2012), and eligible applicants can gain admission to another campus even if they are not admitted at one or more campuses. As well, eligible undergraduate students who do not achieve admission to any of the UC campuses to which they applied are offered the opportunity to request, and automatically receive, admission to a campus that is not fully subscribed, currently Merced. However, the percentage of students in that category who accept the proffered admission to Merced has so far been small, well under 5 percent, presumably because most of those students prefer opportunities that they have received at other universities rather than what they may perceive as the more limited offerings of a new campus. However, one can anticipate that this percentage will increase as the Merced campus further matures. In addition, the increasing denial rates for eligible applicants at other campuses have produced a significant decrease in the participation rate, the percentage of graduating high school senior

---

[87] Student Academic Support, California State University, "CSU Campus Impaction Information 2016–17," https://web.archive.org/web/20160505191851/http://www.calstate.edu/sas/impaction-campus-info.shtml.
[88] "California State University," *Wikipedia*, https://perma.cc/EL6S-E43M.
[89] California State University, "Enrollment," https://perma.cc/8J4D-YXQ4.

who actually enroll at UC. That figure stood at 7.3 percent for 2012, the lowest level since the early 1980s. It had been at or above 8.0 percent in the intervening years. In simpler terms, the access provided by UC and CSU, while still optimized in view of the state funding available, has resulted in more students deciding that they will be best served elsewhere rather than by the UC and CSU systems.[90]

Another issue is degree-completion rates, a subject that has been analyzed by Bowen et al.[91] for US public universities. The University of California stands relatively high among US public universities, with four- and six-year graduation rates of 63 percent and 83 percent respectively,[92] reflecting in part the high academic caliber of entering students. The California State University has lower success rates, reflecting the greater eligibility rate and more student needs for income from employment. CSU has recently implemented an initiative to raise six-year graduation rates for freshmen from 54 to 60 percent.[93]

Ultimately, campus capacities limit access to UC and CSU. To gain capacity, the two universities must create new campuses, substantially increase the capacities of existing campuses, bring in nonresident (e.g., computerized) methods of instruction to a large degree, and/or lessen degree contents. New campuses are expensive and require considerable time from inception of the project to opening (seventeen years for UC Merced). Maximum campus enrollments have crept upward over the years from Clark Kerr's 27,500 to what is now 36,000 to 45,000 for UCLA, Berkeley, Davis, and San Diego (table 3-1). However, most existing campuses are constrained in enrollment by either geographical factors or community agreements. Instructional

---

[90] See also chapter 15. An analysis of the situation upon which this discussion is based is given elsewhere: Saul Geiser, "Back to the Future: Freshman Admissions at the University of California, 1994 to the Present and Beyond," Research and Occasional Papers Series, no. 4.14, Center for Studies in Higher Education, University of California, Berkeley, 2014, https://perma.cc/PAS4-6NXX.
[91] William G. Bowen, Matthew M. Chingos, and Malcom S. McPherson, *Crossing the Finish Line: Completing College at America's Public Universities* (Princeton, NJ: Princeton University Press, 2009).
[92] "Undergraduate Student Success," chapter 4 in *Accountability Report 2014*, University of California, https://perma.cc/WL8E-LXZ3.
[93] Graduation Initiative 2025," California State University, https://perma.cc/5EDN-5XAP.

technology has come into use and will grow over time, but it is not yet clear to what extent it will reduce costs and release on-campus capacity.

The Master Plan was written in a time of very different demographics in California than exist now. In 1960 the population was overwhelming Caucasian. Over the intervening years, the state has become one without an ethnic majority. The differences in UC and CSU eligibility among ethnic groups are stark, with the last CPEC eligibility study in 2007 having shown UC eligibility rates ranging from 6.9 and 6.3 percent for Latinos and African Americans, respectively, to 29.4 percent for Asian Americans. Corresponding 2007 figures for CSU range from 22.5 percent for Latinos to 50.9 percent for Asian Americans.[94] As is documented by Johnson[95] increasing eligibility levels for UC and CSU should increase ethnic diversity.

The passage in 1996 of the constitutional amendment calling for race-neutral admissions, following the earlier regents' resolutions on the same subject (chapter 15) had a negative effect on diversity in UC admissions, not because of any effect on eligibility criteria but because of lower admissions of Latino, African American, and American Indian applicants to the most selective campuses and removal of the ability of the university to target financial aid toward those students. More UC-eligible students from those categories then chose to go to other universities than had been the case previously. (Private institutions and most public universities in other states have not yet been subject to race-neutral restrictions on admissions and financial aid.)

There is also an unfortunate correlation between various measures of school quality and the ethnic composition of the student body of the secondary schools of California, reflecting geographic, demographic-clustering, and community-wealth factors (i.e., suburbs versus rural and inner-city).[96] This fact feeds the inequalities in eligibility. Any revision of the Master Plan should be sensitive to broad cultural differences among ethnicities.

---

[94] Johnson, 2010, *op. cit.*, p. 14, table 1.
[95] Johnson, 2010, *op. cit.*, p. 15, table 2.
[96] Outreach Task Force, "New Directions for Outreach," p. 16, figure 5, University of California, 1997, https://perma.cc/K8CT-E66T.

The Master Plan and the California Public

Marginson[97] has provided an analysis of the sociological and economic factors which have affected views of the California public on the Master Plan, as well as the ability of the state to carry it out.

The original Master Plan was clear, understandable, and relatively well accepted by the public in California. By virtue of the simple criteria for eligibility, it provided both a clear indication to schools of the college-going course curriculum and the ability for anyone to determine whether or not a particular student was eligible and thereby guaranteed admission to UC or CSU. Because of the clarity and sharpness of the eligibility criteria, people understood the criteria for admission to the two public universities and were generally accepting of them.

The bright line of eligibility and the concomitant guarantee of attendance somewhere within UC or CSU have now been blurred in several ways. The 2012 change by the University of California to extend the possibility of eligibility and admission to more students through the category of "entitled to review" without a guarantee of admission at some campus created a category of students with uncertain eligibility status. Although use of that category was suspended in 2016, it is still something that has been approved by the Academic Senate for use if and when needed. The 2011 elimination of funding for the California Postsecondary Education Commission (CPEC) leaves no mechanism to assure that the Master Plan is enforced or periodically reviewed either directly or through advice to the state government. Another consequence had been that there were no eligibility studies for high school classes graduating between 2007 and 2016, although a 2016 study is being conducted through the Governor's Office of Planning and Research,[98] a body with much wider scope than just higher education and less politically insulated than was CPEC since it reports directly to the governor. As noted by Geiser[99] and others, there are clear signs that UC's effective eligibility rate in 2017 is substantially above 12.5

---

[97] Simon Marginson, "", *Higher Education Quarterly*, v. 71, September 2017.
[98] "SB 103 Higher Education Eligibility Study Information," Governor's Office of Planning and Research, https://perma.cc/CXK2-R4GQ.
[99] Geiser, 2014, *loc. cit.*

percent, perhaps as high as 16 to 20 percent. The expansion in the number of students who have good reason to regard themselves as eligible contrasts with the limitations on the capacities of UC and CSU that stem from budgetary factors. Because of these factors and a general lack of understanding of what is now a much more complex state of affairs, many more California students and their families are likely to believe that they may somehow have been unjustly deprived of a deserved resource. It can appear that admissions of full-fee-paying out-of-state and foreign students are the reason they were not admitted.

The feelings are epitomized by a well-publicized statement from Governor Jerry Brown referring to Berkeley at a UC Regents' meeting in 2015: "It just feels that whatever used to belong to the normal people of California—assuming the Brown extended family is normal—it's not available anymore. And so you got your foreign students and you got your 4.0 folks, but just the kind of ordinary, normal students, you know, that got good grades but weren't at the top of the heap there— they're getting frozen out."[100] An aggressive 2016 report from the California State Auditor serves to stoke the same sorts of feelings.[101] There are, of course, answers, including the fact that the available enrollment capacities at Berkeley and UCLA are probably the smallest percentages of the total state population for a large public-university campus that exist for any of the fifty states. But the perception remains and is therefore a Master Plan issue. The situation cries for analysis and advisory coordination through a revival of the California Postsecondary Education Commission or something similar to it.

OBJECTIVES FOR MODIFICATION

Recently, there has been no shortage of recommendations for changes to the California Master Plan for Higher Education to bring it

---

[100] Ry Rivard, "The New Normal at Berkeley," *Inside Higher Education*, January 23, 2015, https://perma.cc/7LRM-XRJ8.

[101] California State Auditor, "The University of California: Its Admissions and Financial Decisions Have Disadvantaged California Resident Students," Report no. 2015–107, March 29, 2016, https://perma.cc/VA4H-PCRN.

up to date. Sources include the California Office of the Legislative Analyst;[102] the Public Policy Institute of California;[103] the Bay Area Council Economic Institute;[104] the Little Hoover Commission;[105] the Higher Education Policy Institute;[106] the Institute for Higher Education Leadership & Policy of Sacramento State University;[107] the Center for Studies in Higher Education of the University of California, Berkeley;[108, 109] the Institute for Research on Higher Education of the University of Pennsylvania;[110] a joint effort between a former senior analyst of the University of California and an ex-president of UC;[111] a former higher-education reporter for the *San Francisco Chronicle* and program officer for the Hewlett Foundation;[112] and the independent group California Competes.[113] Despite all this interest, as of 2017 there has not yet been any formal effort to revise or rewrite the Master Plan. The last study of the Master Plan at the level of the California Legislature was done in

---

[102] Mac Taylor, "The Master Plan at 50: Assessing California's Vision for Higher Education," Office of the Legislative Analyst, State of California, November 12, 2009, https://perma.cc/4E69-5MDB.
[103] Johnson, 2010, *loc. cit.*
[104] Randolph and Johnson, 2014, *loc. cit.*
[105] Little Hoover Commission, "A New Plan for a New Economy: Reimagining Higher Education," October 2013, https://perma.cc/TYT8-V628.
[106] Callan, 2012 and 2009, *locs. cit.*
[107] Shulock, Moore, and Tan, 2014, *loc. cit.*
[108] John Aubrey Douglass, "From Chaos to Order and Back? A Revisionist Reflection on the California Master Plan for Higher Education@50 and Thinking about Its Future," Research & Occasional Papers Series, 7-10, Center for Studies in Higher Education, University of California, Berkeley, May 2010, https://perma.cc/8JQ2-T3TB.
[109] John Aubrey Douglass, "Re-imagining California Higher Education," Research & Occasional Papers Series, 14-10, Center for Studies in Higher Education, University of California, Berkeley, October 2010b, https://perma.cc/MG3B-GNJL.
[110] Joni E. Finney et al., "From Master Plan to Mediocrity: Higher Education Performance & Policy in California, Institute for Research on Higher Education, University of Pennsylvania, April 2014, https://perma.cc/E39H-S59U.
[111] Geiser and Atkinson, 2012, *loc. cit.*
[112] Pamela Burdman, "Does California's Master Plan Still Work?," *Change: The Magazine of Higher Learning*, July-August, 2009, pp. 28–35. Also published by *CrossTalk*, National Center for Public Policy and Higher Education, https://perma.cc/5NX6-AMEZ.
[113] California Competes, 2014, *loc. cit.*

2002 by the Joint Committee to Develop a Master Plan for Education[114] and covered both higher education and K–12 education. There has been no further effort by the legislature, probably in part due to the defunding of the California Postsecondary Education Commission.

There are indeed continually growing necessities both to monitor and to update the Master Plan. The following discussion outlines what I believe are reasonable objectives for a revised plan and implementations of it, rather than recounting the assortment of recommendations that have been made in the various referenced papers.

Differentiation of Mission and Transfer

In any revision, the differentiation of the missions of the three sectors of public higher education should be retained. The economic efficiency gained by mission differentiation and the ability to focus research upon the University of California have accomplished much for the state and its economy. The resultant quality and utility of University of California research has become the envy of many other states and countries. Transfer education, enabled to work well through sufficient clear information and counseling, is also a vital component since it is less costly for students, families, and the state. Retention of transfer also implies retention of the dual vocational and transfer functions of the community colleges, along with improvement in managing that mix in the community colleges. The transfer system should be designed and supported so that a much higher percentage of students who enter community colleges intending to transfer do in fact transfer.

Coordination

A statewide coordinating body of the general nature of the former Postsecondary Education Commission is also needed. Without it there will be issues stemming from the inherent conflicts among voluntary coordination and the self-interests of the different sectors of public higher education. The present situation of lower state budgets and

---

[114] Joint Committee to Develop a Master Plan for Education, The California Master Plan for Education, 2002, https://perma.cc/8UD4-DECP.

limited capacity for higher education makes coordination an urgent priority.

Eligibility

The bright-line eligibility concept for UC and CSU has served California well historically, providing clear guidance to students and families as to what it takes for a student to be able to attend the University of California, as well as to schools regarding curricula needed for college-bound students. It has also served as a cogent argument over the years for full enrollment funding by the state.[115] A revision to the Master Plan would do well to maintain this concept and to make it as clear as possible what does and does not constitute eligibility.

More Bachelor's Degrees

As has already been noted, the state of California needs to increase the percentage of California residents achieving the bachelor's degree so as to meet the needs associated with the quantity and spectrum of jobs in California. Increasing eligibility percentages for UC and CSU, as was recommended by the Public Policy Iinsitute of California (PPIC), is the best and most direct approach for accomplishing this goal; however, it does necessitate additional funding.

Another approach that has been pushed is to allow the community colleges to give more bachelor's degrees. However, the workforce needs of the state identified by the PPIC[116] relate to the present bachelor's degrees of CSU and UC, and to engender that capability in the community colleges would take extremely large change and expense. It would also result in loss of the financial and mission effectiveness associated with differentiation of missions. It would be much better to increase the effectiveness of transfer education and/or create additional capacity within CSU and UC.

Support and Enhance Transfer Education and Make It More Uniform across the State. It is certainly desirable to keep and further build the concept of transfer education as a way of relieving capacity

---

[115] Pointed out by Saul Geiser, personal communication, September 2016.
[116] Johnson, Cueller Meija, and Bohn, 2015, *loc. cit.*

pressures on UC and CSU, as a way of providing a baccalaureate education with lower overall cost for students and the state, and as a second-chance route for those not admissible to UC and CSU as freshmen. The two largest needs are to make transfer more nearly even across the entire community college system and to reduce the large attrition of would-be transfer students during their community college years. Without these steps, transfer will remain an unhappily inefficient mechanism.

More plentiful and more effective counseling, best carried out as a jointly designed and overseen effort by the community colleges, CSU, and UC, is one obvious and much needed means of enhancing transfer efficiency. Transfer-guarantee programs are effective because they provide a clear path. Those that already exist should be developed further and made as comprehensive as possible. Programs of that sort should be particularly effective for improving transfer from those community colleges that have low transfer yields. Designing student financial support to cover the years both before and after transfer as seamlessly as possible should also be effective.

Increased use of the less expensive transfer route could also be achieved in structural ways, one of which would be to relax the eligibility requirements for transfer to UC and CSU to some degree. To the extent that transfer is more straightforward and attractive, it may be used more even by those students who are eligible as freshmen for UC and CSU. That would be an economically attractive goal if transfer attrition rates can be greatly reduced.

Maintaining the dual mission of the community colleges (vocational and transfer) has presented difficulties. As the ratio of vocational to transfer education has grown overall throughout the community college system, some colleges have directed services proportionately less to transfer. Consideration should be given to how best to reinforce the transfer function within the community colleges, while still recognizing the need for pretransfer education to be distributed geographically around the state.

Satellite Lower-Division UC and CSU Campuses. Another approach could be to build UC and CSU enrollments by creating satellites of existing UC and CSU campuses, as has been suggested by the author,[117] Geiser and Atkinson,[118] and Geiser.[119] The satellite campus would handle some of the undergraduate enrollment of the main campus, most likely in the lower division, with transfer to the main campus for the upper division being automatic and therefore not an issue for the students involved. By being located in different communities, such campuses could overcome any enrollment-limitation agreements of the main campus with its own community. The UC Santa Barbara campus had such a satellite center in Ventura, 1974-2009, and UC Riverside operates a satellite center in Palm Desert, but currently without undergraduate degree programs.

A satellite campus within easy driving distance from the parent campus could utilize parent-campus faculty in its teaching. An example could be the use of the existing Richmond Field Station by the Berkeley campus for this purpose. Use of parent-campus faculty would be less feasible for a more distant satellite campus, but an offsetting benefit for more distant satellite campuses could be the opportunity to extend the reach of the parent campus to other parts of the state, notably those that are not served well by existing campuses. This may be the ultimate approach for UC to serve the large northern portion of California. Converting existing community college campuses to UC/CSU satellite campuses could minimize needs for land acquisition and new capital construction, but it would deplete capacity for vocational education in the area and raise questions of the extent to which existing faculty of the community college could be used effectively for the focused mission of university-level lower division instruction.

Instructional Uses of Information Technology

The rapidly advancing field of information technology has come into use in a variety of ways for university-level instruction. It is still very much a developing area and is continually being assessed in numerous ways. Despite significant successes, much hoopla, and much attention to it by state and federal government officials in searches for

---

[117] C. Judson King, "An Analysis of Alternatives for Gaining Capacity so as to Maintain Access to the University of California", Research & Occasional Papepers, 5-06, Cener for Studies in Higher Education, University of California, Berkeley, March 2006, https://perma.cc/K8BZ-QKKF.
[118] Geiser and Atkinson, 2012, *loc. cit.*
[119] Geiser, 2014, *loc. cit.*

financial panaceas, the use of information technology for instruction is still an evolving area with much uncertainty regarding its future roles. But as more is developed, known, and evaluated, it will certainly be both necessary and desirable to incorporate the educational uses of information technology into planning at higher levels such as a Master Plan. Clearly it will strongly affect matters such as the amount of time that students spend physically on campus and the distribution of needs for off-campus and on-campus instruction and activities. Good uses of information technology may alleviate much of the need for new campuses as the population continues to grow.

Seek Leveraging of Funds

The Master Plan and policies for implementing it should be structured so as to enhance leveraging of state funds to bring in other monies in support of public higher education, notably from private sources and the federal government. Many people and organizations value public higher education as a high priority, and there is consequently significant private money available in support of it. Within the University of California, total private funding now (2017) exceeds state funding for the Berkeley and UCLA campuses. A Master Plan and the implementing policies that surround it should help draw in such funding. State and federal tax policies should promote private giving to not-for-profit universities. There should be no barriers to the use of state funds in support of private fund-raising.

SUMMARY AND CONCLUSIONS

The California Master Plan for Higher Education of 1960 greatly benefitted higher education in California and, within it, the University of California. As a product of negotiation and compromise among the sectors of higher education itself, it was an academically sensible plan that created efficiencies for the state and enabled the University of California to reach the level of academic and research distinction that it has achieved. The benefits of that research in the form of new societal concepts and scientific and technological innovations, as well as corporations and entrepreneurs drawn by the strength of California's

universities, have greatly enhanced the economy of the state. The Master Plan
- identified separate and distinct missions for the three sectors of public higher education;
- placed the research mission almost exclusively with the University of California, meaning that UC would be funded accordingly and that UC would be the de facto research arm of the state;
- created the concepts of eligibility and guaranteed access for UC-eligible freshmen and transfer applicants, which became a "bright line" for eligibility whereby students, parents, schools, and community colleges could readily determine whether or not a student was eligible for freshman or transfer admission to UC and/or CSU, and whereby the secondary schools of the state knew exactly what college preparatory curriculum should be provided;
- set a clear structure and path for transfer bachelor's-level education, which would start with two years at a community college, thereby providing a convenient way of starting baccalaureate education close to home;
- provided that transfer would assume a large portion of baccalaureate education within the state;
- initially provided for public higher education with no tuition, a provision that has severely eroded over time;
- established a program of Cal Grants, which would provide financial assistance for California residents, even for tuition at private universities and colleges; and
- created statewide coordination of public higher education in the form of an independent organization that was advisory to the state government.

Now over fifty years old, the Master Plan has not evolved sufficiently to meet the needs of the times. Some issues have been present from the start, and others have developed over time. Many of these deal with the community colleges and their dual missions of vocational education and transfer. They include
- the fact that the community colleges have absorbed so much of the growth in enrollment in public higher education over the

years, producing a great imbalance in which very high community college enrollments, mostly in vocational programs, contrast with a relatively low production of bachelor's degrees thereby not matching the spectrum of skill levels needed for employment in the state,
- a resultant imbalance between the dual community college missions, with transfer education a much lower percentage of the whole, meaning that less attention is paid to it at many community colleges,
- a large and highly inefficient attrition of would-be transfer students during their community college years, and
- very large differences among community colleges in production and preparation of transfer students.

Other issues are
- dissatisfaction of many faculty members in the California State University with the comprehensive university mission, fed in part by the lack of proliferation of joint doctorate degree programs,
- defunding and hence dissolution of the state-wide coordinating mechanism,
- inability of the state to finance the Master Plan over time, and
- uneven access to higher education over segments of California society, both ethnically and geographically.

There has been a recent profusion of recommendations on how the Master Plan might be altered or evolve. There are, however, some aspects of the Master Plan that are compelling for preservation. These include
- differentiation of mission, which has given financial efficiency and has enabled the quality of research that has served California society and economy so well,
- statewide coordination of an advisory nature in the model that existed until 2011, and
- the eligibility concept, with a clear definition of eligibility that enables students and schools to know what it takes for a student to be eligible for UC or CSU.

There are some additional needs:
- More bachelor's degrees are needed in California because of the employment spectrum needed by the economy. These could be gained by
  - increasing eligibility percentages for UC and/or CSU,
  - supporting and enhancing transfer better so as to make it more effective, with less attrition during the community college years, thereby increasing financial efficiency and ethnic diversity at UC and CSU, and/or
  - creating lower division satellite campuses of existing UC and CSU campuses.
- UC, CSU, and the community colleges must continue to evaluate uses of information technology so as to bring in efficiently the methods that prove most useful.
- State funding for public higher education should be designed so that it will best leverage other sources of funding, for example, through tax policy.

6.
Structure, Organization, and Internal Budgeting of UC: One University, with Campuses Empowered

It was my conviction, both as chancellor and president, that the campus was the basic loyalty unit; that "universitywide" was an essential superstructure in service to the campuses; that we needed "one university" but one university with a pluralistic system of governance; that the campuses should control item-by-item decision making under general policy guidance unless there was a good reason to the contrary; that the chancellors should be the "executive heads" of their campuses as the Board of Regents had decided in 1951.
—*Clark Kerr*[1]

In the best kind of university system, the system office functions as a kind of corporate office and does not become an operating entity. The system does not offer academic programs or engage in research. The system does not confer tenure or award academic degrees. The system does not have a football team. Academic programs and decisions concerning them are campus based. The academic leadership is on the campuses and the [system head] does not function or represent himself or herself to be the chief academic officer of the campuses...In this ideal, the system provides services, including planning, architectural, engineering, budgeting, financial and investment, and legal services. The system undertakes lobbying efforts. It is the continuing responsibility of the chancellor to evaluate the performance of the presidents and maintain a high quality of leadership across the system.
—*Peter Flawn, former president, University of Texas at Austin*[2]

---

[1] Clark Kerr, *The Blue and the Gold: A Personal Memoir of the University of California, 1949–1967* (Berkeley: University of California Press, 2001), p. 193.
[2] Peter T. Flawn, *A Primer for University Presidents* (Austin, TX: University of Texas Press, 1990), p. 178. Note that in this passage the titles Chancellor and President are reversed from how they are used in the University of California,

Continuing struggles between the center and the parts are inevitable. Sheldon Rothblatt has observed that "Any federal system by the facts of its very existence undergo[es] periodic struggles for domination between the center and the parts." So it has been for the University of California.
 —*Clark Kerr*[3]

In my judgment, the pressures for constant extensions of chancellorial dominance have reached the point of challenging the effectiveness of the center in assuring state authorities and the people of the state that their financial support is being used to the maximum benefit of the people of the state. And therefore we need to take a new look at the proper role of the center as well as the autonomy of the parts.
 —*Clark Kerr (in 2001)*[4]

The universitywide system has no alumni, no students, no faculty, no sports teams, no one to cheer for it.
 —*Clark Kerr*[5]

The University of California is a single university within which all campuses have the full public-research-university mission. This structure contrasts with the more usual situations in the United States, where state systems are composed of more than one university or college, or where university systems are composed of campuses having different missions from one another.[6] This chapter concerns the structure, organization, and internal budgeting of the multicampus University of California, how it evolved, and where it is now.

---

[3] Kerr, 2001, *op. cit.*, p. 220.
[4] Kerr, 2001, *op. cit.*, p. 220.
[5] Kerr, 2001, *op. cit.*, p. 192.
[6] Examples of the former are the State University System of Florida, the University System of Georgia, and the Utah System of Higher Education. Examples of the latter are the State University of New York, the University of Texas system, and the University of North Carolina.

ONE UNIVERSITY

The university started with a single campus at Berkeley. As is described in chapter 2, auxiliary operations covering particular areas of instruction (San Francisco) and particular topics of research (San Diego, Davis, Riverside) were then established over the years. A Southern Branch was developed in Los Angeles as of 1919. Later, that Southern Branch became a general campus, a state college in Santa Barbara was switched to UC, and the operations in Davis, San Diego, and Riverside were expanded into general campuses. The San Francisco operations remained dedicated exclusively to the health sciences but became a full-fledged campus. Entirely new grass-roots general campuses were started at Irvine and Santa Cruz in the 1960s and then in 2005 at Merced. With one exception (Santa Barbara), and technically another (Los Angeles), all the campuses beyond Berkeley have developed as growth of satellite facilities toward full and general education or as entirely new campuses spawned from within the university.

The essential history of the University of California is then one of a succession of transitions from a single-location main campus with satellite facilities to the current ten-campus university. As the number of campuses multiplied, the university created chancellor positions to provide leaders for each of the campuses, along with campus administrations to which various administrative functions were delegated. The Academic Senate (chapter 7) divided first into a Northern Division and a Southern Division, and then into separate divisions for the individual campuses. As these changes occurred, the university has never forsaken the status of being a single university, and many aspects of its structure and operation reflect that fact.

As one university, it is one corporate entity and has one mission, one state budget, and one set of dealings with the state government. It also has common standards, policies, and policy envelopes and the ability to grow from within by academic design rather than by amalgamation of preexisting entities.

One Mission

All campuses of the University of California have the same research-university mission integrating doctoral education. The uniformity of mission means that the university can focus upon doing that one mission well and can share best practices internally, rather than having to consider conditions for campuses or universities of several different natures. The single mission has enabled all the campuses to grow toward premier research-university status at whatever rate they can, without being limited by imposed mission constraints. That fact has served the state well.

One Corporate Identity

The university has a single corporate identity as the Regents of the University of California, despite its size and the large number of campuses. This simplifies governance vis-à-vis the state of California and creates a clear chain of responsibility, avoiding any real or de facto existence of multiple masters.

One State Budget

The single-university structure means that there is one state budget for the University of California, as opposed to state structures where individual single-campus universities or university systems compete with one another for budget at the state level. As well, there is one Office of State Government Relations presenting a uniform voice on state legislative and executive matters, and one office for dealing with legislation at the national-government level, again with a single, uniform voice. The distribution of budget among campuses within the university and the formulation of single university stances on government issues are matters for decisions within the university, not for competition among the campuses at the state and national levels. An exception occurs when there is a competition for national institutes or large research operations funded by executive agencies of the federal or state government, industrial corporations, or foundations. For these the campuses do compete with one another.

One Set of Standards, Policies, and Policy Envelopes

Particularly because the university grew by additions of entirely new, or very small existing[7] campuses to the original campus at

---

[7] Los Angeles and Santa Barbara.

Berkeley, the university has successfully spread the academic standards and culture that had developed at Berkeley to all the additional campuses and has benefited by integrating views from all campuses as it has gone further along. It has been important for that purpose that the *Academic Personnel Manual* (chapter 11) has been a university-wide document and that numerous other academic policies establishing or related to academic standards are also university-wide. n som cases, it is policy envelopes that are university-wide, enabling campuses to implement their own specific policies so long as they fall within the constraints set by the policy envelope. An example of a policy envelope is undergraduate admissions policy (chapter 15), where university-wide policy allows the use of the fourteen criteria set by the overall policy of comprehensive review,[8] but individual campuses may choose not to use some of the criteria and can determine their own methods of utilizing the criteria that they do use.

The Ability to Grow New Campuses from within the University

The one-university structure with new campuses being formed de novo or from very small preexisting campuses has meant that there is much involvement of the existing academic enterprise in defining and establishing the academic structure and culture of each new campus. The infusion of academic values has come in several ways, notable among them being the formation of an Academic Senate Task Force to work with the administration on the various aspects of the academic development of the campus, as was done for San Diego, Irvine, Santa Cruz, and Merced. As well, the academic development of new campuses has continually been under knowledgeable academic administrative leadership, starting with the university-wide provost once the project for a campus is approved, and then passing to the chancellor and the provost (or equivalent title) of the new campus.

The Senate Task Force acts effectively as the division council of the Academic Senate for the new campus in shared governance (chapter 7), and establishes senate committees as needed, an early one being the Committee on Academic Personnel, which reviews and advises on

---

[8] UC Admissions, "How Applications Are Reviewed," University of California, https://perma.cc/HZJ6-ELLK.

appointments of faculty for the new campus. Douglass[9] describes the structure and roles of the Academic Senate advisory functions for the three new University of California campuses of the 1960s, for which the senate task forces were called Special Advisory Committees. The charge, membership, and various documents of the Senate Task Force formed in 1998 for UC Merced are available on Internet Archive.[10] The initial members of these committees are drawn from existing campuses. Over time, as faculty members are added to the new campus, the membership combines some members from the new campus with others from existing campuses. Then eventually the membership of senate committees is entirely from the new campus. As of 2015–16, the eleventh year after the 2005 opening of the Merced campus, the Division Council and all but two of the UC Merced senate committees were composed entirely of UC Merced faculty members. However, the Committee on Academic Personnel, which advises on appointments, promotions, and advancements, had six of its eight members from other UC campuses, and the Committee on Privilege and Tenure (dealing with faculty grievances) had the chair and one other member from other UC campuses, and another member from Merced itself.[11]

A certain amount of tension develops naturally between the Academic Senate Task Force and committees, on the one hand, and the administration and faculty of the new campus, on the other hand. The typical issues are whether the campus is being given the latitude that a new campus needs and whether the appointments and standards for new faculty members fulfill the criteria of quality and promise that are sought throughout the University of California. In this regard there is a

---

[9] John Aubrey Douglass, "Planning New UC Campuses In the 1960s: A Background Paper For UC Merced on the Role of the Universitywide Senate," Research and Occasional Papers no. 2.98, Center for Studies in Higher Education, University of California, Berkeley, December 1998, https://perma.cc/XX77-A7X2.

[10] Academic Senate, "Task Force on UC Merced," https://web.archive.org/web/20160103172004/http://senate.universityofcalifornia.edu/ucmerced/.

[11] Academic Senate, "Committees," University of California, Merced, https://perma.cc/Y5AE-5TBM

telling passage in a chapter[12] by the founding provost of UC Merced bemoaning a case where "the Senate Task Force's worry about signs of eminence in initial hired faculty undermined what would have likely been an excellent fit of a potential faculty member's strengths with campus needs." However, he then goes on to say, "In the final analysis, CAP's absolute allegiance to quality was undeniable and will yield the ultimate benefit of creating a coequal UC campus." The founding dean of engineering, who came from another university, observed[13] that the task force "endeavored to impart the culture of UC shared faculty governance to new faculty and administrators, most of them also new to the University of California, and did so with patience and in many cases compassion." But then he goes on to say, "For a start-up campus, the overhead of creating this version of faculty-shared governance combined with the need to create concurrently nearly all administrative and academic functions, resulted in a decision-making environment much less efficient and effective than that within a mature campus." It would be interesting to have related observations from the Senate Task Force or the Committee on Academic Personnel.

It clearly takes constructive administrators and senate leaders to make the shared-governance aspects of the development of new campuses within the university work well. But the challenges of bringing about the culture shifts and other changes associated with bringing a developed university campus from outside into the university as a new campus are much greater. Attesting to that fact are the difficulties encountered in the amalgamation of the Santa Barbara State College (formerly the Santa Barbara State Normal School of Manual Arts and Home Economics) into UC as the Santa Barbara campus, and the fusion of the Citrus Experiment Station and "Watkins College" to become the Riverside campus (both described in chapter 10). The formation of the State University of New York[14] is another

---

[12] David B. Ashley, "Building Academic Distinction in a Twenty-First-Century Research University," in Karen Merritt and Jane Fiori Lawrence, eds., *From Rangeland to Research University: The Birth of the University of California, Merced*, New Dimensions in Higher Education, no. 139 (San Francisco: Jossey-Bass, San Francisco, 2007).
[13] Jeff K. Wright, "Building the School of Engineering," Merritt and Lawrence, 2007, *op. cit.*, p. 54.
[14] W. Bruce Leslie, John B. Clark, and Kenneth P. O'Brien, *SUNY at Sixty: The Promise of the State University of New York* (Albany, NY: SUNY Press, 2010).

example of the difficulties of bringing together disparate existing universities and colleges into a multicampus university.

What Suffers

The model of one university with many campuses all having the same research mission has many benefits, but there are of course some drawbacks, too. These relate primarily to the singularity of the mission. State boards of education and multimission state universities can do overall planning of higher education at the board level. The three public systems of higher education—the University of California, the California State University, and the California Community Colleges—operate under three separate boards, none of which has responsibility to coordinate overall coverage of all higher education. A particular problem is articulation for transfer students between two-year and four-year institutions.

DECENTRALIZATION

Sproul and Corley

The original organization and governance of the University of California was entirely centralized, befitting its structure having a single main campus in Berkeley with several outlying operations. Even though the Southern Branch at Los Angeles had proceeded significantly toward maturity, this structure persisted until 1952, late in Robert Gordon Sproul's presidency. By this point the lack of any appreciable decentralization was considerably impeding the operation of the university. Even though a vice president position, later changed to provost, had been created to oversee the Los Angeles campus, all decisions on personnel or financial matters were made at Berkeley. Stories abound[15] of the hassles and delays that ensued when small matters that needed a decision that had to be transmitted from Los Angeles to Berkeley. The same was true for the main campus at

---

[15] See, e.g., Angus E. Taylor, *Speaking Freely: A Scholar's Memoir of Experience in the University of California* (Berkeley: Institute of Governmental Studies Press, University of California, 2000); Roger L. Geiger, *Research and Relevant Knowledge: America's Research Universities since World War II* (New York: Oxford University Press, 1993), pp. 135–43.

Berkeley. Even seemingly small decisions went to Sproul, whose managerial style was to keep as complete control for himself as possible.

Although the position "provost of the university" had been created in 1931 and filled by Monroe Deutsch, professor of classics at Berkeley, what was delegated to Deutsch was much less than for a provost today. Verne Stadtman observed:[16]

> In practice, the power enjoyed by Deutsch and Moore [Ernest C. Moore, Provost of the University of California at Los Angeles] on their respective campuses was limited. Sproul retained authority in all budget matters and in the appointment of tenured faculty members, department chairmen, and deans. Neither could easily contravene the directives of the comptroller on business matters affecting their campus.

As noted in that quotation, another unusual feature of the Sproul presidency was the amount of latitude given to James M. Corley, who was "variously assistant comptroller, comptroller, university representative in Sacramento, and vice president—business affairs."[17] He had dual reporting lines, both to Sproul as president and to the regents. Before becoming president in 1930, Sproul had held an assortment of positions that collectively were analogous to what became Corley's role. The working arrangement with the two presidents before Sproul—David Barrows and William Wallace Campbell—was that the president dealt with academic matters, and Sproul functioned as vice president for business and financial affairs, comptroller, secretary to the Board of Regents, land agent, and representative for the university in Sacramento. Thus the arrangement between Sproul and Corley in many ways continued what had already existed. As was the case for Sproul, Corley kept tight control on things.

In the 1940s several forces brought about pressures for some decentralization of governance. First of all, as described in chapter 10, several strong Southern California regents and UCLA deans sought both more localized governance and greater status for the Los Angeles

---

[16] Verne Stadtman, *The University of California, 1868–1968* (New York: McGraw-Hill, 1970), p. 272.
[17] Clark Kerr, 2001, *op. cit.*, p. 17.

campus. Secondly, there were rumblings from Berkeley itself, from both deans and in particular the Academic Senate. A speech to the Academic Senate in 1943 by Joel Hildebrand is credited by both Clark Kerr [18] and Eugene Lee [19] as having had considerable influence. Hildebrand, whom we will meet further in chapter 9, was a distinguished physical chemist, a longtime senate leader who had been prominent in the Berkeley revolution in 1919 (chapter 7), and a holder of a number of decanal positions. He was well known as a close associate and strong supporter of Sproul.[20] Clark Kerr considered the speech so important that he transcribed it in an appendix to his memoirs.[21] A passage from that speech follows:

> The fact is that the President divides his attention between seven campuses[22] and numerous public affairs. He has but limited time, therefore, to devote to any one of the scores of departments directly responsible to him. His contacts with members of the faculty are rare. Even a department chairman may have to wait days for an interview and weeks for a decision. The administration seems to be trailing its business rather than steering it. There is little leisure for long-range planning. There is little delegation of authority, even when the President is absent. The government is then carried on by mail. There is no administrative officer whose business is to sit down and discuss with a department chairman the work, welfare, and future of his department…I believe the Senate must take the initiative.

Finally, in 1947, the university chartered a consulting firm, the Public Administration Survey, to examine the administration structure.

---

[18] Clark Kerr, 2001, *op. cit.*, p 43.
[19] Eugene C. Lee, *The Origins of the Chancellorship: The Buried Report of 1948* (Berkeley: Center for Studies in Higher Education and Institute for Governmental Studies, University of California, 1995), p. 7, https://perma.cc/EK5X-E687.
[20] One of pleasures of my life was to preside, as the relatively new dean of the College of Chemistry at Berkeley, over the massive hundredth-birthday celebration for Joel Hildebrand on November 16, 1981. A video of that occasion has been preserved, https://archive.org/details/cubanc_000113.
[21] Kerr, 2001, *loc. cit.*, vol. 1, p. 43, 462–463.
[22] Presumably referring to Berkeley, Los Angeles, San Francisco, the newly acquired campus in Santa Barbara, and the facilities in Davis, La Jolla, and Riverside.

That firm in its report recommended decentralization in a manner much the same as what was eventually done, but still with provost as the title for the primary administrators of campuses.[23] Sproul divided the report into many sections, sending it different places for review and thereby buying more time. Finally, under pressure from regents and faculty, Sproul established chancellor positions for both the Berkeley and Los Angeles campuses to begin in 1952. Clark Kerr and Raymond Allen were appointed to those posts at Berkeley and UCLA, respectively. However, the roles of the chancellors remained ill defined at best. Kerr describes his first days in his new post as finding that he had a small office, nothing that he could do, and a business manager who still reported directly to Vice President Corley rather than to him.[24] Being Kerr, he found an outlet in long-range academic and physical planning and academic leadership directed toward further enhancing the academic stature of Berkeley.[25]

Clark Kerr

Kerr moved from the Berkeley chancellorship to the presidency of the University of California in 1958.[26] Given his experiences as Berkeley chancellor and his view that the Sproul administration was by then overly centralized, Kerr moved promptly to make the major changes in the number and status of campuses that have already been outlined in chapters 2 and 3.

Kerr also worked with the regents to undo the arrangement whereby James Corley had independent authority with a joint reporting line directly to the regents. The functions were separated, and both the new vice president of finance and the person in charge of state government relations now reported directly to the president.[27]

---

[23] Lee, 1995, *loc. cit.*
[24] Kerr, 2001, *op. cit.*, pp. 40–47.
[25] Kerr, 2001, *op. cit.*, pp. 56–128.
[26] Kerr's successor as chancellor at Berkeley was chemistry Nobelist Glenn Seaborg, who has left us what amounts to his diary covering his time in the post up until the point where he was called by President Kennedy to head the Atomic Energy Commission. Glenn T. Seaborg with Ray Colvig, *Chancellor at Berkeley* (Berkeley: Institute of Governmental Studies Press, University of California, 1994).
[27] Kerr, 2001, *op. cit.*, pp. 165, 194, 203–204.

Figure 6-1. Robert Gordon Sproul (*left*) and Clark Kerr at the Inauguration of Kerr as UC President, Septermber 29, 1958[28]

The third set of changes made initially by Kerr was operational. He delegated to the campus chancellors the business affairs of the campus, the selection of department chairs, and oversight of grounds and buildings, architects and engineers, campus public affairs, police, intercollegiate athletics, and alumni associations.

Fourth, as has already been noted, Kerr moved from unitary to pluralistic decision-making.[29] He made consultation with the Academic Senate more meaningful and effective, bringing it to its present status (chapter 7). He initiated the monthly Council of Chancellors meetings that still persist today, bringing major issues to this meeting of chancellors and the more senior vice presidents for discussion. He initiated periodic meetings of administrative officials having like functions on the different campuses with their Office of the President counterparts (chapter 8). He created the post of vice president—

---

[28] Online Photographic Collection, Bancroft Library, University of California, Berkeley, https://perma.cc/EB8J-93ZF.

[29] Kerr, 2001, *op. cit.*, pp. 191–205.

academic affairs to interface more consistently with the Academic Senate. In addition, he created the position of vice president of the university and designated it as most senior vice president position and his second in command. For that position he chose Harry Wellman, who had been vice president for agriculture sciences. Details of these and other associated decentralization actions are given by Furtado.[30]

Given these changes in the administrative structure, the Academic Senate decided to reorganize. In 1933 it had been divided into northern and southern divisions. In 1963 the senate changed from the two divisions so as now to have one division per campus. At this point, the Academic Council became the university-wide executive body of the senate (chapter 7). Concomitant with the reorganization by the Academic Senate, Kerr and the chancellors created deans of the graduate division on each campus, to correspond with the senate structure for consultation on graduate affairs.

There were continued changes during Kerr's time as president, influenced by ongoing considerations, the desires of some chancellors, and a regents' study known as the Byrne Report.[31] In 1964–65 the UC Regents delegated to President Kerr, and Kerr in turn delegated to the chancellors, full authority for faculty appointments and promotion, including tenure decisions and advancement to above-scale salary,[32] as well as approvals for research grants and contracts. Budget transfers were also made to individual chancellors that would give them greater control over personnel actions, budgeting, fund-raising, and admissions. In his memoirs,[33] Kerr notes reservations that he and various regents had at the time about possible uneven approaches among the campuses (notably San Diego) in awarding above-scale

---

[30] Loren M. Furtado, *Budget Reform and Administrative Decentralization in the University of California* (Berkeley: Berkeley Public Policy Press, Institute of Governmental Studies, University of California, 2002), pp. 43–45.

[31] Jerome C. Byrne was an attorney who staffed a regents' committee that examined the structure, organization, and governance of the university in light of the student unrest associated with the 1964 Free Speech Movement at Berkeley. The report recommended more radical changes than were eventually made and was viewed by Kerr and others as having been strongly influenced by Chancellor Franklin Murphy's desire for much increased autonomy (chapter 10). See Stadtman, 1970, *op. cit.*, pp. 471–472, and Kerr, 2001, *op. cit.*, pp. 208–210.

[32] Except for the few very high salaries, most of them in medical schools, that are above a certain dollar value and still require approval by the regents.

[33] Kerr, 2002, *op. cit.*, p. 211.

salaries. He also notes his retrospective belief that removal of the regents from the tenure-approval process should have been treated as a major issue to be given deeper consideration. But he also states his belief that things have worked out well enough over the years since the changes were made.

These changes in the Kerr era transferred the large bulk of administrative functions from the Office of the President to the campuses. From 1957 to 1965, the percentage of all full-time positions in general administration, student services, and institutional services located at the Office of the President decreased from 46 percent to 9 percent, and the percentage of faculty personnel actions with final approval by chancellors rose from 2 to 99 percent.[34]

Further Changes in Budgeting

Even with the 1964–65 budget transfers, the Office of the President still retained substantial resources in state and grant-overhead funds to enable it to launch and support new initiatives within the university. Examples of these initiatives are planning and development of new campuses, major university-wide research initiatives such as the UC share of the operating funds for the twin Keck ten-meter telescopes built and operated jointly with Caltech atop Mauna Kea in Hawaii, and new academic programs such as engineering at Riverside and Santa Cruz.

1996 Budget Decentralization. Up until 1996 there had been guidelines for the distribution of core funding to campuses that were based upon weighted enrollments: on a full-time equivalent basis, lower division students were weighted 1.0, upper division students 1.5, master's and professional students 2.5, and advanced graduate students (i.e., students having passed their PhD qualifying examinations), 3.5.[35]

In 1996, early in his term as president, Richard Atkinson instituted a new scheme for distribution of state funds and student fee revenue to campuses, whereby the allocations to date would be kept in place as a base, and funds for new enrollment growth would be distributed on

---

[34] Kerr, 2001, *op. cit.*, pp. 212–213.
[35] Furtado, 2002, *op. cit.*, p. 14.

an unweighted basis. In addition, the funds passed on to campuses were now allocated on essentially a lump-sum basis, allowing the campus administration much more flexible uses of the funds. In addition Atkinson arranged a return of 94 percent of all University Opportunity Funds (the university share of indirect costs from grants and contracts) to the individual campuses that had generated the funds.[36] The underlying logic was that leaving the existing distribution in place supported the greater concentrations of graduate and professional programs on the Berkeley, Los Angeles, and Davis campuses, while the different allocation of incremental funds still incentivized growth, particularly growth of undergraduate enrollment, in the same way that the state paid for it (i.e., on an unweighted basis). Determination of the portions of graduate-level enrollments on the various campuses would be left to the academic marketplace.[37] Under this approach substantially lesser amounts remained available to the president for large initiatives. The new Merced campus was starting at the time, and care was taken to place start-up funding for it on separate and specific state allocations.

It is significant that the two main occasions on which major decentralization actions took place were also points in time when a new president entered who had until then been a chancellor.[38]

Funding Streams and "Rebenching" Initiatives, 2008–2018. Further review of budget allocations to campuses was started in 2008, with the primary aims of gaining clarity and transparency, incentivizing campuses to raise money in view of state funding reductions, and assuring equity in the distribution among campuses. Two innovations resulted—the Funding Streams Initiative, which was instituted in 2011, and "Rebenching" (i.e., rebenchmarking), which has been brought in over the six-year period from 2012–13 to 2017–18. The implementation of both initiatives is outlined in the *UC Systemwide*

---

[36] Patricia A. Pelfrey, *Entrepreneurial President: Richard Atkinson and the University of California, 1995–2003* (Berkeley: University of California Press, 2012), pp. 63–65.

[37] One result is that the nine general campuses still (2014–15) remain uneven in graduate and professional enrollments as a percentage of total enrollment: UCLA and Berkeley at 28 percent; Davis, San Diego, and Irvine at 21 percent; Santa Barbara and Riverside at 12 percent; Santa Cruz at 9 percent; and Merced at 6 percent.

[38] Kerr in 1958 from Berkeley, and Atkinson in 1995 from San Diego.

Budget Manual,[39] with further background on the rebenching component in a report from the defining committee [40] and commentary[41] from the Academic Senate members of that committee. An article[42] in the media summarizes the initiatives.

The Funding Streams Initiative specified that revenues other than the state allocation should go directly to the campus generating them. This includes tuition and fees, indirect cost recovery, net patent revenues, and investment earnings. There are two exceptions. The first of these is that financial-aid monies, such as from the designated return-to-aid portions that have typically been one-third of all tuition increases, go into the general pool for student financial aid. That pool is then distributed in accord with an education financing model[43, 44] and the funding of the Blue and Gold Opportunity Program (chapter 2). The former allocates financial-aid funding among campuses on the basis of aggregate student need, which does differ from campus to campus. The latter covers tuition and fees for students from families with incomes up to a certain level ($80,000 per year for 2015–16).

Secondly, the operations budget for the Office of the President, formerly a direct allocation, became effectively a tax placed on campus funds, initially uniform at 1.6 percent for 2011–12.[45] As of 2014–15 the

---

[39] "Systemwide Budget Manual," Budget Analysis and Planning, Office of the President, University of California, rev. November 3, 2017, https://perma.cc/YU4Q-W6FW.
[40] University of California Rebenching Budget Committee, *Committee Report and Recommendations*, June 25, 2012, https://perma.cc/8XJR-L4PV.
[41] Susan Gillman and Jim Chalfant, "Rebenching: A Guide and Update," June 2012, https://perma.cc/99F8-TGVY.
[42] Kevin Kiley, "Can Funding Be Fair?," *Inside Higher Education*, January 31, 2013, https://perma.cc/F4R4-BYQE.
[43] "Education Financing Model: Implementing Guidelines for the University of California's Undergraduate Financial Aid Policy, 1998–99," University of California, https://perma.cc/GYE5-MLPN.
[44] "Financial Aid Funding and Allocation," chapter 5 in *Systemwide Budget Manual*, Budget and Analysis, Office of the President, University of California, revised November 2, 2017, https://perma.cc/YU4Q-W6FW.
[45] Debora Obley, "The University Budget," Business Officers Institute, University of California, November 2011, https://web.archive.org/web/20131203231425/http://ucop.edu/ucophome/businit/boi/presentations/2011/07-budget-planning-obley.pdf.

allocation to operate the Office of the President became based equally upon three factors that are presumably more reflective of the actual services received from the university-wide office—the total expenditures from the campus, the total number of employees at the campus (reflecting personnel and benefits services), and the total number of students on the campus. Also included is a relatively small amount ($10 million as of 2016) for new university-wide initiatives at the discretion of the president.

Rebenching[46] was designed to be an equitable redistribution of state funds among campuses, carried out over a period of years so as to enable the redistribution to be done without any campus suffering an actual loss at any point. It distributes state funding on the basis of enrollment, after removing off-the-top of portions to provide (1) $15 million per campus for fixed costs, (2) funding for designated university-wide programs such as the Agricultural Experiment Station and Student Academic Preparation and Educational Partnerships (chapter 16), and (3) funds for the Office of the President, which has no enrollment. Enrollment eligibility for funding is determined with weighting factors of 1.0 for undergraduates and nonresearch graduate students, 2.5 for research doctoral students, and 5.0 for health sciences students. San Francisco and Merced are treated differently, in ways described in the referenced manual, because of the lack of undergraduates at San Francisco and the newness of Merced. The state funding per undergraduate-equivalent student for each of the undergraduate campuses before the rebenching process is shown in table 6-1.

After rebenching, the allocation per undergraduate-equivalent student would presumably be at a uniform level for all eight of these campuses. As can be seen in table 6-1, the net transfers were from campuses with more professional schools to those with fewer or none, reflecting in part that professional schools have more ways of deriving other revenue, such as through executive and continuing education. As noted above, historically enrollments in graduate professional schools

---

[46] "Allocation of State General Funds," chapter 2 in *Systemwide Budget Manual* (Berkeley: Budget and Analysis, Office of the President, University of California, rev. November 3, 2017), https://perma.cc/YU4Q-W6FW.

had been given additional weight. Note also that, going into rebenching, the largest campus per-student allocation of state funds (for UCLA) exceeded the smallest (for UCSB) by 50 percent.

Table 6-1. Funding per undergraduate-equivalent student in 2009, before rebenching[47]

Los Angeles:	$6,413
Davis:	$6,129
Berkeley:	$5,749
San Diego:	$5,499
Riverside:	$5,401
Santa Cruz:	$5,215
Irvine:	$4,975
Santa Barbara:	$4,275

The funding streams and rebenching efforts serve to rationalize funding, subject to the assumptions reflected in the enrollment weightings, but they also do constrain the role of the president. The amount that can be utilized off the top for special university-wide initiatives, such as a new campus or operating costs for a special facility or program, is now limited by the amount of the budgetary allocation for new initiatives and the complications and sensitivities of securing additional funds through further direct assessment of the campuses. The situation can also give the appearance that the campuses are funding the Office of the President rather than vice versa—something of symbolic if not substantive importance.

Equity. At the end of this process or at any other time, there will still be concerns about the equity of the distribution of funds among campuses for many reasons. Those concerns will not be answerable to the satisfaction of all, and contentions will continue within the

---

[47] Kevin Kiley, "University of California Rethinks How It Funds Campuses," *Inside Higher Education*, January 31, 2013 https://perma.cc/FQ4F-F2LZ.

university. Campuses differ in the mix of academic programs that they offer, and different programs can have quite different costs from one another. Professional education tends to be more expensive than general undergraduate education, and among the professions costs vary widely, with engineering being substantially more costly per enrollee than, for example, law. The rebenching allocation is based strictly on instructional enrollment, yet research and tutorial supervision of student research are as much state-chartered missions of a research university as is ordinary instruction. Furthermore, costs of living vary substantially among the different regions of California.

Academic Decentralization

Originally, of course, academic administration and planning were done through the Office of the President. As already noted, the position provost of the university was created in 1931, but what was delegated by President Sproul to Monroe Deutsch in that position was much less than what is in the portfolio of a provost today. With Clark Kerr's decentralization moves of 1958–59 and 1964–65, initiation and definition of academic programs were moved to the campuses, while review and approval functions remained with the Office of the President. Campuses would define their academic programs and their coverage of disciplines. If a new academic program required a new school or college, or if it required budget beyond what the campus already had, the proposal would come to the Office of the President for academic and budget review, the latter carried out by consultation with the Academic Council of the senate. Requests for approval of new colleges, schools, and other major initiatives would then go to the Board of Regents.

In 1972, President Charles Hitch launched the Academic Planning and Program Review Board (APPRB),[48] combining the functions of three separate bodies that had existed within the Office of the President. The APPRB consisted of seven members of the university administration, four faculty members, two undergraduate students, and one graduate

---

[48] "President Hitch Establishes New Academic Planning and Review Board," *University Bulletin* 20 (December 13, 1971), University of California, https://books.google.com/books?id=I_M2AQAAMAAJ&pg=PA27&source=gbs_toc_r&cad=3#v=onepage&q&f=false, p. 61.

student. One of the faculty members was the vice chair of the Assembly of the Academic Senate (university-wide). The other faculty members were nominated by campus chancellors, who may have in at least some cases have consulted with the campus Academic Senate. The charge of the APPRB was to
1. prepare guidelines and review and coordinate academic plans and proposals for new programs,
2. prepare the university Academic Plan,
3. prepare and revise university growth plans,
4. review university academic and professional offerings, and
5. prepare operating and capital budget recommendations for the president.

Pelfrey[49] describes the background that Hitch had with the Department of Defense that led him to this university-wide approach to planning and the tensions that existed with the campuses with regard to the appropriateness of the roles of the APPRB and the means by which it would carry out planning.

The APPRB lasted through the presidencies of Charles Hitch and David Saxon. One of the outgrowths of the APPRB was the university-wide review of programs in education, which led to the examination of the Berkeley School of Education described in chapter 12. Another, fulfilling item number two of the charge, was the 1974 university-wide academic plan.[50]

The APPRB was discontinued when David Gardner became president in 1983. Functions one and three remained with the Office of the President. Function two became campus academic plans with a series of reports to the regents rather than a comprehensive, university-wide plan. Function four was devolved to campuses. Function five became the responsibility of the Budget Office under the direct supervision of the president, in consultation with the campuses

---

[49] Patricia A. Pelfrey, "From the Golden Age to the Age of Austerity: Planning at the University of California, 1968–1983: Research and Occasional Papers Series, no. 8-17, Center for Studies in Higher Education, University of California, Berkeley, July 2017, https://perma.cc/R489-CLSU.

[50] "The University of California Academic Plan, Phase 2, Campus Academic Plans," vol. 1: "The University-wide Perspectives," vol. 2: "The Chancellors' Statements," University of California, https://perma.cc/96SD-M3BQ.

and bodies such as the Council of Chancellors and the Council of (Academic) Vice Chancellors.

In the decades following Kerr's decentralization, the principal university-wide academic position became the senior vice president for academic affairs. Functions kept at the university-wide level under this position were (1) coordination of academic policy development, including the *Academic Personnel Manual* (chapter 11); (2) enrollment and capacity planning and coordination; (3) oversight of eligibility and admissions policies and practices; (4) preparation of comprehensive reports to the UC Regents on university-wide academic matters on an ad hoc basis, and (5) administrative oversight of various university-wide academic programs, including multicampus organized research, the Education Abroad program, the University of California Washington Center, the University of California Press, and Continuing Education of the Bar (legal publishing and postdegree education).

In 1992–93, the university took advantage of a presidential transition (Gardner to Peltason) to create a transition team, chaired by long-term UCLA chancellor Charles Young, to carry out "an examination of the structure and policies of the University's administrative apparatus and organization, especially as they bear upon the relationship between the campuses and the Office of the President, and secondly to make recommendations with regard to the planning and implementation of external and internal communications programs required to obtain the support necessary for success in this effort." [51] The report of this team recommended strengthening academic functions in the Office of the President in various ways, including adding the provost title for the senior vice president—academic affairs, placing the Budget Office under the provost, and adding a vice provost for research.

The changes recommended by the 1993 transition team were made, except that with the arrival of a subsequent president (Atkinson), the budget function was moved again to be a direct report to the president. Two other substantial university-wide academic functions that arose soon thereafter were planning and start-up for the

---

[51] The University of California Transition Team Final Report, September 1993, https://perma.cc/RBX9-DM39.

new Merced campus (chapter 10) and the California Digital Library[52] (chapters 2 and 16), which holds and licenses electronic material for all campuses in a single collection. As well, in the late 1990s, the university started centrally the eScholarship program[53] (chapter 2), an initiative that provides digital, open-access publishing opportunities for UC authors. For reasons of gaining economic efficiency, buying power, and trust among campuses it made sense to carry out these two initiatives centrally on a university-wide basis.

It is important that a sufficiently strong academic presence be kept at the Office of the President. One reason is that there are functions such as policy development for academic personnel and research, eligibility and admission, and other academic areas that must be coordinated university-wide. Another reason is that activities such as the digital library, scholarly publishing initiatives, and various specialized academic programs such as Education Abroad benefit in both academic richness and economic efficiency from being done for the entire university, as amplified below. There is also a need for senior officials at the Office of the President who have in-depth knowledge of the academic enterprise, so that academic knowledge can be built fully into university-wide deliberations and decisions. In addition, a large and complex operation such as the University of California cannot operate effectively and efficiently with academic planning occurring only on the campuses without some university-wide element.

Location of the Office of the President; Symbolism

Historically, the Office of the President of the University of California had been at the Berkeley campus. After Kerr's conversion to the organizational structure with chancellors for all campuses, the Office of the President moved in 1959 to University Hall, a building directly adjoining the Berkeley campus to the west and specially constructed for occupancy by the Office of the President. [54]

---

[52] California Digital Library, University of California, accessed June 3, 23016, http://www.cdlib.org/
[53] eScholarship, University of California, https://www.cdlib.org/services/access_publishing/publishing/escholarship.html.
[54] Harvey Helfand, *The Campus Guide: University of California, Berkeley* (New York: Princeton Architectural Press, 2002), pp. 322–323.

Structure, Organization, and Internal Budgeting of UC: One University, with Campuses Empowered

Subsequently, in 1967, the estate[55] of Anson Blake in Kensington, just north of Berkeley, was acquired by gift from the owners and became the official residence for the president of the University of California, thereby liberating University House on the Berkeley campus to be the residence of the Berkeley chancellor.

The location of the Office of the President, or the equivalent office for any university system or multicampus university, is a sensitive and complicated matter. If it is located on or adjacent to one of the campuses, other campuses will sense that there is favoritism to that campus. On the other hand, the chancellor or president of that campus will likely sense that the president or system head is too close at hand, continually looking over his or her shoulder. There may be rivalries on matters of status and recognition with regard to social affairs and ceremonies on that campus. Such contentions were a large issue between Chancellor Franklin Murphy of UCLA and President Clark Kerr (Chapter 10). There may also be confusion as to who is really in charge of what, as evidenced by the following story from Richard Atkinson:[56]

> In an earlier period, there was a presidential order that the chancellor's letterhead should have the president listed by name and title at the top lefthand corner with the chancellor's name and title immediately below...On one occasion while I was chancellor, an individual came to my office. He handed me a letter that I had written to him and explained that he did not wish to deal with me but rather with the president of UC San Diego.

Yet there are also disadvantages to having the multicampus university or system office away from any campus. First, employees working in that office will not have as many continual reminders of what campus life, values, and needs really are. Second, if the office of the multicampus university president or system head is in the state capital, that may lead to the perception andf/or the reality that the system office is too responsive to the interests of the state government. All these criteria conflict. The common resolutions are to

---

[55] "Blake Family, Biographical Notes, Social Networks, and Archival Context," University of Virginia, https://perma.cc/E62G-V6M9.
[56] Richard C. Atkinson, "20/20, Reflections on the Last 20 Years of the 20th Century," pp. 62–63, Oakland, 2001, Mandeville Special Collections Library, UCSD, https://perma.cc/P8JZ-4Q2U.

place the office in the state capital (State University of New York, State University System of Florida, University of Massachusetts System) or on or near the oldest and most established campus (University of Illinois, University of North Carolina, University System of Maryland) or both, when the oldest campus is in the same city (University of Texas System, University of Wisconsin System).

During the Gardner years, the University of California Office of the President outgrew its quarters in University Hall, Berkeley, and the decision was made to move the headquarters to the Kaiser Center in downtown Oakland, California. The decision process is described by Gardner.[57, 58] The Oakland site was selected for convenient airport access and so that Office of the President employees would not have to relocate their homes. Oakland is about six miles or twenty-five minutes by automobile or rapid transit away from Berkeley.

Working from University Hall adjoining the Berkeley campus, the senior staff of the Office of the President would often go to seminars on that campus, have lunches at the Berkeley Faculty Club, and be included in Berkeley campus social affairs. Thus, they had a feel for campus life and were themselves a part of it. In Oakland that was no longer the case, and therefore Office of the President employees were reminded much less often of campus life and needs. As well, the particular location chosen in Oakland was a large, twenty-eight-story office building (figure 6-2) that had been world headquarters for Henry J. Kaiser's industrial empire—aluminum, steel, ship building, and, for a while, automobiles. Completed in 1960, it was and still is Oakland's tallest building and when built was the largest office tower west of the Rocky Mountains. Both the new location and the operations of the Office of the President caused the words "corporate culture" to be used often on the campuses to describe it, not without basis.

When Richard Atkinson became president in 1995, he indicated at an early press conference a desire to move the UC Office of the President back to the Berkeley campus.[59] The aim was to regain

---

[57] Gardner, 2005, *op. cit.*, pp. 251–252.
[58] Gardner, 1995–96, *op. cit.*, pp. 414–419.
[59] Edward Epstein and Chronicle Staff Writer, "SACRAMENTO—UC President's Office May Move," *San Francisco Chronicle*, *SFGate*, October 31, 1995,
https://www.sfgate.com/news/article/SACRAMENTO-UC-President-s-Office-May-Leave-3021316.php.

closeness to campus life and diminish both the image and the reality of corporate culture. But the idea was not received well by the chancellors. The move away from Berkeley was irreversible.

Figure 6-2. The Kaiser Center (*center*), Oakland, California[60]

When the ten-year lease for the Kaiser Center space was up in 1998, most of the Office of the President moved from the Kaiser Center to a newly constructed building in downtown Oakland. This has not alleviated the corporate image and remoteness from campus life.

DISTRIBUTION OF FUNCTIONS AMONG UNIVERSITY-WIDE AND CAMPUS LEVELS

The distribution of governance activities between the university-wide and campus levels differs according to the nature of the function.

---

[60] "Kaiser Center," *Wikipedia*, https://perma.cc/E28D-DGZH.

What follows is an attempt to summarize broadly the 2017 distributions.

If something is to be a university-wide function, there are several potential ways of doing it. One is to take it into the Office of the President as a role. Another is to designate a lead campus, with the Office of the President retaining any oversight that may be necessary. Yet another is to carry out the function through a committee or commission with representation from the various campuses. A comparison[61] is available of the Office of the President functions at the University of California with the functions of the system or university-wide office for eight other multicampus public universities[62] and the Arizona Board of Regents.

Administrative Appointments

Administrative appointments are made following formal, structured, and consultative search processes and are typically recommended by the person to whom the appointee reports and approved by the person or board the next level up. Thus, the president selects and recommends chancellors and vice presidents, and the Board of Regents approve them. The provost selects and recommends vice provosts and deans, and the chancellor or president approves them. Deans select and recommend, and the provost approves, department chairs.

Academic Matters

Program. As already indicated, selection and definition of academic programs remain with the campuses, and approval by the Board of Regents is needed for new campuses, new schools and colleges, and major initiatives. However, the size and nature of the University of California have enabled it to undertake some academic programs collectively for the entire university that would not be as viable if undertaken by individual campuses alone. Prime examples are

---

[61] "UC's Headquarters Charged with Significant, Wide-Ranging Functions," Office of the President, University of California, https://perma.cc/RH3W-7AWX.
[62] University of Texas, State University of New York, University of North Carolina, University of Q1 Wisconsin, University of Illinois, Texas A&M University, City University of New York, and California State Universities.

the digital library and open-access scholarly publication projects (chapter 2). Another earlier example was the Education Abroad Program (EAP),[63] which was started through the Santa Barbara campus in 1962. EAP continues to operate university-wide, currently with 408 programs in forty-three countries, many of them with resident UC faculty as station directors. Students typically take courses through host universities and have other group academic experiences. The Natural Reserve System[64, 65] is another instance, with the program overseen by the vice president for research and graduate studies at the Office of the President, but with individual campuses overseeing various ones of the thirty-nine individual reserve sites for use by the entire university.

Figure 6-3. The University of California Washington Center (*center of photograph*) adjoins a park with a memorial to Daniel Webster.[66]

---

[63] University of California, Education Abroad Program, accessed September 8, 2016, http://uc.eap.ucop.edu/.
[64] At 756,000 acres (over 3,000 sq. km.), the University of California Natural Reserve System is the largest in the world.
[65] Natural Reserve System, University of California, http://www.ucnrs.org/.
[66] Photo courtesy of Rodger Rak, UC Washington Center, https://perma.cc/SGN2-KSRY.

Another example is the University of California Washington program (UCDC), which draws from all campuses to provide students with a semester or quarter in the nation's capital, with some courses and opportunities for mentored internships. The Washington program joins with the UC Office of Federal Government Relations in the University of California Washington Center,[67] located near Scott Circle in Washington, DC. The eleven-story building (figure 6-3) also provides housing space for students participating in the academic program. Subsequently, a similar Sacramento Center[68] was started, focused on internships in the state capital. It serves students and programs university-wide but is now operated through the Davis campus.

Faculty Hiring and Advancement. As already noted, selection, review, promotion, and advancement of the faculty, including tenure decisions, remain with the campuses. Regental approval is needed only for the highest salaries, which are typically in the medical schools. Academic personnel policies, including review criteria for faculty, are determined by a highly consultative, university-wide process.

Libraries. The digital library (chapter 2) is university-wide, with campus options as to whether to join in licensing of specific material. Print libraries remain at the campuses but with rapid transportation of material among campuses. Less-used materials are kept in regional storage facilities, one for the north at Berkeley's Richmond Field Station and one for the south on the UCLA campus.

Research Oversight. The oversight of the three national laboratories (chapter 13) associated with the University of California is done through the Office of the President, with the Berkeley Laboratory overseen directly by the university and the Los Alamos and Livermore Laboratories managed through two limited liability corporations in partnership with industrial companies.

Proposals for extramural research grants are submitted by individual campuses. Funding from successful proposals is received directly by the campus, subject to campus application of university-wide policy on indirect costs. Indirect-costs rates do vary from campus

---

[67] "University of California Washington Center," https://www.ucdc.edu/.
[68] "About—University of California Center Sacramento," https://perma.cc/XA5T-G328.

to campus.[69] A reduction or waiver of indirect costs counter to established policy requires approval at the university-wide level.

Organized research units on individual campuses typically report to the vice chancellor for research of that campus. Agricultural research funded lhrough block grants to the entire university is overseen by a university-wide vice president. The project for the four Governor Gray Davis Institutes of Science and Innovation (see chapter 14), launched in 2000 through a state budget initiative, was overseen at the university-wide level through the competition that led to the approval of the subjects and locations of the four institutes.

The University of California also has a group of multicampus research units (MRUs), which are similar to organized research units on individual campuses, except that they involve all campuses with research activities in the particular area. Management is accomplished through a lead campus. At the high point, there were about twenty-three MRUs. In 2008, as there were severe reductions in the state budget, the funding for MRUs was lessened considerably, and much of the remaining funding was then converted into two competitive programs: Multicampus Research Programs and Initiatives and the president's Catalyst Awards. For the latter two programs, proposals are sought every several years for planning and program grants for new multicampus research activities. The focus of those programs is on initiation of multicampus research that can become financially sustainable in other ways, rather than on provision of continuing support. As of 2017, thirteen MRUs were still active, and another six were pending approval.[70]

One of the multicampus research units is the University of California Observatories (UCO),[71] which operates the Lick Observatory (chapter 2), which is still functional and useful for research, even after

---

[69] See, e.g., "Annual Report on Newly Approved Indirect Costs and Discussion of the Recovery of Indirect Costs from Research," item F2, Committee on Finance, Meeting of November 17, 2010, Regents of the University of California, https://perma.cc/BRT2-WGU6.

[70] "Multicampus Research Units (MRUs), Research and Graduate Studies, Office of the President, University of California, https://perma.cc/23U7-FDVW.

[71] University of California Observatories, https://perma.cc/9W4B-K46A.

130 years. UCO also provides administrative support for the twin Keck telescopes atop Mauna Kea in Hawaii (chapter 2).

Another MRU is the Humanities Research Institute, started by competition[72] in 1987 and awarded to the Irvine campus, where it remains.[73] UCHRI supports in-residence fellows and hosts working groups, seminars, conferences, and the like on topics traditional to the humanities, with emphasis on multidisciplinary research.

Overall research policy is determined through a consultative process at the university-wide level. Applications of human-subject and animal-usage policies and other aspects of regulatory policy are made on the individual campuses.

Planning. Planning for enrollments and overall enrollment capacity has been carried out university-wide under the auspices of the provost, including negotiations with individual campuses as necessary to accommodate overall enrollment demand from eligible applicants. Programmatic planning is carried out by individual campuses, with approval by the regents needed for major program initiatives. Long-range development plans (LRDPs) are required by law and are drawn up by campuses looking ten or more years ahead on the basis of campus academic plans and overall university needs. Program reviews are carried out entirely by the campuses.

Continuing Education. Continuing education is a self-funded operation under the name University Extension. It is carried out by the individual campuses subject to a university-wide delineation of geographical areas of coverage for each campus. University-wide enrollments are over 500,000 in over 17,000 courses.[74]

Business, Financial, and Administrative

Budget. Budget decentralization over the years was described in previous sections. The campuses receive formulaic, enrollment-based allocations of state funds. Other revenues, which are composed mainly of monies from tuition and fees, research grants, private gifts, and

---

[72] David P. Gardner, *Earning My Degree: Memoirs of an American University President* (Berkeley CA: University of California Press, 2005), pp. 228-31.
[73] "UCHRI: University of California Humanities Research Institute", https://perma.cc/7BQM-VKGW.
[74] "University Extension," University of California, https://perma.cc/FG5U-UQRT.

auxiliary enterprises, are received at the campus level. Campuses have wide authority to transfer funds among different usage categories.

Audit. Audit is a corporate responsibility of the UC Regents. There is a chief compliance and audit officer, which is one of three senior positions[75] that report jointly to the regents and the president. That office is responsible for internal audit university-wide. There are also campus-level audit offices, reporting jointly to the chief compliance and audit officer and the chancellor of that campus.

Benefits and Retirement. Employee benefits and retirement are handled university-wide. The university has its own retirement system, described in chapter 2.

Investment. The chief investment officer handles the investment of the endowment and retirement funds university-wide, as well as the short-term investment pool. Originally this was done through investment processes supervised in-house, but now most of the investment is contracted to large investment firms. The individual campuses have their own foundations with separate management of investments. Donations made to campuses can be designated for either the campus foundation or the main investment pool of the university.

Procurement. Purchasing is carried out by campuses, now with fully computerized systems for requests, approvals, and the purchasing itself. Large purchasing agreements are negotiated at both the university-wide and campus levels so as to gain purchasing power.

Accounting and Human Resources. Both of these services are carried out at the campus level.

Facilities and Real Estate. In early days many university buildings were funded privately for construction. During the 1900s state funds paid for much construction, especially in the decades immediately following World War II. The state then swung to issuing bonds for construction. Now the state is no longer funding buildings except for a few seismic projects. Campuses must, for the most part, fund new buildings through private donations and debt financing (i.e., bonds approved and issued by the UC Regents). The campuses provide maintenance and repairs to their own buildings. Campuses have

---

[75] The other two are the general counsel and the chief investment officer.

significant real estate operations, dealing in purchases and sales of buildings and acquisition of rental properties.

External Relations
   Media. Relations with the media are carried out university-wide for university-wide matters and by individual campuses for campus matters.
   Federal Government. The Washington, DC, headquarters of the university (figure 6-3) houses the Federal Government Relations office along with the university-wide Washington academic program.
   State Government. The university maintains one Office of State Government Relations in Sacramento. Both the Office of Federal Government Relations and the Office of State Government Relations are parts of the Office of the President.
   Local Governments. Campuses deal directly with their own local (city, county) governments. Being a state agency, the university and its campuses are tax-exempt. However, on various occasions campuses have purchased items for the local government that relate to services to campuses (e.g., a new fire engine). These items have at times been the subject of negotiation, or an *exaction*,[76] when a permit is sought from the city.
   Development. Development, or private fund-raising from alumni, friends, corporations, and other donors, has become a major operation even for public universities. Development operations for the University of California are done almost exclusively at the campus level, and at Berkeley, for example, are decentralized further to the level of individual colleges and schools, with the central development office serving the chancellor's priorities and providing services such as donor research and databases for the operations of individual colleges and schools. The reason for the high degree of decentralization is that many alumni, especially those with graduate and professional degrees, feel more attachment to their campus and even their college, school, or department than to the university as a whole, and corporations are closest to the academic unit(s) from which they hire graduates.

---

[76] Exactions are requirements that a local government places on an entity to pay for related costs as a condition of permitting.

Alumni Relations. Alumni relations (events for alumni, alumni magazines, summer camps, group trips, etcetera) are carried out at the campus and academic-unit levels separately from development. Alumni associations provide alumni with publications and events, as well as collecting information on the subsequent careers of graduates.

Technology Transfer, Patent Licensing, and Relations with Industry
These operations are now highly decentralized to campuses, as described in chapter 18.

Legal
Regents General Counsel provides institutional legal services to the university as a whole and reports jointly to the regents and to the president. The university maintains one centralized legal office in Oakland at the Office of the President, so that legal advice is coordinated and hopefully uniform. Individual campuses have their own counsel, typically one or two persons, who report jointly to the chancellor and the Regents General Counsel. Specialized external legal services are procured ad hoc as needed.

Information Technology
Management of computing and information technology services has had a varied history within the University of California as computing has gone through successive generations involving mainframe computers, personal computing, networking, and cloud technology. The bulk of academic and administrative computing has been campus based. The university-wide office works toward common standards and interchangeable software that will allow data to be collected consistently among campuses and is also undertaking to lead cybersecurity efforts. Desktop support has traditionally been highly localized. As part of its Shared Services initiative (see below), the Berkeley campus centralized oversight of desktop support while providing the services locally. Because of the very rapid advances of technology, the effectiveness of the organization of computing services has often lagged behind the realities of usage.

Health Sciences

UC has six schools of medicine—San Francisco, Los Angeles, San Diego, Davis, Irvine, and, as of 2013, Riverside. The university owns the associated hospitals or hospital systems, except in the case of Riverside. These belong to the particular campuses and are administered through them. At the university-wide level, UC Health, headed by an executive vice president, provides coordinating services and financial oversight for these operations as well as for the university's two schools of public health (Berkeley, Los Angeles), two schools of dentistry (San Francisco, Los Angeles), four schools of nursing (San Francisco, Los Angeles, Irvine, and, as of 2010, Davis), two schools of pharmacy (San Francisco, San Diego) and school of optometry (Berkeley).

Student Affairs

All campuses have vice chancellor offices overseeing student affairs. These are large and very multidimensional service operations, including oversight of admissions, the registrar, student housing and eating facilities, financial aid, the dean of students, the career or placement center, student conduct, student activities centers, health services, and ombudsman services. As already noted, at the university-wide level, financial aid is coordinated across campuses following an education financing model that gauges need-based aid. Also at the Office of the President, an admissions office oversees and coordinates eligibility policy and the envelope of admissions policies for the university and provides what coordination there is with other sectors of California higher education on admissions.

Athletics

For most campuses intercollegiate athletics is a very large undertaking, with much interest on the parts of students and local supporters. It is also a very large enterprise financially, and much national concern today deals with the financial dominance of intercollegiate athletics and its effects upon the rest of the academic enterprise at universities and colleges within the United States.

Intramural athletics, sports, and recreation are quite different and are supported by student fees on campuses. Intramural activities are designed for all students and in many cases faculty, staff, and even local constituents as well. Both intercollegiate and intramural athletics are entirely decentralized to the campus level.

Competition among Campuses

Contrary to the situation for many other multicampus universities or university systems around the world, the University of California campuses compete directly against one another in several ways. Even though competition can bring economic inefficiencies, the overriding benefit is that competition hones quality and enables campuses to reach for high attainment, thereby greatly enhancing the overall quality of the university. Campuses compete against one another in recruitment of faculty, staff, and students. Campuses can recruit faculty members from other UC campuses. Limits are placed upon the amount of salary increase and the size of recruitment packages for intercampus recruitments.[77] Campuses often compete against one another for federal government grants and major institutes and for industrial grants and contracts. The selection of the four Governor Gray Davis Institutes for Science and Innovation (chapter 14) was a large internal competition within UC, overseen by the Office of the President and utilizing outside reviewers and panels.

THE OPTIMAL DEGREE OF DECENTRALIZATION

There are many differences among public-university systems and multicampus universities with regard to what is centralized and what is not. There have also been large changes in that balance within the University of California over time, and, as noted in the quote at the start of this chapter, Clark Kerr did in 2001 express the view that what was the situation at that time may have gone too far in the direction of decentralization. Yet decentralization has proceeded further since then. It is therefore logical to ask the question, "What is the optimal degree of decentralization?"

---

[77] "Guidelines for Intercampus Recruitment," Academic Personnel Office, University of California, Berkeley, https://perma.cc/PQU6-DUG9.

Subsidiarity

The term *subsidiarity*[78] connotes that decisions should be handled by the smallest, lowest, or least centralized authority capable of handling the matter effectively. Among the results should be more informed and expedited decisions and less remoteness of governance. Subsidiarity is an explicit organizing principle of the European Union,[79] the Catholic Church,[80] and a variety of other multitiered organizations. Although the word was caught up in politics in the United States recently with rhetoric that strayed from the basic concept, the essential sense of the concept of subsidiarity is still valid.[81] It has particular relevance to institutions where the principal strength lies at the grass-roots level (i.e., the faculty in universities). It has the greatest implications for large and complex organizations, which include many universities, multicampus universities, and university systems.

Optimal Decentralization

As we have seen, administrative decentralization has already proceeded to a large extent for the University of California through a series of changes over the years. There is continual interest in more decentralization, and there are also cogent arguments for recentralization of some functions so as to exercise responsible oversight for the state or other funding entities and/or so as to gain economic efficiencies and consistency in decisions that affect the edges of overall policy. What is optimal will change over time and will be continually open to deliberation and dispute.

One can consider at least five aspects of decentralization—administrative decision-making, budget control, academic program, services, and board-level governance.

Administrative Decision-Making. On the whole, it appears that the degree of decentralization of administrative decision-making

---

[78] Andreas Føllesdal, "Survey Article: Subsidiarity," *Journal of Political Philosophy* 6, no. 2 (1998): pp. 190–218.
[79] George Bermann, "Taking Subsidiarity Seriously: Federalism in the European Union and United States," *Columbia Law Review* 94, no. 2 (1994): pp. 331–456.
[80] Robert K. Visher, "Subsidiarity as a Principle of Governance: Beyond Devolution," *Indiana Law Review* 35 (2001–02): pp. 103–142.
[81] Visher, 2001-02, *loc. cit.*

currently operative within the University of California is about right in terms of the subsidiarity concept. A problem that does arise by virtue of the size of the university and the division (some might say stovepiping) of functions among many offices is a sort of paralysis brought about by different offices having responsibility for different parts of a matter that requires a single overall decision.[82] It is difficult to generate a decision when those involved have different views of the elephant, tend to take strict yes-no positions that they believe are imposed on them from above, and/or are in reporting lines within the university that are separate from the decision-maker.

Budget Control. As described above, there is now a large decentralization of the University of California budget to the campuses as well as further down the administrative line on campuses. This is healthy in terms of giving budgetary flexibility to chancellors, provosts, vice chancellors, and deans. However, the changes in budgeting within the university over the years have now placed the University of California in a situation where the president now holds a much smaller amount flexibly to support major university-wide initiatives, such as new campuses or major new programs (e.g., schools of medicine or law, or energy, climate, and water institutes) to be carried out on still-developing campuses. Yet the population of California continues to increase substantially, the vast northern portion of the state has no UC campus, and the new Merced campus needs the ability to undertake large initiatives. The starts of major new initiatives must now be funded by increased "taxation" of the campuses, privately, and/or by the full load of political negotiations and give-and-take in Sacramento. In the latter case, the university loses control, and some of the key advantages of constitutional autonomy are lost through the lack of flexible, central budget.

As former Irvine chancellor and UC president Jack Peltason said in his oral history, "The Office of the President has to champion the new campus. I now know that from my own experiences three decades

---

[82] I can recall situations when, in my various administrative positions, I was at the table with perhaps eight other people, all representing different aspects of the issue. An example would be a personnel matter with legal implications, where the group would represent Regents General Counsel, risk management, the status of women and minorities, labor relations, and human-relations offices at the campus, vice-chancellor, and unit levels. Each member of such a group tends to view the issue primarily from his or her own standpoint.

later. Existing campuses don't understand the need for new campuses."[83] To which his interviewer replied, "They're a competitive threat, aren't they?"

Academic. The UC academic program is decentralized to campuses and on campuses further decentralized very largely to academic departments. New programs are initiated by campuses, reviewed university-wide with involvement by the Academic Council's Coordinating Committee on Graduate Affairs (for graduate programs) or Committee on Education Policy (undergraduate programs), then approved by the provost and then the president, and finally approved by the UC Regents if the program involves creation of a college or school or represents a major academic or budgetary initiative.[84] Historically, this process has been entirely bottom-up; academic programs have not been "assigned" to campuses. There have not yet been many issues of program elimination or consolidation within the university, and those that have arisen have been handled locally on campuses. Examples where these actions have been considered or done are criminology, education, biological sciences, and library and information studies at Berkeley (all four described in chapter 12); the elimination of the nascent School of Architecture at San Diego; and the Professional Schools Restructuring Initiative at UCLA.[85, 86] The latter two and the Berkeley School of Library and Information Studies occurred during the state budget crisis of the early 1990s. Complete attention to the academic menu of the university does also require that there be a

---

[83] Jack W. Peltason, interview by Ann Lage, "Political Scientist and Leader in Higher Education, 1947–1995: Oral History Transcript; Sixteenth President of the University of California, Chancellor at UC Irvine, and the University of Illinois," Regional Oral History Office, Bancroft Library, University of California, Berkeley, http://www.archive.org/details/leaderinhigher00peltrich.
[84] "Compendium: University-wide Review Processes for Academic Programs, Academic Units, and Research Units," University of California, September 2014, https://perma.cc/X46V-T9CR.
[85] Ralph Frammolino and Marina Dundjerski, "Plan to Dismantle 4 UCLA Schools Protested; Students, Faculty Resist a Proposal to Cut Several Graduate Programs; Chancellor Says Across-the-Board Reductions Would Be More Harmful," *Los Angeles Times*, October 15, 1993, https://perma.cc/Q2KU-EKSV.
[86] Suzanne Muchnic, "UCLA Merges Architecture and Arts Into a New School," *Los Angeles Times*, October 14, 1994, https://perma.cc/H8R5-WBJJ.

mechanism for examining the full panoply of academic offerings among campuses to see where there may be inadequate coverage, excess capacity, or opportunities for fruitful collaboration among campuses. This was a function of the Academic Planning and Program Review Board during the Hitch and Saxon administrations. A university-wide mechanism for those purposes is needed, and the present full decentralization of the academic program makes it difficult to achieve. The university-wide Academic Planning Council, which has existed since 1994, is more of a consultative and informational body than an actual planning body. Program elimination will become more of a necessity to the extent that campus budgets tighten further.

A challenge for all universities is getting faculty members from individual academic departments to participate in general-education and multidisciplinary courses and degrees (chapter 14). This need calls for incentive and reward structures that act across departmental boundaries. In these senses the curriculum can no longer be delegated fully to the level of academic departments. This issue is academically important and is not limited to the University of California.

Services. With the exception of retirement, benefits, the digital library in its wider contexts, and areas such as large procurement contracts, support services to the academic enterprise are almost entirely at the campus level. On the campuses, the tension in the design of support services is between centralization on the campus to gain efficiency, on the one hand, and expertise and placement locally in units so as to gain closeness and responsiveness to the needs of faculty and other users, on the other hand. A classic example of this tension has been in the area of computing services, as documented in a 2006 report of a UC Berkeley external/internal review committee chaired by the author.[87] Tracing back to the days of mainframe computers, the Berkeley campus has had a large centralized computing operation, now known as Information Services and Technology, under an associate vice chancellor who was also chief information officer. Over the years, computer support systems had been built up by the various units of the campus, academic and nonacademic, providing services that often

---

[87] "Information Technology at UC Berkeley, Governance, Funding, and Structure: Final Report and Recommendations," University of California, Berkeley, January 18, 2006, https://perma.cc/3XLY-88PK.

went well beyond desktop support and had been direct and specific to the needs of the units. Reasons for the units developing localized services themselves were the seeming remoteness of the centralized staff and the problem of a "computer-ese" communication barrier.

As part of a drive to reduce overall costs, the Berkeley campus commissioned a study by Bain and Associates focused upon administrative efficiency and carried out from 2009 to 2010.[88] This study led off an initiative denoted Operational Excellence, the design and operation of which are described by Szeri et al.[89] A major component of that initiative has been shared services.[90] The general goal of shared services is to gain economic efficiency, greater depth of knowledge by service performers, and operational effectiveness by centrally providing and coordinating services that have been at the individual-unit level. Areas covered have been research administration, information technology including desktop computer support, human relations and academic personnel support, and business and financial services. This has been one of several such efforts at UC campuses (five others so far) and other universities.[91]

These endeavors have been controversial, with a significant number of misfires in early years. One large issue is whether the employees of the shared-services unit are truly responsive to those in the units that they serve, since their reporting relationships are now outside the unit. A second issue is whether there is an added load upon the staff employees who remain in the unit stemming from needs to nurse along the shared-services effort in order to make it work for the

---

[88] University of California, Berkeley and the Bain Corporation, "Achieving Operational Excellence at University of California, Berkeley," Final Diagnostic Report–Complete Version, April 2010 https://perma.cc/G35S-5CFG.

[89] Andrew J. Szeri, Richard Lyons, Peggy Huston, and John Wilton, "Doing Much More with Less: Implementing Operational Excellence at UC Berkeley," Paper no. CSHE.10.13, Research and Occasional Papers, Center for Studies in Higher Education, University of California, Berkeley, June 2013, https://perma.cc/TZE5-7U7E.

[90] Campus Shared Services, University of California, Berkeley, https://perma.cc/74KP-ZUQZ.

[91] See, e.g., a list and associated references at "Shared Services Elsewhere," Shared Services, University of California, Berkeley, https://web.archive.org/web/20170726010840/http://sharedservices.berkeley.edu/shared-services-elsewhere/.

unit. The answers to such questions and the extent to which such shared efforts will indeed make substantial cost savings are still not clear. In the case of Berkeley shared services, units were initially placed in a location about 2.5 miles and twenty to thirty minutes (allowing for parking) from the campus. As it became apparent that this geographical remoteness compounded the problems of remoteness of allegiance of the staff, shared-services activities were moved back and distributed to various locations on the main campus itself. As of 2017, the campus was rethinking the entire idea and trying some efforts to centralize services for groups of similar units (e.g., physical sciences). This is a step in between a single set of campus shared services and full distribution of services to the level of individual units.

SUMMARY CONCLUSIONS

The structure of the University of California as one university with multiple campuses provides many advantages, including
- a single mission upon which the university can focus,
- a single corporate identity—one state budget to the university as a whole rather than to individual campuses,
- one set of standards, policies, and policy envelopes, and
- the ability to grow new campuses from within with standards and policies extant from the start and with oversight and guidance from faculty from existing campuses through the Academic Senate structure.

What can suffer, on the other hand, is coordination among the three segments of higher education, especially articulation for transfer.

Decentralization of governance has continued at intervals over time, with state funding now being allocated to campuses almost entirely formulaically. Decentralization of budget has now gone far enough so that the president does not have as much ability to nurture new initiatives directly from discretional funds as was the case in earlier years. The degree of decentralization and relocations of the Office of the President have also created more tendencies for it to be viewed as a "corporate" rather than academic function.

The academic program belongs to the individual campuses, with the exception of certain activities that benefit in terms of academic efficiency and/or critical size from being at the university-wide level. Academic programs at the university-wide level include Education Abroad, the Washington and Sacramento Centers, the California Digital Library, services for open-access publishing, the University of California Press, and large, shared facilities such as the Natural Reserve System and the Keck ten-meter telescopes.

During the presidencies of Charles Hitch and David Saxon, university-wide academic planning was overseen by the Academic Planning and Program Review Board. There remains an Academic Planning Council, university-wide, but with a weaker and more generally consultative role. Planning for needed university-wide initiatives should be strengthened in a way that still recognizes the individual determinative roles of the campuses.

For such a large organization as the University of California with its programmatic strength dispersed at the level of individual departments and faculty members, the concept of subsidiarity in governance is valuable. Following it, decision-making should be placed at the lowest level possessing the requisite information to make the decision.

7.
Shared Governance

The two greatest gifts to the University of California have been the institutional autonomy given to its Board of Regents in the Constitution of 1878 and the unprecedented grant of authority the board assigned to the Academic Senate in 1920. These two gifts constitute the institutional foundation for the growth in distinction of the University of California.
　—*Clark Kerr*[1]

Faculty governance is rarely simple, is frequently ponderous, and is sometimes frustratingly ineffective. The degree of faculty participation may be low and variable. Overall, however, it has served the universities well, and it remains an essential factor in the vigour of university life.
　—*Frank H. T. Rhodes*[2]

At its core, shared governance is simply a methodology for managing a particular kind of diverse and complex organization, and like any methodology, it can go awry if implemented poorly.
　—*James C. Garland*[3]

The contemporary university is too complex and fragmented to allow for substantive faculty involvement in the broader governance of the university.
　—*James Duderstadt and Farris Womack*[4]

---

[1] Clark Kerr, foreword to Angus E. Taylor, *The Academic Senate of the University of California: Its Role in Shared Governance and Operation of the University of California* (Berkeley: Institute of Governmental Studies Press, University of California, 1998), https://perma.cc/HU3G-KUTX.

[2] Frank H. T. Rhodes, "Governance of U. S. Universities and Colleges," in Luc E. Weber and James J. Duderstadt, eds., *Reinventing the Research University* (London: Economica, 2004), p. 224.

[3] James C. Garland, *Saving Alma Mater: A Rescue Plan for America's Public Universities* (Chicago: University of Chicago Press, 2009), pp. 84–85.

[4] James J. Duderstadt and Farris Womack, *Beyond the Crossroads: The Future of the Public University in America* (Baltimore, MD: Johns Hopkins University Press, 2003), p. 166.

Faculty in their collective behavior have a tendency to be individualistic, self-centered, and short-sighted; therefore, they should not have any decision power regarding strategic issues.
—*Luc Weber*[5]

The term "shared governance" denotes participation of the faculty in the governance of a university. The practice is widespread in name, particularly in public universities, but it is very different in practice from one university to another. Because of its wide-ranging implementations and degrees of effectiveness from institution to institution, shared governance is controversial and is often denigrated. That fact explains, in part, the very different attitudes expressed in the quotations above, which come from former presidents of the University of California, Cornell University, Miami University of Ohio, the University of Michigan, and the University of Geneva, respectively.

The University of California is probably the institution in the United States where shared governance is most developed, structured, and well regarded. It is one of the keys to the success of the university and therefore is worthy of detailed examination. The approach of this chapter is to start by considering the ways in which shared governance developed at the University of California and then how it operates there in practice. We then look more generally at shared governance—the reasons for having it, what it takes in order to work well, what can go wrong, and ways in which it needs to evolve with the times.

SHARED GOVERNANCE AT THE UNIVERSITY OF CALIFORNIA

How It Developed

An Academic Senate was established in the Organic Act of 1868 (chapter 2) that originally established the University of California.

---

[5] Luc Weber, "Critical University Decisions and Their Appropriate Makers," in Werner Z. Hirsch and Luc E. Weber, eds., *"Governance in Higher Education: The University in a State of Flux"* (London: Economica, 2001), p. 84.

However, the Academic Senate had limited and ill-defined responsibilities, which resulted in it being relatively ineffective. The presiding officer was the president of the university, and thus delineation between the senate and administration was indistinct, and the senate was largely a means for the president to consult with the faculty if and when he chose to do so. The history of the Academic Senate during the period before 1919 is outlined by Stadtman.[6]

As we have seen in chapter 2, President Benjamin Ide Wheeler took many steps during his administration (1899-1919) that set the University of California on the road to greatness. However, he operated in largely dictatorial fashion. Examples of his approach were hiring, promoting, and dismissing faculty without consultation; making his own appointments to committees of the Academic Senate; and, when he did consult, seeking and taking counsel largely from those who would agree with him.

As the Wheeler presidency ended in July 1919, the Board of Regents chose not to appoint a new president immediately but instead placed the administration of the university temporarily under a three-man administrative board while a more thorough search was made for a new president. As is the case for most attempts to carry out administration by troika, the administrative board did not work well. It was plagued by members working at cross-purposes and seeming to seek and value the views of the faculty even less than had been the case while Wheeler was president.

The Berkeley Revolution.[7, 8, 9] The methodology used by Wheeler during his years and the situation with the new administrative board caused the faculty, working through the Academic Senate, to seek meetings of their leaders with the regents so as to effect change. The

---

[6] Verne A. Stadtman, *The University of California, 1868–1968* (New York: McGraw-Hill Book Co., 1970), pp. 239–241.
[7] Arthur E. Hutson, "Faculty Government" in Verne E. Stadtman, ed., *The Centennial Record of the University of California, 1868–1968* (Berkeley: University of California Printing Dept., 1967), pp. 288–291, https://perma.cc/8Q7G-8MKA.
[8] Angus E. Taylor, *The Academic Senate of the University of California: Its Role in Shared Governance and Operation of the University of California* (Berkeley: Institute of Governmental Studies Press, University of California, 1998), https://perma.cc/XTW4-VCAD.
[9] Stadtman, 1970, *op. cit.*, pp. 239–249.

faculty initiated the process by adopting a memorial[10] to the regents, outlining their desires. The aim was to work out a better form of governance and in particular more structured and effective roles for the faculty. On the basis of extensive interviews that he conducted much later with Hildebrand and Louderback, Hutson[11] reports that the leaders of the faculty group within the senate were Joel Hildebrand and Gilbert Lewis of chemistry, Armin Leuschner of astronomy, and Frank Louderback of geology, with Andrew Lawson, also of geology, as floor manager and strategist. What is very significant here is that all five of those individuals were renowned scholars who had key roles in building the University of California to eminence (see chapter 9). They were true intellectual leaders of the faculty. Coincidentally or not, all five were physical scientists, leaders of an area that was then developing to national research prominence (also see chapter 9).

The faculty group ultimately meeting with the regents was Lawson, Lewis, and Louderback, along with George Adams of philosophy and Orrin McMurray of law. The latter two were also recognized intellectual leaders and served to widen the disciplinary base across the campus. The negotiations of this group with an ad hoc committee of the regents brought about a set of agreements relating to the roles of the Academic Senate that are essentially what is in place today and is described in the following sections.

In December of 1919, the UC Regents selected as the new president David Barrows, former dean of the faculties of the university, who had been on leave for eight months as an intelligence officer with the Allied Expeditionary Forces in Siberia. Barrows was given the opportunity to review what had been worked out by the regents with the faculty leaders, and he found it to be acceptable, although he did later object that those faculty members who had opposed the new arrangements were being shut out of committee membership. The senate then took steps to remedy that perception. Then in March 1920, the regents formally adopted the portion of their standing orders pertaining to the Academic Senate. Through this sequence of events,

---

[10] Bylaws of the Academic Senate, section 90, "Memorials," University of California, accessed https://perma.cc/WY3V-LP34.
[11] Hutson, 1967, *loc. cit.*

often called the "Berkeley Revolution,"[12] the roles, structure, and influence of the present-day Academic Senate came into being.

Figure 7-1. The newly empowered Academic Senate meets in the Faculty Club, 1920.[13]

The Roles of the Academic Senate in Governance

Standing Orders 105.1[14] and 105.2[15] of the regents delineate the roles of the Academic Senate. They specify that the Academic Senate

---

[12] Taylor, 1998, *op. cit.*, p. 1.
[13] "History and Discoveries," University of California, Berkeley, https://perma.cc/9BY3-MTMV.
[14] Standing Order 105.1: Organization of the Academic Senate, Regents of the University of California, https://perma.cc/Y5QW-TZRG.
[15] Standing Order 105.2: Duties, Powers, and Privileges of the Academic Senate, Regents of the University of California, https://perma.cc/4ZD9-VMF4.

- may determine its own membership within constraints, its own organization, its own officers and committee memberships, and how it wishes to delegate responsibilities internally;
- subject to the approval of the Board of Regents, shall determine the conditions for admissions of students and for degrees and certificates and shall be consulted in connection with the award of honorary degrees;[16]
- authorizes and supervises all courses and curricula;
- may select committees to advise chancellors on campus budgets and to advise the president on the university-wide budget;
- may present to the Board of Regents, through the president, its views on any matter pertaining to the conduct and welfare of the university;
- should advise the president and chancellors on the administration of the libraries; and
- should select a committee to approve the publication of manuscripts by the University of California Press.

Another major role of the Academic Senate stemming from the 1919 negotiations is review, evaluation, and recommendation of faculty members for promotion and advancement along the professorial scale of ranks and salaries.[17] This process, in which the administration has final approval authority but the Academic Senate has the primary role, is described in chapter 11. Only rarely does the administration decide counter to the recommendations from the

---

[16] Honorary degrees were suspended, by presidential policy in 1972. The triggering event was the refusal of the regents to approve an honorary degree for Mayor John V. Lindsay of New York City, which had been recommended by the Berkeley campus with Academic Senate consultation. There were apparent political reasons for the regental nonapproval, since Lindsay was a very liberal Republican, of different politics from the more conservative members of the board. (See, e.g., Martin Snapp, "Honor Roll: Colleges Dole Out Honorary Degrees for Star-Studded, Curious Cast," *California*, California Alumni Association, May 12, 2016, https://perma.cc/54F3-H3PS.) An exception to that policy was made in 2009 when retroactive honorary degrees were given to Japanese-Americans who had been University of California students at the time of relocations and incarcerations of Japanese-Americans during World War II. (See Judy Sakaki and Daniel Simmons, "Conferring of Honorary Degrees and Suspension of Bylaw 29.1," PowerPoint, presented at Regents Meeting, University of California, July 16, 2009, https://perma.cc/4MQ2-JKB8.)

[17] Stadtman, 1970, *op. cit.*, p. 248.

senate faculty review process, and then only after further consultation with the senate.

In practice, the administration brings virtually all major matters pertaining to the governance of the university to the leadership of the Academic Senate for its advice. The senate may also bring up issues of its own. Senate advice in these other areas is taken seriously but is not as controlling in administrative decisions as it is in the area of promotion and advancement of faculty.

The chair and the vice chair of the Academic Council (the university-wide executive body of the Academic Senate) take part in regents' meetings, sitting at the table with the regents and speaking when they wish. In line with the desires of the Academic Senate, they have no vote, following the rationale that they would not be able to represent the senate membership on issues that have not yet been taken up formally by the senate.

University of California practice is for deans, provosts, chancellors, and the president to undergo formal but confidential reviews of performance at five-year intervals. There is a role for the Academic Senate in all of these reviews, with a selected committee and/or the senate leadership receiving review materials and advising for both initial appointments and the five-year reviews. If a high administrator is not working out well on a campus, it is usually the senate that most effectively communicates the point in a review, and in some cases without waiting for a review.

Functionally, the Academic Senate has direct authority for courses, curricula, the conditions for admission of students, and for self-organization. It has the primary influence, but without actual decision authority, for promotion, advancement, and dismissal of faculty, and for program review. It has "soft" power—that is, the right to be consulted but not to decide, on other major issues, including appointments and reappointments of senior administrators.

How the Academic Senate Works

All tenure-track faculty (i.e., assistant, associate, and full professors) are members of the Academic Senate, along with *emeriti*[18]

---

[18] The title professor emeritus is granted to all faculty members who retire in good standing.

holding those titles, certain high administrative officers, and holders of a few other academic titles. The Academic Senate exists both at the all-university level and as divisions on each campus. One feature of the Academic Senate that stands in contrast with some other research universities is that all faculty members—junior as well as senior and from professional schools as well as academic disciplines—have the opportunity to become equally involved with campus-wide issues. Thus the views from the senate reflect faculty from the entire campus.

There are a few meetings of the full senate membership on the campuses each year. These regular meetings are usually mostly informational and attended by a small portion of the faculty, although attendance will rise substantially if there is a major issue on the agenda. Special meetings can be called when large issues arise, and those meetings are typically much better attended. For example, meetings of membership of the Berkeley Division were frequent during the Free Speech Movement and other crises during the 1960s and were attended by a majority of the faculty.

The main body at the all-university level is the Academic Council, composed of the chairs of the campus divisions, chairs of major university-wide senate committees, and the chair and vice chair (incoming chair) of the Academic Council, who are elected by the Academic Council itself. Similar bodies exist for each of the ten campus divisions, typically called the Division Council. The ultimate university-wide legislative body for the senate is the Assembly of the Academic Senate, comprised of elected representatives from the campuses along with the chairs of the campus divisions and the university-wide senate officers. In a sense, the Academic Council is the executive arm of the assembly.

Both the Academic Council and the divisions have large numbers of committees on various subjects. The 2015 Committees of the Academic Council are shown in table 7-1. Those for the Berkeley Division are shown in table 7-2. These committees typically meet monthly, or more often if the timing associated with particular issues warrants.

Table 7-1. Committees of the Academic Council, 2016-7[19]

Academic Computing and Communications
Academic Council (executive body)
Special Committee on [National] Laboratory Issues
Academic Freedom
Academic Personnel
Affirmative Action, Diversity, and Equity
Board of Admissions and Relations with Schools
Committees
Coordinating Committee on Graduate Affairs
Editorial
Education Policy
Faculty Welfare
    Task Force on Investment and Retirement
    Task Force on the Future of UC Health Care Plans
International Education
Intersegmental Committees of the Academic Senates
Library and Scholarly Communication
Planning and Budget
Preparatory Education
Privilege and Tenure
Research Policy
Rules and Jurisdiction

---

[19] "Academic Senate Committees," https://web.archive.org/web/20170116011125/https://senate.universityofcalifornia.edu/committees/index.html

TABLE 7-2. Committees of the Berkeley Division of the Academic Senate, 2015[20]

Academic Freedom
Academic Planning and Resource Allocation
Admissions, Enrollment & Preparatory Education
American Cultures
Assembly Representation
Budget and Interdepartmental Relations
Committees
Courses of Instruction
Demonstrations and Student Actions
Diversity, Equity, and Campus Climate
Divisional Council (the executive body)
Educational Policy
Faculty Awards
Faculty Research Lectures
Faculty Welfare
Graduate Council
Library
Memorial Resolutions
Ombudspersons
Panel of Counselors
Privilege and Tenure
Prizes
Research
Rules and Elections
Senate Athletics Council
Teaching
Undergraduate Council
Undergraduate Scholarships, Honors, and Financial Aid

---

[20] "About the Committees: Academic Senate", https://web.archive.org/web/20151219044042/http://academic-senate.berkeley.edu/senate-committees

The Committees on Committees, at both the campus and university-wide levels, have the function of identifying and selecting members for the various other committees, as well as gaining the acceptance of those selected. The members of the campus Committee on Committees and those positions on the campus Division Councils that are not filled ex officio are elected by the division (campus) membership of the senate. Those are typically the only senate positions elected by the full membership.

Here are some responsibilities of committees at the university-wide level:

- The Board on Admissions and Relations with Schools (BOARS) has the role of determining the conditions (requirements) for eligibility and admissions (chapter 15), subject to approval by the Academic Assembly and then the Board of Regents.
- The Editorial Committee works with the University of California Press and exercises final approval for publications brought in through the various subject-matter editors of the press.[21]
- All three sectors of public higher education (UC, CSU, and the community colleges) have academic senates, and the Intersegmental Committees of the Academic Senates provide liaison among the sectors at the senate level.

Committees for the Berkeley Division of the Academic Senate have the following responsibilities:

- The Committee on Budget and Interdepartmental Relations carries out the processes of review and evaluation for promotions and step-level advancement of Berkeley faculty. The analogous committees on all other campuses are known as Committees on Academic Personnel. The university-wide Committee on Academic Personnel coordinates policy, most notably having a substantial role with regard to changes in the *Academic Personnel Manual*.
- The Committee on Academic Planning and Resource Allocation provides consultation to the chancellor and vice chancellors on matters of budget, planning, and associated policies. At the

---

[21] This is an unusual, and possibly even unique, structure among university presses.

university-wide level, the Committee on Planning and Budget has the same role with respect to the President.
- The Committee on Admissions, Enrollment, and Preparatory Education deals with the criteria for campus-level admissions, including choosing among UC-eligible applicants.
- The American Cultures Committee oversees the American Cultures requirement for bachelor's degrees.[22]
- The Committee on Courses of Instruction evaluates all courses proposed by individual departments and must approve a course in order for it to be offered.
- The Committee on Privilege and Tenure (P&T) hears and recommends actions to the administration on complaints received from faculty members regarding matters of academic privilege, appointment, tenure and promotion, and works with the Panel of Counselors, which is available to advise faculty members having issues that are considered by the P&T Committee.

Many faculty members are members of at least one committee.[23] The involvement of so many different faculty members and the layered structure of responsibility within the Academic Senate are both designed to discourage undue influence from any one or a small group of people on the outcomes of senate deliberation processes.

University-wide senate bodies are composed of one member from each of the campuses plus any ex officio members. This seemingly democratic aspect of the senate, which works very much by consensus, has been a source of tension at times. Larger and older campuses can believe that their interests are being outvoted by newer and smaller campuses, and vice versa. It is therefore important that the senate evaluate the issues that are taken up at various levels to determine which issues are indeed university-wide and which are appropriately left to campuses. This division of issues should also correspond to the

---

[22] "American Cultures Requirement," *Berkeley Academic Guide*, University of California, Berkeley, https://perma.cc/4D9Q-3TBE.

[23] See, e.g., the roster of committee membership for the Berkeley Division available by sublink at "About the Committees," Academic Senate, University of California, Berkeley.

administrative division of issues between campus and university-wide administrations.

For those who would like to dig deeper, the nature of shared governance within the University of California has also been discussed by Taylor,[24] Douglass,[25] Simmons,[26] Switkes,[27] and Hollinger.[28] The system is well entrenched and generally understood and accepted by both faculty members and administrators. It makes for decisions that are consultative, well considered, and recognized as valid. The process also has its difficulties and potential dangers, which I will consider in the following discussion of shared governance in universities in general.

SHARED GOVERNANCE IN RESEARCH UNIVERSITIES

Why Have It?

Universities are unusual, but not unique, in having shared governance. A search on the term "shared governance" will turn up at least as many entries for nursing management as for academic governance. But the approach is very different from what is normally done in the world of business and thus can strike people as a slow and very cumbersome way of doing things. Why have shared governance?

---

[24] Angus E. Taylor, *The Academic Senate of the University of California: Its Role in Shared Governance and Operation of the University of California* (Berkeley: Institute of Governmental Studies Press, University of California, 1998), https://perma.cc/CDV5-27NH.

[25] John Aubrey Douglass, "Shared Governance at the University of California: An Historical Review," Research and Occasional Papers Series, CSHE.1.98, Center for Studies in Higher Education, University of California, Berkeley, CA, 1998, https://perma.cc/3NTL-FV7H.

[26] Daniel L. Simmons, "Shared Governance at the University of California: A Review," 1995, https://perma.cc/4VDR-KU4G.

[27] Ellen Switkes, "Governance at the University of California: An Example of Faculty Involvement," in *Comparison of University Governance USA, UK, France, and Japan*, RIHE International Seminar Reports, no. 19 (Hiroshima, Japan: Research Institute for Higher Education, 2013), pp. 1–22, https://perma.cc/L2QC-EUDA.

[28] David A. Hollinger, "Faculty Governance, the University of California, and the Future of Academe," *Academe* 87, no. 3 (2001): pp. 30–33.

In research universities faculty members are selected on the bases of creativity and knowledge of specific subject matter. It makes sense to make use of that expertise in decision processes and governance.

There are other, more pragmatic reasons for shared governance as well. Involving the faculty in governance has the result that faculty members appreciate and care for the university as an institution. It increases faculty allegiance to the university, something that can be of considerable value in retaining faculty members who receive job offers from other institutions, and sustains care and concern for the university as a whole. Also, with effective shared governance, serious breaks between the faculty and university leadership are much less likely.

Shared governance tends to be stronger in public universities than in private universities. Concomitantly, more crises of leadership (e.g., petitions from the faculty to have the president replaced) occur in private universities than public universities. If the voice of the faculty has been sought and demonstrably considered in administrative decision processes, potential breaks between the faculty and the administration will usually have been recognized and resolved before reaching the stage of public accusations and lines drawn in the sand.

Service in the Academic Senate provides a good way for members of the faculty to find and come to know one another. One of the major changes in research universities over the past fifty years has been the tendency for faculty members, even ones in the same department, to drift apart. In the sciences, engineering, and some social sciences, a cause has been the extensive time and care required for funding, supervising, and securing the future of faculty members' individual research enterprises. Service together in the Academic Senate builds bonds and appreciation for the institution as a whole. Multidisciplinary research and teaching collaborations among faculty members have been launched by service together within the Academic Senate.

Examples. Shared governance, if structured and operating well, provides an established, clear, understandable, and accepted path for dealing with complex and difficult issues. Several examples from this book help show this. Two of the points in the history of the University of California where the availability of shared governance was essential and highly useful were in devising ways to absorb the major

Depression-era budget cuts of the early 1930s (chapter 2) and bringing the university into compliance with the regents' 1995 resolutions limiting affirmative action (chapter 15), while at the same time preserving the core values of the university as best possible. The roles of the specially established ad hoc Academic Senate committees for consultative academic oversight of the San Diego, Irvine, Santa Cruz, and Merced campuses when they were initiated were invaluable in establishing University of California standards from the start (chapter 10). The role of the Academic Senate in helping define the continual, most productive paths ahead is apparent from the discussion of the creation of the School of Information at Berkeley (chapter 12). Senate reviews of UC management of the Los Alamos and Livermore national laboratories were helpful to the university for establishing contract conditions that would enhance the quality of science at those laboratories (chapter 13). More effective use of the Academic Senate also accounts for the much more favorable Berkeley campus reaction to the agreement with BP for the Energy Biosciences Institute in 2007 than had been the case for the hotly contested agreement with Novartis Corporation in 1998 (chapter 18).

What Is Necessary for Shared Governance to Work Well?
There are several essentials for shared governance to work well.
- There should be a faculty culture where institutional needs and building and preserving academic quality are the highest shared values.
- A large majority of faculty members, including the intellectual leaders within the faculty, should have the interest and willingness needed to participate actively.
- The campus leadership and administration should work constructively and effectively with the faculty in ways such that it is clear that faculty views and advice are given full consideration in the decision process. Consultation should occur before decisions are made, not after.

It was particularly important for the establishment of the present-day roles of the University of California Academic Senate for the intellectually most respected members of the faculty to have taken the lead roles in meeting with the regents in 1919 and designing shared governance. That involvement gave shared governance the impetus and level of respect from the faculty that has helped it work well. A sense of hard-won victory also probably instilled satisfaction and pride, which helped and enabled shared governance to come into being effectively.

What Can Go Wrong with Shared Governance?

Much will be lost if an Academic Senate functions more like a labor union for faculty than as a positive force for academic quality and institutional strength. The senate is then being used in an adversarial fashion, seeking job benefits that can readily clash with, and submerge, the pursuit of academic quality. An academic senate should be hatched with a culture and goal of seeking academic excellence, with the senate being an important path for doing so. An effective senate can reduce interest among the faculty in having a labor union, and it has done so at the University of California, where the only campus with a faculty union is Santa Cruz, even though in the 1970s Governor Jerry Brown authorized union elections on all campuses of the university. The faculty of the California State University is unionized.

In a related vein and as has already been noted, shared governance works best when the respected intellectual leaders of the campus are interested and take active parts. A lack of participation, or worse yet disdain, from the most respected faculty members carries a message that the work of the senate is not regarded as sufficiently important and is something best left for those who have idle time available. If faculty participation in shared governance is low, then there is a greater chance that individuals with personal agendas will come to dominate the senate, not reflecting general faculty views and impeding constructive progress.

Confrontation is not beneficial to shared governance. The administration and senate should both strive to work together positively, recognizing that solutions to problems and constructive progress are both needed and that these can best be gained by working together in a respectful fashion. It is important that the Academic Senate leadership be well aware of faculty views and the breadth of those views. A classic University of California example of the senate leadership not being sufficiently aware of faculty views occurred in the loyalty oath controversy of 1949–50 (chapter 2), when the senate leadership communicated a degree of acceptance of the proposed loyalty oath that was quite different from the actual run of faculty opinion.

Attitudes within Universities and Colleges toward Shared Governance, Nationwide

Surveys have been made periodically to ascertain how faculty members and administrators within universities view shared governance. One example is a survey made by Tierney and Minor[29] covering 1,199 department chairs, 411 academic vice presidents or provosts, and 400 Academic Senate leaders from four-year universities and colleges in the United States.

The following passages from their report summarize results from the survey. First, faculty senates are commonplace: "A total 93 percent of doctoral institutions, 90 percent of master's institutions, and 82 percent of baccalaureate institutions have such senates, while only 13 percent of surveyed schools do not."

Second, there is widespread concern about the effectiveness of, and faculty interest in, shared governance:

> At those institutions that had faculty Senates, 22 percent of respondents reported that the Senate was not an important governing body, 53 percent indicated a low level of interest in Senate activities, 43 percent stated that involvement in the Senate was not highly valued, and 31 percent felt the goals of the Senate were not clearly defined, even though there appeared to be clarity about the domains of faculty influence—that is, there was clarity about areas of decision-making where faculty have authority. This dissatisfaction was particularly strong at doctoral universities, where only 19 percent of respondents agreed that the faculty had high levels of interest in Senate activities. By contrast, 54 percent of respondents from baccalaureate institutions and 39

---

[29] W. G. Tierney and J. T. Minor, "Challenges for Governance: A National Report," Center for Higher Education Policy Analysis, University of Southern California, Los Angeles, CA, 2003, https://perma.cc/K5UD-RHL3.

percent of respondents from master's institutions reported high levels of interest in Senate activities.

These results underscore the first need stated above for shared governance to work well—a faculty culture where institutional needs and academic quality are the highest shared values.

Another extensive survey, the 2001 Survey of Higher Education Governance, was made by Kaplan,[30] and covered a wide variety of US academic institutions. Attitudes on various aspects of shared governance clustered toward the middle of the scale, avoiding extremes of enthusiasm or concern. The survey found that Academic Senate influence is mostly over policy development.

A recent survey by the Association of Governing Boards[31] obtained the views of presidents and chancellors, as well as governing board members, primarily from nonpublic institutions, on shared governance. While the results were generally accepting of shared governance and its utility, the wide swath of institutions covered makes it difficult to discern attitudes and effectiveness in any detail. A large shortcoming of these general surveys is that many different types of colleges and universities are lumped together and therefore many different forms of shared governance are lumped together. Some are intense and active; others are pro forma. Research universities, comprehensive universities, liberal arts colleges, and sometimes community colleges, public and private, are pooled.

Although I am not aware of quantitative data on attitudes toward shared governance within the University of California, fifty-five years of UC experience and myriad conversations during that time have given me the sharp impression that both attitudes toward and participation in shared governance are much more positive for UC than are expressed for the nation as a whole in the nationwide surveys.

What Is Inherently Problematic in Shared Governance?

Many views have been expressed about shared governance by present and former university administrators. These range from rather

---

[30] Gabriel E. Kaplan, "How Academic Ships Actually Navigate," in Ronald G. Ehrenberg, ed., *Governing Academia* (Ithaca, NY: Cornell University Press, 2004), pp. 165–208.
[31] "Shared Governance: Is OK Good Enough?," Association of Governing Boards, 2016, https://perma.cc/9F2S-GJ9Z.

monolithic condemnations by authors such as Duderstadt and Womack,[32] to a collection of varied views in a volume emanating from one of the Glion Conferences,[33] and to in-depth analyses such as those in books authored by Bowen and Tobin[34] and by Garland,[35] among others. In their book, Bowen and Tobin also trace the development of shared governance in the United States and the issues that surround it and examine shared governance in more depth for four quite different institutions—Princeton University, the University of California, [36] Macalester College, and the City University of New York. In their chapter 4, they consider shared governance in each of six different areas: (1) selection and tenure of the president, (2) the faculty appointments and dismissals process, (3) advice on matters of all kinds, (4) budgetary and staffing questions including non-tenure-track faculty, (5) academic standards in admissions, and (6) curricular content, grading, and authority to determine teaching methods.

Typical concerns raised about the value and effectiveness of shared governance are the following:

- It is a slow process that may inherently not be able to keep up with the needs of fast-changing times.
- Faculty members represent only one of the interest groups within the university, albeit a very important one. Faculty members cannot recognize and balance needs across groups, and/or they are self-interested and will serve their own interests.
- Faculty members are typically conservative, well satisfied with the status quo, and reluctant to change.
- Shared governance tends to draw a cadre of faculty members who are less active in research and/or have particular issues

---

[32] James J. Duderstadt and Farris Womack, *Beyond the Crossroads: The Future of the Public University in America* (Baltimore: Johns Hopkins University Press, 2003), pp. 166–169.
[33] Werner Z. Hirsch and Luc E. Weber, eds., *Governance in Higher Education: The University in a State of Flux* (London: Economica, 2001.
[34] Willam G. Bowen and Eugene M. Tobin, *Locus of Authority: The Evolution of Faculty Roles in the Governance of Higher Education* (Princeton, NJ: Princeton University Press, 2015).
[35] Garland, 2009, *op. cit.*, pp. 81–103.
[36] The author consulted with Bowen and Tobin at some length regarding the University of California.

other than academic quality. The busiest faculty members, who tend also to be the most respected, see shared governance as an ineffective use of their time.
- Current needs are for changes so great that they cannot be accomplished by traditional means of governance.
- Times have changed, such that faculty now have much more allegiance to their disciplines than to their institutions. They thus cannot, or will not, see the broader picture beyond their disciplines.
- Shared governance, because it reflects so many different interests and requires frequent and thorough consultation, can be dysfunctional and lead to inabilities to confront and solve problems and to move with the needs of the times.
- Shared governance, even if done well, is inherently expensive in its use of faculty time. Garland presents results of an effort to calculate the cost of shared governance for Miami University of Ohio, concluding that the cost was about 15 percent of faculty time, or $13 million per year.[37] A national 1993 survey by the National Center for Education Statistics cited by Lyall[38] concluded that 11 percent of faculty time goes to operations of shared governance.

It is instructive to read the various discourses on shared governance in terms of what they imply about the management styles of the author of the paper, who is much more often than not a former university president or provost.

Many who have expressed concerns have done so in the context of a belief that shared governance is still needed and valuable. Because of the very nature of outstanding research faculty, it is difficult to conceive of an effectively operating research university of high caliber where shared governance is absent. Faculty members do not care for situations where there is no mechanism for them to be heard, and without shared governance it becomes too easy for the top administration to get too far out in front of the faculty.

---

[37] Garland, 2009, *op. cit.*, pp. 100–101.
[38] Katharine C. Lyall, "Recent Changes in the Structure and Governance of American Research Universities," in W. Z. Hirsch and L. E. Weber, eds., *Governance in Higher Education: The University in a State of Flux* (London: Economica, 2001).

Ways of Nurturing Shared Governance[39]

There are a number of different ways in which concerns about shared governance can be mitigated or overcome.

Have Structure with Clarity on Roles, and Use the Process. A clear structure for shared governance and an established and agreed-upon delineation of the responsibilities of the different parties guard against misunderstandings and confusion.

Weingartner[40] defines three different types of collaborative decision-making: (1) *consultative decision,* where the faculty should be consulted, but the administration is determinant, (2) *codeterminative decision,* for which the faculty organization should advise and consent (as is the role for the US Senate in certain presidential appointments), and (3) *all but determinative decision,* where a faculty decision is overruled by the administration only for strong reasons explicitly stated. To this could be added cases where the faculty senate has *full determinative authority,* such as for courses, curricula, and the conditions for admission within the University of California. What forms of governance and what decisions are in which category should be well understood. An explicit written document can serve as a continual point of reference and should minimize misunderstandings of roles. Clark Kerr[41] noted a need for such a document even for the University of California, despite it being a university where shared governance is more structured and for which some written descriptions do exist. Vagueness generates misunderstanding and controversy.

A related concept is that senate functions should be real and have clear impact, as has also been observed by Weingartner.[42] Not only does this promote the goals of shared governance; it also provides a strong and attractive rationale for participation in shared governance.

---

[39] What is expressed in this section works forward from a previous paper by the author: C. Judson King, "Tailoring Shared Governance to the Needs and Opportunities of the Times, Research and Occasional Papers, no. 13-13, Center for Studies in Higher Education, Berkeley, CA, November 2013, https://perma.cc/3YNP-RHL7.
[40] Rudolph H. Weingartner, *Fitting Form to Function: A Primer on the Organization of Academic Institutions,* 2nd ed., American Council on Education (Lanham, MD: Rowman & Littlefield, 2011), p. 9.
[41] Kerr, 2001, *op. cit.,* pp. 228, 230.
[42] Weingartner, 2011, *op. cit.,* pp. 35, 39.

It is also important to recognize and avoid situations where problems can occur because shared governance, although established, has not been used in the intended way. The UC Online initiative, discussed in chapter 12, is a case in point. There the university-wide administration implemented a top-down initiative that left the Academic Senate in a reactive mode instead of working with the senate to create a jointly defined effort on an inherently academic matter.

Involve the Most Respected Faculty Members and Intellectual Leaders of the Campus. Personal requests to faculty members from the president, provost, or respected leaders of the faculty can be effective for this purpose. It will help for it to be abundantly clear and accepted that the faculty senate has meaningful roles in governance and that its contributions are valued by the campus leadership. Respected but busy faculty members may respond to requests for them to take on the project of working collectively to build an Academic Senate into a more meaningful body with the specific overriding goal of promoting and maintaining academic quality. After all, the academic quality of the institution is very important to faculty members personally. In comparing shared governance at Michigan and Berkeley, David Hollinger[43] notes both the involvement of the most respected faculty members at Berkeley, and the boost that gives to senate activities.

Serving as a principal officer of the Academic Senate is both time-consuming and filled with pressures because of the large number of constituents and highly varied issues. It is a small and very worthwhile investment to provide temporary released time from teaching to these officers so that they can do their jobs most efficiently and effectively.

Faculty Senate Positions Should Turn Over and Not Be Sinecures. Scheduled turnover, through means such as one- or two-year terms of office, should be the norm or even required for Academic Senate positions. This lessens the impact of situations where a faculty member with a particular agenda—or one who is unsuited to effective committee work or is underperforming—becomes ensconced in a senate position. It also increases the number of faculty members who participate in shared governance and thereby enables more faculty

---

[43] Hollinger, 2001, *loc. cit.*

members to be aware of governance and to meet and work with other faculty members outside their disciplines.

Make Full Information Available to All Parties. Again, to avoid misunderstandings and enable advice to be fully informed, both the senate and the administration should have access to full information on subjects being considered, except for information protected for personal privacy. This is all the more possible today because of computerized databases and websites that can be password protected. An open environment with all information available also builds trust and an understanding of the pressures that bear upon either party.

Seek Ways to Expedite the Consultation Process. One of the hindrances to effective shared governance is that events and needs for decisions can move faster than does the consultation process, especially if there are successive layers of consultation or multiple relevant committees. There are several approaches that can be pursued to speed things up. First, modern information technology can be used to the full extent of its capabilities, not only for making background information available to all but also for overcoming hurdles of scheduling, geographical separation, and differences in time zones. When there are successive layers of consultation (e.g., both all-university and campus levels within the University of California), simultaneous rather than sequential processing can be utilized. This applies to considerations internally within both the administration and the senate, as well as to interactions between the administration and senate. In that way, concerns expressed by those involved at the higher levels can be known and taken into account more efficiently by those in the process at lower levels.

For particularly fast-moving issues, it can help to establish a joint administration-senate body to carry out consultation in real time. As noted in chapter 15, that approach was used to bring the University of California into compliance in the difficult and fast-moving situation that followed the regents' motions in 1995 relating to affirmative action.

From time to time, it has been advocated within the University of California Academic Senate that the senate should maintain a fully arms-length relationship with the administration so as to assure independence. That approach leads to the senate operating on the basis of less information and slower consultation, and there is a greater likelihood of a sense of obstruction. It does not fit today's world well.

Enable Academic Choices to Be Made with Budgetary Awareness. Bowen and Tobin[44] note the tendency for faculty evaluations and advocacy on academic matters to be done without awareness or consideration of budgetary implications. This may also be inferred from discussions within the recent book by Smelser.[45] The best solution is to make relevant budgetary information available to Academic Senate faculty as they consider academic matters and for the administration continually to reference budgetary issues when communicating with the Academic Senate. The senate members can then have budgetary trade-offs in mind as they consider issues and provide advice.

Enable and Engender Changes to Meet Evolving Needs and Opportunities. The Academic Senate and the administration should continually work together to identify changes in their approaches and modes of interaction that can better meet evolving needs and conditions. As Neil Smelser[46] wrote and has also been quoted by Bowen and Tobin,[47] "Given *both* the value and indispensability of shared governance *and* its deterioration, the only proper course is for administration and faculty to confront one another openly and frankly about their values and frustrations, about what is working and not working in shared governance, and initiate joint efforts to diagnose problems, identify points of vulnerability, and attempt to overhaul and streamline archaic structures."

A fully candid discussion among principals of the senate and administration expressly for that purpose at the beginning of each academic year would be a useful mechanism. As circumstances and opportunities evolve, it is important to examine modes of operation and interaction. Some examples of current relevant major changes that afford both needs and opportunities include the expanding capabilities of information technology, state-funding stringencies for public universities, the resultant diversification of the base of finances and

---

[44] Bowen and Tobin, 2015, *op. cit.*, pp. 177–181.
[45] Neil J. Smelser, *Dynamics of the Contemporary University: Growth, Accretion, and Conflict* (Berkeley: University of California Press, 2013).
[46] Smelser, 2013, *op. cit.*, p. 66.
[47] Bowen and Tobin, 2015, *op. cit.*, pp. 211–212.

constituents of the university, and the very different habits and uses of social media by succeeding generations of faculty and students.

Functional Correspondence. The delegation of functions from the university-wide level to the campus level within the Academic Senate should correspond to board and administrative delegations, so that consultations occur at the appropriate level. For the University of California, the last major changes in Senate organization were made in 1963, when the move was made to convert from the then-existing Northern and Southern Divisions to individual campus divisions of the Academic Senate,[48, 49] and when division councils and various committees were then created on the campuses. The senate should continually examine its structure, delegations, and roles at various levels in light of the administrative decentralization that has occurred during recent decades. As well, the senate should examine continually ways in which it can enable its leaders to act in an informed fashion for the senate when time is short.

Interactions between Administration and Senate. The most common stereotypical negative views about shared governance are that the administration tries to stiff-arm the senate and that the senate is inherently naysaying to change. For effective shared governance, these descriptions will not pertain. However, both parties must take steps to avoid either the reality or the perception of these images. The administration should bring important current issues of governance to the senate, but the senate should also take the initiative in raising issues that the members believe are important for shared governance but which the administration has not yet brought to them. The senate should seek to respond on issues in ways that provide avenues to go forward as opposed to an impasse.

Within the University of California, substantive senate communications with the administration have traditionally been accomplished by memo, although there are also meetings for discussion between the senate chairs and vice chairs and administrative officers. Memos do serve to create a useful written record of interactions, but they are not as efficient as conversation, nor

---

[48] Taylor, 1998, *op. cit.*, pp. 53–58.
[49] Clark Kerr, *The Gold and the Blue: A Personal Memoir of the University of California, 1949–1967. vol. 1., Academic Triumphs* (Berkeley: University of California Press, 2001, p. 199.

do they clear up misunderstandings or assure that both parties have a good familiarity with all the background that might bear upon a decision. One way of enabling both parties to have sufficient knowledge of the factors involved in a decision is to use the information bank described above. But conversational interaction is vital, including meetings between senate principals and individual administration leaders.

There are additional steps that can be taken to increase the familiarity of the senate leadership with the breadth and depth of administrative matters and their dimensions. At the Office of the President of the University of California, the chair and vice chair of the Academic Council occupy offices on the same floor of the building as the president and the provost and meet with them regularly. In addition the president and provost and some other administrative leaders meet with the full Academic Council monthly. During most of the time that I served as university-wide provost (1995–2004), at the initiative of President Richard Atkinson, the chair of the Academic Council participated in the president's weekly meeting with the senior members of the administration.[50] This was a two-hour period during which all major current issues were taken up. It therefore provided a very effective way of keeping the senate leadership up on things.

For issues where the senate role is advisory rather than determinative, the senate should make any substantially held minority positions within the senate known to the administration as part of consultation. The reason is that complex situations should not be reduced to a single senate point of view. That is only fair to significant minorities within the senate. As well, the administration should be made aware of the full spectrum of opinion within the faculty so as not to be blindsided on issues. At UC, numerical votes at full meetings of the campus divisions and votes of the Assembly of the Academic Senate generally become known; however, the Academic Council and corresponding division councils act as executive bodies taking single stances, and votes within them are typically not known. It would help if those votes were disclosed and substantial minority positions relayed

---

[50] Richard C. Atkinson, "20/20: Reflections on The Last 20 Years of the 20th Century," p. 14, August 2000, https://perma.cc/2KNU-KNHS.

and explained. This could be viewed as reciprocity for the inclusion of the senate chair in meetings of bodies such as the president's cabinet and/or the various other means by which the spectrum of views within the administration becomes apparent to the senate.

SUMMARY AND CONCLUSIONS

Shared governance, meaning participation of faculty in university governance, exists in many forms in universities and colleges around the United States. Surveys show that attitudes toward its effectiveness, overall, are often tepid. However, there are great advantages to shared governance done well, including involvement of outstanding minds and increased faculty satisfaction and allegiance. The University of California is an example of an extensive, highly structured, and generally effective system of shared governance. Although shared governance was nominally present from the start of the university, it was greatly enhanced and brought into the present form in the so-called Berkeley Revolution of 1919, during which the intellectually most respected members of the faculty dealt directly with the regents during an interregnum in the presidency.

The essential roles of the faculty Academic Senate in shared governance at the University of California include
- full responsibility for courses, curricula, and the conditions for admission of student applicants;
- responsibility for determining its own membership and organization;
- rights of presenting faculty views directly to the regents, including having its two primary leaders participating (but not voting) at the meeting table with the regents;
- carrying out reviews of faculty members for appointment, promotion, and advancement along the professorial scale;
- participating in reviews of programs and for appointment or continuation of academic administrators;
- approval of manuscripts for publication by the university press; and
- provision of advice to the administration on budget, libraries, and virtually any other important administrative matter.

The Academic Senate exists at the levels of both the university-wide administration and individual campuses. On campuses, there is typically a division council, composed of both elected and ex officio members. There are many committees, members of which are selected and secured by the Committee on Committees, an elected nominating committee. A similar structure exists university-wide, where there is an executive Academic Council and a legislative Assembly of the Academic Senate, along with many committees, one of which is the Committee on Committees. Faculty members from professional schools are every bit as involved in campus and university-wide shared governance, as are faculty members from the academic disciplines.

There are several ways in which effective shared governance can be nurtured. These include

- defining a meaningful structure and clear roles, and using the resultant process,
- seeking to interest and involve the most respected intellectual leaders on campus,
- designing the senate so that positions turn over regularly,
- making full information on any issue under consideration available to both the senate and the administration,
- carrying out regular evaluations, joint between the senate and the administration, of how to make consultation more effective and efficient and to move with the times,
- enabling academic decisions to be made with relevant budgetary information in mind,
- assuring equivalent delegation within the senate and the administration, and
- continually seeking positive and constructive interactions between the administration and the senate.

8.
Operational Governance of the Multicampus University

While not technically part of management, the Senate plays an indirect part in virtually every major decision within the university. Funding of new academic initiatives for example, funding for the construction of new or the renovation of older facilities, for our libraries, computer centers, clinics, and hospitals and the like; issues of compensation for all personnel, allocation of faculty positions across the university, fellowship funds and so forth, all involve consultation with the Senate.
—*David P. Gardner*[1]

The University of California is among the more difficult systems to govern effectively because it is among those most subject to internal and external tensions. It is one of the larger systems and the most academically prestigious of them all, with individual campuses of national and international standing and proud of their positions. It has, along with the University of Michigan, the most autonomous Board of Regents, the most empowered Academic Senate...and a highly competent and somewhat arrogant student body...Yet the University of California has become academically supreme above all other systems. If the measure of the quality of governance is not internal tensions but academic results, then the University of California has had superb governance despite its inherent handicaps, as I think it mostly has.
—*Clark Kerr*[2]

---

[1] David P. Gardner, "The California System: Governing and Management Principles and Their Link to Academic Excellence", Twenty-fifth David Dodds Henry Lecture, University of Illinois at Chiago, October 20, 2005,
http://web.archive.org/web/20130606071116/http://www.uic.edu/depts/oaa/ddh/25th_DDH.pdf.

[2] Clark Kerr, *The Gold and the Blue: A Personal Memoir of the University of California, 1949–1967. vol. 1., Academic Triumphs* (Berkeley: University of California Press, 2001, pp. 226-7.

Chapter 8

The two previous chapters have dealt with the organization and governance structure of the university with its multiple campuses (chapter 6) and the system of shared governance that was launched in 1919 and has developed into what may be the most structured and truly involved such systems in existence anywhere in the academic world (chapter 7). The tiered organization, the shared-governance structure, and the sheer size of the university make for a very complex governance situation. The complexity begs the question of how it really works in practice. This chapter addresses that question.

GOVERNANCE MECHANISMS

Formal Mechanisms. Figure 8-1 shows components of academic governance for the University of California. The central, vertical stream shown in roman capitals depicts the administrative reporting structure, with the downward, unidirectional arrows showing who reports to whom. On the left side, in italic capitals, is the Academic Senate, with horizontal, bidirectional arrows showing pairings for consultation. The divisions of the senate on the campuses have consulting relationships with the campus administrations, and the university-wide Academic Senate has them with the university-wide administration. In the second column from the left is a standing university-wide joint administration-senate committee, the Academic Planning Council. It and an Executive Budget Committee were both started as a result of the transition team report[3] of 1993. These two bodies were created to enable a continuing consultative dialog between the administration and the Academic Senate and included chancellors and vice chancellors from campuses as well as university-wide officials. As of 2017 the Academic Planning Council still exists[4], while the Executive Budget Committee does not. The lines without arrows denote individuals composing a formal group.

---

[3] University of California Transition Team Report, September 1993, https://perma.cc/WK7N-5APA.
[4] Academic Planning Council, Institutional Research and Academic Planning, Office of the President, University of California, https://perma.cc/U6BH-T8A7.

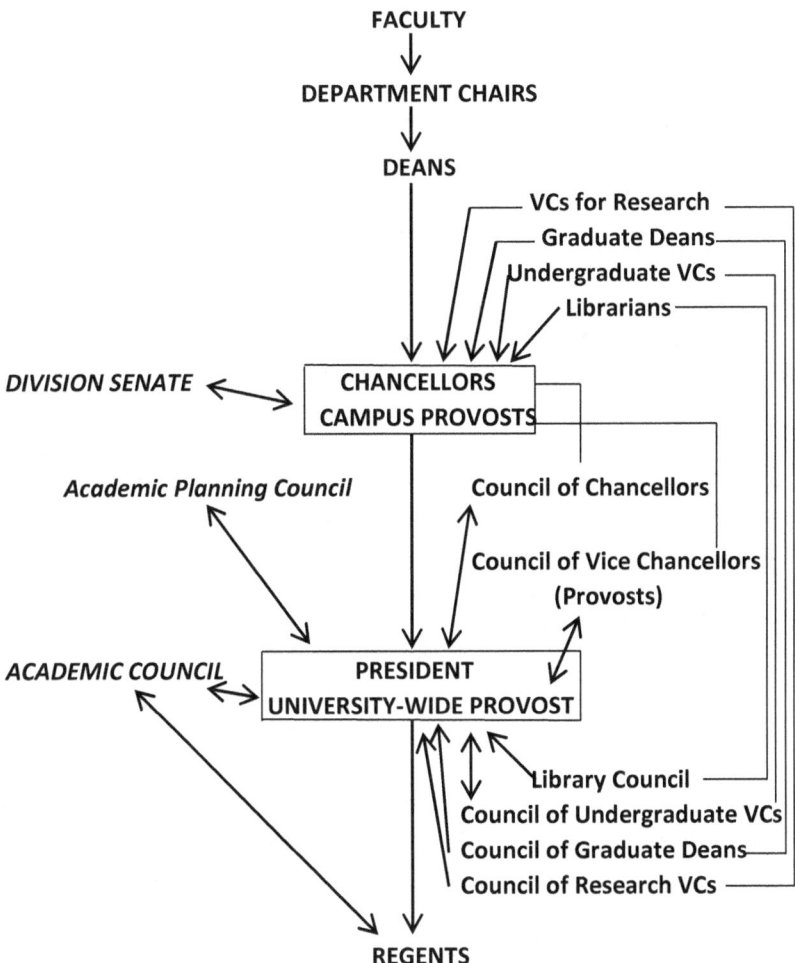

Figure 8-1. Academic governance structure of the University of California

This structure enables senate consultation at both the campus and university-wide levels, and it has enabled both joint reflection and more rapid action when needed through ad hoc joint senate-administration bodies, which are not shown. Care must be taken by the participants to deal with university-wide issues at the university-wide level and campus issues at the campus level, not to mix the two levels, and to avoid a campus issue being brought to the university-wide level before it is appropriate to do so. This could happen, for example, if a division senate took a concern to the Academic Council and from there to the president before the chancellor and the division senate had dealt with the matter.

Informal Mechanisms. The lower right-hand side of figure 8-1 shows the various meetings of persons with like responsibilities on campuses with their Office-of-the-President counterparts. These were started in the days when Clark Kerr was president. The figure shows several groups of an academic nature, but there are also many more. Virtually every group with like administrative functions on the various campuses meets with regularity somehow—personnel managers, labor-relations managers, affirmative-action officers, planning and budget officers, risk-management officers, those involved with the many student-support services, and so forth.

These meetings enable those with like roles on campuses and in the university-wide administration to share best practices and address common problems. They serve as key mechanisms for keeping university-wide officers aware of what the issues on the campuses are and how those issues are seen by the campuses. They build bonds and friendships, such that an administrator on one campus is comfortable calling up a counterpart on another campus or university-wide to discuss a thorny issue. Alternatively, such an issue can be taken up within the university-wide group.

These groups should not be viewed as being controlled or even chaired by the university-wide official. They are in no way top-down. Usually one of the campus officers is chair, facilitator, or convener, and the agenda is set by all participants through that person. They represent an entirely different dimension of governance, in that a campus participant may even use discussion in the group to derive arguments to use in considerations of a contended policy issue on that participant's campus.

Historically, the Council of Chancellors (campus chancellors plus executive and/or senior vice presidents) has met monthly all day on first Wednesdays and for dinner the evening before Board of Regents' meetings. These meetings enable chancellors to bring issues to other chancellors and the president and executive/senior vice presidents, and they often identify needs for administrative studies or problem solving to be done. By contrast, the Council of (Academic) Vice Chancellors and other councils of vice chancellors (Administration and Finance, University Relations, etc.) are more in nature problem-solving groups, endeavoring to identify and create the actual paths forward.

In addition to formal and informal structures, contacts and good will among people are essential for effective academic governance. Full awareness and understanding of the roles of the Academic Senate on the parts of both the administration and the senate are important. As described in chapter 7, things are at their best if both the administration and the Academic Senate regard each other positively and with interest and respect, rather than with suspicion. Similarly, an open, transparent atmosphere of governance is best. The same needs exist for relations between campus and university-wide officials.

Academic Departments. Definition and delivery of the academic curriculum are left almost totally to the academic departments. The one exception is the need for review and approval of proposed courses by the campus Committee on Courses of the Academic Senate; however, in practice, very few courses are turned down, although aspects of them are questioned. The campus-wide committee does not have much basis for disagreeing with the collective academic judgment of a department. This practice enables the curriculum to be guided by a deep understanding of the subject matter in a discipline but hampers multidisciplinary instruction (chapter 14).

PAROCHIALISM, UNDERSTANDING, AND RESPECT

A challenge with which academic governance, or almost any governance, must deal is the natural tension among different levels of governance and administration. Department chairs view the world from the standpoint of their own discipline and the health and standing of their department within it. Deans of colleges must take a broader view, looking across their disciplines and being concerned with building, preserving, and enhancing their colleges as a whole, as well as encouraging interactions among the departments within the college. Provosts concern themselves with building, preserving, and enhancing the entire academic enterprise and seek synergies and cooperation among their units. Chancellors must balance the needs of nonacademic operations with academic ones and must seek and choose those relatively few major initiatives that are most critically needed for the campus as a whole. Within the multicampus university, the president must evaluate the needs and opportunities for the entire university and will often find it necessary to do things that will build and enhance newer campuses but that the more mature campuses may not see as serving their own needs well. For a public university or university system, regents represent the public and cannot as readily be cheerleaders for the university as are trustees of private universities.

To the extent that these tensions can be overcome or eased, governance will work better. To the extent that the persons interacting among the different tiers of governance understand one another's situations and needs, governance should work better. For example, it is beneficial for the provost to meet with the full ensemble of deans to discuss common concerns and crosscutting campus issues. Deans will thereby have an awareness of campus-wide needs and tensions. As well, it is good for a provost to meet frequently with individual deans so as to be fully aware of the pressures on them and their own needs and concerns.

WHAT CAN GO WRONG

There are, of course, many things that can go wrong with university governance, even despite the best of structures. Some of the most common problems within the United States are the following.

The President Gets Too Far Out in Front of the Faculty

The most common high-visibility problem is for the president to get too far out in front of the faculty on one or more major initiatives. If the president then encounters active resistance or votes of no confidence from the faculty, the trustees are put in a difficult situation. Often the ultimate result is a negotiated departure of the president. After all, the faculty is the heart of the university, and there are no straightforward steps to change the composition of the faculty, other than very slowly over time through retirements, resignations, and so on. Situations of this sort have been rare at the University of California because the Academic Senate's consultation mechanism serves to identify potential problems of this sort before they develop to crisis stage. The senate mechanism also provides a formal way to discuss and resolve contentious issues internally. The very fact that formal consultation has occurred and the faculty organization has been heard is itself a defusing mechanism.

One of the important roles of deans—and of provosts in particular—is to be on the lookout for situations where the president or chancellor of the campus may be getting too far out in front of the faculty and then protect the president by keeping keep him or her aware of the situation and working to smooth things out.

The President and Board Members Work without Sufficient Synergy or Even at Cross-Purposes

Public flare-ups between board members and presidents are generally counterproductive. It is much better that such matters be solved or at least ameliorated within the university through effective governance practices.

Three examples discussed in chapter 2 reflect the entry of state politics into board governance of the University of California, and all three also set members of the Board of Regents against the president publicly: (1) the loyalty oath controversy of 1948–50, (2) the dismissal of Clark Kerr as president in 1967 following incoming governor Reagan's campaign promise to "clean up the mess at Berkeley," and (3) the passage in 1995 of the two Board of Regents' resolutions precluding attention to race, gender, etcetera, in university admissions and employment. The last of these three events occurred during a primary campaign by the governor of California for the Republican nomination for the US presidency. In another example from the University of California, some years after the aforementioned regents' resolutions of 1995 and a subsequent successful state ballot proposition on the same subject, the chair of the Board of Regents wrote a leaked report and then an article[5] in the national press accusing the Berkeley campus of applying favoritism to the admission of underrepresented minority students, thereby circumventing state law and the regents' resolutions. In this case a result was a breach between this regent and most of the rest of the board, which ultimately led to censure of that regent by the board and a subsequent resignation of the regent before his term had been completed.

Public flare-ups of this sort are not unique to the University of California, but are much more characteristic of public universities than of private ones, both because of the different natures of the boards and because of public-records laws that make documents, e-mails, and the like, from public institutions much more readily available to the media. Another prominent example of public conflict between a board and a president was the 2012 dismissal of the president of the University of Virginia by the Board of Visitors of that university over the issue of not moving fast enough on online instruction. The dismissal was followed by reinstatement of the president in response to pressures from the faculty and the public, the latter generated by the attention given in the media.[6] In another conspicuous recent (2014) case, there was an ongoing, very public, politically driven dispute on faculty tenure, admissions, and other issues between regents of the University of Texas and the Governor of Texas, on the one hand, and the president of the flagship Austin campus and much of the UT-Austin faculty, on the other hand.[7]

---

[5] John Moores, "College Capers", *Forbes*, March 29, 2004, https://perma.cc/EQZ5-DLG4. See also "UC Berkeley Responds to Regent Moores Report on Admissions", University of Clifornia, Berkeley, October 31, 2003, https://perma.cc/VH6A-2EZX.
[6] Andrew Rice, "Anatomy of a Campus Coup," *New York Times Magazine*, September 11, 2012.
[7] Scott Jaschik, "Battle for Texas," *Inside Higher Education*, July 7, 2014, https://perma.cc/X938-LUS3.

The Faculty Senate Does Not Act Constructively

As noted throughout chapter 7, it has been vital for the success of shared governance at the University of California for the Academic Senate to draw the involvement and leadership of respected faculty members whose allegiances to the institute outweigh any personal agendas. This feature is crucial for developing trust in the governance process by both the faculty as a whole and the administration. If not guarded carefully, the situation can go astray.

Busy faculty members join into shared governance if they conclude that their involvement will be meaningful and truly important for overall governance. Thus, having effective shared governance becomes a criterion for drawing capable and very active faculty members to shared governance, and drawing such faculty is in turn a criterion for the effectiveness of the governance. Building successful shared governance requires both from the start.

The Faculty Does Not Act Cohesively

Faculty lives are busy and full of pressures. In the world of academic science and engineering, teaching responsibilities are coupled with supervision of graduate students and postdocs and the need to nurture what may be three or even four major sources of external financial support for research. Department-chair positions have become less attractive. They require capable, institutionally oriented people who will generate the time needed to do the job well and are capable of gaining the respect and confidence of the faculty members of the department and drawing them together. However, because of the many pressures upon faculty members, community-minded individuals with good leadership qualities seem to be much rarer now than they were forty or fifty years ago. That sort of person may simply not exist in a department, or the faculty members who do have those attributes may be unwilling to take on the job or not be able to generate the time needed to do the job well. Even with a capable and dedicated chair, department dynamics may deteriorate because everybody leaves it all for the department chair to do. These factors, economic efficiency, and the negative effects of narrow disciplinary or subdisciplinary interests are strong reasons for encouraging larger department sizes and recognizing and rewarding service as a department chair.

Morale Suffers

If faculty members are not motivated to do their best or conclude that they are not being well supported by their department or institution, both performance and quality will suffer. As a result, the education of students and the reputation of the institution will also suffer. A vital role of university governance is to support and incentivize the faculty so that they will remain motivated toward their careers and their students. The administration must have the ability to sense morale continually and address it effectually when necessary. An effective Academic Senate can be a useful avenue toward that understanding.

9.
Creating Research Excellence: Physical Sciences at Berkeley

[Armin] Leuschner has done more than almost any other single person to make this a great university, although few people know it. He knew what a university should be.
—*Joel H. Hildebrand[1]*

There are ancient cathedrals which, apart from their consecrated purpose, inspire solemnity and awe. Even the curious visitor speaks of serious things, with hushed voice, and as each whisper reverberates through the vaulted nave, the returning echo seems to bear a message of mystery. The labor of generations of architects and artisans has been forgotten, the scaffolding erected for their toil has long since been removed, their mistakes have been erased, or have become hidden by the dust of centuries. Seeing only the perfection of the completed whole, we are impressed as by some superhuman agency. But sometimes we enter such an edifice that is still partly under construction; then the sound of hammers, the reek of tobacco, the trivial jests bandied from workman to workman, enable us to realize that these great structures are but the result of giving to ordinary human effort a direction and a purpose. Science has its cathedrals, built by the efforts of a few architects and many workers.
—*Gilbert Newton Lewis[2]*

I shall always be grateful for the wise and generous guidance and help that our work has received from the University Board of Research, and

---

[1] Joel H. Hildebrand, interview by Edna Tartaul Daniel, "Chemistry, Education, and the University of California," oral history, p. 132, Regional Oral History Office, University of California, Berkeley, 1962, https://perma.cc/PW5V-4QUC.

[2] Gilbert N. Lewis, preface to Gilbert N. Lewis and Merle Randall, *Thermodynamics and the Free Energy of Chemical Substances* (New York: McGraw-Hill, 1923).

Chapter 9

especially from Professor Leuschner, Chairman of the Research Board, in the early years of organization of the laboratory, and above all may I acknowledge my deep appreciation of the support of the President of the University [Robert Gordon Sproul], who whole-heartedly has been all along such a stimulus to our activities. It may truly be said that this Nobel Award is yet another tribute to his great academic leadership.
—Ernest O. Lawrence, Nobel Prize Acceptance Speech[3]

Chemistry was a "college," not a department, as it remains to this day...It has been, and still is, in my judgement, the outstanding unit within the University of California—superb in research, superb in the teaching of both undergraduate and graduate students, and superb in the contributions of its faculty members to university governance.
—Clark Kerr[4]

Research excellence has been at the heart of the reputation of the University of California, starting with the original Berkeley campus and going forward to the newer campuses. This chapter and the succeeding three explore how that excellence came about both initially and then university-wide, and how it is sustained.

In order to understand research excellence, we need to define it. The appendix explores that issue, utilizing both qualitative and quantitative approaches, including many surveys and rating systems that have appeared within recent decades. Many of the quantitative measures have to do with research. The quantitative approaches can and should be challenged, but they do provide a view of what is considered important.

Respected research hardly ever results from happenstance. In order to have well recognized and highly effective research, an institution must devise and carry out a workable plan to identify outstanding or potentially outstanding people, attract those people or

---

[3] Ernest O. Lawrence, Nobel Prize Acceptance Speech, Berkeley, CA, 1940, https://perma.cc/5GZ6-M6W5. The prize was presented in Berkeley rather than Oslo because of the onset of World War II.

[4] Clark Kerr, *The Gold and the Blue: A Personal Memoir of the University of California, 1949–1967,* vol., 1, Academic Triumphs (Berkeley: University of California Press, 2001), p. 61.

grow them de novo, and fully enable and support them in their careers. The institution must draw effectively upon distinguished researchers in the selection and evaluation of other researchers, and it must spread and maintain a culture of research excellence throughout the institution. By contrast, it is next to impossible to convert a midcareer person into an outstanding researcher.

In the present chapter, we explore how that culture and the tradition of excellence were initially built at the University of California in the physical sciences. Chapter 10 then examines how that culture spread to the other campuses of the University of California as they came into being. Next, chapters 11 and 12 deal with ways in which that culture has been supported and maintained through assessment of people and through reviews and changes in programs.

I have chosen the physical sciences to illustrate the initiation of research excellence at Berkeley for several reasons. First, the physical sciences are to a large, but by no means exclusive, extent where the move to research excellence at the University of California was launched. Second, the physical sciences have contributed much of the stature of the Berkeley campus, although, as is underscored by reputational surveys, that stature is remarkably widespread across the disciplines. Third, the development of the physical sciences is relatively well documented and presents a clear path of development displaying the interconnectedness of the people involved and mutual support among disciplines. Finally, it is what I am most familiar with myself, having now spent fifty-five years as a chemical engineering faculty member within Berkeley's College of Chemistry.

ASTRONOMY, THE LICK OBSERVATORY, AND ARMIN LEUSCHNER

The Lick Observatory

An act of serendipity coupled with the talents of Daniel Coit Gilman began the rise of the University of California to research eminence. James Lick,[5] a wealthy San Francisco businessman, decided

---

[5] "James Lick the 'Generous Miser,'" Lick Observatory Historical Collections, https://perma.cc/83M5-BKMM.

in 1873, toward the end of his life, that he wanted to use a substantial amount of his fortune to enable construction of the world's most powerful telescope. As he worked with various advisors, including President Gilman,[6] the project underwent many major changes. The site was originally intended to be in downtown San Francisco, then at an altitude of 10,000 feet (3,000 meters) in the Sierra Nevada mountains, then near Lake Tahoe, and finally atop Mount Hamilton at 4,360 feet (1,329 meters) above San Jose, California. The gift and hence the project budget started at $1.2 million but then came down to $700,000. Several types of telescope were considered, with the ultimate choice being a thirty-six-inch refracting telescope. The original idea was to give the telescope, once built by the Lick Trust, to the California Academy of Sciences in San Francisco. However, when the final trust was established in 1875 a year before his death, Lick had been persuaded by Gilman and others to entrust the telescope upon completion to the University of California.[7]

The Lick Observatory brought fame, interest, and highly capable people, among them two presidents of the University of California. Edward S. Holden, the original director of the Lick Observatory, was identified for the post as early as 1874 by Simon Newcomb of the US Naval Observatory in Washington, DC. Although still employed elsewhere, he was involved with the Lick project during the fourteen years of planning and construction. When the presidency of the University of California became open in 1885, UC Regent John Hager, Daniel Coit Gilman (now president of Johns Hopkins University), and President Charles Eliot of Harvard all recommended Holden to become president of the University of California. In an unusual move, Holden was recruited as both director of the Lick Observatory and UC president, with the understanding that he would assume the Lick directorship full-time upon completion of the telescope, which indeed

---

[6] Stadtman, 1970, *op. cit.*, p. 108.
[7] F. J. Neubauer, "A Short History of the Lick Observatory," *Popular Astronomy* 58 (1950); part 1: no. 5, pp. 201–221; part 2: no. 7, 318-333; part 3: no. 8, pp. 369-387.

occurred in 1888.[8] Lick's body was reburied at the foot of the telescope one year earlier.[9]

With the approval of the regents, Holden established a graduate school in astronomy at the Lick Observatory. Equipped with that opportunity and what was then the world's most capable telescope, he was able to recruit top-notch astronomers. Among these were William W. Campbell,[10] who became a noted astronomer in his own right, the third director of the observatory (1901–30), and ultimately president of the University of California (1923–30) while still retaining the directorship of the Lick Observatory. Campbell later served as president of the National Academy of Sciences. Campbell had a number of important accomplishments in astronomy.[11] He was a major figure in the quest to confirm Einstein's theory of relativity through astronomical observations.

Armin Leuschner

The University of California more systematically started its rise to research eminence during the twenty years that Benjamin Ide Wheeler was president, 1899–1919. Much of the credit for guiding the initial years of that rise goes to Armin Leuschner. For example, Paul Herget,[12] in his biographical memoir of Leuschner for the National Academy of Sciences, observes, "It was his insight and perseverance, perhaps more than any other individual, who raised the University of California to the level of a great university." In addition to his quote at the beginning of this chapter, Joel Hildebrand stated about Leuschner from firsthand experience, "He knew what a university should be and the kind of men who should constitute its faculty. He had attended a German

---

[8] This arrangement was made even though Holden's only administrative position had been the directorship of the Washburn Observatory in Madison, Wisconsin. It is symbolic of the UC presidency having been a relatively weak position in the latter half of the nineteenth century.
[9] Neubauer, 1950, *loc. cit.*
[10] W. H. Wright, "William Wallace Campbell, 1862–1938," Biographical Memoirs, National Academy of Sciences, 1947, https://perma.cc/JR6S-ZEMT.
[11] Wright, 1947, *loc. cit.*
[12] Paul Herget, "Armin Otto Leuschner, 1868–1953," Biographical Memoirs, National Academy of Sciences, 1978, https://perma.cc/9X43-LNJQ.

university, he was a distinguished astronomer, he knew how to apply high standards to graduate study, he was a very patient man, but very persistent. If he didn't win his point on one attempt he would return to it at the next opportunity. He was reasonable and sympathetic. He was a most valuable counselor." Hildebrand indicated as well that Leuschner "helped a great deal to educate Wheeler in what a real university should be."[13] To Wheeler goes the credit for selecting growth toward research eminence as a prime goal and for recognizing that Leuschner should take a key role.

Figure 9-1. Armin O. Leuschner ("Armin Otto Leuschner," *Wikipedia*, https://perma.cc/MD8F-F37R.)

Leuschner was born in the United States in 1868, but moved to Germany with his mother for his precollege schooling after the early death of his father. He returned to the University of Michigan, from which he graduated in 1888. From there he became one of the first graduate students hired by Holden for the Lick Observatory, which had opened that same year. He then became instructor (1890) and assistant professor (1892) of mathematics at Berkeley, before converting to assistant professor of astronomy and geodesy in 1894. He went next to the University of Berlin for an unusually rapid PhD, 1896–97 and then returned to his position at Berkeley.[14]

---

[13] Hildebrand, 1962, *op. cit.*, pp. 132, 140.
[14] S. Einarsson et al., "Armin Otto Leuschner, Astronomy, Berkeley," In Memoriam, University of California, Berkeley, 1958, https://perma.cc/Y3DU-EJA3.

Astronomy at Berkeley had been separate from the graduate program at the Lick Observatory. The subject was originally taught at Berkeley by George Davidson, chief of the Pacific Division of the US Coast and Geodetic Survey, and then by Frank Soulé, who housed it within Civil Engineering until the subject was turned over to Leuschner in the early 1890s. During Leuschner's long tenure (1907–38) as department chair, astronomy at Berkeley achieved distinction in the field, both by producing students who would go on to postgraduate work and for Leuschner's own work on the discovery of orbits of comets and asteroids. Under Leuschner, the astronomy programs at Berkeley and Lick were progressively interwoven. Students received instruction at Berkeley but did much of their actual observation work using the facilities at Lick. Of those graduates awarded PhDs by the Department of Astronomy between 1898 and 1965, about half held fellowships at Lick.[15]

A person blessed with sharp insights and great energy, Leuschner was also a noted effective leader on the national scale. He took the initiative[16] in convening the meeting of presidents and other leaders of US universities in 1900 in Chicago that resulted in the founding of the Association of American Universities (AAU). He was active in the National Research Council and in 1919 was both executive secretary and chairman of its Division of Physical Sciences. He was also President of the American Association of University Professors (AAUP), 1923–25. Within the university he served as dean of the Graduate Division (1913–18, 1920–23), as founder and long-term chairman of the Board of Research (1915–35), and as one of the faculty members who met with the Board of Regents in 1919–20 to establish the current roles of the Academic Senate (see chapter 7).

Further State-of-the-Art Astronomy Facilities

The University of California has continued to have state-of-the art astronomical observing facilities over the years. That fact has helped the university recruit faculty members whose work has kept the UC astronomy departments at the top ranks. The Hat Creek Radio

---

[15] "UC Berkeley Astronomy Department History," https://perma.cc/T848-GRXP.
[16] Einarsson et al., 1958, *loc. cit.*

Astronomy Laboratory was completed in 1958 and produced important discoveries. Management of it was passed to SRI International in 2012. The twin ten-meter Keck optical telescopes (chapter 2), built and administered jointly with Caltech atop Mauna Kea in Hawaii, were put into scientific use as of 1993 and 1996. The National Aeronautics and Space Administration (NASA) later joined as a third partner. The Keck telescopes use a segmented-mirror design developed by Jerry Nelson of UC. They also utilize a complex adaptive-optics system to compensate for turbulence in the boundary layer of earth's atmosphere, thereby sharpening images. A design using interferometry enables the two telescopes to operate together to provide some features of a telescope almost an order of magnitude larger. As of 2017 a partnership composed of UC, Caltech, and the national astronomical societies of China, Japan, India and Canada was working to obtain final permits to initiate construction of the Thirty-Meter Telescope, also atop Mauna Kea, with the Canary Islands as a back-up site. This too uses segmented mirrors and adaptive optics.

THE BOARD OF RESEARCH

As dean of the Graduate Division in a governance system in which the provost position had not yet been established, Leuschner had the key leadership role in building the research faculty and serving as a close academic advisor to Presidents Wheeler, Barrows, and Campbell. He also had strong influence through his chairmanship of the Board of Research,[17] which was formed by the regents upon Wheeler's request in 1915. This board was chartered to use funds in support of the best research within the university, especially at critical early points in faculty careers. The amount was initially not large, $2,000 in 1915–16, growing to $4,000 in 1917–18.[18] The purpose, since the beginning, has

---

[17] Victor H. Henderson, "A Board of Research," University Record, *University of California Chronicle*, vol. 18, p. 80, January 1917,.
https://books.google.com/books?id=Ik8MAQAAIAAJ&pg=PA72&source=gbs_toc_r&cad=4#v=onepage&q&f=false.

[18] Recognize, however, that there has been considerable inflation since this era. The sum of $4,000 at the start of 1917 is equivalent to $83,000 one hundred years later (InflationData.com, https://perma.cc/CL3M-7H24.

been to help cover incidental expenses associated with research, such as travel. The board was, and still in its present form is, entirely a faculty-run operation, following the belief that distinguished researchers among the faculty would know how best to use the funds.

The rationale for creation of the Board of Research is reported by Raymond Birge,[19] who was a member of the board for sixteen years and chair of it for the last eight of those years, succeeding Leuschner in 1935. Specifically, it was to enable faculty members to apply for scarce funds in support of their research directly, without the need of seeking those funds from, or even obtaining the approval of, the department chair. For departments with a strong sense of cooperation, there could be a departmental request for a block grant to be administered by a committee or even by the department chair, but the approach of individual applications and grants also dealt with situations in which a chair was not particularly friendly to research.

The funding for the Board of Research grew substantially over the years, from the initial 1915 annual allocation of $2,000 to over $200,000 in 1951. Even allowing for inflation, the amount of funding probably seems small by today's standards, but it was crucial in the days before massive support of research by the federal government. Birge indicates that the major portion of the research funds of the physics department, for many years, came from just this one source. The Board of Research launched both G. N. Lewis and Ernest O. Lawrence on their ways (see below). It also helped overcome the problem of distance from other leading research universities by enabling trips that Birge, Loeb, Hildebrand, and others made to the East Coast of the United States to present papers at meetings of scholarly societies and simultaneously to learn of faculty prospects. The board supported numerous other faculty members at critical points in their careers. In 1938, when UCLA was given its own equivalent of the board, the names of the boards for both campuses were changed to Committee on Research. These committees, now as formal committees of the Academic Senate, continue to this day on all UC campuses and provide enabling, flexible annual grants to faculty members. For

---

[19] Raymond T. Birge, *History of the Physics Department,* vol. 1 (Berkeley: University of California, 1966), p. vi (14). Available through HathiTrust Digital Library.

Berkeley in 2014, grants of $4,000 were available to all research-active faculty members.[20]

THE COLLEGE OF CHEMISTRY AND GILBERT NEWTON LEWIS

Early Days

The early years of Berkeley's College of Chemistry saw a succession of colorful figures, who are described in more detail by Jolly.[21] Robert A. Fisher was appointed as professor of chemistry, mining, and metallurgy in the founding year of 1868 and learned from the newspaper of his dismissal by the regents for budgetary reasons in 1870. Ezra Carr was appointed to the imposing position of professor of agriculture, chemistry, agricultural and applied chemistry, and horticulture in 1869. Chapter 2 gives a summary of his actions with the legislature in contention with President Gilman, which led to his dismissal by the regents in 1874. Willard Rising was appointed professor of chemistry in 1872 by Gilman and effectively led chemistry at the University of California for the rest of the nineteenth century. Rising doubled as state analyst for the State Board of Health, working effectively on improvement of drinking water around the state. He was not designated as dean of the College of Chemistry until 1896. The decanal role had fallen instead to Irving Stringham of mathematics (see below), who had a position known as dean of the College of Letters and the Colleges of Science.

Edmond O'Neill was appointed to the chemistry faculty in 1879 and served as dean from 1901 until the arrival of Lewis in 1912. He was a marvelous citizen of the university and the broader community, working with many of the student honorary societies, cofounding the Faculty Club and serving as its president for a decade, co-organizing and being president of the California Alumni Association, chairing the Faculty Committee on Athletics, and leading the movement to create a chapter of the American Chemical Society in the Bay Area. In his estate,

---

[20] "Indirect Cost Recovery (ICR)," Berkeley Executive Vice Chancellor and Provost, https://perma.cc/8BQR-3UX8.

[21] William L. Jolly, *From Retorts to Lasers: The Story of Chemistry at Berkeley* (Berkeley: College of Chemistry, University of California, 1987).

he left an endowment for the purchase of an organ (now several organs) and support for the university organist. A new chemistry facility was built during O'Neill's time and opened in 1897 (figure 9-2).[22]

Figure 9-2. An 1899 photo of the Old Chemistry Building at Berkeley[23]

Frederick Cottrell

Through these early years, some research of an applied nature was present here and there, but no concerted effort was made to develop research. The notable exception was Frederick Cottrell, who served on the chemistry faculty from 1903 to 1911. While he was at Berkeley, he consulted with the DuPont Corporation at its plant in nearby Pinole, California, on the problem of mist formation associated with the contact process for making sulfuric acid. In connection with that effort, Cottrell invented the extremely successful *electrostatic precipitator*, which has become universally used for the removal of particles and mists from effluent gases.

---

[22] When I arrived as an assistant professor in January, 1963, this building was still standing for a few months until it was taken down to provide the site for Hildebrand Hall.
[23] Bancroft Library, Online Archive of California, https://perma.cc/AME3-UJGY.

Cottrell was a brilliant and accomplished man who could have had an illustrious academic and research career and might himself have been the initiator of distinguished research within the College of Chemistry. However, with the clear success of the precipitator, he decided to move on to other ventures. One was a career with the US Bureau of Mines, of which he eventually became director, and the other was to launch an innovative corporation to utilize the royalty income from the patents on the electrostatic precipitator. The Research Corporation[24, 25] devoted the patent proceeds and their growth through investment to the support of scientific research. It was a vital source of support for scientific research before the large growth in government sponsored research following World War II. The Research Corporation still exists, now as the Research Corporation for Scientific Advancement. Upon coming to Berkeley, G. N. Lewis urged that Cottrell remain associated with the university as a "nonresident professor," and Lewis did seek and rely upon Cottrell's counsel, an example being in the recruitment of Joel Hildebrand (below).

The Hiring of Gilbert Newton Lewis

Benjamin Ide Wheeler, president of UC from 1899 to 1919, recognized the need to build chemistry. Upon the recommendations of both Armin Leuschner and Edmond O'Neill,[26] he contacted Gilbert Newton Lewis, a rising star, who was part of an outstanding group of physical chemists at MIT that had been put together under the leadership of Arthur A. Noyes in the Research Laboratory of Physical Chemistry, which operated on the German model of research.[27] Still a young man at the age of thirty-six, Lewis was invited by Wheeler to come to Berkeley in December 1911 to look over the situation and make recommendations. The recommendations, which are contained in a report letter from Lewis to Wheeler that is cited in full by Jolly[28],

---

[24] David C. Mowery et al., *Ivory Tower and Industrial Innovation: University-Industry Technology Transfer before and after the Bayh-Dole Act* (Stanford University Press, 2004), pp. 58–84.
[25] T. D. Cornell, *Establishing Research Corporation: A Case Study of Patents, Philanthropy, and Organized Research in Early Twentieth-Century America* (Tucson, AZ: Research Corp., 2004).
[26] Jolly, 1987, op. cit., p. 28.
[27] Roger L. Geiger, *To Advance Knowledge: The Growth of American Research Laboratories, 1900–1940* (Oxford University Press, 1986), pp. 87–88.
[28] Jolly, 1987, pp. 50–52.

were well designed, ambitious, and seemingly unlikely to be accepted. However, they were almost fully accepted by Wheeler and resulted in Lewis coming to Berkeley. Among the commitments were the opportunities to hire and dismiss faculty, several new faculty positions and a substantial support budget, a free hand in defining the development of the department, and a new building. This building became Gilman Hall[29], named for Daniel Coit Gilman. Gilman Hall is both one of the least imposing and one of most successful science buildings of all time, anywhere.[30]

Contention at MIT

There is a story behind the recruitment of Lewis to Berkeley, told in more detail by Servos,[31] Geiger,[32] and Weber.[33] Within the Research Laboratory of Physical Chemistry, there was a Research Laboratory of Applied Chemistry, organized and headed by William H. Walker, which eventually formed the basis for the Department of Chemical Engineering at MIT. There was bitter tension between Walker and Noyes, with Walker pushing for closer ties with industry, which he needed to fund his operation. Noyes, on the other hand, valued pure science and resisted influences from industry. The fact that Lewis shared Noyes's views on these matters and that Walker seemed to have the upper hand no doubt contributed to Lewis's willingness to move to Berkeley in the fall of 1912. His experience at MIT also left Gilbert Lewis with a lifelong aversion to ties with industry, a factor that substantially delayed the introductions of both organic chemistry and chemical engineering at Berkeley.

---

[29] Harvey Helfand, *University of California, Berkeley: The Campus Guide* (New York: Princeton Architectural Press, 2002), pp. 93–95.
[30] The American Chemical Society has also designated Gilman Hall as a National Historic Chemical Landmark. Room 307 in Gilman Hall, where Seaborg and associates first isolated plutonium, is both a US Historic Landmark and a National Nuclear Landmark of the American Nuclear Society.
[31] J. W. Servos, "The Industrial Relations of Science: Chemical Engineering at MIT, 1900–1939," *Isis* 71, no. 4 (1980): pp. 530–549.
[32] Geiger, 1986, *op. cit.*, pp. 177–191.
[33] Harold C. Weber, "The Improbable Achievement: Chemical Engineering at MIT," in W. F. Furter, ed., *History of Chemical Engineering*, Advances in Chemistry Series, vol. 190, American Chemical Society, Washington, DC, pp. 77–96, 1980; republished in book form, Dept. of Chemical Engineering, Massachusetts Institute of Technology, Cambridge, MA.

The president of MIT, Richard Maclaurin, found himself with an impossible situation and a fear that he would lose both Walker and Noyes.[34] In the spring of 1919, Walker threatened to resign if Noyes was not removed as head of the chemistry department, under which the two laboratories fell. Since Maclaurin felt a need for strong industry relations to support overall MIT finances, he did remove Noyes, and adopted a plan that was designed to bring considerably more funding from industry. A Division of Industrial Cooperation and Research was formed to cement these ties, and Walker was put in charge of it.

This action hardly ended Noyes's career. He left MIT to join the Throop Institute of Technology in Pasadena, California, and had a major role, along with George Ellery Hale and Robert K. Millikan, in leading the conversion of it to the California Institute of Technology (Caltech).[35] Walker too left MIT in the early 1920s, thereby bearing out Maclaurin's fear that he would lose both men. Finally, in 1930 the trustees of MIT concluded that the institute had lost too much ground in academic science through its heavy orientation toward industry and selected a distinguished physicist from Princeton, Karl T. Compton, to become president and rebuild the sciences. Compton was President of MIT for eighteen years, until 1948.

Lewis's Methods and Style

When G. N. Lewis (figure 9-3) arrived at Berkeley in 1912, he started a deanship of the College of Chemistry that lasted virtually continuously for thirty years until 1941. That deanship was much more a role of strong intellectual leader than the administrative role of which that one would think today.

Intellectual leadership was manifest in Lewis's approaches to research, building the faculty, and encouraging research and interactions of ideas among his colleagues. Administration was done through a very capable assistant, Mabel Kittredge (later Wilson), who literally would come to Lewis's side as he stood in the laboratory or in another conversation, tell him what needed to be done or decided, and either await his decision or be told to come back later after Lewis had

---

[34] Weber, 1980, *loc. cit.*
[35] Judith R. Goodstein, *Millikan's School: A History of the California Institute of Technology* (New York: W. W. Norton, 1991).

been able to think about the matter.[36] This form of multitasking sometimes led to important matters falling between the cracks. For example, Jolly notes that Berkeley lost Linus Pauling as a potential graduate student due to administrative delay.[37]

Figure 9-3. Gilbert Newton Lewis, 1925 (courtesy College of Chemistry Photo Archive, University of California, Berkeley)

Lewis himself did not teach undergraduate courses. He also saw to it that there were no graduate-level courses, per se, in chemistry, although there were a few senior-level undergraduate honors courses that were, in fact, mostly taken by graduate students.[38] Lewis believed that graduate education was best accomplished and creativity fostered through the intensive interactions of doing research and in research discussions without the distraction of courses.

The main event of the week and Lewis's only real personal teaching activity was the research conference, described by Jolly,[39]

---

[36] Jolly, 1987, *op. cit.*, p. 60.
[37] Jolly, 1987, *loc. cit.*
[38] Kenneth S. Pitzer, interview by Sally Smith Hughes and Germaine LaBerge, *Kenneth Sanborn Pitzer: Chemist and Administrator at UC Berkeley, Rice University, Stanford University, and the Atomic Energy Commission, 1935–1997*, pp. 51–52, oral history, Regional Oral History Office, University of California, Berkeley, 1999,
http://content.cdlib.org/view?docId=kt3s20030f&query=&brand=calisphere.
[39] Jolly, 1987, *op. cit.*, pp. 62–63.

Hildebrand,[40] Pitzer,[41] and Coffey.[42] There were two components to the research conference—a review by a graduate student of a published paper and then a presentation by a faculty member, postdoc, or advanced graduate student of a paper nearly ready for publication. Lewis led the discussion and asked intensely penetrating questions. In the research laboratory and in encounters around Gilman Hall as well, Lewis also invited and stimulated debate on research matters.[43] New ideas, cross-fertilization, and challenges abounded. Thus, graduate education was accomplished in the real world of continual awareness of, and wrestling with, current research issues.

Interestingly, Lewis himself did not supervise many research students. However, he often had a personal research assistant to whom he would assign research. Among these, over the years, were Melvin Calvin, Glenn Seaborg (two future Nobelists), Merle Randall, Samuel Ruben (a near Nobelist), and Philip Schutz, who later was hired to bring chemical engineering to Berkeley.

Lewis personally built chemistry at Berkeley around his own widespread interests generally focused upon physical chemistry, a field that was in an era of rapid expansion of knowledge.[44] He seems to have had his design for Berkeley chemistry in mind when he arrived in 1912. From the Research Laboratory of Physical Chemistry at MIT, he brought with him William Bray and Richard Tolman (later with a very distinguished career at Caltech) as assistant professors and Merle Randall as a personal research assistant.[45] The preexisting professorial faculty members at Berkeley were encouraged to depart, or they assumed subsidiary roles, except for O'Neill, who ably aided Lewis in administration of the department as director of the chemical laboratories.[46] In the year following his arrival at Berkeley, Lewis hired

---

[40] Joel H. Hildebrand, "Gilbert Newton Lewis, 1975–1946: A Biographical Memoir," *National Academy of Sciences Biographical Memoirs*, vol. 31, pp. 225–235, 1958; https://perma.cc/2VPH-H6GC.
[41] Pitzer, 1999, *op. cit.*, pp. 48–50.
[42] Patrick Coffey, *Cathedrals of Science: The Personalities and Rivalries That Made Modern Chemistry* (Oxford: Oxford University Press, 2008), pp. 124–125.
[43] Pitzer, 1999, *op. cit.*, p. 50.
[44] Coffey, 2008, *loc. cit.*, gives a description of the main actors of the day and the synergies and rivalries among them.
[45] Jolly, 1987, *op. cit.*, p. 54.
[46] Jolly, 1987, *op. cit.*, p. 28.

Joel Hildebrand as assistant professor and George Gibson [47] as instructor.

Joel Hildebrand

Hildebrand[48, 49] (figure 9-4) put his own stamp on the college in concert with Lewis. In addition to being an accomplished researcher in his own right, Hildebrand authored an extremely successful and long-used freshman textbook, *Principles of Chemistry* (seven editions, 1918 through 1964), was a classroom teacher extraordinaire who taught an estimated forty-thousand-plus students in freshman chemistry in memorable style,[50] was a prime actor in the Academic Senate, and held a variety of administrative posts, including being a dean three times (twice for chemistry during absences of Lewis and once for letters and science) "for periods as short as I could decently make them."[51] He also had wider interests, having been president of the Sierra Club (1937–40) and manager of the 1936 US Olympic skiing team.[52, 53] With his daughter, he coauthored a widely used book[54] on camp cooking. He was a prime contributor, as were two of his sons, to a how-to book on mountain travel.[55] Hildebrand was a nearly perfect complement to Lewis in the building of the chemistry program.

How Hildebrand was found and recruited is revealing. Apparently Bray had heard a paper that Hildebrand presented before the American

---

[47] Jolly, 1987, *op. cit.*, pp. 87–88.
[48] J. H. Hildebrand, "Joel Hildebrand, Described by Himself," *Perspectives in Biology and Medicine* 16, no. 1 (1972): 88–111.
[49] Hildebrand, 1962, *loc. cit.*
[50] Kenneth S. Pitzer, "Joel Henry Hildebrand, 1881–1993," National Academy of Sciences Biographical Memoirs, 1993, https://perma.cc/9G6N-9LUY.
[51] Hildebrand, 1972, *op. cit.*, p. 99.
[52] Wallace Turner, "Joel Hildebrand, 101, Chemist—Joined U. of California in 1913," *New York Times*, May 3, 1983.
[53] Robert Livermore. "Notes on Olympic Skiing: 1936," *Atlantic Monthly*, May 1936, https://perma.cc/VCG7-HYLC.
[54] Louise Hildebrand (Klein) and J. H. Hildebrand, *Camp Catering or How to Rustle Grub for Hikers, Campers, Mountaineers, Packers, Canoers, Hunters, and Fishermen* (Brattleboro, VT: Stephen Daye Press, 1938; Whitefish, MT: Kessinger Publishing Co., 2010).
[55] D. R. Brower, ed., *Going Light with Backpack or Burro* (San Francisco: Sierra Club, 1951). This book and *Starr's Guide to the John Muir Trail and the High Sierra Region* were the first books that I bought on the subject and used as I started my own lifetime of hiking in the Sierra Nevada mountains upon my arrival in California in 1963.

Chemical Society in 1912 and was favorably impressed. Frederick Cottrell, no longer on the faculty but in continued close contact with Lewis, was then asked by Lewis to pay a visit to Hildebrand at the University of Pennsylvania in Philadelphia so as to size him up further. Cottrell did so and returned a favorable report.[56, 57] Hildebrand was then invited to come to Berkeley for a visit in March 1913 "to inspect and be inspected,"[58] greatly liked what he found there, made a continued strong and positive impression on Lewis, and received an offer of an assistant professorship at an annual salary of $2,000 per year. He turned down a competing offer of $3,500 from the National Bureau of Standards and accepted Berkeley.

Figure 9-4. Joel H. Hildebrand, 1924 (courtesy College of Chemistry Photo Archive, University of California, Berkeley)

Hildebrand's rationale for coming to Berkeley is also pertinent to the story. At Penn he had taught eighteen hours per week[59] and was not allowed to supervise research students of his own. The research conference at Penn, such as it was, was conducted by a professor who did no research.[60] Hildebrand wrote, "Arriving in Berkeley, I felt like I had escaped from a dungeon into sunshine."[61]

---

[56] Hildebrand, 1962, *op. cit.*, p. 38.
[57] Jolly, 1987, *op. cit.*, p. 91.
[58] Hildebrand, 1962, *op. cit.*, p. 39.
[59] Hildebrand, 1962, *loc. cit.*
[60] Jolly, 1987, *loc. cit.*
[61] Jolly, 1987, *loc. cit.*

Further Building of the Faculty

Lewis then grew the faculty of the chemistry department by a form of inbreeding that was eminently successful at the time but would no longer be looked upon with favor in the United States. After 1913, all new faculty appointments were filled with Berkeley graduates until the appointment of Melvin Calvin as instructor in 1937. Many of the hires from within during that period proved to be outstanding (e.g., Gerald Branch, Wendell Latimer, William Giauque, Willard Libby, and Kenneth Pitzer), for all of whom Jolly[62] provides brief biographies. Although Gerald Branch was in a sense a theoretical organic chemist, his interests were close to those of Lewis and on the border with physical chemistry. There was no other organic chemistry and, in line with Lewis's experiences at MIT, no applied chemistry, analytical chemistry, or chemical engineering.

Nobel Prizes

Remarkably, the research atmosphere during Lewis's time produced six recipents of the Nobel Prize, a feat that has not been duplicated. Those six were the following (all in Chemistry):

- 1934: **Harold Urey** (Berkeley PhD, 1923 with Lewis), "for his discovery of heavy hydrogen (deuterium)"; work done subsequently at Columbia
- 1949: **William Giauque** (Berkeley PhD, 1922 with Gibson), "for his contributions in thermodynamics, particularly concerning the behavior of substances at extremely low temperatures"; work done at Berkeley
- 1951: **Glenn Seaborg** (Berkeley PhD, 1937 with Gibson; research assistant with Lewis), "for his discoveries with Edwin McMillan in the chemistry of trans-uranium elements"; work done at Berkeley
- 1960: **Willard Libby** (Berkeley PhD, 1933 with Latimer), "for his method to use carbon-14 for age determination in archaeology, geology, geophysics, and other branches of science"; work done subsequently at University of Chicago
- 1961: **Melvin Calvin** (UC Berkeley instructorship, 1937, carrying out research with Lewis, 1937 through about 1944, and then UC

---

[62] Jolly, 1987, *op. cit.*

Berkeley professorship; PhD at University of Minnesota), "for his research on carbon dioxide assimilation in plants"; work done at Berkeley
- 1983: **Henry Taube** (Berkeley PhD, 1940, with Bray), "for his work in the mechanisms of electron-transfer reactions, especially in metal complexes"; work done subsequently at Uiversity of Chicago

In addition, Samuel Ruben, who died as the result of an unfortunate laboratory accident in 1943, would otherwise have been a strong contender for sharing the carbon-14 Nobel Prize with Libby, based upon his pioneering important work in that area with Kamen.[63]

Lewis himself never received the Nobel Prize but was nominated and considered often. Coffey[64] explores this matter in detail, reporting and speculating on the politics and rivalries that surrounded the issue.

University Service

Finally, it is worth noting that Lewis and his colleagues also had strong and very positive roles within faculty governance, thereby spreading their influence and affecting matters of academic quality at Berkeley in other ways. As was noted in chapter 7, Lewis had a prime role in stimulating the actions that led to the Berkeley Revolution establishing the role of the Academic Senate, and he led the committee that negotiated directly with the regents on behalf of the Academic Senate in 1919–20.[65, 66] This was only six years after Lewis had come to Berkeley. Lewis also proposed, and succeeded in having set up, a faculty search and recruiting effort cutting across the university, which consisted of sending the best researchers to meetings of scholarly societies and to other universities seeking promising young prospects.

Hildebrand was also very active in the Academic Senate in the crucial period of the Berkeley Revolution[67] and throughout his long career. He chaired a special committee of the Academic Senate that took on the thorny problem of salary reductions in the Depression era of the early 1930s (chapter 2). As was described in chapter 6, he had a

---

[63] Jolly, 1987, *op. cit.*, pp. 151–153.
[64] Coffey, 2008, *loc. cit.*
[65] Stadtman, 1968, *op. cit.*, pp. 254–255.
[66] Robert W. Seidel, "Physics Research in California: The Rise of a Leading Sector in American Physics," (PhD dissertation, History, University of California, Berkeley, 1978), pp. 85–88.
[67] Hildebrand, 1962, *op. cit.*, pp. 129–148.

key role in the decentralization of authority within the university that led ultimately to the creation in 1952 of chancellor positions for the individual campuses. Hildebrand was still a leader of the Academic Senate at the time of the loyalty oath crisis of the late 1950s and had a prominent and somewhat controversial role in the senate's initial responses to it.[68, 69, 70]

Post-Lewis

After Lewis was required to step down as dean in 1941 because he had reached age sixty-five, Wendell Latimer became dean. Lewis died in 1946 in a laboratory accident. With the transition in authority, several substantial changes came about. One was that faculty hiring moved beyond Berkeley and became largely extramural. Second, Latimer expanded the disciplinary coverage of the college and moved hiring into two fields not previously well represented on the faculty—organic chemistry and chemical engineering. The method of selecting faculty to be hired continued to be personal evaluations by one or relatively few people. Kenneth Pitzer, who was dean from 1951 to 1960, described the method in his oral history.[71] Essentially, Pitzer would rely on his own judgment or that of a trusted colleague, typically Robert Connick for chemistry and Charles Wilke for chemical engineering. Their judgments would be based on personal contacts with the individual and recommendations from people whose acumen they respected. This worked very well for the development of organic chemistry and chemical engineering in particular, but would not stand scrutiny today because of the lack of opportunity for equal inputs from the rest of the faculty and the lack of a widespread search.

Chemical Engineering

Despite Lewis's disinterest in the field as a discipline within itself, there had been some earlier elements of applied chemistry or chemical engineering in the College of Chemistry dating all the way back to

---

[68] David P. Gardner, *The California Oath Controversy* (Berkeley: University of California Press, 1967).
[69] Bob Blauner, *Resisting McCarthyism: To Sign or Not to Sign California's Loyalty Oath* (Stanford University Press, 2009).
[70] Stadtman, 1970, *op. cit.*, pp. 319–339.
[71] Pitzer, 1999, *op. cit.*, pp. 288–294.

Frederick Cottrell, who was followed with applied and engineering interests by Randall and Giauque. However, their activities were specific to particular areas of research rather than in the discipline per se or in providing degrees within the field. As one of the two areas started in earnest by Latimer and the college after the death of Lewis, chemical engineering was launched within the College of Chemistry as a full-fledged program at Berkeley as of 1946. In Lewis-like fashion, Philip Schutz, who had been research assistant with Lewis, had obtained his PhD with Latimer, and then had helped start chemical engineering at Columbia University, was hired to guide the development of the program; however, Shutz tragically died in 1947. The other five founding members of what became the Department of Chemical Engineering were hired by Latimer and Pitzer, following the methodology just described. Subsequent faculty recruitments were made in the same personal way by Charles Wilke, one of the five, after he became division head in 1953 and then department chair in 1957.

Interestingly, even though there had been a College of Engineering going back to 1931, with roots in three colleges (Mining, Mechanical Arts, and Civil Engineering) going back to the start of the university, there had been no serious effort to start chemical engineering in that college before World War II. An interdepartmental Graduate Group in Chemical Engineering was formed in 1942 and could give the master of science degree in chemical engineering, but fell into contention between the College of Chemistry and the College of Engineering over issues of domain. In 1945 Provost Monroe Deutsch relayed an administrative decision, involving shared governance, to place chemical engineering within the College of Chemistry. Subsequent negotiations dealt with splitting the subject matter, placing those subjects shared with mechanical engineering (e.g., heat transfer and fluid dynamics) into the College of Engineering under the name process engineering and the remainder of the curriculum under the name chemical engineering into the College of Chemistry. This history is summarized by Jolly[72] and Lostuvali.[73] The Dean of the College of Engineering, Morrough (Mike) O'Brien, went ahead with process engineering as a

---

[72] Jolly, 1987, *op. cit.*, pp. 199–201.
[73] Elif Kale Lostuvali, "A Brief History of Chemical Engineering at Berkeley", draft unpublished manuscript, August 2008.

degree curriculum within the College of Engineering, as did the College of Chemistry with chemical engineering. These two programs existed in parallel and competition, and for a time (1949–51), both had accreditation from the American Institute of Chemical Engineers.

In 1954 chancellor Clark Kerr set up a committee to adjudicate the conflict and, following their recommendation, chartered the program in the College of Chemistry to continue as the official and accredited program, while Mechanical Engineering could continue to teach courses emphasizing the mechanical engineering aspects of process engineering. Process engineering then withered away within the College of Engineering.

Why was that decision made in favor of the College of Chemistry? In his memoirs[74] Clark Kerr observed, "He [O'Brien] was, however, very unhappy that I had decided to leave chemical engineering in the College of Chemistry where it had an outstanding record and where its faculty members were very satisfied. A hot dispute, but Mike reluctantly accepted my decision."

In his oral history, Pitzer[75] observes, "By that time, our chemical engineers had made quite a name for themselves nationally, and the people that were appointed under the term 'process engineering' had essentially done their job locally but didn't have a national reputation. So they were allowed to serve out their careers in the Department of Mechanical Engineering. The Department of Mechanical Engineering has various sub-groups in it, so that they were not completely out of place there. But that's all developed very successfully, and in the last national survey,[76] our chemical engineering was number three in the country." In fact, Chemical Engineering was rated number five in the country in the first such survey, carried out in 1966 for the American Council on Education,[77] just twenty years after its start—a substantial credit to the hiring and start-up practices of the College of Chemistry.

---

[74] Kerr, 2001, *op. cit.*, p. 66.
[75] Pitzer, 1999, *op. cit.*, p. 100.
[76] M. L. Goldberger, B. A. Maher, and P. E. Flattau, eds., *Research-Doctorate Programs in the United States* (National Research Council, National Academy Press, 1995), appendix table P-8, p. 500.
[77] A. M. Cartter, *An Assessment of Quality in Graduate Education* (Washington, DC: American Council on Education, 1966).

Jolly[78] notes some other factors that may have contributed to the decision to sustain chemical engineering within the College of Chemistry. The program there attracted substantially more students than did the one in the College of Engineering; it had teaching assistantships in freshman chemistry available for the support of incoming graduate students; and it had a block-grant program for chemical engineering set up within the Lawrence Berkeley Laboratory, administered by Wilke for start-up of the research of new faculty members. That block grant program was very helpful at the start, and lasted into the mid-1960s.

Why a Separate College?
It is also striking that the College of Chemistry has remained in place as the structure over time, whereas there is no other College of Chemistry, per se, in the United States, and nearly everywhere chemistry is part of a college of arts and sciences or simply a college of sciences, and chemical engineering is part of a college of engineering. That fact begs the question "Why?" The short answer is that the College of Chemistry was created by the legislature at the request of President Gilman in 1872,[79] and it never changed. Chemical engineering was originally placed with chemistry at the University of Illinois at Urbana-Champaign and still is part of a Division of Chemistry and Chemical Engineering at Caltech, but there is no other structure at a university in the United States putting the two disciplines together into an actual college. Although the separate college, having the same status as the College of Letters and Science and the College of Engineering, can be regarded superficially as administrative inefficiency, it affords the College of Chemistry a unique ability to govern and control its own affairs. In reviewing the advantages of this situation, Pitzer[80] observed, "Over the long period of time…[this structure has] helped Chemistry; the College of Chemistry has prospered. One of the things that Hildebrand used to say, and I've said many times, is that it's very important that we continue to manage our own affairs so that we don't cause any problems elsewhere on the

---

[78] Jolly, 1987, *op. cit.*, pp. 200–201.
[79] Jolly, 1987, *op. cit.*, p. 19.
[80] Pitzer, 1999, *op. cit.*, pp. 56–57.

campus. Then we can always use that argument, as I've said before, 'If it ain't broke, don't fix it.'" It hasn't been, and is unlikely to be, "fixed."

As part of an abortive, top-down academic reorganization effort of 2015–16, a number of restructuring proposals were placed on the table by a relatively new campus administration in which the chancellor and provost both came from careers elsewhere. One of these proposals was to eliminate the College of Chemistry, probably by placing the Department of Chemistry with the Division of Physical Sciences within the College of Letters and Science and the Department of Chemical (now Chemical and Biomolecular) Engineering with the College of Engineering. This proposition received attention in the press and led to a student-generated online petition[81] in opposition to the proposal which drew forty-five hundred signatures within ten days. The proposal was withdrawn by the administration when it became apparent that the proposal did not meet any academic needs and would do little, if anything, to improve the budget situation of the Berkeley campus.[82]

PHYSICS, RAYMOND BIRGE, ERNEST LAWRENCE, AND THE LAWRENCE BERKELEY LABORATORY

Despite a history tracing back to John LeConte, one of the first faculty members and an early president of the university, physics at Berkeley in the early 1900s was a relatively ordinary department with

---

[81] "Petitioning Chancellor Nicholas Dirks: Prevent the College of Chemistry from Being Dissolved" https://perma.cc/EAD5-2MRC.

[82] I have had many relationships of my own to the story of the College of Chemistry, having grown up intellectually in the MIT chemical engineering tradition that was initiated by Walker and then having gone in 1963 from MIT to a faculty position in the Berkeley College of Chemistry, where I stayed for the rest of my career, fifty-five years so far. I took graduate thermodynamics from Harold Weber at MIT; knew Seaborg, Pitzer, Connick, and Calvin well; and hold the William H. Walker Award of the American Institute of Chemical Engineers. I was recruited in the exact way described by Pitzer. I was visited for two days by Charles Wilke in 1960 while I was a term-appointment assistant professor and director of the Bayway (New Jersey) Station of MIT's School of Chemical Engineering Practice. He came ostensibly to see the Practice School Station and the Bayway Refinery. I had been recommended to Wilke by Thomas K. Sherwood, who knew me at MIT and had spent a sabbatical leave at Berkeley. I had my offer of an assistant professor position and accepted it without either having visited Berkeley or having been interviewed by anyone else in the department or college. I started my research at Berkeley with the support of the block grant through the Lawrence Berkeley Laboratory.

distinguished research not having yet flowered. Research eminence developed following the appointments of Raymond T. Birge (figure 9-5) and Leonard Loeb.

Raymond Birge

Birge, who was appointed as instructor in 1918, became the first member of the National Academy of Sciences from Berkeley physics (1932) and showed strong management and leadership ability as chair of the Physics Department from 1932 to 1955. One manifestation of Birge's accomplishments in building and leading physics at Berkeley is that by the time of his death in 1980, the Berkeley Department of Physics had moved to a position where it had more members in the National Academy of Sciences than any other university physics department in the United States.

Birge's life, research, and administrative and leadership abilities are well documented by Helmholz,[83] in Birge's own oral history,[84] in a dissertation by Seidel,[85] and even in a thorough and detailed history[86] of the Berkeley Department of Physics that Birge himself wrote. The latter work covers the period from 1868 up to 1932, when Birge became department chair.

Finding Birge and getting him to accept a faculty position were not challenges. He had been at Syracuse University for five years, serving as instructor and then assistant professor, after his graduation with a PhD from the University of Wisconsin. He had not found the atmosphere at Syracuse to be sufficiently stimulating intellectually, and so he applied for one of two open instructor positions at Berkeley. Recognizing the attraction of Birge as an established researcher in his own field of spectroscopy, E. S. Lewis (no relation to G. N.), then chair of the

---

[83] A. Carl Helmholz, "Raymond Thayer Birge, 1887–1980," Biographical Memoirs, National Academy of Sciences, 1990, https://perma.cc/XDG4-GD6M.
[84] Raymond T. Birge, interview by Edna Tartaul Daniel, *Raymond Thayer Birge, Physicist,* oral history, Regional Oral History Office, University of California, Berkeley, 1960, https://perma.cc/TAP3-36NZ.
[85] Seidel, 1978, *op. cit.*
[86] Birge, 1966, *op. cit.*

Berkeley Physics Department, upgraded the salary of one of the positions and offered it to Birge, who accepted and arrived in 1918. Thus both Birge in physics and Hildebrand in chemistry were attracted to Berkeley because they had reasons to believe that the world of research at Berkeley would be much more stimulating and offer more opportunities than would be case where they had been.

Figure 9-5. Raymond T. Birge at his desk, circa 1920[87]

Although G. N. Lewis had undertaken a number of actions to build research in physics, and perhaps also to extend the influence of chemistry over physics,[88] there had been very little interaction between the chemistry and physics departments before Birge's arrival. In a very real sense, the two departments were competitors, with physics envying the status that had been given to chemistry through the conditions to which the university administration had agreed in the recruitment of Lewis. Birge overcame that barrier by choosing to attend the weekly research conference in chemistry held by G. N. Lewis.[89] Lewis welcomed him and made what was probably his first entry into a physics building for many years in order to attend a seminar given by Birge on the determination of Planck's constant.

---

[87] https://perma.cc/G444-UM5Q, courtesy of Bancroft Library, University of California
[88] Seidel, 1978, *op. cit.*, pp. 89–90.
[89] Birge, 1966, *op. cit.*, vol. 2, pp. vii (11–12).

Differing theories of the atom and discussion over them also provided an avenue for intellectual interactions between Birge and Lewis. The Bohr theory of the atom was relatively new, and Birge was a proponent of it. However, Lewis had his own cubic theory of the atom, which had been the subject of considerable controversy between Lewis and Irving Langmuir over credit for the origination of the model.[90] Birge considered one of his greatest accomplishments to have been eventually winning Lewis over on the subject of the Bohr atom.[91, 92]

Leonard Loeb

Leonard Loeb was hired by E. S. Lewis and Armin Leuschner in 1923. He had been a Berkeley undergraduate student and was the son of a former head of the Department of Physiology there. After receiving his PhD at the University of Chicago with Robert Millikan, he had returned as a National Research Council Fellow to Chicago, where his research concerned electrical phenomena in gases. He saw the position at Berkeley as a way to participate centrally in the development of an outstanding physics department.[93] A factual summary of Loeb's career is given by Birge.[94]

Upon the death of E. S. Lewis in 1926, Armin Leuschner was asked by then-president Campbell to chair the search committee to find a new chair for the physics department, with the intention of hiring someone from outside who could build research further.[95] G. N. Lewis was also a member of that committee.[96] Following an effort to hire Arthur Compton[97] of Washington University and subsequently the University of Chicago and a Nobelist (1926), Campbell then settled upon Professor Elmer E. Hall from within the department, who served as chairman until his death in 1932. At that point, Birge was the obvious choice and was chairman for the next twenty-three years.

---

[90] Coffey, 2008, *op. cit.*
[91] Birge, 1960, *op. cit.*, pp. 130–134.
[92] Helmholtz, 1990, *loc. cit.*
[93] Seidel, 1978, *op. cit.*, p. 94.
[94] Birge, 1966, *op. cit.*, vol. 2, pp. vii (10–12).
[95] Birge, 1966, *op. cit.*, vol. 2, pp. vii (23–24).
[96] Seidel, 1978, *op. cit.*, p. 97.
[97] Brother of Karl T. Compton, previously mentioned as president of MIT. See Figure 13-1.

During the period in which Hall was department chairman, Birge and Loeb handled matters of faculty recruitment because it was recognized that they were most intimately involved with the physics research arena and could best judge research. Hall, on the other hand, was near retirement and not current in research.[98] Birge and Loeb settled upon a strategy of seeking promising researchers at earlier points in their careers when they were not yet embedded securely at their present institutions. One promising source was National Research Council fellows, who were drawn from among the top 5 percent of science PhDs.[99] During this time and as a result of this strategy, the addition of Ernest O. Lawrence was made.

Ernest O. Lawrence

Lawrence had an enormous effect upon physics, upon the development of large-scale science at Berkeley and elsewhere, and on government support of science and science policy. Much has been written about him, and here I shall concentrate only upon the way in which he was attracted to Berkeley and retained in the face of outside offers, the ways in which he derived financial support for his research, and the ways in which the university and others supported him in those endeavors. He was the quintessential self-initiator and driver.

Lawrence had grown up in rural South Dakota and was drawn to physics research through his association as a student with W. F. G. Swann, a pioneer in cosmic-ray research. As Swann moved from the University of Minnesota to the University of Chicago and then on to Yale University, Lawrence followed him, obtaining his PhD with Swann at Yale in 1925. A year later, while Lawrence was still a National Research fellow at Yale, Loeb "found" him and was highly impressed.[100] Birge and Hall agreed with Loeb that they should offer Lawrence a faculty position at the higher of what were then the two steps of assistant professor (see chapter 11 for the step system). Yale countered with an offer of an assistant professor position, and Lawrence then chose to accept the Yale offer, probably on the bases of Yale's prestige and Swann still being at Yale. Birge and his entire family (wife and

---

[98] Seidel, 1978, *op. cit.*, pp. 98–99.
[99] Hiltzik, 2015, *op. cit.*, p. 41,
[100] Hiltzik, 2015, *op. cit.*, pp. 33–38.

three- and five-year old children) then visited Lawrence in New Haven,[101] and Birge was similarly impressed firsthand. At the initiative of Loeb and Birge, Berkeley then decided to offer Lawrence an associate professor position, something most unusual for someone at such an early career stage. This set off a large effort to convince Lawrence to accept. The written correspondence between Birge and Lawrence, which is quite extensive, is given in full by Birge[102] and is summarized by Heilbron and Seidel.[103] The salary offered was increased substantially during the recruitment. Key factors in Lawrence's decision to come to Berkeley were Yale's reluctance to provide an associate professor position so early in his career; the opportunities to supervise graduate students in research and teach graduate-level courses, which were not yet open to him at Yale; and his perceptions of the atmosphere and upward vector of the Berkeley department.

Only six months after arriving in Berkeley, Lawrence conceived the principle of the cyclotron, upon which he built his scientific career. The cyclotron was an original invention, building upon the idea of Norwegian physicist Rolf Wideröe that ions can be accelerated in a straight line through a linear series of charged electrical gaps. Lawrence's essential invention was that the same thing could be accomplished in a much more compact form by using magnetic fields to create a circular path in which charged particles would pass repeatedly through such gaps. The compact circular path could then be the equivalent of an extremely long ion accelerator. Lawrence recognized that with the right design, it should be possible to reach very high energies for the particles, thereby greatly increasing the ability of experimenters to bring about reactions within atomic nuclei. The sketch of the operating principle from the original patent application is shown in figure 9-6. Heilbron and Seidel[104] describe the physics involved in more detail and analyze the scientific advances as Lawrence developed the concept further and implemented and tested

---

[101] Birge, 1966, *op. cit.*, vol. 3, p. ix (5).
[102] Birge, 1966, *op. cit.*, vol. 3, pp. ix (5–11).
[103] John L. Heilbron and Robert W. Seidel, *Lawrence and His Laboratory: A History of the Lawrence Berkeley Laboratory*, vol. 1 (Berkeley: University of California Press, 1990), pp. 21–24, https://publishing.cdlib.org/ucpressebooks/view?docId=ft5s200764&brand=ucpress.
[104] Heilbron and Seidel, 1990, *loc. cit.*

it over the years in successively larger devices. Hiltzik[105] describes the more sociological aspects of recognizing the idea and building upon it.

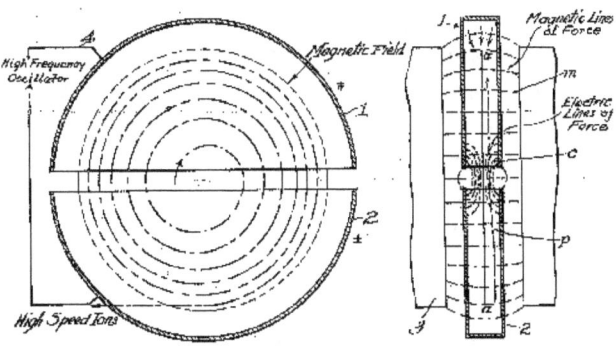

Figure 9-6. Sketch of the operating principle of the cyclotron, from the original patent application[106]

Upon arrival in Berkeley in 1928, Lawrence lived at the Faculty Club on campus, as did Gilbert Lewis at the time. The two became well acquainted and traded thoughts in discussion over nightly dinners there.[107] Thereby Lewis became familiar with Lawrence's interests and became a strong supporter of him. The two were also occasional collaborators, most notably on research relating to heavy water and the deuteron, which went too rapidly down a path that proved to be erroneous.[108, 109]

Lawrence's cyclotrons, with their very large magnets, high voltage requirements, and needs for skilled and capable staffing were expensive. It is therefore instructive to examine how Lawrence got his money in the 1930s, which was before the era of big support of science by the US government. His entrepreneurial methods utilized a wide variety of sources, most of which were private foundations.[110] The

---

[105] Hiltzik, 2015, *loc. cit.*
[106] Ernest O. Lawrence, Method and apparatus for the acceleration of ions," US Patent 1,948,384, January 26, 1934.
[107] Heilbron and Seidel, 1990, *op. cit.*, p. 24.
[108] Heilbron and Seidel, 1990, *op. cit.*, pp. 153–182.
[109] Hiltzik, 2015, *op. cit.*, pp. 105–121.
[110] Heilbron and Seidel, 1990, *op. cit.*, p. 212, table 5.1.

staffing for the cyclotron project grew from ten people to fifty-six between 1932–33 and 1939–40.[111] In line with the purposes of Leuschner's Board of Research, Lawrence's first funding came from that board.[112] Lawrence also made effective use of coworkers funded by a variety of extramural means. For example, in 1937 there were seventeen postdoctoral fellows in physics on his staff, but he paid the salaries of only two of them from his own funds. The others were sustained on stipends from external entities such as the National Research Council and the Rockefeller Foundation.[113] Lawrence's laboratory was innovative in another way, by bringing together teams of researchers from several different disciplines to address complicated issues. In this way he was a pioneer of University of California efforts to foster multidisciplinary research (chapter 14).

Frederick Cottrell, the former Berkeley faculty member in chemistry who had invented the electrostatic precipitator, became both a supporter and an ambassador for Lawrence. Starting early on, Cottrell's Research Corporation supported Lawrence's research, and in return Lawrence (in the absence of any University of California patent policies) assigned the patents to the Research Corporation in the same way that Cottrell himself had done for the electrostatic precipitator. Cottrell was also the path to funding of Lawrence's research by the Chemical Foundation, which had been set up in 1918 by the US government to administer five thousand German patents that had been appropriated at the end of World War I.

Still later (1935–36) Lawrence obtained funding from the Josiah Macy, Jr. Foundation to initiate work relating to the use of radiation in medicine. Over his career, Lawrence recognized the value of research on medical applications of the cyclotron as an effective lure to obtain financial support from foundations with medical interests. That goal meshed well with the fact that Lawrence's younger brother, John Lawrence, was a medical researcher with interest in using high-energy beams for treatment of conditions such as cancers. John Lawrence joined Ernest Lawrence's team in 1937, spearheaded the Donner Laboratory which opened in 1942 on the Berkeley campus, was a

---

[111] Heilbron and Seidel, 1990, *op. cit.*, p. 223, table 5.2.
[112] Heilbron and Seidel, 1990, *op. cit.*, p. 98.
[113] Hiltzik, 2015, *op. cit.*, p. 74.

founder of the Medical Physics Program at Berkeley in 1947, had a significant research career of his own, and eventually was one of the few faculty members of the university ever to move on to become a regent of the University of California, 1970–83.[114]

Then, in 1937, as Ernest Lawrence moved toward his ultimate 184–inch cyclotron, he obtained support in the amount of $1.15 million from the Rockefeller Foundation, an amount far greater than any of his other grants and extremely large by the standards of the time.[115] In 1939, Lawrence also began a very productive relationship with Albert L. Loomis (figure 13-1), a wealthy investment banker who was also trained in mathematics and became a scientist through interest, collaboration, and an apprenticeship of sorts with the distinguished physicist Robert W. Wood of Johns Hopkins University. That connection led to large direct funding from Loomis for Lawrence's work. It also led to the launching of the radar-development laboratory at MIT, which was spurred by Lawrence and Loomis and deceptively given the name Radiation Laboratory, the same name as that of Lawrence's laboratory at Berkeley, for purposes of wartime secrecy. The career of Loomis and the interactions between Lawrence and Loomis are engagingly described by Conant.[116] Lawrence's relationship with Loomis is further described by Hiltzik.[117] Lawrence also obtained some funding for staff support from the Works Progress Administration of the US government and other Depression-relief agencies that were active as the Great Depression proceeded during the 1930s.

As the cyclotrons became larger and staff for the laboratory grew, space, location, and the status of Lawrence's laboratory were ever-present issues. As his space needs outgrew those in LeConte Hall, where physics was housed, Lawrence was assigned the Civil Engineering Test Laboratory, a wooden building nearby located just

---

[114] John H. Lawrence, interview by Sally Smith Hughes, *John H. Lawrence, 1904–1991, Nuclear Medicine Pioneer and Director of Donner Laboratory, University of California, Berkeley*, oral history, Regional Oral History Program, University of California, Berkeley, 2000, https://perma.cc/B5D2-E3AM.
[115] Heilbron and Seidel, 1990, *op. cit.*, pp. 220–221, 480–483.
[116] Jennet Conant, *Tuxedo Park* (New York: Simon & Schuster, 2002). See also Figure 13-1.
[117] Hiltzik, 2015, *op. cit.*, pp. 191–210

north of chemistry's Gilman Hall. This building received the name "Radiation Laboratory" from the regents in 1932.[118] The much larger Crocker Radiation Laboratory was built nearby for medical physics, 1936–39, through a gift from William Crocker, a regent of the university.[119]

With the new Rockefeller Foundation grant for the 184-inch cyclotron, the sheer physical size of the operation required space off the main campus, and with that the laboratory and its new cyclotron moved to Charter Hill behind the Berkeley campus, where it remains today. The World War II activities of the laboratory, its conversion to a national laboratory, its development of other fields of scientific and engineering activities, and its relationship and synergies with the Berkeley campus are taken up in chapter 13.

As the success and fame of Lawrence and his activities grew, other universities, of course, tried to recruit him away from Berkeley. The first such attempt came early on from Northwestern University in 1930. With advice and urging from G. N. Lewis,[120] Leuschner and then-president Robert Sproul shepherded the process by which Lawrence was retained, in large part through promotion to full professor at the tender age of twenty-nine and with a substantial increase in salary. So as to assure a favorable outcome in the promotion review process, Sproul appointed a group composed entirely of very distinguished science faculty members, including G. N. Lewis as chair, to be the faculty ad hoc committee that would review the case. Because of the prestige of those on the committee, more traditional faculty members who would object to such a promotion and salary for such a young individual were, in effect, silenced.[121]

The most serious threat came from Harvard in 1936, with Lawrence still at the comparatively young age of thirty-five. Harvard, whose president at that time was chemist James B. Conant, boldly struck out to hire Lawrence as dean of engineering and applied science, and along with him, Edward McMillan[122] and Robert Oppenheimer.

---

[118] Heilbron and Seidel, 1990, *op. cit*, p. 113, footnote 30.
[119] Heilbron and Seidel, 1990, *op. cit.*, p. 122.
[120] Heilbron and Seidel, 1990, *op. cit.*, p. 99.
[121] Heilbron and Seidel, 1990, *op. cit.*, p. 208.
[122] Lawrence's physics colleague and successor as director of the laboratory (see chapter 13), as well as a future Nobelist. Lawrence and McMillan married sisters from New Haven, CT.

Despite the fact the university's budget was under severe stress as the Depression continued, Sproul pulled out the stops and responded by offering independent identity for the Radiation Laboratory, substantial monies for the operating budget of the laboratory, and a promise to work with Lawrence in obtaining the funds and facilities (which became the Crocker Laboratory) for Lawrence's nascent program in medical physics. [123, 124] Birge [125] noted that he and Oppenheimer worked continually to convince Lawrence to stay and concluded that the ultimate deciding factor was the fact that it would have taken several years of construction and acquisitions to duplicate at Harvard the facilities that Lawrence had already at Berkeley and that the pace of Lawrence's research could not afford that delay. Lawrence stayed at Berkeley.[126]

Finally, in 1939 the University of Texas made a strong play for Lawrence to become a vice president of the university and lead a movement of that university, backed by its oil money, into the first ranks of academic science. Sproul again moved energetically and promptly. From this retention came matching monies and work by Sproul himself in synergy with Lawrence toward the large grant from the Rockefeller Foundation and the designation of Charter Hill as the site for the 184-inch cyclotron and the future home of the Radiation Laboratory.

Robert Oppenheimer

After Lawrence, the Berkeley Department of Physics made a number of outstanding hires, probably the best known of which was Robert Oppenheimer. [127, 128, 129] Oppenheimer came in 1929, splitting

---

[123] Heilbron and Seidel, 1990, op. cit., p. 208–209.
[124] Hiltzik, 2015, op. cit., pp. 145–151.
[125] Birge, 1966, op. cit., vol. 3, pp. 15–16.
[126] It is also interesting to speculate how Lawrence might have functioned as an engineering dean. The offer itself displays the wavering attitudes and concepts surrounding engineering that Harvard and Yale had until recent decades. When engineering was revivified at Yale in 1994, the dean chosen was D. Allen Bromley, a high-energy physicist like Lawrence.
[127] Ray Monk, *Robert Oppenheimer: A Life inside the Center*, 1st American edition (New York: Doubleday, 2013).
[128] Kai Bird and Martin J. Sherwin, *American Prometheus: The Triumph and Tragedy of J. Robert Oppenheimer*, 1st ed. (New York: Alfred A. Knopf, 2005).

his time between Berkeley and Caltech. He was the department's first exclusively theoretical physicist, developed a strong reputation, and became close to Lawrence. Lawrence had a major role in the selection of Oppenheimer to lead the scientific aspects of the Manhattan Project, as described in chapter 13. Birge[130] recounts many interesting aspects of Oppenheimer's academic life. Herken[131] explores the lives of Lawrence, Oppenheimer, and Edward Teller and their interactions.

Figure 9-7. Oppenheimer (*left*), Seaborg (*center*), and Lawrence examine controls associated with a cyclotron.[132]

Physics Nobelists

Lawrence received the Nobel Prize in Physics for 1939, the first Berkeley faculty member to do so. The list of Nobelists associated with Berkeley physics is comparably impressive to the above list of those

---

[129] Jennet Conant, *109 East Palace: Robert Oppenheimer and the Secret City of Los Alamos* (New York: Simon & Schuster, 2005).
[130] Birge, 1966, *loc. cit.*, vol. 3, pp. ix, 25–37.
[131] Gregg Herken, *Brotherhood of the Bomb: The Tangled Lives and Loyalties of Robert Oppenheimer, Ernest Lawrence, and Edward Teller*, 1st ed. (New York: Henry Holt & Co, 2002).
[132] https://perma.cc/B749-TNBE (Courtesy of Lawrence Berkeley National Laboratory, © 2010 The Regents of the University of California, through the Lawrence Berkeley National Laboratory.)

from Berkeley Chemistry.[133] All prizes are in physics, except that for McMillan, which is in chemistry. The list through the Lawrence era includes the following persons:
- 1939: **Ernest Lawrence** (Berkeley faculty member), "for the invention and development of the cyclotron and for results obtained with it, especially with regard to artificial radioactive elements"; work done at Berkeley and Radiation Laboratory
- 1951: **Edwin McMillan** (Berkeley faculty member), "for discoveries (with Seaborg) in the chemistry of the trans-uranium elements"; work done at Berkeley and Radiation Laboratory
- 1959: **Emilio Segré** and **Owen Chamberlain** (Berkeley faculty members), "for their discovery of the antiproton"; work done at Radiation Laboratory in Berkeley
- 1960: **Donald Glaser** (Radiation Laboratory and later Berkeley faculty member), "for the invention of the bubble chamber"; work largely done earlier at University of Michigan
- 1964: **Charles Townes** (Berkeley faculty member), "for fundamental work in the field of quantum electronics, which has led to the construction of oscillators and amplifiers based on the maser-laser principle"; work done earlier at Bell Labs and Columbia
- 1968: **Luis Alvarez** (Berkeley faculty member), "for his decisive contributions to elementary particle physics, in particular the discovery of a large number of resonance states, made possible through his development of the technique of using hydrogen bubble chamber and data analysis"; work done at Radiation Laboratory and Berkeley

---

[133] Berkeley Nobel Prizes are of course not limited to the Physics and Chemistry Prizes of the Lewis and Lawrence eras. The *Wikipedia* "List of Nobel Laureates by University Affiliation," https://perma.cc/LZY9-36ZM lists seventy-two persons having affiliations with UC Berkeley as faculty, academic staff, or alumni who have received the Nobel Prize. Other faculty members winning the prize beyond those listed here and earlier in this chapter for the Lewis era include Yuan T. Lee (1986) in chemistry; George Smoot (2006) and Saul Perlmutter (2011) in physics; Randy Schekman (2013) in physiology/medicine; Czeslaw Milosz (1980) in literature; and Gerard Debreu (1983), John Harsanyi (1994), Daniel McFadden (2000), George Akerlof (2001), and Oliver Williamson (2009) in economic sciences. See "History and Discoveries, Faculty Nobels" University of California, Berkeley, https://web.archive.org/web/20170421063230/https://www.berkeley.edu/about/history-discoveries.

Figure 9-8. A 1960 photo of seven Berkeley/LBL Nobelists in front of the thirty-seven-inch cyclotron magnet in front of the new Lawrence Hall of Science. *Left to right:* Chamberlain, McMillan, Segré, Calvin, Glaser, Alvarez, Seaborg.[134]

MATHEMATICS AND GRIFFITH EVANS

Major, uprooting actions were taken to upgrade the Department of Mathematics on two occasions. The situations and the steps taken are described by Calvin Moore in his history of the Berkeley Mathematics Department.[135]

The original professor of mathematics for the university had been William Welcker, a graduate of the US Military Academy at West Point, who instituted basic courses in mathematics, but without advanced mathematics or research. After the departure of Daniel Coit Gilman as

---

[134] https://perma.cc/8G3U-SHZT (Courtesy of Lawrence Berkeley National Laboratory, © 2010 The Regents of the University of California, through the Lawrence Berkeley National Laboratory.)
[135] Calvin C. Moore, *Mathematics at Berkeley: A History* (Wellesley, MA: AK Peters, 2007).

president in 1875, the UC Regents sensed that the university was drifting academically and in 1880–81 created a Committee on Instruction and Visitation composed of regents chartered to dig into the leadership, management, academic structure, and curriculum of the university, and to recommend needed steps. The report, reproduced in its entirety by Moore[136] was far-reaching, quite critical, and highly specific. It included a recommendation for the removal of the president (John LeConte) and the separation of the Office of the President from professorial functions. This committee targeted mathematics as well and recommended the dismissal of Welcker, apparently linking that step with a finding that "in some of the departments outgrown methods are still adhered to." After substantial discussion the regents voted 11–6 to dismiss Welcker.

Paralleling what had been done earlier by Erza Carr (chapter 2), in the year (1882) following his dismissal, Welcker ran for the office of superintendent of public instruction in California. After winning that election, he became a regent ex officio, and through that post eventually succeeded in having the regents eliminate the Committee on Instruction and Visitation that had initiated his dismissal.[137]

The report, the dismissals, and the entire process are prime examples of the very strong role of the regents in the early years and the lack of organized faculty roles. As well, they may also reflect at least some intrusion of politics. The regents who had created the Committee on Instruction and Visitation were mostly Republicans, and LeConte and Welcker were Democrats.

The Committee on Instruction and Visitation conducted the search for a replacement for Welcker. (This again underscores the lack of established roles at the time for faculty in academic appointments.) Irving Stringham was strongly recommended by former UC president Daniel Coit Gilman, who was by then the founding president of Johns Hopkins University, where Stringham had obtained his PhD. Stringham was also endorsed by President Charles Eliot and Professor Benjamin Pierce of Harvard, where he had done his undergraduate work in mathematics under Pierce. Stringham had just completed two years of

---

[136] Moore, 2007, *op. cit.*, appendix 2, pp. 316–319.
[137] Moore, 2007, *op. cit.*, 27.

postdoctoral work at Leipzig, as well. He was hired. Stringham effectively modernized the curriculum and created advanced studies, but, while remaining highly respected within the field, did not do much research himself. Instead, he moved to academic administration.

Stringham held decanal positions of several kinds, starting in 1886. As noted above, he was dean of both the College of Letters and the Colleges of Science for many years and then Dean of the Faculties under President Wheeler. This was a position with functions similar to those of a provost today and a precursor to the Dean of the Graduate Division position held later by Leuschner. It was Stringham who recognized and hired Leuschner as an instructor in Mathematics.[138]

Fifty years after the crisis of 1881, it was again concluded that mathematics at Berkeley was much in need of reinvigoration and new leadership. But the way in which it happened and what was done about it stand in marked contrast to the regents-dominated process of 1881, reflecting the 1919 Berkeley Revolution which established the roles of the Academic Senate, as well as the arrival of figures such as Leuschner, Lewis, Hildebrand, and Birge. The process is again described by Moore.[139] In 1927 a consensus grew among the faculty, primarily in physical sciences, that the mathematics department was insufficiently distinguished and did not effectively serve the needs of the physical sciences, which were then developing much more of a mathematical basis. The mathematics department had stagnated in part as a result of inbreeding (i.e., hiring its own graduates as faculty members).[140] The conclusion was that an outstanding new professor of mathematics was needed to lead the renaissance of the program.

The Committee on Budget and Interdepartmental Relations of the Academic Senate created an ad hoc Committee on a Professorship of Mathematics. Two members were drawn from the mathematics department and three, including G. N. Lewis and Armin Leuschner, from outside that department. This committee settled upon Griffith Evans, who had joined Rice Institute (now Rice University) in 1912 as its

---

[138] Moore, 2007, *op. cit.*, p. 34.
[139] Moore, 2007, *op. cit.*, pp. 51–54.
[140] This downhill result from inbreeding in mathematics stands in sharp contrast to the strong results obtained by Gilbert Lewis in chemistry using an inbreeding approach. Lewis obviously had much the better eye for researchers and exercised much higher standards.

first faculty member, declining offers from Yale, MIT, and the University of California. Evans declined the Berkeley offer because of his continuing strong feelings for Rice. He had also declined a 1925 offer from Harvard following the same rationale.

As the stock market crash (1929) and Depression came along, nothing further was done about mathematics at Berkeley until 1932, when the existing department chair reached retirement age. The new Berkeley provost, Monroe Deutsch, doubtless relying upon input from senior physical sciences faculty members, convinced the new president, Robert Sproul, that something must be done to invigorate the Department of Mathematics. Sproul concurred, and Deutsch asked the Academic Senate Committee on Budget and Interdepartmental Relations to propose a committee for an intensive study of the department and its needs. Members named by the Budget Committee were once again Gilbert Lewis as chair, along with Birge, Leuschner, Hildebrand, and two members of the engineering faculty, Charles Derleth and Baldwin Woods.[141] The committee's recommendations were drastic, including terminations of existing nontenured faculty members, a search for a new chair from outside, and a proposal that Hildebrand be tasked with visiting leading institutions elsewhere in the United States to search for both the new chair and new faculty members. The recommendations were accepted by the administration. Hildebrand, who describes his role in his oral history,[142] returned from his extensive tour of other universities with the renewed recommendation that Griffith Evans (who was now much less enamored of Rice and therefore more interested) be appointed professor and chair, and with a list of other persons who should be considered for appointment.

Evans was pursued, and, after communication back and forth on salary,[143] which could be vulnerable during the Depression years, accepted and came to Berkeley in July 1934. Hildebrand's very positive evaluation of him was verified when Evans was elected to the National Academy of Sciences in 1933, as the negotiations with Berkeley were proceeding. There was an interim year before the actual arrival of

---

[141] Moore, 2007, *op. cit.*, p. 55.
[142] Hildebrand, 1962, *op. cit.*, pp. 58–60.
[143] Moore, 2007, *op. cit.*, pp. 58–60.

Evans, and for that time Hildebrand was formally designated by the administration as advisor to the acting chairman—that is, to stay in contact with Evans so that Hildebrand would know Evans' desires and make sure that they were followed.

Figure 9-9. Evans Hall, named for Griffith Evans, frames the Berkeley campus campanile in this photograph[144]

Griffith Evans chaired Mathematics at Berkeley from 1934 through 1949. Brief biographies of him are available as a National Academy of Sciences biographical memoir[145] and a short memorial piece written by

---

[144] Photograph © 2003 by Alan Nyiri, courtesy of the Atkinson Photographic Archive https://perma.cc/7A6H-2NTU.
[145] Charles B. Morrey, "Griffith Conrad Evans, 1887–1973," Biographical Memoirs, National Academy of Sciences, 1983, https://perma.cc/T2XX-F3QK.

Berkeley colleagues.[146] He systematically built the department into its present preeminent status.[147] Working with the list that Hildebrand brought back from his travels on behalf of the committee and other contacts, Evans oversaw twenty-one appointments to the mathematics faculty during his fifteen years as department chair. Among his most notable hires was Jerzy Neyman, who built statistics, which eventually (and against Evans's desires) became a separate department. It too is one of Berkeley's outstanding fields.

GEOLOGY AND GEOPHYSICS

In the case of the geological sciences, the richness of the geology of California itself was a large stimulating force, and the field grew up at Berkeley essentially independently from the other physical sciences. Geologic interests in California had been set in motion by the needs generated by the gold rush of 1849 and the associated great surges of settlement, population, and interest in natural resources. These concerns set in motion the California Geological Survey of 1860 to 1864 (figure 9-10), known more familiarly as the Whitney survey after its leader, Josiah D. Whitney, who had been appointed state geologist. The field leader of that survey was William H. Brewer, who recorded many of the events in a well-read book still available today.[148] Some of the other members of the survey were Clarence King,[149] a future head of the US Geological Survey; William Gabb,[150] who became a noted paleontologist and member of the National Academy of Sciences; and William Ashburner, who was subsequently associated with the

---

[146] C. B. Morrey Jr. et al., "Griffith Conrad Evans, Mathematics: Berkeley," In Memoriam, University of California, Berkeley, 1977, https://perma.cc/Z4WJ-PQL7.
[147] Moore, 2007, *op. cit.*, pp. 62–89.
[148] William H. Brewer, *Up and Down California in 1860–1864* (Berkeley: University of California Press, 2003).
[149] Robert Wilson, *The Explorer King: Adventure, Science, and the Great Diamond Hoax—Clarence King in the Old West,* Scribner, New York, 2006).
[150] William H. Dahl, "William More Gabb, 1839–1878," Biographical Memoirs, National Academy of Sciences, 1908, https://perma.cc/7WRF-24JR.

University of California as of 1874 as professor of mining engineering, then honorary professor, and then regent (1880–87),[151] another of the few faculty members who have become regents. Extensive fossils and other geological material were collected by the survey and, through Gabb, became the founding collection for what is now the Museum of Paleontology on the Berkeley campus.[152]

Figure 9-10. The California Geological Survey, December 1863: from left, Chester Averill, assistant; William M. Gabb, paleontologist; William Ashburner, field assistant; Josiah D. Whitney, State Geologist; Charles F. Hoffmann, topographer; Clarence King, geologist; and William H. Brewer, botanist.

As noted in chapter 2, one of the founding faculty members of the University of California was geologist Joseph LeConte[153, 154] (figure 9-

---

[151] Horace Davis, "Memorial of William Ashburner," *The Overland Monthly* (Samuel Carson, August 1887), pp. 219–221.
[152] "The foundations of paleontology in California and at Berkeley (1843–1874)," Museum of Paleontology, University of California, Berkeley, https://perma.cc/GR6S-6A5D.
[153] LeConte, Joseph, The Autobiography of Joseph LeConte, electronic edition, https://perma.cc/MU84-A26J.
[154] "The Impact of Joseph LeConte (1869–1901)," Museum of Paleontology, University of California, Berkeley, https://perma.cc/F9S2-AR9C.

11), a charismatic and learned individual who was a well-known proponent of evolution, made early trips to Yosemite Valley, and was a cofounder and early director of the Sierra Club. He did much to raise interest in the scientific method, geology, evolution, and fieldwork.

Figure 9-11. Joseph LeConte, 1875[155]

Andrew Lawson,[156] a native of Scotland, was appointed to the Berkeley faculty in 1890 at the invitation of Joseph LeConte as an assistant professor of mineralogy and geology. He was the first to identify the San Andreas Fault and wrote in 1908 what was at the time the definitive analytical report on the 1906 San Francisco earthquake. Seismology quite naturally became a major emphasis within Berkeley geology and geophysics, given California's location astride several major faults. Lawson was also floor manager and strategist for the faculty in the Berkeley Revolution of 1919 (chapter 7).

---

[155] "The Impact of Joseph LeConte [1869–1901]," University of California Museum of Paleontology, University of California, Berkeley, https://perma.cc/F9S2-AR9C.
[156] Perry Byerly and George D. Louderback, "Andrew Cowper Lawson, July 25, 1861–June 16, 1952, *National Academy of Sciences Biographical Memoirs* 37 (1964): 185–204, https://perma.cc/DYA6-GCBJ.

Research and teaching at the highest level in paleontology were set in motion by the arrival on the faculty in 1894 of John C. Meriam,[157] who had been drawn to Berkeley as an undergraduate by LeConte's textbook on geology and then had taken his PhD in Munich with noted paleontologist Karl Zittel. With the financial sponsorship of his patron, Annie Alexander,[158] Meriam carried out landmark research including studies of the fossils from the La Brea Tar Pits in Los Angeles.

Another prominent faculty member arriving shortly thereafter was George Louderback, geologist, mineralogist, and seismologist, who became an assistant professor in 1906.[159] In addition to his teaching and scholarship, Louderback was also distinguished through his service to the university in important roles. He too was a member of the Academic Senate committee that met with the regents in 1919–20 to establish the present roles of the Academic Senate. He was Dean of the College of Letters and Science for two periods, 1920–22 and 1930–39. He was active in many leadership roles with the Academic Senate, including being chair of the Budget Committee for eight years (1923–31), and a member of two of the initial advisory committees (1943 and 1945) for the Santa Barbara campus when it was first brought into the University of California.[160]

SUMMARY OBSERVATIONS

Several key factors can be identified from this survey of how the University of California was initially able to build research excellence and stature in physical sciences.

First of all, the process had to start with bringing in people who were known nationally or internationally to be strong or very promising researchers. These intellectual founders had to be located, identified,

---

[157] "A Paleontology Program Develops (1894–1950)" and "John C. Meriam (1869–1945)," Museum of Paleontology, University of California, Berkeley, https://perma.cc/MYK9-L4LS and https://perma.cc/3YH3-XAAD.
[158] "Annie Montague Alexander, 1867–1950," Museum of Paleontology, University of California, Berkeley, https://perma.cc/QA3Q-UPJZ.
[159] N. Taliaferro, T. Buck, and V. F. Lenzen, "George Davis Louderback, Geological Sciences: Berkeley," In Memoriam, University of California, 1959, https://perma.cc/MG3J-W9AB.
[160] Stadtman, 1970, op. cit., pp. 245, 249, and 347.

and selected by people who could judge research well and they had to be hired with very attractive packages (Lewis, Lawrence, and Evans) or arrive serendipitously and be recognized and fully supported for their talents (Leuschner, Birge, and Meriam). They had to obtain and retain the trust and confidence of the university administration and other faculty members, so that they could define recruitment plans and carry out searches, evaluations, and recruitments (Lewis, Hildebrand, and Birge). These approaches follow the principle that top-flight researchers are best equipped to identify outstanding research and to recognize, evaluate, and identify the people who can best do it.

Notice also the involvement of relatively few people in the process of developing research excellence as it flowed through chemistry to physics to mathematics. Note also Pitzer's description (which also applies to Lewis, Hildebrand, Birge, and others) of how he relied on his own judgment and the judgments of a certain few people upon whom he depended heavily to assess quality. That was clearly a very successful approach in developing the research stature of Berkeley, but it does not fit well with today's concepts of broad searches and inclusiveness. The approach today at any major research university is for academic departments to propose definitions of positions for recruitment of faculty. Then, if the recruitment is authorized, the department creates a search committee, advertises and solicits nominations widely, invites multiple candidates in for visits and seminars, compares among candidates, and then by a collective process picks the actual person to recruit.

It was also important that many of the principal actors had institution-wide interests at heart and were willing to give time and effort to building quality across the institution, recognizing that the success of any one discipline depends as well on the success of other disciplines. One can see a network of quality recognition and university-wide concern stemming from Leuschner to and through Lewis, Birge, Hildebrand, Evans, and even Lawrence.

The development of research excellence was very much driven and fostered by intellectual interactions themselves. Lewis's weekly research conference is a prime example, as is the involvement of Lewis and Birge in arguing concepts of the atom. Intellectual excitement, controversy, and even disagreement (as for the Bohr atom) actually generated intellectual cohesion and cross-disciplinary interests.

The Lick Observatory, as the most capable telescope in the world when built, provided a lure for leading astronomers, one of whom (Leuschner) was a leader in the building of research in general at Berkeley, another of whom (Holden) was both observatory director and president of the university, and a third of whom (Campbell) became observatory director, then president of the university, and then president of the National Academy of Sciences.

It was important that salaries could ignore seniority and that special arrangements could be made for recruitments (Lewis) or retentions (Lawrence), even though these usual steps could generate resentment and disapproval among the rank-and-file faculty.

Finally, it is worth noting that many of the principals in the development of Berkeley toward research excellence had studied in Germany (Stringham, Lewis, Hildebrand, Evans, and Leuschner in his early education). It was Germany that had developed the modern concept of a research university, and by being there, one could soak up the concepts behind an outstanding research university.

10.
Spreading Excellence: Developing New Campuses

The eye-catching additions to the Research I ranks in our classification of research universities, however, are the UC campuses at Santa Barbara, Riverside, and Santa Cruz. The speed with which these institutions rose from modest beginnings is astonishing.
   —Hugh Graham and Nancy Diamond[1]

During the seven years from 1955 and 1961 I experienced the fierce joys of helping to found a new university. As with most things one does for the first time—making love, becoming a father, getting a Ph.D.—this task was approached with more enthusiasm than knowledge...We decided...to build our first "little university" from the top down, or, if you like, to lay the roof first. We started to build a series of graduate research and teaching departments, one at a time, first in physics and chemistry, then in the earth sciences and biology, mathematics and engineering, and in linguistics, philosophy, comparative literature, and economics. In each department we aimed for a critical mass of faculty who would be able to give a doctoral program right from the start.
   —Roger Revelle[2]

I...conceived of myself as someone who really had to project the image of UCLA—in the community, within the regents—and to carry the UCLA message right directly head on to the Berkeley administration. I also conceived of myself as a person...who somehow had to convince the UCLA community that they were as good as I knew they were. They had so long been Berkeley's little brother. And, you know, sure, Berkeley has nine Nobel Prize winners, and we'll never have any sort of thing; and

---

[1] Hugh D. Graham and Nancy Diamond, *The Rise of American Research Universities* (Baltimore: Johns Hopkins University Press, 1997).
[2] Roger Revelle, "On Starting a University," unpublished paper, circa 1983, Scripps Institution of Oceanography Archives, https://perma.cc/V2J4-9K5Q.

when you talk about the University of California in London or New York or something, they say, "Oh, yes, you mean Berkeley." So I conceived early on that this image had to be changed.
—*Franklin Murphy*[3]

We would always end up after our discussions and disputes saying, "Would it not be nice someday to combine the advantages of the big campus providing the library, the research facilities, the cultural programs, and the small campus intimacy among students and among faculty members?"
—*Clark Kerr*[4]

As described in chapter 2, decisions were made by degrees over the years that resulted in the University of California becoming one university with multiple campuses with equal opportunity to develop, something that was unique at the time within the United States. UC is still the research university with by far the most campuses with the same, single mission. The quality and norms that had developed at Berkeley spread very effectively to the newer campuses as they were developed. The purpose of this chapter is to outline how that happened, what the key steps were, and how the different campuses undertook initiatives for academic development.

UC LOS ANGELES (UCLA)

During most of the latter half of the nineteenth century, the population of California was largely in the northern part of the state, with the greater San Francisco area being the largest settlement. It was

---

[3] Franklin D. Murphy, interview by James V. Mink, "My UCLA Chancellorship: An Utterly Candid View," tape 1, side 2, October 18, 1973, Oral History Program, University of California, Los Angeles, 1976, https://archive.org/details/myuclachancellor00murp; http://oralhistory.library.ucla.edu/viewFile.do?itemId=29627&fileSeq=3&xsl=http://oralhistory.library.ucla.edu/xslt/local/tei/xml/tei/stylesheet/xhtml2/tei.xsl.

[4] Clark Kerr, quoted by Kay Mills, "Changes at 'Oxford on the Pacific': UC Santa Cruz Turns to Engineering and Technology" *National CrossTalk*, Spring 2001, https://perma.cc/6ACP-4UVW.

logical, therefore, that when the University of California was initially established, it was situated in the San Francisco Bay area. However, the shift of population toward the southern part of the state with the arrival of the twentieth century created a demand for university-level public education in the south. Faced with the alternatives of acquiescing to there being a second, independent public university in the Los Angeles area or spreading the University of California itself to the south, the university leadership took the latter path. The Los Angeles Normal School was brought into the University of California in 1919 as the Southern Branch, offered a full four-year undergraduate education, and then in 1927 became the University of California at Los Angeles, now known familiarly as UCLA.

Figure 10-1. Aerial View of the UCLA Westwood Campus Site, shortly before the opening of the campus, 1929[5]

The Los Angeles campus moved from the Vermont Street location of the normal school to essentially bare land (Figure 10-1) at the

---

[5] https://perma.cc/QL2R-5VQU. Courtesy, Regents of the University of California.

present Westwood site in 1929. Governance of the campus at that time stemmed from Berkeley and was for the most part located at Berkeley. As of 1931 there were two provost positions within the university: one held by Monroe Deutsch as "provost of the university" at Berkeley, and the other held by Ernest Moore as "provost of the University of California at Los Angeles," the highest position resident in Los Angeles. Moore had been the last president of the normal school.[6] Over time, the Los Angeles campus developed a modest graduate program. It was first authorized in 1936 to give the PhD[7] and awarded its first PhD degree in 1938[8] to one of Vern Knudsen's PhD students in acoustics (see below). However, there were continued feelings in the south, backed up by fact, that UCLA was being held back from moving toward the status that Berkeley had in terms of faculty and programmatic distinction and budget. For example, Taylor describes the spartan situation for a research-oriented assistant professor of mathematics.[9]

During his presidency Robert Gordon Sproul kept tight administrative control over the Los Angeles campus, frustrating later UCLA provosts, such as Clarence Dykstra (provost, 1945–50), who had been president of the University of Wisconsin before coming into the UCLA position. However, there were also a growing number of long-term and strong regents from the south. The first of these had been journalist (*Los Angeles Express*) Edward Dickson, who was a twice-reappointed regent for forty-three years, from 1913 until his death in 1956, and was chair of the UC Regents from 1948 until 1956. Other later and similarly influential, long-term southern regents were oil-magnate Edwin Pauley (1940–72) and Edward Carter of Carter Hawley Hale stores (1952–88).[10] This situation brought about a complex

---

[6] Verne A. Stadtman, *The University of California, 1868–1968* (New York: McGraw-Hill, 1970), p. 272.
[7] Angus E. Taylor, *Speaking Freely: A Scholar's Memoir of Experience in the University of California, 1938–1967* (Berkeley: Institute for Governmental Studies Press, University of California, 2000), p. 23.
[8] Clark Kerr, *The Gold and the Blue: A Personal Memoir of the University of California, 1949–1967, vol., 1, Academic Triumphs* (Berkeley: University of California Press, 2001), p. 18.
[9] Taylor, 2000, *op. cit.*, pp. 9–16.
[10] These remarkably long terms of service—forty-three, thirty-two, and thirty-six years, respectively—were the result of what were at the time appointment terms of sixteen years, followed by reappointments. The very long cumulative terms were hallmarks of an era now past.

triangle of influence and governance wherein the UCLA administration reported to the president and the president to the regents, but Dickson and other southern regents engaged key deans socially and worked with them to accomplish desired ends.[11, 12]

Research and graduate work began to take form at UCLA around 1930. Vern Knudsen[13] joined the institution in 1922, developed his own interests and research in acoustics within physics, and became UCLA's first graduate dean (1934–58). He describes how Armin Leuschner, then graduate dean for the university, came to UCLA from Berkeley starting in 1929 in his capacity as chair of the Board of Research to meet with a local committee to determine awards of research grants for the Los Angeles campus. Knudsen attributes the initial establishment of high standards at UCLA to Leuschner and Charles Lipman, who was Leuschner's successor as graduate dean for the university.[14] The start of UCLA's research prominence came with Knudsen and a few other faculty members of that era. In the case of Knudsen, graduate students in physics at Berkeley who were interested in acoustics came to Los Angeles to work with him. These included Norman Watson, the initial UCLA PhD recipient and subsequently a UCLA faculty member, and Richard Bolt,[15] later cofounder of Bolt, Beranek and Newman, Inc.[16] Kerr[17] stresses that Deans Gordon Watkins (1936–45) and Paul Dodd (1946–60) from letters and science also had

---

There have been some regents reappointed recently, but now with twelve-year terms, full service upon reappointment amounts to at most twenty-four years.

[11] Roger L. Geiger, *Research and Relevant Knowledge: American Research Universities since World War II* (Transaction Publishers, 2004), pp. 135–146.

[12] Kerr, 2001, *op. cit.*, vol. 1, pp. 328–329.

[13] Vern O. Knudsen, interview by James V. Mink, "Teacher, Researcher, and Administrator: Vern O. Knudsen," Oral History Program, University of California, Los Angeles, 1974, http://oralhistory.library.ucla.edu/permissionPop.jsp?forward=viewTextFile.do?itemId=29607&fileSeq=1.

[14] Knudsen, 1974, *op. cit.*, pp. 856–858

[15] Leo J. Beranek, "Gold Medal Award, 1979: Richard Henry Bolt," Acoustical Society of America, https://web.archive.org/web/20170621000819/http://acousticalsociety.org/about/awards/gold/12_10_10_bolt.

[16] Knudsen, 1974, *op. cit.*, pp. 852–863.

[17] Kerr, 2001, *op. cit.*, vol. 1, p. 330.

much to do with stimulating high-quality research at UCLA. Neil Jacoby[18] and Franklin Murphy[19] also note the contributions of Dodd.

After World War II, the interests of the southern regents and community leaders in the Los Angeles area centered on vigorous development of professional schools.[20] The initial push came with the medical school, for which Stafford Warren[21] was recruited from the University of Rochester as dean when the school was founded in 1947. Warren, who brought a team of researchers with him, had been a medical advisor to the Atomic Energy Commission on the Bikini Atoll atomic bomb tests and thereby had contacts that could and did lead to substantial research funding from the federal government.[22] Warren used this federal funding to leverage money for facilities from the university administration and the state government. In order to do this, he had to overcome substantial resistance from James Corley, UC vice president for business affairs and government relations, who, as already noted in chapter 3, had a large degree of independence in Sacramento and did not want to see an expensive research-based medical operation in the south. Warren also developed a support base of his own in Sacramento and elsewhere, using the entrée that he had been appointed by Governor Earl Warren to establish a state commission on radiological defense. That gave him opportunities to tour the state, linking awareness of civil defense with the UCLA medical school.[23] The UCLA School of Medicine has become a prominent and thriving operation in patient care and forefront research and is a world leader in, among other areas, joint replacement.[24]

Also impressive was the development of a research-based School of Management, which underwent large changes from its initial form as

---

[18] Neil H. Jacoby, interview by James V. Mink, "The Graduate School of Management at UCLA: 1948–1968," p. 35, Oral History Program, UCLA, 1974, http://digital2.library.ucla.edu/viewFile.do?contentFileId=2289890.
[19] Murphy,1973, op. cit., tape 1, side 2.
[20] Geiger, 1993, op. cit., p. 140.
[21] W. P. Longmire Jr., J. F. Ross, and Robert Vosper, "Stafford L. Warren, Biophysics: Los Angeles," In Memoriam, University of California, 1985, https://perma.cc/24BY-9DSE.
[22] The year 1947 was still a very early point in government support of university research in general. Government support became widely available only with the establishment of the National Science Foundation in 1950.
[23] Geiger, 1993, op. cit., pp. 138–139.
[24] Jonathan R. Cole, The Great American University (New York: Public Affairs, 2009), p. 224.

the College of Commerce[25] when it was founded in 1935. Neil Jacoby[26] was hired as dean in 1948 from the University of Chicago, where he had been secretary, vice president, and professor of finance. Jacoby's stated reasons for the move were to gain a favorable climate for his son's health and the opportunity to build a major school of management.[27] During a visit to Los Angeles ten years earlier in 1938, he and his wife had decided, "This is where we want to live."[28] Jacoby was available by virtue of a loss in his rapport with Chicago president Robert Hutchins and his own feelings of a decline in the physical environment at the University of Chicago and its surroundings.[29]

During Jacoby's first four years as dean, the faculty grew by a factor of four from eleven to forty-four, with Jacoby doing the recruitment, negotiations, and preparation of appointment cases for senate review and then ultimate approval by Sproul in Berkeley.[30] The more pedestrian programs within the school were discontinued, and the associated faculty members were replaced by others highly capable in research and research-based instruction. Much of that recruiting was done from the University of Chicago itself, akin to what Roger Revelle at UC San Diego would do subsequently. The recruitment process made heavy use of the salubrious Southern California climate.

Jacoby built the present School of Management and enjoyed considerable support from the Los Angeles professional community in doing so. A key step was gaining a large grant in the late 1950s from IBM Corporation, creating the Western Data Processing Center, and thereby using the capabilities of then-new digital computers for business research. That in turn led to a major grant from the Ford Foundation, establishing the Western Management Science Institute. Undergraduate education in business was then phased out in the mid-1960s, leaving a well-respected, research-based graduate program,[31]

---

[25] The same name, "College of Commerce," had originally been used for the program at Berkeley.
[26] J. F. Weston et al., "Neil H. Jacoby, Management: Los Angeles," In Memoriam, University of California, 1980, https://perma.cc/Y52B-ZVRG.
[27] N. H. Jacoby, interview by James V. Mink, "The Graduate School of Management at UCLA, 1948–1968," Oral History Program, p. 11, University of California, Los Angeles, CA, 1974, http://digital2.library.ucla.edu/viewFile.do?contentFileId=2289890.
[28] Jacoby, 1974, *op. cit.*, 1973, p. 29.
[29] Jacoby, 1974, *op. cit.*, pp. 36–37.
[30] Jacoby, 1974, *op. cit.*, p. 54.
[31] Geiger, 1993, *op. cit.*, pp. 138–139.

which today as the Anderson School of Management (Figure 10-2) is comparably high ranked to the Haas School of Business at Berkeley.

Figure 10-2. Anderson School of Management, UCLA[32]

The Law School and College of Engineering had rockier roads at the start, for reasons that differed greatly between the two cases. The founding dean of the Law School was Dale Coffman, who came from Vanderbilt in 1946. Politically conservative and thereby in tune with the conservative southern regents, he was a strong anticommunist and was also accused of being anti-Semitic.[33] He was a strong and vocal proponent of the loyalty oath (chapter 2), which fact put him politically at odds with many of his faculty; he referred to the Law School as "an island in a red sea."[34] As well, he was a relatively ineffective administrator and resisted the roles of the Academic Senate in shared governance. His removal in 1956 was, because of his connection with regents, a sensitive matter that was carried out through a review by

---

[32] Photograph © 2003 by Alan Nyiri, courtesy of the Atkinson Photographic Archive, http://www.lib.berkeley.edu/uchistory/archives_exhibits/campus_planning/atkinson_archive/ucla/anderson1.html.
[33] Geiger, 1993, *op. cit.*, p. 137.
[34] Kerr, 2001, *op. cit.*, p. 141.

three other deans.[35, 36, 37] The climb of the UCLA Law School to prominence was thereby delayed.

The College of Engineering was started in 1944 with the recruitment of L. M. K. Boelter[38] as the founding dean. Boelter's career until then had been at Berkeley, where he had become prominent in the field of heat transfer through the development of the widely used Dittus-Boelter equation and other accomplishments. His decanal appointment at UCLA became his opportunity to put into practice his ideas on engineering education, which called for a unified engineering curriculum, built around the science of engineering without division into the classical engineering disciplines (electrical, civil, mechanical, and so on). He also favored having graduate students in engineering who were at the same time working at full-time or nearly full-time engineering jobs in industry.[39] A thorough analysis of Boelter's approach and activities in launching engineering at UCLA is given by Akera,[40] who also points out that Boelter's different approach to engineering education was in part driven by the desire that he and his former superior, Berkeley dean Morrough P. (Mike) O'Brien, had to differentiate the UCLA and Berkeley programs so that they would not directly compete.

Boelter was dean for twenty years until his death in 1965, and during that time the College of Engineering at UCLA had a single Department of Engineering with Boelter as both dean and department chair. This structure[41] matched some of the needs of the aerospace

---

[35] Geiger, 1993, *loc. cit.*
[36] Jacoby, 1974, *op. cit.*, pp. 102–104.
[37] Taylor, 2000, *op. cit.*, p. 35.
[38] G. J. Maslach, S. L. Warren, and J. W. McCutcheon, "Llewellyn Michael Kraus Boelter, Engineering: Berkeley and Los Angeles, In Memoriam, University of California, 1968, https://perma.cc/CGD7-D2AF.
[39] Taylor, 2000, *op. cit.*, p. 34.
[40] Atsushi Akera, "Engineering 'Manpower, Regional Economic Development, and the 1960 California Master Plan for Higher Education," paper no. AC 2010-724 presented at session on Historical Perspectives for Engineering Education, Annual Conference, American Society for Engineering Education, 2010, https://perma.cc/52Q9-TCD5.
[41] See, e.g., R. L. Perrine, "Unification in Engineering Education and the Petroleum Engineer," absteract, paper no. SPE-620-MS, Fall Meeting of the Society of Petroleum Engineers of AIME, New Orleans, LA, 1963, https://perma.cc/PT2K-P53M.

industry but substantially held back appreciation of UCLA engineering within the classical engineering disciplines, which are the loci of academic recognition for both United States and world engineering. The unified structure has now been abandoned, with a return to conventional disciplines. As one example of this history, the tortured path for chemical engineering went from the undifferentiated Department of Engineering (1944), to a Chemical, Nuclear, and Thermal Division within that department in the early 1960s, to an Energy and Kinetics Department within the College (1968–69), to a Chemical, Nuclear, and Thermal Engineering Department (1976–77), and finally to a Chemical Engineering Department (1983).[42]

Given the unusual administrative structure for UCLA within the University of California before the era when Clark Kerr was president, it was the deans and the academic-personnel review functions of the Academic Senate that did most of the building of high-quality academic research.[43] The deans drove selective faculty recruitment, as we have seen for Warren (medicine) and Jacoby (business/management). Effective senate review of appointment and advancement cases drove quality, as did the overall participation of the Academic Senate in governance. As at Berkeley, outstanding UCLA faculty scholars participated conscientiously in senate work. There were also two important periods (1943–45 and 1950–52) before and after Dykstra's provostship when the on-site administration of UCLA was carried out by committees of deans.[44] Enrollment grew tremendously, from ten thousand before World War II to fifteen thousand in the early 1950s after the end of the surge from the GI Bill and then to twenty thousand in 1960. The size of the faculty grew by an even greater percentage,

---

[42] See timeline table, pp. 22–23 of Ken Nobe, "Douglas Bennion's Contributions to Electrochemistry at UCLA," in J. S. Newman and R. E. White, eds., *Proceedings of the Douglas N. Bennion Memorial Symposium, Proceedings of the Electrochemical Society* 94-22 (1994), https://perma.cc/ZLX4-NUTD.
[43] Geiger, 1993, *op. cit.*, pp. 136–137, 141.
[44] Kerr, 2001, *op. cit.*, p. 330.

from 220 in 1940 to over 900 in 1960. Graduate students were one of every eight students in 1940 and had become one in three by 1960.[45]

Perhaps the strongest rise of an academic department at UCLA during the period between World War II and 1960 was that for chemistry. Here too the building was done by an energetic department chair who was well able to gauge talent. William G. Young became chair in 1940, shortly before the PhD program was established in chemistry at UCLA. He was himself a distinguished physical organic chemist, and he assembled outstanding faculty colleagues such as Saul Winstein and Donald Cram (Nobel Prize in Chemistry, 1987) in that area and built other subfields of chemistry. Young's abilities were recognized and utilized at UCLA as he went on to become dean of physical sciences in 1948 and then vice chancellor for planning, 1957–70. In the latter position, he was influential in establishing the Center for Health Sciences, now a badge of distinction at UCLA.[46, 47]

Chemistry at UCLA was largely built by promotion of assistant professors from within, rather than recruitment of senior faculty from outside. Hires would be made at the assistant professor level, with high standards and considerable selectivity being exercised in tenure decisions.[48] The large exception was Willard Libby, former faculty member at Berkeley (1933–45) and Chicago (1945–59), coworker with Harold Urey on gaseous diffusion for separation of uranium isotopes at Columbia during World War II, and commissioner of the Atomic Energy Commission (1955–59).[49] Libby selected UCLA from among five academic offers as he left the AEC in 1959, declining a return to the University of Chicago, a department-chair position at Stanford, and what would have been one of Roger Revelle's initial faculty positions in La Jolla (see UC San Diego, below). He had also been approached for the presidency of Rice University. In his oral history,[50] he indicates that

---

[45] Geiger, 1993, *op. cit.*, p. 138.
[46] J. D. Roberts, "William Gould Young, 1902–1980," Biographical Memoirs, National Academy of Sciences, 1998, https://perma.cc/3K2Q-6DLL.
[47] Geiger, 1993, *op. cit.*, p. 140.
[48] Geiger, 1993, *loc. cit.*
[49] C. R. Berger, Leon Knopoff &, W. G. McMillan "Willard Frank Libby, Chemistry: Berkeley and Los Angeles", In Memoriam, University of California, 1980, https://perma.cc/2UZ3-LH8Z
[50] W. F. Libby, interview by Mary Terrall, "Nobel Laureate: Willard F. Libby," Oral History Program, University of California, Los Angeles, CA, 1978,

he came to UCLA because his then-wife wanted to live in Los Angeles. He accepted the UCLA offer even though at the time in his view Chicago was "four orders of magnitude better than UCLA...[At UCLA] there were some chemists who were pretty good, and the chemistry department was the best in the university. But it was nothing like what it is now."[51] Libby received the Nobel Prize in Chemistry in 1960—the year after his arrival at UCLA—for his earlier work on dating with carbon-14. During his twenty-year career at UCLA, he was highly active in research and directed the university-wide Institute of Geophysics and Planetary Physics, corresponding to his interests at that time in aspects of chemistry bearing on space.[52]

During Sproul's last year as president (1957–58), intense negotiations between longtime Southern California regent Edward Carter and Sproul, amplified by an Academic Senate planning study, had resulted in a plan to provide "equal opportunity" to UCLA. The substance of the proposal was embedded in a statement from the senate Committee on Educational Policy: "Plans for the future and budget allocations for the Berkeley and Los Angeles campuses should be comparable in size and have equal opportunities for developing programs which, although not identical but rather complementary, are of equal quality."[53] This confirmation of equal opportunity, adopted by the Board of Regents in Kerr's first year (1958) upon Kerr's recommendation, was vital for continued academic development at UCLA.

As was noted in chapter 2, chancellorships had been established in 1952 at Berkeley and UCLA under the overall supervision of the president, who at the time was Sproul. The initial Berkeley chancellor was Kerr. After an earlier effort from Southern California regents seeking the appointment of World War II General Mark Clark[54] (a person with no academic background but seen as someone who could

---

http://oralhistory.library.ucla.edu/permissionPop.jsp?forward=viewTextFile.do?itemId=29649&fileSeq=1.
[51] Libby, 1978, op. cit., pp. 134–137.
[52] Libby, 1978, op. cit., pp. 143–146.
[53] Kerr, 2001, op. cit., pp. 332–334.
[54] See, e.g., Kerr, 2001, op. cit., p. 335; Taylor, 2000, op. cit., pp. 77–78.

and would stand up to Sproul), the first chancellor selected for UCLA was Raymond Allen, who had been president of the University of Washington. After gaining experience with him, Kerr and many regents and UCLA faculty members thought that Allen was insufficiently dynamic, and so, following a search, Kerr and the regents replaced Allen with Franklin Murphy, who had until then been president of the University of Kansas.

Murphy, who served from 1960 to 1968, energetically and capably established the separate identity of UCLA. He also built relationships with the Los Angeles community; the fine arts, both academically and through the cultural life of Los Angeles; and rapport with the students in what could have been a difficult time for student relations given the Free Speech Movement and its aftermaths at Berkeley.[55] Murphy has left an oral history[56] that is quite critical of Kerr on matters relating to the independent identity of UCLA and the relative roles and visibility (what Kerr calls "regal matters" or "symbolic functions") of the chancellor vis-à-vis the president. Kerr gives his own, more moderate views of the same matters.[57] Related to this controversy, it should be noted that Sproul as UC president had kept a firm and near-total grip on the reins. Kerr decentralized governance in function and form considerably, but the transition to the present high degree of autonomy of the individual campuses was not yet complete.

The contributions of Murphy during his eight years and of Charles ("Chuck") Young during a remarkable twenty-nine years (1968–97) as UCLA chancellor were heavily directed to building UCLA in all the various ways that are needed, placing it on a firm and diverse base of financial, community, and regional support, thereby assuring its future. The leadership and stability provided by those two leaders were vital.

As the other side of the coin, Kerr cites the statements of Vern Knudsen in his oral history: "I would say if there's any shortcoming with the Murphy administration it was the failure to press sufficiently for the recruitment of top scholars...I believe that if you look at the number of distinguished professors that we have here [1973], you will

---

[55] Margaret L. Davis, *The Culture Broker: Franklin D. Murphy and the Transformation of Los Angeles* (Berkeley: University of California Press, 2007).
[56] Murphy, 1973, *op. cit.*
[57] Kerr, 2001, *op. cit.*, pp. 214–218.

find that we haven't been as ardent in pressing that very important requirement as took place in the earlier years."[58]

The rise of UCLA in academic rankings from 1936, when it had no PhD programs, to 1957 is impressive. The Keniston survey of 1957, cited by Kerr[59] and Geiger,[60] placed UCLA fourteenth among US research universities. Subsequent surveys have placed UCLA in about the same position. This does not at all reflect the campus having stood still academically, since the general tide of quality within US research universities also rose during the more recent period. Even during the Murphy years, most faculty hiring was at the assistant professor level. Under Young, the campus made greater ventures into the national hiring market for senior faculty.

As of 2015 UCLA had six faculty Nobelists, fifty-two members of the National Academy of Sciences, twenty-six members of the National Academy of Engineering, and thirty-nine members of the National Academy of Medicine.[61, 62] The Nobelists are/were:

- 1960, Chemistry: **Willard Libby**, "for his method to use carbon-14 for age determination in archaeology, geology, geophysics, and other branches of science"; work done earlier at the University of Chicago
- 1965, Physics: **Julian Schwinger**, "for fundamental work in quantum electrodynamics, with deep-ploughing consequences for the physics of elementary particles"; work done largely at Harvard
- 1987, Chemistry: **Donald Cram**, for "development and use of molecules with structure-specific interactions of high selectivity"; work done at UCLA
- 1997, Chemistry: **Paul Boyer**, "for elucidation of the enzymatic mechanism underlying the synthesis of adenosine triphosphate (ATP)"; work done at UCLA

---

[58] Knudsen, 1974, *op. cit.*, vol. 3, pp. 1290–1292.
[59] Kerr, 2001, *op. cit.*, pp. 340–341.
[60] Geiger, 1993, *op. cit.*, pp. 131, 141.
[61] "Selected Major Awards to UCLA Faculty," University of California, Los Angeles, https://web.archive.org/web/20160605055137/http://www.ucla.edu/about/awards-and-honors/faculty-honors.
[62] For purposes of comparison with these figures for UCLA and for other campuses, as of 2015 the Berkeley campus had 143 members of the National Academy of Sciences and 73 members of the National Academy of Engineering.

- 1998, Physiology or Medicine: **Louis Ignarro**, "for discoveries concerning nitric oxide as a signaling molecule in the cardiovascular system"; work done at Tulane and UCLA
- 2012, Economic Sciences: **Lloyd Shapley**, "for the theory of stable allocations and the practice of market design"; work done largely at RAND Corporation.

In summary, given the handicap of initial second-class status that UCLA had to overcome in order to become an academically distinguished institution, how did the university do it? A first answer is the instillation of the standards and structure of the University of California during the 1930s and during the decade following the end of World War II in 1945. The standards were manifest in the attention given by Berkeley graduate deans Leuschner and Lipman to the development of graduate studies at UCLA, by the existence of the Academic Senate structure and the active participation of the best scholars in the senate's work, and by the standards and quality-seeking values of deans such as Dodd, Knudsen, Warren, and Jacoby.

Another vital ingredient was the general political muscle of Los Angeles, which resulted in the selection of long-term and effective Southern California regents such as Dickson, Pauley, and Carter; their drive for equal opportunity for UCLA; and their synergy with the deans.

Also very important were the general attributes of the Los Angeles and Southern California area. The very attractive climate brought faculty members such as Libby and Jacoby to UCLA and served as a general incentive for faculty recruitment. The cohesion and synergy established by Chancellors Murphy and Young with the community brought cultural events, large community support, and the strongest private fund-raising among the general UC campuses.

UC DAVIS

As we have seen in chapter 2, two large issues in the 1870s at the start of the University of California were the degree of emphasis on agriculture and mechanics as opposed to higher education in general and the nature of instruction in agriculture. Although Gilman's view of a more classical and comprehensive university eventually won out, the university retained substantial interest in agriculture and particularly science-based agriculture. The UC pioneers in agricultural research were Eugene W. Hilgard and Edward J. Wickson, who arrived in 1875 and 1878, respectively. Hilgard, in particular, was a leader in scientifically based agriculture.

Agricultural research required land, which became less and less available around the Berkeley campus. After some continued controversy in Sacramento as to whether practical agriculture would be better situated in a separate public university, a bill was passed in 1905 through the advocacy of Judge Peter Shields to seek and create the University Farm (figure 10-3) as part of the University of California.[63] A year later in 1906, a site was selected and acquired in Davisville in Yolo County, about seveny-five miles northwest of Berkeley and fifteen miles west of Sacramento. Soon thereafter courses of instruction were offered along with the research operations.

Thomas F. Hunt, who became dean of agriculture in 1912, the year that G. N. Lewis arrived at Berkeley, launched an effort to make the University of California agriculture program the best in the country. In doing so he had the strong support of President Wheeler and the California legislature. During the decade preceding 1915, agriculture enrollments grew from 4.2 percent of the Berkeley student population to 11.7 percent.[64]

The location of the University Farm in Davis, so near the state capital in Sacramento, was important. As was pointed out by California historian Kevin Starr,[65] the University Farm, *en route* to becoming the University of California at Davis, would never lose that vital political connection. For the first half of the twentieth century, in fact, rural California held a disproportionate authority at the capitol, especially in the state Senate; and two generations of rancher-legislators understood as a matter of lifetime recognition the importance of the Davis enterprise to the development of rural California.

---

[63] Ann F. Scheuring, *Abundant Harvest: the History of the University of California, Davis*, pp. 13–15, UC Davis History Project, Regents of the University of California, 2001.
[64] Scheuring, 2001, *op. cit.*, p. 31.
[65] Kevin Starr, Foreword to Scheuring, 2001, *op. cit.*, p. xiv.

The University Farm was situated on 776 acres in Davisville, Yolo County — 75 miles north of Berkeley. Three buildings from this image, circa 1910, are still in use at UC Davis: North Hall, South Hall and the Cottage.

Figure 10-3. The University Farm in Davis[66]

The link between the agricultural interests in the legislature and those in the University of California has been vital for both California agriculture and the University of California over the years. The university has performed research and Cooperative Extension services (see chapter 16) that have enabled modern agriculture to thrive in the state, including the establishment of major subindustries such as wine making and viticulture. Agricultural interests in the legislature have, in turn, been a steady source of support for the University of California in all respects, not just agriculture.

In 1921, soon after the arrival of the Southern Branch in Los Angeles in 1919, agriculture was reorganized so that there were two branches, Northern and Southern, under the College of Agriculture which was still headquartered at Berkeley. The University Farm at Davis became the Northern Branch and now had a resident director of the branch, Claude Hutchison, who was later (1955-63) mayor of Berkeley.

---

[66] "UC Land Grants: A Photo History," *California Agriculture*, v. 66, no. 2, University of California, https://perma.cc/ZQL3-F4SB.

The Southern Branch included the Riverside Citrus Experiment Station as well as activities that could be developed in Los Angeles. At this point a four-year agriculture degree program was started at Davis. Science and humanities programs were started during the 1920s to support the four-year degree, and several more specific agriculture fields were started in the 1930s and 1940s. The Davis enrollment exceeded one thousand for the first time in 1937.

For World War II (1943–45), the campus at Davis was converted to a Signal Corps training camp for the US Army. With the surge from returning war veterans, the Davis campus grew considerably following the war. In the late 1940s and the 1950s, several steps were taken that served to move the balance of emphasis on agricultural matters from Berkeley to Davis. Four departments that had been split between Berkeley and Davis were moved to Davis—Poultry Husbandry and Food Technology in 1951, and Home Economics and Soils and Plant Nutrition in 1955. Home Economics was later disbanded in the early 1960s, with remnants becoming part of Nutritional Sciences and Agricultural Economics.[67]

The School of Veterinary Medicine had formally been established at Davis in 1948, building on and pulling together elements of veterinary medicine that were already there. It became and has remained an outstanding school, being consistently named top in the country in various surveys.[68]

The first UC Davis PhD was awarded in 1950 in botany, and, as described in chapters 2 and 3, in 1959 the Board of Regents designated Davis to become a general campus.[69]

Stanley Freeborn had been made provost for the Davis campus when that position was established for the smaller campuses in 1952. Freeborn served one year as chancellor after that position was established in 1958, but for all intents and purposes, the founding chancellor was Emil Mrak, who served from 1959 through 1969. Mrak had been chair of the Department of Food Technology and had moved from Berkeley to Davis with that department in 1951. Mrak was approachable, gregarious, an excellent politician, and a builder, with an

---

[67] Scheuring, 2001, *op. cit.*, p. 118.
[68] Scheuring, 2001, *op. cit.*, pp. 231–241.
[69] Scheuring, 2001, *op. cit.*, pp. 300–301.

ability to recognize quality. He was an excellent fit for a campus embarking on the ambitious path toward being a full general campus of the University of California. He has also left us a substantial oral history.[70]

One important undertaking early in Mrak's term was restructuring and further building the College of Agriculture, linking to advances in biology and bringing in environmental issues, particularly those that interface with agriculture. Over the years, ongoing efforts of this sort have kept UC Davis at the forefront of agriculture research and education. That has been important for sustaining the very high reputation that the campus has in fields relating to agriculture.

The agricultural heritage of Davis made it receptive to professional schools, a situation different from what prevailed at Riverside, Santa Barbara, and Santa Cruz, where there was appreciable resistance among core academic faculty against the establishment of professional schools.[71] This fact coupled with the considerable interest of political figures in Sacramento in having core professional schools established near Sacramento at Davis, or even within Sacramento itself. As a consequence, Davis has the greatest density of professional schools among the campuses other than Berkeley and UCLA—Medicine, Law, Management, Veterinary Medicine, Education, and Nursing, as well as the College of Engineering and the College of Agriculture and Environmental Sciences, both of which also have undergraduate programs.

The School of Law was secured through the help of both a university-wide planning process for legal education[72] and legislative ties and interest.[73, 74] Approved by the regents in May, 1963, the school admitted its first class in 1966, just as student activism was burgeoning

---

[70] Emil F. Mrak, interview by A. I. Dickman, *A Journey through Three Epochs: Food Prophet, Creative Chancellor, Senior Statesman of Science*, UC Davis: Shields Library, Oral History Program, 1974.
[71] Kerr, 2001, *op. cit.*, vol. 1, p. 306.
[72] Scheuring, 2001, *op. cit.*, pp. 133–134.
[73] Mrak, 1974, *op. cit.*, pp. 275–276.
[74] Harry R. Wellman, interview by Malca Chall, "Teaching, Research, and Administration, University of California, 1925–1968, p. 165, oral history, Regional Oral History Office, University of California, 1976, https://perma.cc/66EU-V3N2.

within the university. Despite a somewhat rocky start resulting from the activism, the school is now being placed in the top twenty-five nationally in rankings by lawyers, judges, deans, and professors.[75]

The UC Regents also approved a medical school for Davis in 1963. Again, this was encouraged by Sacramento-area legislators and was acceded to by Kerr, vice president of the university Harry Wellman, and Mrak, despite the young age of the general campus, recognizing the good that the political partnership could do for university needs in general.[76] Pending construction of a hospital on the Davis campus, the school affiliated with the Sacramento County Hospital in southeast Sacramento for its clinical element.[77] The first class of medical students was admitted in 1968.

The school encountered several difficulties upon start-up. The failure of a statewide bond issue in 1970 made funding for both a hospital ($56 million) and a veterinary hospital ($22 million) unavailable. The veterinary hospital was eventually built on the campus, and it is both regionally recognized and a vital component of the School of Veterinary Medicine. But for hospital facilities, the campus eventually had to go the route of taking ownership of the Sacramento County Hospital in 1972, thus leaving the UC Davis Medical School with on-campus medical-science facilities and a hospital half an hour away by automobile. That situation was eventually remedied by constructing additional facilities at the Sacramento hospital site in the early 2000s and moving the entire medical school to that location.

Other difficulties in the early years of the UC Davis Medical School had to do with the school being the focus of what became the 1977 Bakke decision of the US Supreme Court on affirmative action (see chapter 15) and in 1980 public attention to an in-house controversy between faculty cardiologists and UC Davis Medical Center heart surgeons who were accused of having high rates of mortality and complications.[78] Despite its difficult beginning, the UC Davis Medical School and Medical Center have developed well over the years.

---

[75] "UC Davis School of Law Improves Five Slots in Latest *U.S. News & World Report* Rankings," University of California, Davis, March 10, 2015, https://perma.cc/JJ5B-PXJF.
[76] Wellman, 1976, *op. cit.*, p. 167; Mrak, 1974, *op. cit.*, pp. 244–246, 267–268.
[77] Scheuring, 2001, *op. cit.*, p. 139.
[78] Scheuring, 2001, *op. cit.*, pp. 252–254.

In the early days of the Lawrence Livermore National Laboratory, Edward Teller (see chapter 13), who was then a professor of physics at Berkeley, strongly urged creation of a joint graduate program between Berkeley and the Livermore Laboratory relating to applied sciences. Teller's well-known strident manner and in particular his aggressively negative testimony against Berkeley/Caltech physicist Robert Oppenheimer in the 1954 hearings that resulted in the nonrenewal of Oppenheimer's security clearance led many Berkeley scientists to oppose this relationship vigorously. Teller then turned to the Davis campus. Again, many chemists and physicists at Davis opposed a relationship with Teller and Livermore. However, a new College of Engineering had been formed at Davis in 1961 to branch out into other areas of engineering from agricultural engineering, which had already existed at Davis. The Dean of Engineering, Roy Bainer, with the encouragement of Kerr and Mrak, agreed to form such a program, which opened in 1963 as the Graduate Program in Applied Science. The Applied Science emphasis fit with the trends of the time to bring more science base into engineering. More informally known as "Teller Tech," this program continued with facilities at both Livermore and Davis until 2011, when it was discontinued in a time of budgetary stringency. Mrak describes the controversies at the start of the program.[79]

A more recent addition to the Davis campus is the magnificent Robert and Margrit Mondavi Center for the Performing Arts (figure 10-4), which forms an entry to the campus and is a legacy of Larry Vanderhoef, who served as chancellor from 1994 to 2009. The Mondavi Center serves to make the Davis campus a prime cultural center for the Sacramento state capital area.

As of 2103 the Davis campus had twenty members of the National Academy of Sciences, eleven members of the National Academy of Engineering, and thirteen members of the National Academy of Medicine. It is top ranked in most fields relating to agriculture, including the School of Veterinary Medicine and the Department of Viticulture and Oenology, which has had an enormous influence on the success of the California wine industry (see chapter 18).

---

[79] Mrak, 1974, *op. cit.*, pp. 170–174.

Figure 10-4. The Robert and Margrit Mondavi Center for the Performing Arts, University of California, Davis[80]

UC SANTA BARBARA

The Santa Barbara and Los Angeles campuses are the two cases in which a state college or normal school campus was transformed into a University of California campus. Santa Barbara State College had started in 1909 as the Santa Barbara State Normal School of Manual Arts and Home Economics and had added the typical normal school function of teacher education.[81] Now renamed Santa Barbara State

---

[80] Photograph © 2003 by Alan Nyiri, courtesy of the Atkinson Photographic Archive, https://perma.cc/K9SK-6MCE.

[81] Robert L. Kelley, *Transformations: UC Santa Barbara, 1909–1979* (Santa Barbara: Associated Students, University of California, 1981), pp. vii, 2.

College and with a pre–World War II enrollment of about nineteen hundred students, it was brought in the University of California in 1944 as a result of a series of political actions and responses that are described by Douglass,[82, 83] Kelley,[84] and Stadtman.[85] This episode and similar unsuccessful efforts by legislators elsewhere in California are among the factors that led to recognition of the need to develop what became the 1960 Master Plan for Higher Education in California (chapter 5).

As the University of California came out of World War II, the enrollment at the still-unchanged Santa Barbara campus grew to almost 2,700 students.[86] The nature and status of this very different campus within the University of California were then evaluated seriously by the university. As a new site at a former US Marines air base in nearby Goleta became available, attention turned to the concept of a small liberal arts college on the model of Reed, Bowdoin, or Williams, and a plan to that end was adopted by the UC Regents in 1953 promising "instruction and activities worthy of a liberal arts college of the highest quality enabling it to become a distinguished unit of the university."[87] In a sense this Santa Barbara plan paralleled that for Watkins College at UC Riverside (see below) and was a precursor of the eventual model for the Santa Cruz campus when it was founded later.

There was considerable tension between the faculty members of the old state college and those who favored the transition to a liberal arts college. Probably as a result of that tension, the industrial arts program stayed at the original site in Santa Barbara itself, but it could

---

[82] John A. Douglass, *The California Idea and American Higher Education*, pp. 157–163 (Stanford: Stanford University Press, 2000).
[83] John A. Douglass, "On Becoming an Old Blue," *Coastlines*, pp. 6–11, 37, September 1994.
[84] Kelley, 1981, *op. cit.*, pp. 4–6.
[85] Verne A. Stadtman, *The University of California, 1868–1968* (New York: McGraw-Hill,1970), pp. 340–348.
[86] Kelley, 1981, *op. cit.*, p. 8.
[87] Nancy C. Diamond, "Engineering the Leap: The University of California, Santa Barbara, in the Postwar Era," in *New Models of Excellence: Rising Research Universities in the Postwar Era, 1945–1990* (PhD dissertation, University of Maryland, Baltimore County, 2000), p. 187.

not sustain itself in isolation and withered away.[88] The remaining faculty members from that program were placed in other positions within the university, through the guidance of the vice president of the university, Henry Wellman.[89] The buildings released by the demise of the industrial arts program eventually formed the core for the present-day Santa Barbara City College, which is one of the more active and effective sites for transfer of community college students to UC. Placement of what remained of the industrial arts program within the community college system was also in accord with the Master Plan when it was formulated soon thereafter. Contention remained within the university as a whole over whether or not the Santa Barbara faculty should be admitted to the Southern Branch of the Academic Senate,[90] which did not happen until 1956.[91, 92]

Some individuals who were associated with the state college were very positive forces in the subsequent transitions through the liberal-arts-college model to full research-university status. Both Clark Kerr[93] and Robert Kelley[94] praise the contributions of Elmer Noble, who was dean of liberal arts and then acting provost in the days before general-campus status, and Russell Buchanan, who became dean of letters and science and then vice chancellor for academic affairs as Vernon Cheadle became chancellor. Enlightened and willing individuals of that sort are extremely helpful for difficult transitions.

As described in chapter 2, when Clark Kerr became UC president in 1958, he recognized the need for large forthcoming growth of the university to meet the coming "baby boom" enrollment, the children of returned World War II veterans. The short-lived plan for a small liberal arts college was abandoned in favor of Kerr's proposal that UC Santa Barbara, along with Davis and Riverside, should become general campuses of the university (i.e., undertake the research mission with a

---

[88] Kelley, 1981, *op. cit.*, p. 9.
[89] Kerr, 2001, *op. cit.*, p. 309.
[90] One of the delegations from the regents directly to the Academic Senate is the right to determine its own membership (see chapter 7).
[91] Kelley, 1981, *op. cit.*, p. 9.
[92] Diamond, 2000, *op. cit.*, p. 188.
[93] Kerr, 2001, *op. cit.*, vol. 1, p. 312.
[94] Kelley, 1981, *op. cit.*, p. 99.

full panoply of programs and both undergraduate and graduate education). That plan was adopted by the regents in 1958.

With the determination that Santa Barbara should be a general campus came the need for it to have a chancellor. (It had had only a provost theretofore.) The first chancellor (1959–62) was Samuel Gould, former president of Antioch College, who involved himself personally and energetically in the process of building toward a general campus. In 1961 Gould secured the formation of the College of Letters and Science and the School (later College) of Engineering and placed teacher education in the School of Education, all approved in 1961.

Gould's major coup was to attract as the first dean of engineering Albert G. Conrad, a distinguished electrical engineer who could well have been the next dean of engineering at Yale University. However, in 1961 Yale had eliminated its School of Engineering, converting it into a single department within Yale College.[95, 96] Gould recognized the unhappiness created at Yale by this action and moved to recruit Conrad, who came to UCSB together with Philip Ordnung, another distinguished Yale engineering professor, who became the initial chair of the Department of Electrical Engineering.[97]

Another innovation was the Education Abroad Program (EAP),[98] implemented in 1962 by William Allaway, who then led the program for twenty-seven years.[99] A pioneer program of its sort at the time, EAP operates on a university-wide basis, establishing study centers at many universities overseas, some with resident UC faculty directors. UC students go to the study centers and can take courses at the host university. There is a system for establishing credit for these courses at the home campus. Allaway was succeeded in 1989 by John Marcum, a

---

[95] William J. Cunningham, "Engineering at Yale: School, Department, Council 1932–82," pp. 65–74, *Transactions Connecticut Academy of Arts and Sciences*, 1992.
[96] "Yale School of Engineering & Applied Science," *Wikipedia*, https://perma.cc/LTM7-ULQU.
[97] "Electrical and Computer Engineering," *Santa Barbara: Departments*, University of California History Archives, https://perma.cc/Q8WF-STNJ.
[98] University of California, "Education Abroad Program," https://perma.cc/CF7C-4MGA.
[99] William H. Allaway, *The Global Campus: Education Abroad and the University of California* (Berkeley: Institute of Governmental Studies, University of California, 2002).

distinguished scholar and former academic vice chancellor from the Santa Cruz campus, who led EAP for another eighteen years until 2007.

Gould tended to be self-driven and nonconsultative. He came into conflict with the Academic Senate in many ways, the most difficult of which concerned the initial appointments in engineering, where Gould operated on his own, seemingly ignoring the senate roles in review of new faculty members.[100, 101] Those faculty appointees were very strong; hence preventing the senate from carrying out its role was an unnecessary red flag. The break with the senate became so severe that Kerr asked Vice President Harry Wellman to ease the situation through personal intervention. Shortly thereafter, Gould left to become head of the Educational Broadcasting System in New York, and then president of the State University of New York.

As the next chancellor, Kerr chose Vernon Cheadle, a distinguished botanist who at the time was academic vice chancellor of the Davis campus. Cheadle had been in many Academic Senate positions during his career and was regarded as a fully consultative administrator, factors that were clearly important in his selection. Cheadle served as chancellor for fifteen years, 1962–77. On the basis of a number of interviews, Diamond [102] reports that Cheadle remained highly consultative and liked by the faculty in his role as chancellor. Kelley observes, "Vernon Cheadle was not an eloquent man, nor a charismatic one. His strength lay rather in his integrity, his firm scholarly values, and in his readiness to speak and act for his principles. His personal capacity for extraordinary endurance, for bearing the continuing burden of indignity and frustration all administrators must face—especially was this true in the 1960s—without losing his civility, were remarkable gifts to a campus going through wrenching changes and, in crisis years, violent and debilitating controversies."[103]

Kerr indicates that as UCSB became a general campus in 1958, "One urgent issue, or at least policy action, was to expand [UCSB] as fast as possible so that the new 'university' faculty would overwhelm

---

[100] Kelley, 1981, *op. cit.*, p. 18.
[101] Diamond, 2000, *op. cit.*, p. 189.
[102] Diamond, 2000, *op. cit.*, p. 199.
[103] Kelley, 1981, *op. cit.*, p. 101.

the old 'college' faculty."[104] During Gould's era (1959–62), fall enrollment grew from 2,380 to 4,780, 5 percent of whom were graduate students. During Cheadle's period there was extremely rapid growth to a fall enrollment of 10,833 in fall 1966 and then a percent-wise lesser rate of growth to 14,588 in fall 1977, 13 percent of whom were graduate students.[105] The period of extremely rapid growth coincided with the onset of the surge in demand from children of returning World War II veterans (the baby boom) and migration to California. To obtain this rate of growth Cheadle aggressively recruited students including "redirects"—UC-eligible students whose first choice had been another UC campus to which they had not been admitted.[106]

There was a continuing and pressing need for growth and building academic quality. In addition to increasing enrollment so as to provide the wherewithal for adding faculty, challenges included building research quality, securing extramural grants, creating support systems, and enhancing the library, which in 1958 had included only 150,000 volumes.[107]

Cheadle personally involved himself in faculty promotion and tenure processes, working collaboratively with the Academic Senate to raise the bar in reviews and actually participating in some faculty searches as well.[108,109] Academic quality was the criterion for allocations of budget and faculty-recruitment authorizations. He emphasized disciplines such as physics and religious studies in which quality had already taken hold. The National Defense Education Act of 1958 provided national government support in the form of fellowships and other academic resources that could be used effectively to build. The number of graduate students grew from 123 in 1960 to 624 in 1964 and over 2000 in 1969. The first two doctorate programs, history and biological sciences, had been approved in 1961, and the UCSB's first two PhD degrees were awarded at end of Cheadle's first year (1963) to students who had been admitted with advanced standing.[110]

---

[104] Kerr, 2001, *op. cit.*, p. 309.
[105] Kelley, 1981, *op. cit.*, pp. 135–142.
[106] Diamond, 2000, *op. cit.*, p. 190.
[107] Diamond, 2000, *op. cit.*, p. 189.
[108] Kelley, 1981, *op. cit.*, p. 26.
[109] Diamond, 2000, *op. cit.*, p. 193.
[110] Diamond, 2000, *op. cit.*, p. 191.

Academic Senate review of the proposed programs was carried out through the Southern Division of the Academic Senate, the structure that existed until 1963, when it was changed to individual campus divisions within a university-wide Academic Senate (see chapter 7). That senate review system included faculty members from UCLA and Riverside as well as Santa Barbara. Advice on the actual setup of new programs would typically be provided by faculty members drawn from existing UC campuses.[111]

In 1966 the regents approved growth to a target goal of twenty-five thousand students, a full-sized UC campus. Cheadle, working closely with the Academic Senate, developed proposals for new schools of Law, Administration, Preclinical Medicine, Architecture and Regional Planning, Library and Information Science, and Creative Studies.[112] However, as of 1968, state budgets for the university—and hence, the rate of growth of the campus—sagged, and only three of these proposed schools (Law, Administration, and Creative Studies) were approved by the university-wide administration and the regents, and only one of those (Creative Studies) was actually funded and came into being. Even today, UC Santa Barbara has only one professional school—the Bren School of Environmental Science and Management, established in 1993. The College of Creative Studies has remained a small but viable program over the years. It is designed to serve the needs of unusual students who are highly gifted and well along in particular fields of endeavor, who engage in small seminar settings with advanced faculty—a sort of personally adapted graduate school for undergraduates.[113]

In the period 1969–72, the Santa Barbara campus underwent intense and almost continual student unrest, built around protesting the Vietnam War and other student issues of the time. These protest activities brought in many nonstudents. They were follow-up waves to the activism at Berkeley that had begun with the Free Speech Movement in 1964 (chapter 2). The base for the activism was the

---

[111] For example, upon my own arrival at Berkeley in 1963, I found that my department chair, Charles R. Wilke, was actively involved in setting up the curriculum for the new chemical engineering program at UCSB.
[112] Diamond, 2000, *op. cit.*, pp. 191–192.
[113] Kelley, 1981, *op. cit.*, p. 30.

community of Isla Vista, adjoining the campus and housing many students outside any oversight from the university. A culmination of the activism that received major national media coverage was the burning and total destruction of the Bank of America branch building in Isla Vista on February 25, 1970.

The student unrest had several negative effects—diversion of the campus from academic building, diversion of the attention and energies of Chancellor Cheadle, and a reputation for the campus that was discouraging to many students and families. As of 1973 Cheadle promoted economist Alec Alexander from dean of the College of Letters and Science to vice chancellor for academic affairs. His intent was that Alexander would continue to pay close attention to academic development as Cheadle had done but no longer could do because of these other needs.[114] It turned out to be an inspired choice. Alexander worked synergistically with the Academic Senate in academic planning and allocation of faculty recruitments, including launching a program of senior appointments for distinguished individuals who could spark their disciplines to greater academic heights.[115, 116] Faculty positions were reallocated to areas with research potential, strong job markets, or both, the aim being to sustain and build academic enrollment despite the image issues that had come with the Isla Vista problems. Tenure decisions became more selective. During the period from 1968 to 1971, there was a 60 percent concurrence between favorable recommendations of departments and recommendations of senate review committees. For 1971–4 this figure fell to 48 percent. As of 1978, one in five tenure-track faculty members had been hired in the previous three years, and 35 percent of these 128 new appointments were at the rank of professor.[117]

Still, with this boost in size and faculty quality, UCSB's extramural support in 1978 was less than 25 percent of the volume on the other UC general campuses, excluding Santa Cruz and Riverside.[118] The campus still had a substantial way to go in building to the stature of

---

[114] Diamond, 2000, *op. cit.*, p. 197.
[115] Kelley, 1981, *op. cit.*, pp. 66–67.
[116] Diamond, 2000, *op. cit.*, pp. 200.
[117] Diamond, 2000, *op. cit.*, pp. 197–202.
[118] Diamond, 2000, *op. cit.*, p. 207.

most other UC campuses. However, major strides were made in the next fifteen years, despite campus leadership that was troubled in several ways.

With the age-related mandatory retirement of Vernon Cheadle in 1977, Robert Huttenback, a historian of science from Caltech, was chosen as the next chancellor and served until his resignation in 1986. His time with the campus was turbulent. There were some strong accomplishments, but his manner and style occasioned the resignation of several top campus officials, including Alexander, another vice chancellor for academic affairs, and a dean of letters and science.[119, 120] Huttenback was also viewed by the Academic Senate as dismissive of faculty consultation. In addition, he got into legal and ethical difficulties[121, 122] that resulted in his becoming the first faculty member to be formally dismissed by the Regents of the University of California.

In 1979 the investment of the campus in building academic strength in physics paid off as the campus won a competition held by the National Science Foundation to establish an Institute of Theoretical Physics. The request for proposals had drawn fifteen proposals from major universities.[123, 124] The founding director of that institute was Walter Kohn, a theoretical physicist who subsequently won the Nobel Prize in Chemistry in 1998. The award of the institute also drew to UCSB Robert Schrieffer of the University of Pennsylvania, who had already received the Nobel Prize in 1972 for the development of the theory of superconductivity. The Institute of Theoretical Physics served as an effective catalyst for further academic development of the campus in related areas. Schrieffer became the second director. The institute is now the Kavli Institute for Theoretical Physics (figure 10-5), supported by the Kavli Foundation,[125] and continues to be a highly visible pillar of strength for the campus.

---

[119] Diamond, 2000, *op. cit.*, p. 213.
[120] Kelley, 1981, *op. cit.*, p. 122.
[121] Diamond, *loc. cit.*
[122] Judith Cummings, "Ex-University Chief and Wife Held in Fraud Case," *New York Times*, March 17, 1987.
[123] Kelley, 1981, *op. cit.*, pp. 115–118.
[124] Diamond, 2000, *op. cit.*, pp. 204–306, 215–217.
[125] Kavli Institute for Theoretical Physics, The Kavli Foundation, https://perma.cc/KW7B-TF5P.

Spreading Excellence: Developing New Campuses

Figure 10-5. Kohn Hall, Home of the Kavli Institute for Theoretical Physics, UCSB[126]

The continued academic-building strategy was to invest selectively in those areas that matched Santa Barbara's attributes with federal research funding sources and the availability of outstanding faculty. This approach paid off during the 1980s as multiple areas grew in distinction, including marine sciences (a strength continuing from early days, figure 10-6), materials science, chemical and nuclear engineering, remote sensing and other areas within geography, and multidisciplinary humanities activities., including award of the Interdisciplinary Humanities Center in 1987, where Santa Barbara was chosen over other UC competitors.[127]

Another important development during Huttenback's time was the hiring of Robert Mehrabian from the National Institute of Standards and Technology as dean of engineering in 1983, coupled

---

[126] Photograph © 2003 by Alan Nyiri, courtesy of the Atkinson Photographic Archive, https://perma.cc/X3SC-SWNK.
[127] Diamond, 2000, *op. cit.*, p. 223.

with a big push for building engineering. During the 1980s, through Mehrabian's efforts, the engineering faculty increased from fifty-four to ninety-five, and there was a major push toward multidisciplinary research activities and a consequent large increase in government-funded organized research activities. In addition, a poll of engineering deans nationally recognized the program as being the number-one up-and-coming engineering program. Engineering accounted for 21 percent of UCSB's extramural funding in the late 1980s.[128] Mehrabian subsequently became president of Carnegie Mellon University and then CEO of Teledyne.

Figure 10-6. Marine Biotechnology Laboratory, opened 1964, UCSB.[129]

After the resignation of Huttenback in 1986, UC president David Gardner took a healing step by appointing as interim chancellor Daniel Aldrich, the founding chancellor at Irvine (see below) and a person respected throughout the university. The search for a permanent chancellor then led to Barbara Uehling, chancellor at the University of Missouri, Columbia, who served as UCSB chancellor from 1987 until 1994, when she was succeeded by Henry Yang, who now (2017) has

---

[128] Diamond, 2000, *op. cit.*, p. 220–221.
[129] Photograph © 2003 by Alan Nyiri, courtesy of the Atkinson Photographic Archive, https://perma.cc/DG8S-Y53U.

been chancellor for over twenty years. Uehling encountered difficulties of her own: being arrested the evening before her inauguration for driving while intoxicated, being viewed as having insulated herself from both faculty consultation and criticism as she focused upon external fund-raising, and facing but staving off a vote of no confidence from the faculty in 1993.[130]

Despite these administrative issues, the rises across the board in academic quality and recognition during the 1980s placed the University of California at Santa Barbara in a prominent and highly respected position. It was elected to the American Association of Universities (AAU) in 1995, the fourth UC campus to be so recognized after Berkeley, Los Angeles, and San Diego. (The Davis and Irvine campuses were elected a year later, in 1996.) In a ranking of research quality carried out by Graham and Diamond looking at data from the late 1980s, UC Santa Barbara and the Stony Brook campus of the State University of New York tied for second place behind UC Berkeley among Carnegie classification Research 1 public universities.[131]

UC Santa Barbara now has the following impressive array of Nobel Laureates, some of whom did their prize-winning work while at UCSB and others of whom came subsequently to UCSB:

- 1972 Physics: **J. Robert Schrieffer** with John Bardeen and Leon Cooper, "for their jointly developed theory of super-conductivity, usually called the BCS-theory"; work done at the University of Illinois at Urbana-Champaign
- 1988 Chemistry: **Walter Kohn**, "for his development of the density-functional theory"; work done at Carnegie Mellon, UC San Diego, and UC Santa Barbara
- 2000 Chemistry: **Alan J. Heeger**, "for the discovery and development of conductive polymers"; work done at University of Pennsylvania and UC Santa Barbara

---

[130] Diamond, 2000, op. cit., p. 215.
[131] H. D. Graham and Nancy Diamond, *The Rise of American Research Universities: Elites and Challengers in the Postwar Era* (Baltimore, MD: Johns Hopkins University Press, 1997), table 6.7, p. 167. The method used per capita indices of numbers of papers published in certain selective, leading journals in both (a) sciences (including some engineering) and (b) social sciences, as well as (c) the number of fellowships won in arts and humanities from certain prestigious organizations. Universities were ranked in order of the values of each of these three indices, and the resultant three individual ranks were added to produce a combined index.

- 2000 Physics: **Herbert Kroemer**, "for developing semiconductor heterostructures used in high-speed and opto-electronics"; work done at several institutions in Germany and the United States
- 2004 Physics: **David J. Gross**, "for the discovery of asymptotic freedom in the theory of the strong interaction"; work done largely at Princeton
- 2004 Economic Sciences: **Finn E. Kydland**, "for contributions to dynamic macroeconomics: the time consistency of economic policy and the driving forces behind business cycles"; work done in Norway and the United States
- 2014 Physics: **Shuji Nakamura**, "for the invention of efficient blue light-emitting diodes, which has enabled bright and energy-saving white light sources"; work done in Japan

Four of these prizes are in physics, and a fifth winner (Kohn) was a physicist. Three of them (Kohn, Schrieffer, and Gross) were directors of the Kavli Institute, thereby reflecting the importance of UCSB's early emphasis on physics and the 1979 award of the Institute of Theoretical Physics in the National Science Foundation competition.

As of 2014, UC Santa Barbara had thirty-nine members of the National Academy of Science and twenty-four members of the National Academy of Engineering.

UC Santa Barbara has succeeded despite some major obstacles, overcoming the handicaps associated with beginning as a very different sort of institution, difficulties in style and other factors associated with three chancellors, and the negative images associated with the student unrest of the late 1960s and early 1970s. The success can be attributed to several factors, among them being the inherent strength of the University of California system and its methods and culture, some excellent strategic choices, an outstanding location and environment, and the steady and effective leadership at critical early times by persons such as Vernon Cheadle and Alec Alexander.

At the conclusion of her examination of UCSB, Nancy Diamond[132] concludes that these factors were crucial for the rise of UCSB:

---

[132] Diamond, 2000, *op. cit.*, pp. 224–231.

1. The successful exploitation of the natural advantage of a unique California location (through emphasis on marine sciences, geography, and engineering)
2. An inherited UC research-doctorate mission
3. An ability to absorb a tidal wave of enrollments during the 1960s, thus assuring the size necessary to support a significant program of research
4. Effective leadership from UC president Clark Kerr, campus chancellor Vernon Cheadle, vice chancellor Alec Alexander, and the Academic Senate
5. The development of unique research niches in marine sciences, theoretical physics, and engineering that matched federal funding priorities; and establishment of the NSF-sponsored Institute for Theoretical Physics (ITP) and subsequent national research centers
6. Campus adaptability and nimbleness

With regard to factor two, one should really cite the entire structure, culture, and traditions of the University of California. Factor three gave the ability, through numbers of faculty hires, for a rapid transition from the original state college to a research culture. Although size per se is certainly helpful, it is not a sine qua non, a fact witnessed by the success of Caltech, which has remained a very small institution. Factor six is particularly pertinent for UCSB.

UC RIVERSIDE

The Riverside campus had two precursors, an agricultural research facility and a small, liberal arts college. The Citrus Experiment Station[133] (figure 10-7), founded in 1907, was recognized throughout the world for its research on citrus fruit trees. That research evolved into other agricultural products as well. The liberal arts college, a College of Letters and Science known colloquially as "Watkins College" after its

---

[133] "The Citrus Experiment Station," University of California, Riverside, https://perma.cc/GX2V-SHFY.

founder, Gordon Watkins, a former UCLA dean of Letters and Sciences, was authorized by the Board of Regents of the University of California in 1949 and opened in 1954. Future vice president of the university Harry Wellman, [134] who was on the university committee that recommended the college, describes the intent as "to create a "Swarthmore of the West" where undergraduate instruction of the highest quality in the liberal arts would be preeminent."[135]

Figure 10-7. Citrus Experiment Station. ca. 1916.[136] This building, refurbished, is now home to UC Riverside's A. Gary Anderson Graduate School of Management.

In the years immediately after its founding, the UC Riverside liberal arts college functioned impressively. It drew a capable faculty committed to undergraduate teaching in the spirit of the college. The high school grade point averages of students upon entry exceeded even those for Berkeley, and the college was the only public college ranked in the top ten of US liberal arts colleges in a national survey. Among its first graduates was Charles (Chuck) Young, who became a

---

[134] L. Furtado, C. Kerr, and G. Rowe, "Harry Wellman, Agricultural Economics: Berkeley," In Memoriam, University of California, 1997, https://perma.cc/8QQW-DCCF.

[135] Harry R. Wellman, interview by Malca Chall, "Teaching, Research, and Administration, University of California, 1925–1968, p. 67, oral history, Regional Oral History Office, University of California, Berkeley, 1976, https://perma.cc/5EK3-H5DU.

[136] University of California Citrus Experiment Station, *Wikipedia* https://perma.cc/7ADX-VZDU.

legendary figure, serving twenty-nine years as chancellor at UCLA (Chapter 10) and then as the president of the University of Florida.[137]

As of the mid-1950s, demographic projections, which later turned out to be overestimated (see chapter 3), led to the decisions to create three new campuses and to convert Santa Barbara, Davis, and Riverside to general campuses. Thus, in April 1959 upon Clark Kerr's recommendation, the UC Regents approved the conversion of the Riverside campus into a general campus. The goal then became to convert it to a research university with both undergraduate and graduate study and with a much larger ultimate enrollment.[138]

On the surface it might appear than the combination of the well-recognized agricultural research station and the liberal arts college might be a good starting point for evolution to a general campus, but that was not the case. First of all, the faculty of the liberal arts college had not been hired on the basis of being suitable for a research university; in fact, the college had drawn faculty members who wanted to focus solely upon undergraduate teaching and took pride in that fact. Secondly, the staff members of the Citrus Experiment Station were not the same sorts of researchers and were less suited to the needs of a general campus than were the Scripps researchers in the case of the founding of UC San Diego (see below). In the classical mode of agriculture research, they were much closer to the farmers and ranchers who made use of their work, and they were on full-year salaries, whereas the college faculty members were paid for only their academic-year instructional work. The college faculty members had nothing in common with the Experiment Station faculty and were even of a different age group, since nearly all the college faculty members had been hired at the entry level. The two groups looked down upon one another.

The difficulties became manifest in 1956, when Gordon Watkins, who had been given the provost title as on-site head of the campus, retired, and it was necessary to find a successor. As the only Academic

---

[137] Charles E. Young, interview by James V. Mink and Dale E. Treleven, "Oral history with Charles E. Young: Oral History Transcript, 1984–1999," Oral History Program, University of California, Los Angeles, 2002. Available from both UCLA and the Bancroft Library, Berkeley, currently available in print only.

[138] Kerr, 2001, *op. cit.*, p. 315.

Senate members, the college faculty populated the faculty search committee and steadfastly provided only one name, in violation of a university policy that required search committees to forward more than one name. That one person was the dean of the College of Letters and Science of the college, who was vigorously opposed by the scientists of the Citrus Experiment Station, who would of course also come under the provost. Sproul resolved this impasse by naming as provost the dean of biological sciences within the college, Herman Spieth.[139] Spieth and most other biologists in the college were interested in research, as were many of the physical scientists. Also biology, albeit a fundamental science, was as close to the interests of the Experiment Station scientists as one could get within the college. Spieth had seven difficult years as chancellor as moves to graduate education and expanded enrollment were made. The Graduate Division at Riverside was established in 1960.

In hindsight, one can question the original decision to create the small, liberal arts college. The experiment was appealing as a way of emphasizing undergraduate education and individualized attention to undergraduate students. A similar short-lived experiment was being made at Santa Barbara at the same time from a different starting point, and a much grander experiment of a similar sort would be made at Santa Cruz a few years later. But why endeavor to maintain a small fifteen-hundred-student liberal arts college as part of the public research university, which would have to do its part in educating the children of the postwar baby boom and the surge of immigration to California? Why do it in a location so close to the successful private Claremont Colleges complex in Pomona? And why do it on a campus with such an unnatural coinhabitant as the Citrus Experiment Station?

In 1964 Chancellor Spieth resigned and transferred to the Davis campus so as to continue his teaching and research. Without a search, President Kerr recruited as replacement Ivan Hinderaker, who as academic vice chancellor had for two years been planning and recruiting the initial leaders for the new Irvine campus (see below). In

---

[139] Kerr, 2001, *op. cit.*, pp. 315–316.

his oral history,[140] Hinderaker describes the invitation and his decision as follows:

> The Irvine dedication [took] place on June 20, 1964. At eight o'clock the next morning in my office, Harry Wellman came in without any preliminaries or anything and said, "Clark and I want you to go to Riverside as Chancellor." It was a complete surprise...Why I did go? Ok, it was a part of the University of California. I just kept the great seal of the university polished and clutched it tightly to my breast at all times. (chuckle) And I was being asked by the President and the Board of Regents, and I hadn't applied for the job. OK. Getting UCR well established on a track consistent with the Master Plan was one of the critically important things for the university to do. That was a feeling expressed by the President, but rather generally throughout all of the campuses of the university. And, I just found it difficult to resist that challenge. My experiences as administrator, as chairman of the department at UCLA and Vice Chancellor here led me to feel that I might be able to handle what was then regarded as a very difficult problem. I liked administration, so I had to give it a try. And furthermore, my leaving was not creating a problem, because Peltason had been recruited as a Dean.

Although Kerr does not state it explicitly, one can presume that Hinderaker was chosen in substantial measure because of his abilities to calm troubled waters.

In addition to the college-versus-experiment-station issue and the needs to initiate a graduate program and convert both preexisting entities into a single research university, Hinderaker inherited another problem and had yet another major one soon to arrive. The other inherited problem had to do with the fact that the founding college faculty members had all been hired at the entry level. Arthur Turner, who was somewhat more senior than the other college faculty and was

---

[140] Ivan and Birk Hinderaker, interview by Jan Erickson, "Transcription of an Oral History Interview with Ivan and Birk Hinderaker, June 5, 1998," pp. 28–29, University of California, Riverside, https://perma.cc/7NQQ-QUAK.

hired as associate professor and chairman (later dean) of social sciences, described some of the difficulties:

> Not only in the Division of Social Sciences, but all the divisions on the whole campus, the level of initial appointment was extraordinarily low, and I think it was technically a mistake because we had extremely few people at a senior level. Hardly any people except the division chairmen, in fact, had tenure...This was an astonishingly low level of appointment and gave a certain kindergarten air to not only the students but the faculty. And of course it was a great consequence later on that people moved upwards into the various stages of promotion in step with each other. So instead of having almost everybody assistant professors, you had some years down the line everybody being associate professors and everybody being full professors and eventually everybody retiring at once, which was not good from any point of view. It would have been much better to do, as in fact the early chancellors at San Diego did, to have a decent distribution of positions over the various levels and ranks and to enable, therefore, the campus to get older in a more orderly and distributed manner among the various levels.[141]

Hinderaker carefully pursued a path of consolidation to get the college and the experiment station working together. In an approach that is seen again in the reorganization of biosciences at Berkeley fifteen years later (see chapter 12), Hinderaker started by appointing a special committee of six respected senior faculty members, three from the Citrus Experiment Station and three from the College of Letters and Science. After examining the issues involved, this committee recommended that the Division of Biological Sciences be removed from the College of Letters and Science and merged with what were then the nine departments in agriculture to form a new College of Biological and Agricultural Sciences.

This recommendation was substantially opposed within the College of Letters and Science, which would be broken up, and by many

---

[141] Arthur Turner, interview by Jan Erickson, "Transcription of Videotape with Arthur Campbell Turner, April 20, 1998," oral history interview, University of California, Riverside, 1998, https://perma.cc/CB9B-3E72.

of the senior scientists in the Citrus Experiment Station, who now had senate membership by virtue of partial faculty appointments for their teaching. The recommendation was nonetheless endorsed by the two pertinent Academic Senate committees, Education Policy and Budget, which were both chaired by distinguished faculty members who could see the issues on a broader scale. The proposal went to a formal vote of the Letters and Science senate faculty, where it was opposed by a vote of 62 to 16 with 10 abstentions. From there it went to a full Senate vote, where it was opposed 101 to 31. However, in shared governance such Senate votes are advisory, and Hinderaker was able to trade upon the considerable respect and liking for him across the campus as well as the cover afforded to him by the special committee of senior faculty members and the two senate Committees. By "sailing tight to the wind," as he described it, he was able to accept the proposal and institute the change in 1968, with the chair of the Division of Biological Sciences being named dean and the director of the Citrus Experiment Station being associate dean for research.[142] In 1974 the physical sciences were brought into this college too, with the name then being changed to College of Natural and Agricultural Sciences.[143]

The major problem that arrived while Hinderaker was chancellor related to smog, publicity for it, and the resultant effects on student enrollment. Riverside is located such that the terrain and the generally west-to-east flow of air off the Pacific Ocean funnel the air from both the Los Angeles Basin and the Orange County area into Riverside. Following the morning-commute traffic, the resultant photochemical smog would flow to, and intensify in, Riverside in the early afternoon. Thus, although Riverside was not the primary generator, it was the recipient of the smog. The public relations problem for the campus was so severe that Hinderaker kept a collection of newspaper headlines from 1972 and 1973,[144] which convey the picture:

Toronto Star, "City Being Strangled by Smog"

---

[142] Hinderaker, 1998, *op. cit.*, pp. 41–43, 79–80.
[143] Kerr, 2001, *op. cit.*, p. 318.
[144] Hinderaker, 1998, *op. cit.*, pp. 59–61.

Chapter 10

Washington Post, "Smog Peril Spreads to Riverside California" (with photo of jogger wearing gas mask)

New York Times, "Smog Alerts Blight Life in Riverside California. Angry Citizens Urge Drastic Action on Befouled Air"

Los Angeles Times, "Riverside, A Black Eye for Fighting Smog"

Honolulu Star Bulletin, "The Smog Capital of the World"

San Francisco Chronicle, "Riverside's War on Its Smog Image"
(The lead paragraphs of each of the last three stories were about a senior professor who decided not to come to Riverside after reading the *New York Times* headline.)

New York Times, "'The Town That's Choking to Death, Riverside California" ["The air is so bad that kids can't play outdoors. The sun is rarely seen and they are beginning to grow oranges in oxygen tents. Riverside smog has become the object of national attention…"]

Riverside Press-Enterprise, "Millions of Ill Persons in the U.S. Are Made Sicker by Smog"

Oxnard Press Courier, "Prediction: The World's Next Great Smog Disaster May Strike Riverside. Experts Believe Riverside Will Fall Victim of Smog"

Torrance South Daily Breeze, "You Need To Feel Your Way To Class in Riverside"

Los Angeles Times, "Regents Ponder UC Riverside's Future as Enrollment Dips"

San Francisco Chronicle, "UC Regents Try to Revive Riverside Campus"

Los Angeles Herald Express, "Smog Location Blamed for UC Riverside Decline"

Oakland Tribune, "Enrollment Drop Alarms Regents"

Pasadena Star News, "Students Decline Mystery. UC Riverside Rolls Drop"

Anaheim Bulletin, "UC Riverside Budget Cut"

The last six of these headlines refer to the natural result of the earlier headlines and stories. The enrollments at the Riverside campus actually dropped from 6,200 in 1971 to 4,600 in 1978 and then stayed essentially flat at 4,600–4,800 for another six years.[145] Since funding was based on enrollment, budget dropped too. This situation led to widespread rumors that the Riverside campus would be closed.

There were some other facts besides smog that contributed to the enrollment issue. Kerr notes that "the city of Riverside, with its Victorian ambience, proved to be something of a cultural desert from a 1960s student's point of view."[146] Further, Hinderaker,[147] Turner,[148] and Kerr[149] all note the effects of competition from the nearby Irvine campus, less than an hour away by automobile.

The Riverside campus itself actually contributed to the ultimate solution to this problem. Control of photochemical smog was a major scientific and technological accomplishment. The sources and mechanisms of formation of photochemical smog were worked out by Arie Haagen-Smit and associates of Caltech during the 1950s and 1960s.[150] At UC Riverside the Statewide Air Pollution Research Center had been founded in 1961 by James N. Pitts, an original faculty member. Upon his death in 2014, the chair of the California Air Resources Board said, "Jim Pitts was probably the single person most responsible for the understanding of what strategies we need to clean up Southern California's air. He was able to explain all of this in English to policymakers so that they would be able to accept that it was going to take extensive and difficult actions to control emissions."[151]

---

[145] Kerr, 2001, *op. cit.*, pp. 470–471.
[146] Kerr, 2001, *op. cit.*, p. 317.
[147] Hinderaker, 1998, *op. cit.*, p. 59.
[148] Turner, 1998, *op. cit.*, pp. 60–61.
[149] Kerr, 2001, *loc. cit.*
[150] James Bonner, "Arie Jan Haagen-Smit, 1900–1977," Biographical Memoirs, National Academy of Sciences, 1989, https://perma.cc/JXV7-2A7E.
[151] Mary Nichols, quoted in Tony Barboza, "James Pitts Dies at 93; His Research Led to Cleaner Air in California," *Los Angeles Times*, https://web.archive.org/web/20160306062039/http://www.latimes.com/local/obituaries/la-me-james-pitts-20140626-story.html.

Ultimately, positive crankcase ventilation (1961), the requirement of catalytic converters for automobiles (1975), and the elimination of lead in gasoline (1976) led to near elimination of the smog problem for Los Angeles and Orange Counties and thereby Riverside. The understanding of the mechanism of photochemical smog and the ensuing work with government and industry to develop methods to control it are prime examples of the contributions of academic research to improving modern life.

The Statewide Air Pollution Research Center later became part of CE-CERT, the Bourns College of Engineering Center for Environmental Research Technology (figure 10-8). In 2016 UC Riverside was chosen by the State of California Air Resources Board for a $366 million investment as the new home of its motor vehicle and engine emissions testing and research facility.[152] This is a striking case of making a silk purse (outstanding research accomplishments that serve the state) out of a sow's ear (the smog problem).

Figure 10-8. Center for Environmental Research and Technology (CE-CERT), University of California, Riverside, courtesy of CE-CERT[153]

The first PhD program at Riverside began in chemistry in 1960. By the end of Hinderaker's fifteen years as chancellor in 1979, there were twenty-nine PhD programs and thirty master's programs. Over a

---

[152] Sara Nightingale, "California Air Resources Board Chooses Riverside for $366 Million Facility," *UCR Today*, March 24, 2016, https://perma.cc/GU5L-TPCY.

[153] "Center for Environmental Research and Technology," Bourns College of Engineering, University of California, Riverside, https://perma.cc/DN2G-VE6T.

thousand PhDs and twenty-five hundred master's degrees had been awarded, and the student body had become 25 percent graduate students.[154] But perhaps Hinderaker's main contribution, noted by many, was simply to keep the campus going and improving during the difficult period in which he was chancellor.

Hinderaker's chancellorship was followed by a rather tortured thirteen years, during which there was frequent turnover due to deaths and other reasons. Tomás Rivera, a noted Mexican American author and poet who had been executive vice president of the University of Texas at El Paso (UTEP) succeeded Hinderaker in 1979 but died unexpectedly in 1984. He was succeeded by Theodore Hullar, a biochemist who had come to UCR that same year as executive vice chancellor after being director of the Agricultural Experiment Station at Cornell. In 1987, President Gardner moved Hullar from Riverside to the chancellorship of the Davis campus. At the same time he appointed as Riverside Chancellor Rosemary Schraer, a biochemist who had come from Pennsylvania State University in 1985 to be executive vice chancellor under Hullar. Schraer died unexpectedly in 1992, a few months before her term was to end, at a time when Raymond Orbach, a physicist who had been provost for letters and science at UCLA, had already been selected as the next UCR chancellor.

The image that Hullar was apparently being upgraded in his move from Riverside to Davis and the appointment of Schraer without a search were both seen as degrading to the campus by many faculty members at Riverside; see, for example, reflections by Carney[155] and Turner.[156]

Orbach served a stabilizing ten-year period as chancellor, from 1992 until 2002, during which time the campus advanced in both distinction and enrollment. When Orbach left in 2002 to become director and then under secretary for science in the US Department of Energy, Executive Vice Chancellor David Warren was acting chancellor until a search yielded the appointment of France Córdova, a physicist

---

[154] Hinderaker, 1998, *op. cit.*, p. 45.
[155] Francis M. Carney, interview by Jan Erickson, "Transcription of Video Interview with Francis M. Carney, July 20, 1998," p. 41, University of California, Riverside, 1998, https://perma.cc/8UJP-MBWX.
[156] Turner, 1998, *op. cit.*, p. 61.

who had been chief scientist at NASA and then vice chancellor for research at UC Santa Barbara. Córdova served from 2002 to 2007, when she became president of Purdue University and then later director of the National Science Foundation. Robert Grey, former executive vice chancellor at UC Davis, then served as interim chancellor for somewhat over a year while a search was done to recruit Timothy White, president of the University of Idaho and former Berkeley faculty member. White served, again in an effective and stabilizing capacity, for four and a half years through December 2012, when he became president of the California State University system. He was then followed by an eight-month interim chancellor, Jane Close Conoley, who had been dean of the Graduate School of Education at UC Santa Barbara. The current chancellor (2017), who started in January 2014, is Kim Wilcox, who had been provost of Michigan State University.

From this synopsis, one can see that the leadership of the Riverside campus over the past thirty-six years has been an up-and-down affair, with some very effective longer-term chancellors, most notably Hinderaker and Orbach, interspersed with shorter-term chancellors, some of whom have been lured to other major universities.

Nonetheless, the Riverside campus is now fully established and secure and is steadily making inroads. There are now six members of the National Academy of Sciences and two of the National Academy of Engineering[157] on the faculty. The enrollment for fall 2015 was 21,539, a notable recovery from the depressed-enrollment situation with which Ivan Hinderaker had to cope in the 1970s. In fact, the campus has become selective, in the sense that more UC-eligible students now apply than can be admitted.

---

[157] Engineering was a latecomer at Riverside, reborn in 1989 after an abortive start in 1967 under the deanship of Seymour Calvert, also a noted air-pollution researcher (see "In Memory of A&WMA Member Seymour Calvert, Ph.D. 1924 — 2002," obituary, Air & Waste Management Assn., 2002, https://perma.cc/HVT8-WCME. The delay was for the same reasons as for the Santa Cruz campus (see below).

UC SAN FRANCISCO

The San Francisco campus of the University of California underwent extremely rapid development of research stature, going from a situation as late as 1964, when it was a relatively conventional but undistinguished medical school and a minor player in research, to worldwide recognition achieved during the 1970s and multiple Nobel Prize winners on the faculty. (Two of its faculty members received the Nobel Prize in 1989, and other Nobel Prizes were awarded in 1997, 2009 and 2012.) How did this happen?

As described in chapter 2, a number of professional schools of various sorts were established in San Francisco in the last part of the nineteenth century and were affiliated with the University of California. Several of these—the Tolman Medical College (later known as the Medical Department), the California College of Pharmacy, and the Department of Dentistry—became the basis for what is now the San Francisco campus of the University of California.[158, 159] The original affiliations were on a self-sustaining basis financially, meaning that the Board of Regents of UC appropriated no funding to them. From the standpoints of these school and departments, the stature achieved by affiliation was enough of a gain.

When a tract of thirteen acres of land on Parnassus Heights south of Golden Gate Park was donated to the University of California in 1895 by San Francisco mayor Adolph Sutro for the purpose, the three colleges moved to that location and became known as the Affiliated Colleges.[160] A building was also created there for the Hastings College of Law, but Hastings never moved to it from its downtown San Francisco site. That building was then used to hold the extensive worldwide archeological collections that had been acquired and donated to the university by Phoebe Apperson Hearst (see chapter 2).

The Affiliated Colleges lost building space in downtown San Francisco in the great fire that stemmed from the earthquake of 1906. This loss required more space for clinical operations at Parnassus

---

[158] Stadtman, 1970, *op. cit.*, pp. 125–136.
[159] "UCSF History," University of California, San Francisco, https://perma.cc/LQH6-DBWN.
[160] Stadtman, 1970, *op. cit.*, pp. 136–138.

Heights, which was generated by the move of the basic science departments (pathology, anatomy, physiology) of the medical school to the Berkeley campus. The first two years of medical education were then being taken at Berkeley.[161] This arrangement served to strengthen academic ties for the clinically oriented Medical Department. However, over time it weakened the appreciation for science and engagement in research by the medical faculty in San Francisco.

The establishment of the UC Training School for Nurses in 1907 added a fourth professional school to the Affiliated Colleges. During his time as UC president, Benjamin Ide Wheeler persuaded the Board of Regents to accept full financial responsibility for the Medical and Dental Departments, including meeting the payroll. Thus, affiliation ended for these units and subsequently pharmacy and nursing, and they became integral parts of the university.[162] In 1949 the regents renamed the Parnassus Heights campus the UC Medical Center in San Francisco. Until 1954 the deans of what had been the Affiliated Colleges had all reported independently and directly to the UC president, but in that year they became the Executive Committee with the dean of medicine as chair of that committee and chief executive officer of the Medical Center.[163] As Clark Kerr became University of California president in 1958, he gave the dean of medicine the title provost, and in 1965 the provost title was changed to chancellor.[164]

Also in 1958, Kerr ended the arrangement whereby the basic sciences supporting medical education and hence the first two years of medical school had been at Berkeley. Physiology, biochemistry, and anatomy were moved back to the Parnassus Heights site in San Francisco.[165] Pathology had moved back earlier, and pharmacology and bacteriology were already at Parnassus Heights.[166] The space enabling the remaining basic science departments to move back was freed by a decision of Stanford University to consolidate its medical education in

---

[161] Stadtman, 1970, *op. cit.*, p. 197.
[162] Stadtman, 1970, *op. cit.*, p. 198.
[163] Stadtman, 1970, *op. cit.*, p. 404.
[164] Kerr, 2001, *op. cit.*, vol. 1, p. 319.
[165] Kerr, 2001, *op. cit.*, vol. 1, pp. 350, 369.
[166] Henry R. Bourne, *Paths to Innovation: Discovering Recombinant DNA, Oncogenes, and Prions, in One Medical School, Over One Decade* (Berkeley: University of California Medical Humanities Consortium and University of California Press, 2011), p. 9.

Palo Alto. Stanford had until 1958 been using clinical facilities at Parnassus Heights in San Francisco. However, Bourne[167] notes that many of the most distinguished researchers in those scientific disciplines that were moved back from Berkeley to UCSF chose to stay at Berkeley, which they saw as providing a richer intellectual climate. Bourne also observes that the research of those who did move to San Francisco "proved more sleepy than exciting."

Thirteen years later, in 1971, a joint medical program was created between UC San Francisco and UC Berkeley, whereby about 10 percent of the students in the incoming class in medicine for USCF take the first three years of a five-year program at Berkeley, obtaining a master's degree (originally in any of various disciplinary areas but now in the Health and Medical Sciences at UC Berkeley's School of Public Health) on their way to the MD degree.

Kerr's structural changes in 1958 set the stage for the subsequent rise of UCSF in research stature, but changes in leadership, outlook, and hiring practices were also needed before the ascent could start in earnest. The culture and leadership at UCSF were still heavily clinically oriented and generally did not recognize the value of research supporting and being integrated with clinical practice. This outlook was particularly true for the initial chancellor, John Saunders. There were, however, pockets of research activity and belief in its value. A "coup" of sorts occurred in 1964 when a group of research-valuing leaders from the campus sought a meeting with Kerr to push for the removal of Saunders. This group was led by the director of the Cardiovascular Research Institute, Julius Comroe, and included both Dean of Medicine William Reinhardt and chair of the Department of Medicine L. H. (Holly) Smith. Kerr arranged for the vice president of the university, Harry Wellman, to meet with the group and upon finding that there was much substance to the complaints, consulted widely and made the difficult decision to remove Saunders. So as to calm the troubled waters as much as possible and minimize perceptions of winners and losers, Kerr also arranged the resignation of Reinhardt as dean of medicine, and for a new Chancellor he took the unusual step of

---

[167] Bourne, 2011, *op. cit.*, pp. 2, 8.

selecting the dean of dentistry, Willard Fleming, who was a respected and a capable healer.[168, 169]

Henry Bourne[170] has explored the specific careers of four of the most important individuals in the rise of UCSF to preeminent research distinction during the 1970s—three Nobel Prize winners (J. Michael Bishop,[171] Harold Varmus, and Stanley Prusiner) and the co-inventor of recombinant DNA and cofounder of Genetech Corporation,[172] Herbert Boyer.[173] Bourne has sought to identify the ways in which particular structures, policies, and leadership at UCSF affected their selection and growth as faculty members and the development of their careers and accomplishments. He cites a "Great Man Theory of History" that pervades UCSF, involving as heroes "a pioneering scientist with a brilliant mind and fiery temperament" (Comroe) and "a shrewd, charismatic physician, skilled in the magic of persuading others" (Smith). There is a "dastardly villain" (Saunders). These heroes, plus others, constitute the "aces, kings, queens, and jacks ('face cards') that always appear to dominate history's otherwise anonymous deck." Finally there are the four scientists about whom he writes, who "arrived on the USCF scene unheralded and obscure, but quietly became wild cards with unexpected transformative qualities."[174] He then explores the question of what the face cards (leaders) had to do with the discoveries made by the particular wild cards (scientists) and finds the answer to be surprisingly little. The scientists arrived upon their own volitions, researched in remarkably confined and unequipped space, and largely on their own hit upon great ideas and discoveries.

But there is indeed a strong connection between the leadership, structure, and culture of UCSF and its rise toward outstanding science. In a penultimate chapter entitled, "Something in the Water: Can We

---

[168] Kerr, 2001, *op. cit.*, pp. 319–325.
[169] Bourne, 2011, *op. cit.*, pp. 30–40.
[170] Bourne, 2011, *op. cit.*
[171] J. Michael Bishop, *How to Win the Nobel Prize: An Unexpected Life in Science* (Cambridge, MA: Harvard University Press, 2003).
[172] Sally S. Hughes, *Genentech: The Beginnings of Biotech* (Chicago: University of Chicago Press, 2011).
[173] Herbert W. Boyer, interview by Sally Smith Hughes, oral history, 1996, http://content.cdlib.org/ark:/13030/kt5d5nb0zs/; https://archive.org/stream/dnaresearchucsf00boyerich#page/n7/mode/2up.
[174] Bourne, 2011, *op. cit.*, p. 4.

Bottle It?," Bourne concludes that UCSF supplied three essentials toward the careers of these outstanding researchers: "(1) the opportunity for adventures at a new frontier; (2) freedom to apply skill and passionate effort to asking questions, without unnecessary constraints from funding sources, supervisors, and pressures for quick results or conformity to prevailing views; and (3) material resources adequate to the task."[175] The first factor relates to the excitement of someone from the eastern United States coming to California to find a new and more open society, encouragement of experimentation, and the lure of a glorious outdoors capped by the Sierra Nevada mountain range.[176] With regard to the second factor, he notes the importance of a benevolent mentor, Leon Levintow, whom Bishop had followed from the National Institutes of Health to UCSF, as Varmus followed Bishop.[177] Bourne notes that the same enabling factor applied strongly to the accomplishments of James Watson and Francis Crick as they unraveled the double-helix structure of DNA[178] and cites a quote attributed to Watson, "It is necessary to be slightly underemployed if you are to do something significant." Boyer, on the other hand, found himself stifled, especially by space limitations, in the Department of Microbiology, which he did not find to provide a welcoming atmosphere. At his own instigation, he transferred to the Department of Biochemistry and Biophysics in 1975, as he recognized the very different environment provided by the approaches of William Rutter and Gordon Tompkins in that department,[179] now to described.

The actual building of the science enterprise to excellence was launched with the 1968 recruitment of William Rutter as chair of the Department of Biochemistry and Biophysics. Securing Rutter was the result of a long and arduous search that was led by Holly Smith, Bert Dunphy (head of surgery), and William Reinhardt, who was now in the position of associate dean of medicine. After a search in which "probably every good scientist in the United States had been asked to

---

[175] Bourne, 2011, *op. cit.*, chapter 11, pp. 204–228.
[176] Bourne, 2011, *op. cit.*, p. 158.
[177] Bourne, 2011, *op. cit.*, pp. 134, 145, 158.
[178] James D. Watson, *The Double Helix: A Personal Account of the Discovery of the Structure of DNA* (New York: Touchstone, 1968).
[179] Boyer, 1996, *op. cit.*, pp. 24–27.

take that job,"[180] Rutter, who at the time was professor in both genetics and biochemistry at the University of Washington, was persuaded to accept. In doing so, he indicated that he was moved in large measure by the strong interests of the clinical leaders in developing research of the highest quality in the science departments and the availability of what became twenty open faculty positions to fill.[181] Also important was a dinner set up to include Rutter and Gordon Tompkins, a capable and inspiring biochemist at the National Institutes of Health who had previously been approached for the UCSF position. Rutter and Tompkins effectively recruited one another (i.e., each was attracted by the opportunity to work with the other as a team).

A striking feature of UCSF in comparison with other medical and health science institutions became the close cooperation and valuing of one another by the research and clinical enterprises, forming "a genuine partnership that made each partner stronger."[182] There are several striking manifestations of the partnership. One was an unusual use of a "dean's tax" on clinical income that was used to support basic science.[183] Another was the involvement of three top clinicians (Smith, Dunphy, and Reinhardt) in leading the UCSF search that obtained Rutter to fill the biochemistry post, a very important position in fundamental science. A third was the prominent involvement of clinicians (Reinhardt, Smith, and others) in the effort to convince Kerr and Wellman to replace Saunders as chancellor. Rutter explains that at the time "it was unpopular to do basic science in a medical school. The best science was really being practiced outside medical schools. The relationship between the clinical sciences and the basic sciences in medical schools generally was strained, perhaps because of consistently diverging interests. There was no easy way to address mechanistically and from a molecular point of view the most important problems of clinical medicine. Science had not progressed far enough

---

[180] W. H. Rutter, interview by Sally Smith Hughes, *The Department of Biochemistry and the Molecular Approach to Biomedicine at the University of California, San Francisco: Volume 1*, p. 15, oral history, 1992, https://perma.cc/22FN-9PEZ.
[181] Rutter, 1992, *op. cit.*, p. 16.
[182] Bourne, 2011, *op. cit.*, p. 227.
[183] Bourne, 2011, *op. cit.*, p. 61.

to be able to ask sophisticated questions about complex physiology and clinical phenomena."[184]

Bourne,[185] building upon earlier observations by Smith,[186] notes that the creation of the synergistic partnership between the clinical and scientific research sides of the house required a major shift in institutional culture at UCSF that began with the transfer of the science departments back across San Francisco Bay from Berkeley to Parnassus Heights, followed by eight key developments that helped to bond the partners. Those developments were

1. Construction of both hospital and research facilities at the Parnassus site
2. Medicare, which reimbursed cost of care for many more patients and allowed recruitment of first-rate clinicians
3. Early replacement of the old guard (Saunders and others) by new leaders who valued both research and patient care
4. Early models of research excellence provided by Comroe's CVRI and William Rutter's rejuvenation of the Department of Biochemistry (see below)
5. Increasing cooperation and synergy between clinical and basic science departments
6. The fundamental discoveries of Boyer, Bishop, Varmus, Prusiner, and others, which opened avenues to understanding disease mechanisms and developing effective new therapies
7. The birth of Genentech and the biotech industry
8. Continually increasing National Institutes of Health funding.

In his introduction to Rutter's oral history, Holly Smith writes:

> Leadership is difficult to define but easy to recognize in action. There is no single style that makes effective academic leadership, which has been defined as the singular ability of an individual to stand up and pull the rest of us over the horizon. Suffice it to say that the

---

[184] Rutter, 1992, *op. cit.*, p. 16.
[185] Bourne, 2011, *op. cit.*, p. 227.
[186] L. H. Smith, introduction to oral history of H. W. Boyer, 1996, https://perma.cc/MG7C-DHR3.

arrival of the Rutter-Tomkins team almost immediately began to transform the climate of the whole basic science community at UCSF. New standards of performance were both exhibited and demanded. Bill had then, and still retains, an innate and uncanny ability to judge people. It has been said that horse sense is the good sense horses have not to bet on people. But academic leadership depends, in considerable measure, in betting on people, especially during the ascending curves of their respective careers. The appointments in Bill's department were astutely made and many of these individuals remain today as leaders of our campus. Fortunately, Bill Rutter fostered lateral dendrites as well, such that UCSF's whole basic science community synaptically improved in parallel with the transformations that were so evident in the Department of Biochemistry and Biophysics.

Several aspects of Rutter's approach and leadership at UCSF are evident in those remarks and can be summarized as follows.

- **The intellectual atmosphere that Rutter and Tomkins created and sustained.** Working with and through Tompkins, Rutter built a culture of free and open intellectual exchange where scientists would discuss problems and needs together.[187] To quote Rutter,[188] "We began developing an intensively interactive culture. We got together as a group to talk science. We developed an active seminar program." There are strong shades here of the intellectual atmosphere that arrived at Berkeley with Gilbert Lewis in 1912. Tomkins died in 1975 as a result of a tragic illness, but his style and contributions to science at UCSF survived him.
- **Building the faculty through a complementary, multidisciplinary approach.** While recognizing that faculty would need to build strong research programs of their own, Rutter and Tomkins sought and fostered collaboration and multidisciplinary approaches and focused the activities of the department broadly upon the

---

[187] Bourne, 2011, *op. cit.*, pp. 52–59.
[188] Rutter, 1992, *op. cit.*, p. 26.

structural-functional aspects of fundamental genetic macromolecules, nucleic acids, and proteins relating to human genetics. As Rutter noted, "One didn't know from which branch of science the solutions would come. The issues were multidimensional; there wasn't just one simple solution. There had to be chemical solutions, genetic solutions, structure solutions, biological solutions. If you didn't have all these approaches working collectively, the risk would be higher."[189] This emphasis fit in a very timely fashion with the explosion of fundamental knowledge and capabilities in molecular biology that was occurring at the time and placed UCSF in a prime position for discovery and accomplishment. Rutter's approach here is again reminiscent of Lewis's approach of focusing Berkeley chemistry on broad and current issues of the rapidly developing field of physical chemistry, where faculty members could reinforce one another while still having independent programs and not being so different in interests and expertise that interactions and mutual reinforcement would not be possible.

In moving toward these capabilities, Rutter generated still more open positions by encouraging those faculty members who did not fit the plan or who were unproductive or problematic in other ways to leave. He even expended considerable effort in working to get them good positions elsewhere.[190] Building a multidisciplinary team working on molecular issues of human genetics from a variety of directions was enabled by the unusually large number of faculty recruitments that could be made over a relatively short time. Rutter's personal style generated a wide spread of reactions among the faculty, particularly the younger ones,[191] but the value of his approaches and goals was so widely appreciated that he stayed on as chair of biochemistry and biophysics until 1982, a tenure of fourteen years. Joint appointments were used more sparingly, but Michael Bishop, Leon

---

[189] Rutter, 1992, *op. cit.*, p. 54.
[190] Rutter, 1992, *op. cit.*, p. 34.
[191] Bourne, 2011, *op. cit.*, pp. 56–57.

Leventow, and Herbert Boyer of Microbiology were all brought into biochemistry and biophysics through joint appointments.[192]

- **Astute judgment and assessment of the research potential of scientists.** Echoing Holly Smith's comments above, Julius Krevans, who was dean of medicine from 1971 to 1982, and chancellor from 1982 to 1993, noted that Rutter "was blessed with a sommelier's taste in judging scientific promise."[193] Rutter and Tompkins worked as a team in aggressively going out and finding and recruiting outstanding new, usually early-career, faculty members.[194] This too evokes the practices of Lewis, and later Pitzer, at Berkeley.
- **Enabling and facilitating the spread of the biochemistry and biophysics approaches to other departments.** Julius Krevans indicated that, in his role as dean of medicine, he would not release a faculty position for recruitment to other science departments unless they had someone from biochemistry and biophysics on their recruitment team. This, of course, was an effort to spread the values and judgments of Rutter, Tompkins, and their colleagues beyond their own department. That insistence initially caused resentments; for example, pharmacology simply decided not to recruit.[195] Recognition of that issue and perceptions that biochemistry/biophysics was being greatly favored budgetarily led Rutter to work to transform "ourselves from a position of being somewhat antagonistic towards the other groups to a position of helping others to develop their programs in order to develop a more distinguished scientific community." Asked if that meant that he and the department became, in effect, a catalyst, Rutter replied that was true.[196]

Another perspective on Rutter and his influence comes from Edward Penhoet, who followed Rutter as a student and coworker from the University of Illinois to the University of Washington, was close to him in the UCSF years, and then cofounded Chiron Corporation with him. Penhoet observes that Rutter has always had an intense work ethic.

---

[192] Rutter, 1992, *op. cit.*, p. 30.
[193] Bourne, 2011, *op. cit.*, p. 63.
[194] Rutter, 1992, *op. cit.*, pp. 28, 38–39.
[195] Bourne, 2011, *op. cit.*, p. 63.
[196] Rutter, 1992, *op. cit.*, pp. 31–32.

Speaking of the Rutter lab at UCSF, he says, "I've never known a place in which people worked so hard, and I think it's the main reason it's been successful. I don't think the raw talent of that group of people at UCSF in the seventies was any greater than any other place. I respect them all tremendously; that's not the point. They were a somewhat above-average group of scientists who were way above average in terms of productivity, in large part because everybody in the place worked seven days a week, eighteen hours a day. And that still exists today to some degree."[197, 198]

It is interesting to contrast Rutter's opportunity to build a cohesive, interactive, and multidimensional molecular approach to modern biology with the situation in which the Berkeley campus found itself in the late 1970s, when aspects of biology were spread out over many different departments that were divided by types of organism. Although elements of modern biology had entered many of those departments, those faculty members did not have such facile ways to interact across department lines. Berkeley's massive reorganization of biology in the early 1980s (chapter 12) was carried out so as to achieve the kind of organizational structure that Rutter and Tompkins had already been able to create, bottom up, at San Francisco. Thus the northern University of California story begins with the sciences underlying medicine being at Berkeley since shortly after the 1906 earthquake and fire and then continues with the strongest aspects of those sciences remaining at Berkeley as the science departments themselves were moved back to San Francisco in 1958. This was followed by UCSF, through Rutter and Tompkins, building a highly synergistic, multidisciplinary enterprise at UCSF, which in turn provided both the need and a key model for Berkeley to undergo its large reorganization in 1980 and subsequent years to reach the sorts of capabilities that then already existed at UCSF.

---

[197] E. E. Penhoet, interview by Sally Smith Hughes, in "Regional Characteristics of Biotechnology in the United States: Perspectives of Three Industry Insiders," p. 78, Regional Oral History Office, University of California, Berkeley, 2001, https://perma.cc/8MDR-4RC8.
[198] This same work ethic was a marked characteristic of the College of Chemistry at Berkeley that I noticed upon my arrival there in 1963. It, too, still exists today "to some degree."

The nature of the Rutter-Tompkins design for biochemistry and biophysics at UCSF positioned it well for UCSF people to take a lead role in the nascent biotechnology industry, which had and still has its major hubs of activity in California in the areas of San Francisco and San Diego (see chapter 18). Penhoet[199] summarized his views on why that was as follows:

> I think the move to the University of Washington was a crucial move for Bill in the sense that it started this whole era of the integration of biochemistry and medicine, which was [later] fully developed at UCSF. The other reason that UCSF was so powerfully involved in the early days of biotechnology was because it was pregnant with people who were really interested in gene structure and gene function. So once Herb [Boyer] and Stan [Cohen] had done the cloning experiments, their application to medicine went *whoosht*, just like that, like wildfire through UCSF. Because the place was ready to do it.

The key experiments establishing recombinant DNA technology were carried out in 1973 by Boyer and his collaborator, Stanley Cohen of Stanford, and were published in 1974. Later in 1974 Niels Reimers, heading the patent office at Stanford, filed the application for what would become the most fundamental patent for the new biotechnology industry. Following an initial meeting initiated by twenty-eight-year-old venture-capital entrepreneur Robert Swanson with Boyer in January 1976, the two of them cofounded Genentech Corporation in that same year to exploit the technology commercially.[200] In March, 2009, Genetech became part of the Roche Group for an acquisition price of $46.8 billion[201] for the outstanding shares (Roche already held shares) and has been number one in US sales of oncology products since 2006. Five years later, in 1981, Rutter, Penhoet, and Pablo Valenzuela (also a faculty member in biochemistry and biophysics at UCSF) founded Chiron Corporation, which also succeeded handsomely and is now part of Novartis.

---

[199] Penhoet, 2001, *op. cit.*, p. 79.
[200] Sally Smith Hughes, *Genentech: The Beginnings of Biotech* (Chicago: University of Chicago Press, 2011).
[201] Hoffmann–LaRoche, Ltd., "Roche and Genentech Reach a Friendly Agreement to Combine the Two Organizations and Create a Leader in Healthcare Innovation," March 12, 2009, https://perma.cc/M55V-2KYL.

Throughout the development of research stature in the 1970s and on into the 1980s and 1990s, the Parnassus Heights UCSF campus had very limited space, particularly prime research space, even though the campus did build upward there (figure 10-9). The campus acquired additional sites elsewhere in San Francisco at a former Fireman's Fund office building at Laurel Heights (1985)[202] and a complex around the existing Mount Zion hospital (1990).

Figure 10-9. Aerial view of UCSF Parnassus Heights campus, the cluster of higher buildings below Mount Sutro[203]

Finally, in 2003, an additional campus in the Mission Bay area south of downtown San Francisco was opened (figure 10-10). The site is much larger than the Parnassus Heights campus and the other sites and

---

[202] The Laurel Heights site was planned as the site for pharmacy school laboratory research and instruction, but the environmental review process evoked neighborhood concerns about laboratory projects and resulted in UCSF being restricted to nonlaboratory uses.
[203] Color photographs © 2003 by Alan Nyiri, courtesy of the Atkinson Photographic Archive, https://perma.cc/UN6W-5PNP.

has been developed by UCSF working in concert with a private developer (Catellus Corporation) and the city of San Francisco. The overall site design has been to have a central campus core of molecular biology research surrounded by hospitals and clinical services as well as by corporate laboratories and other biotechnology facilities that value proximity to UCSF Mission Bay research. There are also living accommodations for UCSF Mission Bay personnel.[204]

Figure 10-10. The initial UCSF building at Mission Bay (Genentech Hall) under construction, 2002[205]

As of 2014, UCSF had forty-nine members of the National Academy of Sciences and ninety-two members of the National Academy of Medicine. There have been five Nobel Prize winners, all in physiology or medicine:

---

[204] "The Mission Bay Campus," University of California, San Francisco, https://perma.cc/7BUP-45EH.
[205] Photograph © 2003 by Alan Nyiri, courtesy of the Atkinson Photographic Archive, https://perma.cc/Q74A-3PXK.

- 1989: **J. Michael Bishop** and **Harold Varmus**, "for their discovery of the cellular origin of retroviral oncogenes"; work done at UCSF
- 1997: **Stanley Prusiner**, "for his discovery of Prions—a new biological principle of infection"; work done at UCSF
- 2009: **Elizabeth Blackburn**, "for the discovery of how chromosomes are protected by telomeres and the enzyme telomerase"; work done at Yale, UC Berkeley, and UCSF
- 2012: **Shinya Yamanaka**, "for the discovery that mature cells can be reprogrammed to become pluripotent"; work done at the UCSF-affiliated Gladstone Institute and in Japan

Beyond its medical services to the community, UCSF has had very large beneficial effects on the economies of San Francisco, the Bay Area, and California (chapter 14). Those benefits have been achieved through catalytic leadership that capitalized on the wave of advances in molecular biological sciences that led to the biotechnology industry, as well as some very specific actions, such as the creation of the Mission Bay campus.

UC SAN DIEGO

The presence of the University of California in the San Diego area began with studies of marine biology and then oceanography. William Ritter, professor and department chair of zoology at Berkeley in 1903, developed a research tie with the Marine Biological Research Association of San Diego. Together they gained funding from the Scripps newspaper publishing family and with it in 1905 built a laboratory by the ocean shore in La Jolla, north of San Diego. The University of California took over responsibility for that laboratory in 1912, and in 1925 changed the name from Scripps Institution for Biological Research to Scripps Institution for Oceanography (SIO) to recognize the evolving mission. Over the years, the institution attracted outstanding scientists and leaders, including the following, who served as directors: oceanographers Harald Sverdrup (1936–48) and Roger Revelle (1951–61), Berkeley physicist William Nierenberg (1961–86), and astrophysicist Edward Frieman (1986–98). SIO gave UC San Diego a robust starting point by being a preexisting, first-class component, with strong scientists and leaders who could join in on designing and developing UCSD.

Roger Revelle (figure 10-11) was the major figure in the academic design and initial recruitment for UC's San Diego campus. An outstanding scientist, he was one of the first to recognize that carbon dioxide released to the atmosphere through the use of fossil fuels would bring about global warming.[206] He realized the value of bringing the science and engineering disciplines together as needed to address complex issues and did so very effectively. In the words of Clark Kerr,[207] "his great strengths were in identifying talent and recruiting it." For those interested in learning more about him, a four-volume oral history of Revelle exists[208] but unfortunately does not cover his roles in the founding of the San Diego campus of the University of California.

Figure 10-11. Roger Revelle at the Scripps Institute of Oceanography Pier[209]

---

[206] T. F. Malone, E. D. Goldberg, and W. H. Munk, "Roger Randall Dougan Revelle, 1909–1991," Biographical Memoirs, National Academy of Sciences, 1998, https://perma.cc/V8BT-K6M3.
[207] Clark Kerr, 2001, op. cit., p. 248.
[208] Roger Revelle, interview by Sarah L. Sharp, Oceanography, Population Resources, and the World, oral history, Regional Oral History Office, University of California, Berkeley, CA, vols. 1–4, 1988,
http://vm154.lib.berkeley.edu:3002/searchinterview/display?q=Roger+Revelle&commit=Search.
[209] https://perma.cc/V8JG-QL97.

As SIO director during the 1950s, Revelle urged that a full-fledged University of California degree-granting program come to San Diego in the form of an ultra-select graduate program in science and engineering at La Jolla. In this he gained the support of many leaders of the San Diego community, who saw it as a path to economic development and diversification of an economy that had been focused heavily upon military needs during World War II and thereafter.

The plan proposed by Revelle as his "Cathedral on a Bluff" had several unusual components.[210, 211, 212, 213] One was that the campus should be relatively small and directed toward multidisciplinary science and engineering, on the model of a graduate-level-only Caltech. The campus should be built from the top down, in the sense that outstanding established stars would be hired as the initial faculty. These faculty members would be hired without regard to any specific design as to which fields should be built initially; the flexibility to hire outstanding, accomplished, well-regarded people was more important. The campus would also be built from the outside in, meaning that there would be no effort to provide comprehensive coverage among disciplines or even within a discipline. The campus would be built one academic field, or a small number of fields, at a time in order to create a stimulating critical mass of scholars in each. The fields in which the initial hires were made would drive the academic direction of the campus. Academic instruction would be through multidisciplinary "divisions of instruction," and research would be carried out through three multidisciplinary institutes—the Benjamin Franklin Institute directed toward societal problems; the Alfred North Whitehead Institute which would address pure reason; and the Charles Darwin Institute devoted to the study and description of the physical world.

---

[210] Roger Revelle, "On Starting a University," unpublished paper, Scripps Institution of Oceanography Archives, circa 1983, https://perma.cc/8CEN-EP6C.
[211] Nancy S. Anderson, *An Improbable Venture: A History of the University of California, San Diego* (La Jolla, CA: UCSD Press, 1993), pp. 37–47, https://perma.cc/VE7P-KXWT.
[212] Clark Kerr, 2001, *op. cit.*, pp. 256–257.
[213] Judith Morgan and Neil Morgan, *Roger: A Biography of Roger Revelle* (San Diego, CA: Scripps Institution of Oceanography, 1996), pp. 60–61.

In 1956 the Revelle plan was reviewed by two University of California committees. In addition to review by the Academic Senate Education Policy Committee, which would occur anyhow, President Sproul appointed a university-wide committee, possibly to help offset an anticipated negative review from the senate committee. The special committee was chaired by Berkeley chemist Glenn Seaborg. It also contained Vice President James Corley, Ernest Lawrence, Joel Hildebrand, and engineering dean "Mike" O'Brien from Berkeley, as well as engineering dean L. M. K. Boelter, physicist Joseph Kaplan, and Institute of Geophysics director Louis Schlichter from UCLA. All these members were distinguished scientists or engineers except for Corley),[214] The select committee endorsed the plan, with the important exception that the members believed that the organization of the campus should be with along conventional departments rather than the institutes.[215] Despite what did turn out to be objections from the Education Policy Committee of the Academic Senate after their deliberations, described by Taylor,[216] Sproul transmitted the modified plan to the regents, who approved it in August 1956 as "a graduate program in science and technology, with such undergraduate instruction as is essential to support the graduate program."[217] With this endorsement, General Dynamics, a large employer in the area, pledged $1 million to support recruitment of faculty, and the city of San Diego voted to transfer a large tract of land near the SIO site to the university for the project.[218, 219]

The approach taken by Sproul here can be seen as another form of the strategy undertaken by Hinderaker at UC Riverside to consolidate biological sciences and agriculture into a single college (see above), and

---

[214] Angus E. Taylor, *Speaking Freely: A Scholar's Memoir of Experience in the University of California* (Berkeley: Institute of Governmental Studies Press, University of California, 2000), p. 93.
[215] Anderson, 1993, *op. cit.*, pp. 41–42.
[216] Taylor, 2000, *op. cit.*, pp. 92–104.
[217] Stadtman, *op. cit.*, p. 408; Anderson, 1993, *op. cit.*, p. 43.
[218] H. R. Wellman, interview by Malca Chall, *Harry R. Wellman, Teaching, Research and Administration, University of California, 1925–1968*, oral history, Regional Oral History Program, p. 178, University of California, Berkeley, 1976, https://perma.cc/W3U6-2Q52.
[219] Stadtman, 1970, *op. cit.*, p. 408.

that taken by Heyman and Park to restructure biological sciences at Berkeley (see chapter 12). The use of a select committee of intellectually highly respected faculty served to offset anticipated negative reactions from the Academic Senate, thereby enabling a controversial decision to be made.

The new campus opened in 1957 as the Institute of Science and Engineering, later called School of Science and Engineering at La Jolla.[220] Because of growing undergraduate enrollment pressure for UC as a whole, the Board of Regents almost immediately augmented the mission to evolve over time to "a large campus...fulfilling the functions of a major university including both undergraduate and graduate instruction..."[221] Revelle was made director of the new campus as well as of SIO, and dean of the new school.

Equipped with the plan, the regents' authorizations, and the $1 million from General Dynamics, Revelle went energetically about hiring faculty. Atkinson[222] observes that Revelle would sometimes recruit faculty before he had actual authority to do so, paying them with federal research funds and promising that when the school was officially established, they would receive their appropriate academic appointments. Several prominent Scripps Institution of Oceanography researchers became founding faculty members and were effective lieutenants to Revelle in identification of prospects and recruitment. Among them were Carl Eckart, Walter Munk, Leonard Liebermann, Ed Goldberg, Harmon Craig, and Hans Suess.[223] Among the criteria for identifying the first faculty members were a top-notch established reputation or equivalent promise and effectiveness as faculty recruiters themselves.

Revelle's first hire was indeed eye-catching—Harold Urey, the G. N. Lewis Berkeley chemistry graduate who had won the Nobel Prize in 1932 for his work on deuterium and had been at Columbia and then

---

[220] Kerr, 2001, *op. cit.*, p. 256.
[221] Stadtman, 1970, *op. cit.*, p. 408.
[222] Richard C. Atkinson, "UCSD: From Field Station to Research University," *The Journal of San Diego History* 58, no. 3 (Summer 2012): p. 156, https://perma.cc/N4KD-489M.
[223] Anderson, 1993, *op. cit.*, p. 67.

Chicago.[224] During World War II, Urey had led the scientific portion of the Manhattan Project for creation of the gaseous-diffusion process for enrichment of uranium-235. The fact that at Chicago Urey would have had to retire at age sixty-five provided the opportunity for Revelle.

Also in 1958 came James Arnold, a noted chemist who had worked on the Manhattan Project and with Willard Libby at Chicago. He had joined the Princeton faculty in 1955. Urey and Arnold were both very active in further recruiting. Keith Brueckner, a young physicist, so impressed Revelle at their first meeting that he was hired on the spot to build the physics program, which he did energetically and very effectively, as he describes in a 1994 memoir.[225] In 1960 came David Bonner from Yale, who with similar energy built the biological sciences, with emphasis on the budding and then burgeoning field of molecular biology. Arnold recruited physical chemist Joe Mayer from Chicago, who arrived in 1960 as part of a husband-wife team with physicist Maria Goeppert-Mayer, who soon thereafter received the 1963 Nobel Prize in Physics for her work on proposing the nuclear-shell model of the atomic nucleus. Indicative of the provinciality of San Diego at the time, the San Diego *Union-Tribune* ran a headline banner, "La Jolla Housewife Wins Nobel Prize." Maria Mayer had not had a faculty position while the Mayers were at Chicago because of an antinepotism policy.[226]

The University of Chicago and Bell Laboratories were particular targets for UCSD faculty recruitment. Revelle's recruitment techniques, described by Anderson,[227] made full use of the beautiful natural setting, climate, and ambience of La Jolla, as well as the excitement of his plans for the university. UC procedures required submission of appointment cases for review to the Committee on Academic Personnel of what was then the Southern Division of the Academic

---

[224] James R. Arnold, Jacob Bigeleisen, and Clyde A. Hutchinson Jr., "Harold Clayton Urey, 1893–1981, Biographical Memoirs, National Academy of Sciences, 1995, https://perma.cc/49BS-7BSV.
[225] Keith A. Brueckner, "First Years at the University of California at San Diego, 1959 to 1965," unpublished typescript, 1994, https://perma.cc/A7GV-5QV2.
[226] Richard C. Atkinson, "20/20, Reflections on the Last 20 Years of the 20th Century." Oakland, 2001. Mandeville Special Collections Library, UCSD, https://perma.cc/6JN5-22JU.
[227] Anderson. 1993, *op. cit.*, p. 73.

Senate, but the appointments were so strong that the faculty review was almost an afterthought.[228] Fifty percent of initial faculty appointments at San Diego were made at the full professor level, as opposed to 15 percent for the University of California as a whole. Many of those appointments were made at very high step levels or above scale (see chapter 11). As of 1960–61, 57 percent of the ladder (tenure-eligible) faculty members at San Diego were full professors, and 67 percent of those full professors were above scale. The 50 and 67 percent figures compared at the time with 43 and 29 percent at Berkeley and 40 and 32 percent at UCLA.[229]

This unusual and highly disproportionate emphasis on the new campus in San Diego caused much concern among leaders and faculty members at the other campuses. Although Revelle stressed that such outstanding senior faculty members would bring their own graduate students and postdoctoral scholars and be able to support their research through substantial extramural grants, it was apparent that resources were being selectively diverted to San Diego. Clark Kerr chose to resist those pressures and sustain the Revelle plan.

In 1958–60 the land of the La Jolla site was transferred to the Board of Regents. This included Camp Mathews, a US Marine Corps rifle-range base from World War II, which became the main-campus site. As the first graduate students were admitted to the campus in fall of 1960, the name was changed from School of Science and Engineering at La Jolla to University of California, San Diego.

A chancellor was then appointed later in 1960, to begin July, 1961. To the surprise of many, especially the founding faculty, that chancellor was not Roger Revelle. Instead it was thirty-nine-year-old Herbert York, who had obtained his PhD with Emilio Segre at Berkeley and had then become a Berkeley physics professor. Already with a meteoric career, he had been at age thirty the founding director of the Lawrence Livermore Laboratory (1952–58) and then had held major government posts, including chief scientist of the Advanced Research Projects Agency and director of Defense Research and Engineering within the Department of Defense, being the first occupant of both those posts.

---

[228] Anderson, 1993, *op. cit.*, pp. 72–73.
[229] Kerr, 2001, *op. cit.*, p. 255.

The faculty role in the selection process for chancellor is described by Taylor.[230] He notes that the faculty advisory committee—of which he was a member along with Glenn Seaborg, Harold Urey, and others—put forward six names, with Kenneth Pitzer, Revelle, and York among them. Kerr[231] indicates that an appointment of Revelle would have had to contend with several problems. First, Revelle had gotten into a major public dispute with Edwin Pauley, a long-time regent and a powerful force within both the state and the nation, over the matter of a site for the campus. As is described by Revelle,[232] Kerr,[233] Anderson,[234] and others, Pauley favored Balboa Park in downtown San Diego and was very negative on the La Jolla site. (Atkinson indicates that in addition, or possibly instead, Pauley favored taking over San Diego State University,[235] a possibility that may also have been favored by President Malcolm Love of SDSU.[236]) Second, there were strong opinions from civic leaders in both San Diego and La Jolla that Revelle was out of step politically with the relatively conservative community, that he was too outspoken and too radical. He had taken a vocal and public-leadership role against the loyalty oath in the late 1950s (see chapter 2), and he had worked to eliminate a La Jolla Real Estate Brokers Association ban on deeds to anyone "whose blood is not entirely that of the Caucasian race."[237] Finally, there was opposition from other chancellors because Revelle stood for something different and highly resource-intensive in La Jolla.

While none of these factors, in themselves, would have been an absolute reason for bypassing Revelle, Kerr perceived that the main overall difficulty was that Revelle could come across as contemptuous of his opponents and unable to show "any empathy toward the other's feelings." He was not a diplomat. Kerr[238] concluded, "Roger Revelle was

---

[230] Taylor, 2000, *op. cit.*, pp. 131–132.
[231] Kerr, 2001, *op. cit.*, pp. 247–250.
[232] Revelle, ca. 1983, *loc. cit.*
[233] Kerr, 2001, *op. cit.*, pp. 241–243.
[234] Anderson, 1993, *op. cit.* pp. 59–61.
[235] Atkinson, 2012, *op. cit.*, pp. 158–159.
[236] Taylor, 2000, *op. cit.*, p. 95.
[237] Morgan and Morgan, 1996, *op. cit.*, pp. 57–58.
[238] Kerr, 2001, *op. cit.*, p. 250.

the creator of the San Diego campus; Herb York was its builder as a fully operational campus. The university needed both of them."

Herb York was chancellor for three years, from July 1961 through June 1964. He succinctly labeled his initial chancellorship as "not my cup of tea."[239] He indicates that he accepted Revelle's plans virtually in their entirety. In his previous administrative posts, he had been accustomed to what was to him a straightforward authoritarian style of leadership, and thus the roles of the Academic Senate, particularly in faculty hiring and review and in curriculum development, were new to him, and he saw them as limiting his authority. There was an initial tendency for the faculty to be antagonistic, given York's background in nuclear-weapons work at Livermore and in the government.[240] Anderson assesses the situation as York "working with a collection of faculty members described in scholarly circles as a gifted group of outlaws who saw in San Diego the chance to shed the constraints of ordinary university life."[241] Although respect was gained on both sides over time, York in late 1963 asked Kerr to initiate a search for a successor. York then went on to become vice chair of the US President's Scientific Advisory Council (PSAC) and then returned to UC San Diego as professor and director of the Institute on Global Conflict and Cooperation for the remainder of his career. He was acting chancellor at UCSD from 1970 to 1972 (see below), as the campus recovered from a period of intense student agitation over the Vietnam War and related issues, and he served as US ambassador to the Comprehensive Test Ban negotiations in Geneva from 1979 to 1981.

Plans for undergraduate education and the organizational structure surrounding it were developed by a committee spearheaded by Jim Arnold. This committee produced the concept that UCSD would be composed of a series of separate colleges containing two thousand to twenty-five hundred students each. There would be both undergraduate and graduate students in the colleges, and faculty members would be associated with individual colleges as well. Each college would be headed by a provost and would provide the

---

[239] Herbert F. York, *Making Weapons, Talking Peace: A Physicist's Odyssey from Hiroshima to Geneva* (New York: Basic Books, 1987), pp. 206–217.
[240] Anderson, 1993, *op. cit.*, pp. 84–89.
[241] Anderson, 1993, *op. cit.*, p. 84.

atmosphere of a smaller institution, including social life and sports. Much, then later some, of the instruction that students would take would be provided within the college, and the colleges would have different academic emphases reflected in their general-education requirements.[242, 243] That approach is, in effect, the Oxford and Cambridge model that was earlier implemented in the United States at Harvard, Yale, and Princeton through houses, residential colleges, and eating clubs, respectively. It would be instituted at the Santa Cruz campus of UC in a different form (see below).

The first college, ultimately named for Revelle, was formed from the preexisting School of Science and Engineering and opened in 1964 with an entering class of 180 students. All were freshmen, since transfer students would not have met the Revelle College requirements.[244] The college system continues in existence to this day, now with twenty-five thousand undergraduate students distributed among six colleges. The current individual emphases and requirements of the different colleges (Revelle, John Muir, Thurgood Marshall, Earl Warren, Eleanor Roosevelt, and Sixth) are described on the UCSD website.[245] The histories of each are reviewed by Anderson.[246]

Kerr[247] observes that the colleges "became successful residential and social communities for students and centers for organized activities by students, but they did not become as successful as centers for faculty-student intellectual life as had first been hoped. Faculty members, by and large, did not enter into college activities." The same can be said for the equivalent structures at Harvard, Yale, and Princeton.

There were three relatively public disputes between the campus leadership and the university-wide administration during the early years, all described by Kerr[248] and Wellman[249] from their own

---

[242] Brueckner, 1994, *loc. cit.*
[243] Anderson, 1993, *op. cit.*, pp. 85–87.
[244] Wellman, 1976, *op. cit.*, p. 177.
[245] "Welcome to UC San Diego: A Guide to Understanding the College System," https://web.archive.org/web/20171213130750/http://provost.ucsd.edu/colleges/.
[246] Anderson, 1993, *op. cit.*, pp. 189–208.
[247] Kerr, 2001, *op. cit.*, pp. 273–276.
[248] Kerr, 2001, *op. cit.*, pp. 257–259.
[249] Wellman, 1976, *op. cit.*, pp. 179–180.

viewpoints. One concerned the medical school, both its size and the desire of David Bonner and others to emphasize research, particularly in molecular biology.[250] In this sense, UC San Diego was ahead of both UC San Francisco and Berkeley in recognizing the importance of molecular and structural biology to medicine and as an extremely rapidly developing field. The medical school did come into being and both had and still retains a strong, molecular research base, with multidisciplinary approaches and close integration between research and clinical operations. In this and other ways UCSD has had strong and supportive intellectual ties over the years with its two neighbors on the Torrey Pines mesa that emphasize medical biology—the Salk Institute for Biological Studies[251] and the Scripps Research Institute.[252] The second dispute concerned whether there would be a third great library within UC, in addition to those at Berkeley and UCLA.[253] John Galbraith, the second chancellor, played his demands out in the media and even delayed his inauguration in an effort to get Kerr to supply the desired large acquisitions budget. The third confrontation concerned moving along construction of the library building itself and led to a Galbraith's resignation, which he subsequently reversed at Kerr's request.[254]

UC San Diego had relatively rapid turnover of chancellors in early years, attributable to personal characteristics, the fact that managing such a distinguished assemblage of academic stars was no easy thing, and student unrest. As already noted, York asked to be replaced after only two years. John Galbraith, who followed York, lasted three years and publically squabbled with the university-wide administration, using the threats noted above in efforts to get what he wanted. He was, in effect, negotiated out of office by Kerr. Following Galbraith, an effort was made to get Berkeley chemist Kenneth Pitzer as chancellor, but Pitzer, who had been president of Rice University from 1961 to 1968, was already in negotiations with Stanford University for its presidency and declined the UCSD opportunity.[255] That search then turned to William McGill, who was at the time chair-designate of the San Diego

---

[250] Anderson, 1993, *op. cit.*, pp. 154–180.
[251] "Salk Institute for Biological Studies," accessed May 21, 2016, http://www.salk.edu.
[252] "The Scripps Research Institute," accessed May 21, 2016, http://www.scripps.edu.
[253] Anderson, 1993, *op. cit.*, pp. 91–97.
[254] Anderson, 1993, *op. cit.*, pp. 97–103.
[255] Anderson, 1993, *op. cit.*, p. 115.

Division of the Academic Senate. McGill's tenure from 1968 to 1970 was marked by the arrival of massive student unrest and protest about the Vietnam War and related issues, which clashed strongly with the largely conservative values of the San Diego community.[256] The story of that period has been engagingly recorded by McGill.[257] McGill was then recruited away to become president of his alma mater, Columbia University, where he also had to deal with student protest.

Herb York was brought back as acting chancellor from 1970 to 1972, during which period the university waited for the campus to regroup following the protests before seeking a permanent chancellor. The person eventually recruited was biologist William McElroy, who had been director of the National Science Foundation. McElroy was chancellor from 1972 through 1980. However, toward the end of his time as chancellor, while McElroy also dealt with personal problems, there had been a major squabble within the administration, a perceived lack of consultation with the Academic Senate, and an informal vote of no confidence at an Academic Senate meeting. McElroy's private indications to faculty leaders that he would resign shortly did not forestall the faculty senate seeking a mail-ballot vote. Equipped with the negative formal vote, faculty leaders went to then-president Saxon seeking McElroy's removal.[258, 259]

To replace McElroy, Saxon and the regents chose Richard Atkinson, who, like McElroy, had also been director of the National Science Foundation. Atkinson was a strong stabilizing force. He was well liked and had a very successful chancellorship from 1980 to 1995, when he became president of the University of California. His approach to dealing with the situation that he found at UCSD is told by Pelfrey[260] and at greater length in his own memoir.[261] First and foremost, he gave attention to the faculty and the culture of excellence. He took a direct interest in faculty recruitments, mentioning an approach that he had learned from Fred Terman, long-time Stanford provost. The idea was to

---

[256] Anderson, 1993, *op. cit.*, pp. 113–129.
[257] William J. McGill, *The Year of the Monkey* (New York: McGraw-Hill, 1982).
[258] Atkinson, 2001, *op. cit.*, pp. 6–7.
[259] Patricia A. Pelfrey, *Entrepreneurial President: Richard Atkinson and the University of California, 1995–2003* (Berkeley: University of California Press, 2012), pp. 30–31.
[260] Pelfrey, 2012, *op. cit.*, chapter 3, "The Education of a Chancellor," pp. 29–37.
[261] Atkinson, 2001, *op. cit.*, pp. 10–11, 13–15, 24–30.

pay careful attention, as a member of the National Academy of Sciences, to the names that had just missed election to the academy in a given year. Recruitment of those faculty members would lead to excellent faculty members as well as a strong likelihood that they would be elected to the academy soon after their arrival at UCSD. Secondly, Atkinson moved promptly and with respect for people in making the changes in senior administrative positions that were needed following the very public squabbles at the end of McElroy's time. Third, to enhance relations with the faculty, he established a full-time position of associate to the chancellor, filled for one- to three-year periods by senior faculty members who participated in all Chancellor's Office activities, giving a direct faculty viewpoint. He met regularly with the chair of the San Diego Division of the Academic Senate, included that person in the Monday morning meetings of the chancellor's council, and made efforts to respect and utilize shared governance.

With regard to his position vis-à-vis the faculty, Atkinson cites[262] in translation a passage on leadership from the *Tao Te Ching* of Lao Tzu, a sixth-century BC Chinese philosopher:

> He does not make a show of himself
> Hence he shines
> Does not justify himself
> Hence he is glorified
> Does not boast of his ability
> Hence he gets his credit
> Does not brandish his success
> Hence he endures
> Does not compete with anyone
> Hence no one can compete with him.

This is good counsel for any university administrator. Related to that advice, the San Diego campus maintains an extremely unpretentious Chancellor's Office complex consisting of a group of small and low Californian buildings among much larger and architecturally imposing

---

[262] Atkinson, 2001, *op. cit.*, p. 25; see also Richard C. Atkinson, preface to C. Stewart Gillmor, *Fred Terman at Stanford: Building a Discipline, a University, and Silicon Valley* (Stanford University Press, 2004).

buildings used for other purposes. These buildings are left over from the US Marines base that preceded the campus.

Figure 10-12. Jacobs School of Engineering, UC San Diego[263]

Although engineering had existed at UC San Diego as of the hiring of Sol Penner in 1964,[264] it had not been placed into a school or college. After Atkinson's arrival as chancellor, it became first the Division of Engineering and then the School of Engineering.[265] An interesting family tree[266] shows the evolution of engineering at UCSD through 2005. By design, academic coverage has not been comprehensive, concentrating instead, à la Revelle, on applied science, areas of opportunity, and interdisciplinary activity. For example, there is currently a Department of NanoEngineering. As is the case for the rest of UCSD, the engineering school (figure 10-12), now named after

---

[263] Photograph © 2003 by Alan Nyiri, courtesy of the Atkinson Photographic Archive, University of California, https://perma.cc/RSP8-LC6L.
[264] Anderson, 1993, *op. cit.*, p. 143.
[265] Atkinson, 2001, *op. cit.*, pp. 30–31.
[266] "Jacobs School Family Tree," *Pulse*, Spring 2005, https://perma.cc/AV5R-PFEZ.

Qualcomm founder Irwin Jacobs (chapter 18), is highly ranked nationally and internationally.

Through Atkinson, Mary Walshok, and others, UCSD has had a particularly catalytic and synergistic relationship with the San Diego business community in support of technological innovation and new business enterprises. This too is described in chapter 18.

Achievements and Summation

Clark Kerr[267] observed, "San Diego was an instant success. It came to be one of the four American research universities that started out in the front ranks. The three others were Johns Hopkins in the 1870s, and Stanford and Chicago in the 1890s." This is a remarkable accomplishment for a public university. The other three universities that Kerr identified are all private and were well endowed from the start. This result testifies directly to the strength of the Revelle plan.

Anderson notes that by the late 1980s, not yet thirty years after the first graduate students entered, UCSD had sixty-four members of the National Academy of Sciences and eight Nobel laureates. Winners of six National Medals of Science, two Pulitzer Prizes, two Fields Medals in mathematics, and six MacArthur Foundation fellowships had taught at UCSD, and the faculty had collectively received over one hundred Guggenheim Fellowships.[268] As of 2014–15 there have been sixteen Nobel Prizes associated with the UCSD faculty, and there are eighty-five UCSD members of the National Academy of Sciences,[269] twenty-three members of the National Academy of Engineering, and thirty-eight members of the Institute of Medicine. There are five current (2016) members of the UCSD faculty who are winners of Nobel Prizes:[270]

- 1990 Economic Sciences: **Harry M. Markowitz** with Merton H. Miller and William F. Sharpe, "for their pioneering work in the

---

[267] Kerr, 2001, *op. cit.*, p. 254.
[268] Anderson, 1993, *op. cit.*, p. 1.
[269] "UCSD Faculty Members of the National Academy of Sciences," Academic Affairs, University of California, San Diego,
https://web.archive.org/web/20170124153620/https://academicaffairs.ucsd.edu/faculty/awards/nas.html.
[270] "UCSD Faculty Winners of the Nobel Prize," Academic Affairs, University of California, San Diego,
https://web.archive.org/web/20171011142219/https://academicaffairs.ucsd.edu/faculty/awards/nobel.html.

theory of financial economics"; work done at University of Chicago and RAND Corporation
- 1995 Chemistry: **Paul Crutzen and Mario Molina**, Scripps Institution of Oceanography, joint with F. Sherwood Rowland, "for their work in atmospheric chemistry, particularly concerning the formation and decomposition of ozone"; work done at Stockholm University by Crutzen and at UC Irvine by Molina
- 2003 Economic Sciences: **Robert Engle** with Clive W. J. Granger, "for methods of analyzing economic time series with time-varying volatility (ARCH)"; work done at UC San Diego
- 2008 Chemistry: **Roger Tsien** with Osamu Shimomura and Martin Chalfie, "for the discovery and development of the green fluorescent protein, GFP"; work done at UC San Diego

In addition to these active faculty members, other Nobelists with UCSD connections[271] are Harold Urey and Maria Goeppert-Mayer (both already mentioned), Hannes Alfven (Physics, 1970), Walter Kohn (Chemistry, 1998), William Moerner (Chemistry, 2014), Francis Crick (Chemistry, 1962), George Palade (Physiology or Medicine, 1974), Renato Dulbecco (Physiology or Medicine, 1975); Robert W. Holley (Physiology or Medicine, 1968); Roger Guillemin (Physiology or Medicine, 1977); Sydney Brenner (Physiology or Medicine, 2002), and Clive Granger (Economic Sciences, 1990).

UC San Diego was admitted to the Association of American Universities (AAU) in 1982, the shortest time since founding for any AAU member university. Atkinson describes the strategy and process for achieving that membership.[272]

Kerr[273] states the reasons for the success of UCSD as follows:
> It had the reputation of the University of California; the resources of a then-prosperous state of California; access to the federal funds that followed Sputnik; and an original building block in the world-famous Scripps Institution of Oceanography; the charismatic leadership of Revelle, who

---
[271] "List of Nobel laureates by University Affiliation," *Wikipedia*, accessed May 21, 2016, https://perma.cc/QU5K-43SB.
[272] Atkinson, 2001, *op. cit.*, p. 22.
[273] Kerr, 2001, *op. cit.*, pp. 254–255.

had a gift for identifying and recruiting academic talent, as well as clear preference in the assignment of new resources (for faculty appointments and book acquisition funds) from the regents and from the president of the university—preference over the two other new campuses [Irvine and Santa Cruz], over the metamorphosing campuses of Davis, Santa Barbara, and Riverside, and even over Berkeley and UCLA. No vote had established this preference. It was the result of an unspoken agreement.

Unquestionably, the start from the highly respected Scripps Institution of Oceanography was important, if for no reasons other than establishing values and a culture of excellence. The exquisite Revelle plan was critically important too, emphasizing as it did hiring target-of-opportunity faculty stars of the first magnitude who would in turn attract other faculty members with strong accomplishments or high potential. The start with the graduate program was effective for establishing the importance of research and enabling a start in selected fields (those corresponding to the faculty targets of opportunity) without necessitating the broad coverage needed for the subsequent undergraduate program.

The Revelle plan had to be enabled through funding, which was available from California's thriving economy, strong state support of the university, and presidential decisions that gave San Diego high priority. Other key enabling factors were the dynamic enthusiasm of Revelle and his initial senior hires and the magnificent La Jolla Torrey Pines setting above the Pacific. Another vital factor was a vibrant and supportive community that included leaders who saw the values of both an outstanding research university and valuable companion institutions such as the Salk Institute and the Scripps Research Institute.

The undergraduate colleges have worked out well at UCSD, providing more cohesive social, sports, and living activities for students, even though they have not been able to hold as much independent intellectual life as originally planned.

The faculty has been a constant and stabilizing strength, offsetting what was a relatively volatile turnover of chancellors in the early years. When leadership was needed it was there, notably during the student unrest of the late 1960s, when there was a large need to retain the bond with, and the support of, the politically conservative San Diego community. Chancellors McGill, York (during his second, acting, term), and Atkinson were particularly important for that purpose.

UC IRVINE

Irvine was another of the three new campuses of the 1950s. Like Merced and Santa Cruz, it started from nothing—no preexisting program or even physical structures. It was part of the general development of the huge Irvine Ranch, 480 square kilometers (185 square miles) of what is now Irvine, California, and vicinity. The city of Irvine is also a planned community that started de novo from land of the Irvine Ranch.

Clark Kerr picked Daniel Aldrich to be the founding UC Irvine chancellor. Aldrich had started with UC as a soil chemist at the UC Citrus Experiment Station and subsequently became professor and then chairman of the combined Berkeley/Davis Soils Department. Following that, he was university-wide dean for agriculture, having succeeded Harry Wellman when Wellman was moved to the position of vice president of the university by Kerr.[274] Aldrich's disciplinary background was not a match to the new general campus, but his manner and effectiveness both as a leader and in dealing with people were strong matches.

---

[274] Samuel C. McCulloch, *Instant University: The History of the University of California, Irvine, 1957–93* (Irvine, CA: University of California, 1994), pp. 7–9.

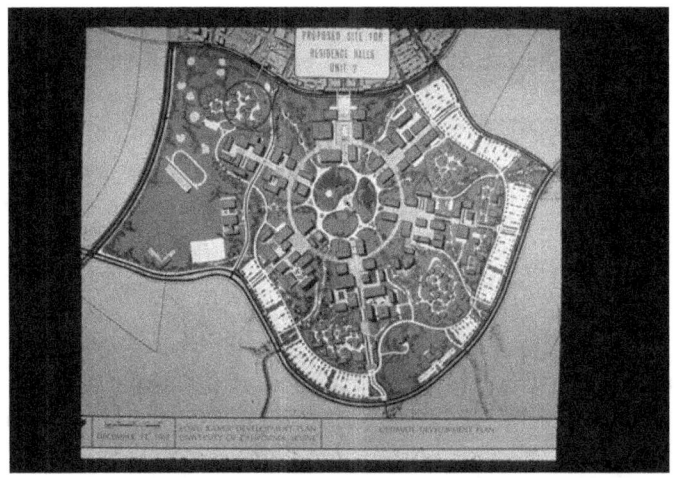

Figure 10-13. (a) Original 1962 plan for the Irvine campus of the University of California (above)[275]; (b) aerial view of Irvine campus, circa 2006 (below)[276]

---

[275] https://perma.cc/R8KD-HX6K.
[276] "University of California, Irvine," *Wikipedia Commons*, Poppashoppa22 at en.wikipedia, https://per3ma.cc/JV92-DWZM.

Starting from undeveloped, bare land presented an opportunity for an innovative physical plan for the campus. The striking plan that came into being (concentric circles with paths and roadways as radial spokes) was suggested by Kerr himself, drawing from his memory of the plan for a model city from Johann Heinrich von Thünen's *Der isolierte Staat*, 1863.[277] The original plan[278] for the layout of the campus is shown in figure 10-13a, paired with an aerial view of the nearly fully built-out campus in figure 10-13b. One goal of the design is to make pedestrian circulation throughout the campus more efficient. Another is to maximize opportunities for interaction among the disciplines.

The principal architect for the campus was William Pereira, who had also worked on the San Diego campus and elsewhere within UC. Pereira's design of the Irvine campus is regarded as one of his principal works, along with the Transamerica Tower in San Francisco, the Geisel Library at UC San Diego, and the Dickson Art Center at UCLA. The design remains striking and effective now that the campus is essentially built out. The innermost circular core is a tranquil park of twenty-one acres, denoted as Aldrich Park, where campus events such as inaugurations of chancellors are held. Additional description and photographs of the initial construction are given by Masters.[279] The campus was dedicated in June, 1964 (Figure 10-14).

Among the three new UC campuses of the 1960s, UC Irvine deviated the least from the standard academic model of a research university. San Diego had followed the Revelle plan, and Santa Cruz was a bold experiment of a different sort, as described below. Aldrich's initial plan was that the campus should open as a full university, enabled by both physical and academic design to grow to the then-contemplated maximum UC campus enrollment of 27,500 students. Aldrich wanted to start with some professional schools as well, for balance and in recognition that the political dynamics, both inside the

---

[277] Johann Heinrich von Thünen, *Von Thünen's Isolated State: An English Edition*, translated by Carla M. Wartenberg (New York: Pergamon, 1966).
[278] "Phsical Design Framework: A Vision for the Physical Environment at the University of California, Irvine", pp. 10-12, University of California, Irvine, January 2019, https://perma.cc/XQN8-3KKN.
[279] Nathan Masters, "Terraforming the Irvine Ranch and the Construction of UC Irvine," KCET Public Television, November 3, 2015, https://perma.cc/44WX-59VX.

campus and within UC, for adding professional schools later on could be difficult.

Figure 10-14. President Lyndon B. Johnson (*center*) at the site dedication[280] for the Irvine campus, June 20, 1964. Others (*left to right*) are Vice Chancellor Ivan Hinderaker, Chancellor Dan Aldrich, UC president Clark Kerr, and California governor Edmund G. ("Pat") Brown.[281]

Fleshing out and implementing this general plan was left to the initial vice chancellors for academic affairs, Ivan Hinderaker (1962–64) and then Jack Peltason (1964–67), who was selected for the position when Hinderaker became chancellor of the Riverside campus on short notice in 1964 to deal with the difficult situation there. Early in his career, Hinderaker had been in the Minnesota State Legislature.[282] He had then been professor and chairman for a few years of the Political

---

[280] Joseph N. Bell, "25 Years Ago, Lyndon Johnson Came to Irvine," *Los Angeles Times*, June 24, 1989, https://perma.cc/36ZW-6GQD.
[281] Courtesy of Regents of the University of California, IC Irvine Archives, https://perma.cc/N7VG-EAUJ.
[282] Kerr, 2001, *op. cit.*, p. 317.

Science Department at UCLA. He was recommended by Dean McHenry at UCLA through Kerr to Aldrich, who met with Hinderaker and appointed him.[283] Peltason had been dean of liberal arts at the University of Illinois. Despite an original decision to separate the traditional College of Arts and Sciences into physical sciences, humanities, and so on, a super-dean position, dean of arts, letters, and science, was created for Peltason so as to draw him to the campus.[284] When he actually arrived a year later in 1964, that position was abolished, and he became vice chancellor for academic affairs, succeeding Hinderaker.

A distinguished political scientist, Peltason was the author of a widely used textbook, *Government by the People*, which went through many editions. He returned to Illinois as the first chancellor of the Urbana campus in 1967, when the University of Illinois became a multicampus university, staying until 1977, when he became president of the American Council on Education (ACE) in Washington, DC. In 1984 he returned to Irvine as chancellor and occupied that position until 1992, when he became president of the University of California, 1992–95. With regard to why he came to Irvine, Peltason noted that he and his wife had always wanted to live in California and that he had said to his good friend Austin Ranney, later a Berkeley political science professor, while they sat together on the beach there, "If you ever start a university in Newport Beach, California, count me in."[285, 286] Newport Beach directly adjoins Irvine.

Several innovations were attempted as Aldrich, Hinderaker, and Peltason drew up plans for academic development. Aldrich wanted to stress activities on campus that would be relevant to needs of society. This led to early development of cultural programs for the community and university extension for continuing education. Emphasis on

---

[283] McCulloch, 1994, *op. cit.*, p. 20.
[284] Ivan Hinderaker, interview by Samuel C. McCulloch, pp. 20–22, 1974, https://perma.cc/3PAF-B8B7.
[285] Jack W. Peltason, interview by Ann Lage, "Jack W. Peltason, Political Scientist and Leader in Higher Education, 1947–1995: Sixteenth President of the University of California, Chancellor at UC Irvine and the University of Illinois," oral history, p. 155, Regional Oral History Center, University of California, Berkeley, 1998, https://perma.cc/Q9YF-JXVR.
[286] Hinderaker, 1998, *op. cit.*, p. 26.

environmental concerns was sought in program design. The builders also wanted to become leaders in the use of information technology for instruction, but they were too far ahead of the time when much could be done. There were also several innovations in academic organizational structure. One already noted was the use of divisions with deans for physical sciences, biological sciences, social sciences, humanities, and fine arts, without an overall college of Letters and science structure. Another was the division of biological sciences into departments by the level of organism, as was also done at UC San Diego and would come much later at Berkeley through a difficult reorganization (chapter 12). Psychology was divided into social psychology and neuropsychology. The former later became the innovative School of Social Ecology. This feature was placed into Hinderaker's own initial draft for the academic plan based upon comments that he had heard at UCLA.[287] Instead of a classical school of business or management, the School of Administration was created, covering administration of all sorts, including the public arena, as has also been tried at Yale. Over time, however, that school has morphed into a more conventional business-management school.[288] A single Department of Comparative Literature was created, as opposed to individual departments covering literature on a language-by-language basis.[289] This latter aspect of the plan did not work out well and was later abandoned.[290]

The academic recruitment plan adopted and pursued by Hinderaker and Peltason was to hire deans first, then chairs, and then faculty, taking advantage of the more specific knowledge and contacts of the deans and chairs to locate and select faculty members.[291] This approach was used in all cases but one. The founding department chairs in physical sciences—Sherwood Rowland, chemistry (recommended by Willard Libby of UCLA); Kenneth Ford, physics (recommended by Herb York); and Bernard Gelbaum, mathematics, from the University of Minnesota—were hired before the founding

---

[287] Hinderaker, 1974, op. cit., p. 5.
[288] Peltason, 2001, op. cit., p. 185.
[289] Kerr, 2001, op. cit., pp. 260–261, 270–272.
[290] Peltason, 2001, op. cit., p. 169.
[291] Peltason, 2001, op. cit., p. 176.

physical sciences dean, Frederick Reines, and took part in the search that led to Reines.[292] For the other dean recruitments, Hinderaker and Peltason looked within UC, used contacts around the country, and followed up on leads from Kerr and others. The other founding deans were

- Biological Sciences: Edward Steinhaus, chair of the Division of Invertebrate Pathology at UC Berkeley,
- Director of Special Studies and then also dean of the Graduate Division: Ralph Gerard, international authority on brain function,
- Humanities: Samuel McCulloch, dean of the college at San Francisco State College (later University),
- Social Sciences: James March, professor of psychology at Carnegie Institute of Technology,
- Fine Arts: Clayton Garrison, chair of drama at UC Riverside,
- Graduate School of Administration: Richard Snyder, chair of political science at Northwestern University, and
- School of Engineering: Robert Saunders, chair of electrical engineering at Berkeley.[293]

Others whom Hinderaker[294] mentions unsuccessfully trying to recruit are George Pimentel of the Berkeley chemistry department, for dean of physical sciences;[295] William Bowen of Princeton and Richard Lyman of Stanford, each subsequently president of those respective institutions; and Charles Hitch, the assistant secretary of defense, who became Kerr's successor as UC president.

Peltason observed that when he arrived in 1964, there were seven academics, and then there were 157 faculty members appointed as of a year later when the campus opened,[296] 119 of whom were on hand on opening day. These faculty members had an average rank at the mid-associate-professor level and an average age of thirty-six.[297]

---

[292] Peltason, 2001, *loc. cit.*
[293] McCulloch, 1994, *op. cit.*, pp. 27–30.
[294] Hinderaker, 1974, *op. cit.*, p. 17–18, https://perma.cc/H2RY-N9K3.
[295] Ivan Hinderaker, interview by Jan Erickson, "Transcription of an Oral History Interview with Ivan and Birk Hinderaker, June 5, 1998,"p. 24, https://perma.cc/E3Y7-GPXZ.
[296] Peltason, 2001, *op. cit.*, p. 164.
[297] McCulloch, 1994, *op. cit.*, pp. 21, 55.

The UC Irvine approach of hiring deans first, then chairs, and then faculty contrasts sharply with the Revelle plan for UC San Diego. At UC San Diego, superstar faculty were sought and hired first, thereby letting initial fields and emphases be defined by who those faculty members turned out to be. Irvine covered fields broadly and by design, having both undergraduate and graduate education at the start. San Diego made no attempt for comprehensive coverage at the start and enabled that choice by starting graduate education before undergraduate education. The San Diego plan was pitched almost exclusively toward outstanding research, while the Irvine plan sought both teaching coverage and excellent research at the start. San Diego sought research stardom from the start and counted on those stars to attract high-quality faculty and graduate students, while Irvine counted on its ability to select promising initial faculty members who were earlier in their careers but held the potential for growth toward star status.

Both campuses succeeded in their very different ways. San Diego made the larger initial splash and has continued to ride the momentum of it with great success. But the Irvine strategy has clearly led to a reputational success too, although longer in coming. Two manifestations of the worth of the Irvine strategy were Sherwood Rowland[298] and James McGaugh, who were hired at ages thirty-seven and thirty-two, respectively, both arriving in 1964 as founding faculty members. Rowland won the Nobel Prize in Chemistry in 1995 for his work at Irvine identifying chlorofluorocarbons as the major cause of destruction of ozone in the stratosphere, while McGaugh won many national and international honors, became a member of the US National Academy of Sciences (1989) and the equivalents in Mexico and Brazil, succeeded Steinhaus in 1967 as dean of the School of Biological Sciences, and then went on to become vice chancellor and executive vice chancellor. He also founded and for many years directed the Center for the Neurobiology of Learning and Memory. Frederick Reines, who came in 1966 as the initial dean of physical sciences, also won the Nobel Prize in Physics (1995) for his lifelong work on the neutrino. He came from Case Institute of Technology, where he was

---

[298] Regarding the hiring of Rowland, see Ivan Hinderaker, 1998, *op. cit.*, p. 24, https://perma.cc/E3Y7-GPXZ.

chair of the Physics Department, and had spent World War II at Los Alamos.[299]

Peltason himself,[300] upon reflection years later, observed, "That's one of the best recruiting jobs I know of...I'm very proud of the recruiting job we did: one of the largest numbers of people recruited in the shortest period of time who turned out subsequently to be distinguished academics. The only other [such successful] recruiting task I know of was Woodrow Wilson's famous recruitment of fifty preceptors to Princeton[301] at the turn of the century."

All three of the campuses that were new in the 1960s were equipped with Advisory Committees, composed of faculty members from other campuses.[302] This approach and its utility are explored by Douglass.[303] The membership was determined by Kerr[304] in consultation with the Academic Senate, and the committees acted in a number of senate roles, interfacing with the rest of the UC Academic Senate structure. The committee would be consulted on initial appointments to both administrative and faculty positions, serving as the Budget Committee (Berkeley) or Committee on Academic Personnel (other campuses) would function on an established campus. At times the committee members would also assist with recruitments themselves. The importance and help of this committee for the initial development of the Irvine campus are stressed by both Peltason and Hinderaker.[305] The approach did much to instill the culture, value systems, and respect for excellence of the university as a whole into these new campuses.

Another person who helped greatly in recruitment was the architect Willam Pereira. Peltason[306] notes, "Bill Pereira and Dan

---

[299] McCulloch, 1994, *op. cit.*, p. 70.
[300] Peltason, 2001, *op. cit.*, p. 163.
[301] John M. Cooper, *The Warrior and the Priest: Woodrow Wilson and Theodore Roosevelt* (Cambridge, MA: Harvard University Press, 1983), pp. 93–95.
[302] For the compositions of these committees, see Kerr, 2001, *op. cit.*, vol. 1, p. 487.
[303] John A. Douglass, "Planning New UC Campuses in the 1960s: A Background Paper for UC Merced on the Role of the Universitywide Senate, Center for Studies in Higher Education (CSHE)," https://perma.cc/B68X-6GLN.
[304] Peltason, 2001, *op. cit.*, p. 165.
[305] Hinderaker, 1974, *op. cit.*, pp. 10, 23.
[306] Peltason, 2011, *op. cit.*, p. 165.

[Aldrich] had the physical plan, and when you're recruiting people you can't show them anything, and there aren't any students, and there are no alums; you're selling them a dream. Bill Pereira was a very persuasive salesperson, as was Dan...We'd bring in the recruits, and this very sophisticated, world-famous planner spent a lot of time helping us recruit faculty. Although he built the Transamerica building and a lot of famous buildings, I think building the Irvine campus was one of the things of which he was proudest."

Academic recruitment continued under subsequent vice chancellors James McGaugh and William Lillyman, filling out the faculty. One important joint recruitment was that in 1989 of Ralph and Carol Cicerone, a distinguished atmospheric chemist from the National Center for Atmospheric Research and a distinguished psychologist from the University of Colorado, respectively. Ralph Cicerone became UCI chancellor (1998–2005) and then president of the National Academy of Sciences (2005 until his death in 2016).

One important aspect of the academic development of the Irvine campus did not come by design, but instead by serendipity and politics. The California College of Medicine, a private institution in Los Angeles, had until recently been focused on osteopathic medicine. It was in a failing financial position but was supported strongly by the one physician in the state senate, who was also in a very strong position as chair of Senate Committee on Finance. Adequate state funding for the development of UC's other medical schools thereby became linked with UC taking over the California College of Medicine, staff and all. Such an agreement was made in 1963, and the transfer was made at the request of the university through action of the state legislature. There were then protracted negotiations both inside and outside the university over the affiliation and then a relocated site for the newly acquired college of medicine. Finally, it was determined that it would be best to move the college administratively to UC Irvine, and in 1966 Chancellor Aldrich agreed with some reluctance.

Acceptance by the Irvine campus had been debated intensely within the Irvine Academic Senate, which had, however, neither supported nor opposed the addition to the campus. The acquisition was also disturbing to the initial fundamental-biology faculty, and it contributed to a decision by one of the best known of them to transfer to UC San Diego. In hindsight, this was probably the only way in which Irvine would have gotten a medical school, since four others (San Francisco, Los Angeles, Davis, San Diego) were already in existence within UC. But the campus received a relatively undistinguished organization with no hospital and a bundle of problems along with a need to provide facilities for the existing school at the Irvine campus.[307]

Years later and following much controversy, the issue of a hospital for the Irvine campus was finally resolved in a semisatisfactory way that also had large political overtones: the university acquired a county hospital in Anaheim, twelve miles away from the campus.[308]

The following Nobel Prize recipients were or are with UC Irvine:
- **F. Sherwood Rowland**, Chemistry, 1995, jointly with his UCI postdoctoral associate, Mario Molina, "for their work in atmospheric chemistry, particularly concerning the formation and decomposition of ozone"
- **Frederick Reines**, Physics, 1995, "for the detection of the neutrino"
- **Irwin Rose**, Chemistry, 2004, "for the discovery of ubiquitin-mediated protein degradation"

As of 2015, UC Irvine had twenty-five members of the National Academy of Sciences,[309] eight members of the National Academy of Engineering, and six members of the National Academy of Medicine.[310]

In his comments looking back on the academic building of UC Irvine, Peltason reflected:

> It's a miracle that major campuses were built in such a short time. It was the genius of the University of California and the wealth and the strength of the state of California that you could do so. There was the excitement of one of the world's greatest universities giving you a fresh start to go out there and start over...We received [positive support] both from the

---

[307] McCulloch, 1994, *op. cit.*, pp. 90–103; Kerr, 2001, *op. cit.*, pp. 370–371; Peltason, 2001, *op. cit.*, pp. 186–187; Wellman, 1976, *op. cit.*, pp. 168–170.
[308] Peltason, 2001, *op. cit.*, pp. 322–336.
[309] Pat Brennan, "UCI's Shaul Mukamel Elected to National Academy of Sciences," University of California, Irvine, https://perma.cc/S5ME-GDBN.
[310] "Wallace Elected to Institute of Medicine," University of California, Irvine, https://perma.cc/J6BL-GKBU.

faculty senate and from the Office of the President...They had been supportive without trying to be controlling. I think that's very important in the development of new campuses. It helps explain why the University of California has been so successful in permitting new campuses to develop and in maintaining quality...The Office of the President was very helpful. Clark was always available...The Office of the President has to champion the new campus. I now know that from my own experiences three decades later. Existing campuses don't understand the need for new campuses. [311]

UC SANTA CRUZ

The third new campus opening in the 1960s was innovative and experimental in several ways. The driving idea pushed by Clark Kerr and Dean McHenry, the founding chancellor (1961–74), was to create a campus that could sustain the approach and benefits of small-college education as the campus grew to what was to be the 27,500-student enrollment then contemplated for all campuses. As such, it was much more designed and sustained than were the short-lived attempts at Santa Barbara and Riverside in the 1953–58 period. Emphasis was to be on undergraduate instruction and the student experience.

The Approach

The initial guiding concepts for the campus are described by McHenry[312] and Kerr.[313] McHenry also describes the process by which these guidelines were formulated, including examination of Oxford, Cambridge, Harvard, Yale, Princeton, the Claremont Colleges, and the newer British universities built on the residential college model. The essential concept was to have an assemblage of small colleges, each overseen by a provost and with student populations averaging seven

---

[311] Peltason, 2001, *op. cit.*, pp. 165, 171, 174.
[312] Dean E. McHenry, "Academic Organizational Matrix at the University of California, Santa Cruz," in Dean E. McHenry and Associates, eds., *Academic Departments: Problems, Variations, and Alternatives* (San Francisco: Jossey-Bass, 1977), pp. 86–116.
[313] Clark Kerr, 2001, *op. cit.*, pp. 261–266.

hundred, which together would compose a full-size University of California campus. Given the target of ultimately enrolling 27,500 students, of which perhaps 70 percent would be undergraduates in the arts and sciences and 50% of those would be housed on campus, there would then be about fourteen such colleges eventually.[314] Initially, they would be built, staffed, and opened at a rate of one per year. Each college would have its own particular emphases and would have a multidisciplinary collection of faculty associated with it according to the academic design and emphases of the college.

Among the complex realities to be dealt with for any model of this sort are
- the division of functions, both academic and nonacademic, between the levels of the individual colleges and the overall campus;
- the means of gaining the additional revenue needed for the greater costs associated with repetitive functions within the colleges and for a lower student-to-faculty ratio to promote high-quality undergraduate education; and
- the ways in which a greater emphasis on, and quality of, undergraduate education can be achieved within the context of what is still a research university, in recognition of the natures of the entire university system and the Master Plan.

The site chosen for the campus provided both opportunities and limitations. It was land of the Cowell Ranch above the beachside city of Santa Cruz on the north side of Monterey Bay in central California. The other site under serious consideration had been the Almaden Valley area, just south of San Jose in Santa Clara County. However, for the latter site, many different properties would have had to be acquired from different owners, and the known interest of the regents in the area had caused property values to increase considerably. Interest therefore shifted to the Cowell Ranch site, which was a magnificent setting of a redwood forest surrounding grassland with sweeping views down to Monterey Bay. That site was purchased from the S. H. Cowell

---

[314] Dean E. McHenry, "University of California, Santa Cruz," in V. Ray Cardozier, ed., *Important Lessons from Innovative Colleges and Universities*, New Directions for Higher Education, no. 82 (San Francisco: Jossey-Bass, Summer 1993).

Foundation, which also provided a grant of over $900,000 toward ongoing support of the first college, to be known as Cowell College. The university thereby gained a handsome site but lost an opportunity to have a campus directly adjoining what was to become Silicon Valley in the fast-growing South Bay.[315, 316] The less urban character of the site that was chosen bolstered the part of the plan that called for accommodating 50 percent of undergraduate students on campus residentially in the colleges, as opposed to the 20 percent figure typical for other UC campuses.

The academic case for the Santa Cruz college approach is presented by Kerr,[317] McHenry,[318] and Noreña,[319] among others. The realities and difficulties associated with the plan and encountered in practice are outlined starkly by Robert Sinsheimer,[320, 321] who was the fourth Chancellor (1977–87).

What Happened over Time

Clark Kerr classifies four successive eras in the development of the Santa Cruz campus—the neoclassical, the countercultural, backlashes, and stabilization.[322] The reasons for those names should become apparent from this narrative.

Originally the plan was that all academic functions would belong to the colleges as they were built. However, in its review of the original academic plan, the Committee on Education Policy of the university-wide senate noted, "A college transmits knowledge; a university creates it" and then urged "more formal organization of faculty by

---

[315] Stadtman, 1970, *op. cit.*, p. 413.
[316] Kerr, 2001, *op. cit.*, pp. 245–246.
[317] Kerr, 2001, *op. cit.*, pp. 261–266.
[318] McHenry, 1977, *loc. cit.*
[319] Carlos G. Noreña, *The Rise and Demise of the UCSC Colleges* (Berkeley: Public Policy Press, Institute for Governmental Studies, University of California, 2004).
[320] Robert L. Sinsheimer, *The Strands of a Life: The Science of DNA and the Art of Education* (Berkeley: University of California Press, 1994), https://publishing.cdlib.org/ucpressebooks/view?docId=ft5j49p04r&chunk.id=d0e4022&toc.depth=1&toc.id=d0e3458&brand=ucpress.
[321] Robert L. Sinsheimer, interview by Randall Jarrell, "The University of California, Santa Cruz during a Critical Decade, 1977–1987," oral history, University of California, Santa Cruz, 1996, https://escholarship.org/uc/item/0mp6n2rx.
[322] Kerr, 2001, *op. cit.*, pp. 280–283.

departments."[323] During the first year of operation of the campus (1965–66) the Academic Senate put forth a plan where there would, in addition to the colleges, be boards of study in each disciplinary area that would set requirements for the major, provide for a comprehensive examination, and propose graduate degrees.[324] Faculty members would have joint appointments—50 percent associated with the college and 50 percent associated with a board, and thereby the discipline. A position for recruitment was then determined by a college and a board getting together and agreeing to combine their respective half positions. Given the nature of the faculty positions, academic reviews and requests for advancement or promotion were done by both the college and the board. About twenty-three boards were established, all thinly and unevenly staffed with faculty.[325]

Another innovation from early on was the use of a narrative evaluation system (NES) for grading of courses. This was introduced by Page Smith, the initial provost of Cowell College and was adopted the next year by the Santa Cruz Division of the Academic Senate.[326] Instead of receiving a letter grade, a student would receive either a pass or a fail (later changed to no report), together with a narrative evaluation of performance. This approach was believed to be more nuanced and useful than a simple letter grade. Students in science courses could receive a letter grade if they petitioned for it, but petitions were rare.[327] The NES was controversial, to say the least, with concerns that it would handicap students who would seek graduate work elsewhere, especially in professional schools. Also, in practice the narratives were inconsistent in quality and conscientiousness. Through the Academic Senate, the faculty reviewed this policy and tweaked it in various ways over the years, moving generally toward letter grades. In 2001 the use of letter grades for all courses became mandatory.[328]

---

[323] Kerr, *op. cit.*, p. 278.
[324] McHenry, 1977, *op. cit.*, pp. 101–102.
[325] Sinsheimer, 1994, *op. cit.*, p. 168.
[326] Noreña, 2004, *op. cit.*, pp. 76–77.
[327] McHenry, 1977, *op. cit.*, p. 111. McHenry notes that for an academic quarter in the mid-1970s, only 0.003 percent of the grades issued were letter grades.
[328] M. R. C. Greenwood, interview by Randall Jarrell and Irene H. Reti, "From Complex Organisms to a Complex Organization: An Oral History with UCSC Chancellor M. R. C. Greenwood, 1996–2004," oral history, University of California, Santa Cruz, 2014, https://escholarship.org/uc/item/9hv2j5t9.

Spreading Excellence: Developing New Campuses

Figure 10-15. Aerial view of Crown (*left, upper*) and Merrill (*right, lower*) Colleges, the third and fourth of the UC Santa Cruz colleges, showing the typical setting among the redwood trees[329]

The colleges, years of opening, and initial emphases have been
    Cowell, 1965, world civilization;
    Stevenson, 1966, self and society;
    Crown, 1967 (figure 10-15), science, culture, and man;
    Merrill, 1968, (figure 10-15) poverty at home and abroad;
    Porter, 1969, visual and performing arts;
    Kresge, 1970, educational innovation;
    Oakes, 1972, skills and community service;
    Eight, 1972 (figure 10-16), the environment;
    Nine, 2000; and Ten, 2002 – no emphases yet
Among the first four colleges, Cowell College received over $900,000 from the S. H. Cowell Foundation, Crown College received an

---

[329] Photograph © 2003 by Alan Nyiri, courtesy of the Atkinson Photographic Archive, https://perma.cc/RGS4-8APP.

endowment of $500,000 from the Crown-Zellerbach Foundation, and Merrill College $650,000 from the Charles Merrill Trust. The Stevenson name was sought by the initial provost, in honor of two-time presidential candidate Adlai E. Stevenson, without a corresponding endowment. In hindsight, these endowments were much too low to address the extra expenses associated with the college model.

Figure 10-16. College Eight, UC Santa Cruz.[330]

The designs and emphases of the colleges were left to the initial provosts to formulate, with quite varied results, as is evident from the list above. Kerr[331] and Sinsheimer[332] both describe the problematic situation that involved Kresge College and a provost who established sensitivity training, as well as courses where students took the lead

---

[330] Photograph © 2003 by Alan Nyiri, courtesy of the Atkinson Photographic Archive, University of California, https://perma.cc/5WYJ-JRQW.
[331] Kerr, 2001, *op. cit.*, pp. 281–282.
[332] Sinsheimer, 1994, *op. cit.*, p. 169.

with faculty in the role of facilitators, an approach known now as a form of the flipped classroom.

The original plan for the Santa Cruz campus entailed engineering, and early steps were taken in that direction, including the recruitment of Francis Clauser, a distinguished aeronautical engineer at Johns Hopkins University, as dean. However, the California Coordinating Council for Higher Education (the forerunner of the Postsecondary Education Commission—chapter 5) chartered Frederick Terman, then ex-provost of Stanford, to carry out a major study of engineering education within California.[333] Terman's report,[334] released in the spring of 1968, maintained that small engineering programs were economically inefficient and specifically recommended that the nascent programs on two UC campuses (Riverside and Santa Cruz) should not be pursued.[335] In accord with this recommendation, President Hitch decided that both programs should be abandoned. This episode, with unfortunate timing and result, cost the Santa Cruz campus its one professional school, a solid tie with the community, and what would have been an early, crucial link with Silicon Valley as it developed over the hills to the north. Santa Cruz was not able to initiate engineering until thirty years later in 1997. In 2003 UCSC opened a University-Affiliated Research Center (UARC) jointly with the Ames Research Center of the National Aeronautics and Space Agency at Moffitt Field at the northern edge of Silicon Valley.[336] The UARC has served to enhance engineering education and foster ties with Silicon Valley companies.

Several other problem areas developed as the number of colleges multiplied and the population of Santa Cruz evolved. The most fundamental academic problem stemmed from the roles of the

---

[333] This was the second study made by Terman of engineering education needs in California. The first, in which he chaired a committee commissioned by the then-existing Liaison Committee in the early 1950s, addressed the interests of the state colleges for providing engineering education (see chapter 5).

[334] For the background, development, and general content of the report, see C. Stewart Gillmor, *Fred Terman at Stanford: Building a Discipline, a University, and Silicon Valley* (Stanford University Press, 2004), pp. 455–459.

[335] Sinsheimer, 1994, *op. cit.*, pp. 174–175. For Richard Atkinson's comments on the implications of this report for the San Diego campus, see Atkinson, 2001, *op. cit.*, pp. 30–31.

[336] "Welcome to the University Affiliated Research Center (UARC)," University of California, Santa Cruz, https://perma.cc/Z5Z8-BZ4U.

colleges and the boards and the duality of the faculty appointments between the two. Simsheimer[337] described the situation succinctly:

> Conceptually, the boards of study were to be merely coordinating bodies. But, inevitably, the demands of disciplinary education and the need for provision of an appropriate range and depth of courses within each field began to be felt. Although a faculty member nominally held a 50 percent appointment in a board and a 50 percent appointment in a college, educational control gradually but inexorably shifted to the boards. Disciplinary pressures increased within the boards and courses given by faculty within the colleges became for the most part increasingly peripheral and "Mickey Mouse," and their requirement increasingly resented by many faculty members. And, inevitably, since the boards and colleges competed for the same always inadequate pool of funds, the tension between these two organizational sets, with their nearly orthogonal missions, increased...The college-board structure was supposed to produce "creative tension"; instead it produced deadlock. This became particularly manifest in the recruitment and promotion of faculty.

> With their "themes," the colleges had their own recruitment agendas. But each faculty appointment had to be in a board as well, which had *its* recruitment agenda. Frequently, these requirements were in conflict, for which there were three possible solutions. In times of rapid growth, two appointments could be made available, one to satisfy each agenda. As growth slowed, this option became unavailable. Or sometimes the board's first choice and the college's first choice could be bypassed in favor of a second-choice candidate, probably inferior to either first choice but more broadly acceptable. Peace was preserved, but at a price. Or, finally, the issue could be passed up to the central campus administration for resolution, which left one side happy and the other bitter. Faculty promotions and

---

[337] Sinsheimer, 1994, *op. cit.*, p. 168.

particularly tenure reviews brought these conflicts to a head. The boards and the colleges simply had different missions and correspondingly different criteria. The board valued scholarship, research, and professional teaching and was generally in accord with the system-wide UC standards. The college valued service in the college, counseling and working with students, teaching in interdisciplinary college courses, and participation in "college building" (especially in the early years). The college functioned more like a club. Junior faculty, who often had been encouraged to devote their energies to collegiate affairs at the expense of their research and scholarship, now found themselves caught. Tenure decisions for a member of the faculty were made in both one's board and one's college. Understandably, these frequently diverged. Indeed, individual senior faculty, members of both the board and the particular college, were known to vote oppositely in the two circumstances using different criteria. The divergent votes would then be reviewed by the Academic Senate Committee on Academic Personnel, a six-person body and, depending on their inclinations preferentially to value board or college service, they would frequently produce a split vote. Which left the decision to the central campus administration—that is, the chancellor. Most often, the chancellor tended to uphold the disciplinary or board standard as most consistent with broad UC standards, from which Santa Cruz had never been exempted. Then, as such negative tenure decisions most often resulted in the departure of an often well-liked member of a college, faculty and students in the college were outraged. Thus, "creative tension" became a constant irritant, a boil on the campus ambience.[338]

Compounding this problem, as had been the case for the original Riverside college, most of the initial Santa Cruz faculty members had

---

[338] Sinsheimer, 1994, *op. cit.*, pp. 169–170.

been hired at the entry level, and thus progressed into tenure and promotion decisions more or less together.[339, 340]

The primary external issues related to the changing population of the city of Santa Cruz during the late 1960s and early 1970s. Originally, the university campus had been a major attraction, seen as a way of reviving a sagging beach-resort economy. The population trends included several very different factors.[341] First there was an influx of the hippie culture that had developed in the San Francisco Bay Area in the 1960s. Second, there was substantial influx of persons whose employment was to the north, over the hills in Silicon Valley, and who valued the semirural aspect of Santa Cruz and Aptos. The third factor was the growth of the university population, most notably the students themselves, who along with other college and university students in California were enabled by a 1971 California Supreme Court decision to vote in the communities where they resided as students. These three factors, each in their own way, created a considerable problem of town-gown relations—one that still exists.

Another pervasive problem was budget, or really the lack of it. Simply put, the funding for the campus was in proportion to enrollment, as it was for other campuses, and yet the Santa Cruz campus had to deal with the added costs associated with distribution of academic functions and services to the colleges. As already noted, the initial endowments made for colleges were not large enough to make much difference.

Faced with these problems, in his last year (1973) as chancellor, McHenry went to the UC Regents requesting that the growth plan for the campus be scaled back to a cap of 7,500 students for at least the next decade.[342] This request was not approved, given the overall enrollment pressure then foreseen for the university.

The person chosen as McHenry's successor as chancellor was Mark Christensen (1974–76), who had been academic vice chancellor at Berkeley. He was unable to come up with, or steer through,

---

[339] Sinsheimer, 1994, *op. cit.*, p. 224.
[340] Kerr, 2001, *op. cit.*, p. 290.
[341] Sinsheimer, 1994, *op. cit.*, p. 176.
[342] Sinsheimer, 1994, *op. cit.*, p. 177.

solutions to the problems.[343] Sufficient unhappiness prevailed so that then-president Saxon asked Angus Taylor, the former vice president for academic affairs, to go to Santa Cruz as chancellor for a year to settle the waters, start on needed changes, and serve until the time was right for a search for a new chancellor to be engaged. Taylor did so effectively, although he could not and did not make major changes. He describes his time at Santa Cruz in an engaging oral history.[344]

The new chancellor, starting in 1976, was Robert Sinsheimer, a Caltech molecular biologist who had headed the Division of Biology at Caltech. In both an autobiographical book[345] and an oral history,[346] Sinsheimer describes the situation as he saw it and what he decided to do about it.

First, a new, menacing problem raised its head—declining enrollment. For the first few years after opening in 1965, Santa Cruz had drawn outstanding students (the highest SAT scores among UC campuses) and was oversubscribed. But several factors soon combined to start a noticeable decline in applications for admissions as of 1971, which became a 22 percent decline in 1975.[347] The Berkeley campus, which was a direct competitor geographically, recovered from its student-unrest problems of the mid-1960s, and a substantial amount of the radical student element found its way to Santa Cruz, in part because of the general environment and the attractions for radical elements on campus such as the nature of Kresge College, described above. Sinsheimer[348] described what happened as follows:

> This "radical" image combined with the soft "no-grade" image to create a vision of Santa Cruz as a far-out, laid-back campus where one went to flake out and smoke pot under the redwoods, not a serious academic locale. While doubtless attractive to some, this image further deterred many more

---

[343] Daniel H. McFadden, interview by Randall Jarrell, "The Chancellor Mark Christensen Era at UC Santa Cruz, 1974–1976, University of California, Santa Cruz, 2012, https://escholarship.org/uc/item/98s606j3.
[344] Angus E. Taylor, interview by Randall Jarrell, "UCSC Chancellorship, 1976–77," oral history, University of California, Santa Cruz, 1998, https://escholarship.org/uc/item/42j3c98r.
[345] Sinsheimer, *op.. cit.*, 1994.
[346] Sinsheimer, *loc. cit.*, 1996.
[347] Randall Jarrell, preface to Taylor, *loc. cit.*, 1998.
[348] Sinsheimer, *op. cit.*, p. 172, 1994.

prospective students...And then, in the early 1970s, the Santa Cruz community was the scene of several shocking murders, two involving a campus employee. Santa Cruz became known as the "murder capital," and enrollment applications plummeted.

Sinsheimer took two main steps to deal with the enrollment matter. First, he hired Richard Moll, formerly of Bowdoin College, who was an energetic and effective,[349] albeit controversial,[350] admissions director, a forerunner of the enrollment-management directors now common in private higher education. Second, he made an arrangement with Berkeley whereby Berkeley would refer to Santa Cruz UC-eligible freshman applicants whom they had no room to admit, with the commitment that with satisfactory performance in the first two years they could then transfer to Berkeley as juniors. Sinsheimer[351] notes that about half of such students who did come to Santa Cruz in that way chose to stay rather than transferring to Berkeley as juniors.

Still, the largest issues requiring attention were the conflict in values between the colleges and the boards, its effect upon faculty recruitment and promotion, and how the structure could be adapted to a UC budgeting process that did not allow for the extra costs associated with the college setup. This then led in 1978 to what became known as the Rearrangement, the essential elements of which[352] were (1) placing faculty recruitment, promotion, and advancement completely with the boards rather than split between the boards and the colleges; (2) reclustering faculty members among the colleges so as to aggregate kindred interests in one or several colleges, thereby creating affinity groups that did not exist when the faculty members were fully dispersed among colleges; and (3) cutting the courses within the colleges back to just a core set so as to improve the budgetary situation. The plan was essentially Sinsheimer's own design. There was an elaborate process, including a large multifaceted campus committee

---

[349] Sinsheimer, *op. cit.* pp. 189–190.
[350] Michael Cowan, interview by Irene Reti, "It Became My Case Study: Professor Michael Cowan's Four Decades at UC Santa Cruz," p. 209, 2013, https://escholarship.org/uc/item/3j5438d7.
[351] Sinsheimer, 1994, *op. cit.*, p. 193.
[352] Sinsheimer, 1996, *op. cit.*, pp. 22–27; Cowan, *op. cit.*, pp. 212–213.

that is described by Cowan[353] and senate roles, by which the plan was assessed and eventually accepted with a 75–80 percent positive faculty vote.[354] Sinsheimer[355] describes his guiding concepts as follows:

> Academic standards are the *sine qua non* of a major university. To maintain and improve the standards of the disciplines was a primary step in the recovery of the image of Santa Cruz. To accomplish this, the diversion of resources into second-rate college courses had to be stopped. The influence of the colleges had to be removed from personnel decisions so that the faculty had a clear set of academic goals. The vitiation of the intellectual life of the disciplines caused by the dispersion of faculty among all eight colleges had to be ended by establishing intellectually coherent groups of faculty in each discipline in at most two or three colleges.
>
> At the same time, I wished to maintain the colleges as intellectual and cultural centers in the liberal arts tradition, as well as residence facilities. There would be several diverse groups of faculty in each college and a mix of students with varied interests. Each college would be required to provide a freshman "core" course on some broad topic of interest to its faculty—funds would be provided for this purpose. As available, funds might also be provided for other college-based endeavors that fell outside the scope of any discipline.

Robert Stevens, who as chancellor from 1987 to 1991 succeeded Sinsheimer, added the fine-tuning of increasing the academic budgets for the colleges but to nowhere near their original levels, while focusing student services to a greater degree centrally.[356] Stevens had from 1978 to 1987 been president of Haverford College, a prominent private liberal arts college with 1,300 enrollment. He had difficulties meshing into the system of shared governance of the University of California, and upon his departure, a longtime UC person, Karl Pister, who had been dean of engineering at Berkeley, was brought in, first as

---

[353] Cowan, 2013, *op. cit.*, p. 214.
[354] Sinsheimer, 1996, *op. cit.*, p. 26.
[355] Sinsheimer, 1994, *op. cit.*, pp. 187–188.
[356] Robert B. Stevens, interview by Randall Jarrell, "Robert B. Stevens: UCSC Chancellorship, 1987–1991," pp. 30, 41–46, 1999, https://escholarship.org/uc/item/95h8k9w0.

interim chancellor and then as chancellor following the expressed desires of the Santa Cruz faculty. Pister indicates that he endeavored to resuscitate some of the originally intended academic aspects of the college system further but that faculty sentiment was by then generally too much opposed for that to happen.[357]

The structure and academic nature of the campus have remained largely unchanged since the rearrangement. The boards are now simply called departments. The colleges parallel the Harvard houses and the Yale residential colleges, in that the provosts now equate roughly comparably in function to the masters[358] of those bodies, and the college activities are very largely directed to sports, organizations, and social functions. Under Chancellor Stevens an agreement was reached with the city of Santa Cruz to limit the enrollment to fifteen thousand, a figure unusually low for UC campuses. That figure was subsequently raised to seventeen thousand, which is the approximate present enrollment of the campus. Of this enrollment, only 9 percent in 2014 was at the graduate level, the lowest percentage for any UC campus other than Merced, which in 2014 was at 6.1 percent. Riverside and Santa Barbara, the next lowest, were at about 12.5 percent. One of the purposes of budgetary "rebenching" within the university (chapter 6) was to enable growth in the percentage of graduate students enrolled at the Santa Cruz campus.

In terms of current academic recognition, UCSC has achieved preeminence in astronomy[359] through an outstanding collection of faculty members and its stewardship of the UC participation in the Keck ten-meter telescopes atop Mauna Kea in Hawaii, the Lick Observatory, and the current project for a thirty-meter telescope (chapter 2). The stature of UCSC in astronomy can be traced back to Clark Kerr's decision[360] to place the Lick Observatory above San Jose with the new Santa Cruz campus, so as to give it a unique focus for academic development. As of 2014, fourteen members of the National Academy

---

[357] Karl S. Pister, interview by Randall Jarrell, "Karl S. Pister, UCSC Chancellorship, 1991–1996," pp. 52–54, 2000, https://escholarship.org/uc/item/7pn93507.
[358] The use of the title *Master* was discontinued at both Harvard and Yale in 2016.
[359] See, for example, A. L. Kinney, "The Science Impact of Astronomy PhD Granting Departments in the United States," https://arxiv.org/ftp/arxiv/papers/0811/0811.0311.pdf.
[360] Kerr, 2001, *op. cit.*, p. 266. This decision was of course strongly resisted at the time by the Berkeley astronomy faculty.

of Sciences are associated with UCSC. A recent study[361] using data compiled by Thomson-Reuters in *University Science Indicators* [362] reviewed the average number of times that faculty research papers are cited in papers by other researchers and found that, overall, UC Santa Cruz was the top public university, behind only Harvard, Caltech, and MIT.

Retrospectives

Many people have looked back over the history of the Santa Cruz campus seeking lessons to be learned. Kerr himself dwells upon the balance of factors, recognizing that the initial objective was probably too much of a dream and wishing that he had been able to be more involved himself in the initial implementation.[363] An early comparative analysis by Grant and Riesman[364] was generally quite favorable toward the concept academically, painting a picture of probable success in a niche market. The initial UCSC chancellor, Dean McHenry, who worked with Kerr on the concepts and was on the ground for the implementation, has left us much in the way of retrospectives.[365, 366, 367] Noreña[368] has provided a thorough introspective on the colleges approach, arguing that the Sinsheimer Rearrangement went much too far. Sinsheimer [369, 370] is the most succinctly critical—for example, in the following passages:

---

[361] "University of California, Santa Cruz, Accountability Profile," University of California, https://perma.cc/HA7K-YQTF.
[362] See Thomson Reuters, INCITES, https://perma.cc/9537-CVWN.
[363] Kerr, 2001, *op. cit.*, vol. 1, pp. 293–301.
[364] Gerald Grant and David Riesman, "To Seem Small as It Grows Large," in *The Perpetual Dream: Reform and Experiment in the American College* (Chicago: University of Chicago Press, 1978), pp. 263–290.
[365] McHenry, 1977, *loc. cit.*
[366] McHenry, 1993, *loc. cit.*
[367] Dean McHenry, interview by Elizabeth Spedding Calciano, *Founding Chancellor of the University of California, Santa Cruz* (3 vol.), oral history, UC Santa Cruz, University Library, Regional History Project, vol. 1: 1972; vol. 2: 1974; vol. 3: 1987 (coeditor, Randall Jarrell), https://escholarship.org/uc/item/34r6t4d5.
[368] Noreña, 2004, *loc. cit.*
[369] Sinsheimer, 1996, *op. cit.*, p. 94.
[370] Sinsheimer, 1994, *op. cit.*, pp. 167, 272–273.

I feel [UC] Santa Cruz was betrayed in three ways. It was betrayed by Kerr and McHenry because...they had this great vision and they simply did not think through how they could do this within the University of California....In an experimental lab, the *E. coli* aren't going to complain if there is a fault in the experiment and they are wasted. But people are. UCSC was betrayed by the community which invited it here and then turned on them.... And third, in a sense it got betrayed by the system in that after Kerr left...nobody in the system felt any obligation to foster this experiment.[371]

The question is how to implement the original concept of having a group of four-year liberal arts colleges—a cluster of colleges. Quite aside from the question of how you would integrate such a structure internally, how do you do this within the UC system and under the Master Plan, which says the UC system is a research university, which has quite different demands on its faculty than the demands made on the faculty at Swarthmore or Haverford. How do you do this within a system which is geared to kind of large, mass undergraduate education with the economies that that provides, again compared to a good first-rate liberal arts college, which operates at a much higher cost per student? You don't have the money. So where is that money supposed to come from? To illustrate, again, it doesn't square with the Master Plan.[372]

Tapper and Palfreyman[373] have examined the UCSC experiment in some depth, concluding, among other things, that the difficulties and failures result from an inability to couch in the American context the values that have driven and supported Oxford and Cambridge in the United Kingdom. They conclude that neither a public-funded collegiate university independent of UC nor direct public funding of UCSC's college system makes practical sense. Similar viewpoints are offered by

---

[371] Sinsheimer, 1996, *op. cit.*, pp. 38–39.
[372] Simsheimer, 1996, *op. cit.*, p. 94.
[373] Ted Tapper and David Palfreyman, "Pragmatic Reformer as Romantic Radical? Clark Kerr and the University of California at Santa Cruz," in Sheldon Rothblatt, ed., *Clark Kerr's World of Higher Education Reaches the 21st Century: Chapters in a Special History* (Berlin: Springer, 2012), pp. 183–205.

Duke.[374] Finally, there are many oral histories available,[375] most notably the insightful reflection by Cowan.[376]

Concluding Thoughts

The University of California, Santa Cruz, has been an experiment in public higher education that has been much analyzed and evaluated. While conclusions and opinions certainly vary, the most common view is that the original design, providing education in small colleges placed together within a large university-campus framework, was a goal that had large difficulties fitting within a public research university such as the University of California. If the goal was to have a high-stature research faculty, the structure of joint appointments in colleges and disciplinary boards severely hampered the recruitment, nurturing, and evaluation of faculty. If the goal was to de-emphasize the research roles of the faculty, then, following Sinsheimer, the campus design was not consistent with the California Master Plan for Higher Education or the natural value system of a research university.

However, the fact that the colleges do exist today in the setting of a major public university is itself an accomplishment not to be belittled. The colleges provide a situation where the students within them know one another and socialize together. This goes a long way in overcoming the usual, largely nonresident, nature of public research universities and is a particular strength of both the Santa Cruz and San Diego campuses of the University of California.

The Santa Cruz campus was started in an era of abundant public funding for public higher education but encountered difficulties in accommodating the more intensive college type of instruction within the standard state budgetary framework of the University of California. Since then we have entered an era of declining public financial support and a need for public universities, particularly major research universities, to develop additional sources of funding from diverse private sources. Would this move to new funding models better enable

---

[374] Alex Duke, "The University of California, Santa Cruz: The City on a Hill" in *Importing Oxbridge* (New Haven, CT: Yale University Press, 1996).
[375] "Institutional Oral History of the University of California, Santa Cruz," University of California, Santa Cruz, https://perma.cc/35B7-36XX.
[376] Cowan, 2013, *loc. cit.*

the success of the original Santa Cruz design? Put another way, could the Santa Cruz college model draw endowment and other sustaining private funding particularly well? Currently the emphases of major foundations run to matters of access and throughput in higher education. However, some large private donors might be captivated by an opportunity to make the college model work, following the thoughts of Rhoades[377], Grant and Riesman[378] and Tapper and Palfreyman[379] that a UCSC could effectively serve a niche market. There would still be the issue of sustaining the remaining public funding as lawmakers question the more expensive type of education.

The major design and leadership issues associated with the Santa Cruz campus have been compounded by four instances when emergency interim or new leadership was needed in connection with the turnover of chancellors. Specifically there was the 1976 interim chancellorship of Angus Taylor to recover from the difficulties of the Christensen era, the 1991 appointment of Karl Pister in the wake of severe governance issues that developed during the Stevens era, the appointment of Martin Chemers as acting chancellor following the departure of M. R. C. Greenwood to become provost and senior vice president of academic affairs of the University of California in 2004, and the appointment of the current chancellor, George Blumenthal, following the suicide of Chancellor Denice Denton in 2008.[380]

UC MERCED

Timing and Securing Land Use

As described in chapter 2, the site for Merced campus was chosen by the Board of Regents in July 1995 following an extensive site-selection process. The original 1988 proposal from President Gardner

---

[377] Gary Rhoades, "Distinctive Choices in Intersecting Markets: Seeking Strategic Niches," in R. L. Geiger, C. L. Colbeck, R. L. Williams, and C. K. Anderson, eds., *Future of the American Public Research University* (Rotterdam: Sense Publishers, 2007), pp. 121–143.
[378] Grant and Riesman, 1978, *loc. cit.*
[379] Tapper and Palfreyman, 2012, *op. cit.*, pp. 193–195.
[380] See, e.g., Paul Fain, "Too Much, Too Fast," *Chronicle of Higher Education*, January 19, 2007.

had a new campus opening in 1998. What then occasioned the delay, such that the new campus opened seven years later in 2005? The answers are the volatility of the state's economy, a variety of political factors, and environmental permitting issues. As is explained in chapter 2, the California state budget is highly subject to changes in the economy. The economy took sharp downturns in both the early 1990s and the early 2000s. These downturns fed political positioning with respect to the campus. Politicians who were opposed would point toward the expense of a new campus. Largely lost in that battle was the fact that the capacity was needed to enable the University of California to meet its Master Plan enrollment obligations, given the fact that, one way or another, all existing campuses were subject to enrollment limitations included in long-range development plans that had been worked out with their surrounding communities. The legally mandated environmental review process provided avenues for groups opposed to the project for any reason, environmental or otherwise, to slow or stop the development of the campus. A particular environmental issue for the Merced project involved vernal pools and fairy shrimp. Founding chancellor Carol Tomlinson-Keasey described the situation:[381]

> A year after the site was selected, a tiny fairy shrimp that lives in seasonal vernal pools was added to the federal endangered species list. A vernal pool...emerges from the depressions in the land where there is clay hardpan soil. For a brief period during the winter rains, these dips retain water, allowing the dormant fairy shrimp and other animal and plant species adapted to ephemeral wetlands to go through the active phase of their life cycle. As the pools dry up in March and April, the fairy shrimp burrows into the mud and resumes the dormant phase of its existence. Fairy shrimp can remain in this dormant phase for decades if there is a drought. Vernal pools exist only where the soil has not been seriously disturbed by farming, orchards, vineyards and development, which all break up the hardpan, leading to the disappearance

---

[381] Carol Tomlinson-Keasey, "A Delicate Dance," in Karen Merritt and Jane Fiori Lawrence, eds., *From Rangeland to Research University: The Birth of University of California, Merced*, New Directions for Higher Education, no. 139 (San Francisco: Jossey-Bass, 2007), pp. 21–22.

of vernal pools. For this reason there are only a few areas in California where significant vernal pools remain. Furthermore, as the federal Clean Water Act has been extended over the years, vernal pools have been included among the waters of the United States and now come under the jurisdiction of the U. S. Army Corps of Engineers [as inland waterways].

Figure 10-17. A vernal pool in Merced Vernal Pools and Grassland Reserve[382]

Thus, a difficult permitting process with the US Army Corps of Engineers came into play. The complications from that process eventually led to relocation of the campus site from its original intended location within the donated land to adjacent land that had already been developed as a municipal golf course. This required acquisition of both the golf course and adjoining private property, which would be used for development of a neighborhood community to support the campus. For that purpose a grant from the Packard

---

[382] "Merced Vernal Pools and Grassland Preserve, Natural Reserve System," University of California, https://perma.cc/QL4X-RN5K.

Foundation was secured in support of both the campus development and the opportunity to lessen impacts on vernal pools.[383]

As the campus was further developed, and in accord with the Packard Foundation grant, a Merced Vernal Pools and Grassland Reserve was created and added to the University of California Natural Reserve System, thereby setting aside a substantial portion of the Virginia Smith Trust lands for preservation and scientific study.

The permitting, legal, and land-acquisition processes associated with the Merced campus and the long time for carrying them out stand in marked contrast to the relatively uncomplicated processes involved in the start-ups of the San Diego, Irvine, and Santa Cruz campuses in the 1960s. The differences also display the changes that occurred in US environmental and legal permitting requirements over the intervening forty years. As well, they have strong implications for what would be required for development of new campuses in the future.

Oversight and Leadership

As was the case for the starts of the Irvine and Santa Cruz campuses, the Merced project originated in the Office of the President. In the case of UC Merced, the foundational work took place from 1989 until the appointment of the first chancellor, which happened in 1999. In 1997 as the site had been selected and development was clearly getting underway, a position called vice provost for academic initiatives was created within the university-wide provost's office, with the principal initiative in the portfolio for the position being the new campus. In 1999 a full search for a chancellor was carried out, and Carol-Tomlinson-Keasey, who had been vice provost for academic initiatives, was selected. Also, the Academic Council was asked to appoint a Faculty Advisory Committee for the new campus, as had been done for the new campuses in the 1960s. The first chair of that committee was Fred Spiess,[384] a longtime distinguished scientist with the Scripps Institution of Oceanography at UC San Diego. The Faculty Advisory Committee was closely involved in academic planning, the

---

[383] Lindsay A. Desrochers, "A Fragile Birth," pp. 32–35, in Merritt and Lawrence, *op. cit.*
[384] "Obituary Notice Pioneer in Ocean Technology: Fred N. Spiess," Scripps Institution of Oceanography, University of California, San Diego, September 11, 2006, https://perma.cc/9Y6P-TB3Y.

appointment of academic officers, and in the normal Academic Personnel Committee role for appointments of faculty.

Academic Planning and Start-Up

As it started, the Merced campus was faced with a much more stringent funding environment than was the situation for the new campuses of the 1960s.

Early in the academic planning for the Merced campus, the decision was made to have no academic departments, but instead to place faculty within one of three colleges: Social Sciences, Humanities, and Arts; Natural Sciences; and Engineering. In addition to fitting better with funding and overall growth prospects, the aim was to avoid the allegiances and limitations of horizons associated with departments and to stress interdisciplinary study and multidisciplinary interactions.[385] Undergraduate majors would grow in number and become more field-specific as adequate numbers of faculty members became available. As of 2018 there are twenty-three different undergraduate majors available.[386]

There are, of course, some difficulties associated with the approach that was taken, as is the case for any start-up strategy. There were dangers of spreading the faculty too thin and having incomplete coverage of material within a major. This concern then led to the concept of building affinity clusters of faculty with a variety of disciplinary backgrounds. One cluster, early on, was environmental sciences. Others that have now (2017) been added include sustaining the planet; computational science and data analytics; adaptive and functional materials; innovation and entrepreneurship; precision agriculture; human health science[387]; inequity, power, and social justice; and anthropology and archaeology.

It was felt desirable to seek research distinction in some cluster areas from the start. Therefore the initial faculty hiring was to be at the

---

[385] Tomlinson-Keasey, 2007, *op. cit.*, p. 25.
[386] "Majors and Minors," University of California, Merced, https://perma.cc/HC5W-Y7H3.
[387] Intended to lead eventually to a medical major, which would fill a void in the San Joaquin Valley.

senior level,[388] although subsequently a large number of junior hires have been made (see below). Two research institutes were planned from the start—the Sierra Nevada Research Institute and the World Cultures Institute. The former[389] takes advantage of the unique location of the Merced campus near the Sierra Nevada Mountains, along with formal partnerships with Sequoia-Kings Canyon and Yosemite National Parks, to address specific research issues associated with the mountain environment and the parks. It has been an impressive success. The World Cultures Institute was to address the multicultural makeup and history of the San Joaquin Valley. It did not materialize as such for a number of reasons, one of them being the predominance of individual, rather than collaborative, research within the social sciences, humanities, and arts.

One helpful feature toward the start-up of UC Merced was an alliance with UC's Lawrence Livermore National Laboratory, which enabled research partnerships and the actual location of the research of some science faculty members to be at Livermore (one hour away by automobile) in the early years. Early on, the campus also obtained use of facilities at nearby, recently decommissioned Castle Air Force Base.

The initial undergraduate class for UC Merced entered in 2005, and the first commencement (figure 10-18) was in 2009.

Current Status

The current (2017) tenure-track faculty, on a headcount basis, numbers 221 individuals, of whom 15 are in the lecturer (potential security of employment) series, 57 are full professors, 69 are associate professors, and 95 are assistant professors.[390] The large proportions of assistant and associate professors correspond to the fact that recent hiring preferences have been at the entry level. That trend can lead to a version of the past Riverside and Santa Cruz situations in which large cohorts of faculty members moved through the ranks more or less together. The Merced campus also has an unusually high proportion of

---

[388] David B. Ashley, "Building Academic Distinction in a Twenty-First-Century Research University," in Merritt and Lawrence, 2007, *loc. cit.*

[389] Sam Traina, "Creating a Research Signature: The Sierra Nevada Research Institute," in Merritt and Lawrence, 2007, *loc. cit.*

[390] "Faculty Directory," University of California, Merced, https://web.archive.org/web/20170508040828/https://www.ucmerced.edu/faculty-directory.

non-tenure-track faculty, 194 headcount, almost as great as the number of tenure-track faculty members.[391] The lecturers enable coverage of fields for which tenure-track faculty members have not yet been hired.

Figure 10-18. First Lady Michelle Obama speaks at the first commencement of the Merced campus, May 16, 2009, courtesy of UC Merced[392]

As of 2017, UC Merced had 7,336 students, of whom 7.1 percent were graduate students.[393] It is the one University of California campus that is available to fulfill the Master Plan promise of a place for every eligible California-resident applicant to the University of California (chapters 5 and 15). The student body at Merced is remarkably diverse ethnically. As of 2017, 51 percent of undergraduate students were Hispanic, 22 percent Asian or Pacific Islander, 11 percent Caucasian, 5

---

[391] "Lecturers," University of California, Merced,
https://web.archive.org/web/20170503093845/http://www.ucmerced.edu/lecturers.
[392] The Senate Source, Academic Senate, University of California, June 2009,
https://perma.cc/DH86-TD4B.
[393] "Fast Facts," University of California, Merced, accessed April 13, 2017,
https://web.archive.org/web/20170501140129/https://www.ucmerced.edu/fast-facts.

percent African American, and 7 percent nonresidents of California.[394] Among the undergraduates, 71 percent are first-generation students in the sense that neither parent holds a four-year degree.[395] Thus, the new campus more than does its part to maintaining access to UC-quality higher education throughout the diverse population of California.

Less than a decade after the first graduating class, it is still too early to judge the academic and research success of the campus, although there are promising signs. The two largest winners of the 2015 university-wide Multicampus Research Initiatives competition were the UC Advanced Solar Technologies Institute,[396] Roland Winston of UC Merced, lead investigator, and the UC Water Security and Sustainability Research Institute,[397] Roger Bales of UC Merced, lead investigator.

Future Growth

Growth and academic development of the Merced campus are vital for the University of California to meet its access obligations under the California Master Plan. However, in a stringent budget climate, that is much more difficult than it was for campuses before 1990. The regents have approved an innovative project, dubbed Merced 2020, that will enable the campus "to attain self-sufficiency and function effectively as a world-class, but highly focused, research university."[398] The project enables academic development, a doubling of physical capacity, and growth of enrollment to ten thousand students as of the

---

[394] "Fast Facts," University of California, Merced, loc. cit.
[395] "Merced 2020 Project," University of California, Merced, https://perma.cc/7VFT-553Z.
[396] University of California Advanced Solar Technologies Institute (UC Solar), https://perma.cc/7ZT4-NRZX.
[397] UC Water Security and Sustainability Research Initiative, https://perma.cc/4JVV-453R.
[398] "UC Merced 2020 Project," briefing memorandum for July 2017 regents meeting, University of California, https://perma.cc/GQ69-WHGX.

year 2020.[399, 400] The project funds both academic buildings and student housing.

In recognition of the fact that the state no longer finances facilities projects other than for some seismic purposes and no longer issues construction bonds for the university, the financial and organizational plans for the project are innovative. There is a public-private operation known as an availability-payment concession in which a single development team designs, builds, and heavily finances the entire project and then operates and maintains the resultant buildings through a thirty-nine-year, performance-based project agreement.[401] The cost of nearly $1.3 billion is financed by a combination of $600 million long-term regents' bonds and $738 million of debt and equity financing arranged by the private development team. In addition to very beneficial decompression of facilities use, the project increases enrollment capacity by twenty-seven hundred students for the campus, raising the campus capacity by 36 percent, but only increasing the capacity of the University of California as a whole by a bit over 1 percent. However, the project should really be viewed as setting the necessary stage for the campus to develop over time to a capacity similar to those of the other campuses.

SUMMARY COMPARATIVE ANALYSES

Differences in Starting Points

The eight newer general campuses reflect three different ways of adding campuses to an existing university or university system: (1) building upon an existing specialized operation to form a general campus (Davis, Riverside, San Diego), (2) acquiring an existing university or college (Los Angeles, Santa Barbara), and (3) a de novo start from no existing base (Irvine, Santa Cruz, Merced). Each of these has its own features, opportunities, and problems.

A start from an existing specialized base is beneficial if the culture and values of that base effectively establish and readily transition to

---

[399] Merced 2020 Project, *loc. cit.*
[400] UC Merced 2020 Project, briefing memorandum for July 2017 regents meeting, *loc. cit.*
[401] Merced 2020 Project, *loc. cit.*

the standards and goals for a more general campus. Starting from the Scripps Institution of Oceanography clearly did this for the San Diego campus, given the strong emphasis of SIO on science of the highest quality. The preexistence of the University Farm did this in a different way for the Davis campus, setting traditions of service to the state and valuing professional education. However, given the unique situation surrounding agricultural research (year-round appointments, guaranteed research support), it was more difficult to transition to a more general standard of the highest quality as other disciplines were built. In the case of the Riverside campus, the start was an unlikely combination of a very specialized agricultural research station on the one hand, and a college focused upon high-quality, liberal undergraduate education without much attention to research on the other hand. Both of these preexisting structures were rather far removed from the ultimate goal of establishing a research-university general campus, and the start was therefore difficult. With the development of mass higher education and research universities around the world, conversions of previously specialized academic institutions have been happening on a large scale, notably in China (e.g., Beijing Forestry University, Nanjing University of Posts and Telecommunications, and Shaanxi Normal University). The nature of the starting point has been or becomes a major factor in each case.

A start from an existing university or college of a different sort is generally a substantial handicap, because of the need for transitions in culture and probably also replacement of faculty. Only very rarely do nonresearchers transition to become strong researchers. The approach that was used and ultimately worked for converting the state college campuses at Los Angeles and Santa Barbara to general research-university campuses in the University of California was essentially one of dilution through rapid growth. Program elimination (e.g., industrial arts at Santa Barbara) was also used. But the need to deal with inherited faculty and traditions did make the starts of these two campuses more difficult, and resources were needed for the conversion. The difficulties would be even greater and would require at least thirty or forty years for turnover of faculty through attrition if dilution through rapid growth were not possible.

The same sort of institutional transformation took place in a different way for the San Francisco campus. There it was necessary to infuse research values into a medical school that had been built upon traditional medical education and clinical practice and where the value of research had not been appreciated except in a few isolated areas. The change was accomplished by faculty leaders who recognized the need for strong research and persuaded the university-wide administration to go in that direction through a change in campus administrative leadership, with consequent changes in the value system and faculty reward structure. For UC San Francisco, serendipity and the general attractiveness of the location then served to bring in highly capable young researchers.

A "grassroots" or bare-land start from no preexisting university operation provides the least encumbrance and the most opportunity for innovation through an unconstrained fresh start. It may also be the most expensive route because of the lack of inherited academic buildings and the need to build all support services. The Irvine, Santa Cruz, and Merced campuses of the University of California are all examples of that sort. The Santa Cruz project enabled the campus to try a system of small-college education within a large campus. The Merced project has allowed that campus to try structures without actual academic departments, as was also done in a different way at Santa Cruz. The value of a fresh start rather than an inherited institution is a rare opportunity. That fact was also recognized by the Olin Foundation when it chose to foster innovation in engineering education by starting an entirely new institution (Franklin W. Olin College[402]), rather than trying to influence or cause evolution of engineering education in an existing university.[403]

Transitions in Responsibility and Leadership

The new campuses in the 1960s (San Diego, Irvine, Santa Cruz) and the new Merced campus forty years later all "belonged" to the Office

---

[402] "About Olin," Olin College of Engineering, https://perma.cc/PE3A-V3K6.
[403] Richard K. Miller, "From the Ground Up: Rethinking Engineering Education in the 21st Century," Proceedings of 2010 Symposium on Engineering and Liberal Education, Union College, Schenectady NY, 2010, https://perma.cc/MZQ7-H6QE.

of the President and its staff for the first six or seven years after the projects were chartered until a chancellor was be named to fill out resident staff.[404] This was necessary in order to give proper attention to, and have proponents for, the new campuses from the start. The chancellors then oversaw their own buildups, 1961–68 and 1999–2006. Similarly, Academic Senate committees were formed by the university-wide Academic Council with the approval of the president for each of the new campuses from the start and took the Academic Senate shared-governance roles. These committees were composed of respected and capable faculty members from existing campuses.[405]

Building from Within

All University of California campuses have been developed largely by building from within the existing university rather than through incorporation of already well-developed other universities or college campuses into the UC system. This is true even for UCLA and Santa Barbara, because of the large dilution effects when they were built. There are several significant advantages to creating new campuses from within a university or university system. Most notably, the university or university system can generate its own design and impose its own values, standards, and approaches from the start, especially by using wisdom and personnel from existing campuses. For example, for a new campus, all faculty members can be hired with review and recommendations from a Committee on Academic Personnel that is initially composed of faculty members from preexisting campuses. There is no inherited different culture, value system, or work ethic to overcome.

Strategies for Academic Building

A new campus by definition opens with a small contingent of faculty. Who should those faculty members be? Should a campus build initially across the entire range of disciplines or area by area? Should a campus start with primarily senior faculty members, primarily junior faculty members, or a spread across ranks? Should the start be with

---

[404] Kerr, 2001, *op. cit.*, p. 235.
[405] Kerr, 2001, *op. cit.*, p. 487.

undergraduate education or with graduate education or both? Should extensive use be made of lecturers or other temporary faculty to provide coverage before ladder-rank faculty can be hired? There were different answers to these questions among the new campuses.

The conventional approach is to start undergraduate education first, while having enough graduate education to draw research-oriented faculty. This is what was done at Santa Cruz, Santa Barbara, and Merced, and to a significant extent at Irvine. For a public university, undergraduate education visibly satisfies the political supporters of the campus. However, starting with undergraduate education also calls for a sufficient distribution among disciplines and potential majors at the start to accommodate the varied interests of undergraduates. It thereby spreads the faculty thin. In the affluent time of the 1960s, the Irvine campus was able to ameliorate this challenge with a large burst of initial faculty hiring—the addition of 150 faculty members in the single year 1964, described by Peltason, above. In order to effectively nurture the academic quality of a campus, such a large amount of hiring cannot be allowed to exceed the supply of highly promising potential faculty members. The Merced campus, opening later at in a time of severe budgetary constraints, has been fiscally limited in its ability to hire tenure-track faculty members. As noted, it is providing adequate initial coverage of fields through the use of a large number of non-tenure-track faculty members.

The San Diego approach was to start by hiring faculty stars of the first magnitude and offer study in such fields as they turned out to represent, with only graduate education initially. As Revelle predicated, this was indeed a path to early and rapid academic distinction. However, the San Diego approach entails a serendipitous arrival of research fields and a delayed inception of undergraduate education. Typically, a public university has more political support for undergraduate education than it does for research, despite the ultimate contributions of research to the economy and human betterment. More constituents are visibly and directly affected by undergraduate education. What was different in San Diego was that the community saw the university campus as a key and necessary factor in economic redevelopment following the military-related economy of World War II.

The two efforts to start largely with entry-level faculty did not work well. The Riverside "college" faculty were hired very largely at the entry level and progressed through the ranks together, as was also the case for the start of UC Santa Cruz. This approach had several problems, as youth and then various degrees of age and experience prevailed at various points in time, lessening the breadth of experience of the faculty and concentrating periods of faculty renewal rather than spreading them evenly over time. At San Diego, star-quality senior faculty prevailed at the beginning, and at Irvine and UCLA the spectrum of experience of faculty was, by design, widespread from the start. The current distribution of faculty ranks at Merced is closer to the Riverside and Santa Cruz situations, given the unusually high proportions of associate and assistant professors (33 and 46 percent, respectively).

Stars as Magnets

The Revelle plan for building the research stature of the San Diego campus worked admirably. Revelle himself and the initial star-quality faculty such as Urey, Arnold, Bonner, and Goeppert-Mayer did indeed draw other distinguished senior faculty members, junior faculty members, and graduate students who wanted to work with and near these people. San Diego could build in this way, deferring attention to an undergraduate program, because of the strong interest of the San Diego community in the research base, the strong intellectual leadership of Revelle himself, the relatively affluent state of the California treasury, and the fact that the regents were developing several other new campuses, such that San Diego's different path would not draw as much attention at the state level. Strikingly, the faculty members that Revelle and York assembled provided a strong base for generating the undergraduate program when it did come.

A Sommelier's Taste

Above all else, examination of the developments of the various UC campuses reveals the extreme importance of the faculty being built not by top administrators and not by sitting back and waiting for applications from prospective faculty members. Instead, it is most effective for unique intellectual leaders, probably distinguished researchers themselves, to get out and actively seek the best and the brightest. What is needed, as was described by Julius Krevans for William Rutter in the case of UCSF, is the rare people who have "a sommelier's taste" in recognizing quality research and talent and promise for it. In addition to Rutter at UCSF, we have seen this for Lewis, Birge, Hildebrand, Pitzer, and Evans at Berkeley; for Revelle and Brueckner at San Diego; for Young and Jacoby at UCLA; and for the founding deans and department chairs at Irvine (two themselves future Nobelists).

Organizational Structures

Two significant categories of organizational innovation have been devised and tested in the development of University of California campuses. They are ways of securing a small-college experience within a large research university and ways of overcoming the constraints associated with academic departments. Toward the first goal, residential colleges were created from the start at San Diego and Santa Cruz, among the first efforts to do so within public universities. In line with what has happened at Harvard, Yale, and elsewhere, these have proven to be successes in terms of focusing the social lives, recreational sports, and other events for students. The Santa Cruz effort to center intellectual life and instructional courses within the colleges was less successful and has been largely abandoned. With regard to the second objective, the original design for Santa Cruz called for no academic departments. Boards of study were introduced as weaker forms of departments to coordinate curricula, and now UCSC has actual departments. The newer Merced campus also was started without departments, having just the three academic schools. Organization without formal departments may indeed be a good way to start a new campus with a small faculty size. However, as the campus grows, as faculty multiply in number, and in view of recognition and academic stature occuring within the disciplines, department structures become increasingly compelling.

Initial Research Signature

We have seen a number of instances where distinction in a focused area of research early on has been a very positive factor. One example, of course, is the start that the Scripps Institution of

Oceanography gave to the distinction of the San Diego campus. The same can be said of the strong standing of the Davis campus in agricultural research before it became a general campus. Landing the National Science Foundation's Institute of Theoretical Physics was a plum for Santa Barbara and has led to considerable distinction for UCSB in physics. The creation of the Air Pollution Research Center at Riverside was important, both intellectually and in creating a positive image to counter the negative publicity from the smog problem. The Sierra Nevada Research Institute has been a very positive early accomplishment for the Merced campus.

Campus Site

The geographical siting of a campus has a very important effect. This is true in terms of the appeal of the surroundings, such as access to recreational opportunities, cultural events, and delightful living in general, and it can be important in terms of what linkages there are for the campus with the community or other nearby institutions. Seven of the UC campuses (all except Riverside, Davis, and Merced) are in coastal regions near the Pacific Ocean and therefore have a pleasant and moderate Mediterranean climate. The major metropolitan areas surrounding Los Angeles and San Francisco have many cultural activities. San Francisco has extremely progressive (some would say left-wing radical) politics, which appeal to some potential faculty members. The state of California has an extremely beautiful and accessible mountain range, the Sierra Nevada, and attractive desert locales. As Bourne reported, the San Francisco climate and range of activities and interests figured prominently in attracting the four research luminaries-to-be (Boyer, Bishop, Varmus, Prusiner) who came to UCSF early in its development of research.

Nearby and allied institutions that have been important for drawing faculty members include the Scripps Research Institute and the Salk Institute in La Jolla (San Diego); marine research facilities in San Diego, Santa Barbara, and Santa Cruz; Silicon Valley for Berkeley and Santa Cruz; the biotechnology industry for UCSF and Berkeley in the San Francisco Bay Area and for San Diego; and the proximity of the Sierra Nevada for Merced and Davis.

Chapter 10

The Radicalism of the 1960s

Campus unrest in the 1960s caught different campuses in different stages of development and was of different natures and intensities on the various campuses because of different political environments. The initial Free Speech Movement started at Berkeley and caused a major crisis that led to the removal of a chancellor, much negative publicity, and eventually the dismissal of Clark Kerr as president by the Board of Regents. Clark Kerr devotes the second volume of his memoirs[406] largely to these matters. These events brought Berkeley a radicalized political image and had a negative effect upon applications to the campus, since overcome many times over.

A counterpart countercultural movement some years later in San Diego, largely in resistance to the Vietnam War, is described by then-chancellor William McGill[407] and was particularly stark because of the contrast with the politically quite conservative San Diego and La Jolla communities. At this still early stage in the development of the campus, the campus leaders—McGill and interim successor Herb York—were almost fully diverted for two years to repairing relationships with the community and regaining equilibrium on campus.

A similarly highly disruptive series of events was generated by the protest activities in Isla Vista, the student residence area adjoining UC Santa Barbara, culminating in the burning of the Bank of America building in Isla Vista in February 1970. These events created genuine concern about the safety of students attending UCSB and surely had their impacts on enrollments. As well, they consumed much of the time of Chancellor Vernon Cheadle. Unfortunately, such concerns were stoked again by a rapid sequence of six murders perpetrated by a demented nonstudent in Isla Vista in May 2014.

There were also instances in which faculty members prompted political concerns and headlines. Herbert Marcuse, a philosopher of the far left, was a San Diego faculty member who drew national attention during the period of student activism and was in various ways a thorn

---

[406] Clark Kerr, *The Gold and the Blue: A Personal Memoir of the University of California, 1949–1967, vol. 2, Political Turmoil* (Berkeley: University of California Press, 2003).
[407] William J. McGill, *The Year of the Monkey: Revolt on Campus, 1968–69* (New York: McGraw-Hill, 1982).

in the side of William McGill during the 1968–69 year.[408] Angela Davis, a radical activist, was an acting assistant professor at UCLA in 1969–70 and drew so much attention that the regents chose to dismiss her, over the protests and challenge of then-new-chancellor Charles Young. Davis was reinstated by court action. Subsequently, Davis became a professor at UC Santa Cruz from 1991 until her retirement in 2008.

Student unrest and the images associated with it were factors in the enrollment problems at UC Santa Cruz in the early 1970s.

Learning and Adjusting to the University of California

The University of California has its own ways of governance and operation. These are often markedly different from the experiences of a campus or university leader coming from outside the university. Most new leaders from outside can adjust to the ways of UC, but some do not, and there can also be difficulties encountered during a period of learning and adjustment. There were a number of instances during the formative years of campuses when setbacks came because of crises of governance associated with the lack of attunement of leaders to the systems and traditions of the university.

Times to AAU Membership

Membership in the Association of American Universities is by invitation only and is highly sought. As of 2017 there are sixty-two member universities, of which thirty-four are public, twenty-six are private, and two are in Canada. University of California campuses make up 10 percent of the US membership and 18 percent of the US public-university membership.

Repeating the statistics from chapter 1, it is interesting that it has taken about the same lengths of time after embarking on the general-campus research-university mission for the various University of California member campuses to achieve AAU membership. This speaks to the general strength of the structural and operational principles of the university as a whole. Davis, which awarded its first PhD (botany) in 1950, was established as a general campus in 1959 and achieved AAU membership in 1996, thirty-seven years later. Irvine, which opened in

---

[408] McGill, 1982, *loc. cit.*

1965, also became a member of the AAU in 1996, thirty-one years later. Santa Barbara, which was chartered as a general campus in 1958 and conferred its first PhD in 1963, became a member in 1995, thirty-seven years later. San Diego was on yet a faster track in its rise, achieving AAU membership in 1982, only twenty-two years after admitting its first graduate students in 1960. The shortness of that period further attests to the worth of the Revelle approach as a way of moving an institution as fast as possible to distinction. UCLA was admitted to the AAU in 1974, thirty-six years after giving its first PhD in 1938, and only sixteen years after being accorded "equal opportunity" by the UC Regents and Clark Kerr in 1958. That too is impressive.

The other AAU member is Berkeley, which, as the University of California, was a founding member of the AAU in 1900. That is only thirty-two years after the founding of the university as a very small institution in 1868. But the interval cannot be compared, since research distinction was not as large a criterion for the AAU in 1900 as it is at present.

The three potentially eligible UC campuses that are not yet members of the AAU are Santa Cruz, Riverside, and Merced. Santa Cruz was held back in research growth until the Sinsheimer Rearrangement of 1978. As of 2017, thirty-nine years have elapsed since that time, and Santa Cruz is now regarded as a strong contender for AAU membership. (Whether or not the AAU will choose to allocate over 10 percent of its US membership to University of California campuses is another matter, however.) Riverside was held back in development by the conflicts that existed in the early years and by the smog infamy of the early 1970s but has developed well in recent decades. Merced opened in 2005 and is still a new campus.

11.
Sustaining Excellence: Faculty Appointments and Advancement

The quality of the faculty of the University of California is maintained primarily through objective and thorough appraisal, by competent faculty members, of each candidate for appointment or promotion. Responsibility for this appraisal falls largely upon the review committees nominated by the Committee on Academic Personnel or equivalent Committee and appointed by the Chancellor or a designated representative. It is the duty of these committees to ascertain the present fitness of each candidate and the likelihood of the candidate's pursuing a productive career...Superior intellectual attainment, as evidenced both in teaching and in research or other creative achievement, is an indispensable qualification for appointment or promotion to tenure positions.
—Academic Personnel Manual, *University of California*[1]

The Committee on Budget and Interdepartmental Relations (Budget Committee)...is the most potent expression of the egalitarian philosophy of "faculty governance," which has fostered and safeguarded the academic distinction of our institution for almost a century.
—Committee on Budget and Interdepartmental Relations[2]

[At the University of California[3]*] academic quality is elevated to a priority and even a collective obsession that pursues every academic all*

---

[1] *Academic Personnel Manual*, University of California, Section 210-1(a), https://perma.cc/N6JD-VGVN.
[2] Committee on Budget and Interdepartmental Relations, "Introduction to the Budget Committee," Academic Senate, University of California, updated August 2017, https://perma.cc/63UW-N958.
[3] These authors studied Berkeley, but their conclusions can be extended to the other UC campuses as well by virtue of the spread of common practices and a common academic culture throughout the campuses of the University of California.

along his/her academic career...Evaluation is on-going throughout an academic's lifetime. It never seems to come to an end. Faculty members are submitted to reporting requirements all along their career, from recruitment to retirement, whether as junior or senior professor.
—Jean-Claude Thoenig and Catherine Paradeise[4]

At the heart of a distinguished research university is a culture of faculty excellence in research, teaching, and service. The concept of academic excellence should underlie everything that is done, ranging from the evaluation of faculty for promotion and advancement throughout their careers, to the choice and piloting of research by the faculty, to initiatives and priorities within the administration, to the coverage and emphases within teaching, and to attitudes and habits transmitted to students. Given a culture of excellence and practices that stem from it, all else will follow.[5]

MAINTAINING THE CULTURE

Chapters 9 and 10 have explored ways in which academic excellence was initially built at the various campuses of the University of California. We now turn to how that excellence has been, and can be, effectively nurtured and sustained over time.

Excellence is embedded in faculty values and capabilities. Sustaining excellence requires serious involvement of the most accomplished and most capable faculty members of the institution in program review, planning for evolution of program areas, and evaluation of fellow faculty members for appointment and throughout their careers. Key roles for the university administration are to identify

---

[4] Jean-Claude Thoenig and Catherine Paradeise, "Organizational Governance and the Production of Academic Quality: Lessons from Two Top U. S. Research Universities," *Minerva* 52, no. 4 (2014): pp. 381–417.

[5] Through extensive interviews Thoenig and Paradeise, 2014, *loc. cit.*, have examined both the Berkeley campus of the University of California and the Massachusetts Institute of Technology (MIT) from this standpoint and have stressed how a strong devotion to principles of academic quality influences all that is done.

and place excellence as the highest priority; to foster methodologies that enable identifying, recruiting, and sustaining the best and brightest faculty; and to enable the faculty to define and pursue outstanding research and teaching with as few institutional constraints and diversions as possible.

If the quest for excellence does not yet pervade the faculty culture of a mature university, it will be nearly impossible for the university administration to create it. If the university is small in comparison with its intended ultimate size, then the approach of dilution with waves of new faculty members who are strongly oriented toward quality can be used, as was done by UC in the development of both the Los Angeles and Santa Barbara campuses (chapter 10). But without the opportunity for growth and a dilution approach, it may well make better sense to create an entirely new university as the approach for creating academic quality and stature, rather than trying to upgrade the concern for academic quality in an existing university.

This chapter concerns the unique University of California system of reviewing faculty members for appointment and advancement throughout their careers with emphasis on the ways in which the process stresses and secures academic quality. This established mechanism is probably the single most identifiable and important reason for the standing that has been achieved by the university. Program reviews and changes and evolution of program have also been important and are a subject of the following chapter.

PRINCIPLES USED IN THE UNIVERSITY OF CALIFORNIA

Reviews

All initial appointments and increases in rank and/or salary[6] come as the result of reviews of the recent performance and accomplishments of individual faculty members. These reviews are carried out at the time of initial hire and then typically every two to four years, continuing throughout the entire career of a faculty member. The intervals between reviews become longer, the criteria

---

[6] Except for cost-of-living increases. See the next section.

applied become greater, and the bar to be cleared for advancement becomes higher as a faculty member moves further along in her or his career. The reviews are conducted by a thorough and structured process involving first faculty members in the candidate's own department and then faculty members campus-wide. At key points in the career of a faculty member, written, confidential evaluations are solicited from national and international peers who are closely familiar with the accomplishments of the candidate. The process is designed to involve a large number of reviewers with no one or even a few particular reviewers dominating the process, thereby helping to assure fairness and increase objectivity. The ultimate decisions are made by the administration, typically the provost or a vice provost, but the recommendations of reviewers are highly influential in these decisions and are almost always controlling.

Salaries

The University of California establishes salary scales[7] for academic titles, corresponding to advancement through the ranks by means of steps within rank. Currently these scales entail six steps for assistant professor, two of which overlap in salary with the first two of the five steps for associate professor. The top two steps for associate professor overlap in salary with the first two of the ten steps for professor. The overlapping steps offer some latitude to provide continual advancement before the next promotion in rank. When a faculty member is promoted, the overlapping steps are generally not repeated so that the professor does receive continual salary increases upon advancement. For the most distinguished faculty members, there are above-scale appointments, which allow continual recognition of accomplishments beyond the top of the established salary scale. In years of sufficient state budget, cost-of-living adjustments (COLAs) are applied to all the steps and are automatically received by all faculty members.

---

[7] "Academic Salary Scales, Effective July 1, 2017," Office of the President, University of California, https://perma.cc/H2T2-KZKS. See the indicated subpages for the scales for different types of appointment. The scales are updated whenever cost-of-living increases are applied.

Under California law, salaries of all University of California employees are publicly available within a database maintained by the university[8] as well as a database maintained by the *Sacramento Bee* newspaper[9] covering all California public employees.

Historically, the set scales served a valuable purpose of maintaining equity in salaries among disciplines; however, market forces have grown substantially over the past half century and do differ considerably among disciplines and also professions. Two additional approaches have been taken to recognize that fact. One of these is the establishment of special higher scales for certain disciplines—one for law and another for business, economics, and engineering[10]. There iis also a different approach to salaries within the health sciences, where compensation for practice occurs through the university as well. The second change is more frequent use of higher, off-scale salaries, which are still determined through the standard review process.

Up through professor, step 4, the academic salary scales specify "normal" intervals for advancement: two years through associate professor, step 3, and three years beyond that level. Depending upon performance, a faculty member may receive accelerated advancement at periods shorter than the stated normal period, be advanced at the normal interval, be advanced at a slower rate than normal, or not be advanced at all. In any event the interval between reviews cannot be more than five years.[11] Above professor, step 4, there is no normal period, connoting that some faculty members will not advance further and that typical periods within step will be longer.

Major Reviews

Reviews are in-depth at all levels of advancement, but for certain advancements they are more thorough. These special advancements include the award of tenure, which equates to promotion from assistant professor to associate professor; promotion from associate

---

[8] "Compensation at the University of California: University of California Employee Pay", https://perma.cc/X8KM-ASLP.
[9] "State Worker Salary Database," *Sacbee*, https://perma.cc/T9GH-D47C.
[10] The latter special scale was established in 1981.
[11] Section 200-0, "Policy," *Academic Personnel Manual*, University of California, https://perma.cc/X2AZ-E8U8..

professor to professor; advancement to step 6 professor; and advancement above scale (i.e., beyond step 10).

The tenure review is of course particularly important. That review is preceded by a midcareer appraisal,[12] which at Berkeley occurs in the seventh semester of employment. The purpose of the midcareer appraisal is to provide information that can help an assistant professor gauge the likelihood of achieving tenure and make any desirable adjustments in his or her approach. Following that, the tenure review is typically started in the eleventh semester (the start of the sixth year) of employment as an assistant professor. The University of California extends to eight years the recommendation[13] of the American Association of University Professors that employment in a pretenure position should be limited to seven years. The review in the sixth year enables a year for re-review if that is needed for procedural reasons while still leaving a year for the candidate to arrange relocation if not awarded tenure.

BUDGET COMMITTEE/COMMITTEE ON ACADEMIC PERSONNEL

As of the Berkeley Revolution of 1919 (chapter 7) and the consequent increase in the roles and formal structure of the Academic Senate, the Board of Regents established a policy that the Academic Senate should be consulted by the president on all "appointments, promotions, demotions, and dismissals" of faculty members in professorial positions.[14, 15] The Academic Senate then established the Committee on Budget and Interdepartmental Relations, known familiarly as the Budget Committee, to advise the president on those matters. Berkeley

---

[12] "Procedure for the Formal Appraisal of an Assistant Professor," Academic Personnel Manual, Section 220-83, University of California, https://perma.cc/6Z7A-B7UL..
[13] "1940 Statement of Principles on Academic Freedom and Tenure: AAUP," https://perma.cc/6P3F-3SN5.
[14] Standing Orders of the Regents, no. 105.2, "Duties, Powers, and Privileges of the Academic Senate," University of California, https://perma.cc/T9SP-8FRM..
[15] Angus E. Taylor, "The Academic Senate of the University of California: Its Role in Shared Governance and Operation of the University of California," p. 3, Institute of Governmental Studies, University of California, Berkeley, CA, 1998, https://oac.cdlib.org/ark:/13030/hb896nb4tk/?brand=oac4.

chemist Joel Hildebrand, who was often a member of that committee in its early years, indicated that among the first things that the committee did was to "set up criteria for the ranks in the academic ladder" and "what the criteria and length of periods of [service as] instructor, assistant professor, [and] associate professor are." He further indicated that there had previously (i.e., during the Wheeler era and before) been no regular plan or approach and that promotion and salary increases had simply been presidential decisions without clearly identified criteria.[16]

As campuses came into being beyond Berkeley and then UCLA, the Academic Senate divided into Northern and Southern Divisions, and each of the divisions had a Committee on Budget and Interdepartmental Relations with the same functions. Subsequently the structure changed to there being divisions of the Academic Senate on each campus, and the names of the campus committees were changed to Committee on Academic Personnel (CAP) on all campuses except Berkeley, where the committee retains the original name. Operations and membership of the CAP or Budget Committee and its interactions with the administration vary among campuses, but for all campuses the CAP or Budget Committee is the focal point of the process for faculty review and advancement. At some campuses (e.g., UCLA) CAP does not review advancements at normal rates within ranks and/or initial appointments, leaving these to deans. At some campuses, CAP audits reviews of routine advancements after the fact.[17] At UCLA, CAP reviews and recommends the appropriate step and then the salary, if off scale, is determined by the administration. At Berkeley, on the other hand, the Budget Committee reviews and recommends both step and salary for all cases.

For Berkeley, the Budget Committee is composed of nine faculty members, appointed by the Committee on Committees of the Berkeley Division for three-year overlapping terms, so that there are three new appointments per year. The faculty members are drawn from

---

[16] Joel H. Hildebrand, interview by Edna Tartaul Daniel, "Chemistry, Education, and the University of California," oral history, p. 155, Regional Oral History Office, University of California, Berkeley, 1962, https://perma.cc/PW5V-4QUC.

[17] Ellen S. Switkes, personal communication, June 2016.

disciplines throughout the campus, including the professional schools. The chair is one of the third-year members.

So as to even out the work of the Budget Committee over time, there is a published schedule[18] giving due dates for various categories of advancement requests. It is also possible to submit a request off cycle at any other time of year if that is needed because of the timing of a recruitment or retention.

METHODOLOGY

The sequence of events by which an advancement review occurs has been described by Switkes[19] and by the Berkeley Budget Committee[20] for the Berkeley campus and is summarized here.

At the end of each academic year, faculty members complete a statement of activities and accomplishments known as the Annual Supplement to the Bio-bibliography.[21] Equipped with this information, and if there is a possibility that an advancement request could be appropriate, the department chair meets with faculty members individually to discuss objectives and accomplishments and to determine whether or not an advancement request is indeed in order.[22] An advancement review begins with the candidate assembling a full dossier covering research (accomplishments, extramural grants, publications, and presentations since the last review, as well as research plans for the future); teaching (creation of courses, syllabi, online material, and textbooks); and service activities to the department, the university, professional societies, government, and

---

[18] "APO Deadlines for Deans: Cases with July 1, 2019 effective date," Academic Personnel Office, University of California, Berkeley, https://perma.cc/Y36F-YZ5H. These are updated annually.
[19] Ellen Switkes, "University of California Peer Review System and Post-Tenure Evaluation," *Innovative Higher Education* 24, no. 1 (September 1999): pp. 39–48, https://perma.cc/2YJY-G4FY..
[20] "Introduction to the Budget Committee," Academic Senate, University of California, Berkeley, updated August 2017, https://perma.cc/CA88-8J73.
[21] Annual Supplement to the Bio-bibliography, University of California, Berkeley, https://perma.cc/Y7BP-JBX6.
[22] An advancement request and review may also be initiated by the faculty member, even if the department chair concludes that such a request would not be timely.

community. Student evaluations of teaching from each course are collected directly in the department office, and those for the candidate are added to the dossier. The emphasis is on activities since the last review, except for the major reviews described above, where everything since the last major review is considered.

For initial appointment, for promotion to associate professor and professor, for advancement above scale, and optionally for advancement to professor step 6 or advancement above scale, letters of evaluation are solicited and are included with the case for review. These letters are sought from respected scholars and other leaders who are familiar with the specific field(s) in which the candidate in engaged and who should therefore be able to assess the work and its impact upon, and standing within, the field. The letters are solicited on a confidential basis, with the understanding that it may ultimately become necessary to release the language, without identifiers of the letter writers. That fact is pointed out to those from whom letters are requested, with a request that they put any information identifying their relationship with the candidate in a protected passage below the signature line. The Berkeley campus furnishes extensive guidelines[23] for the solicitation of these letters. Candidates may make their own suggestions regarding persons to be consulted for letters and are encouraged to do so. However, there should be a department list of potential reviewers prepared in advance of receipt of the candidate's list, and Berkeley campus policy is that at least half of the letters should be requested from persons on that department list. Candidates may also submit a list of names of persons they believe should not be contacted, along with the rationales for those requests.

For key advancements and optionally for other advancements, there should be consultation with departmental faculty at the rank or step proposed and above as well as a report by the department chair of the vote and views expressed. There may also be reports of departmental evaluation committees, which are required for promotions and for advancement to professor step 6. Members of

---

[23] Academic Personnel Office, "External Letters," University of California, Berkeley, December 9, 2009, https://web.archive.org/web/20170731221254/http://apo.berkeley.edu/external_letters_guidelines_12.09.pdf.

these committees must be faculty members of the rank proposed or higher. Berkeley campus checklists show the content requirements for submitted faculty advancement requests at various levels.[24] The candidate has the right to review the personnel file, with external letters redacted of the below-the-signature information that could identify the reviewer. The candidate may provide a written response to the departmental analysis and recommendation. That response, if made, is included with the case as it proceeds to further review.

The case assembled by the department chair, together with the chair's analysis and recommendation and any response to letters or other evaluations from the candidate, is forwarded to the dean,[25] who reviews and adds her or his own analysis and recommendation. The full case then goes to the central-campus Academic Personnel Office, which refers it to the CAP or Budget Committee. For Berkeley, if the case involves promotion from assistant professor to associate professor (tenure) or promotion from associate professor to professor, the Budget Committee submits nominees for a special ad hoc committee of reviewers to the vice provost, who selects from among these and may add others to form the committee. The ad hoc committee has three or five members, with two of three, or three of five, members including the committee chair being from outside the candidate's department(s). Five-member committees are typically used for situations where the recommendation from the department is substantially mixed, and then the two departmental members would reflect differing viewpoints. The ad hoc committee produces a report and a recommendation, which become part of the case reviewed by the Budget Committee and the administrative decision-maker. The membership, the deliberations, and the report of the ad hoc committee are all confidential.

The Budget Committee or CAP now examines the full case, typically making use of a lead reviewer from its own ranks. The full committee then deliberates and recommends an action, which, for Berkeley, is embedded in a two- or three-page "minute" that is transmitted to the vice provost for the faculty. For tenure decisions,

---

[24] Academic Personnel Office, "Checksheet for Preparation of Academic Personnel Actions," University of California, Berkeley, https://web.archive.org/web/20180611185158/https://apo.berkeley.edu/check-sheets.

[25] For single-department schools, the dean fulfills the role of the department chair.

promotions, and some other appropriate cases, the vice provost for the faculty will consult with and gain the agreement of the provost and chancellor to make the ultimate determination. The chancellor's decision on promotion and tenure is final. Although the regents had to approve tenure decisions during the early history of the university, since 1964–65 that is no longer the case, as noted already in chapter 3.

CRITERIA

The criteria that are sought for performance and for various appointments are delineated in the *Academic Personnel Manual* (APM),[26] which is maintained at the university-wide level, and which is continually updated and modified as needed by extensive and formalized procedures involving university-wide Academic Senate committees in consultation with both campus and university-wide administrations and Academic Senate divisions on the campuses. Specifically, Section 210-1(d)[27] of the APM gives the evaluation criteria for use by personnel review committees. Key passages include the following:

> The review committee shall judge the candidate with respect to the proposed rank and duties, considering the record of the candidate's performance in (1) teaching, (2) research and other creative work, (3) professional activity, and (4) University and public service. In evaluating the candidate's qualifications within these areas, the review committee shall exercise reasonable flexibility, balancing when the case requires, heavier commitments and responsibilities in one area against lighter commitments and responsibilities in another. The review committee must judge whether the candidate is engaging in a program of work that is both sound and productive. As the University enters new fields of

---

[26] "Academic Personnel and Programs," Division of Academic Affairs, Office of the President, University of California, https://web.archive.org/web/20170606030317/https://www.ucop.edu/academic-personnel-programs/academic-personnel-policy/index.html.
[27] "Review and Appraisal Committees," Section 210-1(d), *Academic Personnel Manual*, University of California, https://perma.cc/7RND-K9HK.

endeavor and refocuses its ongoing activities, cases will arise in which the proper work of faculty members departs markedly from established academic patterns. In such cases, the review committees must take exceptional care to apply the criteria with sufficient flexibility. However, flexibility does not entail a relaxation of high standards. *Superior intellectual attainment, as evidenced both in teaching and in research or other creative achievement, is an indispensable qualification for appointment or promotion to tenure positions.* Insistence upon these standards for holders of the professorship is necessary for maintenance of the quality of the University as an institution dedicated to the discovery and transmission of knowledge. Consideration should be given to changes in emphasis and interest that may occur in an academic career. The candidate may submit for the review file a presentation of his or her activity in all four areas.

The University of California is committed to excellence and equity in every facet of its mission. Contributions in all areas of faculty achievement that promote equal opportunity and diversity should be given due recognition in the academic personnel process, and they should be evaluated and credited in the same way as other faculty achievements. These contributions to diversity and equal opportunity can take a variety of forms including efforts to advance equitable access to education, public service that addresses the needs of California's diverse population, or research in a scholar's area of expertise that highlights inequalities. Mentoring and advising of students and faculty members, particularly from underrepresented and underserved populations, should be given due recognition in the teaching or service categories of the academic personnel process.

The criteria set forth in the following passages from the *Academic Personnel Manual* are intended to serve as guides for minimum standards in judging the candidate, not to set boundaries to exclude other elements of performance that may be considered:

Teaching — Clearly demonstrated evidence of high quality in teaching is an essential criterion for appointment, advancement, or promotion. Under no circumstances will a tenure commitment be made unless there is clear documentation of ability and diligence in the teaching role. In judging the effectiveness of a candidate's teaching, the committee should consider such points as the following: the candidate's command of the subject; continuous growth in the subject field; ability to organize material and to present it with force and logic; capacity to awaken in students an awareness of the relationship of the subject to other fields of knowledge; fostering of student independence and capability to reason; spirit and enthusiasm which vitalize the candidate's learning and teaching; ability to arouse curiosity in beginning students, to encourage high standards, and to stimulate advanced students to creative work; personal attributes as they affect teaching and students; extent and skill of the candidate's participation in the general guidance, mentoring, and advising of students; effectiveness in creating an academic environment that is open and encouraging to all students, including development of particularly effective strategies for the educational advancement of students in various underrepresented groups...

Research and Creative Work — Evidence of a productive and creative mind should be sought in the candidate's published research or recognized artistic production in original architectural or engineering designs, or the like. Publications in research and other creative accomplishment should be evaluated, not merely enumerated. There should be evidence that the candidate is continuously and effectively engaged in creative activity of high quality and significance. Work in progress should be assessed whenever possible. When published work in joint authorship (or other product of joint effort) is presented as evidence, it is the responsibility of the department chair to establish as clearly as possible the role of the candidate in the joint effort...

Professional Competence and Activity — In certain positions in the professional schools and colleges, such as architecture, business administration, dentistry, engineering, law, medicine, etc., a demonstrated distinction in the special competencies appropriate to the field and its characteristic activities should be recognized as a criterion for appointment or promotion. The candidate's professional activities should be scrutinized for evidence of achievement and leadership in the field and of demonstrated progressiveness in the development or utilization of new approaches and techniques for the solution of professional problems, including those that specifically address the professional advancement of individuals in underrepresented groups in the candidate's field...

University and Public Service - The faculty plays an important role in the administration of the University and in the formulation of its policies. Recognition should therefore be given to scholars who prove themselves to be able administrators and who participate effectively and imaginatively in faculty government and the formulation of departmental, college, and University policies. Services by members of the faculty to the community, State, and nation, both in their special capacities as scholars and in areas beyond those special capacities when the work done is at a sufficiently high level and of sufficiently high quality, should likewise be recognized as evidence for promotion.

Performance in teaching, research and creative work, and university and public service are evaluated for all faculty members. Professional competence and activity is also evaluated for faculty where indicated, but does not replace or lessen evaluation in the other categories.

Recommended methods for assessing teaching include evaluations by current students (required for all courses and collected independently), former students, faculty colleagues through methods such as co-teaching or course visitations, and alumni evaluation.[28]

As is noted in the quoted APM passages, the evaluation of research and creative activity (as opposed to professional competence) can have different dimensions for professional schools. For twenty-two

---

[28] "Policy for Evaluating Teaching (for Advancement and Promotion)," University of California, Berkeley, April 1987, accessed May 28, 2016, https://perma.cc/VZQ2-94H4.

years, 1972–94, the Berkeley campus had an unusual administrative structure that involved two provosts. One had responsibility for the Letters and Science departments and had the additional title, Dean of the College of Letters and Sciences. The other provost had responsibility for the other four colleges[29] and nine professional schools,[30] carrying the title Provost—Professional Schools and Colleges. In that the shared-governance functions of the campus involve academic disciplines and professions working together, the provost—professional schools and colleges (of which the author was the last of three) had the role of representing the unique attributes of the professions, including reflecting the unique and different aspects of creativity in the professions, in reviews and actions on faculty advancement and promotion cases.[31]

QUALITY VERSUS QUANTITY

In both the statement and the application of the standards, quality is stressed above quantity. Originality and innovation are sought and rewarded. There is no quantitative measure or even an estimate of the number of papers or books required for various levels of advancement. Rather, the questions focus on how much impact the research has had, whether the candidate leads the field intellectually, and what the candidate has done that is truly original.

Innovation and being at the forefront of one's field are valued sufficiently highly so that the advancement system is designed and implemented to enable and provide encouragement for faculty members who wish to switch fields within a discipline as that discipline evolves. As but one example, such was the case for Charles Wilke, mentioned in chapter 9 as a founder of the chemical engineering program at Berkeley. At age fifty, midcareer, he was at the top of his field of mass transfer but recognized the potential of the incipient field

---

[29] The Colleges of Engineering, Chemistry, Environmental Design, and Natural Resources.
[30] The Schools of Law, Business, Public Health, Education, Optometry, Social Welfare, Information (formerly Library and Information Studies), Public Policy, and Journalism.
[31] C. Judson King, "A Provost for Professional Schools and Colleges," Research and Occasional Papers Series, no. 3-13, February 2013, https://perma.cc/FD3Q-5KLH. .

of biochemical engineering. He took the time to learn the associated concepts of biology and bacteriology, invited visitors to Berkeley who were already active in the field, and thereby opened both a second research career and a new field in which the Chemical (now Chemical and Biomolecular) Engineering Department has excelled.[32] This transition and its importance were taken into account in the advancement system.

Similarly, as is also noted by Thoenig and Paradeise,[33] the criterion for hiring entry-level assistant professors to the faculty is promise for a productive, creative, and innovative career, rather than the amount of accomplishment already, or number of publications, or even the quality of previous mentors, although the recommendations of others with high standing in the field do carry considerable weight. At Berkeley, if a candidate of the quality and promise sought cannot be found in a given year's search, the recruitment authorization is automatically carried over for another year. That policy removes any incentive to fill a position just to avoid loss of the position.

RESOLVING DISAGREEMENTS

Again using the Berkeley campus as an example, if the vice provost upon reviewing the "minute" of the Budget Committee concludes that the recommendation does not reflect the evaluation or that additional factors when brought into the evaluation may lead to a different conclusion, the vice provost writes back to the Budget Committee expressing these concerns and offering any pertinent additional thoughts. The Budget Committee then reevaluates the case and submits a new minute, which may, but usually does not, contain a different recommendation. If upon reviewing this second minute, the vice provost leans toward a decision that differs from the action recommended by the Budget Committee, the vice provost requests a meeting in person with the Budget Committee. In the case of a tenure

---

[32] John Prausnitz and Harvey Blanch, "Charles R. Wilke, Professor of Chemical Engineering, Emeritus, Berkeley, 1917–2003," In Memoriam, University of California, https://perma.cc/49X4-LTK6.

[33] Thoenig and Paradeise, 2014, *loc. cit.*

decision or if the Budget Committee so requests, the chancellor and/or provost join that meeting. If the higher officers are to join, the provost or vice provost of course first makes sure that the administrators are in essential agreement. Following the in-person meeting, the Budget Committee furnishes yet another minute, conveying their current recommendation. The administration then makes its decision.

Tradition has it that ultimate disagreements will be few and far between. The number of ultimate disagreements for the year is reported by the Budget Committee in its annual report and is typically quite small, having averaged over the period from 2004 to 2013 about three out of a total on the order of about nine hundred cases per year (circa 0.3 percent).[34]

The decision is relayed in a memo from the provost or vice provost to the dean, with that memo typically containing much of the language in the Budget Committee minute. The action memo, redacted if necessary to protect confidentiality of reviewers, is relayed to the department chair and the candidate, thereby providing explicit feedback to the candidate. If the candidate, department chair, or both believe that the rationale or process is somehow flawed, there are avenues for appeal.

COMPARISON WITH OTHER UNIVERSITIES

The faculty advancement system of the University of California differs from those of all, or very nearly all, other US universities. The more common approach in the United States is for intense reviews to be attached only to promotions—associate professor, professor, and tenure, if that is a separate review. Salary increases in between promotions from rank to rank are more commonly determined annually by the department chair or possibly a dean, sometimes with the assistance of an internal departmental or college committee, but without the depth of review that occurs within the University of

---

[34] Annual Reports, Committee on Budget and Interdepartmental Relations, Academic Senate, University of California, Berkeley,
https://web.archive.org/web/20160510183333/http://academic-senate.berkeley.edu/committees/BIR.

California and usually without any systematic post-tenure peer review. By contrast the University of California carries out in-depth reviews not only for promotions but also for all salary increases other than cost-of-living adjustments, before and after tenure is granted.

WHAT IS GAINED BY THE UC METHODOLOGY?

The nature, intensity, and thoroughness of the University of California reviews accomplish a number of desirable objectives, both directly and indirectly, as follows.

Rigorous, Objective, and Even Application of High Standards

Standards are kept high by virtue of the culture of excellence that pervades the university, the system of multiple levels of review, and participation in those reviews by many faculty members and faculty administrators. Any introduction of lower standards, bias, prejudice, or campus politics would be exposed to others on review committees or at other levels of review. That fact provides a strong deterrent against any lowering of standards. The campus-wide aspects of the Budget Committee or CAP, the multidisciplinary composition of ad hoc committees when they are used, and the final decision-maker(s) ensure that the same high standards are applied evenly to all academic areas of the university. Members of the faculty tend to support these standards strongly, since they appreciate the value of being associated with an institution of the highest standing.

All Disciplines and Professions Are Reflected in the Review Process

The way that the University of California has fully integrated professional schools into the review and advancement processes and all essential academic functions of the campus stands in contrast to the situations of the professional schools at many other leading universities, such as Harvard and Yale, where the professional schools stand alone, making their own determinations internally.

The variety in disciplinary backgrounds of members of the campus committees means that the differences among the academic natures of the disciplines must be recognized and taken into account, albeit by what can be difficult discussions in individual cases. Faculty members from academic disciplines must think together about what constitutes creativity and original accomplishment in the professions and vice versa.

Incentives for Faculty Members throughout Their Careers

The system of continual reviews and the fact that rank and salary are directly tied to the reviews provide strong incentives for continual strong performance throughout a faculty member's career. For most universities elsewhere in the United States and many others throughout the world, the lack of, or weakness of, post-tenure review is a major issue.[35] There is a perception that faculty members can coast once they have tenure, and that does indeed happen for what is hopefully a small fraction of faculty members. The issue carries across to the general public, where there can be perceptions and even political stances that tenure for faculty in universities, as well as for teachers in schools, leads to suboptimal performance.

The University of California review system provides incentives that discourage coasting. In addition to continued strong performance being the route to higher salary, it is embarrassing for a faculty member to have subpar performance revealed to colleagues within the department and throughout the campus. Most faculty members would not want to be exposed in that way. That fact is probably also the reason why the relatively very few nonperforming faculty members have retired or left the University of California rather than suffering the embarrassment associated with the many-step process for dismissal for incompetent performance (see below).

Equal Opportunities for All Faculty Members

The University of California makes it clear that every faculty member, regardless of discipline or other factors, has the same opportunities. The same review systems and campus-wide standards apply to all. Faculty appointments are made with the understanding that tenured positions are available to assistant professors if they meet

---

[35] See, e.g., Gabriela Montell, "The Fallout from Post-Tenure Review," *Chronicle of Higher Education*, October 17, 2002.

the absolute standard. There is no quota on the overall number of tenured faculty positions nor is there any need to wait until a tenured position becomes available.

An Understandable and Generally Accepted Salary System

The clarity, objectivity, and relative openness of the system mean that faculty members generally understand their circumstances with regard to advancement. Any faculty member interested in the salaries of other faculty members can gain that information from the public posting of salaries, mentioned earlier. These factors serve to minimize suspicions of unfair or partisan treatment.

Nurturing the Culture of Excellence

The involvement of faculty members from many disciplines on CAP or the Budget Committee, the involvement of faculty members from other disciplines on ad hoc committees, and indeed the involvement of so many faculty members throughout the continual advancement and promotion processes all make the process widely owned and valued by the faculty. The continual discussions and assessment of quality among faculty at the departmental level also maintain a continual awareness of the issue of academic quality among the faculty.[36]

The Quality Standards of Any One Department Are Seen by Others

Higher-level reviewers continually see the ways in which faculty members in different departments interpret and exercise quality standards. Positive recommendations from a department for tenure or other advancement can fail under higher-level review. When this happens, it reflects negatively on the initiating department. Repeated situations of that sort can be negative factors when the CAP or Budget Committee comments in programmatic reviews of departments.

Many Academic Administrators Maintain Research and Even Teaching

Nearly all department chairs, many deans, some provosts and chancellors, and even one recent president of the University of

---

[36] Thoenig and Paradeise, 2014, *loc. cit.*, elaborate upon these factors.

California have maintained some research and/or teaching while in their administrative positions. In addition to reflecting a love for those activities, keeping active in academic matters affords a way to experience firsthand the factors affecting the faculty. As well, all administrators drawn from the faculty retain a shadow professorial salary to which they will return when they complete their administrative service. That shadow salary continues to receive reviews and advancements while the faculty member is an administrator.

Faculty Members Find One Another

As a side benefit, as faculty members from different disciplines work together in carrying out academic reviews, they may find aspects of the work of other faculty members that are interesting and useful to them. Multidisciplinary research and teaching teams have come together as a result of participation in the review process. It is also beneficial for faculty members simply to gain some understanding and appreciation of other disciplines on the campus.

CHALLENGING ASPECTS

Speed

The multiple layers of review and the various safeguards mean that the process can be slow and is a burden on a number of people: departmental colleagues, department chairs, internal reviewers, external referees, and decision-makers. Faculty members do generally value the process and are accepting of the impositions on their time. From an administrative standpoint, the faculty time consumed, although substantial, is a vital component of building and maintaining the high quality and stature of the university.

An obvious question is how well the system can respond to the need for a quick review that could lead to a salary increase to counter a recruitment offer from another institution. In practice, the answer has been that this can be done surprisingly well. It is a matter of giving top priority for such cases in the queue for review and actions.

Lack of Administrative Discretion

In meetings of UC chancellors and provosts, one does hear complaints that the nature of the review system prevents administrative leaders from making appointments, advancements, or promotions that they would otherwise want to do. That is a natural result of the multiple participants and tensions associated with the process. Academic Senate review does serve as a brake or a checking mechanism. If one believes in administrative checks and balances and that the involvement of multiple minds makes for better decisions, this factor can be viewed as a strong advantage rather than a disadvantage.

Differences in Applications of Standards on Different Campuses

Reviews are carried out and decisions are made on the individual campuses, with no coordination other than the multifaceted review process for additions and changes to the university-wide *Academic Personnel Manual* (APM). Despite the detailed wording of the criteria and procedures in the APM, the fact that the campuses function separately holds the potential that standards and their application may drift apart among the campuses. Several factors serve to counteract that possibility. There is a university-wide Committee on Academic Personnel reporting to the Academic Council, and the chairs of the campus CAPs and the Berkeley Budget Committee are members of it. That committee considers policy matters, standards, and applications of standards. The existence of multiple reviewers at various levels of review serves to even out extremes on a campus.

During my service as university-wide provost and senior vice president—academic affairs, I noticed that campuses differed as to whether the CAP/Budget Committee or the administration tended to be stricter in cases of disagreement. That factor too serves to even things out among the campuses. Finally, the fact that new campuses initially have Committees on Academic Personnel composed of faculty from existing campuses means that the standards and approaches of the existing campuses are imbued into new campuses from the start.

Departures from the Salary Scale

As already noted, in recent years market forces have brought about more and more upward departures from the set salary scale.

Off-scale or "decoupled" salaries have become much more common. In part this phenomenon reflects market forces that vary considerably from one discipline to another, and that factor was initially addressed by the creation of the higher salary scales for law and for business, economics, and engineering. Since these scales were created, the marketplace has intensified further, and there has been reluctance, especially on the part of the Academic Senate, to make further across-the-board adjustments applying to all faculty members in a discipline or subdiscipline. The result has been a continual increase in the use of off-scale salaries. However, the step system continues to serve as a valuable measure of accomplishment.

COMMENT

In any academic advancement system, there is a balance to be made between intensity and frequency of review, on the one hand, and the burden of work that is placed upon extramural evaluators, internal reviewers, and administrative decision-makers, on the other hand. The University of California is clearly on the extreme high side with regard to the burden, but through all the opinions that I have heard expressed during what is now a career of fifty-five years in many different positions within the university, I know that the strong belief of those who have been involved with the system is that, in general, the results warrant the burden. Specific arguments can be made and are made continually as to whether various individual facets of the system might be streamlined, but the general conclusion regarding the worth of the system as a whole remains strong.

OTHER FACETS

Family-Oriented Policies

A number of policies and procedures have been invoked so as to make the academic promotion and advancement system accommodating for childbearing, child-rearing, and family issues. These are outlined in the *Academic Personnel Manual*[37] and include stopping the tenure clock for one year for childbirth or a total of two years for multiple children, childbearing leave with or without pay, active service with modified duties, and reduction in time to accommodate family needs. These policies are not gender dependent.

Mentoring

Formal mentoring of pretenure faculty members by senior faculty is encouraged and often set up formally within departments. An aim is to keep the junior faculty member aware of what is sought in advancement considerations, how proposals to funders of research can best be made, how the various services at the university function and can best be used, and other matters of importance to the career of the junior faculty member.

Dismissal

Coupled with the requirement for reviews at least every five years, there is are criteria for determining incompetence and an established procedure that can ultimately lead to dismissal of a tenured faculty member for incompetent performance.[38] This procedure involves a departmental recommendation, responses by the professor, multiple reviews, specifications of what improvement is needed, opportunities between reviews to make that improvement, provision for an evidentiary hearing before the Committee on Privilege and Tenure of the Academic Senate, an ultimate recommendation by the chancellor of the campus, and then transmission via the president to the regents for action. In practice the existence of the process has been valuable for convincing poorly performing faculty members to retire or otherwise voluntarily depart from the university. Only a very unusual faculty member would be willing to go through the exposure and intense review that the policy involves.

---

[37] "Benefits and Privileges: Family Accommodations for Childbearing and Childrearing," Section 760, *Academic Personnel Manual*, University of California, https://perma.cc/23DX-26JA.
[38] "Termination for Incompetent Performance," Section 075, *Academic Personnel Manual*, University of California, https://perma.cc/5ZL6-ZHXV.

Sanctions up to and including dismissals of faculty members can also occur for willful misconduct. The Faculty Code of Conduct[39] gives criteria to be used, and the *Academic Personnel Manual*[40] gives procedures and types of sanctions that may be applied. In practice there have been dismissals for reasons such as unethical actions in medicine and sexual misconduct.

SUMMARY CONCLUSION

Many faculty members and leaders of the University of California believe that the system of faculty review for appointment, promotion, and advancement is the single most identifiable factor underlying the success and stature of the university. Throughout their careers, faculty members are reviewed in depth by their peers on research and other creative activities, teaching, professional competence (if applicable), and service. The intervals for these reviews are typically two to four years. Salaries and rank advancements are tied to the reviews.

Teaching abilities and accomplishments are evaluated in a variety of ways. Research is evaluated for quality more than quantity, with well-recognized external reviewers asked for evaluations at several points along a career. Service activities that are considered include contributions to the university, the discipline or profession, national and state bodies, and the community.

The intensity and frequency of reviews give a faculty member continual valuable feedback and serve as prime performance incentives because of the reluctance of faculty members to appear less than first class to their reviewing peers. It has been noted by many observers that a culture of quality pervades the University of California. In addition to the reviews themselves, the participation of so many faculty members and faculty administrators in the reviews serves to reinforce the importance of academic quality continually.

---

[39] "Faculty Code of Conduct," Section 015, *Academic Personnel Manual*, University of California, https://perma.cc/YK95-N44A.

[40] "University Policy on Faculty Misconduct and the Administration of Discipline," Section 016, *Academic Personnel Manual*, University of California, https://perma.cc/KZY5-CDF9.

Faculty members from professional schools and academic disciplines participate together on review committees. The many review committees also provide a useful mechanism for faculty members from different parts of a campus to come to know one another. These contacts have occasionally led to collaboration in research and teaching.

12.
Sustaining Excellence: Program Review, Planning, and Change

About eighty-five institutions in the Western world established by 1520 still exist in recognizable forms, with similar functions and with unbroken histories, including the Catholic church, the Parliaments of the Isle of Man, of Iceland, and of Great Britain, several Swiss cantons, and seventy universities. Kings that rule, feudal lords with vassals, and guilds with monopolies are all gone. The seventy universities, however, are still in the same locations with some of the same buildings, with professors and students doing much the same things, and with governance carried on in much the same ways. There have been many intervening variations on ancient themes, it is true, but the eternal themes of teaching, scholarship, and service, in one combination or another, continue. Looked at from within, universities have changed enormously in the emphases on their several functions and in their guiding spirits, but looked at from without and comparatively, they are among the least changed of institutions.
      —*Clark Kerr*[1]

In universities, sunset is an hour that almost never arrives.
      —*Donald Kennedy*[2]

The glacial pace of university decision making and academic change simply may not be sufficiently responsive to allow the university to control its own destiny.
      —*James J. Duderstadt*[3]

---

[1] Clark Kerr, *The Uses of the University*, 5th ed. (Cambridge, MA: Harvard University Press, 2001), p. 115.
[2] Donald Kennedy, "Making Choices in the Research University," *Daedalus* 122, no. 4 (Fall 1993): p. 139.
[3] James J. Duderstadt, "Fire, Ready, Aim! University Decision-Making during an Era of Rapid Change," in W. Z. Hirsch and L. E. Weber, eds., *Governance in Higher Education: The University in a State of Flux* (London: Economica, 2001), p. 41.

Chapter 12

No man should tamper with a university who does not know and love it well.
—Lord Chesterfield, cited by Frank T. Rhodes[4]

The preceding chapter dealt with the ways in which the University of California evaluates, advances, and incentivizes faculty members so as to assure that they have creative and productive careers at the tops of their fields. It is, of course, also vital to assure that entire academic programs of teaching and research are similarly distinguished and are current with respect to the needs of students, society, and opportunities for research and teaching. That topic, too, fits in with a general culture of academic excellence and is one of the key ways in which that culture is both exercised and maintained. This chapter explores that topic both for the University of California and in a more general context, along with some specific examples.

CHANGE

Accomplishment of change at universities, and particularly research universities, is a subject that is much discussed and often maligned. The review and decision-making processes that would lead to change are usually complex and involve multiple layers, consultation, and checks and balances. The inherent conservatism of the faculty—that is, their usual preference to keep doing what they have been doing—is frequently cited as a limitation. The facts that consensus-building processes can be drawn out and tend toward the status quo are often cited as other factors inhibiting change. Anything that is threatened will have its supporters, and those supporters will generally have ways to influence the decision process. Administrators from department chairs on up may choose to abate conflicts by finding avenues that cause the least collective unhappiness.

---

[4] Frank H. T. Rhodes, "Reinventing the University," in Luc E. Weber and James J. Duderstadt, eds., *Reinventing the Research University* (London: Economica, 2004), p. 13.

As a consequence of these factors, change in universities tends to be unidirectional, in that change that adds functions is much easier than change that deletes functions. Smelser[5] examined this situation at length and gave the phenomenon the name *accretion*. It works well in times of expansion and growing budgets. It is not well attuned to times of budget stringency and contraction.

Following his well-known observation that leads off this chapter, Clark Kerr elaborates on the durability of "the eternal themes of teaching, scholarship, and service," and then observes that research universities are the least fundamentally changed portion of higher education over what is now almost 150 years since Daniel Coit Gilman built Johns Hopkins on the German model. Kerr's statements and his surrounding analysis[6] can be cited as a manifestation of the difficulty of accomplishing change in universities. But his words can just as readily be read to indicate that universities have been sufficiently resilient and successful in evolving over the years and centuries so that they have survived over such long times without having been replaced by entirely new or different institutions. They have been adaptable.

There are those who postulate that universities are now subject to *disruptive innovation*,[7] whereby if they do not change to a large enough degree and sufficiently rapidly, they will be put out of the market. The quote from James Duderstadt at the start of this chapter reflects that viewpoint.

Are research universities in a period of such disruptive innovation? What are the extents and rates at which research universities can change by evolution? Do particular types of change occur more readily than other types? Do certain approaches toward accomplishing change work better than others? In addressing these and similar questions, it is useful to drill down into the specifics of actual case studies, which can reveal what has actually enabled and restricted substantial changes in the research university setting. I first outline the program-review and academic-planning processes of the University of California and then

---

[5] Neil J. Smelser, *Dynamics of the Contemporary University: Growth, Accretion, and Conflict* (Berkeley: University of California Press and Center for Studies in Higher Education, 2013).
[6] Clark Kerr, 2001, *op. cit.*, pp. 114–120.
[7] Clayton M. Christensen and Henry J. Eyring, *The Innovative University: Changing the DNA of Higher Education from the Inside Out* (San Francisco: Jossey-Bass, 2011).

examine four cases of actual and potential significant change for the Berkeley campus. None of the changes in these cases are as dramatic as the more draconian predictions of disruptive innovation, but they do provide insights into adaptability, governance, and what will and will not work. I then draw some generalizations from them. I then return to the question of the abilities of universities in general and the University of California in particular to accomplish needed changes.

PROGRAM REVIEWS

The main mechanism by which the University of California assesses the quality, issues, and needs of existing academic programs is regular program review. The results of these reviews feed into academic planning processes that can lead to change. University-wide policy calls for regular reviews of both academic departments and organized research units.[8]

The Berkeley campus carries out program reviews at intervals of eight[9] years for its roughly sixty-five academic departments. Reviews of organized research units have been suspended since the early 2000s for budgetary reasons; it is both desirable and intended that they be started again at some point. The current Berkeley review procedure is laid out in detail in the *Academic Program Review Guide*[10] and is summarized here.

The review process at Berkeley is overseen by the Program Review Oversight Committee, a joint committee of the administration and the Academic Senate.[11] The reviews of individual departments are carried

---

[8] Compendium: University-Wide Review Processes for Academic Programs, Academic Units, & Research Units, University of California, September 2014, https://perma.cc/7LYX-K9DH.
[9] Extended to nine years for the currently undefined duration of budget stringency.
[10] UC Berkeley Guide for the Review of Existing Instructional Programs, rev. June 2015, https://perma.cc/4QRJ-Y6Q6.
[11] "Program Review Oversight Committee, Vice Provost for Academic and Space Planning," University of California, Berkeley, https://perma.cc/D4W2-NTBT.

out on a fixed cycle.[12] As of 2016 the process begins with preparation of a packet of data by the campus Office of Planning and Analysis, including information on peer comparison departments at other institutions. The department being reviewed uses this information to prepare an extensive self-study report. The department also provides nominations for members of the External Review Committee, an academic senate liaison, and appropriate comparison departments on the Berkeley campus. From these nominations the External Review Committee of three to five members is created. One senate liaison is selected with the participation of the Committee on Committees of the Berkeley Division Senate. The senate liaison is a source of consultation for the External Review Committee with regard to Berkeley campus and University of California matters, serves as the senate's general overseer of the review, and evaluates the general environment of the department. The External Review Committee receives the data and the self-study, comes to the campus for a multiday visit, and prepares a report. The department then comments on the reports of the External Review Committee and the senate liaison. These materials are then passed to five different Berkeley Division Senate committees[13] for consideration. Analyses and recommendations from these committees feed to the Division Council of the Academic Senate, which adds comments. There is then a wrap-up meeting of the Program Review Oversight Committee, senate liaison, and dean, followed by transmission of a formal feedback document to the department. The department then supplies a response to that document indicating what steps it intends to take.

As for the evaluations of individual faculty members described in chapter 11, the fact that faculty members from many different departments are involved in these reviews serves to bring the different disciplines together and create a shared sense of pride and collective ownership of the academic quality of the campus. Again, the professional schools and colleges are involved proportionately, bringing the professions and the academic disciplines together.

---

[12] Academic Program Reviews Expanded 9-Year Cycle, https://perma.cc/6XMB-TAAN.
[13] Budget and Interdepartmental Relations; Academic Planning and Resources Allocation; Educational Policy; Diversity, Equity, and Campus Climate; and the Graduate Council.

Historically, academic program reviews started in 1971 and have taken various forms over the years.[14] At the times of the reviews considered in the cases analyzed below, there were campus review committees composed of faculty members from other departments, chosen by the administration on the basis of nominations from the Academic Senate. An external review committee could also be chosen and utilized. The review process began with the unit assembling information, followed by visits by the external review committee (if used) and the campus review committee, then a report from the external committee that would be input to the campus committee, then a report from the campus committee, then reviews of that report by committees of the Academic Senate, and then advice from the senate committees to the administration, who would determine the path of action.

Follow-ups on reviews are ad hoc to the issues uncovered and can feed into the planning processes described below. Examples are given in the case studies.

For comparison with the Berkeley process, the program review processes of the Los Angeles,[15] Davis,[16] Santa Cruz,[17] and other campuses are available.

ACADEMIC PLANNING PROCESSES

Since the time of Clark Kerr as president, it has been University of California policy for campuses to select and define their own academic programs, with review university-wide including the Academic Council of the Academic Senate and its committees, and then approval by the regents for proposals of new schools and colleges, and for new

---

[14] UC Berkeley Guide for the Review of Existing Instructional Programs, *loc. cit.*, June 2015, appendix I: "Historical Background."
[15] Academic Program Reviews, Academic Senate, University of California, Los Angeles, https://perma.cc/9HSH-F7QK.
[16] Graduate Program Review Guidelines, 2016–17, Program Review Committee, University of California, Davis, https://perma.cc/E2VM-U7D7.
[17] Academic Program Reviews, University of California, Santa Cruz, https://perma.cc/2FFC-FBNC.

programs with major budgetary impact. The university does not assign particular new programs to individual campuses, although the politically driven negotiation processes in the 1960s that paired medical schools with the Davis and Irvine campuses and a law school with the Davis campus (chapter 10) were exceptions to a degree. Campus enrollment targets have historically been determined through a process of university-wide coordination by the Office of the President, with proposals from individual campuses adjusted when needed by working with the campuses interactively to meet the overall Master Plan enrollment requirements. During the administrations of UC presidents Hitch and Saxon (1968–83), there was an Academic Planning and Program Review Board (APPRB) university-wide, as described in chapter 6 and by Pelfrey.[18]

Campuses typically prepare strategic academic plans at intervals of about ten years. Links to current campus plans are provided on the website of the UC Office of Enterprise Risk Management.[19] These strategic academic plans are quite broad. Among their purposes is to feed into the campus long-range development plans (LRDPs), which are legally required environmental-review documents for physical planning purposes. The LRDPs are subject to formal public review and input. In between strategic academic plans, identification of planning and programs needs stems continually from the ongoing program-review process.

Other than establishing and disestablishing academic colleges, schools, and departments, which are treated in the cases below, the primary mechanisms for implementing planning recommendations and for adjusting from year to year at Berkeley are the annual allocations of faculty recruitment authorizations,[20] All vacated faculty positions revert to the Chancellor's Office for evaluation and reassignment to units in

---

[18] Patricia A. Pelfrey, "From the Golden Age to the Age of Austerity: Planning at the University of California, 1968–1983," Research and Occasional Papers Series, no. 8-17, Center for Studies in Higher Education, University of California, Berkeley, July 2017, https://perma.cc/ZB43-GGH5.

[19] "Defining Objectives: Strategic Planning," Office of Enterprise Risk Management, University of California, https://web.archive.org/web/20180611201917/https://www.ucop.edu/enterprise-risk-management/procedures/objective-setting/strategic-planning.html.

[20] "Search Guide for Senate Faculty Recruitments: Policies, Procedures and Practices," Office for Faculty Equity and Welfare, University of California, Berkeley, https://perma.cc/EVL7-UAWP.

an annual planning exercise that includes formal faculty-recruitment requests from departments. An exception is made for positions vacated by an assistant professor; these stay with the department so as to remove any concerns that the department could have during the tenure-evaluation process about the retention of the position if tenure were not to be granted. In addition to advising and usually determining the ultimate decision on faculty promotions and advancement, the Berkeley Committee on Budget and Interdepartmental Relations advises the provost on the allocations of faculty positions for recruitment. The specific information sought for the process of allocating faculty positions on the Berkeley campus is available.[21] That information is extensive and consists of analysis of departmental strengths and needs, the relationship of the request(s) to the academic plan developed in connection with the last departmental review, and justifications of the request(s).

Historically, the Berkeley campus and most of the other campuses have emphasized recruitment of entry-level faculty. Thus, in the annual Berkeley process for faculty recruitment allocations, most authorizations are for recruitment at the assistant professor level, and strong justification is required when a more senior recruitment is to be considered. The university has been very successful in selecting and nurturing entry-level faculty members who become stars in their fields. There is also a more subtle process at play whereby entry-level faculty members naturally attune to the culture of an academic department, while senior additions from elsewhere can be more disruptive to that culture. On the other hand, at the start of a new campus, a more even distribution of hires among grades of the professorship is important, as is attested by the issues described in chapter 10 for the early years of the Riverside, Santa Cruz, and Merced campuses, when large blocks of entry-level faculty members moved through the ranks more or less simultaneously.

The reason that the annual allocation of authorizations for recruitment of faculty is such an important component of academic planning is that it is the mechanism by which the collective expertise of

---

[21] Faculty FTE Request Template, TY 2017–18, https://perma.cc/F4LQ-6TVZ.

the faculty changes and is thereby a prime method by which the university continually modernizes its programmatic coverage. The career span for an entry-level faculty member who is successful in making tenure is typically of the order of thirty-five to forty years; so the search and selection processes for every faculty recruitment are critically important and require a long-range viewpoint.

The more formal academic planning processes are supplemented by a number of less formal consultative mechanisms, notably the university-wide Academic Planning Council and the regular meetings of chancellors, various sorts of vice chancellors, campus librarians, etcetera (chapter 8).

FOUR CASES OF CHANGE IN ACADEMIC PROGRAMS AT BERKELEY[22]

The purpose of the analyses presented in this section is to examine the roles of governance in four instances of change at the Berkeley campus[23] of the University of California. In all of these cases, the ongoing program-review process was a critical element in initiating the consideration of change. The outcomes differ among the four cases. One (the third) led to a large reorganization of structures and

---

[22] I originally discussed these four cases in C. Judson King, "Change and Governance at the University of California: Comparative Case Studies," Research and Occasional Papers Series no. 11-14, November 2014, https://perma.cc/3TLG-U4S9.

[23] There are, of course, examples of major academic change at other University of California campuses as well. Two that are described in chapter 10 are the "Rearrangement" at the Santa Cruz campus, carried out through a multifaceted process culminating in 1978, and the creation of the College of Biological and Agricultural Sciences, later the College of Natural and Agricultural Sciences, at Riverside during the time that Ivan Hinderaker was chancellor. A major example at UCLA is the Professional Schools Restructuring Initiative, coordinated during the 1990s by Executive Vice Chancellor Andrea Rich (see, e.g., Marina Dundjerski, "UCLA: The First Century," (London: Third Millennium Publishing, 2012), pp. 218–219; Ralph Frammolino and Marina Dundjerski, "Plan to Dismantle 4 UCLA Schools Protested: Students, Faculty Resist a Proposal to Cut Several Graduate Programs," *Los Angeles Times*, October 15, 1993, https://perma.cc/6U3AA-KHF2. More broadly, the response made in 1995 and later conforming to both regents' resolutions and state law that precluded considerations of race and several other faxtors in admission and employment resulted in major changes in admissions (chapter 15) and development of large special outreach programs relating to both schools and precollege students (chapter 16). Finally the entire process of devolving governance to the campuses in the time of Clark Kerr (chapters 2, 3, and 6) involved major changes.

affiliations. For another (the first), a professional school was closed. In yet another case (the fourth), a professional school was discontinued and another was started with a much wider and more modern scope. In the other case (the second), a professional school was assessed at length and a decision was ultimately made to retain it, while seeking a much more professional bent.

A common denominator for three of these examples (the Schools of Criminology, Education, and Library and Information Studies) is the tension that exists in professional schools between educating practitioners, on the one hand, and engaging in research and other creative activities of a sort that will carry intellectual weight in a distinguished university, on the other hand. I have addressed that subject elsewhere[24] in more depth; it is a fundamental challenge to many professional schools in major research universities.

Closure of the School of Criminology at Berkeley (1972–76)

Berkeley and the University of California had lead roles in launching criminology as an academic field. That history is told by Morn.[25] August Vollmer[26] was police chief for the city of Berkeley and a leader in developing education for law enforcement, corrections, and forensics. He defined needs and worked closely with the University of California to launch criminology instruction in 1916 in the form of summer-session courses. Vollmer led and developed a school of thought on criminology education that spread throughout the country through so-called "V-Men," who had been trained by Vollmer and/or believed strongly in college-level education for police and related professions. With Vollmer's active participation, the University of California program at Berkeley developed into a full curriculum and degree program over the years, and became a separate professional

---

[24] C. Judson King, "A Provost for Professional Schools and Colleges," Research and Occasional Papers Series, no. 3-13, Center for Studies in Higher Education, University of California, Berkeley, CA, February 2013, https://perma.cc/3CDM-2CS9.

[25] Frank Morn, *Academic Politics and the History of Criminal Justice Education* (Westport, CT: Greenwood Press, 1995).

[26] Willard Oliver, *August Vollmer: The Father of American Policing* (Durham, NC: Carolina Academic Press, 2017).

school in 1950. The program served to train law enforcement professionals in law enforcement, corrections, and criminalistics.

Throughout its existence, the program and school were subject to a tension between needs for instruction for practicing professionals, on the one hand, and desires for pertinent research of an intellectually high caliber on the other. Initially, the school stressed training of professionals and did so through the deanship of O. W. Wilson (1950–60).[27] However, the relative absence of research was continually noted by both the administration and the Academic Senate and was out of step with trends throughout the rest of the university, particularly after World War II. In 1961, in a deliberate move to increase the research roles of the school, the Berkeley campus appointed as dean Joseph D. Lohman, who was highly respected as both a professional and an academic. Lohman introduced a program of research in the school, but of a sort that was viewed by many within the campus and elsewhere as being more in the "job shop" vein rather than addressing fundamental intellectual questions.[28] Unfortunately, Lohman died unexpectedly in 1968.

There were two trends that affected the School of Criminology contemporaneously with the student unrest (chapter 2) of the mid- to late 1960s and early 1970s. One was the growth, particularly within the Berkeley school, of a field that came to be known as radical criminology. The field was and is much more concerned with social justice than with the classical elements of law enforcement, forensic science, and corrections. The growth of this field within the school created tensions between the school and its various supporters and potential supporters, substantially lessening the interests that the law enforcement and corrections communities had in the school. Matters came to a head with the unsuccessful 1969 tenure case of Anthony

---

[27] Arthur H. Sherry, Milton Chernin, and Austin MacCormick, "Orlando Winfield Wilson, Criminology: Berkeley," In Memoriam, July 1975, University of California, https://perma.cc/9ZVW-RZJ3..

[28] Editors, "Editorial: Berkeley's School of Criminology, 1950–1976," *Crime and Social Justice* 6 (Summer 1976): pp. 1–3, https://perma.cc/AG5P-RXU8.

Platt, a Marxist radical criminologist.[29, 30, 31] The denial of tenure to Platt and a subsequent denial to another radical-criminology scholar, Herman Schwendinger in 1973, became celebrated causes.

A second major trend during the same period was a large shift in enrollment in the school from the graduate (professional) level to the undergraduate level. Would-be professional students saw the school as not meeting their needs well as a stepping-stone toward professional jobs, while undergraduates saw the school as being in line with social concerns of the times and a path toward one of the easier degrees on campus. Enrollment in the school became 68 percent undergraduate in 1969–70 and 82 percent in 1971–72.[32]

Shifts in deans for the school and the growth of related but competing interests on campus also became important. For three years after the death of Lohman, there were acting deans, the first of whom resigned during the 1968–69 year in sympathy with campus student strikers. Finally Sheldon Messinger was appointed dean in 1971. Messinger was a respected sociologist with scholarly interests in aspects of social justice. He had been among those involved in the 1961 formation of the Center for Law and Society, an organized research unit affiliated with the School of Law at Berkeley that took a more research- and discipline-based approach to social issues and the law.[33]

In the mid-1960s, the Berkeley campus, through the dean of the Graduate Division working with the Academic Senate, devised and launched[34] what became the regular program of reviews of academic departments and schools. This program had been developing for several years when the School of Criminology was selected, along with

---

[29] Richard Schauffler, "Criminology at Berkeley: Resisting Academic Repression," *Crime and Social Justice* 1, no. 1 (1974).
[30] Albert H. Bowker, oral history, pp. 16–17, Regional Oral History Office, University of California, 1995, https://oac.cdlib.org/ark:/13030/hb1p3001qq/?brand=oac.
[31] George J. Maslach, oral history, pp. 429–430, Regional Oral History Office, University of California, Berkeley, CA, 2000, https://archive.org/details/aeronoticaleng00maslrich..
[32] Morn, 1995, *op. cit.*, p. 112.
[33] Jerome H. Skolnick et al., "Tribute: Retirement of Sheldon L. Messinger," *California Law Review* 80, no. 2 (1992): pp. 307–316.
[34] Sanford S. Elberg, oral history, pp. 202–211, Regional Oral History Office, University of California, Berkeley, 1990, https://archive.org/details/graduateeducation00elberich.

other units, for review in 1972. The review committee was formed in December 1972 and reported in June 1973. The committee recommended disestablishment of the school, with a primary reason being that it was "a professional school without a professional commitment or program, or without effective links to its professional constituencies." [35] The recommendation of the committee was reviewed and supported by the relevant Academic Senate committees, and passed on to the administration, who made the decision to close the school. The administrative decision process is described by Albert Bowker, [36] Sanford Elberg, [37] and George Maslach, [38] who were chancellor, dean of the Graduate Division, and provost—professional schools and colleges, respectively, at the time. The school would admit no new students and would close when the last students graduated in 1976. Substantial demonstrations and a building occupancy by supporters of the school ensued, but the decision held.

No tenured faculty members were dismissed as a result of the closure. Several of them went to a new Jurisprudence and Social Policy Program within the School of Law, which was formed around them and which also gives an undergraduate degree within the College of Letters and Science. The Law School has proven to be a good academic home for this program, and the program has provided an effective link from the Law School to the scholarly work of the rest of the campus, supporting the Berkeley concept that the professional schools and academic departments are involved on equal bases in research, the Academic Senate, and the academic operation of the campus. Those faculty members involved with criminalistics (forensic science) went to the School of Public Health and formed a small subprogram there. There were no substantial budgetary savings associated with the closure other than administrative staff savings.

Another way of looking at the fate of the school was provided by Sheldon Messinger in a memo to his faculty in 1973,[39] indicating that the former programs of the school had been "displaced by the

---

[35] Morn, 1995, *op. cit.*, p. 113.
[36] Bowker, 1995, *op. cit.*, pp. 17–19.
[37] Elberg, 1990, *op. cit.*, pp. 209–211.
[38] Maslach, 2000, *op. cit.*, pp. 420–423.
[39] Morn, 1995, *op. cit.*, p. 111.

development of criminal justice programs in other institutions. The vocational program of the first years is now offered by police and other academies. The vocationally oriented academic program that followed is now offered by the community colleges. The agency-oriented but more generalized academic program that came later is now the staple of the state colleges[40]—and, if my guess is correct, the state colleges will be moving into the area of management education." In that sense, the closure of the Berkeley School of Criminology can also be regarded as a logical consequence of the distribution of missions among the sectors of public higher education occasioned by the California Master Plan for Higher Education of 1960. Criminal justice or related programs are now offered at nine California State University campuses.[41]

Review, Evaluation, and Ultimate Retention and Reorientation of the School of Education at Berkeley (1978–82)

Schools of education often have difficult situations within major research universities, for they are probably the academic units most torn by the competing forces of accomplishing professional instruction and seeking incisive research of the highest intellectual caliber. The Berkeley School of Education is no exception. The histories of the Berkeley and UCLA Schools of Education are outlined and contrasted by Clifford and Guthrie.[42]

In 1976 a series of events started that ended up putting the Berkeley School of Education under intense scrutiny with closure of the school being a distinct and even likely possibility. The process again started with a scheduled review, this time by the university-wide Academic Planning and Program Review Board (APPRB), which is described in chapter 6. The review by the APPRB covered all schools of education within the University of California, and the recommendations regarding the Berkeley School are reported by

---

[40] That is, the California State University, which was formed from state colleges in the 1960 Master Plan for Higher Education.
[41] "Criminal Justice Schools in California,", https://perma.cc/CR6B-XDKN.
[42] Geraldine J. Clifford and James W. Guthrie, *Ed School* (Chicago: University of Chicago Press, 1988), chapter 7.

Smelser.[43] These recommendations were sufficiently critical to spur the Berkeley campus to initiate in 1978 one of the now-regular Berkeley campus program reviews. The recommendations of the report from that campus review, which was both intensive and critical of the School in a number of ways, are also given by Smelser.[44] The review report was then analyzed and commented upon by three committees of the Academic Senate.

By this time the criticism of the School of Education had become fundamental in many ways, and among the possibilities brought forward were reorganization of the school, integration of the school more intimately with the rest of the Berkeley campus, and closure of the school with distribution of key functions to the rest of the campus. At that point (1980–81), the chancellor decided to request a study by a specially formed commission to examine "how the study of Education, both as a field of scholarship and an area of professional practice, should be pursued on the Berkeley campus." The commission, chaired by Neil Smelser, consisted of three distinguished faculty members and one graduate student, all from other areas of the campus but with knowledge of the School of Education.

Compounding the situation was the fact that during the review period, the school had no permanent dean. The last dean, Merle Borrowman, had left the position in 1977. There was an unsuccessful search for a new dean, following by a series of seven(!) acting deans as the matter of a permanent dean was put on hold during the review and decision periods. A new dean eventually arrived in April 1983. There was also an erosion of regular faculty positions during this time, since recruitment authorizations were largely held back until the review issues were resolved by decisions.

Multiple problem areas were identified surrounding the school and are described by Smelser,[45] from the standpoint of a major reviewer, and by Clifford and Guthrie,[46] from the standpoint of two school faculty

---

[43] Neil J. Smelser, *Reflections on the University of California: From the Free Speech Movement to the Global University* (Berkeley: University of California Press, 2010), pp. 268–269.
[44] Smelser, 2010, *op. cit.*, pp. 269–273.
[45] Smelser, 2010, *op. cit.*, pp. 238–251.
[46] Clifford and Guthrie, 1988, *op. cit.*, pp. 305–311.

members at the time who were also both among the acting deans. The issues included the following:

- **Ineffective Internal Governance and Internal Fragmentation by Divisions.** The school was divided into five divisions, which were relatively autonomous and had substantial difficulty working together either for the common good or even to identify and fulfill a common mission for the school. The divisions did not collectively cover the field in a comprehensive way, and the whole was, in these senses, less than the sum of the parts.
- **A Bifurcated Faculty.** Teacher education was not carried out by the professorial faculty members of the school but instead by a separate set of supervisors of teacher education. Consequently, the professorial faculty members were not concerned with the principal professional function, and the opportunity was missed for having a teacher education program closely informed by research. The situation was also beset by issues typically associated with a body of adjunct faculty who see themselves as second-class citizens in some respects relative to the tenure-track faculty.
- **Perceptions and Stature of Research.** By doing research more in the vein of what might be done in the social science disciplines rather than on the profession itself, faculty members set themselves up for comparison in research with faculty from the social science departments, leading to perceptions of lower academic quality.
- **Relatively low national ranking.** The school was ranked number ten in the Ladd-Lipset survey of 1977, a relatively low ranking for a Berkeley academic unit.[47]
- **Role vis-à-vis the California State University.** The California State University has the largest role in teacher education within the state of California. The school had not determined its own best roles in view of that fact.
- **Balance of EdD and PhD Degrees.** The EdD degree was developed and used at an early stage historically at Berkeley. It had been a focal point of the educational efforts of the school. However, with the removal of the foreign-language requirement for the PhD

---

[47] Smelser, 2010, *op. cit.*, pp. 239–240.

degree at Berkeley in 1966 and with what Clifford and Guthrie call the "prestige gradient" associated with the PhD, the balance of degrees awarded by the school swung heavily from the EdD to the PhD. As a result, there became only a hazy difference in content between the two degrees.

- **Diffusion of Education Research outside the School.** The APPRB report of 1976 had found that 88 percent of education research on the Berkeley campus was done outside the School of Education.[48] Yet there was relatively little interaction of the school with other professional schools or academic departments.

The report of the ultimate Smelser Commission on Education is available in its entirety.[49] It offered a number of structural and organizational options, with comparative discussion. One theme was to find ways to foster intellectual ties pertaining to education throughout the campus. Closure of the school with redistribution of its more essential elements throughout the campus was presented as a serious option.

The chancellor throughout the period of the earlier reviews was Albert Bowker, who later observed[50] that he was inclined toward abolishment of the school. However, as of July 1980, the chancellor became Ira Michel Heyman, who chartered the Smelser commission, received its report, submitted it to the Academic Senate for review, and appointed an acting dean from outside the school (Steven Weiner), who would also work with him to analyze the possibilities presented by the commission. Despite the fact that the advice from the pertinent Academic Senate committees tended toward elimination of the school, Chancellor Heyman made the decision in January 1982 to retain the school and to seek changes in its orientation so as to revitalize it professionally. Much of the concern about primary and secondary education in the United States that was reflected soon thereafter in the national report *A Nation at Risk*[51] was already in existence at that time. Heyman cited as his reasoning that he believed that the Berkeley

---

[48] Clifford and Guthrie, 1988, *op. cit.*, p. 310.
[49] Smelser, 2010, *op. cit.*, chapter 8.
[50] Bowker, 1995, *op. cit.*, pp. 49–51.
[51] David P. Gardner et al., *A Nation at Risk: the Imperative for Educational Reform*, National Commission on Excellence in Education, April 1983, https://www2.ed.gov/pubs/NatAtRisk/index.html.

campus "had an obligation to deal with problems besetting elementary and secondary education" and that "progress was more likely in the context of a school than in a number of disassociated departments."[52]

In addition to the negative public image that would come from closure of the school, Heyman may also have been influenced by the stark difficulties associated with dismissal of tenured faculty members or placement of them in other departments.[53] Heyman also indicated a belief in three missions for the School—"training new teachers, providing advanced education for those in the profession, and carrying on relevant research"—and emphasized two goals—"the provision of good teachers by enlarging the certificate program and recruiting within the student body at Berkeley" and "reorientation of the faculty to treat the school more as a professional school than as a pale mirror of departments in the College of Letters and Science."[54]

A widespread search was carried out for a new dean who would reflect and implement these goals, with the eventual appointment of Bernard Gifford, who started in 1983. A PhD biophysicist, Gifford had been deputy chancellor of the New York City school system and at the Russell Sage Foundation before becoming vice president and professor of public policy at the University of Rochester. During his six years as dean, Gifford did move in new directions, building a very well-regarded program in STEM (science, technology, engineering, and mathematics) education and through that and other means increasing the amount of extramurally funded research in the school.[55] However, in later, long-term reflection, Heyman was more pessimistic, saying, "Unfortunately, my vision was not followed and I am sure that someday in the future the problems will be revisited."[56]

---

[52] Ira Michael Heyman, oral history, pp. 64-65. Regional Oral History Office, University of California, Berkeley, 2004, accessed May 30, 2016, https://archive.org/details/heymaniramchanc00heymrich.
[53] Clifford and Guthrie, 1988, *op. cit.*, p. 311.
[54] Heyman, 2004, *op. cit.*, p. 65.
[55] Educom Staff, "Bernie Gifford on the Changing Educational & Technical Landscape," *Educom Review* 31, no. 4 (July/August 1996).
[56] Heyman, 2004. *op. cit.*, p. 65.

Reorganization of the Biological Sciences at Berkeley (1978–90)

Biological sciences underwent rapid advances and large changes in the 1970s, as progress on the molecular scale and in genetics, cloning, and recombinant DNA opened new and powerful knowledge and avenues for much deeper understanding and radical innovation. The intellectual affinities, methodology, and laboratory techniques for research at the forefront now related much more to scale (molecular, cell, whole organism, ecology or groups of organisms) than to the classical divisions by classes of species and by application (e.g., zoology, botany, physiology, entomology). At the beginning of this period, Berkeley had preeminent ranking in the various fields of biology. These activities were divided among about twenty different departments, located primarily in the College of Letters and Science and the College of Natural Resources, the latter having been formed in 1974 by merger of the College of Agriculture and the School of Forestry. These departments were delineated in the classical way, by classes of species and applications.

As we have seen in chapter 10, these changes struck the San Francisco and San Diego campuses of the University of California at early points in the research development of both campuses, and those two campuses were able to do their initial academic building effectively so as to be well positioned in these new approaches to biology from the start. Berkeley, by contrast, was hampered by preexisting structure that did not fit the new directions of the field well.

As the revolution in biological research brought about change, Berkeley started slipping in the ratings. An external review in 1981 observed the slippage and attributed it to "a failure to develop strong faculty groups in newer subject areas."[57] As well, laboratory facilities had deteriorated, were constrained, and were not well suited to the newer areas of biology where the greatest breakthroughs were likely to occur. The same 1981 external review observed substantial duplication in expertise among the existing departments as each tried in its own

---

[57] Martin A. Trow, "Biology at Berkeley: A Case Study of Reorganization and Its Costs and Benefits," Research and Occasional Papers Series, no. 1-99, Center for Studies in Higher Education, University of California, Berkeley, CA, 1999, https://perma.cc/BU73-4KWB..

way to cover the new dimensions of biological research. The situation described by this review and some antecedent studies led to a major reexamination of the structure, affinities, and plans for the biological sciences at Berkeley, leading eventually to rearrangement and consolidation of the twenty departments into four, along with modernized laboratory facilities in two new buildings and a thoroughly renovated third building. The challenge was then how to bring the changes about, given the relatively entrenched interests of the existing departments and the possible, even likely, strong effect of those departmental concerns on deliberations in the Academic Senate. An earlier article [58] by Trow analyzes the origins, development, and leadership aspects of these changes up to 1983. This was followed by his 1999 analysis.[59] Park[60] subsequently reflected on the process from the standpoint of his own close involvement in it. An oral history volume[61] on the subject of the reorganization contains recorded interviews with three principal participants—Daniel Koshland, Roderic Park, and Louise Taylor, who staffed the process.

As already noted, Ira Michael Heyman became chancellor of the Berkeley campus in 1980, having previously been vice chancellor for academic affairs. The Vice Chancellor[62] Roderic Park, whom Heyman appointed as his replacement, was a botanist, had molecular interests, had a full appreciation for the rapid changes in biology, and had until then been serving effectively as dean of the College of Letters and Science. Park and Heyman engaged the leadership of Dan Koshland,[63] an eminent biochemist who had large stature in research, was well respected on the campus, and had a strong sense of intellectual

---

[58] Martin A. Trow, "A Matter of Leadership: Reorganizing the Biological Sciences at Berkeley," *Change* 15, no. 8 (Nov.–Dec. 1983): pp. 28, 44–53.
[59] Trow, 1999, *loc. cit.*
[60] Roderic B. Park, *It's Only the Janitor: A Handbook for New Academic Administrators* (Geyserville, CA: Rockpile Press, 2010), chapter 10.
[61] Regional Oral History Office, "The Reorganization of Biology at the University of California, Berkeley, an Oral History Project of the Regional Oral History Office, conducted 1998 and 1999," Bancroft Library, University of California, Berkeley, 2003, accessed May 30, 2016, https://archive.org/details/reorgbiounical00hughrich.
[62] This position was the one to which the two provosts in the dual-provost system reported (see the following case). It also had responsibility for academic activities beyond the colleges and schools (e.g., the library, summer session, and university extension).
[63] Randy Schekman, "The Nine Lives of Daniel E. Koshland, Jr.," *Proceedings of National Academy of Sciences* 104, no. 37 (2007): 14551–14552.

leadership. After an initial inventory of biology faculty and their interests and expertise, the administration in spring 1980 appointed a special Internal Biological Sciences Review Committee of faculty members (Koshland, Alex Glazer, Milton Schroth, and David Wake) to evaluate "the programs in the biological sciences on the Berkeley campus" and analyze "the space needs of these sciences." This was an administrative committee, not a senate committee (i.e., it was appointed by the administration). The committee recommended (August 1981) the creation of a Chancellor's Advisory Council on Biology (CACB) to point the way toward reshaping and upgrading biology at Berkeley and to develop a comprehensive assessment of space needs.

The chancellor created that council, composed of nine distinguished Berkeley biology faculty members with modern research interests covering a spectrum of expertise, and with Koshland as the initial chair. The council had several roles, which in effect expanded upon the funcions of the Review Committee—advising on the nature of new faculty appointments and in what areas they were most needed, effectively naming the members of the search committees for these recruitments, and generating an overall space plan. That space plan involved an intensive renovation of the Life Sciences Building (figure 12-1, the largest university building west of the Mississippi River), completed in 1994, and the construction of two new buildings—the Life Sciences Addition (1988) and the Plant Biology Building (1990), which later became Koshland Hall. The space plan became the basis for the first large capital campaign of the Berkeley campus,[64] so as to obtain private monies to supplement state building funds and assure the priority of the three building projects within the overall University of California queue for state building funds.

The role of the Chancellor's Advisory Council in faculty appointments effectively supplanted the usual department roles, since the Budget Committee of the Academic Senate and the provosts

---

[64] Until 1983 the Berkeley campus had the modest fund-raising activities then characteristic of public universities, although some units, notably business, law, and engineering, had launched significant private fund-raising activities of their own. As a vice chancellor for development was added in 1983, definition of an initial capital campaign became one of his earliest priorities. This campaign became at that time the largest ever undertaken by a public university.

generally followed the advice of the Chancellor's Advisory Council on Biology in reviewing and granting recruitment authorizations and in reviewing and approving appointments. (The Budget Committee was less influenced than was the Academic Senate as a whole by the desires of faculty in the existing departments and of course has a primary adherence to academic quality.) It was important that CACB reported directly to the chancellor and vice chancellor, since this gave the council leverage with respect to the departments.

Figure 12-1. The Valley Life Sciences Building, with Life Sciences Annex in the shadow to its right[65]

The role of the Academic Senate was a concern, and the approaches taken with the senate are reported in the aforementioned oral history. The process was not carried out in the traditional fashion

---

[65] Photograph © 2003 by Alan Nyiri, courtesy of the Atkinson Photographic Archive, University of California, https://perma.cc/UF7T-E8N8..

of posing issues to the senate for review and advice and then garnering the senate comments before proceeding. The principals believed that these more usual processes with the Academic Senate would impede matters to such an extent that the reorganization would not be achieved. Instead, the process was led intellectually by the Chancellor's Advisory Council. Documents and plans, as they came into existence, were then sent to the Academic Senate and its pertinent committees to keep them informed, and it was then incumbent upon the senate to take the initiative to question actions or raise issues. As a result, the involvement of the Academic Senate was significantly less than it might otherwise have been.

Almost half of the biology-related efforts on campus were in the College of Natural Resources (CNR), stemming from previous College of Agriculture and School of Forestry functions. For several reasons, faculty members and departments in that college were much warier of the reorganization effort than were the faculty members in the College of Letters and Science. Being on the applied end of things, many of the CNR faculty sensed that the ascendancy of molecular biology would lessen their roles and positions. Also the faculty members in CNR had very different situations from faculty elsewhere on campus, since they had year-round appointments, split between regular campus instructional and research (I&R) funds, on the one hand, and Agricultural Experiment Station (AES) funds, on the other hand.[66] They also received sustained research support through the AES. The year-round appointments obviated the need for extramural research grants to provide summer salary, and there was little incentive for the CNR faculty to seek outside research funding. Since the AES funding was limited, this situation led to research programs of modest size relative to those of the biology faculty members outside CNR. Because of the stronger reluctance of the CNR faculty and their different situation, the CACB and administration decided to leave CNR out of the initial round of reorganization and out of the new facilities as well. The one exception was for the departments dealing with plant biology or botany, for which there had been two separate departments in the two colleges. In the initial round of changes, those two departments were

---

[66] This situation has now changed to more conventionasl academic appointments.

combined into one, located now in CNR with a new building of its own and with conventional faculty appointments.

The development of the space plan and the definition of the building projects preceded decisions on the specifics of departmental organization. The rationale was to let the space plan define natural affinity groups for colocation in the new facilities, based upon the nature of laboratory needs and desirable working adjacencies, and then to use the desirability of the new space to mobilize faculty interest in the new affinity groups. The new departmental organization followed the establishment of affinities and the space plan and resulted in the collapse of the biology departments involved into three large departments: Molecular and Cell Biology within the College of Letters and Science, Integrative Biology within the College of Letters and Science, and Plant Biology within the College of Natural Resources.

Matching faculty members with departments went through four iterations from 1984 to 1986. Each iteration consisted of a proposed set of assignments devised by the CACB, followed by both a town-hall meeting for affected faculty and an opportunity for submission of written comments. The initial plan met with much concern and strong objections, including feelings on the part of many faculty members in the Department of Integrative Biology that the molecular biologists were "taking over." But over the course of the iterations and a few adjustments made by the CACB, objections diminished, and there was ultimately widespread acceptance of the final plan. The new space markedly helped this process.

It should be noted that the entire reorganization process did have strong faculty guidance, but it came from a special faculty council, developed by the administration and with concurrence from the Academic Senate that was often tacit, in the form of not challenging or offering substantial additional input on the various decisions that were made.

Subsequently, the College of Natural Resources reorganized, merging a number of smaller departments (Plant Pathology, Entomology, Forestry, Soil Science, Conservation, and Resource Studies) to form a large Department of Environmental Science, Policy, and Management (ESPM) as of 1993, the last step in the overall process. This process was also contentious, but was facilitated by the visible success of the biology reorganization and now by a greater involvement of the Academic Senate, which became a positive force in the reorganization. Emulating the new structure of the biological sciences, the ESPM department has three divisions based upon scale: Ecosystem Sciences, Organisms and Environment, and Society and Environment.

From Librarianship to Information Management and Systems at Berkeley (1989–1995)

In 1918 Berkeley established within the College of Letters and Science a Department of Library Science, which became the professional School of Librarianship in 1926 and then was renamed the School of Library and Information Studies in 1976.[67] Although the "Information Studies" component of the name connoted information systems beyond libraries themselves, the school's main concerns remained the education of professional librarians and research related to libraries.

An essay[68] accompanying a past Berkeley campus accreditation report identifies the steps that led to the closing of the School of Library and Information Studies and to the opening of the new professional School of Information Management and Systems in 1994.[69]

A regular Academic Senate/administration program review occurred for the School of Library and Information Studies in 1989–90. The report observed some troubling signs in the school and in the profession as a whole. Among the points raised were that there were few linkages with the rest of the campus, that the tenure-track faculty members were directed mainly toward the doctorate program, leaving the professional MLS to the non-tenure-track faculty, that the school had relatively low support from extramural grants, and that there was

---

[67] University of California, Berkeley, "UC Berkeley School of Information: History," https://perma.cc/3JZW-QNHX..
[68] University of California, Berkeley, "UC Berkeley Accreditation: 4(b) Program Review," accessed May 30, 2016, https://web.archive.org/web/20141130101706/http://vcue.berkeley.edu/accreditation/pr_essays_4b.html.
[69] The name of the new school was subsequently changed to School of Information in 2006, without any further change in its essential mission.

no compelling academic plan or vision of the scope and future of the professional field. (Note the similarity of these issues to those for the School of Education.) The report recommended the hiring of a permanent dean.[70] With a new dean, the school should assess the future directions of the field and develop a well-reasoned academic plan.

Up to this point, the process was normal for a program review. Beyond this point, the process was designed for the situation at hand. This design and oversight of the process were done by the provost—professional schools and colleges (PS&C)[71] in consultation with the leadership of the Academic Senate.

Building upon advice from the Graduate Council and the Academic Senate from their considerations of the review report, the administration asked the school to proceed with the preparation of a vision statement before a dean search was considered, the rationale being that the vision statement and the review of it would be valuable in determining the qualities that would be sought in a dean.

The faculty of the school produced the vision statement in December 1991. It indicated desires to expand the scope of the school to information systems beyond those of libraries, increase the research base, and enhance interactions with the rest of the campus. Again in consultation with the senate with regard to both purpose and membership, the provost—PS&C created a Special Evaluation Committee to review the vision statement. The April 1992 report of that committee affirmed the importance of information studies for Berkeley; indicated that the status quo was unacceptable; recommended the appointment of a new dean with a clear, well-focused vision; and recommended that if such leadership were not available, "only then should [the school] be reexamined with serious consideration being given to its permanent closure." Senate review agreed that the status quo was unacceptable and indicated that "the preferred result is to rebuild the school along the lines recommended by the Evaluation Committee." Since rebuilding the school implied a

---

[70] For several years there had been an interim dean, who was primarily a member of the law faculty and functioned also as law librarian.
[71] The author at the time.

substantial commitment in a time of very constrained resources, the matter was referred to the relatively new Academic Planning Board.

The Academic Planning Board (APB) had been established for the Berkeley campus in spring 1992 as a joint senate-administration group to enable the two bodies to work together to implement overall academic planning in response to the severe state budget crisis in the early 1990s.[72] The APB was composed of equal numbers of members from the Academic Senate leadership and the administration. Upon receiving the results of the reviews and the commentary, the APB in March 1993 chartered a planning group. This group was charged with developing a viable definition of the field to be served, identifying and assessing potential leadership, and assessing external resources and support to help determine whether the new direction would be economically feasible given the budgetary stress. The APB also suspended admissions to the existing school and determined that financial support to the existing school should be limited to the current level. The resultant planning group was chaired by the provost—PS&C and had a diverse, knowledgeable membership approved by the Academic Planning Board.

The December 1993 report[73] of the planning group laid out a new professional School of Information Management and Systems, which would "advance, through teaching and research, the organization, management and use of information and information technology, and enhance our understanding of the impact of information upon individuals, institutions, and society." It addressed the justification and drivers for such a school, the degrees that it would offer (MS and PhD), the desirable components of the faculty (highly multidisciplinary), likely students and their career opportunities, and the alternatives to this path of action along with the reasons that they were not recommended. It delineated potential classes of employers, job functions, and research opportunities, along with potential federal and private funding sources and an economic justification.

---

[72] Usually the senate and the administration work separately from one another, as described in chapter 7, but in particularly difficult or fast-moving times, joint groups have been formed to enable fuller interchange and more rapid progress.

[73] University of California, Berkeley, "UC Berkeley School of Information: Proposal for a School of Information Management and Systems," https://perma.cc/9DFS-PZT9.

Chapter 12

Figure 12-2. South Hall, one of the two original buildings on the Berkeley campus and now the home of the School of Information[74]

The recommendations of the planning group were endorsed by the Academic Planning Board and adopted by the administration. The necessary actions were embedded in a resolution enacted by the Regents of the University of California in May 1995 discontinuing the School of Library and Information Studies and forming the new School of Information Management and Systems. The first dean for the new school, Hal Varian, a distinguished economist of information, was found through a comprehensive search and was appointed in July 1995, with the new school formally being launched as of fall 1995.

The plan envisioned that the faculty would grow soon to ten FTE (full-time equivalent), of whom three would be carried forward from the old school. Other ladder faculty members from the old school

---

[74] Photograph © 2003 by Alan Nyiri, courtesy of the Atkinson Photographic Archive, University of California, https://perma.cc/GA8K-EUD2.

elected retirement, and one was transferred to another department. As of 2014 there were sixteen tenure-track faculty members (fourteen FTE) drawn from a diverse range of disciplines. There were joint faculty appointments with a wide variety of other departments, including Computer Science, History, Industrial Engineering, Law, Education, and City and Regional Planning. MS and PhD degrees are given in information management and systems, along with a master of science in information and data science.

The venture to create the new school was also a case of recognizing the probable development of a new professional field, which has now been borne out. The result is that the Berkeley campus is well positioned academically to take full advantage of the research and educational opportunities afforded by the rapid development of capabilities and usages of information technology. To get to that point required the new start; a process of evolution in the old school would have been much slower and most likely would not have gotten as far. Students interested in library fields can still apply and receive a pertinent and useful education that equips them well for the still rapid advances in information technology that lie ahead.

Some important components of the process leading to the end result were the strong cooperation and positive contributions of Acting Dean Nancy Van House of the School of Library and Information Studies, the quality of the program review process that flagged the issues in the first place, and the close working relationship of the Academic Senate and the campus administration. Finally, as the process was going on, there was a large letter-writing campaign from librarians in the state to government and university officials, protesting closure. However, there were a few contacts made by legislators with the university, and because of UC's constitutional autonomy no legislation was introduced that would affect the process or the result.

The knowledge base for information technology and its uses continues to grow rapidly. As of 2017 there are strong interests at Berkeley in developing and coordinating the growing field of data science, but there are also strong differences and contentions as to how that should be done. A different approach has been taken to this matter, namely creating a dean for a Division of Data Science. The dean does not yet have units or a program; instead, that dean is asked to work synergistically with others on campus to define what program and organization will work best.[75]

Comparative Analysis of the Four Case Studies

Accomplishing Programmatic and Structural Change. The four cases show that the system for change does work within the University of California for situations where programmatic or structural change is driven by academic and quality considerations stemming from advances in knowledge, perceptions of suboptimal overall performance, or new research capabilities. That is, quality control is accomplished well. The four cases also show that successful change is a deliberative and multifaceted process requiring skilled leadership.

The role of the Academic Senate in programmatic change at the University of California is vital because it is, after all, the faculty who best know the program and programmatic needs. Because of the inherently conservative natures of most faculty members, the faculty role can be viewed as an impediment as well, as is reflected in some of the quotes at the start of this chapter. However, in the final analysis, the role of the Academic Senate gives a gravitas and imprimatur that establish the validity of adopted changes and facilitate acceptance. The senate is thereby a steadying and stabilizing force for accomplishing change. Shared governance is a valuable tool and should operate and be used in the most constructive ways to address needs for change.

It is instructive to examine the various cases in terms of the roles of the Academic Senate and the ways in which the administration worked with the Academic Senate. For the Schools of Criminology and Library and Information Studies, the process was built heavily around program reviews and Academic Senate evaluations of points raised in those reviews, and the administration role was more in the design of the process and in the ultimate decision and implementation. The same can be said for the case of the School of Education, except that there was the added dimension of changing from a chancellor who would probably have decided to eliminate the school to a new chancellor who ultimately decided not to do so. The case of Biological

---

[75] Nicholas Dirks, Carol Christ, and Paul Alivisatos, "Campus Leadership Announces New Division of Data Science," December 20, 2016, https://perma.cc/9TVE-X89L.

Sciences stands in contrast to these other three cases and shows how the process can be guided by the administration in different ways. The senate mechanism can be used heavily for change that is generally perceived within the senate as being needed. Other forms of intellectual leadership can be brought into play when senate views would be more divided.

For cases of programmatic change, displacement of tenured faculty can be a dominant issue. It is probably not coincidental that the three cases that worked through to actual structural change (criminology, library, and biological sciences) did not ultimately require dismissals of faculty members or relocations of tenured faculty members far outside their disciplines, whereas the one case that did not result in structural change (education) would have had large issues of that sort if the change had been made. Although it could do so, the University of California has not yet chosen to dismiss tenured faculty members for programmatic reasons without providing relocation opportunities elsewhere on the campus or university-wide. Members of terminated departments or schools have been relocated either on the affected campus or to other campuses. Both of these approaches were taken, for example, when the nascent UC San Diego School of Architecture was terminated in the early 1990s. Even the initial faculty members for the new Merced campus were assured that they would have positions at other campuses if the Merced campus did not ultimately materialize.

The cases of the Schools of Criminology, Library and Information Studies, and Education are also instructive with regard to the effects of suspending searches for deans and holding back faculty recruitment authorizations, both of which often occur with situations of protracted and/or difficult review. Both steps are rational as holding actions until new directions are defined as a result of the review process, but they also serve to weaken the academic unit. Therefore decisions to withhold dean searches and/or recruitment allocations should be regarded as tantamount to a decision that fundamental changes must and will be made in the unit.

Intellectual Leadership. The value of proven intellectual leadership is exhibited by the roles of Daniel Koshland and the Chancellor's Advisory Council in the reorganization of the biological sciences. They commanded a level of academic respect that strengthened their roles vis-à-vis the affected faculty and those in the Academic Senate who would be concerned about the reorganization. In any administration-driven effort for change, it is vital that intellectual leadership of that sort be identified and take clear and major roles.

Professional Schools. Professional schools in research universities must serve the needs of the profession effectively through both education programs and research and other creative endeavors. The pressures to do outstanding research are strong and can be difficult to reconcile with the needs for professional education. This tension can lead to two undesirable situations. First, a bifurcation can occur where those teaching for the profession are not ladder faculty who also do research. Second, the ladder faculty may pursue research that is more in the line of that done by academic departments than being matched to research needs of the profession. In the former situation, the university loses the opportunity for education for the profession to be done by research-informed faculty, which should be a major advantage of research universities. The latter easily leads to a situation where the research of the faculty in the professional school is regarded as second-rate by the more classical academic departments. Elements of these factors are found in the cases of the Schools of Education, Library and Information Studies, and Criminology. Among the other professions, engineering, medicine, and law are less affected by these tensions.

ADAPTATIONS OF RESEARCH UNIVERSITIES TO MAJOR FORCES OF CHANGE

The four cases considered so far are all programmatic in nature and can be considered as evolutionary rather than radical upheaval. Although three of them also led to structural change that included elimination or wholesale transformation of academic units, none of them led to substantial downsizing. In that way these changes are consistent with Smelser's aforementioned thesis that change at universities tends to go in the direction of structural accretion, rather than removal of functions,[76] and Donald Kennedy's comment cited at the start of the chapter regarding sunset being "an hour that almost never arrives" in universities.

But what about change that is more disruptive? Can research universities adapt sufficiently rapidly to the forces generated by advances in information technology and globalization, by new market competition, and by financial stresses that include diminished state funding for public higher education? Do other types of change, in particular those that may require downsizing, have characteristics that make the change much more difficult, or even impossible, to achieve?

As Clark Kerr noted in his quote cited at the start of this chapter, universities "have changed enormously in the emphases on their several functions and in their guiding spirits." Frank Rhodes[77] observes that there have been major changes in universities within the United States as results of the following:

- the Land Grant (Morrill) Act of 1862, which "changed forever the role of the nation's great public institutions"
- the GI Bill of 1945, which "changed forever the accessibility of America's universities and colleges"
- the Vannevar Bush report to President Roosevelt in 1945, which "changed forever the relationship between science in the academy and sponsorship by the federal government"
- the executive orders from Presidents Kennedy and Johnson in the 1960s instituting affirmative action requirements and then the subsequent actions through regents' actions, ballot initiatives, legislative action, and court decisions in California, Washington, Texas, Florida, and Michigan placing limits on affirmative action criteria and procedures
- the Bayh-Dole Act of 1980, which gave research universities clear roles and incentives in the arena of technology transfer

The first three and the last of these factors all presented opportunities for universities, to which they rose. The fourth factor (affirmative action) has presented a world of challenges for universities and must

---

[76] Smelser, 2013, op. cit., pp. 12–22.
[77] Frank H. T. Rhodes, 2004, op. cit., p. 12.

still be regarded as an unsettled issue; however, universities have proven to be resilient on the subject.

Reactions to Current Forces of Change

Drivers that are often cited as potentially disruptive are online instruction, massive open online courses (MOOCs), competency-based degrees, and reduction of the nominal time for the baccalaureate from four years to three. Another issue that could be added to this list is career-oriented higher education as opposed to the more classical US concept of a broad liberal education. Markets will eventually resolve these issues. Vendors will offer, employers will recognize, students and families will seek, and universities will create and offer entirely online degrees to the extent that they find them to be useful and effective. More likely, online instructional mechanisms will become integrated into conventional academic degrees, rather that leaving students with a stark choice of going all one way or the other. This is already happening.

Competency-based degrees will require respected certifiers. It is unlikely that the brand-name positions of Harvard, Yale, Stanford, Berkeley, UCLA, Michigan, and the like will be overtaken by start-up or less distinguished certifiers. More likely, the possibilities and alternatives will continue to grow for degree programs of respected existing universities to credit demonstrable mastery of knowledge gained elsewhere. As has already become the case, online learning will be a large component of continuing education.

The Faculty

For academic changes, no matter how large, to work, it is essential that the faculty enter the picture early and fully, because the faculty will have to be the ones to subscribe to a new concept and carry it out and because at least some faculty members will have insights that are valuable in assessing and defining the initiative. Two recent, unsuccessful efforts in California in the area of online instruction illustrate this point. Both were cases where the top administration got too far out in front of the faculty. There was also an ingredient in both cases of trying to please the governor of the state (Jerry Brown), who has pressed his belief that online instruction will substantially decrease costs of higher education—now.

The first case was an effort[78, 79] at San Jose State University that took the form of a large partnership with a Silicon Valley firm (Udacity) to provide open-access, online, entry-level courses for both SJSU students and enrollees elsewhere. The project was launched with considerable fanfare by the president of San Jose State in January 2013 at a press conference involving Governor Brown. However, there had been little faculty involvement in the formulation of the initiative; instead it had the appearance of being a personal initiative of the SJSU president. The launch of the initiative resulted in substantial faculty controversy and objection on many different grounds, most of which were academic. Then, results for the first offerings showed very low rates of successful completion. Six months after its start, the project with Udacity was "paused" and has not been restarted. More successful has been the effort at San Jose State to make use of the courses put online for open-access usage by edX,[80] formed by MIT, Harvard, UC Berkeley, and other universities to share course content around the world. SJSU uses these courses largely in a hybrid format (i.e., as one component of classroom instruction).

The second example occurred within the University of California itself and is described by Wu.[81] A July 2009 op-ed piece in the *Los Angeles Times*[82] was authored by the dean of the Law School at Berkeley who was at the same time also a 50 percent time senior advisor to the president of the University of California. This proposal urged creation of an entirely "virtual" eleventh University of California

---

[78] "San Jose State University and Udacity Announce Partnership to Pilot For-Credit Online Courses to Expand Access to Higher Education", *Business Wire*, January 15, 2013, https://perma.cc/B7MR-NQDJ.
[79] Ry Rivard, "Citing Disappointing Student Outcomes, San Jose State Pauses Work with Udacity," *Inside Higher Education*, July 18, 2013, https://perma.cc/2TQJ-CC3Z.
[80] "edX," https://perma.cc/XNR7-9YQW.
[81] Derek Wu, "The University of California Online Education Initiative," in William G. Bowen and Eugene M. Tobin, *Locus of Authority: The Evolution of Faculty Roles in the Governance of Higher Education* (Princeton, NJ: Princeton University Press and ITHAKA, 2015), pp. 251–260.
[82] Christopher Edley Jr., "Building a New UC—in Cyberspace," *Los Angeles Times*, July 1, 2009, https://perma.cc/Q2U8-E6ZF.

campus to expand capacity of the University of California. The prospect of such a massive movement into online education for the entire content of degrees and the fact that it came from a source so close to the UC president triggered a large backlash and much discussion within the faculty. It also led to a generally negative reaction from the Academic Senate. Even so, the Office of Programs and Planning at the UC Office of the President was charged to pursue the initiative.

As the proponents met with Academic Senate committees, one of the suggestions that arose from campuses was to develop a set of online versions of "gateway" courses (i.e., courses that are on the prescribed paths for large-enrollment majors and are frequently oversubscribed). This proposal was incorporated into a presentation of the broader promise of online education made at a regents meeting in July 2010.[83, 84] A pilot project to create such courses was then created by the Office of the President, an RFP was issued, and a review process was used to pick twenty-nine course proposals. These courses were to be funded through a budget totaling $7–8 million, for which extramural funding would be garnered. However, the only funding gained was $750,000 from an EDUCAUSE initiative that had been funded by the Gates and Hewlett Foundations. An internal loan of $7 million was then made to complete the funding with the idea that it would be repaid by sales of the product outside the university. This too drew substantial criticism from faculty members when extramural sources to repay the loan did not materialize. Six years later, the initiative was redefined again more generally and is broader, more modestly funded, and much more faculty driven.[85]

While the original intent may have been simply to stir the pot and get things going, the initial media splash, the top-down aspect, and the unrepayable internal loan were not useful for winning the faculty over

---

[83] "Undergraduate Online Instruction Pilot Project," Regents Item E-5, Regents of the University of California, July 14, 2010, https://perma.cc/C89P-SHZP.
[84] Nanette Asimov, "UC Regents Endorse Test of Online Instruction," *San Francisco Chronicle*, July 15, 2010,
https://web.archive.org/web/20150719164841/https://www.sfgate.com/education/article/UC-regents-endorse-test-of-online-instruction-3181427.php.
[85] "Innovative Learning Technology Initiative" and "UC Online," Office of the President, University of California, https://web.archive.org/web/20160522231414/http://ucop.edu/innovative-learning-technology-initiative/index.html.

to the project. A more suitable approach is to seed the garden, water the flowers, and support those that bloom best, which is better reflected in the current definitions of the UC Online project. A number of different campus approaches flesh out this line of attack. For example, the Berkeley campus has created the Resource Center for Online Education,[86] which provides a variety of support services for faculty and for departments that want to create clusters of courses or degree programs.

The importance of approaching change through early and genuine consultation with the faculty and through prominent roles for intellectual leadership from within the faculty cannot be stressed too highly. Getting too far out in front of the faculty and/or seeming not to value the views of the faculty are probably the two most common causes of involuntary departures from university presidencies. In this regard the formal structure provided by the Academic Senate has been vital for the University of California.

Efficiencies in Services

Change in nonacademic aspects of universities can be handled through mechanisms that are more typical of corporate management. For example, a more managerial approach has been taken in recent movements toward shared administrative services (chapter 6) at Yale, UC Berkeley, the University of Michigan, the University of Texas at Austin, and a number of other universities. However, for services that support faculty in their academic work, consultation and faculty involvement are still essential.

Reflective Thoughts

On the matter of disruptive innovation and the threatened plight of universities, in the end—and perhaps not surprisingly for a lifelong University of California person—I find myself with Clark Kerr. In the final preface[87] to *The Uses of the University*, he observed "that new knowledge still makes the world go round and that the university is still

---

[86] "What We Do," Berkeley Resource Center for Online Education, University of California, Berkeley, https://web.archive.org/web/20160602001456/http://online.berkeley.edu/what-we-do/.
[87] Clark Kerr, 2001, op. cit., p. x.

its main source." And in a chapter written in 1982,[88] he concluded that "the research university in America still has a long way to go" (i.e., it will endure for a long time). Research universities very synergistically combine education with active research, continual critical thinking, and creativity. Faculty members are chosen and evaluated on the bases of those criteria of creativity and critical thinking. Methods of research continually change as faculty members individually and competitively determine the best paths ahead. Some recent examples are use of online methodologies in research, creation and use of very large databases enabled by the growing capabilities of information technology, increasing collaboration among researchers worldwide, and honing of research results through working papers, preliminary communications, and online feedback. There is continual feedback from research into teaching. It is no surprise that educational innovations such as Coursera and edX have come out of research universities.

In sum, research universities can and do change, and there are good reasons why that happens, relating to the inherent creativity of the faculty. By contrast, education that is more directly oriented toward vocations and careers and is less tied in with research does not have these paths toward continual innovation and improvement and may be more directly subject to the forces of disruptive innovation.

SUMMARY CONCLUSION

Much has been written about difficulties of accomplishing change in universities, including how it is easier to add functions (accretion) than to eliminate them and how faculty members are inherently conservative with regard to change. Yet on the other hand, Clark Kerr's observation that universities are primary among the longest-lived institutions of the world and that much change has been accomplished over the years to enable that longevity is also striking. The five examples of relatively recent major changes in research universities

---

[88] Kerr, 2001, *op. cit.*, p. 140.

cited by Frank Rhodes also clearly show major changes over time stemming from opportunities and needs.

Within the University of California, program-review mechanisms have decentralized over time, and now regular program reviews at the campus level are the usual mechanism for monitoring program quality along with needs and opportunities for program change. Valuable adjuncts to these procedures have been the continual reviews of faculty members (chapter 11) and the participation of respected external reviewers. The Academic Senate has major roles in the process.

Academic planning itself is also carried out on regular bases and by a variety of means, such as campus academic plans associated with campus long-range development plans; annual faculty recruitment plans, reviews of them, and authorization of recruitments; and various less formal consultation mechanisms.

Four instances of programmatic change at Berkeley have been described as case studies. These include (1) the elimination of the School of Criminology in the 1970s, (2) the intense review of the School of Education around 1980, which almost led to the closure of the school and did lead to a reemphasis on the profession itself, (3) the major rearrangement of the biological sciences and related fields in the 1980s to recognize the large changes and opportunities within the field of biology itself, and (4) the closure of the School of Library and Information Studies in the 1990s and the establishment of the School of Information Management and Systems (now simply School of Information) to replace it. An analysis of these cases shows important programmatic change, skilled oversight and management in various ways, the importance of intellectual leadership, and some of the particular issues associated with professional schools in research universities.

Faculty creativity and faculty competition for innovation are particular advantages for research universities in generating change. Academic change in research universities works best when faculty members are the ones to inspire it and carry it out. It works much less well when attempts are made to impose it from above.

13.
National Laboratories

The day when the scientist, no matter how devoted, may make significant progress alone and without material help is past. This fact is most self-evident in our work. Instead of an attic with a few test tubes, bits of wire and odds and ends, the attack on the atomic nucleus has required the development and construction of great instruments on an engineering scale.
—Ernest O. Lawrence, Nobel Prize acceptance speech[1]

There was some very informal discussion after that with Dr. Oppenheimer, and it is my understanding that as a preliminary matter we were to provide personnel service, traveling expenses and to cover charges then being expensed by Princeton University under a similar letter of intent. It was some time later before permission was granted to inform me as to where this project would be located, my only knowledge up to that time being that it would not be in the State of California. It very definitely seemed to be that the University, as a corporation, was to be almost a straw man in the proceedings, but to this the University never agreed.
—Robert M. Underhill, reflecting upon the Manhattan Project[2]

If we get rid of bomb-making, plutonium, and New Mexico, I would be very happy.
—Robert Gordon Sproul (1946)[3]

---

[1] Ernest O. Lawrence, Nobel Prize Acceptance Speech, February 29, 1940, Berkeley, CA, https://perma.cc/KG4Y-RQLN.
[2] Robert M. Underhill, cited by the Manhattan Project Heritage Preservation Association, Inc., "Manhattan Project History: You Know What They're Doing Down in Los Alamos? UC's First Contract to Operate the Laboratory," https://web.archive.org/web/20130501214816/http://mphpa.org/classic/HISTORY/H-06c11.htm.
[3] Peter J. Westwick, *The National Labs: Science in an American System, 1947–1974* (Cambridge, MA: Harvard University Press, 2003), p. 47.

An earlier university president [Holden] *once complained that the university had three presidents: "the president* eo nomine, *the secretary of the regents, and the professor of agriculture"; in 1958, the triumvirate was the president, the vice president-business affairs,[4] and the professor in charge of atomic energy projects.*
—*Clark Kerr*[5]

In chapter 9 we left off on the story of the University of California Radiation Laboratory with the grant obtained by Ernest Lawrence from the Rockefeller Foundation in 1937 for $1.15 million to enable the construction of the 184-inch cyclotron. That project was begun but was interrupted before completion by the onset of World War II.

WORLD WAR II, THE BERKELEY RADIATION LABORATORY, AND NEW MEXICO

With the onset of World War II, the university, Ernest Lawrence, and Robert Oppenheimer entered into a monumental endeavor leading to the development of the most powerful and destructive weapon the world had known to that point—the atomic bomb. The story of the Manhattan Project has been told in many forms[6] and will not be repeated here except for those elements relating to the University of California and its future roles.

Discovery and development of understanding of the fissile properties of the 235 isotope of uranium stimulated interest in a military weapon that would exploit that property. An additional route to a fission bomb became available as the unstable transuranium

---

[4] See chapter 6 regarding the relationship between Kerr and James Corley.
[5] Clark Kerr, *The Gold and the Blue: A Personal Memoir of the University of California, 1949–1967,* vol. 1, *Academic Triumphs* (Berkeley: University of California Press, 2001), p. 191.
[6] See, e.g., Richard Rhodes, *The Making of the Atomic Bomb* (New York: Simon & Schuster, 1986); Gregg Herken, *Brotherhood of the Bomb* (New York: Holt, 2002); Atomic Heritage Foundation, accessed October 3, 2017, http://www.atomicheritage.org/ (formerly Manhattan Project Heritage Preservation Assn., Inc.),
https://web.archive.org/web/20150226110315/http://www.mphpa.org/classic/HISTORY/ERC-1.htm).

element plutonium was created at the Radiation Laboratory and isolated by Glenn Seaborg and associates in Room 307 of Gilman Hall on the Berkeley campus in February 1941. Ernest Lawrence had a lead role in national considerations of how best to proceed, because of his stature, forcefulness, and familiarity with the subject.[7]

Figure 13-1. A meeting in Berkeley in March 1940 regarding the 184-inch cyclotron project. The same group would very soon be involved in initial scientific definition of the Manhattan Project.[8] (*Left to right*: Ernest Lawrence, Arthur Compton, Vannevar Bush, James Conant, Karl Compton, and Alfred Loomis, all of whom appear in various ways in this book)

---

[7] See, e.g., Verne A. Stadtman, *The University of California, 1868–1968* (New York: McGraw-Hill, 1970), p. 306; Herken, 2002, *op. cit.*, pp. 35–51.
[8] "Breaking Through: A Century of Physics at Berkeley, 1868–1968," Bancroft Library, University of California, Berkeley, https://perma.cc/3WTP-C5SV.

Calutrons

The need to isolate uranium-235 from the much more plentiful uranium-238 in order to enable a critical explosive mass for the uranium bomb called for innovative means of large-scale separation, since that separation could not be accomplished on a production scale by any method that was already developed. Among the approaches explored in depth were ultracentrifugation, gaseous diffusion, thermal diffusion, and electromagnetic separation. The latter approach utilized principles of the mass spectrometer, related to those of the cyclotron, and was pushed intensely by Lawrence in national considerations. The project for construction of the 184-inch cyclotron was redirected, and the other cyclotrons were adapted as well, so as to investigate the principles of electromagnetic separation on a large scale at the Berkeley Radiation Laboratory.

Substantial and ever-growing government funding came for these purposes. The Radiation Laboratory on Charter Hill above the Berkeley campus grew rapidly in size—buildings, projects and personnel—commensurate with the increased government funding. Stadtman[9] notes that the university's income from government contracts grew from $1.56 million for the fiscal year 1941–42 to $8.25 million for 1942–43, to almost $23 million for 1943–44, to $25.95 million for 1944–45. Nearly all of this federal support focused on the Radiation Laboratory. Needs for security grew by leaps and bounds as well, with all the issues and needs associated with a classified program within a university setting.[10]

Eventually, the electromagnetic process for separating uranium isotopes was sufficiently developed so that the resultant device, dubbed the *calutron* (*Ca*lifornia *U*niversity-*tron*, see figure 2-4), was used for the initial large-scale separation of uranium isotopes at the Y-12 plant in Oak Ridge, Tennessee.[11] An interesting sidelight to this story is that the amount of copper needed for the windings of the magnets for the many large calutrons at Oak Ridge was so great that, when

---

[9] Stadtman, 1970, *op. cit.*, p. 311.
[10] Westwick, 2003, *op. cit.*, pp. 75–76.
[11] Manhattan Project History: Electromagnetic Separation of U235, Manhattan Project Heritage Preservation Assn., accessed June 8, 2016,
https://web.archive.org/web/20150226110326/http://www.mphpa.org/classic/HISTORY/H-06b2-1.htm.

coupled with the general shortage of copper, it required the "loan" of fifteen thousand tons of silver bullion from the US Treasury to serve as a substitute for copper in the windings.

The calutrons had operational difficulties all along, requiring much interaction between the Radiation Laboratory in Berkeley and the plant in Tennessee with urgent needs to be addressed.[12] As the large gaseous-diffusion plants came on line at Oak Ridge in 1945 and subsequently in Paducah, Kentucky, and Portsmouth, Ohio, the use of calutrons for uranium enrichment was phased out, and the silver was returned to the US Treasury. But the calutrons at Y-12 did their job in creating the enriched uranium-235 for the first bombs, and residual calutrons were used for many years for other isotope production needs, such as for medical purposes.

The fact that calutrons, rather than one of the other methods, were used for accomplishing enrichment in the critical few years before August 1945 reflects two aspects of Ernest Lawrence. One is his forceful and compelling argumentation. The other is his strong perseverance through difficult situations. Electromagnetic separation was not the most economical and reliable method of separation. As soon as they came on line, the gaseous-diffusion plants displaced the calutrons. Subsequently ultracentrifugation has become the method of choice. Currently uranium enrichment is done by ultracentrifugation or atomic-vapor laser isotope separation (AVLIS).[13] The laser had not been invented, but ultracentrifugation was known at the time of the Manhattan Project and was actively investigated and developed by Jesse Beams at the University of Virginia. Interestingly, Beams had been a colleague of Lawrence at Yale. He was, however, a reserved and much less forceful individual.

Los Alamos

As the Manhattan Project got under way, it became necessary to identify leadership, select a team, and choose and develop a site for the actual design, testing, and manufacture of the two types of bombs. The project now fell under the US Army Engineers and specifically Maj.

---

[12] Michael Hiltzik, *Big Science: Ernest Lawrence and the Invention That Launched the Military-Industrial Complex* (New York: Simon & Schuster, 2015), pp. 237–258.

[13] Developed at the Lawrence Livermore National Laboratory.

Gen. Leslie R. Groves and what was code-named the Manhattan Engineer District. Initial conceptual work was carried out at the Berkeley Radiation Laboratory as well as other locations. It had been necessary to utilize theoretical physics heavily in predicting needs and capabilities for a uranium-235 bomb since enriched uranium was not yet available in quantity for experimentation and measurements until it could be obtained by electromagnetic separation in the calutrons. The situation for the plutonium bomb was similar. Because of the importance of theory, Lawrence had brought in Robert Oppenheimer, the preeminent theoretician in the Berkeley physics department (chapter 9). As General Groves became familiar with the various players, he settled upon Oppenheimer as his choice to be scientific project leader.

The site for the bomb project was a remote mesa in the Jemez Mountains of New Mexico, northwest of Santa Fe. That site was recommended by Oppenheimer himself, who had been aware of it from summer vacations spent at a nearly location.[14] The site became known as Los Alamos, named after the Los Alamos Ranch School (figure 13-2) for boys, which had been the one occupant of the site. Both the site location itself and the developments there were kept at the highest level of secrecy.

There then came the need for obtaining the services of an impressive array of physicists and other scientists and engineers. Groves and James Bryant Conant[15] (figure 13-1), a prominent chemist who was president of Harvard University and chairman of the S-1 (nuclear weapons) committee of the Office of Scientific Research and Development, recognized the likely reluctance of such persons to work directly for the military and decided to obtain a civilian contractor. The scientists would work under the employment and oversight of the contractor, thereby insulated to some degree from the military. This approach was also used for the other Manhattan Project laboratories being set up at locales such as Oak Ridge and Argonne. The most attractive contractor for this purpose would be a university. Given the

---

[14] "Oppenheimer's Better Idea: Ranch School Becomes Arsenal of Democracy," Los Alamos National Laboratory, https://perma.cc/7FE7-EEKH; Herken, op. cit., pp 73–74.

[15] Jennet Conant, *Man of the Hour* (New York: Simon & Schuster, 2017)

size and reputation of the University of California and the affiliation with it of Lawrence, Oppenheimer, and a number of the other senior scientists, the University of California became the target.[16]

Figure 13-2. General Leslie Groves (*center*) presenting the Army-Navy "E" Award Flag to Robert Oppenheimer (*left*) and UC president Robert Gordon Sproul (*right*) in October 1945, in front of the Los Alamos Ranch School building[17]

Lawrence arranged and participated in discussions that Oppenheimer and Groves had in February 1943 with UC president Sproul and the secretary and treasurer of the Board of Regents, Robert Underhill. Very little was disclosed to Sproul and Underhill, including at first not even the location of the laboratory, other than that it would be in "the Rocky Mountains area."[18] Sproul and Underhill nonetheless agreed to create a letter of intent for the University of California to

---

[16] Herken, 2002, *op. cit.*, pp. 75–77; P. J. Westwick, 2003, *op. cit.*, p. 31.
[17] https://perma.cc/W575-NNG9.
[18] Herken, 2002, *op. cit.*, p. 76.

manage Los Alamos. Eventually, nine months later in November 1943, Lawrence came to Underhill's office, shut the door, told Underhill that the project was for an atomic bomb and what that was, and told him that he must not pass that information onward even to UC president Sproul or to the regents.[19] Thus UC became involved with what has, as of 2018, been a seventy-five-year history of managing nuclear weapons laboratories.

The Manhattan Project succeeded in its monumental mission and produced the "Little Boy" uranium bomb that was dropped on Hiroshima on August 6, 1945, and the "Fat Man" plutonium bomb that was tested at the Trinity site in New Mexico on July 16, 1945, and then dropped on Nagasaki on August 9, 1945.

AFTER WORLD WAR II

By the end of the war, the Radiation Laboratory in Berkeley had grown to employ over twelve hundred scientists, technicians, and engineers.[20] Lawrence had put all his focus on the defense-related programs and the calutrons during World War II. As the end of the war approached, he directed his attention again to the future of his laboratory, anticipating in correspondence with President Sproul a decrease in operating budget by as much as 99 percent—from $692,000 per *month* at the height of the wartime activities to $85,000 per *year*,[21] built around a reversion of the 184-inch cyclotron to its original research purposes. But his entrepreneurial spirit was irrepressible, and he secured very substantial project funding from Groves and the Manhattan Engineer District during the time when the formation of the Atomic Energy Commission (AEC) as a nonmilitary

---

[19] Robert M. Underhill, interview by Verne A. Stadtman, *University of California: Lands, Finances, and Investments*, oral history, 1967, Regional Oral History Office, The Bancroft Library, University of California, Berkeley, 1967, https://perma.cc/8M5D-NHUN. This oral history also recounts several other aspects of the very meager knowledge provided to the University of California institutionally.

[20] Robert W. Seidel, "Accelerating Science: The Postwar Transformation of the Lawrence Radiation Laboratory," *Historical Studies in the Physical Sciences* 13, no. 2 (1983): pp. 375–400.

[21] Hiltzik, 2015, *op. cit.*, p. 304.

successor body to the Manhattan Engineer District was under deliberation and before the AEC came into existence at the start of 1947.[22, 23] This funding focused upon Edwin McMillan's synchrotron, Luis Alvarez's projects for linear accelerators that would be still more capable, and the further development of supporting engineering capabilities. Thus, when the AEC did take over, it already had very substantial ongoing activities at Berkeley.

The University of California also did its part to keep the wave of outstanding research in the laboratory going after the war. For example, Glenn Seaborg was brought back to Berkeley's College of Chemistry when Sproul countered a recruitment effort by the University of Chicago, where Seaborg had been in the Metallurgical Laboratory during much of the war. UC gave Seaborg a full professorship at the then relatively young age of thirty-four as well as funding for his laboratory assistants, and Lawrence added a promise to find outside funding for Seaborg's laboratory.[24] This then led to Seaborg's work creating and confirming heavy elements (chapter 9). Another signal component of the joint efforts of the laboratory and the university was the Nobel Prize work of Melvin Calvin on the mechanisms of photosynthesis, with support arranged by Lawrence through the laboratory.[25] In recognition of the prize and the importance of the photosynthesis work, a special building was created on the Berkeley campus for the Calvin laboratory.[26]

The Atomic Energy Commission faced issues of how best to oversee and manage the Manhattan Project laboratories, what programs would be appropriate for them now that the war had ended, and how large the laboratories should be in terms of staff, facilities, and budget. The research policy of the AEC was guided by the General Advisory Committee (GAC), which was chaired by Oppenheimer and

---

[22] Hiltzik, 2015, *op. cit.*, chapter 15, pp. 303–324.
[23] Westwick, 2003, *op. cit.*, pp. 36–37, 139.
[24] Roger L. Geiger, *Research and Relevant Knowledge: American Research Universities since World War II* (New York: Oxford University Press, 1993), pp. 76–77.
[25] Geiger, 1993, *op. cit.*, pp. 78–79.
[26] The building is circular in footprint, following Calvin's expressed desire that scientists should interact, with no one being able to hide in a corner.

had Seaborg as a member. The deliberations and decisions of that era are chronicled by Seidel[27] and Westwick,[28] among others.

The approach of operating the AEC laboratories through contractors was continued, using contractors that were universities or corporations, depending upon the nature of the laboratory and local conditions. Two reasons for the contractor approach were that it was more attractive to scientists who would fulfill the missions of the laboratories and that it was desirable to use established management organizations rather than having to build such capabilities fully and rapidly within the AEC. For the Berkeley laboratory, contracting was the only option.

Sustained operation of the Los Alamos facility was a particular problem. The University of California was reluctant to continue management of Los Alamos, but the AEC recognized the need for university management as a way of attracting and retaining excellent scientists and engineers.[29] UC, with urging by Lawrence, accepted continued management upon achieving satisfactory terms.

It is interesting to compare the approaches in the postwar years of the two universities that were most involved in the Manhattan Project—the University of California and the University of Chicago.[30] During the war, the University of Chicago held the contract for the Clinton Laboratory, which subsequently became the central part of the Oak Ridge National Laboratory. In 1945 Chicago left that arrangement, and the management was contracted to Monsanto until 1947, when the AEC tried to reestablish university management through the University of Chicago. This led to a lack of convergence on both terms and selection of a laboratory director. Later in the same year (1947), the AEC put the contract with Union Carbide Corporation, which also operated the Y-12 (calutron) and K-25 (gaseous diffusion) production facilities for enriched uranium-235 at Oak Ridge. The University of Chicago had started its own in-house laboratory for nuclear physics after the war, contemplating an end to its management of the wartime

---

[27] Robert W. Seidel, "A Home for Big Science: The Atomic Energy Commission's Laboratory System," *Historical Studies in the Physical and Biological Sciences* 16, no. 1 (1986): pp. 135–175.
[28] Westwick, 2003, *loc. cit.*
[29] Westwick, 2003, *op. cit.*, pp. 46–48.
[30] Seidel, 1986, *op. cit.*, 1986, pp. 139–40; Westwick, 2003, *op. cit.*, pp. 53–55.

33Metallurgical Laboratory, which became the Argonne National Laboratory nearby in Illinois. However, that competitive arrangement did not persist, and Chicago has retained the management of Argonne, now in partnership with Jacobs Engineering Group, Inc.[31]

By contrast, the Radiation Laboratory at Berkeley after World War II was, by virtue of its prewar existence, both an arm of the University of California and a laboratory of the Atomic Energy Commission.[32] The differences in situations for Berkeley and Chicago may also have been related to the fact that Berkeley people such as Oppenheimer, Pitzer, and Seaborg were at times in official government roles—Oppenheimer as chair of the General Advisory Committee of the AEC (1947–54), Pitzer as director of research for the AEC (1949–51), and Seaborg as chairman of the AEC (1961–71).

The division of management responsibilities between the government and its contractors was a subject of contention in the early postwar years, and has remained a source of tension throughout the subsequent histories of these laboratories. The early tensions concerned determination of program. For Berkeley, through the various roles of Lawrence, it was clear that the program was largely to be determined by the laboratory itself[33]; for the other AEC laboratories, that was less clear.[34] More recently, the program-determination process, while still complex, has become better defined, and the tensions surrounding who is responsible for what in management have swung more toward matters that are highly charged politically (see, e.g., the Wen Ho Lee matter, below). A white paper[35] prepared by the Special Committee on the National Laboratories of the University of California Academic Council (Academic Senate) outlined the division of management and programmatic responsibilities as of 2004.

---

[31] See UChicago Argonne, LLC, https://perma.cc/PPB8-VEAR..
[32] Westwick, 2003, op. cit., p. 46.
[33] Seidel, 1986, op. cit., p. 149.
[34] Westwick, op. cit., pp. 14, 97–99, 105–109, 111–116.
[35] Special Committee on the National Laboratories, "What Are the Respective Roles and Authority of UC and DOE in the Management of the National Laboratories?," Academic Council, University of California, April 2004, accessed October 3, 2017,
http://web.archive.org/web/20151004023823/http://senate.universityofcalifornia.edu/committees/acsconl/wp_ix.pdf.

Livermore

The unexpected successful test of an atomic bomb by the Soviet Union in August 1949 brought new impetus to the development by the United States of the hydrogen bomb or "super," which had been urged by Edward Teller during and since the Manhattan Project. Lawrence strongly supported Teller in this quest. The General Advisory Committee of the AEC, still chaired by Oppenheimer, resisted the initiative. Lawrence and Kenneth Pitzer, on leave from the Berkeley College of Chemistry as director of research at the AEC, convinced the AEC to commit to development of the hydrogen bomb and to start by funding a materials-testing accelerator (MTA), to be built at a former naval air station in Livermore, about one hour from Berkeley. Although the MTA itself did not last long, the Livermore site persisted as the locale for the development of the "super." Teller, agonized by the seemingly slow pace of work on the new bomb at Los Alamos, argued for creation of a second weapons laboratory, which could proceed apace on the development of the hydrogen bomb. Another part of the argument was that having two nuclear-weapons laboratories would enable each to review the work of the other.

Figure 13-3. Ernest Lawrence and Edward Teller, founders of the Livermore Laboratory, along with Herbert York, the first director, 1952 (courtesy of Lawrence Livermore National Laboratory)[36]

---

[36] https://perma.cc/R9RR-34LF.

Thus in 1952 the University of California Radiation Laboratory, Livermore Branch was created. The first director of the laboratory was Herbert York, a Berkeley physics faculty member and one of Lawrence's people at the Radiation Laboratory.[37] The Livermore Laboratory has persisted to this day as one of two (Los Alamos and Livermore) nuclear-weapons laboratories.[38] The story of the "super" is told by Rhodes.[39]

TRANSFORMATIONS FOR THE LABORATORIES

In what has as of 2018 been seventy-five years since their origins in World War II, the former Atomic Energy Commission laboratories have undergone many changes in structure, oversight, and program.

Government Reorganization
With the arrival of the Arab oil embargo in 1974, most of the roles of the Atomic Energy Commission were incorporated, along with the AEC laboratories, into the Energy Research and Development Agency (ERDA), broadening the mission of the agency to all aspects of energy. Then in 1977 ERDA was folded into the new Department of Energy (DOE), which took responsibility for nuclear weapons as well as other aspects of energy generation, transmission, storage, and utilization.

Program Diversification
As the years went on after World War II, through the formations of ERDA and DOE, and eventually through the collapse of the Soviet Union in 1991, issues continually surrounded the future and the programs of the national laboratories. Both effective new programs and local political support for the continuance of the laboratories precluded any substantial downsizing. Indeed, the national laboratories as a group have grown, despite budgetary ups and downs relating to

---

[37] York was later the first chancellor of the San Diego campus of the University of California, as described in chapter 10.
[38] Seidel, 1986, *op. cit.*, pp. 151–153; P. J. Westwick, *op. cit.*, pp. 123–128. An engaging history of the Livermore Laboratory is given by C. B. Tarter, *The American Lab: An Insider's History of the Lawrence Livermore Notional Laboratory*, Johns Hopkins University Press, Naltimore, 2018.
[39] Richard Rhodes, *Dark Sun: The Making of the Hydrogen Bomb* (New York: Simon & Schuster, 1995).

such factors as the economy, the onset of nuclear test-ban treaties, and the starts and finishes of hot and cold wars. As the years have gone on, there has been a continual diversification of the programs of the laboratories, with a general theme that the laboratories should undertake programs of national importance that are so large or expensive that they are not likely to be taken up adequately by the private sector. The laboratories have also proven to be effective for large-project research that requires combining multiple disciplines.

The early avenues of diversification at the weapons laboratories related closely to their core mission. The original Manhattan Project had created early forms of nuclear reactors, starting with Fermi's atomic pile at the University of Chicago. Several of the national laboratories had programs relating to power reactors (nuclear energy) after the war, an effort that was more at other laboratories than the UC laboratories. In 1960–61 the AEC decided to create a new Inorganic Materials Research Division at the Berkeley laboratory so as to carry out research that would serve materials needs for nuclear reactors and space vehicles.[40] Materials research spread to the other laboratories as well.[41] Project Plowshare,[42] carried out from 1955 until the early 1970s, principally at the Livermore laboratory, investigated potential peacetime uses of nuclear explosions, such as for power generation, production of tritium and plutonium, excavation, extraction of oil from shale (now done by "fracking"), and mining of copper and other materials. None of these applications have materialized, because of matters of radioactive containment and economics.

As other nations developed nuclear capabilities and concerns developed about "rogue" nuclear weapons being obtained because of insufficient security, the Los Alamos and Livermore laboratories developed programs dealing with nonproliferation and containment. In the 1990s the concept of stockpile stewardship arose, with the objective being assurance of continued working capabilities of weapons th3at had been manufactured in the past. These weapons are subject to decay in various ways and yet could not be subjected to actual performance tests because of test-ban treaties.

---

[40] Seidel, 1986, *op. cit.*, p. 159.
[41] Westwick, 2003, *op. cit.*, pp. 257–266.
[42] Westwick, 2003, *op. cit.*, pp. 231–234.

As environmental concerns reached the forefront, ERDA was created in 1971, and the Arab oil embargo occurred in 1973. The activities of the laboratories grew to incorporate broad issues of energy and environment.[43] In the 1990s the Cooperative Research and Development Agreement (CRADA) program came into full swing, and the laboratories were very active in developing joint programs with industrial companies. More recently, the production of energy from biological sources became another key component of the mission.

These activities served to broaden the mission of the Berkeley laboratory far beyond accelerators, particle physics, and transuranium elements. Over the years, it formed programs in energy, environment, earth sciences, biological sciences, genomics, computation, materials science, and building technology, as well as construction of a well used national Advanced Light Source facility. These developments, in turn, widened the scope of involvement of University of California faculty members (primarily, but not exclusively, from Berkeley) beyond physics and chemistry to various branches of engineering and biological, geological, and computing sciences.

Broadening of mission has affected the Livermore and Los Alamos laboratories too. Somewhat more than half of the program of the Lawrence Livermore National Laboratory is now for purposes other than nuclear weapons, and a substantial fraction of the Los Alamos National Laboratory program is as well. The total operating budgets for the three UC laboratories in 2015 were $2.45 billion for Los Alamos, $1.5 billion for Livermore, and $785 million for Berkeley. By comparison, the total operating budget for the university itself, independent of the laboratories, was about $26 billion.[44] Employment in 2015 was 10,500 at Los Alamos, 6,500 at Lawrence Livermore, and 3,300 at Lawrence Berkeley.

Structures and Names of the Berkeley and Livermore Laboratories

From 1931 until 1959, Lawrence's Charter Hill laboratory at Berkeley was known as the University of California Radiation

---

[43] Westwick, 2003, *op. cit.*, pp. 286–298.
[44] University of California, Budget for Current Operations: Summary and Detail. 2014-15", p. S-5, https://web.archive.org/web/20150905211828/https://www.ucop.edu/operating-budget/_files/rbudget/2014-15budgetforcurrentoperations.pdf

Laboratory (UCRL). Upon the death of Lawrence in 1959, the regents renamed it Lawrence Radiation Laboratory (LRL). When the Livermore Laboratory was formed in 1952, it was a branch of UCRL and then LRL. In 1971 the Livermore laboratory was separated from the Berkeley laboratory and given independent status, so that the Regents of the University of California now contracted with the federal government for the management of three laboratories: Berkeley, Livermore, and Los Alamos. The Berkeley laboratory then became the Lawrence Berkeley Laboratory (LBL) and then in 1995, the Lawrence Berkeley National Laboratory (LBNL). The Livermore laboratory became the Lawrence Livermore Laboratory (LLL) and then subsequently the Lawrence Livermore National Laboratory (LLNL). When the Livermore laboratory was separated from the Berkeley laboratory, classified work then formally ended at LBL.[45]

Contracts and Controversies with the University

Throughout the seventy-five-year management of the nuclear weapons laboratories by the University of California, there has been continual controversy surrounding that management, both within and outside the university and usually swelling toward times of contract renewal. The basic concern has been whether it is an appropriate role for a major research university to manage nuclear-weapons activities.

Contract renewals typically have come at five- to eight-year intervals. The process has begun with a decision by the Department of Energy or one of its forerunner agencies whether to compete or extend—that is, whether to open the contract for competition among potential managers or to negotiate with the current contract holder for an extension of the contract. This decision has been important for the university, because competing is much less in line with being asked to do a public service than is extension. Also, for an extension the university can negotiate specific issues bilaterally with the Department of Energy, as opposed to responding competitively to a set of predetermined criteria in a request for proposals. The university has consistently and appropriately held to the concept of public service as

---

[45] Jeffrey Kahn, "Our History: From Particle Physics to the Full Spectrum of Science," Lawrence Berkeley National Laboratory, January 1989, https://perma.cc/Q4C9-MW2F.

the rationale for managing the Los Alamos and Livermore laboratories. In fact, former UC president David Gardner observes[46] that in 1991, when the secretary of energy contacted him to inform him that the decision would be to compete rather than renew, he responded that in that case the university would not be among those competing. This then led to a response from the secretary indicating that because so much of the nation's defense rested on these contracts, he would then have to "work" the matter at the Department of Energy and Congress so as to extend. Until the 2004–2005 competition, the decision had always been to extend rather than compete.

Various committees have been chartered within the University of California over the years to examine and report on the question of continuing the contract as contract-renewal time approached. In all but one case, the committee was chartered by the Academic Council of the Academic Senate. The committee report would then be followed by an advisory vote of the faculty, carried out by the Academic Senate. These studies included the 1970 report of the Zinner Committee,[47] the 1978 report of the Gerberding Committee[48] appointed by President Saxon in consultation with the Academic Council, the 1989 report of the Jendresen Committee,[49] the 1996 report of the University Committee on Research Policy (UCORP) of the Academic Council,[50] and a 2003 Interim Report to UCORP.[51] Another evaluation and report were supplied in 1996 by the UC President's Council on the National

---

[46] David P. Gardner, *Earning My Degree: Memoirs of an American University President* (Berkeley: University of California Press, 2005), pp. 266–267.

[47] Report of the Special Committee on University Research at Livermore and Los Alamos, Academic Senate, University of California, 1970, https://perma.cc/N7PD-BWFQ..

[48] Report of the Committee to Examine the University's Relationship with the Los Alamos and Livermore Laboratories, University of California, February 10, 1978, https://perma.cc/W2GR-AULX.

[49] M. D. Jendresen et al., "Report of the Special Committee of the Academic Senate on the University's Relations with the Department of Energy (DOE) Laboratories," University of California Academic Senate, November 21, 1989, https://perma.cc/MNS3-HYNA.

[50] University-wide Committee on Research Policy, "Report of the University Committee on Research Policy on the University's Relations with the Department of Energy Laboratories," University of California Academic Senate, January 1996, https://perma.cc/4G75-SCXJ.

[51] Interim Report to the University of California Committee on Research Policy (UCORP), Academic Senate, University of California, 2013, https://perma.cc/YB8Y-DTUK.

Laboratories⁵², and the Academic Council specifically did not endorse the report of the UCORP Committee of that year. Except for the President's Council report of 1996, these reports all recommended either discontinuance of UC management of Los Alamos and Livermore or continuing the contracts with substantial modifications. In all cases the president chose to renew the contracts, but often with some modifications along the lines of the senate recommendations.

Public, National, and Political Issues and Controversies

There are much public concern and political attention directed toward the nuclear laboratories, fueled by the strong public interest and fear about nuclear weapons, existence of numerous "watchdog" operations formed by groups of private citizens, and laws requiring openness and public reporting of incidents regarding nuclear and classified materials.

One case in point was the matter of Wen Ho Lee, who in 1999 was accused of espionage at the Los Alamos National Laboratory. That story broke in a *New York Times* article.[53] The Federal Bureau of Investigation (FBI) had known for over a year that there had been suspicious activity by Lee but had required the laboratory to keep the suspect in place in his employment without informing the University of California while an investigation took place. The university learned of the matter only when the FBI allowed the laboratory director to inform the provost (i.e., the author) just two days before the *New York Times* story ran. The accusations brought on quite aggressive political and legal action within the Department of Energy and FBI against Lee, in a saga that is told in detail by Stober and Hoffman.[54] Lee had clearly violated security rules by taking classified material outside the classified area and indeed outside the laboratory itself. However, it was never proven that he

---

[52] University of California President's Council on the National Laboratories, "Recommendation regarding Continued University of California Management of the Lawrence Berkeley, Lawrence Livermore, and Los Alamos National Laboratories," February 1996, https://perma.cc/BNP2-3B54.
[53] James Risen and Jeff Gerth, "BREACH AT LOS ALAMOS: A Special Report; China Stole Nuclear Secrets for Bombs, U.S. Aides Say," *New York Times*, March 6, 1999.
[54] Dan Stober and Ian Hoffman, *A Convenient Spy: Wen-ho Lee and the Politics of Nuclear Espionage* (New York: Simon & Schuster, 2002).

transmitted sensitive information to a foreign country, and he was convicted on no other charge. The Lee incident was followed in June 1999 by a broad study and report[55] from the US president's Foreign Intelligence Advisory Board that was highly critical of security policy and practice within the Department of Energy and its national laboratories.[56]

In May 2000, a large 48,000-acre (190-square-kilometer) wildfire, known as the Cerro Grande Fire,[57] broke out from what had been a controlled burn by the National Park Service in Bandelier National Monument adjoining the Los Alamos National Laboratory. The fire entered laboratory grounds, causing a two-week closure of the laboratory. Shortly after the laboratory was reopened, it was discovered that two computer hard drives containing classified information were missing from their normal locations within the secure classified area.[58] This again generated much media coverage, attention, and concern. The hard drives were found twelve days later, unscathed and apparently not tampered with, behind a copy machine in the secure area.[59] This incident, the previous Wen Ho Lee matter, and an accusation, ultimately proven erroneous, that an LANL employee used a laboratory credit card to buy a personal automobile[60] were primary reasons why the Department of Energy decided to compete the management contracts for LANL and LLNL in 2004–05 (see also below).

Oversight and Management of the Laboratories within the University of California

The Regents of the University of California have the ultimate authority over the UC management of the national laboratories. The

---

[55] "Science at Its Best, Security at Its Worst: A Report of Security Problems at the U. S. Department of Energy," President's Foreign Intelligence Advisory Board, Special Investigative Panel, June 1999, https://web.archive.org/web/20010119084300/https://fas.org/sgp/library/pfiab/reorg.html.
[56] Patricia A. Pelfrey, *Entrepreneurial President: Richard Atkinson and the University of California, 1995–2003* (Berkeley: University of California Press, 2012), p. 141.
[57] "Cerro Grande Fire," Wikipedia, https://perma.cc/J3YJ-HVXH.
[58] Pelfrey, 2012, *op. cit.*, p. 143.
[59] James Risen, "Missing Nuclear Data Found behind a Los Alamos Copier," *New York Times*, June 17, 2000.
[60] Pelfrey, 2012, *op. cit.*, pp. 144–145.

University of California administrative management structure for oversight of the laboratories started small and has grown substantially over the years. As has already been noted, the original liaison was the secretary and treasurer of the regents, a role limited by high secrecy and security and acquiesced to by the university because of wartime. With the contract renewal of 1972, the first Science Advisory Committee was created within the university,[61] primarily for the two weapons laboratories. In 1978 the position special assistant for laboratory affairs was established.[62] The senior vice president for academic affairs (later with the added title of provost) oversaw the special assistant, James S. Kane, a Berkeley PhD chemist who had been the founding director of the Basic Energy Sciences Program within ERDA and then the Department of Energy. As well, two scientific advisory committees (advisory to both the president and the laboratory directors) were created—the Scientific and Academic Advisory Committee for the two weapons laboratories and the Scientific and Educational Advisory Committee[63] for the Berkeley laboratory. They would continually review the programs of the laboratories for scientific quality, a role that fits appropriately with university management.

In 1989, two UC positions were created to be resident, one at each of the two weapons laboratories, providing on-site oversight. Then in 1991 the Laboratory Administration Office was created to provide oversight of business, financial, and administrative management matters. This office came under the senior vice president for business and finance. The President's Council on the National Laboratories was created at the same time to provide programmatic review, evaluation, and scientific oversight. It was chaired by Sidney Drell of Stanford University, a prominent physicist and expert on nuclear weapons and arms control, and had members who included scientific and industrial leaders, a retired four-star general,[64] and senior representatives from

---

[61] Jendresen et al., 1989, *loc. cit.*
[62] Jendresen et al., 1989, *loc. cit.*
[63] The author was a member of SEAC.
[64] Andrew J. Goodpaster, who had been staff secretary in the administration of President Eisenhower and supreme allied commander of the North Atlantic Treaty Organization (NATO). See Robert S. Jordan, *An Unsung Soldier: The Life of Gen. Andrew J. Goodpaster* (Annapolis, MD: Naval Institute Press, 2013).

the UC administration and Academic Senate. The full membership is given, and the duties of the President's Council are described in a document[65] from the Academic Senate written in 2000. There were also several committees reporting to the President's Council with responsibilities for reviewing specific aspects of the laboratories. The special assistant for laboratory affairs and programmatic matters remained with the provost/senior vice president for academic affairs, through whom the President's Council also reported.

In 2001 the UC administrative structure was changed again, with the creation of the position vice president for laboratory management (now vice president for national laboratories[66]), which assumed oversight of all aspects of oversight, programmatic and administrative. Occupants of that position were John McTague (2001-03) and then retired four-star admiral S. Robert Foley,[67] former commander-in-chief of the US Navy Pacific Fleet (2003-09). This was a major change from science and university expertise to military expertise in the administrative oversight of the laboratories.

In 2004–05 the Department of Energy did hold competitions for the management contracts for Los Alamos and Livermore National Laboratories. At the same time, the Department of Energy switched the laboratory-management model to a performance-based model that is based upon formal grading, with grade-determined results and a much higher management fee that would be put at risk through the performance-evaluation process. For this purpose the university entered into two limited partnership corporations—Los Alamos National Security, LLC,[68] and Lawrence Livermore National Security, LLC[69]—with Bechtel Corporation, Babcock & Wilcox Technical Services, URS Energy and Construction, and Battelle (for Livermore only). These partnerships won both competitions in 2006 and presently (2017) hold the prime contracts.

---

[65] "Purpose Statement: University of California President's Council on the National Laboratories," University of California, October 2000, accessed July 21, 2017, https://web.archive.org/web/20150921032546/http://senate.universityofcalifornia.edu/reports/presidentscouncil.pdf.
[66] "Office of the National Laboratories," University of California, https://perma.cc/QPW5-MLWA.
[67] "Sylvester R. Foley, Jr., Wikipedia, accessed April 23, 2017, https://perma.cc/6G22-VRF2.
[68] Los Alamos National Security, LLC, https://perma.cc/CSS3-GZ37.
[69] Lawrence Livermore National Security, LLC, https://perma.cc/9QKL-QUBT.

The formal oversight of the Berkeley laboratory under the regents lay with the president of the University of California until the chancellor positions were created in the University of California in 1952, at which time the Lawrence Berkeley Laboratory was placed under the chancellor of the Berkeley campus, at a level equivalent to that of a dean.[70] However, Clark Kerr in his memoirs[71] is quick to say that the arrangement was largely nominal since Lawrence functionally reported directly to the regents. That reporting line, now more than nominal, was changed back from the Berkeley chancellor to the University of California president in 1971 at the time of the administrative separation of the Berkeley and Livermore Laboratories.[72]

Management Fee

Historically and in line with the public-service rationale, UC took much smaller management fees than are typically awarded to industrial contractors for managing national laboratories of comparable size and complexity. The fees were gauged to cover the identifiable costs of management and to provide some funds for joint research between the laboratories and UC campuses. As already noted, the 2004 change in approach by the Department of Energy for what became the 2006 contracts involved a major change to a substantially higher, but performance-based and therefore variable fee.

SYNERGIES BETWEEN THE LAWRENCE BERKELEY NATIONAL LABORATORY AND THE BERKELEY CAMPUS

The Berkeley laboratory has undergone remarkable changes over time, such that it has been transformed by degrees from an extension of the Physics Department of the Berkeley campus into a national laboratory with substantial lines of national government funding supporting a wide range of research on subjects of national importance and with an annual budget now in the range of three-quarters of a

---

[70] P. J. Westwick, 2003, *op. cit.*, p. 50.
[71] Clark Kerr, 2001, *op. cit.*, pp. 134, 195.
[72] University of California, *University Bulletin* 19, no. 30 (June 28, 1971): p. 156, accessed June 9, 2016, https://babel.hathitrust.org/cgi/pt?id=uc1.32106020265879;view=1up;seq=170.

billion dollars. There is no main point of time at which this change happened,[73] but the main causative factors for it were World War II, Lawrence's abilities and zeal for bringing science to bear on wartime and postwar needs in useful ways, and the diversification of the programs within the laboratory that occurred, particularly in the 1970s.

The Lawrence Berkeley National Laboratory is an invaluable adjunct to the Berkeley campus and provides a relationship between a government laboratory and a university that is virtually unique among American research universities. The Applied Physics Laboratory is a comparably large (present annual budget about $500 million[74]) research division of Johns Hopkins University that has origins in World War II with the development of the proximity fuse. It is primarily devoted to defense, space, and homeland-security purposes but is an independent, university-affiliated research center and not a national laboratory.[75] The Lincoln Laboratory of MIT is a federally funded research and development center (FFRDC) of the US Department of Defense also working on national security issues and with an annual budget approaching $1 billion. The Jet Propulsion Laboratory (JPL), a NASA laboratory managed by Caltech, is also an FFDRC and has an annual budget around $1.6 million. Both the Lincoln Lab and JPL are more removed geographically from the managing campuses and have limited, mission-oriented programs. The actual involvements of MIT and Caltech faculty with those laboratories are substantially less than for Berkeley faculty with LBNL, as is also the case for interactions of University of Chicago and University of Tennessee faculty with the Argonne and Oak Ridge National Laboratories. The Stanford Linear Accelerator Center (SLAC) and FermiLab are single-purpose

---

[73] P. J. Westwick, 2003, *op. cit.*, pp. 46, 53–55, etc.
[74] Budgets mentioned here are 2013 figures.
[75] The widely cited reports of government R&D funding for universities published in *Science Indicators* by the National Science Foundation include funding for the Applied Physics Laboratory in the total for Johns Hopkins University but do not include funding for the Lawrence Berkeley National Laboratory for either the Berkeley campus or the University of California, even though a large amount of Berkeley faculty research is carried out through LBNL. The result is that Johns Hopkins consistently has the top spot for universities, while Berkeley is surprisingly low—twenty-third for 2014 and only fourth among UC campuses. See, e.g., "Academic Institution Profiles: Rankings by Total R&D Expenditures," National Science Foundation,
https://web.archive.org/web/20171130174516/https://ncsesdata.nsf.gov/profiles/site?method=rankingBySource&ds=herd.

laboratories of the Department of Energy, managed by Stanford and the University of Chicago, respectively, and with budgets of around $325 million and $375 million, respectively. The other DOE laboratory paired with a university is the much smaller Ames Laboratory at Iowa State University, with a budget of about $50 million per year.

About two hundred Berkeley campus faculty members hold joint appointments as LBNL researchers, and about five hundred graduate students conduct their dissertation or thesis research through the laboratory. The large involvement of Berkeley campus faculty members has been enabled by the breadth of program of the laboratory as well as its adjacency to the campus. The relationship considerably enriches the laboratory's research and provides an additional avenue toward research support for the campus faculty. The laboratory has contributed much to the reputation of the campus. For example, ten of the Berkeley Nobel Prizes have been won by Berkeley faculty members affiliated with the laboratory (Lawrence, Seaborg, McMillan, Chamberlain, Segre, Calvin, Glaser, Alvarez, Lee, and Smoot).

There have been other synergies as well. The nature of the laboratory and its program areas are such that they promote and enable multidisciplinary research, and thus the laboratory is a catalyst for that purpose on the Berkeley campus (see also chapter 14). Finally, when the interests of the laboratory and the faculty-recruitment needs of the campus coincide, the combination of research with the laboratory and a faculty position on campus has been a powerful attractant.

THE RELATIONSHIPS WITH LOS ALAMOS AND LIVERMORE

The value to UC of the university's management roles at Los Alamos and Livermore has to be judged in the light of public service, rather than as a source of revenue or as something that enhances the stature of the university. The amount of revenue is both unstable and not large in comparison with total UC revenue. The university has gained and maintains its stature and distinction through activities that do not involve the weapons laboratories. By the very natures of these nuclear weapons laboratories, UC is subject to great public scrutiny and political winds that can cause conflict among the Department of Energy, Congress, numerous interest groups, and the university and its partners with regard to management responsibilities. Because of these factors, the university as contractor does not have full control of the situation and is often buffeted.

In the past, the weapons laboratories have been a considerable drain on the time of those regents most involved and the top-level management of the university. My own estimate is that, before the management restructuring of 2001, about 25 percent of the time of the senior vice president for business and finance and 15 percent of the time of the provost and senior vice president for academic affairs went to laboratory matters.

It would be difficult to make the case that the university itself derives enough value from the management of Los Alamos to offset the negative publicity that can come from the very sensitive public and internal-university aspects of managing the weapons laboratories. One test of utility to the university is the amount of university research that is collaborative with the laboratories. The Jendresen Committee, in its 1989 report,[76] estimated that 10 percent and 40 percent of collaboration with universities by the Los Alamos National Laboratory and Lawrence Livermore National Laboratories, respectively, was with campuses of the University of California. Those figures are probably still much the same. By various measures the University of California is 8 to 10 percent of the nation's academic research enterprise, so one could conclude that Los Alamos research collaboration is not significantly slanted to the University of California, while that at Livermore is. That would be a natural result of the different geographical locations of the two laboratories.

The present structure involving the two LLC companies insulates the university from the two weapons laboratories more than in the past and provides financial, business, and administrative structures that are more directly founded in industrial practice. By virtue of the formation of partnership LLCs, the employees of the two weapons laboratories no longer work for the university itself, which removes some of the attractions that historically have brought scientists to the

---

[76] M. D. Jendresen et al., 1989, *op. cit.*, p. 10.

laboratories. Also, with the elimination of the President's Council and many of its activities, there is no longer the same degree of involved and knowledgeable programmatic oversight that had been brought by the council.

Unfortunately, there have been two accidents associated with the Los Alamos National Laboratory since the change of management to Los Alamos National Security LLC.[77] In February 2014 an improperly packaged container of transuranic waste from LANL shipped to the Waste Isolation Pilot Plant (WIPP) in Carlsbad, New Mexico, ruptured at WIPP, contaminating several workers and causing a shutdown of WIPP. In May 2015 an electrical accident at a substation at the LANL Neutron Science Center injured nine workers, one of them critically. Factoring these instances into the performance-based management grading has resulted in a decision by the Department of Energy to recompete the Los Alamos contract as of 2018. Operations at Livermore have gone much more smoothly, with good performance ratings and continual extensions of the contract. The university was thereby faced with dual questions. First, should UC enter the new Los Alamos competition (to which the answer was yes), and, if so, with the same or different partners (to which the answer was different partners – Texas A&M System and Batelle)? And second, will current and future management structures still provide the degree of programmatic involvement and oversight that makes the university's role worthwhile as service for the country?

SUMMARY CONCLUSIONS

The University of California entered the era of large university-managed laboratories as Ernest Lawrence built ever-larger cyclotrons and eventually had to create a multifaceted but focused research laboratory on university property on the hill above the Berkeley campus. Lawrence and then his Berkeley physics colleague Robert Oppenheimer assumed lead roles in what became the Manhattan

---

[77] David Kramer, "What Went Wrong with the Los Alamos Contract?," *Physics Today*, pp. 22– 24, March 2016.

Project of World War II. The university itself was somewhat reluctantly recruited to "manage" the US Army's Los Alamos Laboratory, which produced the first atomic bombs. The university's institutional role and knowledge of the project were small, but the government believed that a university was needed to enable recruitment of outstanding scientists to the project as well as to provide scientific oversight and administrative capacity in various ways. President Sproul undertook the role for the university as an act of wartime national service.

After World War II, the Manhattan Project laboratories (Los Alamos, Oak Ridge, Hanford, Argonne, and so forth) were converted to a system of national laboratories along with Lawrence's Berkeley laboratory and others. The University of California has managed three of these laboratories—the Lawrence Berkeley National Laboratory, the Los Alamos National Laboratory, and the Lawrence Livermore National Laboratory. The latter laboratory was formed in 1952, following the desire of Edward Teller and others to guide their own program toward development of the hydrogen bomb and the recognition that it would be desirable to have a second nuclear-weapons laboratory so that one could review the research of the other.

There has been much controversy within the University of California about its continued management of the two nuclear-weapons laboratories. As contract renewals have approached, there have been faculty studies and votes within the Academic Senate that have recommended against renewal or sought major changes. Nonetheless, UC presidents did renew the contracts, viewing them as a matter of service to the nation. Not until the mid-1990s were the faculty more generally supportive. The change reflected the creation of a more diverse array of collaborative research between the laboratories and the campuses and probably also the passing of those faculty mrmbers who had the most concerns about the laboratories arising from the tense years after World War II, when nuclear war seemed imminent.

The initial UC management was modest and was centered upon the senior vice presidents for academic affairs and for business and finance. With pressures from the US Department of Energy and from faculty concerns over the years, much more structure for management and oversight was built up.

The management of the Los Alamos and Livermore Laboratories has always been viewed by the university as a public service. The distinction and stature of the University of California come from other sources than management of these laboratories. The general policy of the US government is that there should be competition for management of national laboratories, as for other contracted government functions. The government's desire that the contracts be competitively bid have been a difficult matter for the university over the years since those desires contrast with the concept of an invited public service role. Competition never became a reality until 2005, when the Department of Energy insisted upon it following very public episodes at Los Alamos. The university then joined in partnerships with Bechtel Corporation and other specialized companies to compete and win the contracts once again. Whether or not there is a sufficiently good rationale for the university to participate in the management of Los Alamos, and possibly also Livermore, under these circumstances is an open question at this point.

The Lawrence Berkeley National Laboratory is a very different matter. It has contributed much to the distinction of the University of California and continues to do so. It is a major asset to both the university and the government.

14.
Promoting and Enabling Multidisciplinary Research and Teaching

[The] new economy is being fueled by exciting scientific developments arising out of basic research in nanotechnology, life sciences, information technology, and telecommunications. And these disciplinary areas are creating a spiral vortex, interpenetrating and changing each other as they themselves change. This is where the opportunity to stay competitive lies.
—*From the website of Calit2*[1]

Calit2…achieved its leadership in taking Internet technologies to the next level because 24 academic departments work across disciplines to tackle complex problems, many of which lead to the movement of intellectual discoveries into the marketplace.
—*Richard Atkinson and Patricia Pelfrey*[2]

[The objectives of education are] to give every citizen the information he needs for the transaction of his own business; to enable him to calculate for himself, and to express and preserve his ideas, his contracts and accounts, in writing; to improve, by reading, his morals and faculties; to understand his duties to his neighbors and country, and to discharge with competence the functions confided to him by either; to know his rights…and, in general, to observe with intelligence and faithfulness all the social relations under which he shall be placed.
—*Thomas Jefferson*[3]

An earlier version of much of this chapter appeared as C. Judson King, "The Multidisciplinary Imperative in Higher Education," Research and Occasional Papers Series, no. 11.10, Center for Studies in Higher Education, University of California, Berkeley, CA, September 2010, https://perma.cc/2ECC-K4KF. It was also an invited paper at the 2010 Beijing Forum in Beijing, China, November 2010.

[1] "Calit2 : California Institute for Telecommunications and Information Technology," accessed October 19, 2015, https://perma.cc/E7H5-ZZE9.

[2] Richard C. Atkinson and Patricia A. Pelfrey, "Science and the Entrepreneurial University," *Issues in Science and Technology*, pp. 39–48, Summer 2010, https://perma.cc/WG8G-5BRL.

When an issue becomes highly controversial—when it is surrounded by uncertainties and conflicting values—then expertness is very hard to come by, and it is no longer easy to legitimate the experts. We cannot settle such issues by turning them over to particular groups of experts. At best, we may convert the controversy into an adversarial proceeding in which we, the laymen, listen to the experts and have to judge between them."
—Herbert Simon[4]

You want the inside of your head to be an interesting place to spend the rest of your life.
—Judith Shapiro,[5] quoted by Andrew Delbanco[6]

Knowledge continually grows and forefronts of it become more and more specialized. Yet societal needs and problems become continually more multidimensional and complex. How can research universities best adapt themselves to these trends?

ROLES OF DISCIPLINES AND ACADEMIC DEPARTMENTS

Over the centuries as knowledge developed at an ever-increasing pace, it became desirable and even necessary to organize and codify it

---

[3] Thomas Jefferson, "Report of the Commissioners for the University of Virginia," August 4, 1818, known also as the Rockfish Gap Report, cited by James J. Carpenter, "The Ultimate Defense of Liberty," in M. Andrew Holowchak, ed., *Thomas Jefferson and Philosophy: Essays on the Philosophical Cast of Jefferson's Writings* (Lanham, MD: Lexington Books, 2013), p. 140.
[4] Herbert A. Simon, *Reason in Human Affairs* (Stanford, CA: Stanford University Press, 1983), p. 87, cited by Michael M. Crow and William B. Dabars, *Designing the New American University* (Baltimore, MD: Johns Hopkins University Press, 2015), p. 144.
[5] President, Teagle Foundation, former president, Barnard College.
[6] Andrew Delbanco, *College: What It Was, Is, and Should Be* (Princeton, NJ: Princeton University Press, 2012), pp. 32–33.

and to seek efficient ways of generalizing and extending it. This need gave rise to disciplines (chemistry, economics, physics, sociology, and so on) and then to subdisciplines within them (physical chemistry, organic chemistry, analytical chemistry, and now even physical organic chemistry and biophysical chemistry). Disciplines have served us very well. They have provided effective and efficient ways of advancing, organizing, conveying, and utilizing knowledge. The disciplines have also developed their own methodologies and internal cultures.

In early days, universities sought to provide a general education, often under rubrics such as "natural philosophy" and often with a strong theological bent. But as knowledge grew and disciplines became established, the mode of education became one wherein students majored in a particular discipline, preceded by what was commonly known as general education. During the twentieth century, for most[7] US universities, the concept of general education gradually changed from a collection of particular specified courses to distribution requirements. Distribution requirements typically mandate that the student take certain numbers of courses from each of several areas, but without the particular courses being specified, with many choices available, and often without there being available courses that are specifically designed for general education.[8] At the postgraduate level specialization becomes even greater and education thereby narrower. Thus we produce graduates who are versed in a specific discipline along with general education or distribution requirements that are modest at best. For a field such as engineering with its professional degree at the bachelor's level, there is usually very little in the way of general-education or distribution requirements.

The organization of universities has followed the disciplinary model, with academic departments corresponding one-to-one with

---

[7] Columbia University still requires a specific set of courses for general education, and the University of Chicago, while offering choices for general education, considerably limits that choice.
[8] Appendices A and C of a report on general education in public research universities from a commission chaired by Michael Schudson and Neil Smelser of the UC San Diego and Berkeley campuses, respectively, summarize the general-education requirements of the different undergraduate University of California campuses and general-education reforms of various universities. (See "General Education in the 21st Century: A Report of the University of California Commission on General Education," Center for Studies in Higher Education, April 2007, https://perma.cc/B46E-UVL2.)

specific disciplines. Academic life for the faculty has also come to be centered on disciplines and departments. Departments are the bases for academic appointments, curriculum organization and delivery, budgeting, governance, space allocation, and faculty life in general. Disciplines are the loci for faculty recognition, national and international awards, presentations of research results, and sharing of approaches to teaching. Many observers have remarked on the fact that, over the years since the 1960s, allegiances of faculty have shifted from the university to the department, and from there to the discipline or subdiscipline itself (i.e., outside the university rather than within it).

MULTIDISCIPLINARY NEEDS AND OPPORTUNITIES

Many of the most exciting challenges, needs, and opportunities for research now deal with areas that are not within a single discipline but instead require complementary efforts from several or even many different disciplines. Often the needs have come about from world population growth. Some examples of the areas that have this highly multidisciplinary characteristic and present both needs and major opportunities for research are the following.

- Global climate change
- Energy resources, generation, storage, and transmission
- Privacy in the era of "big data" and the Internet
- Water supply and reuse
- Lessening poverty
- Food supply and novel food sources
- Social unrest, arms control, terrorism, and war
- Heath care
- Safe uses of biotechnology
- Medical informatics
- Acceptance of nuclear energy

The need for involving multiple disciplines in important areas was increasingly recognized after World War II, although even earlier the concept had been the organizing basis for Bell Laboratories, the research arm of what was then the monopolistic telephone industry in the United States. Bell Labs was focused upon bringing together the full expertise of different disciplines in complementary ways, through the design of the buildings, the organization of project teams, and the general culture.[9] The Bell Laboratories' approach led to many striking developments, such as the transistor, zone refining for purification and controlled doping of semiconductor materials, communications satellites, solar cells, radio astronomy, masers and lasers, and much of information theory underlying digital computation.

After World War II, in recognition of the importance of bringing disciplines together, there were scholars who intentionally became *interdisciplinary*, having expertise in more than one discipline and in areas in which the disciplines would meet or where multiple disciplines would be needed. Several programs built around such faculty members have been quite successful, including one at Berkeley known as the Energy and Resources Group,[10] which gives master's and doctorate degrees as well as an undergraduate minor. Still strong, this program was formed in 1973 around John Holdren, who later became presidential science advisor during the presidency of Barack Obama.

However, as time has gone on it has become apparent that the full power of each of multiple disciplines is needed for progress in many areas such as those listed above, and that this knowledge is more than can be packed into the brain of a single individual. Thus interests in many universities have turned back toward the Bell Labs' concepts for bringing faculty members with different disciplinary backgrounds together in ways that enable them to interact well for progress on research. To accomplish this does require special structures, mechanisms, and incentives, since the natural allegiances of faculty members are to their home departments and disciplines, from whence come their resources and recognition. This general need has also been recognized in an American Academy of Arts and Sciences study,[11] which has given the name transdisciplinary to this concept.

---

[9] Jon Gertner, *The Idea Factory: Bell Labs and the Great Age of American Innovation* (New York: Penguin Books, 2012).
[10] Energy & Resources Group, University of California, Berkeley, https://perma.cc/VN84-RFHW.
[11] Venkatesh Narayanamurti, Keith Yamamoto, et al., *ARISE II:, Advancing Research In Science and Engineering: The Role of Academia, Industry, and Government in the 21st Century*,
American Academy of Arts and Sciences, Cambridge MA, 2013, https://perma.cc/24QR-BPWV..

It does not work well simply to assign faculty members from different disciplines to work together. This is counter to the traditions of the great universities, in which faculty members follow their own leads and interests and select and define their own research. There are good reasons for that tradition. The faculty member knows more about her or his field than anyone else in the university and has the most intellectual resources for finding and choosing promising leads and defining how best to pursue them. The well-honed system that assesses and rewards outstanding creativity through reputation and salary provides ample incentive for faculty members to excel. Outstanding quality and striking innovations come from this tradition. It is part of the reason why many large corporations have, starting in the 1970s, wound down in-house fundamental research activities that often involved assigning research to in-house researchers. Even the Bell Laboratories' approach was based upon individual scientists identifying opportunities and working with one another as they saw fit.

Multidisciplinary needs call for education that enables graduates in different disciplines to work together effectively. This is not a simple matter, given the different methods, concepts, and vocabularies of the different disciplines. Inducing faculty members to work together on multidisciplinary or large-problem courses is also difficult because most faculty members do not know faculty members outside their department well and do not have much understanding of other disciplines. Most faculty members are more comfortable teaching in their own disciplinary areas.[12]

Enabling faculty members from different disciplines who wish to do so to get together in research has proven to be an effective way of encouraging them to work together in instruction. As collaborating researchers discover what others can contribute to multidisciplinary research, they come to see the wherewithal of joint preparation and delivery of multidisciplinary courses of instruction.

---

[12] A survey of some of the efforts over the years to bridge the disciplines has been given by Michael M. Crow and William B. Dabars, *Designing the New American University* (Baltimore, MD: Johns Hopkins University Press, 2015), pp. 183–207.

Finally, strong multidisciplinary research seems to occur more readily in the natural sciences and engineering than it does in the social sciences and humanities. In part this is a result of the much greater traditions of individual research in humanities and many of the social sciences, as opposed to research that is collaborative among faculty members, or even between faculty members and their students. It also reflects the substantial differences in research working methodologies among the different social sciences.

FACILITATION OF MULTIDISCIPLINARY RESEARCH

Overall Leadership, Design, and Building

Motivated and highly effective leaders can build multidisciplinary academic enterprises de novo, if given the resources and appropriate timing to do so. In addition to Ernest O. Lawrence at Berkeley (chapter 9), strong examples are William Rutter at UC San Francisco, Roger Revelle at the Scripps Institute of Oceanography, and David Bonner at the UC San Diego School of Medicine (all chapter 10).

Facilitative Organizational Structures

One of the best-known methods for facilitating multidisciplinary research in research universities is to set up cross-matrix organizational structures dealing with specific broad topical areas of research. This approach came into being as government support of research increased following World War II. The historical development is traced by Geiger,[13] who notes[14] that "Berkeley was the most fertile breeding ground of organized research units, and the initiator of the acronym ORU" (for organized research units). There were several reasons[15] for the blossoming of ORUs at Berkeley, among them

- the boom economy of California after World War II with consequent substantial state funding for UC (see chapters 2 and 17);

---

[13] Roger L. Geiger, *Research and Relevant Knowledge: American Research Universities since World War II* (New York: Oxford University Press, 1993), pp. 48–57, 75–76.
[14] Geiger, 1993, *op. cit.*, p. 75.
[15] Geiger, 1993, *op. cit.*, pp. 74–76.

- the influx of tuition money for surging enrollments of World War II veterans provided by the relatively liberal provisions of the GI Bill;
- a policy of retaining a set portion of overhead monies from federal contracts and grants within the university budget as Regents' (now University) Opportunity Funds even though many of the expenses included in overhead calculations had been covered within the state budget;[16]
- a tacit decision by the university administration, the regents, and the state government to stress and build research stature at UC, in recognition of the benefits that it would bring to the distinction of UC, the economy of California, and society in general; and
- a desire to match research units within the university better with specific federal agencies and other external sources of funding for research.

Although none of these factors, except perhaps the last one, specifically addressed multidisciplinary research, encouragement and facilitation of multidisciplinary research was the result. As is described in chapter 6, there are also multicampus research units (MRUs) and related programs to stimulate research involving multiple campuses.

ORUs and MRUs provide space for research, research interactions, and administrative services. In many cases there is some institutional budget in addition to what is derived from outside grants. Although a few University of California ORUs receive funding through direct line items in the state budget,[17] many of the early ones were launched through the aforementioned Regents' Opportunity Fund. Many of the ORUs formed in more recent years are completely self-funded through outside grants, contracts, and services; however, the ORU structure is still valuable for identity and for bringing together researchers of varied disciplinary backgrounds.

The ORU movement within UC grew rapidly. Geiger[18] points out that by the mid-1960s, there were at least 40 ORUs at Berkeley alone and 131 in the entire University of California. A 2015 count for the Berkeley campus showed that there are forty-four ORUs and fourteen

---

[16] Chapter 17 describes this action in more detail.
[17] Examples are the Institute for Transportation Studies and the Institute for Industrial Relations, established in 1947 and 1945, respectively.
[18] Geiger, 1993, *op. cit.*, p. 75.

museums and field stations,[19] as well as sixty other centers, institutes, and the like,[20] nearly all of which have the character of ORUs. The subject matters of ORUs are extremely varied.[21] Nearly all are multidisciplinary, some less so than others. Within the University of California, at some campuses (e.g., UCLA) portions of faculty positions have been allocated to ORUs, while at other campuses (e.g., Berkeley) that is not done. Many ORUs involve faculty members from both professional schools and academic disciplines, another way in which professional schools and disciplines are brought together academically.

When multidisciplinary activities or would-be ORUs are started, they need a source of support services. Rather than investing in a full array of such services for a nascent unit, one useful approach is to provide support services at the start from another, established unit or parent organization. Several of the newer ORUs at Berkeley were started in that way within existing ORUs. Another approach is to combine support services for a number of different units. Going much further in that direction, the Berkeley campus in 2009 combined administrative services (personnel, purchasing, accounting, etcetera) for nearly all ORUs and some related units, over eighty in all, into one unit known as Research Enterprise Services (RES). A few years later, when it seemed that RES had worked well, a number of core administrative services (human resources, purchasing, accounting, and so forth) for all units on the Berkeley campus, academic and nonacademic alike, were combined into the campus-wide Shared Services Division, with the goal of substantially saving on administrative costs. The results so far are mixed at best (see chapter 6).

On a grander scale, the Lawrence Berkeley National Laboratory (LBNL) is an effective mechanism for bringing faculty members and others together in multidisciplinary projects. The laboratory has grown

---

[19] "Organizational Chart—VC Research," University of California, Berkeley, https://web.archive.org/web/20150929062531/https://vcresearch.berkeley.edu/organizational-chart "Organization Chart—Executive Vice Chancellor and Provost," University of California, Berkeley, accessed October 14, 2015, https://web.archive.org/web/20150905135220/http://www.berkeley.edu/admin/pdf/provost.pdf

[20] "Centers & Institutes by Subject Area," Office of Research, University of California, Berkeley, https://web.archive.org/web/20150929154824/http://vcresearch.berkeley.edu/research-units/centers-and-institutes-by-subject_area.

[21] See also previous footnote.

even more multidisciplinary as the mission has diversified from cyclotrons and high-energy physics into issues of energy, environment, geosciences, and biology. Some of the Berkeley-campus ORUs were started within LBNL. The arrival of so many ORUs within the University of California after World War II helped to extend the multidisciplinary approach of the Lawrence Berkeley Laboratory to many other areas, including the social sciences, arts, and humanities.

There is a thorough system of proposals, review, and evaluation by Academic Senate committees required for the formation of ORUs.[22] This process is complex and time-consuming, so that in some cases faculty members who want to get together for research just simply do so, without going through what is required to become an ORU. An example from Berkeley illustrates this fact in a very positive way. When Berkeley faculty members from several different disciplines (engineering, social sciences, medicine, public health, public policy, and law) found themselves brought in on the analysis of the damages caused by Hurricane Katrina (2005) in New Orleans, they discovered a strong common interest in catastrophic risk management and recognized that expertise from a number of different disciplines was needed in order to approach those issues effectively. What is striking is that it took service on the various Hurricane Katrina panels and committees in order for these faculty members to find one another; they did not intersect naturally on campus. On their own and without university budget for initiating it, they created the Center for Catastrophic Risk Management,[23] which has blossomed. The center has been of substantial use with regard to other disasters and potential disasters, such as the Deepwater Horizon offshore platform collapse and oil release in the Gulf of Mexico (2010) and the risks associated with antiquated levees on California's Sacramento River delta. The collaboration has also led to co-teaching of multidisciplinary courses on aspects of risk management for potential catastrophes. The referenced ORU policy does allow for establishment of non-ORU "centers" upon

---

[22] Administrative Policies and Procedures concerning Organized Research Units, memorandum from President Richard C. Atkinson, University of California, December 7, 1999, https://perma.cc/L2AH-4MXC.
[23] "UC Berkeley Center for Catastrophic Risk Management: Overview," University of California, Berkeley, https://web.archive.org/web/20150920010245/http://ccrm.berkeley.edu/.

campus administrative approval following consultation with the campus division of the Academic Senate, a much less elaborate process.

A different Berkeley move toward multidisciplinary academic programs was the creation of the School of Information, described in chapter 12. However, establishment of a new school as a way to foster multidisciplinary activities necessitates a high degree of confidence that the subject is appropriately chosen and will stand the test of time. Since that is usually difficult to assess at the onset of a program, the structures chosen for new multidisciplinary activities should, for the most part, be fluid and subject to modification and even elimination through subsequent reviews.

Governance, Budgeting, and Empowerment

Given all the forces that draw faculty members to their home academic departments, it is important to devise mechanisms whereby multidisciplinary units can deal with academic departments on an even-up basis. In management terms, it helps for the structure to be brought close to a true cross-matrix model.

One essential requirement is effective and tested leadership. Typically, chairs of academic departments and deans in US universities are chosen through processes that have much input and place great weight on demonstrated leadership ability. A similar process should be followed with respect to directors of multidisciplinary units, so that they have the talents to deal with chairs of academic departments and other administrators effectively. Interests centering on the multidisciplinary field are not enough by themselves.

Again for reasons of leverage with respect to the academic departments, the director of a multidisciplinary unit should have continual access to sufficient resources of budget and space. Even if the full professorial appointment of a recruited faculty member is to be in one or more academic departments, an ORU needs to have the resources to participate in start-up packages for recruited faculty members so that allegiance of the recruited faculty member to the ORU can be developed. As well, the ORU may be able to increase the interest of the department in the appointment, or the ability of the department to fund the recruitment, by participating in the start-up package. The same applies to retentions of faculty members when they are recruited by other universities. To the extent that ORUs have financial resources and able leadership, they can hold their own in dealings with academic departments and gaining allegiance from members of the ORU.

At Berkeley an experiment was carried out in which ten of twenty new faculty positions resulting from a state budget increase in the early 2000s were dedicated to the creation of multidisciplinary research and teaching initiatives. A competition was held with a proposal, review, and selection process. The five winning initiatives were given new faculty positions with which to work, but the faculty appointments had to be in academic departments or fractionally divided among multiple academic departments. Multidisciplinary, multidepartmental search committees were used. The resultant faculty appointments were reviewed and approved at the department and central-campus levels in the established way (see chapter 11), and the initiative director determined the allocation of the faculty FTE among the departments. This gave the directors of the new multidisciplinary initiatives considerable leverage in negotiations at the time that the new faculty members were hired. However, that leverage did not continue once the departmental assignments were made, and the allegiances of some of the faculty members recruited drifted back over time to the departments. It is important that the director of the multidisciplinary unit have continual rather than one-time resources, or the ability to obtain continual resources, as the multidisciplinary unit and the department inherently compete in various ways over time for the attention and involvement of the faculty member.

Integration of Disciplines in Governance

As is described in chapter 7 and elsewhere, the University of California has a strong and well-established system of shared governance. Faculty members participate in governance through many topic-specific committees of the Academic Senate, with committee members chosen to represent a wide spectrum of disciplines across the campuses, including professional schools. Often, faculty members with kindred multidisciplinary interests have found one another through these committees.

INSTITUTES OF SCIENCE AND INNOVATION

One effective way of incentivizing faculty members to join together in well-designed multidisciplinary initiatives is to hold a competition with substantial monetary stakes. A prime example was the establishment of the California Institutes on Science and Innovation. Four major research institutes were launched by the state of California in the year 2000 as a gubernatorial initiative to support the role of innovation in spurring the California economy. The idea originated with Richard Lerner, president of the Scripps Research Institute, and John Moores, a successful entrepreneur and a new regent of the University of California.[24] Both Lerner and Moores were close associates of then-governor Gray Davis. With the approval of UC president Richard Atkinson, they approached the governor, who was enthusiastic. As lieutenant governor Gray Davis had been an active regent for four years and was still a regent as governor; hence he knew the university well and had high regard for its research activities and their effect upon the economy. The basic concept was to create a set of research institutes that would be directed toward future economic opportunities for California and to base these institutes within the arm of the state that is designated for research—the University of California. The model most often cited was Bell Laboratories.

The initiative provided $100 million each for three institutes, spread over four years, with a requirement that the institutes raise even greater funds from other sources as a two-to-one match. Because of the state budgetary situation at that time, the state funding was almost totally for capital expenditures. Since the funds were from the capital budget, there was a restriction that no more than 5 percent of the funding could be used for operating purposes. The matching funds could be from any source outside the university and could be either operating or capital funds. The institutes were to be on University of California campuses and would carry out research in fields believed to be promising for the economic growth of the state. They were envisioned as catalytic partnerships between the university and private

---

[24] Patricia A. Pelfrey, *Entrepreneurial President: Richard Atkinson and the University of California, 1995–2003* (Berkeley: University of California Press, 2012), pp. 110–111.

industry that would "increase the state's capacity for creating the new knowledge and highly skilled people that will drive entrepreneurial business growth and expand the California economy into new industries and markets—and bring the benefits of innovation more quickly into the lives of people everywhere."[25] The institutes were later renamed the Governor Gray Davis Institutes for Science and Innovation in recognition of Davis's key role.[26]

Through the Office of the President and in consultation with the campuses and Academic Senate, the university designed and administered an internal competition, encouraging multidisciplinary approaches and synergistic involvement of multiple campuses. Topics for the institutes were not specified;[27] instead, selection among proposed topics was a part of the competition. Two rounds of judging were used with both individual and panel peer review. The first round reduced the field to a smaller number of finalists. Final proposals were subjected to extensive peer review and were judged by a multidimensional, highly distinguished panel whose members came from outside the university. The use of competition was key for honing the quality of the proposals, since the proposers put great effort into making the proposals convincing and attractive in the competition. Because of the compelling strengths of four of the ultimate proposals, a fourth institute was also funded by the state.

The four institutes are the following:
- California Institute for Telecommunications and Information Technology [Calit2]—San Diego and Irvine campuses[28]

---

[25] "California Institutes for Science and Innovation: A Foundation for California's Future," Office of the President, University of California, Background for Item 304 at July 2006 Regents Meeting, https://perma.cc/DHR3-CFPZ..

[26] "Governor Gray Davis Institutes for Science and Innovation," University of California, Office of the President, https://web.archive.org/web/20170820090333/http://www.ucop.edu/california-institutes/.

[27] The authorization language was that "the concentration of each institute may include, *but shall not necessarily be limited to* [emphasis added], any of the following—medicine, bioengineering, telecommunications and information systems, energy resources, space, and agricultural technology." (California Assembly Bill no. AB 1943, April 3, 2000, accessed June 15, 2016, ftp://www.leginfo.ca.gov/pub/99-00/bill/asm/ab_1901-1950/ab_1943_bill_20000403_amended_asm.html.

[28] California Institute for Telecommunications and Information Technology, https://perma.cc/4ENR-62BP.

- California Institute for Quantitative Biomedical Research [QB3]—San Francisco, Berkeley, and Santa Cruz campuses[29]
- California Nanosystems Institute [CNSI]—Los Angeles and Santa Barbara Campuses[30]
- Center for Information Technology Research in the Interest of Society [CITRIS]—Berkeley, Davis, Merced, and Santa Cruz campuses[31]

The California Institute for Telecommunications and Information Technology is described in more detail in a PowerPoint presentation[32] and two independent case studies[33, 34].

The needed match ($800 million) was a very large sum, yet it was raised and exceeded with the ultimate total match being more than $1 billion. Holding a competition facilitated the acquisition of these matching funds, since it was clear for donors that the match would be required to bring an institute into existence. The fact that the subject matters of the institutes were not specified in the competition provided yet another incentive for corporations to provide funding, since the institute to which the donation would be made would have to be selected in order for there to be an institute matching the interests of the corporation. The matching funds were raised primarily from industry for three of the institutes and primarily as federal government project funds for the fourth (CNSI), reflecting the fact that there was at the time no cohesive, substantial nanoscale systems industry, while there were existing industries for the other three areas.

Since the state funding was almost totally for capital expenditures, it went primarily into building the campus facilities to bring the researchers of an institute together. The researchers must still propose

---

[29] QB3, UCB.UCSC.UCSF, https://perma.cc/B3AF-HAEQ.
[30] California NanoSystems Institute, https://perma.cc/2DFJ-GQRD, https://perma.cc/65D9-8ZU5.
[31] CITRIS and the Banatao Institute, https://perma.cc/9SH6-F3QY.
[32] Larry Smarr, "The UC California Institutes for Science and Innovation," invited talk to seminar on Creating a Regional Innovation Cluster: From Discovery to Application, La Jolla, CA, April 25, 2006, https://web.archive.org/web/20161207002334/http://lsmarr.calit2.net/presentations?slideshow=2865477.
[33] Donald Spicer and Bruce Metz, "Calit2: A Case Study in a Next-Generation Research Environment," EDUCAUSE Center for Applied Research, 2006, https://perma.cc/C37J-4LS3..
[34] Linda A. Hill and Alison B. Wagonfeld, "Calit2: UC San Diego-UC Irvine Partnership," Harvard Business School, 2011, https://perma.cc/G94J-TZMR.

and obtain extramural funding for individual projects. Obtaining core operating funds for administering the institutes was more of a problem. Portions of the allowable 5 percent of the state capital funds were a start, and then some chancellors devoted a portion of the overhead from incremental research grants for the institutes to that purpose. Eventually another $20 million of annual operating funds divided among the four institutes became part of the state operating budget for the University of California.

The institutes have now been in existence for over fifteen years. It has been apparent that on the whole they are large successes. Research volume is high, strong multidisciplinary efforts have come about in several areas, and there are several measures of substantial economic impact, as borne out by an economic impact report[35] produced by CITRIS in 2014–15. Incubators have been key parts of QB3,[36] with over four hundred start-ups[37] as of mid-2017.

Congress and agencies of the federal government have frequently sought to catalyze multidisciplinary research in areas of national importance by designating funds for competitions for large institutes, but usually with the subject matter specified. As was the case for the Governor Gray Davis Institutes for Science and innovation, the lure of large funding in those cases has served as an effective catalyst for bringing researchers from different disciplines together.

UNDERGRADUATE EDUCATION

A world of growing multidisciplinary challenges means that university graduates must be able to work effectively with persons from other disciplines and understand enough of the basic vocabulary and methodologies of other disciplines to enable collaboration. Furthermore, there is an ever-growing need for an informed and thoughtful citizenry who can sift among conflicting arguments on

---

[35] "CITRIS Impact Report, 2014–15," https://perma.cc/2SWC-2PZD.
[36] "Incubators to Accelerate Innovation," QB3, https://web.archive.org/web/20171020213249/http://qb3.org/incubators.
[37] "A Portfolio of Transformation and Innovation," QB3, https://web.archive.org/web/20170614025255/https://qb3.org/portfolio/.

complex situations.[38] The classical American concept of a liberal undergraduate education and its strong component of critical thinking address those needs. The American Association of Schools and Colleges defines a liberal education as follows:

> an approach to learning that empowers individuals and prepares them to deal with complexity, diversity, and change. It provides students with broad knowledge of the wider world (e.g., science, culture, and society) as well as in-depth study in a specific area of interest. A liberal education helps students develop a sense of social responsibility, as well as strong and transferable intellectual and practical skills such as communication, analytical and problem-solving skills, and a demonstrated ability to apply knowledge and skills in real-world settings.[39]

A liberal undergraduate education should encompass courses reflecting different disciplines and combinations of disciplines, including the natural sciences and even some engineering. There should be specially designed courses giving the gist of a discipline rather than providing a foundation for future study in the discipline. There should also be courses that are themselves multidisciplinary, displaying the ways in which knowledge from different disciplines can be brought together to bear upon major issues. Preferably, those should be team-taught by faculty from different disciplines. Yes, these goals can be difficult to achieve, but they are vitally important.

Many studies and experiments have been directed toward ways of best achieving objectives of these sorts. Many universities, particularly private ones, carry out general-education studies with some regularity, and many reports from these are available on the Internet. As was already mentioned, such a study was carried out for public research universities, focused largely on the University of California.[40]

The University of California has not been a particular leader in this area, but faculty and academic leaders within it have devised and

---

[38] Anne Colby, Thomas Ehrlich, Elizabeth Beaumont, and Jason Stevens, *Educating Citizens: Preparing America's Undergraduates for Lives of Moral and Civic Responsibility* (San Francisco: Jossey-Bass, 2003).
[39] American Association of Schools and Colleges, "What Is a 21st Century Liberal Education?," https://perma.cc/UP4Q-HQH6.
[40] Schudson, Smelser et al., Center for Studies in Higher Education, 2007, *loc. cit.*

carried out a number of experiments, some of which have lasted. Two, of course, are the UC San Diego colleges (chapter 10) and the entire history of the UC Santa Cruz campus (also chapter 10), both of which involve a number of separate residential colleges, and in the case of UCSD have general-education requirements specific to the college. The UC Santa Barbara College of Creative Studies, enabling programs of study tailor-fitted to individual students, has persisted since its founding in 1968. Two experiments at Berkeley in earlier days received considerable attention—the Experimental College Program[41] (1965), headed by Joseph Tussman, and Strawberry Creek College,[42] spearheaded by Charles Muscatine, 1974–80.

As of 2018 the College of Letters and Science at UC Berkeley has a small program of "big ideas" courses[43] for partial fulfillment of the breadth requirements of the college. These bring together professors from entirely different disciplines to teach courses dealing with a "big idea." An example from 2016 is Energy and Civilization, co-taught by faculty members from the Departments of Civil and Environmental Engineering, Business Administration, Earth and Planetary Science, and South Asian Studies. The big ideas program has its own budget, provided through support from two foundations, furnishing replacement teaching within the home departments of the faculty members involved.

Another, more common approach toward added breadth can be an undergraduate minor—concentrated study in a particular area, but to a substantially lesser extent than for the undergraduate major. Although most of the minors available at UC are, like the majors, single-disciplinary in nature, some are multidisciplinary. As of 2017 the most popular minor for undergraduate College of Letters and Science students at Berkeley is global poverty and practice,[44] carried out

---

[41] Katherine Trow, *Habits of Mind: The Experimental College Program at Berkeley* (Berkeley: Institute of Governmental Studies Press, University of California, 1998).
[42] Gene Maeroff, "Berkeley Is Trying Informal Approach," *New York Times*, October 9, 1977,.
[43] "Big Ideas UC Berkeley," https://perma.cc/R6JD-8MZX.
[44] Global Policy and Practice Minor, Blum Center for Developing Economies, University of California, Berkeley, https://web.archive.org/web/20170622101220/http://blumcenter.berkeley.edu/education/gpp/..

through the multidisciplinary Blum Center for Developing Economies, which is primarily an ORU.

Stopping short of the concept of a minor, per se, the previously mentioned Schudson-Smelser Commission on General Education in the Twenty-First Century recommended developing structured bundles of interdisciplinary courses on major issues such as environmental sustainability, technology and society, bureaucracy and society, military and society, and political and ethical dimensions of biological knowledge.[45]

Another approach Berkeley takes, primarily to provide small-class experience for undergraduates, is to offer the Freshman and Sophomore Seminars,[46] which focus on specific subjects that are often interdisciplinary or multidisciplinary. These provide a small-class, discussion experience for freshman and sophomore students.

Multidisciplinary courses, by definition, usually belong to no academic department. Since faculty members' teaching obligations are normally to their home departments, it is important to find ways of incentivizing teaching in multidisciplinary courses for both departments and individual faculty members within them. Teaching credit for such courses can be allocated to the home departments of the faculty members concerned, and/or there can be a source of funds that can be used by the departments for replacement instructors, such as the foundation support for the big ideas courses mentioned above.

Majors or other disciplinary specialties for students should be built upon the foundations of broad liberal undergraduate education. Professional degrees are best placed at the postgraduate level, built upon a foundational liberal education. Engineering is the one major profession in the United States for which the professional degree is at the undergraduate level rather than the graduate level. Engineering should join the other professions by changing the professional degree to the postgraduate level and basing it on a liberal undergraduate education.[47]

---

[45] Schudson et al., Center for Studies in Higher Education, 2007, *loc. cit.*, section 5.
[46] "Freshman & Sophomore Seminars at UC Berkeley," https://perma.cc/RMZ2-J5A3.
[47] National Academy of Engineering, "Educating the Engineer of 2020: Adapting Engineering Education to the New Century" (Washington, DC: National Academies Press, 2005); C. Judson King, "Let Engineers Go to College," *Issues in Science and Technology* 22, no. 4 (Summer 2006): pp. 25–28, https://perma.cc/DGR8-AM8V ; James J. Duderstadt, "Engineering for a Changing World,"

AVOIDING DEPARTMENTAL STRUCTURES

Another potential route for encouraging multidisciplinary effort is to avoid the traditional academic department structure altogether. Newly established universities or campuses have no existing interests or structures and hence can favor multidisciplinary approaches from the start. As described in chapter 10, the academic founders of the Merced campus of the University of California chose to encourage multidisciplinary interactions of faculty members by having no academic departments. The UC Santa Cruz campus (chapter 10) is another case, with the initial design placing academics heavily into the individual colleges, linked through boards of study for the various disciplines. That structure was abandoned through the Sinsheimer Rearrangement. Another recent example of a structure without departments is the King Abdullah University of Science and Technology (KAUST) in Thuwal, Saudi Arabia, an institution opened in 2009 and designed to be a graduate-only version of Caltech. KAUST has three divisions, each of which combines science and engineering together, seeking to promote interactions between the two areas. There is a parallel organization by research centers.

An absence of formal academic disciplinary departments is also one way to deal with the small size associated with a start-up university. However, the concept becomes much more difficult to sustain as growth continues and the size reaches such a level that there do have to be knowledgeable evaluation of faculty, effective faculty searches and recruitment, design and coordination of instruction, provision of discipline-specific services, synergy among faculty members, and oversight of research.

Millennium Project, Univ. of Michigan, Ann Arbor, December 2007, https://perma.cc/KS5E-PDEX; Norman R. Augustine, "Re-engineering Engineering," *ASEE PRISM* 18, no. 6 (2009): pp. 46–47,; C. Judson King, "Restructuring Engineering Education: Why, How and When?," *Journal of Engineering Education* 101, no. 1 (2012): pp. 1–5; Domenico Grasso and Melody B. Burkins, *Holistic Engineering Education: Beyond Technology* (New York: Springer, 2010).

SUMMARY CONCLUSION

It is important for research universities to takes steps to encourage and enable multidisciplinary research and teaching. Graduates increasingly need to understand multifaceted issues to be responsible citizens and to work constructively in their employment with people from other disciplinary backgrounds so as to bring the full range of necessary knowledge to bear on those issues.

Present-day structures, both for academic departments within universities and for disciplines on national and international scales, tend to hamper multidisciplinary efforts. There is therefore a need to incentivize multidisciplinary research and take specific steps to facilitate it. Multidisciplinary research can naturally lead to multidisciplinary teaching. Skilled and creative academic leaders can build innovative and effective multidisciplinary research through well-designed faculty additions when given the opportunity.

The University of California was the leader in the formation of organized research units (ORUs), a movement that started soon after World War II as government support of research became more plentiful. Most ORUs are multidisciplinary and are directed toward specific broad needs or the interests of particular government research-supporting agencies. The Lawrence Berkeley National Laboratory has also served as a catalyst for multidisciplinary research. UC's Governor Gray Davis Institutes for Science and Innovation were formed in the year 2000 through a gubernatorial initiative that provided funds for construction of facilities, to be matched at least two to one by other sources of funding for any purpose. Most of the matching funds were industrial. The four resultant institutes were chosen by a peer-review competition, university-wide.

Skilled and adequately funded leadership is needed for multidisciplinary ORUs or other institutes, recognizing the fact that institute or ORU directors will need to negotiate on an even-up basis in many ways with department chairs and deans.

University graduates need to be able to work effectively and synergistically with people from other disciplinary backgrounds so that they, as capable and informed citizens, can address multifaceted issues and evaluate complex issues. Therefore undergraduate education should be broad, in the vein of the traditional US liberal education. Professional degrees should be at the graduate level, as is now the case for all the major professions except engineering.

15.
Providing Access: Eligibility and Admissions

This is the University of California. It is not the University of Berlin or of New Haven which we are to copy; it is not the University of Oakland or of San Francisco which we are to create, but it is the university of this state…It is "of the people and for the people," not in any low or unworthy sense, but in the highest and noblest relations to their intellectual and moral well-being.
　—Daniel Coit Gilman, University of California President, 1872[1]

[It is our] earnest hope and confident expectation that the State of California will forthwith organize and put into operation…a University of California…with courses of instruction equal to those of the Eastern colleges.
　—Trustees of the College of California[2]

Each segment of California public higher education shall strive to approximate…the general ethnic, sexual, and economic composition of the recent high school graduates.
　—California Legislature, 1974[3]

The University seeks to enroll, on each of its campuses, a student body that, beyond meeting the university's eligibility requirements, demonstrates high academic achievement or exceptional personal talent, and that encompasses the broad diversity of cultural, racial,

---

[1] Daniel Coit Gilman, "The Building of the University: An Inaugural Address," November 7, 1872, Overland Monthly Presses, San Francisco CA, 1872, https://perma.cc/7C39-N5F8.
[2] Resolution of the trustees of the College of California, offering the College as the basis of the University of California. From Verne A. Stadtman, *The University of California, 1868–1968* (New York: McGraw-Hill, 1970), p. 31.
[3] *Assembly Concurrent Resolution 151,* cited by John A. Douglass, in *The Conditions for Admission: Access, Equity, and the Social Contract of Public Universities* (Stanford: Stanford University Press, 2007), p. 106.

geographic, and socio-economic backgrounds characteristic of California.
—University of California Regents Policy adopted 1988[4]

Effective January 1, 1997, the University of California shall not use race, religion, sex, color, ethnicity or national origin as a criterion for admission to the university or to any program of study.
—University of California Regents, 1995[5]

The state shall not discriminate against, or grant preferential treatment to, any individual or group on the basis of race, sex, color, ethnicity, or national origin in the operation of public employment, public education, or public contracting.
—California State Constitutional Amendment, adopted November, 1996[6]

Anyone who thinks that he has the solutions to [matters pertaining to affirmative action] doesn't understand the issues, and anyone who understands the problems knows that there are no simple solutions.
—David P. Gardner, President of the University of California[7]

Because of the success and popularity of the University of California, selection among would-be students and provision of access across the various elements of society have been sensitive and ever-growing public issues. Today they are among the most public and difficult matters that the university faces.

---

[4] "Regents Policy 2102: Policy on Undergraduate Admissions," Board of Regents, University of California, adopted May 20, 1988, https://perma.cc/X5L7-CJT2.
[5] Text of UC Regents Resolutions, July 20, 1995, University of California, Berkeley, https://perma.cc/ZT39-FPPC.
[6] California Proposition 209, Digital History, University of Houston, https://perma.cc/T8SF-YV4Z..
[7] Cited by Jean H. Fetter, *Questions and Admissions: Reflections on 100,000 Admissions Decisions at Stanford* (Stanford University Press, 1995), p. 118.

GOALS

From the start, the University of California and the Californians who created it have had three major goals. One, epitomized in the above quote from Daniel Coit Gilman, calls for the university to *serve the particular needs of California*. Another, alluded to in the same quote, is to be a public university in the highest sense of the word and *provide access to all who are deserving and capable of partaking from it*. In that way it should be a prime means for personal improvement and upward mobility in the state. A third goal, embodied in the above quote from the trustees of the College of California as they offered their college as the foundation for the university, is for the university to *have the same high caliber as the noted [private] universities in the eastern United States*. The combination of the second and third goals was nurtured by the fact that respected private universities did not yet exist in California at the time when public higher education became encouraged through the Morrill Act, along with a desire to enable access at costs much less than for the leading eastern private universities. Similar noble language appears in the founding documents of other public universities in other states, but California took these goals very seriously, and that fact has had much to do with the development of the University of California.

In recent times these three goals have led to considerable tension surrounding the matter of who should be able to attend the University of California. The first goal, serving the particular situation of California, brings at least two needs. The first is to recognize the immense demographic shifts that have turned California from a strongly white-majority state into a minority-majority state with a very diverse population, reflecting much immigration from Mexico, other South and Central American countries, China, and other Asian and Pacific-Island countries. Admissions should pay attention to the needs generated by that transition. The second need is to recognize the nature of California's particular economy, which had been dominated by agricultural industry but is now heavily reliant on technology, entrepreneurism and start-ups. That fact says that admissions should seek people who can serve that economy well and accentuates the need to sustain the University of California as a preeminent research university that can effectively stimulate and serve that economy.

The second goal, providing access to all who are deserving and capable of partaking from it, calls for enabling and encouraging access to the university by persons who have the abilities to benefit the most from high-level university education, no matter what their economic and social background. That means encouraging enrollment by all talented people, making that economically feasible for students from economically disadvantaged backgrounds, and recognizing that cultural backgrounds differ.

The third goal, having the same high caliber as the noted private universities in the eastern United States, calls for providing a top-flight education for the most capable people, feeding an elitist concept that UC students are the best and the brightest and will be future leaders of the state. Since much learning within universities comes from students associating with other students, the third goal also calls for providing a student body as well as a faculty who can provide a wide variety of academic and social experiences for one another.

These three goals and their associated needs should guide the answers to questions such as these: what the size of the university should be, what the minimum criteria for entrance should be, how to choose among applicants when there are more who meet these criteria than can be accommodated, how to manage conditions when demand for some campuses considerably exceeds the demand for others, and how to mold an incoming class for which the members can best benefit one another. Determining the answers plays out in arenas of public interest and concern where demand considerably exceeds supply, as well as through the politics of race and class, which Peter Schrag[8] has described well for California. Further, these issues play out in an open-book fashion in which everything should be available and understood by the public, not only because of public-meeting and open-records laws, but also because of widespread interest and simply as good public policy. The issues are complex and readily incite passions.

---

[8] Peter Schrag, *Paradise Lost: California's Experience, America's Future* (Berkeley: University of California Press, 1998); *California: America's High-Stakes Experiment* (Berkeley: University of California Press, 2006).

The open-book aspect of University of California admissions criteria stands in contrast to those of the selective private universities, for which admissions criteria are stated only in general terms. By contrast, University of California criteria are known in detail, are publicly evaluated and discussed, and are subject to legal contentions.

Admissions policies for the University of California have been developed in a national setting of similar admissions concerns in other states. Douglass [9] has reviewed the history of public-university admissions in the United States, with the University of California up through about the year 2000 as his prime example.

SELECTIVE ADMISSIONS

Answers to the questions of the size and degree of selectivity of the University of California were not well defined through the end of the nineteenth century, but in two significant steps in the 1870s, the regents decided that the university would be selective and delegated the determination of standards for admission of students to the faculty of the university. This delegation was confirmed and strengthened in the negotiations of 1919 that defined larger roles for the Academic Senate (chapter 7). The decision to be selective was somewhat unusual for public universities in the United States at the time. Many other public universities were set up to interpret access for all to mean that they should admit all applicants who meet a certain low standard of eligibility and then sort those incoming students out through grades in university-level courses, with many students then leaving.

The decision to be selective led UC to adopt in 1884 a policy of formally accrediting high schools, certifying whether they had content standards high enough to prepare students reliably for university education. Originally graduates of these high schools would be admitted if the principal of the high school so recommended. Later, the need for endorsement by the principal was dropped. The accreditation process for high schools did much to upgrade secondary education in

---

[9] John Aubrey Douglass, *The Conditions for Admission: Access, Equity, and the Social Contract of Public Universities* (Stanford: Stanford University Press, 2007).

California. This effect was further strengthened when the university initiated the concept that students should have completed a set of prescribed high school courses if they were to be admitted to UC. The "A-G" courses, now jointly required by UC and CSU for eligibility, still serve that purpose.[10] Accreditation of high schools by UC lasted until 1963, when it was discontinued by action of the Academic Senate. On behalf of both UC and CSU, the UC Office of the President still reviews and approves courses for A-G, based on faculty guidelines.[11]

THE DEVELOPMENT OF ADMISSIONS POLICIES

Both enrollment pressure and funding for the university began to increase during the presidency of Benjamin Ide Wheeler at the start of the twentieth century. The Progressive movement that took hold in California politics around 1910 also promoted public higher education and steered funding to it. During the first decades of the twentieth century, the tripartite system of public higher education took form. The state colleges started developing curricula beyond teacher education, which had been their original base as normal schools. The existence and availability of the state colleges and the community colleges (at the time called junior colleges), provided additional opportunities in higher education and thus enabled the University of California to continue to be selective. As of 1905 arrangements were established to provide for transfer, wherein a student would take the first two years of college education (the lower division) at a normal school or junior college and then transfer to UC for the last two years (the upper division). The state colleges began sharp increases in enrollment in the 1920s.[12]

By the late 1950s, UC required at least a B average in what were then the A-F college-going high school courses. Ninety percent of admissions occurred via this path. Other routes were admission by examination, admission by class rank, admission by exception, and

---

[10] "A-G Guide," Office of the President, University of California, https://web.archive.org/web/20171104105244/https://www.ucop.edu/agguide/a-g-requirements/index.html.
[11] Stephen J. Handel, personal communication, October 2016.
[12] Douglass, 2007, *op. cit.*, p. 38

transfer at the upper division level. The large surge of enrollment by returning veterans of World War II in the late 1940s was met by temporarily increasing admission by exception to as much as 35 percent of the incoming class.

THE EFFECTS OF THE 1960 MASTER PLAN

The effective eligibility rate for graduates of public high schools for the University of California in the late 1950s was about 15 percent. As the California Master Plan for Higher Education was developed and adopted in 1960 (chapter 5), one of the compromises was that UC would reduce the eligibility rate for public high school students to 12.5 percent and that CSU would reduce its eligibility rate from what had been about 50 percent to 33 percent, with the displaced demand for the bachelor's degree to be met through junior-level transfer from California's community colleges. The Master Plan also established the California Coordinating Council for Higher Education (later the California Postsecondary Education Commission, CPEC). Among the roles of CPEC was to conduct periodic eligibility studies to ascertain whether the eligibility criteria of the Master Plan were being met in practice. The criteria for eligibility were to be determined by UC and CSU themselves; for UC that was in line with constitutional autonomy.

Eligibility for UC has come to be defined through a combination of high school grade point average in the A-G courses and standardized test scores. The SAT came into use for out-of-state students and those with relatively low GPAs somewhat belatedly in 1968. In 1979 it was incorporated into an eligibility index, which combined GPA in the required courses with the SAT as the standardized test for UC admissions and the ACT as an allowable alternative. The eligibility index would be moved up or down after CPEC eligibility studies so as to maintain 12.5 percent eligibility. Over time, first by practice and then by state policy, it became understood that the University of California would admit all eligible students somewhere within the university, although not necessarily at the campus or in the major of first choice (chapter 5).

BALANCE OF ENROLLMENT AMONG CAMPUSES

Along with the decision that there would be multiple campuses of the University of California came the decision, during Clark Kerr's era, that there would be a cap on the enrollment of any one campus. That figure was originally set at 27,500, and has inched up over the years to where the Fall 2016 enrollments for the Los Angeles and Berkeley campuses were 45,000 and 40,000, respectively.[13] As the Berkeley and Los Angeles campuses approached what were then their enrollment caps, the matter of how to handle backup choices for eligible applicants who could not be accommodated at those campuses became important. Beginning in the 1970s, the university asked students to submit a single application for admission, indicating their first, second, and third choices of campus. Eligible applicants not admitted to the first-choice campus were then "redirected" to a campus that would admit them. Then in 1985 UC switched to having independent applications to individual campuses, called *multiple filing*. The campuses each had enrollment targets and chose among eligible applicants to admit a number that, when the anticipated acceptance ratio was factored in, would meet their target. Eligible students who were not admitted to any of the campuses to which they had applied constituted the *referral pool*. The students in that category would be offered admission to those campuses (Riverside and Santa Cruz at the time) that still had available capacity after the first round of admissions. This practice continues in 2018, with the one open campus being the newer Merced campus.

ATTENTIVENESS TO RACE

The United States has a long and complex history with regard to race and ethnicity. It has historically been known to be friendly to, and even dependent upon, immigration—the "melting pot" of the world. Yet at the same time there is a history of marked differences in the

---

[13] "Fall Enrollment at a Glance," University of California, https://www.universityofcalifornia.edu/infocenter/fall-enrollment-glance.

average opportunities and standards of living among people of different ethnicities, stemming from lingering effects of poverty, low education, and discrimination—and from earlier days even the practice of slavery, which existed in the southern states and was eliminated by Abraham Lincoln's Emancipation Proclamation in 1863, only five years before the founding of the University of California.

During the administrations of Presidents Kennedy and Johnson, 1961–69, the concept of affirmative action arose through several executive orders, starting with the requirement that government contractors should "take affirmative action to ensure that applicants are employed, and that employees are treated during employment, without regard to their race, creed, color, or national origin."[14, 15] These orders were interpreted at the University of California to mean that applications should be actively invited and encouraged from all ethnic groups and that processes for selecting among applicants should be visibly without discrimination. These actions led to a number of efforts to redress past injustices through positive actions, while seeking to maintain an overall policy of no racial or ethnic discrimination.

As California's minority populations grew, racial balance within the University of California grew in importance as an issue. The proportions of African Americans, Latinos,[16] and American Indians within the university student body were, and still are, substantially lower than in the college-age population as a whole. Further, the percentage of Latinos within the population of the state grew rapidly. Beginning in 1964 with the Equal Opportunity Program (EOP) and consistent with the executive orders on affirmative action, special outreach efforts were made to these minority communities to try to increase the interest in and preparedness of students for the University of California.[17] By 1981 $47 million annually in state funds, fee revenue,

---

[14] Terry H. Anderson, *The Pursuit of Fairness: A History of Affirmative Action* Oxford, UK: Oxford University Press, 2004), p. 60.

[15] Randall H. Woods, *Prisoners of Hope: Lyndon B. Johnson, the Great Society, and the Limits of Liberalism* (New York: Basic Books, 2016).

[16] For simplicity, the term *Latino* is used throughout this chapter to denote the combination of Chicano, Chicana, Latino, and Latina.

[17] These outreach programs, subsequently called educational partnership programs, grew substantially over the ensuing years, with a very large but short-lived burst of growth following the regents' actions in 1995. The programs are described more fully in chapter 16.

regents' funds, and some private funding was spent on a collection of UC outreach programs.[18] The allowable percentage of special-action admissions—that is, admissions by exception to normal requirements—had been 2 percent since the short-term surge to 35 percent in the years immediately after World War II. It was increased to 4 percent in 1968 and was increased again to 6 percent[19] in 1979.

In 1978 the US Supreme Court decided a legal case wherein Allan Bakke, a white applicant to the University of California at Davis School of Medicine, claimed that his application for admission had been denied on the basis of an explicit consideration of race. In a split (5–4) decision, the court held that the use of numerical quota systems[20] to promote racial balance was unconstitutional but that consideration of race as one of many factors in determining admissions was acceptable. Following that legal interpretation, the regents adopted the policy embodied in the 1988 quotation at the start of this chapter. Guidelines for implementation of the policy indicated that 40 to 60 percent of an incoming freshman class should be admitted on the basis of academic criteria (i.e., grades and test scores) alone, while the remainder could be admitted following both academic and supplemental criteria. These criteria could include extracurricular achievements, leadership, special talents, special circumstances (e.g., low-income, disability, veteran status), and "ethnic identity, gender, and location of residence."[21] This procedure became known as two-tier admissions.

The UC campuses then devised means of deciding among eligible applicants that brought race in as one factor among many. The process at Berkeley involved placing applicants in three groups, effectively dividing the second tier into two subgroups. Decisions for one of these subgroups brought in EOP status and some other criteria as well as

---

[18] Douglass, 2007, op. cit., pp. 108–109.
[19] Currently campuses use only a fraction of the available 6 percent, and then for cases where the arguments for an exception are clear and compelling.
[20] The UC Davis School of Medicine did, at the time, have a specific criterion that sixteen of its one hundred spots in the entering class of the School of Medicine were set aside for ethnic minority students.
[21] Nina Robinson and others, "Undergraduate Access to the University of California after the Elimination of Race-Conscious Policies," Student Academic Services, Office of the President, University of California, March 2003, https://perma.cc/AP5K-6Y47.

academic factors, and decisions for the second subgroup required only UC eligibility as an academic factor to be combined with other criteria, including affirmative action. Functionally, three sorts of applicants—athletes, disabled students, and affirmative-action students—were effectively guaranteed admission if they were UC-eligible. UCLA had a still more quantitative, matrix-based method with essentially the same results.

SURGE OF APPLICATION PRESSURE AND BACKLASH

Up until the early 1970s, Berkeley was able to admit all eligible applicants.[22] Then, as campuses reached their designated capacities or maximum rates of growth from year to year, Berkeley, then Los Angeles, and then other campuses became unable to admit all UC-eligible applicants. As of 2017 all eight undergraduate campuses other than Merced are in the situation of not being able to admit all UC-eligible applicants. Admissions have become highly competitive, especially at Los Angeles and Berkeley, but also at San Diego, Davis, Irvine, and Santa Barbara.

One result of these enrollment pressures has been that the eligibility and admissions policies of the university have become highly contentious. Controversies have played out in public limelight. The introduction of multiple filing in 1985 resulted in a much greater number of explicit denials of student applications by individual campuses, which heightened concerns for families of students who had been rejected. For Berkeley, in 1975 there were 5,035 applicants, of whom 77 percent were admitted; in 1980 there were 9,115 applicants, of whom 54 percent were admitted; and in 1990 there were 19,946 applicants, of whom 38 percent were admitted.[23] For 2015 there were 73,753 applicants, of whom 18 percent were admitted.[24] More denials

---

[22] Committee on Admissions, Enrollment, and Preparatory Education (AEPE), "A Report to the Berkeley Faculty on Undergraduate Admission and Comprehensive Review: 1995–2002," May 2002, https://perma.cc/VY3K-4CNV.
[23] Douglass, 2007, *op. cit.*, p. 127.
[24] Janet Gilmore, "In a Competitive Year, Berkeley Admits 13,321 Prospective Freshmen," *Berkeley News*,

of admission mean more unhappy students and families, who in turn are constituents of legislators who pursue redress of their concerns.

Increased enrollment pressure and heightened concern about admissions brought contention against affirmative action policies and the "thumb on the scale" for admission of underrepresented minority students. One of the first manifestations of that concern was reflected in the Asian American Task Force (AATF). Asian Americans had originally been identified as an affirmative action group, but in 1984 they were removed from that status since they were no longer enrolling in a proportion lower than their proportion among eighteen-year-olds. The resultant drop in the percentage of Asian American applicants to Berkeley that were admitted (34.4 percent in 1984 as opposed to 47.4 percent in 1983) led to the formation of the AATF by members of the San Francisco Bay Area Asian American community to contend that there had, in fact, been discrimination against eligible Asian American applicants at Berkeley. The efforts of that task force led to legislative hearings on admissions to the Berkeley campus, recognition of the problem by Chancellor Heyman[25], and changes in elements of the Berkeley admissions process. Criticism of the admissions processes of the university was now embedded in conflict among races and was coming from both conservatives opposed to affirmative action and liberals who wanted even more emphasis on affirmative action.

UC REGENTS' RESOLUTION SP-1 AND STATEWIDE PROPOSITION 209

On July 20, 1995, the Regents of UC adopted two resolutions[26, 27, 28] barring any use of "race, religion, sex, color, ethnicity, or national

---

https://web.archive.org/web/20150919233132/http://news.berkeley.edu/2015/07/02/berkeley-admits-more-than-13000-prospective-freshmen/.
[25] "UC Berkeley Apologizes for Policy That Limited Asians", *Los Angeles Times*, April 7, 1989 https://perma.cc/8JNR-C9RB.
[26] "Text of UC Regents' Resolutions," July 20, 1995, *loc. cit.*
[27] Patricia A. Pelfrey, *Entrepreneurial President: Richard Atkinson and the University of California, 1995–2002* (Berkeley: University of California Press, 2012), pp. 173–175.
[28] Brian Pusser, *Burning Down the House: Politics, Governance, and Affirmative Action at the University of California* (Albany: SUNY Press, 2004), pp. 229–232.

origin" as criteria for university admissions and employment. Sixteen months later, in November 1996, the voters of California adopted Proposition 209,[29] an initiative constitutional amendment that put effectively the same restrictions into the state constitution. The regents' resolutions contained two other features as well. One was a change to increase the portion of the freshman class admitted on academic criteria (i.e., grades and test scores) alone from what had been 40–60 percent to 50–75 percent. The remainder of an incoming freshman class could be admitted filling the academic criteria out with supplemental criteria, which still should not evidence any preference by race or the other stated factors. The second matter was a statement that a task force should be formed to define programs of outreach that would increase the rates of eligibility of students identified by criteria of disadvantage defined in the resolution (see chapter 16).

The process leading to the regents' resolutions was highly political, occurring, as already noted in chapter 2, at a time when the governor of California, Pete Wilson, was seeking the 1996 Republican nomination for president of the United States. Wilson and his predecessor, also a Republican, had appointed most of the then-current regents, and Wilson himself was also president of the board, ex officio. The events leading to the regents' resolutions are described by Douglass,[30, 31] Pelfrey,[32] and Pusser.[33] The events leading to Proposition 209 are described and analyzed by Chavez.[34]

From the standpoint of university governance, it is important to look at the roles of the three main parties—the regents, the administration, and the Academic Senate—as the regents' resolutions were developed and presented. The resolutions originated within the Board of Regents, specifically from Regent Ward Connerly. The president, all chancellors, and all vice presidents openly opposed the

---

[29] California Proposition 209, *loc. cit.*
[30] John A. Douglass, "A Brief on Events Leading to SP1," submitted to the Task Force on Shared Governance, Academic Senate, University of California, 1997, https://perma.cc/CW2W-N686.
[31] Douglass, 2007, *op. cit.*, chapter 7.
[32] Pelfrey, 2012, *op. cit.*, chapter 3.
[33] Pusser, 2004, *loc. cit.*
[34] Lydia Chavez, *The Color Bind: California's Campaign to End Affirmative Action* (Berkeley: University of California Press, 1998).

resolutions. The standing orders of the regents[35] state, "The Academic Senate, subject to the approval of the Board, shall determine the conditions for admission," but the regents did not ask for senate review of the resolution on admissions when it was introduced at the board meeting, nor did the Academic Senate ask to do so. President Jack Peltason did make such a request ten days before the regents' meeting at which the resolutions were introduced and acted upon, but there was no explicit response to his request.

The regents' resolutions and Proposition 209 attracted great attention and were the cause of heated politics within the California Legislature, where many legislators, including the Latino Caucus, urged the university somehow to find effective ways to maintain ethnically diverse admissions even in view of the limitations that had been imposed. Thus the entire follow-up to the resolutions and Proposition 209 played out in a very public arena with much concern and media coverage. For many reasons the resolutions created a major crisis for the university:

- National and state politics in the forms of a presidential campaign and the prelude to what became Proposition 209 had been thrust upon the university.
- There were intense concerns from both students and faculty. Students were by and large both vocal and passionate in defense of affirmative action. While faculty members were substantially split on the issue, the most vocal elements of the faculty were strongly in favor of affirmative action, with many advocating open defiance against the regents' actions.
- The university was the sole state institution subject to the regents' policy actions and remained in that isolated position for sixteen months until Proposition 209 was passed.
- The Academic Senate had not had its usual role on the matters in the two regents' resolutions. Hence a way had to be found to bring the senate promptly in on the issues.
- Everything that was done would be subject to intense media scrutiny.

---

[35] "Standing Order 105, Academic Senate," Board of Regents, University of California, https://perma.cc/62WR-N3FT.

- Changes to bring the university into compliance for admissions of students entering January 1997 (as stated in the resolution) had to be established as of March 1996 because of the lead time needed for students, families, and counselors to know the requirements that the students would have to meet and the criteria by which they would be judged.

The restrictions applied in Regents' Resolution SP-1 and Proposition 209 did not affect eligibility, because there were no preferences used in the criteria for eligibility. But they did affect the admissions processes of the selective campuses, which had used preferences. Thus the likely immediate consequences were expected to be a shift of underrepresented minority (URM) students from the most selective campuses to the nonselective campuses, along with some decrease in enrollment overall of those URM students who were UC-eligible because of the appearance of an unwelcoming atmosphere resulting from the regents' resolution and then the state initiative. Results over time bore out these predictions.[36]

The steps taken by the university in response to these resolutions are summarized in a 2003 report from the UC Office of the President.[37] Pelfrey[38] and Douglass[39] have also provided discussions of these actions. They are presented here with emphasis on the thinking that led to them and the university-governance aspects.

RETHINKING ADMISSIONS

The two regents' resolutions, followed by the adoption of Proposition 209 by the voters of the state in November 1996, brought about a fundamental rethinking within the university regarding what admissions criteria should try to accomplish. What factors had specific consideration of race been trying to overcome? Were family income, geographical location of residence, or other factors surrogates for the disadvantages that had been attached to race itself? Who is most

---

[36] Robinson et al., 2003, *loc. cit.*; see also figure 15-1, below.
[37] Robinson, et al, 2003, *loc. cit.*
[38] Pelfrey, 2012, *op. cit.*, chapters 5, 6, and 8.
[39] Douglass, 2007, *op. cit.*, chapters 8 and 9.

deserving of public higher education at an elite research university? Changes on two time scales had to be devised. One, immediate for admissions as of January 1997 (which later was delayed for undergraduates to the spring quarter of 1998[40]), was to make changes that would bring the university into compliance with the regents' resolutions and Proposition 209. On the second, longer time scale, there could be the more fundamental thinking associated with the above questions to devise further changes.

Even though the determination of the conditions of admissions is directly delegated by the regents to the Academic Senate, subject to approval by the regents, the university-wide administration and the university-wide Academic Senate concluded that it would be best to work closely together in devising the immediate response to the new limitations. Reasons were the short time scale, the public attention, and the fact that an integral part of the issue was also how admissions were carried out operationally by the administration. The administration and senate therefore promptly created a joint task force to review university admissions policies, determine how to place them in compliance, develop guidelines for campus admissions policies, and recommend avenues for fuller deliberation and improvement in the future. Among the avenues proposed for future consideration was "a more comprehensive approach to reviewing students' academic accomplishments and personal backgrounds."[41] The individual selective campuses were then charged with developing new admissions criteria within the guidelines, eliminating consideration of race and ethnicity, increasing the portion of those students admitted chosen on the basis of academic criteria alone if needed to meet the larger overall target set by the regents, and examining and developing supplemental criteria to be used for the remainder of admissions.

UC deferred its development of further major changes until it had the results of an eligibility study carried out by the California

---

[40] This delay resulted from recognition of the need to give information to students, families, and counselors in a timely fashion but did result in a crisis of understanding between President Atkinson and Governor Wilson, which is described by Pelfrey, 2012, *op. cit.*, pp. 42–46. The date of the change for graduate and professional school admissions remained January 1997.
[41] Robinson et al., 2003, *loc. cit.*

Postsecondary Education Commission in 1997. That study[42] indicated an eligibility rate for UC of 11.1 percent. Thus alteration of criteria to enable a return to 12.5 percent eligibility could afford eligibility to additional students without making any currently eligible students ineligible. That fact was a considerable boon.

Eligibility in the Local Context

Following the enactment of the UC Regents' 1995 resolutions and Proposition 209 in 1996, several elected officials in the state called on the University of California to utilize a plan extending admission to the top percentage of graduates from all public high schools, following the example of the "top 10 percent" plan that had recently been implemented for the University of Texas[43] following the Hopwood v. State of Texas court decision. Staff at the UC Office of the President carried out simulations using a database containing the admissions qualifications of UC applicants and the academic performance upon entering UC by those applicants who were admitted and enrolled. From these studies it became apparent that grade point averages (GPAs) in the A-G courses were substantially better predictors of university performance and persistence than were scores on standardized tests. Hence extending eligibility to those performing at top levels in A-G courses at all high schools, in addition to those eligible by current statewide criteria, should actually enhance the performance at UC of those eligible students who would attend. These and various other analyses were planned with and made available to the Academic Senate's Board on Admissions and Relations with Schools (BOARS).

President Richard Atkinson encouraged the idea of extending eligibility to those students in the top 4 percent of their high school class as ranked by GPA in the A-G courses, which the simulations had shown would make an additional 1.4 percent of graduates from public high schools eligible, thereby returning overall eligibility from 11.1 to 12.5 percent. BOARS was receptive, reached the same conclusion, and

---

[42] California Postsecondary Education Commission, "Eligibility of California's 1996 High School Graduates for Admission to the State's Public Universities," Commission Report 97-9, December 1997, https://perma.cc/QUJ2-UD5U,.
[43] "Admission Decisions," Texas Admissions, University of Texas at Austin, https://web.archive.org/web/20160617040323/http://admissions.utexas.edu/apply/decisions..

made the recommendation, which was then adopted by the Assembly of the Academic Senate for submission to the regents. The regents then approved it in March 1999,[44] to be implemented as of admissions for fall 2001. This program became known as Eligibility in the Local Context (ELC). Students to be admitted through ELC were required to take the full set of A-G courses and the standardized tests required by the university, although the scores on those tests would not be used to calculate ELC eligibility.

Students who appeared to be eligible for ELC after their junior year of high school were sent a letter by the UC president indicating that they were on the track to ELC and urging them to complete the A-G courses, take the tests, and apply, which many of them did. The results of the first two years implementing ELC were reported to the regents in May 2002.[45] An interesting and pleasing result was that the test scores of nearly all the students who were admitted through ELC were high enough to make them eligible by the statewide criteria. Thus the existence of ELC and the president's letter served primarily to increase the applications from students who could become eligible by statewide criteria in the absence of ELC, but who without the president's letter would not have completed requirements and applied. Many of these students were from areas of the state remote from UC campuses. ELC had only a modest effect in reversing the slide in ethnic diversity among entering students.

Comprehensive Review

The introduction of ELC served to expand eligibility back from 11.1 to 12.5 percent, but did not affect the selection among eligible students by selective campuses, which was what had been constrained by Regents' Resolution SP-1 and Proposition 209. Several of the campuses had developed forms of more comprehensive review, in which factors in addition to grades and test scores were considered either quantitatively or holistically for the portion of admissions

---

[44] Kenneth R. Weiss, "UC Regents OK Plan to Admit Top 4%," *Los Angeles Times*, March 20, 1999, https://perma.cc/T367-WJ83.
[45] University of California Eligibility in the Local Context Program Evaluation Report," prepared for May 2002 Regents Meeting, University of California Office of the President, https://perma.cc/3S3R-43UT.

beyond the 50–75 percent that Regents' Resolution SP-1 had specified must be made on the basis of academic criteria alone.

As the composition of the Board of Regents started to change with new appointments following the election of a Democrat (Gray Davis) as governor in 1998, there were prospects for repealing the regents' resolutions. Despite the continued existence of the constitutional change made by Proposition 209, a repeal of the regents' resolutions would have symbolic importance and would eliminate the limitation that 50–75 percent of admissions should be made on the basis of grades and test scores only. President Richard Atkinson proposed combining the elimination of SP-1 with the institution of comprehensive review for admissions by selective campuses. He reached agreement with BOARS on this approach, and BOARS and then the full Academic Senate, with ultimate approval by the regents in November 2001.[46] These actions established fourteen criteria that can be used in comprehensive review. The criteria for freshman admissions are given in table 15-1.[47] A similar set of criteria developed in the same way applies for transfer admissions.[48] Comprehensive review of applications is a more complex process because of the greater number of factors involved. However, increased use of information technology has helped offset that burden.

Testing Policies

President Atkinson's own professional expertise was in psychology and testing. He became concerned that the SAT-1[49] was a test that emphasized vague notions of academic *potential*, whereas it should be more concerned with actual *achievement* in learning. He had particular concerns about the verbal analogy questions and the absence in the SAT of any evaluation of the student's writing.

---

[46] Pelfrey, 2012, *op. cit.*, pp. 95–96.
[47] "Freshmen: How Applications Are Reviewed," Office of the President, University of California, accessed December 2, 2015, https://web.archive.org/web/20151204191124/http://admission.universityofcalifornia.edu/freshman/how-applications-reviewed/index.html.
[48] "Transfer: How Applications Are Reviewed," Office of the President, University of California, accessed October 4, 2016, https://perma.cc/5XH2-SZCV..
[49] SAT-1 denotes the morning part of the SAT tests, once known as the Scholastic Aptitude Test.

Table 15-1. Comprehensive Review Criteria

1. Academic grade point average in all completed "A-G" courses, including additional points for completed UC-certified honors courses
2. Scores on the following tests: ACT with Writing or the SAT Reasoning Test
3. Number of, content of, and performance in academic courses beyond the minimum "A-G" requirements
4. Number of and performance in UC-approved honors, Advanced Placement, International Baccalaureate Higher Level and transferable college courses
5. Identification by UC as being ranked in the top 9 percent of your high school class at the end of your junior year (the current version of Eligible in the Local Context)
6. Quality of your senior-year program as measured by the type and number of academic courses in progress or planned
7. Quality of your academic performance relative to the educational opportunities available in your high school
8. Outstanding performance in one or more specific subject areas
9. Outstanding work in one or more special projects in any academic field of study
10. Recent, marked improvement in academic performance as demonstrated by academic GPA and the quality of coursework completed or in progress
11. Special talents, achievements, and awards in a particular field, such as visual and performing arts, communication, or athletic endeavors; special skills, such as demonstrated written and oral proficiency in other languages; special interests, such as intensive study and exploration of other cultures; experiences that demonstrate unusual promise for leadership, such as significant community service or significant participation in student government; or other significant experiences or achievements that demonstrate the student's promise for contributing to the intellectual vitality of a campus
12. Completion of special projects undertaken in the context of your high school curriculum or in conjunction with special school events, projects, or programs
13. Academic accomplishments in light of your life experiences and special circumstances, including but not limited to disabilities, low family income, first generation to attend college, need to work, disadvantaged social or educational environment, difficult personal and family situations or circumstances, refugee status or veteran status
14. Location of your secondary school and residence.

In an invited lecture[50] to the American Council on Education in 2001, Atkinson expressed these ideas. The lecture caught fire nationally, and led to considerable public controversy about the SAT exams.[51]

Atkinson also recommended to BOARS that UC change its testing policies and use the SAT Achievement Tests (SAT-2) instead of SAT-1 in the criteria for admissions. Studies were carried out to assess whether the SAT-1 or the SAT-2 was the better predictor of performance and showed a clear advantage to the achievement tests. BOARS then recommended a change in requirement from the SAT-1 to the SAT-2, noting also that the changed requirement would emphasize curriculum and learning in the high schools. This change too was enacted by the Assembly of the Academic Senate as a request for what then became approval by the regents. Subsequently the College Board made changes to the SAT-1 tests, dropping the verbal analogies and adding a writing test. UC then kept both the SAT-1 and the SAT-2.[52]

Reflections

All three changes made for adaptation to Regents' Resolution SP-1 and Proposition 209—Eligibility in the Local Context, comprehensive review, and the shift to achievement testing—are cases of presidential leadership carried out through logical and scholarly arguments and accomplished by working in synergy with the Academic Senate to gain enactment.

The regents' resolutions and Proposition 209 created a situation in which constitutional autonomy was greatly important to the university. Without constitutional autonomy, the legislature would surely have made strong efforts to prescribe eligibility and admissions policy and define the nature of the companion outreach component (chapter 16).

---

[50] Richard C. Atkinson, "Standardized Tests and Access to American Universities," Robert H. Atwell Distinguished Lecture, American Council on Education, Washington, DC, 2001, https://perma.cc/PL7Y-2MDV.
[51] See, e.g., "Should SATs Matter?," Education Special Report, *Time*, March 12, 2001, pp. 62–76.
[52] BOARS subsequently dropped the SAT-2 requirement in 2009 and returned to the SAT-1, again with regents' approval. The rationale was that the SAT-1 is more commonly taken and that the requirement of the SAT-2 was producing a set of students who would have been eligible except for the fact that they had not taken the SAT-2 tests.

To what extent did the admissions policies instituted in the decade following the two regents' resolutions serve to replenish the ethnic diversity of the University of California? Figure 15-1 shows the percentages of underrepresented minorities (Latino, African American, and American Indian) among California public high school graduates and among UC freshman and the difference between these two percentages over the years from 1989 to 2008. One can see the drop occasioned by the race-neutral limitation that was adopted in 1995 and went into effect as of 1998 and then the subsequent rise in enrollments that primarily reflect the increase in URMs among high school graduates. The drop in the difference starting in 2005 probably reflects the influence of the new policies.

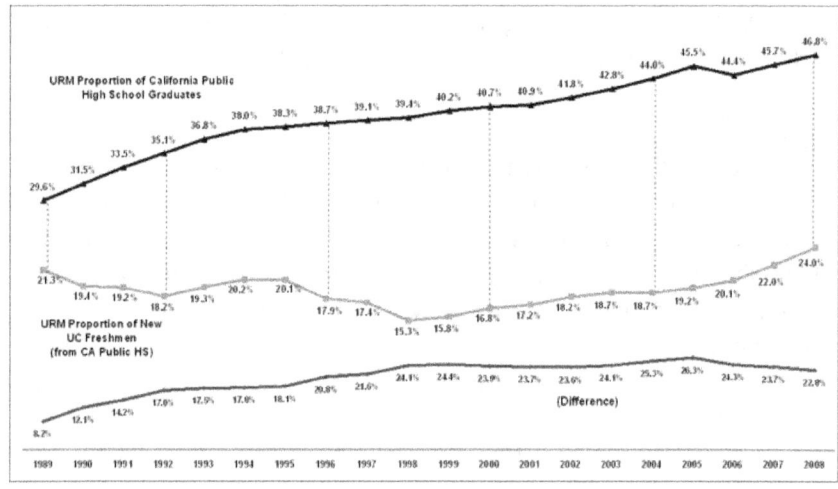

Figure 15-1. Percent of underrepresented minority students in the freshman UC class (*upper curve*) compared to California high school graduates (*middle curve*), fall 1989 to 2008. The lower curve is the difference between the two.[53]

---

[53] *University of California 2009 Accountability Report*, indicator 3.2, https://perma.cc/Z7FD-P2AP.

However, the primary effect of the Board of Regents' resolutions and Proposition 209 was on admission to the most selective campuses rather than on eligibility. At Berkeley and San Diego, the percentage of Latino and African American students is substantially below that at other UC campuses[54]. Geiser[55] has shown that much of the negative effect upon the underrepresented minorities has been that the top-ranking students in those groups tend to a greater extent to go to private or out-of-state institutions, since many of those institutions do offer large financial aid packages on race-attentive bases.

Further Changes and Trends
Redefining Eligibility. In 2009, BOARS and the Academic Senate recommended, and the UC Regents approved, further changes in the determination of freshman eligibility, which became effective for freshman students admitted in fall 2012. The standard based upon the sliding scale of GPA in the A-G courses and score on the SAT or ACT exams would be used to admit the top 9 percent statewide and would be supplemented by the admission of those students in the top 9 percent per high school as measured by GPA in the A-G courses. Students in these categories would receive the Master Plan guarantee of admission to some campus if they were not admitted to any campus to which they had applied. In addition a new category known as eligible to review (ETR) was created, composed of all additional students who had met or exceeded a GPA of 3.0 in the A-G courses. Students in this second category could apply and have their applications reviewed for possible admission, but they would not receive the guarantee of admission somewhere within UC. The rationales for the changes were that the 9 percent/9 percent approach would produce better overall student performance and that the broader ETR pool would enable the

---

[54] Jeremy Askkenas, Haeyoon Park, and Adam Pearce, "Even with Affirmative Action, Blacks and Hispanics Are More Underrepresented at Top Colleges Than 35 Years Ago", *New York Times*, August 24, 2017.
[55] Saul Geiser, "Back to the Future: Freshman Admissions at the University of California, 1994 to the Present and Beyond," Research & Occasional Papers no. 4.14, Center for Studies in Higher Education, University of California, Berkeley, April 2014, https://perma.cc/NPU5-MCBD.

criteria of comprehensive review to be applied to a group that was broader in terms of the index of GPA and test scores.

The analytical methods on which these changes were based predicted that the overlap between the two 9 percent groups would be so great that it would lead to an overall eligibility rate of only 10.5 percent and that the ETR category, while being greater than the additional 2.0 percent that would meet the Master Plan goal of 12.5 percent, could amount to about another 2 percent of admissions selected from that pool. Put another way, 10.5 percent of students would be guaranteed eligibility and admission somewhere at UC, whereas about another 4 percent would be reviewed to determine another 2 percent that would become eligible and be admitted, but without the guarantee. This approach amounted to a decoupling of the earlier Master Plan guarantee that there would be single determination of eligibility for the top 12.5 percent of students, with a guarantee of admission somewhere for the 12.5 percent eligible. With no statewide coordinating body as of 2011, there was no independent assessment of whether this decoupling still comported with the Master Plan.

In practice, the overlap of the two 9 percent pools turned out to be substantially less, such that for 2014 admissions[56] 12.9 percent of the public high school graduates in those pools were eligible, and another 2.4 percent were ETR admits.[57] As of 2016 admissions, the ETR category was no longer mentioned explicitly on the university websites, pending completion of the eligibility study for the high school class of 2016 (chapter 5).

Increasing Campus Selectivity and Its Effects. A detailed analysis of data on UC admissions and enrollments for the period 1994 through 2012 was carried out by Geiser.[58] It shows that all the campuses except Merced became increasingly more selective during that period, and the trend has surely continued since that time. Increasing campus

---

[56] "Annual Report on Undergraduate Admissions Requirements and Comprehensive Review," Board of Admissions and Relations with Schools, Academic Senate, University of California, January 2015, https://perma.cc/3WWB-F3PP..
[57] This result may again have reflected applications being drawn from UC-eligible students who, without receiving the ELC notice, would not have applied.
[58] Geiser, 2014, *loc. cit.*

selectivity for choosing among eligible applicants has led to continuing growth in "cascading" of applicants among campuses, wherein eligible applicants rejected by one or more of the most selective campuses then accept offers from other campuses, thereby displacing eligible applicants from those campuses who take spots at other campuses, and so forth.

All UC-eligible students in the two 9 percent categories, statewide and by school, who are not admitted to any of the campuses to which they applied are offered admission to the Merced campus if they so desire. However, the percentage of such students choosing to enroll at a UC campus to which they did not originally apply has been small—2.1 percent for Merced in 2014[59] and historically rarely over 3 percent. Most of those students choose to attend another institution instead. These factors have combined with the increasing selectivity of oversubscribed campuses so that the percent of California high school graduates actually enrolling at the University of California as freshmen, known as the *participation rate*, declined from 8.8 percent in 2006 to 7.3 percent in 2012—that is, by 17 percent of the total.

As the Merced campus continues to mature, it will become more attractive, and the interest of students in going to Merced should build further. Without increased capacity, admissions selectivity will rise even higher, and it will become impossible to accommodate all eligible California residents. Both the cascading and the decreasing participation rate can feed public impressions that the university is not serving the educational needs of the state fully enough, and unhappiness thereby increases among rejected applicants, their families, and their representatives in Sacramento.

Non-resident Students. One of the ways in which the university adapted to the reduction of state funding in the 2005-15 period was to admit more nonresident students—students from other states and other countries. Since tuition for nonresident students exceeds the average cost of education, enrollments of nonresident students actually bring operating funds that can be used for additional resident students, provided that the physical capacity exists. Crude estimates nationally have been that enrollment of about two full-fee-paying out-

---

[59] Board of Admissions and Relations with Schools, January 2015, *loc. cit.*

of-state students roughly offsets the cost of attendance of one additional in-state student.

For the University of California as a whole, enrollments of students from other states and countries more than doubled over the four-year period from 2011 to 2014.[60] Fall 2015 freshman enrollments university-wide, constituting 71 percent of total new undergraduate enrollments, were 77 percent from California, 14 percent international, and 9 percent domestic out-of-state. Individual campus figures for non-Californian freshman enrollees ranged from just 1 percent for Merced and 4 percent for Riverside up to 29 percent at Berkeley and UCLA and 33 percent at San Diego.[61] New transfer students, constituting the other 29 percent of entering undergraduate students, were 85 percent from California, 15 percent international, and 1 percent out-of-state. Individual campus non-Californian new transfer enrollees ranged from 5 percent at Merced and Santa Cruz up to 11 and 12 percent for San Diego and Berkeley.[62] International students at Berkeley are about one-third from China, followed by South Korea, India, and Canada.[63] The growing percentages of non-resident admissions, especially at the most selective campuses, feed an image that those students are displacing deserving Californians, a point considered further in Chapter 21.

WHITHER THE BUBBLING CAULDRON?

Some of the many intersecting issues that impinge upon University of California admissions are the following
- The requirements of the Master Plan or any successor to it
- Enrollment capacity, both physical and financial
- State financing for the university

---

[60] Board of Admissions and Relations with Schools, Academic Senate, January 2015, *loc. cit.*
[61] "University of California Statement of Intent to Register (SIR) Counts, Freshmen by Campus and Residency, Fall 2013, 2014, and 2015" https://perma.cc/U9W3-NTT7.
[62] "University of California Statement of Intent to Register (SIR) Counts, Transfer by Campus and Residency, Fall 2013, 2014, and 2015" https://perma.cc/4JLQ-SKPN..
[63] "International Student Enrollment Data," Berkeley International Office, University of California, Berkeley, https://web.archive.org/web/20151207232000/internationaloffice.berkeley.edu/students/current/enrollment_data.

- Assuring equivalent access for all elements of society, and the distribution of that access among campuses
- Policies and criteria for university-wide eligiblility and selection among eligible applicants by campuses
- Enrollments of international and other non-resident students, as well as the distribution of those students among campuses
- The differences among campuses in applications pressure[64]

These issues play out within the climate of what has been a serious and probably irreversible reduction in state funding.

Prospects for Increased Enrollment Capacity

The capacity of the University of California for enrolling students is limited by both physical facilities and finances. Existing and potential enrollment capacities reflect land area, availability of operating funds, needs for financing construction and modernization of buildings, and agreements with communities that occur through long-range development plans and environmental impact reports for specific projects. Not keeping up with needed capacity will lessen access by increasing the selectivity of campuses, increasing numbers of rejections of applicants by campuses, and lowering the participation rate. Ultimately it will mean that the university cannot keep up with its Master Plan commitments for access and enrollment. Unfunded increases in enrollment, by themselves, result in decreased quality of education because of increased class sizes, fewer course offerings, and/or less tutorial instruction.

As of 2017 there is not much nominal residual capacity in current campus LRDPs. The Irvine, Riverside, Santa Barbara, and Santa Cruz campuses had combined space left in their LRDPs for about 5 percent overall growth in the university-wide enrollment of about 250,000. The state no longer provides funding for construction of university facilities except for a few projects to address seismic deficiencies, and it no longer puts construction bonding referenda up for voter approval.

---

[64] For decades the administration of the University of California has recognized the desirability of getting the public to accept that the quality of undergraduate education is comparably high on all UC campuses. However, applicants and families often perceive that employers and graduate and professional schools do attach prestige and selectivity to Berkeley, UCLA, and UCSD; thus, those campuses remain particularly attractive.

Bonds must now be issued by the Regents and are subject to campus caps on incurred debt. The current UC Merced expansion project provides about another 1 percent enrollment capacity increase university-wide. Thus, the university is already on the edge of an enrollment-versus-capacity cusp without allowing for what will become increasing attractiveness of the Merced campus or the need for California to increase the percentage of its population that attains four-year degrees (chapter 5). Students are being accommodated by allowing enrollments on individual campuses to creep upward.

Access

As state funding has decreased and tuition has increased, it has been important for the university to guard against a loss of students from families that are less well off financially. So far, as reflected in data on attendance by Pell Grant recipients, the policy of returning one-third of tuition increases to need-based financial aid seems to have worked for this purpose.

Clarity

Clarity, simplicity, and openness are vital for criteria and processes related to eligibility and admissions. They help understanding by the public and government. They help to prevent suspicions that some sort of agenda, hidden or not, is being pursued in eligibility and admissions. Simplicity also enables students, parents, and schools to compute whether or not a student is UC-eligible, and it provides clear guidance as to what schools and students must do in order to enable students to achieve UC eligibility.

ADMISSIONS TO GRADUATE AND PROFESSIONAL PROGRAMS

The discussion in this chapter so far has been entirely about eligibility and admissions of undergraduates, which are handled centrally by UC campuses, although there may also be input from undergraduate deans or advisors of individual colleges. Admissions to graduate and professional schools, on the other hand, are typically handled by the individual schools and departments, subject to review or audit by the office of the graduate dean. For highly competitive schools associated with the high-income professions (e.g., medicine, business, and law) there have been issues similar to those occurring for undergraduate admissions. Indeed, it was admissions to the UC Davis School of Medicine that led to the Bakke decision, and it was admissions to the UC San Diego School of Medicine that were challenged and cited by Governor Wilson and Regent Connerly in the considerations that led to the regents' motions in 1995.

Graduate and professional admissions by departments and schools place strong emphasis on an applicant's record as an undergraduate and on letters of recommendation. There are also standardized tests, such as the Graduate Records Examination (GRE), the Medical College Admission Test (MCAT), and the Law School Admission Test (LSAT).

SUMMARY CONCLUSION

As college going and demand for admission to the University of California have grown over the years, the eligibility and selection processes for admission of freshman and transfer students have become ever more sensitive. UCLA draws the greatest number of applications for admission of all university campuses in the United States. The situation is further complicated by the growing ethnic diversity of California and the great disparities in educational quality among high schools around the state. As a public university, the university has a responsibility to have criteria and processes for making admission decisions that are clear and transparent to the public.

Both the University of California and the California State University utilize the concept of eligibility, whereby students achieve eligibility for admission on the basis of grade point average in specified A-G college-going courses, combined on a sliding scale with standardized test scores. The Master Plan and subsequent amending policies specify that the upper 12.5 and 33 percent are eligible for UC and CSU, respectively, and that all eligible students desiring to come should be accommodated somehow by the two universities. The eligibility concept has brought clarity to students, their families, and the public, as well as guidance to high schools with regard to what college-going courses they should offer.

There have historically been considerable disparities among ethnic groups in achieving eligibility for admission to UC. Recent rates have spread from about 6 percent for Latino and African American students to about 13 percent for Caucasian students, to about 30 percent for Asian American students. In recognition that this situation results in part from disparities among high schools around the state, starting in the 1970s, the university gave attention to race in selections among eligible students for admissions to affected campuses. The UC Regents in 1995 and then the state by a ballot initiative in 1996 precluded any consideration of race, gender, and several other factors in admissions decisions. This situation led to extensive rethinking of UC admissions criteria and led to three innovations—use of GPA rank within school A-G courses by itself as a path to eligibility, comprehensive review considering fourteen different factors for selection among eligible applicants for admission to impacted campuses, and changes in the national SAT tests.

Sharp reductions in state funding have brought additional problems. The state no longer funds the Master Plan. Tuitions have risen in response, but political pressures have kept tuition increases from covering the loss in state funds. Nonetheless, financial aid and access without regard to ability to pay have been retained by devoting one-third of all tuition increases to need-based financial aid.

Since about 2005 there has been an increase of campus selectivities in choosing among eligible applicants for admission, resulting in increased "cascading" of applicants among campuses which has led to a reduction in the overall participation rate, the percentage of UC-eligible students who actually come to UC. This is an indirect capacity and Master Plan issue.

16.
Serving the State of California and the Public

The University of California...must be adapted to this people, to their public and private schools, to their peculiar geographical position, to the requirements of their new society and their undeveloped resources.
 —Daniel Coit Gilman[1]

Napa Valley's success is synonymous with Davis's success.
 —Andy Hoxsey, Napa grape grower and winery owner[2]

The California Digital Library, by transforming a wealth of resources into electronic form, will represent one of the most important doors of the Library of California. We are delighted with this newest library and with the partnership between UC and the California State Library. The people of California will be the beneficiaries of our collaborative efforts.
 —Kevin Starr, California State Librarian[3]

For the University to achieve its aim of enrolling a student body that meets high academic standards and encompasses the broad diversity of California, students from all segments of the state's population must be provided the resources needed for good academic preparation. Ideally, all students, regardless of where they live, and irrespective of race, ethnicity, gender, or family economic circumstance, should have the opportunity to develop their full educational potential.
 —New Directions for Outreach[4]

---

[1] Daniel C. Gilman, "The Building of the University," Inaugural Address as president of the University of California, November 7, 1872, https://perma.cc/W6UM-R2DK..
[2] James Lapsley and Daniel Summer, "We Are Both Hosts: Napa Valley, UC Davis, and the Search for Quality," in Martin Kenney and David C. Mowery, eds., *Research, Public Universities and Regional Growth: Insights from the University of California* (Palo Alto, CA: Stanford University Press, 2014), chapter 7.
[3] Terry Colvon, "UC Announces Founding of the California Digital Library," University of California, October 14, 1997, https://perma.cc/F4FP-L78A.
[4] *New Directions for Outreach*, Report of the University of California Outreach Task Force, July 1995, https://perma.cc/F97X-FTJ9.

The University of California partners with the state of California in many ways, and it is important that it do so. The university should fulfill research needs of the state, and its research should be of genuine use to the state. Furthermore, by virtue of its extreme geographic diversities, its needs for and dependence upon water, and its tendency to be the forerunner of trends in United States, the state of California is itself a valuable laboratory for academic research.

The roles are much wider than just research. Public service is acknowledged in the *Academic Personnel Manual* as an expectation for faculty members and a factor to be evaluated in their promotion and advancement cases. It is, of course, also politically valuable to the university to be seen as valuable in many dimensions and appreciated by people throughout that state so that the public will value the university and their elected representatives will be aware of that fact.

There are many ways in which University of California is meaningful and visible to the citizens of the state other than through its educational and degree-giving functions and its research, both of which are of course prime benefits themselves. Among these added dimensions are

- the six full-function medical centers at San Francisco, Los Angeles, San Diego, Davis, Irvine, and now Riverside, which are prominent primary-, secondary-, and especially tertiary-care centers;
- the Optometry Clinic at Berkeley;
- spectator sports events;
- a massive program of continuing education through university extension;[5]
- music and drama performances;
- museums;
- numerous lectures open to the public;
- the Lawrence Hall of Science[6] at Berkeley, which supports science education in schools, provides continuing education for teachers, and is also open as a participation museum;

---

[5] Among the ten campuses of the University of California, university extension as of 2015 had over 500,000 enrollees in over 17,000 courses each year. It is the largest such operation in the United States and is entirely self-supporting. See "University Extension," University of California, https://web.archive.org/web/20171122213704/http://extension.universityofcalifornia.edu/, and links therein.

- a charter school[7] and the lab school[8] at UCSD and UCLA, respectively, and
- various programs stemming from "practicum" experiences for students in the professional schools, such as free law clinics for the underserved,[9] field placements in social welfare at UCLA and Berkeley, student-run local media in journalism, and summer internships in public policy and many other fields.

The services mentioned so far are common to public research universities in many states. The main purpose of this chapter is to explore five other disparate aspects of the impact of the University of California on the state of California which are distinctive to California:
- influences upon agriculture, including cooperative extension
- the California Digital Library
- education partnerships and outreach
- the California Council on Science and Technology
- general economic impact

AGRICULTURE

The involvement of the University of California with California agriculture is particularly rich and long-standing. California has the largest agricultural industry in the United States. In 2014, it had 13 percent of US cash farm receipts and a 14.3 percent share of total US agricultural exports,[10] as opposed to 12 percent of the population of the United States.[11] As of 2012, one-third of California's $37.5 billion

---

[6] Lawrence Hall of Science, University of California, Berkeley, https://web.archive.org/web/20170830024638/http://www.lawrencehallofscience.org/.
[7] The Preuss School, University of California, San Diego, https://web.archive.org/web/20171226220927/http://preuss.ucsd.edu/.
[8] Welcome to UCLA Lab School, University of California, Los Angeles, https://web.archive.org/web/20170105120327/http://www.labschool.ucla.edu/about/.
[9] For the Berkeley campus, see "Experiential Education" School of Law, University of California, Berkeley, https://perma.cc/4QJB-LLBJ.
[10] California Department of Food and Agriculture, "California Agricultural Production Statistics, 2014," https://web.archive.org/web/20160628185149/https://www.cdfa.ca.gov/Statistics/.
[11] Sumit Passary, "US Population Grows to 320.09 Million: California Still Reigns as Most Populous US State," *Tech Times*, December 30, 2014, https://perma.cc/3HYA-54ZN.

agricultural output was exported abroad.[12] Nationally, the industry itself characteristically has little research in the private sector, with most research being financed by federal and state governments and carried out by universities and government laboratories. From the start, the University of California has had the primary agricultural-research role in California. As was noted in chapter 2, Eugene Hilgard, who succeeded Ezra Carr as professor of Agriculture in 1875, greatly advanced agriculture at the university in support of the state. A pioneering and respected soil scientist himself, Hilgard took many steps to base agriculture more on science. His wine-making activities led the California legislature to formally authorize and commission the university in 1880 to undertake research in support of the development of that industry.[13] Hilgard also created experiment stations that would gauge the suitability of California for various crops and arranged for farmers' institutes for education in agriculture in many of California's counties.[14]

Over the years many advances affecting California agriculture have come from UC research. A few relatively recent examples from among many are current varieties of tomatoes and strawberries; a doubling of yields of almonds (a prime export product at \$3.9 billion in 2011[15]); pest controls of many sorts, including biological (nonchemical) control; and controllable malolactic fermentation and quantitative sensory evaluation methods for wine production. As shown in table 18-1, eight of the twenty-five top-grossing University of California patents as of 2015 were agricultural—six varieties of strawberries and one each of citrus and pistachios. Ninety percent of California's wheat, 65 percent of California's strawberries, and 40 percent of strawberries worldwide

---

[12] "Cultivating California," Division of Agriculture and Natural Resources, University of California, 2012, https://perma.cc/23FN-J9QU.
[13] Maynard A. Amerine, "Hilgard and California Viticulture," *Hilgardia* 33, no. 1 (July 1962), https://perma.cc/PAU3-BVEW..
[14] Verne A. Stadtman, *The University of California, 1868–1968* (New York: McGraw-Hill, 1968), pp. 143–154.
[15] "Investing in California," Division of Agriculture and Natural Resources, University of California, 2012, https://perma.cc/MPR9-PB64.

are University of California varieties.[16] The enormous growth of the California wine industry over the last fifty years to reach wines of the highest quality and worldwide distribution with a huge expansion in sales is directly attributable to research at UC Davis, and that campus has now trained most of the leading viticulturalists and oenologists of California, as well as many around the world.[17, 18] California wine sales in 2016 were 236 million cases with a market value of $34.1 billion.[19]

Cooperative Extension

In agriculture, as in many other areas, there is a vast middle ground between the results of agricultural research and fundamental knowledge, on the one hand, and utilization and successful commercial application, on the other hand. This gap has been very effectively addressed within the United States by the Cooperative Extension System, which was set up through the Smith-Lever Act passed in 1914.[20] For over one hundred years, the University of California has had a very extensive cooperative extension effort. As of 2015 it encompassed 9 research and extension centers, 57 local offices throughout the state in nearly every county, 130 campus-based cooperative extension specialists, and 200 locally based cooperative extension advisors and specialists. These experts work at the interface between research, on the one hand, and growers and processors, on the other hand, to help bring advances and knowledge from research into practice and to enable growers and processors to achieve economies and improved products. They also bring their knowledge of needs and opportunities in the fields back to inform university research. Some of them are researchers themselves.

---

[16] "Investing in California," loc. cit.
[17] See, e.g., Lisa Lapin, "A Fine Blend," *UC Davis Magazine* 19, no.2 (2002), https://perma.cc/9LGR-ZWXP.
[18] Lapsley and Summer, 2014, loc. cit.
[19] "2016 California Wine Sales in U.S. Hit New Record: 238 Million Cases with Retail Value of $34.1 Billion," The Wine Institute, May 1, 2017, https://perma.cc/BJR8-WN95.
[20] Nancy Franz, "Measuring and Articulating the Value of Community Engagement: Lessons Learned from 100 Years of Cooperative Extension Work," *Journal of Higher Education Outreach and Engagement* 18, no. 2 (2014): pp. 5–15,
https://web.archive.org/web/20160513203125/http://openjournals.libs.uga.edu:80/index.php/jheoe/article/view/1231/759.

As but one example of the impact of cooperative extension, Taylor et al.[21] examine the economic impact stemming from the role of cooperative extension in bringing drip irrigation into use in California. Drip techniques were introduced in 1969. By 1988 5 percent of irrigated acreage in California used drip techniques, but as of 2010, almost 40 percent of irrigated land used them. Improved yields, notably of tomatoes, have come from drip irrigation. Taylor et al. conclude that $78 to $283 million per year are now saved in California through the use of drip irrigation. Given the predictions that global warming will accentuate drought conditions in California, research into efficient use of agricultural water will become even more vital.

THE CALIFORNIA DIGITAL LIBRARY

As was noted in chapter 2, when the University of California developed its digital library in the latter part of the 1990s, it took pains to provide the maximum access to the public of California that would be consonant with provisions for licensed content. The library was intentionally designated as the California Digital Library, connoting that it serves the entire state rather than just the university, and it was developed and announced as a joint project of the University of California and the California State Library.[22] Public users can access public material through personal computers and from libraries and schools around the state.

The University of California has been a strong participant in major mass-digitization projects. Supporting the open access movement, UC is a founding partner of HathiTrust[23, 24] and was one of the six universities to join with Google for the creation of the Google Book

---

[21] Rebecca Taylor, Doug Parker, and David Zilberman, "Contribution of University of California Cooperative Extension to Drip Irrigation," Giannini Foundation for Agricultural Economics, 2014, https://perma.cc/FB62-B724.
[22] "UC Announces Founding of the California Digital Library," University of California, October 14, 1997, https://web.archive.org/web/20070609174556/http://www.ucop.edu/news/archives/9697/digital.htm.
[23] "UC Libraries and HathiTrust FAQ," California Digital Library," https://web.archive.org/web/20161009221747/http://www.cdlib.org/services/hathi/faq.html.
[24] "Our Partnership," HathiTrust Digital Library, https://perma.cc/297F-GRQM.

Project[25] and the Google Books Library Project.[26] These projects have created large amounts of digital material for libraries and open access,[27] putting many books in open-access electronic form or partial electronic form and greatly enhancing the abilities of scholars and other users to screen the contents of books.

The public services available through the California Digital Library grow continually and as of June 2016 included the following:

- The **Online Archive of California (OAC)**[28] contains materials placed in the electronic collection by over two hundred different institutions[29] throughout California, including libraries, special collections, archives, historical societies, and museums, as well as collections maintained by University of California campuses. It provides free public access to primary research and record sources, such as manuscripts, photographs, artwork, and scientific data, through more than 38,000 collection guides and 200,000 digitized images and documents from sources throughout the state. It is a primary portal for both general information and scholarly research.
- **Calisphere**[30] is a public gateway to thousands of digitized primary sources, including photographs, documents, newspaper clippings, and works of art from UC museums and libraries and other cultural heritage institutions across California.[31] As of May 2017 there are about 850,000 digital images, texts, and recordings in Calisphere.
- **eScholarship**[32] contains open-access publications deposited by UC faculty members. These include prepublication articles; articles already published for which copyright has been retained; online

---

[25] "About Google Books," https://perma.cc/3KNV-JSQB.
[26] "Google Books Library Project—Google Books," https://perma.cc/85UR-XF75.
[27] As the name indicates, open access provides access for all, irrespective of ability to pay. Of course someone must finance the preparation and publishing of open-access material, and there have been various financial models proposed and used.
[28] "About OAC," Online Archive of California, https://web.archive.org/web/20160303125322/http://www.oac.cdlib.org/about/.
[29] "Contbuting Institutions", Online Archive of California, https://web.archive.org/web/20180331072642/http://www.oac.cdlib.org/institutions/.
[30] Calisphere, University of California, accessed May 8, 2017, https://calisphere.org/.
[31] "Calisphere Web Site Launched: California Digital Library," https://web.archive.org/web/20160415044159/https://www.cdlib.org/cdlinfo/2006/07/13/calisphere-web-site-launched/
[32] "eScholarship," University of California, https://web.archive.org/web/20170329160637/http://escholarship.org/.

journals[33] started by UC faculty, staff, or students; data sets; and even entire books by UC authors that are originally published on the e-scholarship website or which were previously published and for which the author has held or obtained back copyright rights.[34] Many authors are choosing e-scholarship as the primary or only place of publication, counting upon readers using links on the authors' own websites and/or search engines to find the papers readily. Low- or zero-cost (for direct downloads) publication should increase readership. Publishing units within UC can develop hybrid open-access business models for their publications. Books and journals can be freely accessible via eScholarship while being simultaneously offered for sale in print-on-demand and e-book formats at low cost via e-commerce storefronts and retail affiliates providing those services, as is the case for this book.

- The **Web Archiving Service** (WAS) was launched in 2007 as a means of capturing, analyzing, and preserving web (Internet) content, and as of March 2016, 600 million web files had been archived. As of January 2015, WAS became part of the Internet Archive's **"Archive-It,"**[35] also known as the Wayback Machine.[36] A group of leading universities, including UC, is working with the Internet Archive to assure that services there meet the needs of research universities.

The holdings and the services provided by the California Digital Library are growing rapidly. They are increasingly becoming central components of scholarship as well as offering entirely new approaches to scholarship and publication. In the public arena, with the financial pressures on local public libraries, increased digitization, more lenient

---

[33] Such journals can be peer reviewed, if the editors so desire, and many are. Open access does not equate to not peer reviewed; they are different matters.

[34] For example, a widely used chemical engineering textbook, *Separation Processes*, which the author published with McGraw-Hill in 1971 and 1980, went out of print in the early 2000s. The author obtained the copyright back from the publisher and posted the entire book in eScholarship. (The 850-page book had already been scanned by the Google Book Project.) It now receives over 150 downloads per month, a volume somewhat higher than the average monthly sales volume when it was in print with the original publisher, despite that fact that it is now over thirty-eight years old.

[35] "Archive-It—Web Archiving Services for Libraries and Archives," https://perma.cc/Q6ZN-BS36.

[36] Wayback Machine, Internet archive, https://archive.org/index.php.

licensing policies, and the convenience of working from one's computer rather than traveling to sites with different holdings, one can expect this digital library and others like it elsewhere to become the primary library source for the public as time goes on. The digital-library initiative has so far been a major success for UC. Comprehensive digital libraries are among the best services that universities can provide to the public and thereby generate continual recognition and appreciation of the university as a knowledge bank.

EDUCATION PARTNERSHIPS AND OUTREACH

The University of California has long had programs of liaison to high schools and thereby to precollege students. As noted in chapter 15, this began with the 1884 decision to accredit high schools formally, a policy that remained in place for almost eighty years until 1963. Functionally, another relationship grew, also described in chapter 15, whereby the appropriate high school curriculum for college-going students was defined through the A-G courses, which students must take and in which they must achieve a sufficient grade point average in order to be eligible for admission to the University of California or the California State University.

During the second half of the twentieth century, California became much more diverse ethnically, with demographers concluding that the Latino population became larger than the white population as of 2014 (39.0 percent Latino, 38.8 percent white, 13 percent Asian/Pacific Islander, 5.8 percent black; <1 percent Native American).[37] High school completion rates vary sharply by ethnicity, with 2011–12 data for California showing 90 percent for Asians/Pacific Islanders, 86 percent for whites, 73 percent for Latinos, and 66 percent for African Americans.[38] College-going rates also vary considerably by

---

[37] Mark Hugo Lopez, "In 2014, Latinos Will Surpass Whites as Largest Racial/Ethnic Group in California," *Pew Research Center*, January 24, 2014, https://perma.cc/V5L4-KURF.
[38] "State High School Graduation Rates by Race, Ethnicity," https://perma.cc/WX4T-KQKP.

ethnicity and by county within the state.[39] Enrollment of 2008–09 high school graduates in a postsecondary institution within sixteen months of high school graduation ranged from 32 percent in Kern County to 80 percent in San Francisco County, and from 66 percent for Latinos to 86 percent for Asian Americans.

Eligibility rates for the California State University and the University of California also vary greatly, both geographically and by ethnicity. The percentage of high school graduates successfully completing the A-G college-going courses in 2015 (one of the requirements for CSU and UC eligibility) was 43.4 percent statewide, 55 percent in Alameda County, 31 percent in Kern County, and below 25 percent in Mendocino, Mono, Inyo, and some other counties.[40] As noted in chapter 15, there are also huge racial differences in eligibility for UC and CSU.

These disparities and the greater awareness of civil rights issues that arose in the 1960s in the United States led to many efforts by the university as a whole, campuses, and groups of faculty that were started in the 1960s, 1970s, and 1980s and aimed at increasing college-going and eligibility rates among Latinos, Blacks, and Native Americans—the underrepresented minorities. Filipinos and Pacific Islanders have also been included in such efforts. A 1995 report[41] created in the UC Office of the President tallied these programs, finding over six hundred with combined budgets of about $60 million. A history of these efforts up to the year 2000 is also available.[42]

The three largest of these programs are university-wide and have achieved considerable size and renown.

- **Mathematics, Engineering, Science Achievement (MESA)** was founded at Berkeley in 1970 by engineering professor Wilbur Somerton and equal opportunity director William Somerville to

---

[39] Joanna Lin, "College-Going Rates Vary Widely in California," *California Watch*, accessed November 5, 2015, https://web.archive.org/web/20160825175058/http://californiawatch.org/dailyreport/college-going-rates-vary-widely-california-13121.

[40] Lucile Packard Foundation for Children's Health, "College Eligibility in California," https://perma.cc/6XW7-ZU6T.

[41] Leanne Parker, "The Schools and UC: A Commitment to the Future of California," University of California, Office of the President, 1995.

[42] "Outreach at the University of California: A Retrospective," Office of the President, University of California, https://perma.cc/7DAE-VWSR.

generate a support system for minority precollege students who might become majors in STEM (science, technology, engineering, mathematics) fields. The program began at Oakland Technical High School. As of 2010 California MESA served twenty-one thousand students at twenty-two school program centers, thirty-three community colleges, and thirteen four-year universities.[43] In addition to California, MESA now exists in ten other states.
- The **Puente Project**[44] was started in 1981 at Chabot Community College in Hayward, California, and now serves thirty-four high schools, a majority (sixty-four) of community colleges in California, and about fourteen thousand students in all with writing, counseling, and mentoring components. It was headquartered at the UC Office of the President for many years and in 2012 moved to the UC Berkeley campus.
- The **Early Academic Outreach Program (EAOP)**[45] was founded in 1976, operates through individual UC campuses, and has become UC's largest outreach program. It provides four basic types of service: (1) academic advising to help students complete the college preparatory courses and become eligible for admission, (2) academic enrichment to help students with basic skills and study habits, (3) preparation for the standard examinations (SAT or ACT) required for UC admission, and (4) information on financial aid and writing of college applications. Two models are used—working with cohorts of individual students and with entire schools.

As noted in Chapters 2 and 15, in 1995 the Regents of the University of California passed two resolutions barring any use of race, religion, sex, color, ethnicity, or national origin in admissions and employment, and sixteen months later, California voters adopted the

---

[43] "MESA Fall Middle/High School New Advisor Training," University of California, Irvine, undated, https://perma.cc/Q5LA-KR6M.
[44] "Puente," the Puente Project, Center for Educational Partnerships, University of California, Berkeley, https://web.archive.org/web/20161004230256/http://puente.berkeley.edu/.
[45] Brenda Iasevoli, "Making Colleges More Diverse Even without Affirmative Action: Lessons from California's Early Academic Outreach Program," *The Atlantic*, February 28, 2014.

initiative constitutional amendment prohibiting "preferential treatment to any individual or group on the basis of race, sex, color, ethnicity, or national origin in the operation of public employment, public education, or public contracting". These actions necessitated major changes in admissions (chapter 15) and outreach policies. Section 1[46] of the first of the two regents' resolutions stated,

> "The president, with the consultation of the Board of Regents, shall appoint a task force representative of the business community, the university, other segments of education and organizations currently engaged in academic 'outreach.' The responsibility of this group shall be to develop proposals for new directions and increased funding for the Board of Regents to increase the eligibility rate of those currently identified in section four [i. e., disadvantaged students]."

Outreach Task Force

The university then moved to create the Outreach Task Force to identify programs that could increase the eligibility and attendance of disadvantaged students in a race-neutral context. The president and the chair of the regents decided that the task force would be cochaired by the provost (the author) and a prominent person from the private sector. Richard Clarke,[47] an ex-CEO of Pacific Gas and Electric Company, was chosen as that cochair and was both effective and dedicated.

The UC administration decided to recommend a relatively large task force (36 people) that drew from many different backgrounds inside and outside the university so as to obtain trust and respect for the ultimate recommendations of the task force. Through consultation with the chair of the regents, four regents were included on the task force, both to obtain their input early and hopefully to enhance acceptance of the product by the regents.

---

[46] "Text of UC Regents' Resolutions", University of California, Berkeley, https://perma.cc/ZT39-FPPC.
[47] Pacific Gas and Electric Company, "Richard A. Clarke, Former PG&E CEO and Environmental Leader, Dies at 72," December 17, 2002, https://perma.cc/M3L6-D3WA.

Meetings of the Outreach Task Force were construed legally to be public meetings, with the result that several representatives of the media attended and wrote about the first several meetings. Attendance by the media tapered off after a few meetings. The internal dynamics of the task force proved to be challenging, since the entire spectrum of views was present, resulting in tensions among members.

Because of sheer size, cost, and dilution of effort, it would not be possible to have effective outreach programs that extended more or less equally to all school districts and all portions of the state. The deliberations of the task force and the underlying staff work by the Office of the President sought methods of targeting outreach that would reach the most essential sectors and yet be compatible with the regents' resolutions and the constitutional amendment. Addressing this goal required considerable thought about the purposes of outreach and public education. A method of targeting would have to be acceptable to those with views across the spectrum. The task force finally decided to target by *educational disadvantage*—that is, to target the student populations of those schools having low values of various academic measures (enrollment rates in college-going courses, SAT scores, percentage of graduates attending UC, etcetera).

In addition to this recommendation, the report[48] of the task force identified desirable program areas and needs for increases in funding as follows:

- *school-centered partnerships ($27.2 million per year)*, focused upon schools meeting educational-disadvantage criteria and designed to increase preparation and college-going rates from those schools
- *academic development ($17.9 million per year)*, designed to build upon programs such as MESA and Puente to work with individual students from educationally disadvantaged schools
- *informational outreach ($7.9 million per year)*, aimed at students and family to create awareness and understanding of college going
- *research, program evaluation, and information technology capabilities ($7.55 million per year)*

---

[48] Outreach Task Force, "New Directions for Outreach," University of California, July 1997, accessed November 5, 2015, https://perma.cc/6ZNP-2335. The measures of educational disadvantage are on p. 12 of the report.

In all, additional funding of $60.55 million per year was recommended, with primary uses being for school-centered partnerships and student development programs. Those two sorts of programs had political appeal to Republicans and Democrats, respectively. Thereby there was political contention between supporters of the two sorts of programs. Rather than funding at the levels requested, the final resolution between to two political parties was to apply the full funding of $60 million individually to each of the programs, thereby considerably exceeding the university's request. As noted above, funding from a variety of sources for outreach of all sorts before the report had been about $60 million per year. By 2000–01 it had grown to $328 million per year, of which $184 million was from state and UC internal funds.[49]

This rapid escalation of funding created a situation where the university needed to design, institute, and build major new outreach programs over a very short period. This was done remarkably well, considering the challenge. A commissioned evaluation report[50] in 2003 found that the programs had been generally effective in providing educationally disadvantaged and underrepresented students increased access to UC.

The rapid escalation of funding also created expectations for immediate increases in college-going rates that could not be fulfilled. Development of schools and students through outreach are long-term propositions, since work with students in schools must start years before their graduation. In an era of term limits, politicians do not want to wait that long for results. Also, because of the zero-sum aspects of eligibility, students would have to improve enough academically to displace previously eligible students. The outreach programs became the object of sharp differences between the political parties, with the result that the decisions as to whether and how much to fund them would be held hostage until the very final negotiations among the Big

---

[49] Patricia A. Pelfrey, *Entrepreneurial President: Richard Atkinson and the University of California, 1995–2003* (Berkeley: University of California Press, 2012), 83–84.
[50] Strategic Review Panel on Educational Outreach, "Forging California's Future through Educational Partnerships: Redefining Educational Outreach," University of California, February 2003, https://perma.cc/SZE9-HDG6.

Five[51] on the budget. The annual delay and uncertainty in budget determinations created job-security concerns for the employees of the programs. Unfortunately, before the new outreach programs could take root and yield the substantial results that they did eventually produce, state budget stringencies hit again, and funding was greatly reduced. Current (2016) state funding for educational partnerships is about $25 million per year. A description of current university-wide programs is available.[52]

There is, however, one very clear measure of success that became available only after the substantially reduced funding had hit. The CPEC Eligibility Study for the high school graduating class of 2007 (chapter 15) showed eligibility rates of 6.3 and 6.9 percent for black and Latino students respectively, whereas the study for the 1996 high school class[53] had shown 2.8 and 3.9 percent for black and Latino students, respectively. The study for the high school class of 2001[54] had shown 4.3 and 5.5 percent for black and Latino students, respectively. The surge in outreach efforts of the University of California approximately doubled UC eligibility rates for black and Latino students from 1996 to 2007.

The ups and downs of state funding for eligibility-enhancing efforts and the political limelight that fell on these activities both complicated matters considerably. In addition, the university's efforts so far have dealt with school improvement and with counseling and advising students, yet the underlying issues that lead to disparities in college-going rates cover much wider aspects of society, including poverty, cultural traditions, home life, and even public health. For the

---

[51] As the last step in the annual state budget process, the governor, the speaker of the assembly, the president pro tempore of the senate, and the minority-party leaders of the two houses of the legislature work as the "Big Five" to resolve disagreements among the two houses of the legislature, usually by creating deals in which one party yields on an issue so as to gain on another. See "Big Five (California Politics)," *Wikipedia*, https://perma.cc/R4HL-JGJ3.

[52] "Diversity and Engagement," Office of the President, University of California, https://web.archive.org/web/20160815052139/https://www.ucop.edu/diversity-engagement/index.html.

[53] "Eligibility of California's 1996 High School Graduates for Admission to the State's Public Universities," Report no. 97-9, December 1997, California Postsecondary Education Commission, https://perma.cc/SU3T-K7XG.

[54] "University Eligibility Study for the Class of 2001," Report 05-9, September 2005, California Postsecondary Education Commission, https://perma.cc/799G-MALT.

university to try to get operationally into those arenas would be an enormous undertaking.

CALIFORNIA COUNCIL ON SCIENCE AND TECHNOLOGY

The state of California has no equivalents of the presidential science advisor or Office of Science and Technology Policy (OSTP), National Science Board, or National Science Foundation that exist at the national level for the United States. However, in 1988 the California Council on Science and Technology (CCST)[55] was established by legislative resolution.[56]

The roles of the council defined by that resolution are to "identify long-range research needs for sustaining the state's economic development and competitiveness and provide direction for new scientific and technological activities; and...[to] assess private sector/university relations and technology transfer, particularly with respect to California's economic development, leadership in research and development, and capacity to retain vital industries and scientific talent in California."

The council is overseen by a board with members from universities, industry, and national laboratories, appointed and overseen by the president of the University of California, in collaboration with the presidents of the University of Southern California, the California Institute of Technology, and Stanford University and with the chancellors of the California State University and the California Community Colleges.

The council works in ways that are analogous to the functions of the US National Research Council, now known as the Program Units of the National Academies of Sciences, Engineering, and Medicine.[57] Studies are carried out on various subjects by teams composed of California leaders in science, engineering, and science policy. These

---

[55] "California Council on Science and Technology (CCST)," https://web.archive.org/web/20171026155707/https://ccst.us/.
[56] "CCST Legislative Charge," https://perma.cc/3PZQ-SAAM.
[57] "Organization," National Academies of Sciences, Engineering, and Medicine, https://web.archive.org/web/20160623223209/http://www.nasonline.org/about-nas/organization/.

studies are usually requested by an executive agency, legislative committee, or one or more legislators of the state government. Sponsorship through such a request is a mark of true interest in the results. A few studies are done at the initiative of the council itself when there is a strong belief that information and/or interest need to be generated. Studies are of two general types—examination of a specific current subject and examination of the current situation of the state in a broader area.

Funding for the core administrative activities of CCST comes from the six sustaining higher-education members. The contribution of the University of California is twice as large as those of the others, reflecting the size of UC. Project funding comes from state government agencies or appropriations, or from other external entities.

Although the operations of CCST resemble those of the National Academies in many ways, there are two notable differences. One is that CCST as of 2017 has a paid staff of only eleven people. It is highly reliant upon the work of volunteers. Whereas the National Academies staff typically carry out much research for the projects that the academies undertake, CCST is more dependent on the knowledge already acquired by its selected volunteer committee members. The second difference is that the National Academies maintain an arms-length relationship with sponsoring government agencies, having essentially no contact, or very little, with the sponsoring agency during the course of a study. This approach is used to make it clear that the academies are something apart from, and uninfluenced by, the political process. CCST studies do maintain contact with the state agencies or other components of government that are affected by a study, in the belief that the contact is useful so that the study is grounded and has full information.

Examples of recent studies in the more specific arena are "An Independent Scientific Assessment of Well Stimulation in California" (i.e., "fracking"), "Digitally Enhanced Education in California: Creating a Vision for Integrating Digital Media into California's Teacher Preparation System," and "Health Impacts of Radio Frequency from Smart Meters." Examples of those in the more general category are "California Water—Achieving a Sustainable California Water Future through Innovations in Science and Technology," "California's Energy

Future—the View to 2060," and "Innovate 2 Innovation—an Assessment of California's Innovation Ecosystem."

CCST reports have had impact at the state level and do occasionally receive media attention, as was the case for the fracking reports.

The California Council on Science and Technology is relatively unique among state science policy functions. Approaches of the different states within the United States for systematically utilizing science and technology for economic development have been reviewed by Geiger and Sá.[58]

IDENTIFICATION AND DOCUMENTATION OF ECONOMIC IMPACT

The importance of the research mission of research universities for society and the economy is a compelling story that needs to be communicated to the public and governments in clear and engaging ways, as an avenue to public understanding and also as a means for sustaining public funding.

The University of California

The University of California as a whole and the individual campuses have commissioned or carried out numerous studies identifying and documenting the economic impacts of the university and the campuses on the state. Many of these are classical economic-impact reports that deal with employment and spending by the university and university employees without attempting to identify the quantitative impacts of university research and service on industry, economic development, and/or social benefit.[59] A report from the Bay Area Council Economic Institute analyzes the contributions of

---

[58] Roger L. Geiger and Creso Sá, "Beyond Technology Transfer: US State Policies to Harness University Research for Economic Development," *Minerva* 43, no. 1 (2005): pp. 1–21.
[59] See, for example, Economic and Planning Systems, "The University of California's Economic Contribution to the State of California, September 12, 2011, https://perma.cc/FDW8-NCD9, and a listing of such reports given by Innovation Alliances and Services, University of California, https://web.archive.org/web/20171022221435/https://www.ucop.edu/innovation-entrepreneurship/innovation-reports/economic-impact.html.

companies formed by faculty, alumni, and affiliates of the Berkeley campus. [60] Other studies have been aimed at identifying the contribution of university research, graduates, and/or faculty members to the development of specific industries. A portion of the budget of UC's Industry-University Cooperative Research Program (chapter 18) was devoted to determining quantitatively the contributions of University of California research and people to the development of new industries in California. The most attention was given to the biotechnology industry, the results for which are presented by Yarkin[61] and build upon the facts presented in chapters 10 and 18 to demonstrate the vital role of University of California research in the early development of that industry. An oral history collection[62] on the development of the California biotechnology industry contains much related anecdotal information. A similar analysis has been made for the biotechnology industry on a global scale.[63] Working in a more popular vein, Professor Conrad Rudolph of the UC Riverside campus has provided a PowerPoint display of many of the most important and visible impacts of University of California research on society, including, inter alia, flu vaccine, the Internet, the computer CPU, the ground-fault interrupter, the wet suit, the nicotine patch, safer freeways, the bar code scanner, vitamin E, and the beginning of the end of malaria.[64]

---

[60] "Stimulating Entrepreneurship in the Bay Area and Nationwide: An Exploration of the Economic Contributions of UC Berkeley through Company Formations by Alumni, Faculty, and Affiliates," Bay Area Council Economic Institute, San Francisco, CA, 2014, https://perma.cc/96E3-2F8M.
[61] Cherisa Yarkin, "Assessing the Role of the University of California in the State's Biotechnology Economy," chapter 8 in John de la Mothe and Jorge Niosi, eds., *The Economic and Social Dynamics of Biotechnology* (New York: Springer, 2000).
[62] "Program in Bioscience and Biotechnology Studies," Regional Oral History Office, Bancroft Library, University of California, Berkeley, https://web.archive.org/web/20160702051904/http://bancroft.berkeley.edu/ROHO/projects/bio sci/oh_list.html.
[63] Ross DeVol and Armen Bedroussian, *Mind to Market: A Global Analysis of University Biotechnology Transfer and Commercialization*, Milken Institute, Santa Monica, CA, September 1, 2006, https://perma.cc/4JRZ-F9HY.
[64] Conrad Rudolph, "UC We Gave You," PowerPoint presentation, accessed December 3, 2016, http://escholarship.org/uc/item/3ww5g8jj.

Wider Afield

On the national and international scales, beyond just the state of California, a line of economics research over the years has served to give at least semiquantitative insight into the contributions of research—and within it, university research—to economic growth in the United States and the world. This work began with Robert Solow at MIT and Moses Abramowitz at Stanford. It was pursued more deeply by Edwin Mansfield and coworkers at the University of Pennsylvania and then by Paul Romer, who was at the time at UC Berkeley. The body of research has become known as new growth or endogenous growth theory.

Among the conclusions from this line of research are the following:
- Most economic growth, potentially as much as 85 percent, from 1890 to 1950 is attributable to technological progress rather than labor, capital, and other measurable inputs[65, 66, 67]
- The increase of over tenfold in productivity over the past century in the United States, measured as output per worker per unit time, is largely attributable to technological change.[68]
- About 50 percent of the improvement of economic growth in the G-5 emerging-economy countries (Brazil, China, India, Mexico, and South Africa) between 1950 and 1993 can be attributed to increased research intensity, and rising educational attainment of the population accounts for more than another 33 percent.[69]
- The social rate of return from new products and processes (i.e., the return to society as a whole) is much greater than the returns to the individual firms themselves.[70] This result reflects spillover

---

[65] Robert M. Solow, "Technical Change and the Aggregate Production Function," *Review of Economics and Statistics* 39 (August 1957): pp. 312–320.
[66] Robert M. Solow, "Growth Theory and After," Nobel Prize lecture, December 8, 1987, https://perma.cc/76AV-4P9R.
[67] David C. Mowery and Nathan Rosenberg, *Paths of Innovation: Technological Change in Twentieth-Century America* (Cambridge, UK: Cambridge University Press, 1998), p. 4.
[68] Paul Romer, "Endogenous Technological Change," *Journal of Political Economy* 98, no. 5 (October 1990): pp. S71–S103.
[69] Charles L. Jones, "Sources of U. S. Economic Growth in a World of Ideas," *American Economic Review* 92, no. 1 (2002): pp. 220–239.
[70] Edwin Mansfield et al., "Social and Private Rates of Return from Industrial Innovations," *The Quarterly Journal of Economics* 91, no. 2 (May 1977).

benefits from one company's or institution's research to another company's. It also creates the rationale for public funding of research rather than leaving all research to private investment.
- Published estimates of annual return on investment (ROI) for publicly funded R&D are 28 percent for academic science and engineering research aggregated together,[71] from 20 to 67 percent for agricultural research, and over 30 percent for pharmaceutical research.[72]
- In seven major manufacturing areas, including information processing, pharmaceuticals, and petroleum, academic research was directly responsible for about 11 percent of new products and 9 percent of new processes.[73] These estimates are almost surely conservative, since it is very difficult to trace the diffusion of influences from new ideas and the cross flow of ideas from one line of endeavor to another.
- Among metropolitan regions in the United States, 65 percent of the differences in economic growth can be accounted for through "high-tech" developments, with research centers and institutions being the most important factor in incubating high-tech industries.[74]

Overviews of the content and implications of this line of economics research are given by the 2007 *Rising above the Gathering Storm*[75] report of the Committee on Science, Engineering, and Public Policy

---

[71] Edwin Mansfield, "Academic Research and Industrial Innovation," *Research Policy* 20 (1991): pp. 1–12.
[72] Committee on Science, Engineering, and Public Policy, National Academies of Science, Engineering, and Public Policy, *Rising above the Gathering Storm: Energizing and Employing America for a Brighter Economic Future* (Washington, DC: National Academies Press, 2007), p. 48, https://perma.cc/KM2Y-MK9N.
[73] Edwin Mansfield, "Academic Research Underlying Industrial Innovations: Sources, Characteristics, and Financing," *The Review of Economics and Statistics* 77, no. 1 (February 1995).
[74] Ross C. DeVol, *America's High-Tech Economy: Growth, Development, and Risks for Metropolitan Areas*, p. 5, Milken Institute, Santa Monica, CA, July 13, 1999, https://perma.cc/RZX4-KA4N.
[75] Committee on Science, Engineering, and Public Policy, 2007, *op. cit.*, table 2.1, pp. 45–50.

Committee (COSEPUP) of the US National Academies, by Crow and Dabars,[76] and by Pelfrey and Atkinson.[77]

A comprehensive book[78] by former Columbia University provost Jonathan Cole deals with the impacts of university research on life in the United States and explores many specific advances attributable in part or in whole to university research.

The American Academy of Arts and Sciences (AAAS) recently completed the Lincoln Project,[79] which examined the state of public research universities in a time of reduced state funding and made recommendations for their future. One output was an informative report on the contributions of research universities to society.[80]

From this discussion it is apparent that much useful information and good analyses do exist concerning the importance and impact of university research. However, public understanding of these effects is sorely lacking. What has been, and will be, needed, are effective means of conveying the essence of these understandings to voters and thence to their elected representatives in government.

---

[76] Michael M. Crow and William B. Dabars, *Designing the New American University* (Baltimore, MD: Johns Hopkins University Press, 2015), pp. 145–158.

[77] Patricia A. Pelfrey and Richard C. Atkinson, "Science and the Entrepreneurial University," *Issues in Science and Technology* 26, no. 4 (Summer 2010).

[78] Jonathan R. Cole, *The Great American University: Its Rise to Preeminence, Its Indispensable National Role, Why It Must Be Protected* (New York: Public Affairs, 2010).

[79] American Academy of Arts and Sciences, "The Lincoln Project: Excellence and Access in Public Higher Education," https://perma.cc/XQ6P-B948.

[80] "Public Research Universities: Serving the Public Good," Lincoln Project, American Academy of Arts and Sciences, 2016, https://perma.cc/HX8W-2UJT.

17.
Support from the State

The people of California, as much as if not more than the people of any other State, have supported their colleges and their universities and their schools, because they recognize how important it is to the maintenance of a free society that its citizens be well educated.
  —*John F. Kennedy, Address at Charter Day, University of California, Berkeley*[1]

In the decade following the war, the University of California transformed itself from a first-rate regional university into a first-rate world university, and did this, in significant measure, because the taxpayers of California saw in the UC system a vehicle for their own betterment.
  —*Kevin Starr*[2]

It was…a period of prosperity in California and of strong gubernatorial support particularly from Earl Warren and Edmund G. ("Pat") Brown. The spirit was there and also the resources—a happy combination with spectacular results.
  —*Clark Kerr*[3]

The people and the state government of California have been remarkably supportive of the University of California at critical points in its history. They have also reflected confidence in the abilities of the university and California higher education in general to define themselves and carry out their missions in ways that best serve the

---

[1] John F. Kennedy, Address at the University of California, Berkeley, March 23, 1962, John F. Kennedy Presidential Library and Museum, https://perma.cc/T79G-R7LA.
[2] Kevin Starr, *California: A History* (New York: Modern Library, 2005), p. 244.
[3] Clark Kerr, *The Gold and the Blue: A Personal Memoir of the University of California, 1949–1967* (Berkeley: University of California Press, 2001), p. 56.

needs of the state. Seven notable aspects reflect the support and confidence of the state and the public. These factors have all been vital for the development of the University of California to the level of excellence that it has attained. They are also unusual in comparison with the rest of the United States.

- The university has been given rights of self-governance, insulated for the most part from political interests and actions (chapter 4).
- At critical points in its history, particularly in the period following World War II but also in the Progressive era of California in the early part of the twentieth century, the state has given the university high financial priority in ways that have been crucial for enabling its achievement of high academic stature, expanding enrollment, and serving the needs of the state broadly.
- The state accepted the goal that the university should be of a caliber equivalent to the best universities in the country, public or private. This goal has until recently been embedded in the level of financial support and notably in the policy that faculty salaries should be targeted toward the average of eight leading universities, four of them private and four public.
- The state accepted the differentiation of mission that was spelled out in the Master Plan of 1960 and allowed that plan to be created by California higher education itself. As part of the differentiation of mission, the state accepted an eligibility rate of 12.5 percent of graduates of California public schools for the University of California—the lowest of any major public research university in the country.
- In the late 1950s and at the request of the university, the state agreed to there being multiple general campuses of the university, even though this was a more expensive path. Enrollment caps were placed on individual campuses so as to sustain the quality of education and the college experience.
- The state has consistently adopted an enabling, rather than prescriptive, science and technology policy. The University of California has the status of being the research arm of the state. The state therefore supports research at the university at a high level, and places most of its own research with the university.

- As federal support of research grew after World War II, the state agreed to let the university retain a large fraction of overhead funds from extramural grants even though many of the costs which they recognize are funded through the state budget. These monies could be used flexibly as an "opportunity" fund.

The remainder of this chapter explores each of these areas in more depth.

SELF-GOVERNANCE

One of the main outgrowths of the turbulence and contentions surrounding the university in the 1870s (chapter 2) was to embed governance autonomy for the University of California in the 1879 state constitution (chapter 4). This status gives the university a level of independent governance rivaled in the US by only the public universities and colleges in Michigan and the University of Minnesota. The authority for governance lies with the Board of Regents. Although eighteen of the twenty-six members of that board are appointed by the sitting governor with confirmation by the state senate, and four more are elected statewide officials, long terms of twelve years and the checks and balances in the appointment process for the appointed regents have served to remove the political process from the board to a substantial degree. There have of course been some exceptions over time, which are described in chapter 2.

By contrast, in some other states (chapter 4) regents are elected by popular vote (Michigan, Colorado, Nebraska, and Nevada) or by the legislature (e.g., Minnesota). Matters that come before those boards are judged to a greater extent by projections of their appeal to the electorate. Since most other public universities in the United States do not have the degree of constitutional autonomy that the University of California has, the state legislatures in other states are, on the whole, more intrusive into the affairs of their public universities.

HIGH PRIORITY FOR RESOURCES AND INVESTMENT

Until recent decades, the University of California has largely been given high priority for both one-time and ongoing financial support from the state, particularly at two critical times in its history. The first of these periods was the early part of the twentieth century, during the time of the California Progressive movement[4] and the UC presidency of Benjamin Ide Wheeler (chapter 2). One of the foundations of the Progressive movement was belief in the benefits of widespread public higher education.[5]

The time of the Progressives coincided with the latter portion (1912–19) of the period that Benjamin Ide Wheeler was president of the University of California and resulted in both substantial funding for higher education and a major increase in enrollment throughout California public higher education. By 1920 California had the highest public higher-education enrollment in the country, despite being still only tenth in population.[6] Much of Wheeler's building of the University of California to distinction, including the launch of UC into the first tier of academic research through Gilbert Newton Lewis and other faculty recruitments (chapter 9), was enabled by the attention paid by the Progressives to widespread public higher education. Before 1900 annual operating funds provided to UC from the state were no greater than the yield of the endowment for the university. As of 1900 state funding started to grow, and then during the period 1910 to 1920, rose from about $800,000 per year to $3.1 million per year (i.e., by a factor of about four.)[7]

The next great period of investment by the state in the University of California came as a result of World War II and the policies of two forward-thinking governors, Earl Warren and Edmund G. (Pat) Brown,

---

[4] Kevin Starr, *Inventing the Dream: California through the Progressive Era* (Oxford University Press, 1986).

[5] John Aubrey Douglass, *The California Idea and American Higher Education: 1850 to the 1960 Master Plan*, chapter 3, "Progressives and the California Idea" (Stanford, CA: Stanford University Press, 2000a).

[6] John Aubrey Douglass, "Californians and Public Higher Education: Political Culture, Educational Opportunity, and State Policy Making," *History of Higher Education Annual* 16, no. 4 (1996): pp. 71–104.

[7] Douglass, 2000a, *op. cit.*, p. 110.

both of whom gave public higher education great priority. In World War II, there had been much buildup of wartime manufacturing and military bases in California. The change to the state was enormous. Gerald Nash[8] observed, "In four short years the war brought a maturation to the West [and in particular California] that in peacetime might have taken generations to accomplish." The wartime surge also brought a huge surplus to California's state treasury.

After the war there was a large downturn in wartime manufacturing, and a surge of returning veterans needing employment. Earl Warren,[9] who was governor from 1943 until 1953, devoted much attention to postwar planning. Warren was himself a graduate of the University of California, which had provided him the classic public-university route for upward mobility following very humble beginnings as a child of a Norwegian immigrant family in Bakersfield, California. Warren was a UC classmate of UC president Robert Gordon Sproul, with whom he had a longtime association and friendship. He had strong nonpartisan abilities, was a popular and very accomplished governor, and was the beneficiary of the cross-filing initiative of the Progressives when he was nominated for a second term as governor by both major political parties in 1946. He was elected to a third term in 1950 and then left the governorship when he was appointed by President Eisenhower as chief justice of the US Supreme Court. Warren himself was an adherent of the Progressives and their principles as he entered his political career. In 1944 Warren launched the Postwar Reconstruction and Reemployment Commission. Working with the commission and with George D. Strayer, an emeritus professor of education from Columbia Teachers' College, he identified two major "shock-absorber" programs—modernization of infrastructure and enlargement of public higher education—that would bring employment and betterment for the returning veterans and invest in the human infrastructure for the future economic growth of California.[10, 11] At the peak of the enrollment surge of returning

---

[8] Gerald D. Nash, *The American West Transformed: The Impact of the Second World War* (Bloomington, IN: Indiana University Press, 1985), p. vii.
[9] A biography of Warren is given by Jim Newton, *Justice for All: Earl Warren and the Nation He Made* (New York: Riverhead Books, 2007).
[10] John Aubrey Douglass, "Earl Warren's New Deal: Post-War Planning and Higher Education," *Journal of Policy History* 12, no. 4 (2000b): pp. 473–512.

veterans in 1947, veterans constituted just over half of the enrollment of the University of California.[12] Coresponding figures for the state colleges and community colleges were 70% and 36%, respectively.[13]

With the continued support of Governor Warren, the UC Board of Regents and the State Board of Education launched a three-person task force, composed of Strayer and two longtime senior officials from the University of California and California state colleges—Monroe Deutsch and Aubrey Douglass,[14] respectively. The charge to the task force was to outline the ways in which public higher education in California could be sharply increased. The resulting report[15] delineated the functions of the three segments of California public higher education and provided an ambitious road map for the path ahead. It also concluded that the desired expansion was financially feasible, given the resources that the state had at the time.

Between 1942 and 1948, the state had built up a budgetary surplus of $813 million, more than the entire state operations budget for 1948. These accumulated funds went very largely to the two shock-absorber programs, with about one-third going to public higher education to fund the greatly increased enrollments and necessary construction. Enrollment increases in the state colleges were especially large, with state college enrollment surpassing University of California enrollment for the first time in 1954.[16]

There was another large source of financial support for the returning veterans—the GI Bill,[17] which was enacted nationally in 1944

---

[11] Douglass, 2000a, *loc. cit.*, chapter 6, "Postwar Planning and Higher Education."
[12] UC undertook an exceptionally large number of special-action admissions (i.e., admissions in exception to normal eligibility requirements) for returning veterans, rising to nearly 3,000 freshman admissions in 1947 at Berkeley and UCLA (Douglass, 2007, *op. cit.*, pp. 89, 118).
[13] Nancy C. Diamond, "New Models of Excellence: Rising Research Universities in the Postwar Era, 1945–1990" (PhD dissertation, University of Maryland, Baltimore County, 2000), pp. 178–179.
[14] Aubrey Douglass was the grandfather of present-day author and scholar, John Aubrey Douglass.
[15] Monroe E. Deutsch, Aubrey A. Douglass, and George D. Strayer, "A Report of a Survey of the Needs of California in Higher Education, March 1, 1948, https://perma.cc/GS25-6QLT.
[16] Douglass, 2000b, *loc. cit.*
[17] Keith Olson, "The G. I. Bill and Higher Education: Success and Surprise," *American Quarterly* 25, no. 5 (December 1973): pp. 596–610.

as the Servicemen's Readjustment Act. A classic voucher plan, the GI Bill paid the costs of higher education for the large number of returning World War II veterans. California had both the highest percentage and the highest absolute number of veterans in public higher education among the states of the United States. California public higher education was a very large beneficiary of the GI Bill.

As measures of this huge investment and growth, Geiger[18] notes that appropriations by the state to the university increased by an average of 24 percent *per year* between 1946 and 1951; that the amount that UC received from the GI Bill ($11.5 million in 1946–47) exceeded the combined instructional budgets of the two main UC campuses, Berkeley and UCLA; and that the Berkeley instructional budget expressed as spending per enrolled student grew by 56 percent from 1946 to 1950 and then another 45 percent by 1954. As well, the state provided over $120 million of construction funds during the years 1946–50, of which $25 million was spent at Berkeley, much of it to provide modern facilities for the physical sciences.

After the intervening gubernatorial term of Goodwin Knight (1953–59), Edmund G. ("Pat") Brown[19] was governor from 1959 to 1967. His term coincided with the tenure of Clark Kerr as UC president. Although Brown and Kerr started with a tense relationship,[20] they shared the desire for continued growth of higher education and worked together on the two major initiatives: the 1960 California Master Plan for Higher Education and the creation of three new campuses of the University of California in San Diego (La Jolla), Irvine, and Santa Cruz.[21]

Smelser[22] examined the large growth and change in California higher education over the two decades, 1950–70. What had been a

---

[18] Roger L. Geiger, *Research and Relevant Knowledge: American Research Universities since World War II* (Oxford: Oxford University Press, 1993), p. 74.
[19] Ethan Rarick, *California Rising: The Life and Times of Pat Brown* (Berkeley: University of California Press, 2005).
[20] Rarick, 2005, *op. cit.*, p. 145.
[21] Brown liked to tell the fabricated story that in the 1958 gubernatorial election, he failed to carry only three counties—San Diego, Orange, and Santa Cruz—so he decided that the people in those counties should be better educated and hence built UC campuses in each of those counties (Rarick, 2005, *op. cit.*, p. 138).
[22] Neil J. Smelser, "Growth, Structural Change, and Conflict in California Higher Education, 1950–1970," in Neil J. Smelser and Gabriel Almond, *Public Higher Education in California* (Berkeley: University of California Press, 1974)

combined enrollment of 200,000 in all three sectors of public higher education in 1950 became almost 500,000 in 1960 and then over a million in 1970, a huge rate of growth. The level of state support for the three sectors rose by over a factor of ten from $62.6 million in 1950 to $756.8 million in 1970, neither figure counting capital outlay, which was in addition and also large. The budgetary surplus from World War II and the GI Bill covered this growth up to about 1960, when considerations started being made of year-round operations, increased fees, and imposition of tuition as additional ways of addressing the growth financially. The situation was also helped by the fact that external sources, most notably federal research support, assumed a greater portion of financing starting in the 1960s.

Later, Gray Davis, who was governor from 1999 to 2003, made education a high priority, including higher education and research. He brought about the funding for the California (now Governor Gray Davis) Institutes for Science and Innovation (chapter 14).

Financing of public higher education by the state of California is the one of these seven factors that has slipped the most in recent years, an issue that is considered in chapters 2 and 21.

MAINTAINING THE CALIBER OF THE BEST UNIVERSITIES, PRIVATE OR PUBLIC

From the start, California sought for its public university to be the equivalent of the best, with Yale and the University of Michigan being two early role models. Yale had been the institution of many of the university's founders, including Presidents Durant and Gilman. As noted in a quote at the beginning of chapter 15, at the start the Trustees of the College of California made the criterion that courses of instruction should be "equal to those of the Eastern colleges" a condition for merging their institution with the new University of California. Michigan was the model for the incorporation of constitutional autonomy into the constitution of 1879. These aspirations remained largely qualitative until the twentieth century, when they became quantitative in two main ways—faculty and administrative salary scales and the budgeted student-to-faculty ratio.

Faculty Salaries

Since 1920 faculty salaries for the University of California have been established by quantitative comparison with other highly distinguished US universities. The history of the quantitative-comparison methodology for setting University of California faculty salaries is laid out in the appendix to a policy document[23] that was adopted in 1969 by the California Coordinating Council for Higher Education (CCHE, the predecessor body to the California Postsecondary Education Commission, CPEC).

Starting in 1920 the University of California adopted an academic salary scale that was derived from comparison with five other distinguished universities—Chicago, Columbia, Harvard, Michigan, and Yale—denoted as the "Big 5." Note the overall high level of distinction of the comparison universities. Only one of them was public, and even it was generally regarded as the best of the other publics. Faculty salaries are generally higher at the leading private universities than for public universities. These comparisons were the basis for the state budget requests that the university made to the legislature and were generally accepted as a valid approach. In 1960 Chicago was replaced in this group by Princeton.

With the arrival of the California Master Plan for Higher Education in 1960, the matter of the quantitative-comparison methodology became a responsibility of CCHE and then its successor body, CPEC. The principle of comparability as the means for setting salary scales was accepted by CCHE in 1962. There then became concern that there should be a broader group of comparison universities and that public institutions should be better represented within the comparison group. In 1967 the comparison group was expanded in number to eight through the addition of Illinois, Cornell, and Wisconsin, so that publics now constituted three of the eight. In 1968 Stanford and SUNY–Buffalo replaced Columbia and Princeton, so that now there were four publics and four privates.[24]

---

[23] California Coordinating Council for Higher Education, "Review of Procedures to Be Used in CCHE Annual Study of Faculty Salaries and Benefits," Report no. 69-6, May 6, 1969, https://perma.cc/3YJ7-UDEA.

[24] Note also that there was some jockeying regarding the cost of living for the areas represented by the comparison institution. New York, where Columbia is located, was at the time the area with the highest cost of living in the United States.

In the referenced 1969 report, CCHE took the position that the comparison group for UC should be expanded from eight to nineteen, with the nineteen comparison universities being Stanford, Chicago, the entire Big Ten, and the seven Ivy League universities other than Dartmouth—ten public universities and nine private universities.

The Comparison 19 did not last long, and the methodology reverted back to a Comparison 8, which has now for decades been composed of Harvard, MIT, Stanford, and Yale as the four private universities and Illinois, Michigan, SUNY–Buffalo, and Virginia as the four public universities. That set of comparison institutions was developed by an advisory committee that consisted of members from CPEC, the State Legislative Analyst's Office, the State Department of Finance, and administrative and UC Academic Senate leaders from UC and CSU.[25]

What is important to recognize from this history is the principle, formally accepted by the State of California, that the University of California and all its campuses should have parity of faculty salaries with the mean of both the leading private research universities and the leading public research universities. Thereby it would have salaries a cut above the leading public universities. The fact that the resultant salary scales would apply equally on all campuses of the university would underscore the intention that all campuses should be able to rise to top stature.

Figure 17-1 shows the actual trace of faculty salaries over the thirty-year period from 1980 to 2010, in comparison with the averages of the four private and four public institutions. For many years the comparison was made and endorsed by CPEC until CPEC ceased operations in 2011. Historically, including years before the start of the chart, faculty salaries were maintained close to the average of the Comparison 8 institutions, but as of about 2002, they started lagging and are now closer to the average of the four public comparison institutions than to the average of the full Comparison 8. Also apparent from the figure is that faculty salaries for the four comparison private universities have diverged upward from faculty salaries at the four

---

[25] Mercer Group, "Total Remuneration Study for General Campus Ladder-Rank Faculty: Presentation of Final Results," July 30, 2014, https://perma.cc/Z6RT-NLG8.

public comparison institutions during recent decades, reflecting a national trend.

Total compensation, including nonsalary factors such as retirement and other benefits, is also computed and compared periodically through independent studies.[26]

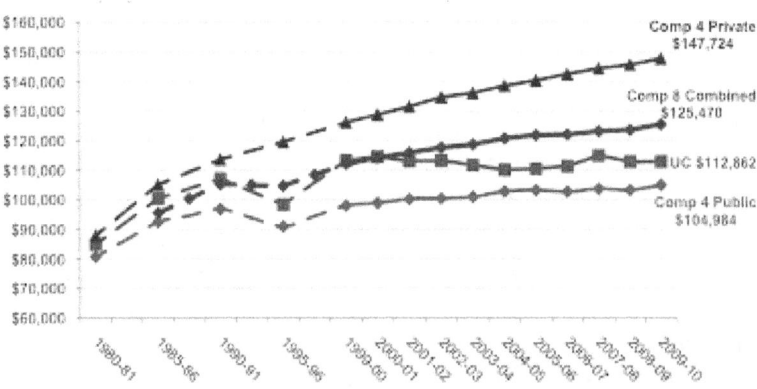

Figure 17-1. Average professorial series faculty salaries (assistant, associate, full), general campus only, University of California and comparison eight universities, adjusted for inflation to 2009 dollars[27]

Administrative salaries

During the years of statewide coordination by CCHE and CPEC, guidelines for administrative salaries were also computed through a similar comparison methodology, as is shown in the last such report from CPEC.[28] From 1992 until this final survey in 2004, there were twenty-six comparison institutions for UC—all leading universities, with fourteen of them public and twelve private. The current (2015)

---

[26] Mercer Group, 2014, *loc. cit.*
[27] Office of the President, University of California, "Biennial Accountability Sub-Report on Faculty Competitiveness," Figure16, discussion item for regents' meeting of January 19, 2011, https://perma.cc/S2CJ-CVGF.
[28] "Executive Compensation in California Public Higher Education, 2003–2004," California Postsecondary Education Commission, https://perma.cc/D67B-A7XS.

guidelines for setting salaries of academic deans within the University of California are available.[29]

State-Budgeted Student/Faculty Ratio and State Funding per Student

Per-student funding from the state, expressed in part by the budgeted student-to-faculty ratio, is an important measure of the commitment of the state to higher education and can be traced through the various periods of the history of the university. As reported by Clark Kerr,[30] the state-budgeted student-faculty (S/F) ratio at Berkeley up to 1950 was typically in the range of 22 to 25 students per faculty member. After a surge due to the postwar enrollment of veterans returning from World War II, the budgeted S/F ratio fell to about 18 students per faculty member in 1953, 16.5 in 1962, and 14.5 in 1966. The 14.5 figure could be compared to the typical private-university S/F ratio of 8 to 12 students per faculty member, and to typical public-university S/F ratios of 18 to 20 students per faculty member at the time—again about halfway in between. Kerr credits both Governor Pat Brown and the Board of Regents as being very supportive of this move toward a lower S/F ratio and hence improved quality of education. This was very tangible strong state support for the university and was of considerable importance for the building of the university through the 1960s and 1970s.

More recently the S/F ratio for UC has slipped back to higher values because of stringencies in state funding. The target ratio agreed to between the university and the state had risen to 17.5 students per faculty member by 1980 and rose further by degrees to about 21 in 2013.[31, 32]

---

[29] "Deans' Salary Structure Analysis," University of California, https://perma.cc/V3YM-4XFL.
[30] Clark Kerr, *The Gold and the Blue: A Personal Memoir of the University of California, 1949–1967*, vol. 1 (Berkeley: University of California Press, 2001), pp. 78–80.
[31] Kerr, 2001, *op. cit.*, fig. 2, p. 80.
[32] University of California, "Budget for Current Operations, 2014–2015," display 10, p. S-16, https://perma.cc/J4JM-8NSH.

DIFFERENTIATION OF MISSIONS

The formal differentiation of missions among the three sectors of public higher education in California, formalized through the Master Plan of 1960, enabled the University of California to be the one designated research university within the public system. The Master Plan focused both the research mission and state research support on the University of California. Because of the role of the California State University (CSU), the Master Plan could fix the eligibility rate of high school graduates for the University of California at 12.5 percent. That low percentage enabled the University of California to develop in research-based graduate and professional education without being flooded with undergraduate students. However, as discussed in chapter 5, the 12.5 and 33 percent eligibility rates for UC and CSU, respectively, now place California very low in the percentage of the population receiving four-year bachelor's degrees, too low for supporting the high-tech economy of the state.

CREATING MULTIPLE CAMPUSES AND CAPPING THEIR ENROLLMENTS

A second general (i.e., all-purpose) campus in Los Angeles was chartered in the early part of the twentieth century because of the growth of the population of the greater Los Angeles area and the distance from there to the original campus in Berkeley. As enrollments grew rapidly after World War II, the obvious question was whether to let these two general campuses grow to the large sizes that would be required to serve the purposes of the public research university in a fast-growing state or to continue to create additional general campuses for a multicampus university. The latter path was chosen, and led to the conversion of Davis, Riverside, and Santa Barbara to general campuses; the development of San Diego, Irvine, and Santa Cruz as new general campuses; and the selection of 27,500 as an enrollment cap for any one campus. That path was followed further with the creation of the Merced campus. The total campus enrollments drifted upwards by 2016 to 40,200 for Berkeley and 45,000 for UCLA. In 2016 Davis was at 35,200, Irvine at 33,500, and San Diego at 35,800. Other general campuses are lower in enrollment, either because of agreements with the community (Santa Barbara, Santa Cruz) or still having capacity left for development (Riverside, Merced).

While part of the motivation for the multicampus approach was clearly political and designed to serve the various populated regions of the state with local campuses of the university, Kerr[33] makes it clear that it was also a matter of avoiding large campus size so as to provide better education to students. From the standpoints of Berkeley and UCLA, the decision to go further down the road toward multiple campuses was enabling for development and enhancement of academic stature, because it relieved them of the very large enrollment burdens that would otherwise have come their ways.

There are multicampus universities in some other states. A few (e.g., Illinois, Nevada) are universities with a common mission and similar expectations for multiple campuses, but none have the large number of campuses with the same research mission that the University of California has. The University of California is unique in that sense.

The multicampus approach was more expensive, but was enabled by the affluent times, the strong support of Governors Earl Warren and Pat Brown for the university, and favorable budget decisions of the state government in the 1950s and 1960s.

AN ENABLING STATE SCIENCE AND TECHNOLOGY POLICY

State policy for science and technology in California has been analyzed by Zumeta[34] and by Geiger and Sá,[35] who compare California with New York, Arizona, and Georgia. The latter book expands upon an

---

[33] Kerr, 2001, *op. cit.*, pp. 78–83.
[34] William Zumeta, "The Public Interest and State Policies Affecting Academic Research in California," in David Dill and Frans Van Vught, eds., *National Innovation and the Academic Research Enterprise: Public Policy in Global Perspective* (Baltimore, MD: Johns Hopkins University Press, 2010). Also appears as Working Paper #2008-01, Daniel J. Evans School of Public Affairs, University of Washington, Seattle, 2008, https://perma.cc/J52X-6V9Q.
[35] Roger L. Geiger and Creso M. Sá, *Tapping the Riches of Science: Universities and the Promise of Economic Growth* (Cambridge, MA: Harvard University Press, 2008), pp. 84–116.

earlier paper[36] by the same authors treating science policies among the states in general. The California Council on Science and Technology (see chapter 16) analyzes the state climate for science, technology, and innovation periodically.[37]

Despite an intense and sometimes heated political climate, California has in various ways over the years seen fit to pursue a multifaceted policy of enablement of research and innovation, rather than a more prescriptive approach. This relatively nonpolitical approach has been of considerable value to both the University of California and the California research community. The partnership of the state with the university and with the research community in these areas has been built on performance, confidence, and trust, recognizing that the institutions themselves can best determine what to do and how to do it. One very auspicious result from these policies and other factors has been that California has more than 20 percent of national R&D expenditures, despite having only 13.5 percent of national gross domestic product (GDP) and 12 percent of the population of the United States.[38]

The initiative in 2000 for the California (now Governor Gray Davis) Institutes of Science and Innovation (chapter 14) left the definitions of the institutes and choice of subject matter to the University of California. The university then solicited proposals with both those aspects remaining undefined and subject to proposals and competition through peer review. Similarly, when Governor Arnold Schwarzenegger worked with the legislature to provide state funds in the amount of $40 million in support of the proposal of the Berkeley-led group for the BP Energy Biosciences Institute (chapter 18), the allocation was made without attempts to influence the content of the proposal. Several

---

[36] Roger L. Geiger and Creso Sá, "Beyond Technology Transfer: US State Policies to Harness University Research for Economic Development," *Minerva* 43 (2005): pp. 1–21.
[37] California Council for Science and Technology, *Innovate 2 Innovation: An Assessment of California's Innovation Ecosystem, Phase II*, 2011, Executive Summary, https://perma.cc/UJ4Z-USSP, *Phase I*, https://perma.cc/7K6V-9MNV; "Science and Technology Innovation in California," 2002, https://perma.cc/5SRK-QZ6Y; "CREST 9, California's Science Base: Size, Quality, and Productivity," 1999, https://perma.cc/ABR8-GEWL.
[38] Geiger and Sá, 2005, *op. cit.*, p. 6.

authors[39, 40, 41] have analyzed policy and implementation of policy in other states. For many states, there have been political definitions of what would be done and who would be selected for large research institutes of similar nature to California's, without the elements of definition by the research community and peer-reviewed competition. California itself is not entirely without that problem, having established the California Institute for Regenerative Medicine (CIRM),[42] a grant-funding entity for stem-cell research, through a 2004 ballot initiative[43] that created a $3 billion bond issue. This was made possible by California's well-used initiative process.

Another aspect of the enablement of the University of California by the state was the *de facto* establishment of the university as the official research arm of the state. In this regard, state funding built the infrastructure that made the University of California highly competitive for federal grants as they grew in the years following World War II.[44] It was a fortunate coincidence for California that the period during which federal funding for research grew so much coincided with both the postwar state budget surplus and the willingness of Governors Warren and then Brown to provide the funds to build the university in both size and infrastructure.

By virtue of the university's role as the research arm of the state, it was natural for the California (Governor Gray Davis) Institutes for Science and Innovation (chapter 14) to be placed within the university when they were formed in the year 2000. As well, the state places a large amount of research of its own in the university, in the forms of support for specific initiatives, seed money, matching funds, and general support for agricultural research. The total amount of state funding designated annually for research projects one way or another in recent years has been about $600 million. Some of the larger specific

---

[39] Geiger and Sá, 2008, *op. cit.*, pp. 84–116.
[40] Stuart W. Leslie, "Regional Disadvantage: Replicating Silicon Valley in New York's Capital Region," *Technology and Culture* 42, no. 2 (2001): pp. 236–264.
[41] Irwin Feller, "American State Governments as Models for National Science Policy," *Journal of Policy Analysis and Management* 11, no. 2 (1992): pp. 288–309.
[42] CIRM, California Institute for Regenerative Medicine, 2017 Annual Report, https://perma.cc/BJ43-R6NQ.
[43] "California Proposition 71, Stem Cell Research (2004)," *Ballotpedia*, https://perma.cc/3YYT-EQL2.
[44] Geiger, 1993, *op. cit.*, pp. 73–75.

items from the 2015–16 budget are $4.8 million of administrative support funds for the Governor Gray Davis Institutes and $11 million each for tobacco-related disease and breast cancer programs administered by UC with grants inside and outside UC. An additional $200 million comes to the university from the budgets of state agencies (notably Health Care Services, Social Services, Transportation, Food and Agriculture, and Education) for specific research areas and projects. State funding accounts for about 13 percent of total research funding within UC, a substantial fraction.[45]

One can view the research funding as a form of support for, and confidence in, the university from the state. However, the research is also an important form of service from the university to the state, a bidirectional partnership.

RETENTION OF A SUBSTANTIAL PORTION OF INDIRECT COSTS FROM CONTRACTS AND GRANTS

As, has already been noted in Chapter 14, as the volume of grants from the federal government to the university grew during and after World War II, the Board of Regents created a special fund to hold the associated indirect-cost revenue, with expenditures from the fund going both to the units generating the projects and a variety of special purposes. In 1954 this special fund had grown to over $13 million annually, and its existence was challenged by Governor Goodwin Knight since the indirect costs, in fact, reimbursed expenses that were already being made largely from the state budget. The regents vigorously defended the fund because of its flexibility and utility for building the quality of the university. In a compromise it was agreed that 55 percent of the net receipts[46] of indirect costs would be used by the university to offset what would otherwise be state-budget expenses and the other 45 percent would remain with the university,

---

[45] University of California, "Budget for Current Operations, 2015–16," pp. 110–118, https://perma.cc/B9F9-KH93.
[46] After off-the-top costs of about 20% for direct support of research, e.g., costs of Sponsored Projects Offices on campuses, are removed.

named the Regents' Opportunity Fund and now renamed the University Opportunity Fund.[47] The Opportunity Fund has been used very effectively over the years for a variety of special purposes including seed monies and faculty start-ups and retentions.

Faculty members sometimes bemoan the "loss" of half the indirect costs from grants to the state, but the nominal commitment for the state might have been to return just those portions of the indirect costs that are not for services that are funded within the state budget or for costs of research administration itself. Because it retains 45 percent of the net revenue from indirect costs, the university does then effectively receive a substantial Opportunity Fund allocation from the state. The net benefit to the university from this agreement has been reduced over the years as a cap on reimbursement of administrative costs by the federal government has come into effect while unfunded administrative needs created by government management and reporting requirements have increased.[48]

The concept and history of indirect costs and policies for both the University of California and the Berkeley campus are spelled out in a summary document.[49]

---

[47] Geiger, 1993, *op. cit.*, p. 75.
[48] Starting in 1993, the Circular A-21 cap on indirect costs for administration is 26%, whereas current Berkeley campus actual administrative expenses for sponsored research are over 36% ("Facilities and Administrative Costs Overview", Office of the Chief Financial Officer, University of California, Berkeley, March 2016, https://perma.cc/Y952-P7QV.
[49] Research Support Policy Committee, Berkeley Campus, University of California, "Indirect Costs at Berkeley: A Primer," November 16, 2004, https://perma.cc/4JGA-L3VS..

18.
RELATIONS WITH INDUSTRY, TECHNOLOGY TRANSFER, AND ECONOMIC DEVELOPMENT

We are just now perceiving that the university's invisible product, knowledge, may be the most powerful single element in our culture, affecting the rise and fall of professions and even of social classes, or regions, and even nations.
　—*Clark Kerr, in 1963*[1]

The most important thing a state government can do to improve local economies is to support research universities.
　—*Gray Davis, Governor of California*[2]

With some of the world's finest universities and research institutions, the Golden State has more scientists, engineers, and researchers and invests more on research and development than any other state. As a leader in developing new technologies, California will reap tremendous rewards for our economy and environment from this investment in our innovation infrastructure.
　—*Arnold Schwarzenegger, Governor of California*[3]

These questions troubled me then. They trouble me still, now that the past decade has brought forth fresh reports of universities partnering with venture capitalists to sell Internet courses at a profit and medical schools taking money from pharmaceutical companies in return for allowing them to help design educational programs for physicians. Observing these trends, I worry that commercialization may be

---

[1] Clark Kerr, *The Uses of the University*, 1st ed. (Cambridge, MA: Harvard University Press, 1963), p. vi.
[2] Comment made in announcing the California (now Governor Gray Davis) Institutes for Science and Innovation. Cited in "3 Research Institutes for California," *New York Times*, December 8, 2000.
[3] Cited in "Gov. Schwarzenegger Proposes $95 Million Innovation Initiative," California Council on Science and Technology, January 2, 2007, https://perma.cc/GEV7-93P7.

changing the nature of academic institutions in ways we will come to regret. By trying so hard to acquire more money for their work, universities may compromise values that are essential to the continued confidence and loyalty of faculty, students, alumni, and even the general public.
—Derek Bok[4]

University research has become increasingly important as a source of new discoveries and inventions that can become commercialized innovations that lead and build the economy as well as aid society. The large magnitude of that effect is documented by the various endogenous-growth studies described in chapter 16. Yet good pathways for bringing university research into social and economic use, which is known as *technology transfer*, are varied and still being developed. California has some remarkable success stories, including Silicon Valley, the hi-tech makeover of the San Diego economy, and the development of the biotechnology industry in both the San Francisco Bay Area and San Diego. The University of California has been a central actor. This chapter is devoted to these topics, along with a trace of how technology transfer has developed in the University of California.

THE CHALLENGES OF TECHNOLOGY TRANSFER FOR UNIVERSITIES

The areas of technology transfer and relations with industry can be complex and challenging for research universities, especially public universities. Many factors are at play. On the positive side, some of them are the following:
- Moving discoveries stemming from university research into commercial use is valuable to the economy and society.
- It is politically effective for a public research university to demonstrate clearly to the government and the populace the

---

[4] Derek Bok, *Universities and the Marketplace*, preface (Princeton, NJ: Princeton University Press, 2003).

ways in which its research has been important to society and the economy of the state.
- In engineering, many sciences, economics, business, and some other fields, close contact with industry provides faculty members with a grounding of realism, awareness of current issues in the industrial world, and a source of ideas for high-impact university research.
- Leaders of industry can be effective for gaining support for a public university at the state level, reflecting their needs for educated manpower and research in their areas of interest. They can also be valuable members of advisory boards and sources of direct support for research of interest to the company.
- There is revenue to be derived from licensing successful patents. That usually comes without restrictions and can therefore be used flexibly for university needs. This source of funds is unpredictable and chancy, but can be particularly valuable in times of budgetary stress.

On the negative side these are some of the issues at play:
- Interactions with industry, and particularly funding to universities from industry, may alter the essential purposes of the university or taint it in other ways. Industrial desires, coupled with industrial funding, may affect administrative decisions, undermine academic needs, and affect choices of research. Bok,[5] Newfield,[6] and Kirp[7] are among those who have explored these concerns. Of course faculty choices of research, particularly in the sciences and engineering, have always been influenced by the availability of funds to finance the research, starting with funding by foundations before World War II, continuing through the large-scale government funding that came into being after World War II, and on through the rise in industrial funding of research that started around 1980.

---

[5] Bok, 2003, *loc. cit.*
[6] Christopher Newfield, *Ivy and Industry: Business and the Making of the American University, 1880–1980* (Durham, NC: Duke University Press, 2003).
[7] David L. Kirp, *Shakespeare, Einstein, and the Bottom Line: The Marketing of Higher Education* (Cambridge, MA: Harvard University Press, 2009).

- Greater relations with, and funding from, industry benefit different disciplines within the academy to different extents, as is also the case for government funding of research. The growth of research funding from government and industry has been challenged as a major factor leading to current concerns about the future of the humanities and liberal education in research universities, particularly public ones.[8]
- If a faculty member or a university administrator has a financial interest in a company (e.g., ownership, consulting, or receiving licensing royalties) and receives funding for and/or carries out research relevant to that company, then a conflict of interest may exist. Furthermore, if a faculty member devotes excessive time, energy, and focus to a corporate interest or is an officer of a company, then a conflict of commitment exists.
- For a publicly funded university, there can be issues relating to whether the university is improperly favoring one or a few companies or industries in the state in comparison with others.

This array of difficult, complex, and overlapping issues calls for structures and policies that enable faculty members to interact synergistically with industry and that enable and promote movement of university inventions and research into the commercial world. There should be mechanisms that enable and facilitate patentable inventions to be disclosed, recognized, written as successful patent applications for optimal coverage, licensed, and moved effectively into and through the marketplace. At the same time, the essential values of the university must be preserved, the marketplace must be treated equitably, and conflicts of interest and commitment must be controlled. Finding the appropriate balance and policies has been a continual part of my own career.[9]

---

[8] See, e.g., Commission on the Humanities and Social Sciences, "The Heart of the Matter: The Humanities and Social Sciences for a Vibrant, Competitive, and Secure Nation," American Academy of Arts and Sciences, 2013, https://perma.cc/CKT5-3GT2.

[9] I have patents secured both before and after the Bayh-Dole Act, with those before belonging to the government and those after belonging to the university; have had research funded by industry; and had both long-term and short-term consulting relationships before moving into the provost position at Berkeley. As a new dean of the College of Chemistry in 1981, I and the higher administration were faced with an almost total lack of existing policy or guidelines when one of my chemical engineering faculty colleagues joined with a colleague from Stanford to create Engenics Corporation, a commercial endeavor that would also support the university research of

WHAT IT TAKES TO "TRANSFER" TECHNOLOGY

Transferring university-generated technology to industry for commercial use is not straightforward. Typically faculty research stops with the discovery of new knowledge or the codification of it. Between that point and commercial usage, there must usually be many back-and-forth steps. These steps include awareness, further R&D heavy on the D (development) side and decisions to fund that R&D, combined technical and commercial evaluation by sufficiently knowledgeable persons, assessment of the likely competition, convincing demonstrations of utility and market, and both decisions and negotiations to license the technology.[10] The word *innovation* is often used in the business world to reflect the totality of these steps. For good reasons this gap between research and implementation has become known popularly as the Valley of Death.

Many mechanisms have been devised and utilized by universities, corporations, and would-be brokers or other middlemen in efforts to bridge this gap effectively. Consulting by faculty with industry is a time-tested and effective method. The flow of people, whereby university graduates go to companies for employment after graduation, is another method. Sometimes the faculty member who is associated with an invention leaves the university temporarily or permanently to start a company, but more often faculty inventors involve themselves with such companies as prime consultants. Academic research may be sponsored by industrial companies, who intend to stay close to the research and continually evaluate possible commercialization. In some cases consortia of companies have funded research, to be close to it but with recognition that no one of the companies enjoys an advantage over the others. Industry-university partnerships may be formed for research that the company believes has potential for innovations, and in some instances colocated university-industry partnerships, such as

---

the faculty founders. (For further information on Engenics Corp., see Martin Kenny, *Biotechnology: The University-Industrial Complex* [New Haven, CT: Yale University Press, 1986], pp. 48–49.) I participated centrally in policy development for these matters for the Berkeley campus and then university-wide. I was also a member of the founding committee of the Council for Chemical Research (CCR) as of 1980 and was subsequently chair of CCR in 1989.

[10] See, e.g., Everett M. Rogers, *Diffusion of Innovations*, 5th ed. (New York: Free Press, 2003).

the BP Energy Biosciences Institute at UC Berkeley described later in this chapter, have come into being.

Starting with the California Institutes for Science and Innovation (chapter 14) in 2000, there has been a wave of major research institutes at universities accompanied by substantial industrial funding and interaction. Some universities have also created industrial parks to bring companies close to university researchers and to facilitate the formation of start-up companies that will utilize university research. A prime example is Stanford Industrial Park (see below). Another within UC is the Irvine Corporation's University Research Park,[11] which adjoins the campus of the University of California, Irvine. Before the Irvine Research Park was formed, Hitachi Corporation's Plumwood House research laboratory became located in the biomedical research complex of the University of California, Irvine,[12] opening in 1990.

More recently, incubator facilities on university campuses have come into vogue, usually as dedicated laboratory space and with available consultants. These incubators are designed as places where ideas from research can be given initial study and tests toward ultimate commercialization. Some universities have created groups of advisors and/or seed-funding programs to help bring university inventions further along to the point where they will be licensed.

National laboratories and the federal agencies overseeing them have seen precommercial development of new technology as one of their roles, particularly through the mechanism of cooperative research and development agreements (CRADAs)[13] with industry. There was particular emphasis on this structure in the 1990s, and the mechanism

---

[11] James Flanigan, "UCI Research Park a Study in Promise," *Los Angeles Times*, April 21, 1999, https://perma.cc/5TMQ-CPWK.

[12] Christina Lee, "Hitachi Goes to College: Technology: The opening of the firm's research facility at UC Irvine heats up a debate over how much access the Japanese should have to American universities," *Los Angeles Times*, April 23, 1990, https://perma.cc/CH7W-5RRL

[13] See, e.g., Kelly Day-Rubenstein and Keith O. Fuglie, "The CRADA Model for Public-Private Collaboration in Agriculture," chapter 8 in Keith O. Fuglie and David E. Schimmelpfennig, eds., *Public-Private Collaboration in Agricultural Research: New Institutional Arrangements and Economic Implications* (Iowa State University Press, now Wiley-Blackwell, 2000); also see "Technology Transfer Cooperative Research and Development Agreements (CRADAs)," US Air Force, https://web.archive.org/web/20160704041735/http://www.wpafb.af.mil/shared/media/document/AFD-070905-013.pdf.

is still very much in use. Some successes have been achieved, but often industry does not see government as a desirable partner in precommercial development.

There is no single answer. What works best is specific to the area of technology and even the characteristics of a particular invention, and what worked well in one case will not necessarily work well for another. One important consideration is the amount of time, effort, and expense needed to bring a product to market. Another is to whom that expense would be an attractive investment.

INDUSTRIAL RELATIONS AND TECHNOLOGY TRANSFER AT THE UNIVERSITY OF CALIFORNIA

In the early days of the University of California, faculty members interacted with industrial companies through public service roles and consulting services. One example is Willard Rising, the initial professor of chemistry after Ezra Carr. Rising specialized in analytical chemistry and performed analyses for industry for a fee that he did not take as personal income. He also helped local communities improve the quality of their water, provided public testimonials for products such as Royal Baking Powder, and was even simultaneously appointed both state analyst and analyst of the State Board of Health.[14] As already noted in chapter 9, chemistry professor Frederick Cottrell invented the electrostatic precipitator while he was consulting with the DuPont Company at its sulfuric acid plant in Pinole, California, in the 1900s under an arrangement that did not give ownership of the resulting patents to DuPont. Rather than capitalizing on the invention himself, Cottrell decided that the proceeds from royalties on licensing of his resulting patents should be plowed back into research, and he therefore formed the Research Corporation,[15, 16] dedicated to that purpose. The Research Corporation handled patents for the University

---

[14] William L. Jolly, *From Retorts to Lasers: The Story of Chemistry at Berkeley* (Berkeley: College of Chemistry, University of California, 1987), pp. 19–20.
[15] David C. Mowery et al., *Ivory Tower and Industrial Innovation: University-Industry Technology Transfer before and after the Bayh-Dole Act* (Stanford University Press, 2004), pp. 58–84.
[16] T. D. Cornell, *Establishing Research Corporation: A Case Study of Patents, Philanthropy, and Organized Research in Early Twentieth-Century America* (Tucson, AZ: Research Corp., 2004).

of California and other universities for many years and also sponsored research itself.

Gilbert Newton Lewis, who arrived in Berkeley in 1912, had negative attitudes toward industrial liaisons. They were colored by the vivid dispute between William H. Walker and Arthur A. Noyes that he had experienced at the Research Laboratory for Chemistry at MIT (chapter 9). He may also have been influenced by the contentions[17] that he had with Irving Langmuir of the General Electric Company concerning attributions of credit within overlapping areas of interest. Lewis therefore discouraged industrial involvements for the College of Chemistry, and that attitude spread to much of the rest of the university. Ernest Lawrence had also not seen interacting with industrial companies as being useful as he built his cyclotrons and his laboratory; his financial support came from foundations and then the government. Consulting with individual companies by individual faculty members did continue to exist, however, particularly in areas such as engineering.

The situation at Berkeley in the first half of the twentieth century with regard to industrial interactions contrasts sharply with that at MIT. There, as described in more detail in chapter 9, the Research Laboratory for Applied Chemistry had been created by William Walker expressly to build and cement ties with industry, and the financial plan of President Richard Maclaurin for the entire institute relied upon relations with industry and consequent financial support. Going back into the late 1800s, relations with industry had been institutionalized through visiting committees [18] reporting directly to both the corporation (board) of the institute and the administration. These visiting committees contained leaders of industry as well as some academics and other alumni. A prime example of industrial innovation resulting from consulting by Walker's successors in chemical engineering at MIT was the contribution of Warren K. Lewis and Edwin R. Gilliland to the invention and development of fluid-bed catalytic cracking while they were consulting with Standard Oil Development

---

[17] Patrick Coffey, *Cathedrals of Science: The Personalities and Rivalries that Made Modern Chemistry* (Oxford: Oxford University Press, 2008), pp. 124–125.
[18] "Visiting Committees of the MIT Corporation," https://perma.cc/9NMG-LDMZ.

Company in the late 1930s.[19, 20] That invention became the backbone of the petroleum-refining industry. The histories of industrial relations at MIT and the University of California, Berkeley, as well as those at Stanford and Penn State, have been contrasted by Matkin[21] in comparing how technology transfer was built at those institutions.

The development of what is now effective patenting and technology transfer at the University of California was late blooming and involved a de facto trial-and-error process with various initiatives along the way. The following sketch of the early history of the University of California patent policy and administration is taken from the report of a 1994 ad hoc committee:[22]

> Since 1926, the University of California has required certain employees to report patentable inventions to the University. Initially the patent program's focus was limited to meeting contractual obligations to research sponsors, and the University had no mandatory assignment policy. Authority over intellectual property was under The Regents at this time, and the Patent Policy was administered by the General Counsel's Office.
>
> The University adopted a mandatory assignment policy in 1963, which required all University employees or researchers using University funds or facilities to assign their inventions to the University. In 1973, responsibility for the administration of the patent program was moved to a Board of Patents, consisting of administrators and faculty appointed by The Regents. As the patent program grew, a more complex administrative structure was required. The UC Patent, Trademark and Copyright Office (PTCO) was founded in 1979

---

[19] Thomas K. Sherwood, "Edwin Richard Gilliland, 1909–1973," Biographical Memoirs, National Academy of Sciences, 1978, https://perma.cc/4WNZ-RDEK.

[20] Arthur M. Squires, "The Story of Fluid Catalytic Cracking: The First 'Circulating Fluid Bed,'" in Prabir Basu, ed., *Circulating Fluidized Bed Technology* (New York: Pergamon, New York, 1985), pp. 1–19.

[21] Gary W. Matkin, *Technology Transfer and the University* (Washington, DC: American Council on Education, 1990).

[22] "Ad Hoc Technology Transfer Advisory Committee, "Report to President Peltason on the University of California Technology Transfer Program," March 8, 1994, https://perma.cc/UN45-HKZK.

to meet the regulatory compliance requirements of sponsoring agencies, primarily the Federal Government, and to assist individual inventors in the commercialization of their patentable ideas. From 1979 to 1985, PTCO reported to The Regents and was advised by the Board of Patents.

The primitive nature of patent oversight at the University of California before 1979 is conveyed by descriptions of the interactions between Stanford and UC as patent coverage for the Boyer-Cohen recombinant-DNA discoveries was being considered and pursued.[23, 24] Niels Reimers, who headed Stanford's Office of Technology Licensing, became aware of the discoveries through a *New York Times* article that was forwarded to him by an administrative colleague in May 1974. When he became interested in securing in patent coverage,[25] he found out from Cohen that Boyer (of UCSF) was a co-inventor, and so he contacted UC's patent office. That office, the precursor to PTCO, was a two-person office that had a substantial number of inventions disclosed from within UC but no way to deal with them effectively and essentially no marketing efforts at all. With regard to the Boyer-Cohen invention, the UC office took the position that it could not participate in the risks associated with seeking patent coverage, not even sharing the filing costs. So an arrangement was made between the two institutions that Stanford would get 15 percent of any revenues off the top so as to recognize that it took the risks by covering patent-procurement and marketing costs, and then after this deduction, the remaining income would be split evenly between the two universities. Given the foundational role of the Boyer-Cohen patent for the

---

[23] Niels Reimers, interview by Sally Smith Hughes, "Stanford's Office of Technology Licensing and the Cohen/Boyer Cloning Patents," 1997, https://perma.cc/SDH6-U9TT.

[24] Sally Smith Hughes, "Making Dollars out of DNA," in *Science and the American Century*, *Isis* 93, no. 3 (2001): pp. 541–575.

[25] Before the passage of the Bayh-Dole Act in 1980 (see below), universities could, through a laborious procedure, conclude institutional patent agreements (IPAs) with individual government agencies. Stanford had such agreements with two of the sponsors of the research, the National Institutes of Health and the National Science Foundation. The third sponsor had been the American Cancer Society, and Reimers eventually was able to get rights from that organization as well (Reimers, 1997, *loc. cit.*).

biotechnology industry, that 15 percent off the top was a large loss of income for UC.

In 1979, Roger Ditzel, who had headed international agricultural business development at Monsanto Corporation and had overseen research and patents at Iowa State University, became UC patent administrator, heading PTCO and still reporting directly to the Board of Regents.[26]

In the period from 1977 to 1983, several important changes occurred in the United States on the national level. First of all, decisions were made by a number of major corporations to wind down or level off in-house research operations and to emphasize to a greater extent new technology that could be acquired elsewhere, including from universities. The consent-decree breakup of the American Telephone and Telegraph Company (AT&T) materialized in early 1982 and created a tenuous situation for Bell Laboratories,[27] which had been the industrial research star of the nation. As a result several organized efforts to facilitate interactions between industry and universities were started in various areas, a prominent example being the Council for Chemical Research,[28] for which discussions were started in 1979 and which came into being in 1981.

The Bayh-Dole Act[29] of 1980 with amendments in 1984 established that universities had ownership rights for inventions stemming from university research carried out under federal government grants and contracts. This was important because previously the government itself would take ownership of patents from such inventions and place them

---

[26] "The University Gets New Administrators for Two Offices—One Heads up Patents and the Other Has Contracts and Grants," *University Bulletin* 27, no. 24 (March 26, 1979), University of California, https://perma.cc/87B9-4QNS.
[27] Jon Gertner, *The Idea Factory: Bell Labs and the Great Age of American Innovation*, reprint edition (New York: Penguin Books, 2012).
[28] J. Ivan Legg, "The Council for Chemical Research," chapter 2, pp. 5–15, in James E. McEvoy, ed., *Partnerships in Chemical Research and Education*, vol. 478, ACS Symposium Series, American Chemical Society, 1992.
[29] "The Bayh-Dole Act: A Guide to the Law and Implementing Regulations," Council on Governmental Relations, October 1999, https://perma.cc/EF3R-PB2U.

in the public domain unless the university had successfully completed an institutional patent agreement with the federal agency concerned. For inventions that have large up-front costs for commercial development, a lack of ability to own or obtain an exclusive license is a major discouragement. Further discussion of the Bayh-Dole Act is given by Mowery et al.,[30] Geiger,[31] and Geiger and Sá,[32] among many others.

Finally, at about this time technology transfer, connoting active efforts to move university inventions out into the marketplace, became an emphasis for many universities, and universities sought to make themselves more active partners with industry and more able to move university discoveries and inventions into commercial use.

The University of California was no exception. In 1985 the reporting line for the patent office was moved from the Board of Regents to the president. In 1985 and again in 1987, the firm Peat Marwick was asked to review PTCO operations and make recommendations. In 1991 the name of PTCO was changed to Office of Technology Transfer to reflect a more active role in moving university technology out into the marketplace and industrial use. The volume of invention disclosures grew substantially, from 134 in 1978,[33] to 345 in 1989,[34] to 865 in 2000,[35] and to 1,769 in 2014.[36]

In 1989, UC hired Carl Wootten to succeed Roget Ditzel, with an understanding that Wootten would considerably increase patent marketing efforts. Wootten had been CEO of University Technology Corporation, affiliated with Georgia Tech, the University of Maryland, Kansas State University, the University of Connecticut, and the University of Iowa. Previously he had directed the Patent

---

[30] Mowery et al., 2004, *op. cit.*, pp. 85–94.
[31] Roger L. Geiger, *Knowledge and Money: Research Universities and the Paradox of the Marketplace* (Stanford, CA: Stanford University Press, 2004).
[32] Roger L. Geiger and Creso Sá, *Tapping the Riches of Science: Universities and the Promise of Economic Growth* (Cambridge, MA: Harvard University Press, 2008).
[33] *University Bulletin*, University of California, 1979, *loc. cit.*
[34] Mowery et al., 2004, *op. cit.*, p. 100.
[35] *Annual Report*, University of California Technology Transfer Program, FY 2000, https://perma.cc/8RTS-B24M.
[36] *University of California Technology Commercialization Report, FY 2014*, https://perma.cc/G73S-ALNM.

Administration Office at Duke University. Wootten's five-year tenure was a time of change and turbulence, as is documented by Matkin.[37] Patent-related revenues rose from $10 million in 1989 to $45 million in 1993. Wootten and Senior Vice President Ron Brady, to whom PTCO reported, advocated creating a not-for-profit foundation to take over the existing roles of PTCO with fewer restrictions from the university legal structure and policies. This foundation would be supplemented by a for-profit corporation to be known as the California Technology Ventures Corporation (CTVC), which would provide both development monies for underdeveloped technologies and venture capital for start-up companies, as well as assembling management teams for new companies. These are now well-established private-sector roles.

As is described by Matkin, these proposals encountered difficulty getting buy-in from the Academic Senate, administrative committees, and the regents. The problems related to both the nature of the proposal and the manner of approach. The proposal also engendered resistance from campuses to the strong centralization of functions within the university that they represented and the evident strong convictions of Wootten in that direction.[38] Even though the university reached an agreement with the state whereby the proposed operations would be funded in part by the state relinquishing what was then its share of patent-royalty income, the proposals never came to fruition.

This situation was further complicated by the involvement of Ron Cowan, the developer of the large Harbor Bay Isle project (near Oakland Airport), to which the Office of Technology Transfer moved in 1989. The distance (eight miles) and travel time (twenty-five minutes) from that location to the Office of the President and the fact that it was still further removed from any campus fed impressions that OTT was working on its own rather than in concert with the rest of the university. There were charges of favoritism to Cowan and others that gave enough appearance of substance to warrant an internal UC

---

[37] Gary W. Matkin, "Technology Transfer and Public Policy: Lessons from a Case Study," *Policy Studies Journal* 22, no. 2 (1994): pp. 371–383.

[38] Ronald W. Brady, interview by Carol Hicke, Germaine LaBerge, and Ann Lage, in *The University of California Office of the President and Its Constituencies, 1983–1995*, vol. 1, "The Office of the President," p. 207, 1997–98, https://perma.cc/Y6DB-KFDK.

investigation. Although Wootten was cleared of most of these charges, he left the university soon thereafter.[39]

About a year before Wootten's departure, ex-chancellor Theodore Hullar of the Davis campus had been brought into the UC Office of the President to review the university's technology transfer efforts. The Ad Hoc Technology Transfer Advisory Committee, referenced above, was formed. Its report[40] carried through with recommendations that had been stirring for some time, namely that many of the functions of the university-wide Office of Technology Transfer should be devolved to technology-transfer offices on individual campuses. The objectives were to place technology-transfer operations in closer proximity to the inventors themselves and to restore a close working relationship with, and confidence within, the academic enterprise. The functions that would remain centralized were legal counsel, policy development and coordination, and other technology-transfer functions for campuses not yet having their own office.

The recommendations from the 1994 report were adopted. Initially two campuses—Berkeley and UCLA, which had already established campus offices in 1990—chose to maximize the allowable distribution of functions to the campuses. By 2002, six campuses (Berkeley, Los Angeles, San Diego, Irvine, Davis, and San Francisco) had independent offices,[41] and now all campuses have them, including the new Merced campus. The university-wide Office of Technology Transfer moved back from Harbor Bay Isle to the Office of the President building in Oakland when its lease at Harbor Bay ended. A president's retreat for senior university administrators and faculty was held in January 1997 and served to help iron out differences. The report from it is available with selected parts online.[42] The reporting relationship of the university-wide office was transferred from the business side to the provost and

---

[39] Ralph Frammolino, "Chief Patent Officer for UC to Step Down: Education: Internal audit had cleared Carl Wootten of conflict of interest a week ago, but raised other questions about his activities," *Los Angeles Times*, July 14, 1994, https://perma.cc/WM2L-SFBV.
[40] Ad Hoc Technology Transfer Advisory Committee, 1994, *loc. cit.*
[41] Mowery et al., 2004, *loc. cit.*
[42] *Proceedings of the President's Retreat: The University of California's Relationships with Industry in Research and Technology* Transfer, January 1997, accessed June 23, 2016, http://web.archive.org/web/20150331173737/http://www.ucop.edu/ott/retreat/tabofcon.html.

executive vice president for academic affairs in 2007, again to reflect the tie with academic functions of the university. In May 2016 it was moved again to report to a new position created by President Napolitano, senior vice president for innovation and entrepreneurship,[43] which added promotional functions and gave industrial relationships and entrepreneurship their own senior position within the university-wide administration.

In 2004, the Berkeley campus office was renamed the Office of Intellectual Property and Industrial Research Alliances (IPIRA), bringing together the support functions for all relations with industry, including establishing research agreements and managing patents and licensing. Other campuses have also moved in this direction, and even the university-wide office is now the Office of Industrial Alliances and Services.

Patent-Related Policies

All employees of the University of California are required to sign and adhere to the UC patent policy.[44] That policy acknowledges that inventions made under university employment or using university facilities belong to the university and indicates that the employee will assist the university fully if it chooses to pursue patent protection. The decision whether or not to patent is made by the university. In some cases the university will release patenting rights to the inventor if the university chooses not to pursue patent coverage.

After the costs of procuring, protecting, and preserving the patent have been recovered, the University of California pays 35 percent of the net royalties and fees per invention to the inventor or splits that amount evenly among inventors. An additional 15 percent of net royalties and fees per invention is allocated to the inventor's campus or national laboratory for research-related purposes. On the Berkeley campus, the latter portion of royalty income is passed on to academic departments.

---

[43] "Office of Innovation and Entrepreneurship," Office of the President, University of California, https://web.archive.org/web/20171209215921/https://www.ucop.edu/innovation-entrepreneurship/index.html.

[44] "Patent Policy," University of California Policy, https://perma.cc/FM6G-3RA2.

Chapter 19

INDUSTRY-UNIVERSITY COOPERATIVE RESEARCH

The Industry-University Cooperative Research Program (IUCRP)[45] of the University of California was set up at the initiative of President Richard Atkinson upon his arrival in office in 1996.[46] It bore similarities to, and held the same name as, a program that had been established at the National Science Foundation in the 1970s during Atkinson's tenure as deputy director and then director of NSF. The program received state funding through a series of budgetary initiatives put forward to the state by the university for consideration as part of the Board of Regents' annual state budget proposals in the era of partnerships and compacts (chapter 6).

IUCRP served to fund research projects for which industrial support would be paired with state support, thereby leveraging both the industrial and the state funds. Projects were selected from annual rounds of proposals through a peer-review process. Four areas were initially identified for the program: biotechnology, telecommunications, digital media, and information technology for life sciences. Over time, the program subsumed the MICRO program (described below) and grew further to add energy, health and wellness, and nanotechnology as eligible fields. At its height, IUCRP drew about $20 million in industrial funds per year, matched with $17 million from the state of California, which in turn were matched by $3 million taken from within the university's general budget. Following university policy, all intellectual property from IUCRP projects was owned by the University of California but could be licensed to firms under standard terms. The MICRO program continued its already-established policy of waiving UC overhead costs, but in the other areas, full indirect costs were recovered. An annual report for IUCRP from 2003 is available online.[47]

---

[45] Lovell Jarvis, "The Industry-University Cooperative Research Program," PowerPoint slides for CUECH workshop presentation, Comptroller General of the Republic and UC Davis, Problems of Implementation of Technology Transfer Mechanisms in the State University System, Consorcio de Universidades del Estado de Chile, October 24, 2014, https://perma.cc/24TB-ARFG.

[46] Patricia A. Pelfrey, *Entrepreneurial President: Richard Atkinson and the University of California, 1995–2003* (Berkeley: University of California Press, 2012), pp. 109–110.

[47] *Annual Report 2003*, University of California Discovery Grant Program, https://perma.cc/XQM8-FB3R (Lower on web page).

The program, by then renamed the Discovery Grant Program, was discontinued in 2008 as a budget cut during a time when state funding for the University of California considerably declined. However, by any measure the program was a considerable success during its era.

REGIONAL INFLUENCES: TECHNOLOGICAL INNOVATION AND ECONOMIC DEVELOPMENT

Two prime examples display the roles that University of California campuses have had in regional economic development stemming from technological innovation. They are Silicon Valley in the San Francisco Bay Area and the San Diego/La Jolla area in southern California.

Silicon Valley

The area generally known as Silicon Valley lies in the southwestern portion of the San Francisco Bay region, roughly from Redwood City on the north to San Jose on the south and incorporating San Mateo and Santa Clara counties. It does not have sharp boundaries. The area is well known as the heart of innovation for the electronics and computing industries. The reasons why Silicon Valley blossomed as it did are complex and have been explored by authors such as Saxenian,[48] Kenney,[49] Lee et al.,[50] Adams,[51] and Isaacson.[52] Saxenian also comparatively examined the dynamics of development and the relative degrees of success of Silicon Valley and Route 128, which surrounds Boston, Massachusetts.

The Early Development of Silicon Valley. Stanford University had the essential and catalytic role in the initial development of Silicon Valley. The area had roots in radio engineering dating back to the early

---

[48] AnnaLee Saxenian, *Regional Advantage: Culture and Competition in Silicon Valley and Route 128* (Cambridge, MA: Harvard University Press, 1994).
[49] Martin Kenney, ed., *Understanding Silicon Valley: The Anatomy of an Entrepreneurial Region* (Stanford, CA: Stanford University Press, 2000).
[50] Chong-Moon Lee et al., eds., *The Silicon Valley Edge: A Habitat for Innovation and Entrepreneurship* (Stanford, CA: Stanford University Press, 2000).
[51] Stephen B. Adams, "Stanford and Silicon Valley: Lessons on Becoming a High-Tech Region," *California Management Review* 48, no. 1 (Fall 2005): pp. 29–51.
[52] Walter Isaacson, *The Innovators: How a Group of Hackers, Geniuses, and Geeks Created the Digital Revolution* (New York: Simon & Schuster, 2015).

days of that field, one of them being the Federal Telegraph Corporation and Lee DeForest's work therein on developing vacuum tubes.[53] One of the people most active in advancing knowledge about radio was Frederick E. Terman, who authored the leading textbook of the time on the subject and carried out research that was both forefront and practical in orientation. Terman was professor of electrical engineering as of 1927, dean of engineering from 1945 to 1955, and then provost (a newly developed post) from 1955 to 1965, all at Stanford University.[54] With the full support of then-president Wallace Sterling, Terman operationally designed and led the building of Stanford as an academic powerhouse.[55, 56, 57] He is also usually given major credit for enabling and indirectly leading the events that primarily led to Silicon Valley. However, Terman's primary endeavor was to build Stanford, and his contributions to the launch of Silicon Valley are in some ways a side benefit of the ways in which he chose to reach that main goal.

One great need for Stanford in the aftermath of World War II was to build revenue, since Stanford held much less endowment and was in a more precarious financial situation than was the case for other major private US universities such as Harvard, Johns Hopkins, and MIT. Terman had carried out his doctoral work with Vannevar Bush at MIT during the 1920s and had spent World War II as director of the Radio Research Laboratory at Harvard. During those periods he had learned about the finances and academic-building approaches of Harvard and MIT. From his relationship with Bush, he recognized that federal government funding of research would probably continue and grow substantially after the war. He directed the building of Stanford toward opportunities for coupling excellent, well-regarded research with areas of available government funding, notably those areas favored by the

---

[53] Timothy J. Sturgeon, "How Silicon Valley Came to Be," in Kenney, *op. cit.*, 2000, pp. 15–47.
[54] For a biography of Terman, see C. Stewart Gillmor, *Fred Terman at Stanford: Building a Discipline, a University, and Silicon Valley* (Stanford, CA: Stanford University Press, 2004).
[55] Roger L. Geiger, *Research and Relevant Knowledge: American Research Universities Since World War II* (Oxford University Press, 1993), pp. 119–135.
[56] Timothy Lenoir, "Inventing the Entrepreneurial University: Stanford and the Co-evolution of Silicon Valley," chapter 5 in Thomas J. Allen and Rory P. O'Shea, eds., *Building Technology Transfer within Research Universities* (Cambridge University Press, 2014).
[57] Jonathan R. Cole, *The Great American University: Its Rise to Preeminence, Its Indispensable National Role, Why It Must Be Protected* (New York: Public Affairs, 2009), pp. 117–134.

Office of Naval Research, which was the largest government funder of academic research immediately after the war.

Terman saw a need for close relations with industry in order to further the goal of building research that was meaningful and informed by possibilities for commercial application. He and others at Stanford recognized the opportunity that would be afforded by creating an industrial park on land owned by Stanford and adjoining the university. An industrial park would make financially beneficial use of Stanford's prime asset, which was 8,200 acres (32.8 square kilometers) of land, much more than was needed for the campus itself.[58] The industrial park would provide rent as income to the university, industrial consulting opportunities for the faculty, and a way of fostering industry that would build upon the knowledge generated at Stanford. The industrial park was opened in 1951 with Varian Associates as the first tenant and Eastman Kodak as the second. As of 2004 the park, which had by then become known as Stanford Research Park,[59] consisted of 700 acres (2.8 square kilometers), which was 8 percent of Stanford's land, with 10 million square feet (930,000 square meters) of building space and 23,000 employees of 150 companies distributed among 162 buildings.[60] A map of Stanford Research Park, built around Page Mill Road in Palo Alto, is available along with a list of current tenants.[61] The success achieved by the Stanford Research Park touched off the creation of numerous university-affiliated research parks elsewhere in the United States and the world. Geiger[62] analyzes university-industry

---

[58] The land was left to Stanford University in the estate of Leland and Jane Stanford, who named the university for their deceased son, Leland Stanford Jr. Leland Stanford was one of the "Big Four" who built the portion of the first transcontinental railroad west of the Rocky Mountains and was also a governor of California. Another substantial use of Stanford land is faculty housing. Today 60 percent of Stanford land remains as open space ("About Stanford," Stanford University, https://web.archive.org/web/20160611003910/http://facts.stanford.edu/about/lands.

[59] "Stanford Research Park," Stanford University, https://web.archive.org/web/20170711214159/http://stanfordresearchpark.com/.

[60] Jon Sandelin, "The Story of Stanford Industrial/Research Park," International Forum of University Science Park, China (2004), https://perma.cc/4PSM-R73X.

[61] "Our Neighborhood," Stanford Research Park, Stanford University, https://web.archive.org/web/20160616114518/http://stanfordresearchpark.com/explore.

[62] Roger L. Geiger, *Knowledge and Money: Research Universities and the Paradox of the Marketplace* (Stanford, CA: Stanford University Press, 2004), pp. 202–213.

clusters elsewhere in the United States in light of the Silicon Valley phenomenon.

Terman also was a leader in the formation of the Stanford Research Institute (SRI), which was created in 1946 to provide more practical services for industry that did not fit with faculty research programs. SRI was so successful that it became independent of Stanford in 1970 and acquired RCA Laboratories in Princeton, New Jersey, in 1988. Now, as SRI International,[63] it is a nonprofit, independent research center serving government and industry, with 2013 revenues in the amount of $540 million.

The result of Terman's policies and initiatives, defense contracting, the Stanford Industrial Park, and the Stanford Research Institute was that by the 1950s a vital nexus had formed among Stanford, the Department of Defense, and the nascent electronics industry nearby, riding the wave of the future in a very fast-growing area of technological and economic development.[64] The timing was vital for what was accomplished.

Another chain of events critical to the emergence of Silicon Valley started with the 1954 departure of William Shockley,[65] one of the inventors of the transistor, from Bell Laboratories in New Jersey to form the Shockley Semiconductor Company, which was also located in the Stanford Industrial Park in Palo Alto. He built a team of top-notch engineers, but his management style was off-putting. Eight of these engineers, including Gordon Moore and Robert Noyce, left in 1957 to launch the Fairchild Semiconductor Company, which developed and marketed the monolithic integrated circuit.[66] Then in 1968 Moore and Noyce, taking Andrew Grove with them, left Fairchild and formed Intel Corporation, which succeeded mightily in its goal of producing large amounts of inexpensive semiconductor memory. [67] Two other

---

[63] SRI International, https://web.archive.org/web/20160621222141/https://www.sri.com/.
[64] Geiger, *op. cit.*, 1993, pp. 119–132.
[65] Jon Gertner, *The Idea Factory: Bell Labs and the Great Age of American Innovation* (New York: Penguin Books, 2012).
[66] Christophe Lécuyer, "Fairchild Semiconductor and Its Influence," chapter 8 in Lee et al., 2000, *op. cit.*
[67] Interestingly, all three of these Intel founders had ties to the UC Berkeley College of Chemistry. Gordon Moore is a BS graduate in chemistry, Donald Noyce (Robert Noyce's brother) was a professor of organic chemistry and longtime associate dean of the college, and Andrew Grove's

companies that also had much to do with the development of Silicon Valley and its culture were Apple Computer and Xerox PARC (Palo Alto Research Center), the latter of which is also located in Stanford Research Park.[68, 69]

Although today Silicon Valley is correctly envisioned as the premier location for corporate start-ups in the world, that was not the focus at the start. Instead, there was a much greater representation of firms headquartered elsewhere that opted to create branches in the Silicon Valley area for proximity to other firms, Stanford, and, in some cases, UC Berkeley.

Sustaining University Roles. There are vigorous, ongoing relationships between Silicon Valley firms and California universities, most notably Stanford and the Berkeley campus of the University of California. The interactions take a number of different forms including
- consulting by faculty,
- licensing by companies of technology stemming from universities,
- participation by faculty and/or alumni in the formation of new companies,
- attracting to the region first-class graduate students who then stay and go to Silicon Valley firms for employment,
- recruitment of faculty from industry,
- continuing education for professionals,
- university advisory boards composed of people from industry, and
- sponsorship of research at universities by industrial companies or groups of companies.

The term *technology transfer* evokes a concept of one-way transfer of university-generated technological innovations and concepts to the world of industry, but the interactions are very much a two-way street. Not only is technology effectively transferred from universities to industry, but university researchers also learn much from their

---

PhD graduation seminar in chemical engineering was the first seminar that I attended upon coming to Berkeley in 1963.
[68] James F. Gibbons, "The Role of Stanford University: A Dean's Reflections," chapter 10 in Lee et al., 2000, *op. cit.*
[69] John Seely Brown and Paul Duguid, "Mysteries of the Region: Knowledge Dynamics in Silicon Valley," chapter 2 in Lee et al., 2000, *op. cit.*

interactions with companies that is useful to their own formulations of research and building of knowledge. Those characteristics are not limited to Silicon Valley. They are features of university-industry interactions in general.

The MICRO Program. An important mechanism for semiconductor research at the University of California was the MICRO (**M**icroelectronics **I**nnovation and **C**omputer **R**esearch **O**peration/**O**pportunities) program. MICRO was started in 1981 as a partnership between the state of California, the microelectronics industry, and the University of California. The state provided funds, ultimately about $5 million per year, to be used to match and lever industrial funding for University of California research projects, which were selected through peer review of proposals. The University of California waived overhead requirements on MICRO grants, thereby indirectly contributing what would otherwise have been its own funds. Jerry Brown, the governor at the time, regarded MICRO as an effective defensive measure against loss of the microelectronics industry from California to other countries. In 2001–02, ninety-six companies invested $6 million in cash and equipment to fund ninety-eight different MICRO projects.[70] As has already been noted, the program was then blended with the Industry-University Cooperative Research Program of the University of California. Along with IUCRP, it was ended in 2008.

UC Berkeley and Silicon Valley. The interactions between the Berkeley campus of the University of California and Silicon Valley are robust and now rival in number and intensity those between Stanford and Silicon Valley.

Lécuyer[71] explores the quite different ways in which semiconductor innovation and entrepreneurship stem from each of three University of California campuses—Berkeley, Los Angeles, and Santa Barbara. He

---

[70] Committee on the Impact of Academic Research on Industrial Performance, National Academy of Engineering, *The Impact of Academic Research on Industrial Performance* (Washington, DC: National Academies Press, 2003), p. 60, http://www.nap.edu/catalog/10805/the-impact-of-academic-research-on-industrial-performance.

[71] Christophe Lécuyer, "Semiconductor Innovation and Entrepreneurship at Three University of California Campuses," in Martin Kenney and David C. Mowery, eds., *Public Universities and Regional Growth: Insights from the University of California* (Stanford Business Books, Stanford University Press, 2014), pp. 20–65.

notes that by virtue of the proximity of Berkeley to Silicon Valley, researchers at that campus focused upon silicon-integrated circuits, especially communications circuits, and on the software tools required to design complex microchips. Because of the proximity of UCLA to large defense-industry firms, researchers there brought in technologies from those companies and developed strengths in chips for broadband communications. Researchers at Santa Barbara, a later and geographically more isolated entrant, concentrated on compound semiconductors, thereby differentiating themselves from the other two campuses.

Kenney, Mowery, and Patton[72] examine the various modes of engagement over the years between the Department of Electrical Engineering and Computer Science (EECS) at UC Berkeley and Silicon Valley industrial firms. They do this through analysis of six specific major research projects that span a period of fifty years, starting with the early history of computing. In so doing, they give a picture of how interactions between EECS and what became Silicon Valley evolved over time. They show as well the importance of three more specific factors—government funding for research that ultimately leads to technological innovation and economic development, the flow of people over time, and the ways in which university-industry interactions have evolved in Silicon Valley. The differences among the projects also display the rapid rate of advances in computing. The six projects are as follows:

- **California Digital Computer Project (CALDIC), 1948–54.** This project, sponsored by the US Office of Naval Research soon after World War II, constructed the first digital computer at a West Coast university. The most important contribution to the economy consisted of the graduates who had worked with the project, several of whom became leaders of the computing industry. Three joined the new IBM research laboratory in San Jose and were key to the development there of IBM's moving-head, hard-disk drive technology.

---

[72] Martin Kenney, David C. Mowery, and Donald Patton, "Electrical Engineering and Computer Science at UC Berkeley and in the Silicon Valley: Modes of Regional Engagement," in Martin Kenney and David C. Mowery, eds., *Public Universities and Regional Growth: Insights from the University of California* (Stanford Business Books, Stanford University Press, 2014), pp. 97–126.

- **Project Genie and Commercial Time Sharing, 1964–68.** The US Defense Advanced Research Projects Agency (DARPA) funded research in EECS at Berkeley to develop time-share computing. This laid groundwork for the Scientific Data Systems (SDS) Corporation in Los Angeles and for Tymshare, a successful time-share company in Cupertino, California. Three of the students involved in the creation of the GENIE software developed in connection with this project went to Xerox PARC to become the core of the firm's computer research group, which in turn developed the first computer workstation.
- **Interactive Graphics and Retrieval System Project (INGRES) and the Relational Database Industry, 1973–80s.** The relational database industry stems from competitive research by the IBM San Jose Laboratory and Berkeley EECS, with the Berkeley work sponsored by the US Department of Defense and the National Science Foundation. The results, which came to fruition during the 1970s, resulted in a tidal wave of new entrepreneurial firms in the San Francisco Bay Area, primarily in Silicon Valley (Oracle, Ingres, Britton Lee, Sybase, PeopleSoft, and so forth). Previously the data-base industry had been on the East Coast of the United States. With the relational database work and start-ups, the industry moved to the West Coast.
- **Reduced Instruction Set Computing (RISC), late 1970s to mid-1980s.** IBM pioneered the concept of reduced instruction set computing as a way of accelerating the processing speed of integrated circuits. Competitive DARPA-funded research by David Patterson at Berkeley and John Hennessy at Stanford (where Hennessey later became president) greatly improved the technology and resulted in large growth of Sun Microsystems (working with Patterson) and the start of Silicon Graphics (working with Hennessey), as well as a number of other start-ups. The technology ultimately led to the ARM microprocessor that has been widely used in cell phones.
- **Berkeley UNIX Software Distribution (BSD), 1973–95.** UNIX is a multi-task, multiuser computer operating system that was initially developed in 1969 at AT&T's Bell Laboratories. Under a

1956 consent agreement stemming from earlier antimonopoly legal considerations preceding those that led to the breakup of AT&T, nontelephone technology of Bell Laboratories was placed in the public domain. UNIX fell in that category and was therefore included. Working closely with Bell Labs, Berkeley EECS greatly improved the UNIX technology to a form known as Berkeley Software Distribution UNIX (BSD UNIX). DARPA made UNIX the standard for the ARPANET computer network that was the forerunner of the Internet. William Joy of Berkeley EECS had worked on BSD UNIX and became a founder of Sun Microsystems in Silicon Valley. Sun adopted BSD UNIX as its operating system, thereby helping to lead BSD UNIX to wide adoption and a foundational position for the Internet. BSD UNIX was made publicly available, so UC received no licensing fees or royalties. However, firms such as Sun have made major donations of research equipment and funding to Berkeley EECS.

- **Redundant Arrays of Inexpensive Disks (RAID), 1987.** Three Berkeley EECS researchers (Randy Katz, David Patterson, and Garth Gibson) developed a methodology for using vast arrays of smaller discs as a superior alternative to very large hard drives for massive data storage. This research was commercialized by several existing large firms (IBM, DEC, and EMC), as well as through at least forty-five start-ups, most of which are in the San Francisco Bay Area.

A seventh case[73] is analyzed by Lécuyer. With support from the Army Research Office, the National Science Foundation, and the MICRO program, software for the design of integrated-circuit microchips was developed at Berkeley by Donald Pedersen and associates in the 1970s. This led to a widely used public-domain simulator known as SPICE (Simulation Program, Integrated Circuit Emphasis). SPICE, evolutions from it, and successors to it became the foundation of microchip design and led to numerous start-up companies concentrated in Silicon Valley.

---

[73] Lécuyer, *op. cit.*, 2014, pp. 33–39.

Chapter 19

Why Does Silicon Valley Surround Stanford and Not Berkeley? Since many faculty members from both UC Berkeley and Stanford have been intellectual partners with Silicon Valley firms going back to early days, it is logical to consider the factors that made Silicon Valley arise in the immediate environs of Stanford, rather than Berkeley. Adams[74] postulates that Terman at Stanford adopted a strategy of business orientation, demonstrating that he understood what would build industry-university interactions and the industrial economy of the Stanford region most effectively. In contrast, the leadership at Berkeley and UC was more oriented toward the politics of Sacramento and preservation of UC's role vis-à-vis other components of the public higher-education sector. Stanford had not yet established a secure financial base, whereas Berkeley and UC had what was, at the time, a comfortable financial base with the state of California. But the most important factor was the fact that Stanford owned land and could readily devote a large tract to the development of an industrial park, which it saw as an immediate source of revenue but also turned out to be the magnetic hub of Silicon Valley. There is little buildable land available in the immediate vicinity of the Berkeley campus and none that would be a large, contiguous block.

Overall Employment Needs. High-technology industries need a spectrum of employee expertise, much more than just the graduates of research universities. Scott, Kirst, et al.,[75] have explored the connection between those needs and San Francisco Bay Area higher education, including California State University campuses, community colleges, private non-profit and for-profit institutions, online institutions, and corporate in-house programs. There have been continual needs for new skills and "reskilling" of employees. The pace of change in the industry has been much faster than the natural capacity of the regional higher education system to respond, making adaptable continuing education more and more of a need.

---

[74] Stephen B. Adams, "Follow the Money: Engineering at Stanford and UC Berkeley during the Rise of Silicon Valley," *Minerva* 47 (2009): pp. 367–390.

[75] W. Richard Scott and Michael W. Kirst, *Higher Education and Silicon Valley*, (Baltimore MD: Johns Hopkins University Press, 2017). See also a ccolloquium by the same title from the same authors, Center for Studies in Higher Education, University of California, Berkeley, February 9, 2017, https://www.youtube.com/watch?time_continue=61&v=ijQIMs9acbU.

Location

San Diego/La Jolla

San Diego is located in the extreme southwest corner of the United States, sufficiently to the south of greater Los Angeles so that it is a distinct and separate region. Historically, the economy of San Diego was centered around tourism associated with the natural beauty and pleasant climate of the area. A large number of military installations came into being in the first half of the twentieth century as the Panama Canal was completed and then as World War II developed in the Pacific arena.[76] An aircraft-manufacturing industry had grown up as well, interacting closely with the military. With the end of World War II in 1945, many of the military operations wound down or ceased, and the area was left with a problematic economy that was in clear need of diversification and rebuilding.

The story of the development of the San Diego campus of the University of California is told in chapter 10. The Scripps Institution of Oceanography provided a strong scientific foundation upon which the campus could grow. Part of the plan for the San Diego campus was for a medical school that would be based heavily upon fundamental scientific faculty research. This portion of the plan enabled UC San Diego to take a strong role at the forefront of the wave of advances in molecular and structural biology that ultimately became the foundation for the biotechnology industry (see section below). The approach of the medical school was also important for the establishment of San Diego's first biotechnology company, Hybritech. The longest-serving (1980–95) chancellor of UCSD, Richard Atkinson, took a particular interest in university-industry relations and their effect upon the economy.[77, 78]

In the 1950s and 1960s, a series of industrial consolidations and redirections also brought important research activities in the private,

---

[76] Mary L. Walshok and Abraham J. Schragge, *Invention and Reinvention: The Evolution of San Diego's Innovation Economy*, chapter 2 (Stanford, CA: Stanford Business Books, Stanford University Press, 2014).
[77] Richard C. Atkinson and Patricia A. Pelfrey, "Science and the Entrepreneurial University," *Issues in Science and Technology*, Summer 2010, pp. 39–48, https://perma.cc/KB25-ZSRH.
[78] Richard C. Atkinson, "20/20, Reflections on the Last 20 Years of the 20th Century," 2001. Mandeville Special Collections Library, UCSD, https://perma.cc/QP8H-7BP6.

commercial sector. Notably, in 1952 General Dynamics Corporation was formed as a merger of several companies that had been involved in military production during World War II, including Consolidated-Vultee and the Aviation Corporation (aircraft), Electric Boat (submarines), and Atlas (guided missiles). The CEO of General Dynamics, John Jay Hopkins, was a major force in recreating the San Diego economy and in working with Roger Revelle to bring about the San Diego campus of the University of California. General Dynamics and Hopkins also spawned General Atomics Corporation, to pursue basic research and development relating to atomic energy and other fields such as medical applications, transportation, and space flight. It too was located on Torrey Pines Mesa in La Jolla. General Atomics proved to be prolific in producing spin-off companies, more than sixty of them by the early 1980s.[79] One General Atomics spin-off was Science Applications International Corporation (SAIC). SAIC, General Atomics, and a number of other companies formed from these roots have been accomplished government contractors and creators of new technology.

Yet another important corporate thread stemmed from Henry Booker, one of the first faculty hires at UCSD and a physicist working in the electronics of radio, communications, systems, and control. One of Booker's early recruitments in that program area was Irwin Jacobs, an associate professor at MIT working on digital communications. Jacobs, in turn, formed Linkabit Corporation together with two UCLA faculty members, Andrew Viterbi and Leonard Kleinrock. Linkabit was initially intended to pool the consulting of the three faculty members, but moved into satellite encryption devices and television scrambling systems.[80] More than seventy-five direct or indirect Linkabit spin-off companies have been identified,[81] a number even greater than for Fairchild Semiconductor in Silicon Valley. One of these spin-offs, founded by Jacobs, Viterbi, and others, was Qualcomm, which achieved a premier position in cellular telephone technology and now (2017) has over $22 billion in annual sales. All told, from 1984 to 2004, more than

---

[79] Walshok and Schragge, 2014, *op. cit.*, p. 122.
[80] Mary Walshok and Joel West, "Serendipity and Symbiosis: UCSD and the Local Wireless Industry," chapter 5 in Martin Kenney and David C. Mowery, eds., *Public Universities and Regional Growth: Insights from the University of California* (Stanford, CA: Stanford Business Books, Stanford University Press, 2014).
[81] Martha G. Dennis, "Linkabit Genealogy," https://perma.cc/U9GB-HN48..

two hundred communications companies were founded in San Diego, the largest concentration in the United States.

There is also a reciprocal relationship between the successes of Linkabit and Qualcomm and the fact that Irwin Jacobs came from UCSD, in that Jacobs has donated hundreds of millions of dollars to UCSD for various purposes, and the School of Engineering at UCSD is now the Jacobs School of Engineering (figure 10-12).[82]

The profusion of expertise and leading-edge technology development in wireless communications in the San Diego area made UCSD a strong contender and a winner in partnership with the University of California, Irvine, in the competition for the California Institutes on Science and Innovation in the year 2000 (chapter 14).

Facilitating Technology Transfer. Walshok and Lee[83] identify five catalytic factors that they believe were preconditions for the rise of high-tech entrepreneurism in the San Diego area, as follows:

- *Regional Land-Use Decisions.* The San Diego City Council designated and donated prime oceanside land on the Torrey Pines Mesa adjoining the existing Scripps Institution for Oceanography for high-tech development. This step joined with the acquisition of a decommissioned US Marines rifle range (Camp Matthews) on Torrey Pines Mesa to create the land that was provided to UC for its San Diego campus and to the Salk Institute, General Atomics, what became the Scripps Research Institute, and the Sanford-Burnham Institute. This foresighted and focused land-use planning contrasts starkly with the more politically contentious and piecemeal approaches that have been taken in many other recent military base-closure and reuse situations in the United States.

---

[82] Paul Jacobs, son of Irwin Jacobs, obtained three degrees in electrical engineering from UC Berkeley and followed his father as CEO of Qualcomm. Following in family tradition, Paul Jacobs was the donor for the Jacobs Institute for Design Innovation, opened on the Berkeley campus in 2015.

[83] Mary Walshok and Carolyn Lee, "The Partnership between Entrepreneurial Science and Entrepreneurial Business: A Study of Integrated Development at UCSD and San Diego's Hi-tech Economy," chapter 6 in Thomas J. Allen and Rory P. O'Shea eds., *Building Technology Transfer within Universities: An Entrepreneurial Approach* (Cambridge University Press, 2014).

Chapter 19

Figure 18-1. Aerial view of University of California, San Diego, campus, with Geisel Library in the upper-left quadrant and the Salk Institute at the top across Torrey Pines Road[84]

- *Building Globally Competitive Research Institutions from the Ground Up.* The Salk Institute and General Atomics were start-ups established in the 1950s and 1960s, as was the San Diego campus of UC. The Revelle plan for UCSD brought in academic superstars from the start, and those faculty members and their initial hires brought an entrepreneurial spirit with them, leading to faculty hires such as Irwin Jacobs and Ivor Royston (Hybritech).
- *A Local Culture of Collaboration among the Academic, Public, and Private Sectors.* In its efforts to redirect and build the economy after World War II, San Diego benefitted greatly from the interest

---

[84] Photograph © 2003 by Alan Nyiri, courtesy of the Atkinson Photographic Archive, University of California, https://perma.cc/VJ7Z-2ZQL.

and willingness of civic, corporate, and university leaders to work together synergistically as a team. This helped greatly in the land-use decisions for the Torrey Pines Mesa, both in convincing the University of California to undertake most of the unusual and expensive Revelle plan to give the San Diego campus a running start at the highest level of academic quality and in adding to the general appeal of the area for research institutions and corporate start-up ventures.
- *Continuous Private-Sector Commitment to Engage with UCSD on Supporting High-Tech Entrepreneurship.* This was primarily carried out through UCSD CONNECT, described in the following section.
- *A Powerful Sense of "Place" That Binds All Inhabitants.* Because of San Diego's location in the extreme southwestern corner of the United States and its geographical separation by mountain ranges and other features, San Diegans have historically had a sense that they are integrally linked and must work together. This gives rise to the culture of collaboration mentioned above.

UCSD CONNECT. The research institutions had important roles in drawing science-based companies to the San Diego area, although there were no programs or priorities of the university or the research institutions toward fostering commercial development until the 1980s. Instead it was more a matter of what individuals did upon their own initiatives. There was also no substantial venture-capital community in San Diego until the 1990s. In part because of this lack, in 1985 UCSD worked with the local community to create UCSD CONNECT. CONNECT is an organization that brings together all participants in the innovation and commercialization process—scientists, corporate pioneers, venture capitalists, law firms, and providers of various other services—with the aims of creating a favorable environment for innovation and formation of new commercial ventures, as well as providing specific advice and help to persons wanting to commercialize technological developments.[85] In 2005, CONNECT, now with about twenty employees and an annual budget of $3 million, was spun off from UCSD to achieve independent status. The university retains the same strong degree of

---

[85] Walshok and Lee, 2014, *loc. cit.*

involvement. Since its founding, CONNECT has assisted more than three thousand start-up companies in attracting over $2 billion of investment capital. CONNECT has achieved a very positive reputation and has been modeled in more than fifty regions worldwide.[86]

BIOTECHNOLOGY

The biotechnology industry stems heavily from California and has a uniquely close involvement with universities. The San Francisco and San Diego campuses of the University of California have both had major roles in the birth and continued development of the industry in their respective regions of the state. Stanford University, UC Berkeley, and the University of Southern California have had significant roles, and there were also contributions from Caltech and other University of California campuses. The three largest clusters of the biotechnology industry in the United States, in order, are the San Francisco Bay area in California, the Boston area in Massachusetts, and the San Diego area in California.[87] That fact is strongly related to the nature of the universities located in those areas and activities within those universities. With regard to other leading universities, Breznitz[88] has provided an analysis of how the technology-transfer operations of Cambridge University (United Kingdom) and Yale University have differed and how they have contributed to the development of the biotechnology industry in those areas.

The biotechnology industry was launched through the technology for recombinant DNA that came from the collaborative research of Herbert Boyer at UCSF and Stanley Cohen at Stanford.[89] As was noted above, that technology was protected jointly by Stanford and the

---

[86] "About CONNECT," https://web.archive.org/web/20160619005725/http://www.connect.org/about-connect/.
[87] Alex Philippidis, "Top 10 U. S. Biopharma Clusters," *Genetic Engineering & Biotechnology News*, May 10, 2014, https://perma.cc/WXT7-BQJW.
[88] Shiri M. Breznitz, *The Fountain of Knowledge: The Role of Universities in Economic Development* (Stanford, CA: Stanford Business Books, Stanford University Press, 2014).
[89] Henry. R. Bourne, *Paths to Innovation: Discovering Recombinant DNA, Oncogenes, and Prions, in One Medical School, over One Decade* (Berkeley: University of California Medical Humanities Consortium, University of California Press, 2011), pp. 67–111.

University of California through a patent that was applied for in 1974 and issued in 1980 and is now among the most licensed of all time.[90, 91] Patenting of such a fundamental biological technique was a novelty at the time and was controversial in several respects.

Here we shall explore the ways in which the biotechnology industry formed around the San Francisco and San Diego campuses of the University of California. Casper[92] provides an insightful analysis of the ways in which these two largest actors participated in the creation of the industry. Interestingly, the methods and dynamics have been strikingly different in the two locales.

UC San Francisco

In chapter 10 the development of research excellence at UCSF was examined, in particular the contributions of the leadership of William Rutter and the research that produced three Nobel Prizes and led to the discovery of recombinant DNA, jointly between UCSF and Stanford researchers. By building a research faculty in the manner that he did, Rutter leapt over the issues that other universities faced in needing to promote transdisciplinary research, expand interests to more complex organisms, and/or integrate with clinical research. Jong[93] analyzes the differences between UCSF, Berkeley, and Stanford in biochemistry and molecular biology at the time of the recombinant-DNA revolution. He contrasts Rutter's approach at UCSF with those at Stanford and Berkeley. At Stanford the disciplines remained separate in research, and the interests of the principal figure, Arthur Kornberg, remained on simpler organisms. At Berkeley developments were hampered by organizational and geographic separation of researchers. Berkeley

---

[90] Hughes, 2001, *loc. cit.*
[91] Maryann Feldman, Alessandra Colaianni, and Kang Liu, "Commercializing Cohen-Boyer 1980–1997," DRUID Working Paper no. 05-21, Danish Research Unit for Industrial Dynamics, 2005, https://perma.cc/C9EU-SSNS.
[92] Steven Casper, "The University of California and the Evolution of the Biotechnology Industry in San Diego and the San Francisco Bay Area," in Martin Kenney and David C. Mowrey, eds., *Public Universities and Regional Growth: Insights from the University of California* (Stanford, CA: Stanford Business Books, Stanford University Press, 2014), pp. 66–96.
[93] Simcha Jong, "How Organizational Structures in Science Shape Spin-off Firms: The Biochemistry Departments of Berkeley, Stanford, and UCSF and the Birth of the Biotech Industry," *Industrial & Corporate Change* 15, no. 2 (2006): pp. 251–283.

ultimately in the early 1980s had to reorganize twenty biological departments that were based on species and applications into three departments based upon structural scale. These changes enabled forefront research, modernized facilities, and sufficient interactions and access to key instrumentation (see chapter 12).

Commercial biotechnology in the San Francisco Bay Area started with the decision by Herbert Boyer of UCSF and Robert Swanson, a young and itinerant venture capitalist, to form Genentech Corporation, which in 1976 became the first substantial biotechnology company.[94] As already noted, Boyer was codiscoverer, with Stanley Cohen of Stanford, of recombinant DNA. The founders of Genentech worked on an open-science model in which research and scientific information were shared freely, through open publication and through close interactions with researchers in universities and elsewhere. This was a natural outgrowth of the atmosphere that Rutter and coworkers had established at UCSF, and which had worked so well for advancing science there. In fact, cofounder Boyer maintained his UCSF professorship and research rather than transferring to Genentech. Open science was the natural way of working in the universities from which the Genentech scientists had come, and it had the added advantage of keeping everyone at the forefront of knowledge without restrictions of secrecy. It leads to a constant flow of ideas and people back and forth between universities and companies.

This nonsecret mode of operation was acceptable and even appealing to the San Francisco Bay Area venture capitalists involved in financing the start of the industry since it was also the working mode of the Silicon Valley electronics industry, with which they were heavily involved and that was already flourishing. From a business standpoint, the idea was to gain fame and start-up investments by exhibiting scientific capabilities and promise. Thus, one of the first undertakings of Genentech was to enter and win in 1978 an open competition held by the Eli Lilly pharmaceutical company for the development of human insulin, the technology for which was then licensed by Lilly.[95]

---

[94] Sally Smith Hughes, *Genentech: The Beginnings of Biotech* (Chicago: University of Chicago Press, 2011).

[95] Stephen S. Hall, *Invisible Frontiers: The Race to Synthesize a Human Gene* (New York: Atlantic Monthly Press, 1987).

Universities now have policies on relations with industry, on what will and will not be done under contracts or grants from industry, and on the uses of space and resources within the university. In the early years of Genentech, experiments for company purposes including the human-insulin work for the Eli Lilly competition were performed in Boyer's UCSF laboratories. Research supporting faculty entrepreneurial ventures was performed in other UCSF laboratories too, leading to controversies within the university, introspection, and eventually policies forbidding use of space and resources for nonuniversity purposes and governing conflicts of interest (see below).[96, 97, 98]

The success of Genentech, the research atmosphere at UCSF, and the fact that both Berkeley and Stanford biological sciences were evolving in the research direction of UCSF resulted in a flood of other new biotechnology companies. At least seventy-nine companies licensing UCSF technology were founded between 1976 and 2003, and UCSF faculty members were directly involved in the founding of forty-one of them.[99] One of these companies, Chiron, was successfully founded by Rutter himself, along with Pablo Valenzuela of UCSF and Edward Penhoet of UC Berkeley. The open-science approach was also followed by most of these other Bay Area biotech start-up companies. One reason is that many of the founders were faculty members. Also, venture capitalists would often seek managers and scientists from firms already in their portfolio to staff new start-up companies. Genentech itself was a particular source of scientists and leaders. Genentech was sold in 2009 to Roche for $46.8 billion,[100] and Chiron was acquired by Novartis in 2006 for $5.4 billion.[101]

Oral Histories. As noted earlier in this chapter, there is a rich collection of oral histories of those connected with the start of

---

[96] Jong, 2006, *op. cit.*, p. 271.
[97] Bourne, 2011, *op. cit.*, pp. 116–117.
[98] Casper, 2014, *op. cit.*, pp. 70–71.
[99] Economic and Planning Systems, *The Power and Promise of UCSF: A Study of the Economic and Fiscal Impact of the University of California, San Francisco*, 2010, https://perma.cc/TJ9B-RUNH.
[100] Hoffmann–LaRoche, Ltd., "Investor Update," March 12, 3009, https://perma.cc/AH9C-VK45..
[101] Novartis Corporation, "Novartis Acquisition of Chiron Approved by Chiron Shareholders," April 19, 2006, https://perma.cc/XP2U-ZF2J.

California biotechnology, especially in Northern California.[102] Those represented include persons from both the business world and universities, with particular emphasis on Genentech and Chiron.

UC San Diego

Due to the timing and nature of the founding of its campus, UCSD was also able to get a running start toward the sort of molecular and structural biology research that would launch the biotechnology industry. Following the Revelle plan, David Bonner, an outstanding molecular biologist from Yale, was hired and arrived in 1960, at the start of the campus. His vision was to build in much the same way that Rutter had at UCSF, with emphasis on bringing the relevant disciplines and subdisciplines together and on integrating modern biology research into what would be the new research-based School of Medicine. UC San Diego actually had ten faculty positions in the School of Medicine that were controlled by the campus Biology Department.[103] As for UCSF, modern biology at UCSD became the catalyst for launching a biotechnology hub within the region.

However, the way in which the industry came about in the La Jolla/San Diego area was substantially different from what happened in the San Francisco Bay area. The industry developed much more on a proprietary model without open science or free flow of information. That ownership approach fits the fact that most products of biotechnology require large up-front investment before there can be sales and revenue, mainly because of the extensive needs for clinical trials preceding approval of the product by the US Food and Drug Administration. In fact, this need has caused the open-science model in San Francisco Bay Area biotechnology to evolve toward a proprietary and ownership model over the years.

The creation of the biotechnology industry in the San Diego area started with the 1978 formation of Hybritech by Ivor Royston, who had that same year joined the UC San Diego School of Medicine as assistant

---

[102] Oral History eLibrary, Program in Bioscience and Biotechnology Studies, Regional Oral History Office, Bancroft Library, University of California, Berkeley, https://perma.cc/TH4S-XFEJ.
[103] Casper, 2014, *op. cit.*, p. 78.

professor.[104] The subject area for Hybritech was molecular medical diagnostics, using target-specific monoclonal antibodies. This technique had come from 1975 work at Cambridge University in England by Cesar Milstein and Georges Köhler that was recognized by the 1984 Nobel Prize for Medicine. Cambridge chose to dedicate that invention to the public domain. Equipped with that knowledge, with cell lines from his postdoctoral work at Stanford, and with the services of his former Stanford associate Howard Birndorf, Royston worked with Brook Byers of the venture-capital firm Kleiner Perkins to form Hydritech and commercialize the technology. Howard (Ted) Greene of Baxter International was hired as CEO and brought with him several other persons from Baxter. The Baxter background was useful because of Baxter's policy of moving employees among positions so as to give them diverse and comprehensive experience;[105] thus, they were versatile.

Hybritech was a large success, so much so that it was bought by Eli Lilly in 1986 for about $400 million. That acquisition was not a happy one, since it generated strong tensions between the conservative, midwestern management of Lilly and the more free-wheeling approach of the Hybritech people in San Diego, leading to the comment of one senior Hybritech scientist that "it was like *Animal House* meets *The Waltons*". That result was unhappy for Lilly and for the future of Hybritech, but it greatly stimulated the biotechnology industry of the San Diego area as former Hybritech managers spread out to form other biotechnology companies, often in concert with scientists from UC San Diego or one of the other strong biotech research institutes in La Jolla.[106] A 2002 study found over forty biotechnology companies in San Diego with a senior manager or board advisor linked to Hybritech.[107]

Large-Scale Research Linkages—UC Berkeley

Another approach that started in the early days of biotechnology was for major corporations to undertake formal, in-depth, and

---

[104] Royston remained on the UCSD faculty until 1990, when he left to spend full time with the venture world.
[105] Casper, 2014, *op. cit.*, pp. 79–82.
[106] Casper, 2014, *op. cit.*, pp. 83–84.
[107] Casper, 2014, *op. cit.*, pp. 82–89.

potentially long-term large-scale linkages with major universities or academic research centers in order to stay close to developments in molecular and structural biology and become aware of new developments earlier than they otherwise might. At first these partnerships were primarily with private institutions in the eastern and midwestern portions of the United States, and in particular Harvard and MIT, although there was also a $30 million research agreement in 1980 between Johnson & Johnson and the Scripps Clinic and Research Foundation in La Jolla directed toward synthetic vaccines. Those early linkages and the Whitehead Institute, a privately funded adjunct of MIT, are described and compared by Kenney.[108] The early approaches had mixed results, and renewals of the relationships were hindered by changes in corporate organization, management, and strategy. Over the years subsequently, large companies have gotten into the biotechnology business more by purchase of successful start-up firms than through large-scale partnerships with universities.

Two more recent large-scale university-industry partnerships on biotechnology research, both centering on the Berkeley campus of the University of California, are agreements with Novartis and with BP, which are described in the following sections.

Berkeley-Novartis Agreement. In 1998, a research agreement was made between the Berkeley campus of the University of California and Novartis, a large Swiss pharmaceutical and biotechnology company. The arrangement was unusual in its design and because it made such a sizeable contract between a commercial firm and a *public* university. The arrangement was controversial, has been thoroughly analyzed by several parties, and is probably the agreement of this nature that is most thoroughly documented in public media. It is therefore both worthy and valuable for consideration as a learning experience. A useful and insightful analysis of the drivers for the arrangement and of the benefits and concerns has been made by Berkeley political science professor Todd LaPorte.[109]

---

[108] Martin Kenney, *Biotechnology: The University-Industrial Complex* (New Haven, CT: Yale University Press, 1986).
[109] Todd LaPorte, "Diluting Public Patrimony or Inventive Response to Increasing Knowledge Asymmetries: Watershed for Land Grant Universities? Reflections on the University of California, Berkeley-Novartis Agreement," in Commission on Physical Sciences, Mathematics, and Applications, *Research Teams and Partnerships: Trends in Chemical Sciences, Report of a*

In the first unusual step, the initiator of the process was not the company but instead the College of Natural Resources of the Berkeley campus, which established a two-year period in which it solicited proposals from six major corporations. Novartis was selected after consideration of more detailed proposals from the four of those companies that responded with interest. By the terms of the ultimate agreement, Novartis contributed $5 million per year for five years, or $25 million total, for support of research in Berkeley's Department of Plant and Microbial Biology (PMB). This turned out to be about 30 percent of the total extramurally funded research budget of the department during those years. The portion of the funds devoted to overhead was 33 percent—that is, a 50 percent indirect-cost rate—covering renovations, support of the general graduate program, and general campus and university overhead. These indirect costs were divided fifty-fifty between the university-wide and campus administrations of UC,[110] with most of the campus portion being used for graduate-student fellowships in the Department of Plant and Microbial Biology.

Another very important component of the agreement was access by Berkeley researchers on a confidential basis to the Novartis agricultural genomic database. This was coupled with the expectation, which never materialized, of $3 million for a Novartis facility near the campus with workstations through which that database could be accessed and advisory Novartis employees who would help with access. The value of this aspect of the arrangement lay in the fact that a substantial amount of genomic data was at the time confidential to large companies. This placed the academic researchers in a situation where they would normally carry out research without full access to the then-existent knowledge base.

In return, Novartis received first rights to license a fraction of inventions from research in the department, whether or not supported with actual Novartis funds. That fraction was the ratio of the Novartis funding to the total departmental extramural research support, cited

---

Workshop (Washington, DC: National Research Council, National Academy Press, 2000), pp. 66–84, https://perma.cc/JCZ5-4RG4.

[110] This was before the 1995 change to distribute 94 percent of indirect costs to the campuses generating them (chapter 6).

as a method of calculation recommended by National Institutes of Health guidelines for arrangements involving both NIH and private support. Novartis also received the conventional thirty-day opportunity to review potential publications for patentable items and an additional sixty days if the decision was made to seek patent coverage.

The project was overseen by a six-member advisory committee with three members from the campus (the vice chancellor for research, the dean of the College of Natural Resources, and a noninvolved faculty member) and three members from Novartis. There was also a five-member research committee, three of whom were from the campus and two from Novartis, to select among proposals and award actual grants.

A number of concerns were expressed at the time and throughout the term of the agreement. These are summarized by LaPorte[111] and in the 2002 report[112] of an internal UC Berkeley administrative review. Many of the concerns dealt with academic freedom, notably the right of faculty members to choose and pursue research as they saw fit. Other concerns dealt with possible influence of corporate interests on the governance and academic workings of the PMB Department and with the possibility of Novartis "cherry-picking" from among all discoveries within the department, whether or not Novartis had actually supported the research. Those concerns eventually formed the lead items for an aggressively hostile story[113] in the *Atlantic Monthly*, which eventually was expanded into a book.[114]

As the controversy continued, there was the aforementioned internal administrative review commissioned by the Berkeley campus, followed by an external review undertaken at the behest of the Berkeley Division of the Academic Senate with the concurrence of the

---

[111] LaPorte, 2000, *loc. cit.*
[112] Robert M. Price and Laurie Goldman, "The Novartis Agreement: An Appraisal," Administrative Review, University of California, Berkeley Office of Research, October 4, 2002, https://perma.cc/6D4A-TJFN.
[113] Eyal Press and Jennifer Washburn, "The Kept University: U. C. Berkeley's Recent Agreement with a Swiss Pharmaceutical Company Has Raised Concerns Over Who Ultimately Directs Research," *Atlantic Monthly* 285, no. 3 (2000): pp. 39–42, 44–52, 54.
[114] Jennifer Washburn, *University, Inc.: The Corporate Corruption of Higher Education* (New York: Basic Books, 2005).

administration. That external review,[115] subsequently published as a book,[116] concluded that academic freedom and the academic conduct of the department had not been seriously compromised. The reviewers also made a number of recommendations, one of which was that the university should consider avoiding industry agreements that involve complete academic units or comparable large groups of researchers. The agreement, the reviews, and lessons learned have also been discussed by Geiger and Sá.[117]

During the five-year period of the agreement, there was a major restructuring of Novartis that eliminated the unit that had made the agreement. Hence renewal of the agreement beyond the five-year period became moot.

In addition to the academic-freedom issue, which was probably well enough addressed with regard to the specifics of research, essential questions surrounding this venture remained: To what extent should public institutions, and entire departments within those institutions, pair themselves with private corporations? Can academic objectivity be maintained amid such a presence? Is it appropriate to "sell" research liaisons with a department competitively to the highest bidder? And is it appropriate for a public institution that derives substantial taxpayer support, including corporation taxes, to match itself so visibly with one corporation? Conversely, it can be argued that a large amount of the total revenue of public universities (on order of 77 percent for the University of California) comes from sources other than the state budget and student fees, and that corporations within the state thereby do receive the benefit of their taxes, even when such arrangements are made with a single corporation. Another substantive issue is how confidential data (in this case, the Novartis agricultural genomic database) can be used in publishable research while fulfilling simultaneously needs for the openness of science and the ability for others to reproduce results.

---

[115] Lawrence Busch et al., "External Review of the Collaborative Research Agreement between Novartis Agricultural Discovery Institute, Inc. and the Regents of the University of California," https://perma.cc/46LS-CG5Q.

[116] A. P. Rudy et al., *Universities in the Age of Corporate Science: The UC-Novartis Controversy* (Philadelphia, PA: Temple University Press, 2007).

[117] Roger L. Geiger and Creso M. Sá, 2008, *loc. cit.*

Institutes for Science and Innovation. The creation and selection processes for the California (subsequently Governor Gray Davis) Institutes for Science and Innovation have been described in chapter 14. One of these (QB3) is in the area of quantitative biotechnology. There has been a very large component of industrial interaction for these institutes, and indeed, most of the matching funds for creating the institutes have been derived from industry. The modes of interaction of these institutes with industry fall within overall University of California policies and include features such as member, affiliate, and partner programs with benefits such as participation in workshops, visiting fellow programs, seats on scientific advisory boards and industrial advisory councils, and collaborative start-up and incubation programs, as well as research grants for individual projects.[118, 119, 120, 121]

Energy Biosciences Institute. In 2006, the multinational energy firm BP (formerly British Petroleum) announced an intention to create a major research operation in conjunction with one or more major universities. After preliminary explorations, BP invited five universities worldwide to form teams to submit proposals to join with BP in an Energy Biosciences Institute (EBI), which would be funded by $500 million spread over ten years. This institute would bring BP researchers together with university researchers and would emphasize innovative means of creating and producing fuels from biological sources. In early 2007, the competition was won by a team headed by the University of California, Berkeley (UCB), which also included the Lawrence Berkeley National Laboratory (LBNL) and the University of Illinois at Urbana-Champaign (UIUC). The proposal submitted by this partnership to BP is

---

[118] "CITRIS Membership Program," Center for Information Technology Research in the Interest of Society, University of California, https://perma.cc/PG87-NCTJ.
[119] "Industry," California Institute for Telecommunications and Information Technology, University of California, https://perma.cc/9CDC-QQMJ.
[120] "Industry Alliances," QB3, University of California, https://web.archive.org/web/20160710110153/http://qb3.org/industry-alliances.
[121] "About CNSI, California NanoSystems Institute," University of California, https://perma.cc/8AHM-BT56.

available online,[122] as is a business-school case study[123] describing the process and the factors surrounding it.

BP spokespersons indicated that important factors in the selection of the Berkeley-led team were the large and diverse array of distinguished researchers, the tradition of technological innovation and entrepreneurship in the San Francisco Bay Area, and the history of successful, large multidisciplinary science projects at LBNL.[124, 125] The existence of QB3 was also important, since it already had a positive reputation and an established team within it that could write the final proposal within the specified short time interval of sixty days. The attention given at the time to the UC Berkeley Artemisinin Project and the firm Amyris Biotechnologies,[126] for which the CEO was a former BP employee, may have been helpful as well. The inclusion of the Lawrence Berkeley National Laboratory served to bring the federal government into the arrangement.

The full agreement between BP and the Regents of the University of California is also available.[127] Elements of the arrangement and governance include the following:
- A new building was built on university-owned land adjacent to the Berkeley campus to house the Energy Biosciences Institute. Construction of the five-story, 112,800-square-foot building ($133 million) was financed by a combination of $40 million dollars in

---

[122] University of California, Berkeley, Lawrence Berkeley National Laboratory, and University of Illinois, Urbana-Champaign, "Energy Biosciences Institute: A Proposal to BP," November 2006, https://perma.cc/P4T4-T8DH.
[123] "EBI Case Study," Corporate Innovations, Haas School of Business, University of California, Berkeley, https://perma.cc/LL99-E5D6.
[124] Robert Sanders, "BP selects UC Berkeley to Lead $500 Million Energy Research Consortium with Partners Lawrence Berkeley National Lab, University of Illinois," News Center, University of California, Berkeley, February 1, 2007, https://perma.cc/VFF2-BRYP..
[125] Bonnie Azab Powell, "Our Generation's Moon Shot: Launching the Energy Biosciences Institute," News Center, University of California, Berkeley, February 1, 2007, https://perma.cc/JXM8-8P7P.
[126] Victoria Hale et al., "Microbially Derived Artemisinin: A Biotechnology Solution to the Global Problem of Access to Affordable Antimalarial Drugs," from *Defining and Defeating the Intolerable Burden of Malaria III: Progress and Perspectives*, supplement to volume 77(6) of *American Journal of Tropical Medicine and Hygiene*, 2007.
[127] "Master Agreement Dated November 9, 2007 between BP Technology Ventures, Inc. and the Regents of the University of California," http://web.archive.org/web/20161227194434/http://www.energybiosciencesinstitute.org/sites/default/files/EBI_Contract.pdf.

state lease-revenue bonds, external financing primarily from British Petroleum, and private gifts.[128] The building belongs to UC and during the EBI project has been a form of state and university cost-matching to the project. It does require substantial debt servicing. There was a similar space provision for the portion of the project at the University of Illinois.
- The building space was to be divided into open and proprietary (BP) research portions, with up to fifty BP personnel doing BP proprietary research accommodated in the building along with UC and LBNL scientists for the duration of the agreement.
- Up to 30 percent of the total funding from BP was to be spent on the BP scientists (i.e., $150 million out of the total of $500 million).
- $100 million of the total funding was to be used at UIUC to fund research on crops for ethanol and other biofuels.
- The director was to be both a UCB faculty member and a faculty senior scientist at LBNL, the associate director a BP employee, and the deputy director a UIUC faculty member.
- A governing board was composed of eight senior persons from the various participating organizations (two from BP; one each from UCB, LBNL, and UIUC; and the director, associate director, and deputy director of the institute).
- There were to be twenty-five themed research teams, with seven of them located at UIUC.
- Full institutional overhead was to be paid to UCB and UIUC on all open research funded by BP, with 75 percent of these indirect costs returned by those institutions to the Energy Biosciences Institute for administrative purposes.
- Intellectual property was to be owned by the participating institution that generated it, with BP having the right to license, royalty-free and nonexclusively, inventions made by researchers supported with BP money. Joint inventions were to have joint ownership.
- BP had the right to take royalty-bearing exclusive licenses on patented inventions in a time-limited fashion.

---

[128] Rebecca Cohen, "Energy Biosciences Building to Open in September," *Daily Californian*, July 22, 2012, https://perma.cc/6L6D-5ZE7.

An apparent motive for BP in setting up such an institute was close access to leading-edge research in an area that was seen as vital to the future of the corporation, with a high premium placed on intimate day-to-day interactions of BP researchers with those from the other institutions. The interest of BP in this form of research relationship was probably stimulated by the fact that the chief scientist of BP at the time was Steven Koonin, a noted physicist, who had been provost of Caltech and was subsequently under secretary of energy for the United States and is now director of the Center for Urban Science and Progress of New York University.

There were a number of concerns to be dealt with in the relationship. One was how to handle proprietary corporate research that is being carried out in close proximity with academic and national-laboratory researchers. The presence of proprietary corporate research on or adjacent to a university campus was not unprecedented, however, having been done, for example, at Hitachi's Plumwood House research laboratory in the biomedical research complex of UC Irvine, mentioned earlier in this chapter. A second concern, familiar from the Novartis agreement described above, was the preferential position given by a public university to a single private corporation with regard to the research of a large number of distinguished faculty members. A third concern was the need to ensure academic freedom in the choice and conduct of research. Recognizing these issues, the Berkeley campus developed both the proposal and the ultimate agreement in close consultation with the leadership of the faculty Academic Senate, something that had not been done for the Novartis agreement. Both the administration and the Academic Senate were usefully informed by the experience gained in the earlier Novartis project. The Academic Senate chartered a special committee to develop a guidance document[129] on university-industry relationships. The document was of considerable use to the administration in the negotiations with BP[130] and provides guidelines for future relationships.

---

[129] Academic Senate Task Force on University-Industry Partnerships, "Principles and Guidelines for Large-Scale Collaborations between the University and Industry, Government, and Foundations," undated, https://perma.cc/D8WK-V3S9.
[130] Beth Burnside, former vice chancellor for research, University of California, Berkeley, personal communication, March 2014.

Although there was predictably some criticism[131] from one of the sources that had criticized the UC Berkeley-Novartis agreement, it was apparent that the university had undergone a learning experience with the Novartis partnership, and this agreement with BP was, on the whole, far less controversial than had been the one with Novartis.

Both the financial circumstances of BP and the world energy situation changed during the ten years of the agreement, 2007–17. BP experienced its Deepwater Horizon oil spill in the Gulf of Mexico in April 2010, leading to major financial liabilities and a much more precarious financial situation for the company. There was also a sharp drop[132] in oil prices associated with developments in pressurized hydraulic fracturing of shale ("fracking") and OPEC (Organization of Petroleum Exporting Companies) policy, deferring the advent of large-scale commercial use of biotechnology for fuels further into the future. BP chose not to renew the contract beyond 2017, also exercising a contract option to reduce its funding by one-third in 2015 to just $5 million per year beyond that, followed by an extra year to smooth the transition.[133]

It is important that universities recognize that industrial needs and financial situations do change and that large-scale industrial partnerships should be viewed as a one-time package when they are established. This factor has been apparent throughout the entire history of large-scale university-industry partnerships. A university cannot hitch its wagon to an industrial star for the long run.

Another aspect to be stressed from a larger view of the Energy Biosciences Institute story is that success breeds success in building research prominence. As noted, the fact that QB3, the Governor Gray Davis Institute, already existed and had already brought together a team greatly facilitated preparation of what became the winning proposal for the Energy Biosciences Institute. The existence of QB3 and

---

[131] Jennifer Washburn, "Big Oil Buys Berkeley," *Los Angeles Times*, March 24, 2007, https://perma.cc/8RXV-E47K.
[132] "Historical Crude Oil Prices and Price Chart", InvestmentMine, https://perma.cc/967R-PTMF.
[133] Erik Neumann, "Not So Fast: At UC Berkeley, Biofuel Research Takes Hit as BP Oil Company Backs Away," *California*, California Alumni Assn., Berkeley, CA, February 2015, https://perma.cc/N4NL-EBWG.

the fact that the Energy Biosciences Institute would be in Berkeley considerably enhanced Berkeley's position in the nearly simultaneous selection by the US Department of Energy of locations for its three Bioenergy Research Centers, which led to the Joint Bioenergy Institute[134] in Emeryville, California, led by the Lawrence Berkeley National Laboratory.

The reduction and then cessation of BP funding left the Energy Biosciences Institute with several challenges. It had excellent biological and chemical laboratory spaces in a new building but a mission that was now hampered by low oil prices and less immediate interests of the business world in biofuels. Meanwhile, it had strong faculties at Berkeley and Urbana-Champaign with wide and diverse capabilities. In that sense it is a good research facility with abilities to involve strong researchers from any of many areas, now assessing its mission and seeking one or more new sponsors.

In 2017 it was announced[135] that Shell had concluded a $25 million partnership with UC Berkeley, $5 million per year for five years with the Energy Biosciences Institute, to "pursue fundamental research in the areas of solar energy transformation, advanced energy storage in novel synthesis routes to create new products, and to leverage new capabilities in computational material science and biosciences and bioengineering." Obviously this commitment and opportunity will draw in a substantially different mix of researchers.

These large-scale arrangements have been followed by additional industry-university arrangements, now tending to be much more targeted and not of such large size. For example, two subsequrnt arrangements involving Berkeley's College of Chemistry have been the California Research Alliance (CARA) by BASF (2014, renewed for five more years in 2017) involving inorganic materials and bioscience,[136] and the Novartis-Berkeley Center for Proteomics and Chemistry

---

[134]"JBEI Overview: From Biomass to Biofuels," *Jbei.org*, https://web.archive.org/web/20160629100030/https://www.jbei.org/about/jbei-overview/.
[135] Brett Israel, "EBI, Shell Sign $25 Million Partnership to Fund New Energy Tech Research," News, University of California, Berkeley, March 15, 2017, https://perma.cc/PFD8-UKT8.
[136] "BASF Launches Inorganics-Focused California R&D Center", CHEManager International, April 4, 2014, https://perma.cc/R8SP-8VP3.

Technologies, aimed at new chemistry directed toward difficult drug targets.[137]

Biotechnology, Agriculture, and Medicine in the University of California Patent Portfolio

The patents from which the University of California derives licensing income are heavily in biotechnology, agriculture, and medicine, with the portion attributable to biotechnology having risen over the years as the field has developed. The twenty-five top-earning inventions for the fiscal year 2015 are shown in table 18-1. As tends to be the case, this list is dominated by a few inventions with very large licensing volume, a feature that makes performance comparison among universities difficult.

The top-earning UC inventions since licensing began were reported in a presentation to the Board of Regents in January, 2012.[138]

---

[137] Ryan Cross, "Novartis, Berkeley sign drug chemistry pact", p. 14, *Chemical and Engg. News*, October 2, 2017.
[138] University of California Technology Licensing Program, presentation to the Committee on Finance, Item no. F9, Regents of the University of California, January 19, 2012, https://perma.cc/B4AG-V36P.

Table 18-1. University of California top-earning inventions, fiscal year 2015[139]
[Invention (Campus), Royalty & Fee Income ($1,000s)]

1. Prostate Cancer Drug (LA)	$65,513
2. Device for the Treatment of Atrial Fibrillation (SF)	$19,518
3. Hepatitis-B Vaccine (SF)	$10,080
4. Bovine Growth Hormone (SF)	$6,697
5. EGF Receptor Antibodies (SD)	$7,058
6. Nephropathic Cystenosis Treatment (SD)	$4,280
7. Chromosome Painting (LLNL)	$3,121
8. Tango Mandarin (RV)	$2,504
9. San Andreas Strawberry (DA)	$2,458
10. Firefly Luciferase (SD)	$2,358
11. Dynamic Skin Cooling Device (IR)	$2,157
12. Detection of Mycoplasma (IR)	$2,141
13. Albion Strawberry (DA)	$1,586
14. Monterey Strawberry (DA)	$1,427
15. Micro Implant for the Treatment of Glaucoma (IR)	$1,375
16. Tear Osmometer for Dry Eye Disease Diagnosis (SD)	$1,139
17. Golden Hills Pistachio (DA)	$1,137
18. Yeast Expression Vector (SF)	$1,030
19. Energy Transfer Primers (BK)	$937
20. Camarosa Strawberry (DA)	$821
21. Macromolecules for Drug/Diagnostic Delivery (SD)	$661
22. Ventana Strawberry (DA)	$637
23. Portola Strawberry (DA)	$611
24. Gate Field Plate Fabrication (SB)	$516
25, Optical Network Switch (DA)	$507

---

[139] "Ideas, Inventions, Impact," *Technology Commercialization Report*, p. 21, University of California, 2015, https://perma.cc/EGM8-W84D.

Chapter 19

UNIVERSITY OF CALIFORNIA POLICIES AND ADMINISTRATIVE STRUCTURES PERTAINING TO RELATIONS WITH INDUSTRY

Institutional Oversight

The University of California develops policies through highly consultative and interactive processes involving the Academic Senate and groups of persons with like administrative functions on the different campuses, coordinated through the administrative chain of leadership (see chapters 6 and 8). University-wide policies are incorporated into the *Academic Personnel Manual* or other compendia. Enforcement of policies is achieved through mandatory disclosure policies, such as the annual *Supplement to the Bio-bibliography*,[140] which is a comprehensive report on activities that each faculty member must make each year. Department chairs are responsible for reviewing the bio-bibliography forms for inclusiveness. Faculty members must also disclose any potential conflicts of interest at the time grant proposals are submitted for campus approval and submission. Situations thereby disclosed are reviewed and judged by specially constituted university committees, deans, and/or department chairs, as appropriate to the situation. The review committees can be either standing or ad hoc.

Many policies or policy envelopes are determined for the entire ten-campus university, while other implementing policies within university-wide policy envelopes are campus-specific. There are two different categories of policies—those for the relationship of the University of California as an institution with industry and those governing relationships with companies by faculty members and other researchers, individually or as groups.

Policies for Institutional Interactions

For years institutional interactions with specific companies were evaluated on an ad hoc basis, following what seemed at the time to make good academic sense. An example was the aforementioned relationship between the Berkeley Department of Plant Biology and

---

[140] Annual Supplement to the Bio-bibliography, https://perma.cc/8QY7-29T8.

Novartis Corporation. Before the subsequent BP agreement was put into place, the Berkeley campus administration worked with the Academic Senate to codify policy ground rules for large-scale campus interactions with industry, thereby producing the document referenced above which now exists as guidance for the future as well.

Policies for Faculty Interactions with Industry

Consulting. The most common form of faculty interaction with industry is private consulting. The Berkeley campus statement of policy for faculty consulting[141] is extensive and includes
- limits on consulting time,
- intellectual property aspects including the opportunity for the university to review disclosures to assess whether to assert ownership,
- a requirement of annual reporting,
- review for conflicts of interest, and
- counsel for the faculty on what to seek in consulting agreements.

Consulting is further restricted for certain health-sciences (e.g., medical) faculty members whose clinical activities are included in a comprehensive compensation plan that includes practice[142] and for those faculty members in agricultural areas whose appointments involve advisory work through Cooperative Extension.[143, 144]

Principles. Several general concepts have driven the generation of University of California policies for interactions with industry.

---

[141] "UC Berkeley Guide to Consulting for Faculty and Academic Employees: Policy & Guidelines," University of California, Berkeley, September 19, 2006, https://perma.cc/AC6M-7AE8.

[142] "Health Sciences Compensation Plan," Section 670, *Academic Personnel Manual*, University of California, https://perma.cc/YZK8-LJLY.

[143] "Academic Personnel and Programs: Cooperative Extension," *Faculty Handbook*, University of California, https://perma.cc/4244-A9TQ.

[144] "Specialist in Cooperative Extension Series, Section 334," *Academic Personnel Manual*, University of California, https://perma.cc/V6GT-7QA6.

- In line with the nature of a public university and to avoid suspicion, the university emphasizes transparency and strong rules on full disclosure. Potential conflicts of interest must be revealed and analyzed. Judgments of potential conflicts are typically done by committees of faculty peers from a variety of disciplines.
- Economic and societal benefits are major outgrowths of a strong public research university. Hence, public service is encouraged, as is consulting, within appropriate limits. Research leaves by faculty for business start-ups are also encouraged, but all these activities are subject to limits.
- Time paid for by the university should be used for purposes that serve the university and a faculty member's roles within it. Leaves without pay can be considered when faculty members are engaged in nonuniversity matters, but should be limited in duration.
- The university is open and, in general, does not engage in secret or confidential research. Both the University of California and its Lawrence Berkeley National Laboratory have no classified (i.e., military secret) research.
- There should be clear rules about graduate student involvement which ensure that students can interact freely with faculty and peers, without information being withheld.

A list of UC policies governing university-industry relations for faculty members is available.[145] Brief descriptions of the most pertinent specific policies follow. (See earlier in this chapter for the patent policy.)

Copyright. Following the tradition that scholars own their own writings or other output subject to copyright, the University of California copyright policy gives ownership to academic employees producing books, papers, works of art, and so forth. For externally sponsored work, the university may assert ownership, but only for reports or other work stemming directly from the sponsored project

---

[145] "UC Policies Governing University/Industry Relations," Vice Chancellor for Research, University of California, Berkeley, https://perma.cc/2J63-4KFN.

and still not for resultant books or journal articles. The university may give its ownership to a sponsoring firm in an agreement.

Conflict of Interest. Conflict of interest falls under an array of policies reflecting university-wide and campus policies, as well as California state law. Any application for approval of a research proposal to an entity in which a principal investigator has a financial interest requires submitting a California state form for review by a campus faculty Conflict of Interest Committee. A determination that there is a conflict of interest does not doom a research project, since there are mechanisms for managing conflicts of interest.

Conflict of Commitment. Policies covering conflict of commitment and faculty leaves are given in Section 025 of the UC *Academic Personnel Manual*.[146] Faculty members on the usual nine-month academic-year appointment are limited to thirty-nine days of outside activities during the academic year (an average of one day per week), and are required to seek and be granted leave without pay when exceeding this limit. That limit becomes forty-eight days for faculty members on year-round appointments. There are no considerations or limits in this policy concerning the amount of compensation that faculty members can receive from external activities. Faculty members cannot, in general, hold an executive or managerial position for a private firm. Leaves of absence without pay may be obtained for purposes such as active participation in the start-up of a company, and are usually granted for the first and even a second year but are normally not approved beyond the second year. The faculty member must then make a basic career decision—company or university.

Use of University Resources. University facilities and resources cannot be used for outside purposes, except for desks, computers, and routine use of telephones.

Publication. It is expected that research results will be published in full without limitations. A sponsor cannot specify that any methodology or results cannot be published, except for the restrictions regarding confidential items described in the next paragraph. A publication delay of up to sixty days is acceptable so that a sponsor may review

---

[146] "Conflict of Commitment and Outside Activities of Faculty Members," Section 025, *Academic Personnel Manual*, University of California, https://perma.cc/QHF5-ANBZ.

publications and offer comments or suggestions and/or determine that proprietary data are not inadvertently disclosed. In either case, the final decision on content must rest with the author. A delay of up to ninety days can be allowed so that the University, the sponsor, or both may screen proposed publications for possibly patentable ideas. If both ninety- and sixty-day delays are applicable, the total period of delay should not exceed ninety days.

Confidential Materials and Information. Access to and/or use of a sponsor's proprietary data or materials are accepted only if regulations regarding access, use, and protection of such data or materials do not restrict the full dissemination of scholarly findings made under the grant or contract or put the University in a position of assuming financial liability.[147]

Licensing. University of California licensing guidelines for intellectual property are posted.[148] In some cases the University of California will take equity in a firm, particularly a start-up firm, instead of a licensing fee. The policy[149] governing such situations is designed to avoid issues of favoritism toward financial gain of a faculty member and any influence of a faculty inventor on the university's decision, and to reduce the amount of risk assumed by the university as well.

MECHANISMS FOR ASSISTING COMMERCIALIZATION OF RESEARCH AND CORPORATE START-UPS

As a public research university, the University of California encourages utilization of its research by industry and the business world, both in California and worldwide. Licensing and technology-transfer policies are designed to maximize commercial and societal uses of research results, rather than maximizing royalty income per se.

---

[147] Note the relation of this policy to the issue of the use of the Novartis agricultural genomic database in the UCB-Novartis agreement described above.
[148] "University Licensing Guidelines," revised February 1, 2012, University of California, https://perma.cc/JE7U-U369.
[149] "Accepting Equity When Licensing University Technology," University of California Policy, June 18, 2008, https://perma.cc/DU6X-W5KZ.

Location

University of California campuses have a number of programs that are designed to assist faculty members and students in developing entrepreneurial skills and bringing their accomplishments and ideas along to commercial ventures. University-wide lists of incubators and accelerators[150] and entrepreneurship[151] programs are available. As an example, the Berkeley campus as of 2017 had the following programs.

SkyDeck[152] is an accelerator program, designed to help faculty and student entrepreneurs move ideas into commercialization effectively and efficiently. A team of consultants is available to advise and help. Elements of the accelerator program include the Product Story, Market Traction, Business Model, Team Development, and a Funding Plan.

The **Coleman Fung Institute for Engineering Leadership**[153] is an arm of the College of Engineering that provides full- and part-time master's programs and continuing education in engineering as linked to entrepreneurship and the business world. The aim is to transform engineers and scientists into leaders who can take risks and develop technical, social, and economic innovations.

The **Berkeley-Haas Entrepreneurship Program** and the **Lester Center**.[154] This program serves as a hub for education and research relating to entrepreneurship in the business world. It is a component of the Haas School of Business.

The **Product Development Program**[155] is a master's degree program provided by the Department of Chemical and Biomolecular Engineering within the College of Chemistry. Students gain knowledge

---

[150] "Incubators and Accelerators," Office of Innovation and Entrepreneurship, Office of the President, University of California, https://web.archive.org/web/20171022221429/https://www.ucop.edu/innovation-entrepreneurship/incubators--accelerators.html.

[151] "Entrepreneurship Programs," Office of Innovation and Entrepreneurship, Office of the President, University of California, https://web.archive.org/web/20171024065339/https://www.ucop.edu/innovation-entrepreneurship/entrepreneurship-programs.html.

[152] "Welcome to SkyDeck," University of California, Berkeley, https://web.archive.org/web/20161123173400/http://skydeck.berkeley.edu/.

[153] Fung Institute for Engineering Leadership, College of Engineering, University of California, Berkeley, https://web.archive.org/web/20140812142700/https://funginstitute.berkeley.edu/.

[154] Berkeley-Haas Entrepreneurship Program, Haas School of Business, University of California, Berkeley, https://web.archive.org/web/20161112003033/https://entrepreneurship.berkeley.edu/.

[155] Product Development Program (PDP), College of Chemistry, University of California, Berkeley, https://web.archive.org/web/20170710194220/http://chemistry.berkeley.edu/grad/cbe/pdp.

and field experience in the complex process of transforming technical innovations into commercially successful products.

Bakar Fellows[156] are selected early-career faculty members whose work shows commercial promise in the fields of engineering, computer science, chemistry, biological sciences, and physical sciences, and in multidisciplinary work in these areas. The fellows receive discretionary research support of $75,000 per year for up to five years and participate in the network of other activities on campus relating to entrepreneurism.

The Foundry@CITRIS[157] is a technology incubator based at the Center for Information Technology Research in the Interest of Society (one of the Governor Gray Davis Institutes) to help entrepreneurs build companies at the intersection of hardware, software, and services. The Foundry provides access to design, manufacturing, and business tools within a community of mentors that transforms start-up teams into founders.

The **QB3 Garages**[158] are similar incubators supporting start-up and commercialization exploration activities in the area of biotechnology, affiliated with the California Institute for Quantitative Biosciences (QB3), another of the Governor Gray Davis Institutes. There are QB3 Garages at UCSF Mission Bay and UC Berkeley, as well as a QB3 East Bay Innovation Center in Berkeley and a larger QB3@953 incubator facility in San Francisco.

Big Ideas@Berkeley[159] is an annual contest designed to provide funding, support, and encouragement to interdisciplinary teams of students who have "big ideas" that could lead to important innovations. The program was founded in 2006 and has a number of sponsors inside and outside the university.

---

[156] Bakar Fellows Program, Vice Chancellor for Research, University of California, Berkeley, https://web.archive.org/web/20170714004556/https://vcresearch.berkeley.edu/bakarfellows/about.

[157] CITRIS Foundry, Center for Information Technology Research in the Interest of Society, University of California, Berkeley, https://web.archive.org/web/20160721200935/http://foundry.citris-uc.org/.

[158] "The QB3 Incubator Network," QB3, https://web.archive.org/web/20161018123352/http://qb3.org/startups/incubators.

[159] Big Ideas@Berkeley, University of California, Berkeley, https://web.archive.org/web/20170818093827/http://bigideas.berkeley.edu/about/.

The **Development Impact Lab**[160] of the Blum Center for Developing Economies provides support to innovators to bring projects to a scale that would server the developing portions of the world.

SUMMARY CONCLUSIONS

One of the most important missions of a major public research university is technology transfer, working cooperatively with industry and entrepreneurs to move inventions based upon university research into commercial use. This is a complex arena and one that universities, including the University of California, have learned by degrees through trial-and-error efforts over the past forty to fifty years. Technology transfer requires mechanisms to move discoveries along the path of initial development, continual synergistic interactions with industry, and a host of policies to avoid favoritism and various conflicts and to keep things generally within ethical bounds. The sequential developments at UC have included a very modest beginning under the direct auspices of the UC Regents, creation of an Office of Technology Transfer within the Office of the President, consideration and then rejection of auxiliary private ventures, decentralization of interactions with industry to the campuses so as to be closer to the faculty, recognitions that licensing should be integrated with other aspects of interactions with industry, and then active efforts to promote the efforts of would-be entrepreneurs in incubators created for that purpose on or near campuses. The MICRO Program developed in the 1970s and the Industry-University Cooperative Research Program (1996–2008) leveraged state funds with industrial funds and thereby facilitated many beneficial relationships.

Two major cases that led to massive high-tech economic communities—Silicon Valley and the Torrey Pines/La Jolla/San Diego area—are described with regard to the forces that brought them about and enabled such success. A similar analysis is made for the development of California's biotechnology industry in the San Francisco

---

[160] Development Impact Lab, Blum Center for Developing Economies, University of California, Berkeley, https://web.archive.org/web/20171012060315/http://dil.berkeley.edu/.

and San Diego areas, the first and third largest, respectively, of such clusters in the United States. University involvements are given particular attention. Two large-scale linkages of the Berkeley campus with industry—those with Novartis and with BP for the Energy Biosciences Institute—are analyzed as well, one serving as a learning experience so that the next could be approached in better fashion.

19.
Location

In what became a set and nationally recognized raiding piece, candidates were lured to La Jolla, where they were given carefully orchestrated dinner parties in faculty homes, including [Roger] Revelle's on the beach in mid–La Jolla and new ones in Scripps Estates...Then it was time for a walk in the eucalyptus groves adjacent to Highway 101 that cut through the piece of Torrey Pines land Revelle wanted for his campus. He would shepherd marks onto the highest point, on Camp Callan land, marked by an "old, fallen brick chimney. I used to take our prospective professors up to this point, climb up on the old chimney, and look around, saying something like, 'Can't you see a great campus arising all around here?'"
—*Nancy Scott Anderson*[161]

The next contact that I had with UCLA came during a visit to the West Coast that my wife and I made in the fall of 1938. I'd recently gotten the Ph. D. degree and received an appointment as assistant professor at the University of Chicago. It happened that the National Tax Association was holding its annual convention in San Francisco...After the convention we came to Los Angeles. Of course, whenever I travel I always go to see the universities, so we came to Westwood. We were simply enchanted with the beauty of the community. At that time Westwood, you know, was a Mediterranean village, a suburban village, very quiet, and altogether delightful. We liked the Italian Renaissance buildings here on the campus. In fact, my wife and I remember saying to each other at that time, "This is where we want to live." We were getting tired of the crush and the grime of Chicago.
—*Neil Jacoby, founding dean of the UCLA Graduate School of Management*[162]

---

[161] Nancy S. Anderson, *An Improbable Venture: A History of the University of California, San Diego* (San Diego, CA: UCSD Press, University of California, 1993), p. 73.
[162] Neil H. Jacoby, interview by James V. Mink, "The Graduate School of Management at UCLA, 1948–1968," Oral History Program, p. 29, University of California, Los Angeles, CA, 1974.

When he [David Saxon] was invited to become a member of the physics faculty at UCLA, he sought the advice of an older colleague. His colleague's view was that UCLA was not a particularly distinguished institution, but it had the advantage of being located in sunny southern California, and if things did not work out he could always play golf. "But everybody says they're going to build a great university and a great physics department out there," David replied, and cast his fate with UCLA.
—Richard Atkinson[163]

They [Mike Bishop, Harold Varmus, Herb Boyer, and Stanley Prusiner] did not choose UCSF because of its excellence as a place to do science— excellence it could not claim at that time, in any case. Instead they chose it because San Francisco and California offered more freedom and more fun—sunshine, Carol Doda, Beat poets, fishing in the San Francisco bay—compared to east coast cities.
—Henry Bourne[164]

In addition to the intellectual, academic, governance, and people factors that constitute the subject of most of this book, the geographical location of California and what has come with it have also been exceedingly important for the development of the University of California.

---

[163] Richard C. Atkinson, "David Stephen Saxon, President Emeritus," In Memoriam, University of California, 2005, https://perma.cc/AX79-SZ3E.

[164] Henry R. Bourne, *Paths to Innovation: Discovering Recombinant DNA, Oncogenes, and Prions, in One Medical School, over One Decade* (University of California Medical Humanities Consortium and University of California Press, 2011), p. 206.

THE EARLY DAYS

It was the gold rush of 1849 that first brought large numbers of settlers from the eastern portion of the United States into California. This was a rough crowd that traded little on knowledge and education and took law and "justice" into its own hands through vigilante groups and kangaroo courts. This setting was not an auspicious one for the development of an outstanding university. However, there were some among this influx of people who did care greatly about education, and the College of California that became the University of California had drawn some of them.

As the new university developed, its California location betokened adventurism and opportunities for entirely new lives. The LeConte brothers, Joseph and John, were two of the ten initial University of California faculty members. As described in chapter 2, they came to the university because it was one of the few places in the United States where former Confederates could have a strong university teaching career. A very similar story, also told in chapter 2, applies to Eugene Hilgard, who placed California agriculture on a scientific basis and was an originator of the field of soil science.

The fact that California was a land of new opportunity and new beginnings was a very important factor in drawing capable people to the university in its early days. But then as of the turn from the nineteenth century to the twentieth, it was primarily the status and promise of the university as a university, rather than the location and nature of California itself, that brought the next wave of intellectual builders, such as Benjamin Ide Wheeler (president, 1899–1919), and then Armin Leuschner, Gilbert Newton Lewis, Joel Hildebrand, and Raymond Birge (chapter 9), who arrived in 1890, 1912, 1913, and 1918, respectively.

LARGE AND CONTINUAL GROWTH

The continual large growth of California has in many different ways been a major enabling factor for the University of California.

Population

California has been in a continual state of large growth over the years, from the gold rush of 1849 through the start of Hollywood as the movie capital of the world in the early twentieth century and on through the influx of those fleeing the Dust Bowl era of the Depression in the 1930s, the great influx of returning World War II veterans to the San Fernando Valley in the late 1940s, the baby boom and its echoes associated with the children of those veterans, and booms and opportunities associated with high-tech industries. Table 19-1 shows US census data[165] for the population at ten-year intervals and the percentage growth during the decades preceding each of those years. These numbers are unparalleled in the United States.

With the growth in population has come corresponding growth in the economy and state revenue, along with needs for services including higher education. This has led to the necessity to create new campuses of the University of California and to increase capacity on existing campuses. Continual growth and building have until recent years brought constantly increasing state budgets for higher education, which have enabled continued improvements and opportunities to do new things. It is much easier to build and improve university education in a time of growth than it is in a time of stasis or contraction.

Economy

The California economy has grown and diversified over the years in what has been a truly synergistic relationship between universities and industry, described in more detail in chapters 16, 17, and 18. Industries have provided employment and stimulated economic growth that have enabled continual building and development of universities, and research universities have provided many of the new ideas, processes, and products that have fueled industry. As well, the industries of California have been a substantial part of the attraction, drawing faculty, graduate students, and postdoctoral researchers to California. Those people who came to California universities have in turn become important founders and hires for industry.

---

[165] "Demographics of California," *Wikipedia*, https://perma.cc/DD5W-VN8P..

Table 19-1. Historical population of California

Census Year	Population	% Growth over Decade
1850	92,597	--
1860	379,994	310.4%
1870	560,247	47.4%
1880	864,694	54.3%
1890	1,213,398	40.3%
1900	1,485,053	22.4%
1910	2,377.549	60.1%
1920	3,426,861	44.1%
1930	5,677,251	65.7%
1940	6,907,387	21.7%
1950	10,586,223	53.3%
1960	15,717,204	48.5%
1970	19,953,134	27.0%
1980	23,667,902	18.6%
1990	29,760,021	25.7%
2000	33,871,648	13.8%
2010	37,253,956	10.0%

The synergy between universities and industry that builds the California economy has gone on through many waves:
- the development and industrialization of California agriculture,
- initiation and growth of specialized agriculture-based industries particularly suited to California such as wine, strawberries, and almonds,
- the oil boom in southern California in the early 1900s,
- the growth of aircraft and other war-related industries in World War II,
- the launch of the movie industry, which then grew further through creation of program content for television and now streaming,
- Silicon Valley and the electronics, computer hardware, and software industries,
- the wireless telecommunications industry in San Diego, and
- the biotechnology industry.

Interestingly, the effects upon the economy and industry have not been uniform around the state of California. Storper et al. compare and contrast the relative economic growths of the San Francisco and Los Angeles areas in recent decades, analyzing the reasons why the San Francisco economy has grown to a much greater extent.[166]

Growth of Funding for the University of California

As already noted in chapters 2 and 17, the booming California economy immediately following World War II provided the financial wherewithal for Governors Earl Warren and Pat Brown to give priority and devote so much of the state budget to the building of the University of California in the 1950s and 1960s, a period that happily coincided with the initial growth in support of university research by the federal government.

THE LURE OF CALIFORNIA LIFE AND CLIMATE

California has many features that are highly attractive for lifestyle and recreation. Seven of the ten campuses of the University of California are located in coastal areas along the Pacific Ocean. By virtue of the Pacific weather patterns and the Alaskan Current, the coastal regions have pleasant, fog-laced Mediterranean climates. Southern California is renowned for its outdoor-living lifestyle, well popularized through entertainment media. There is no snow toward the coast, but one can readily drive to snow and to excellent downhill skiing in the winter months. In the summer, the Sierra Nevada mountain range is John Muir's Range of Light, beckoning for hikes and trips in a land of lakes, open country, and rugged granitic beauty. Sailing and other maritime activities are close at hand. Both the San Francisco and Los Angeles areas have excellent cultural attractions—symphony, art, opera, theater, and more. Santa Barbara is a well-recognized retirement community, as is the Monterey Bay area near Santa Cruz. As is noted in several of the quotes at the beginning of this chapter and in

---

[166] Michael Storper et al., *The Rise and Fall of Urban Economies: Lessons from San Francisco and Los Angeles* (Stanford, CA: Stanford University Press, 2015).

the description of the recruitment of Nobelist chemist Willard Libby to UCLA (chapter 10), these aspects of pleasant living have been vitally important recruitment tools for drawing faculty to the university. University of California faculty members hardly ever move away when they retire.

The more interior campuses have attractions of their own. Merced is only two hours away from Yosemite Valley by automobile. The Davis campus, well known as the capital of knowledge relating to agriculture in California, is a stable and pleasant community. Riverside, the city once plagued by the midday arrival of photochemical smog from traffic in the Los Angeles Basin, has been largely freed of that problem by the catalytic converter and the removal of lead from gasoline, and now is a seat of the vibrant and still developing Inland Empire.

THE SIERRA NEVADA MOUNTAINS AND CONSERVATION

For many the draw was the magnificent natural values and mountains of California. There is a longtime confluence among faculty and graduates of the University of California, the Sierra Nevada Mountain Range, and various conservation movements. The early days of these activities is being documented by Merritt.[167] An original University of California faculty member, geologist Joseph LeConte, led university excursions to Yosemite Valley and environs within the mountains for years. The LeConte Memorial Lodge of the Sierra Club in Yosemite Valley is named for him. The LeConte bond between the university and the Sierra Nevada continued through Joseph LeConte's son, Joseph N. LeConte, who was a professor of mechanical engineering at UC. Joseph N. LeConte and his wife, Helen Gompertz LeConte, were avid explorers and even makers of first ascents.

---

[167] Karen Merritt, *The University of California and the University of the Wilderness: The California Genesis of Outdoor Schools of Discovery in America's National* Parks, book in process, 2017; see also project decription, "A History of Early Educational Connections among the University of California, Sierra Club, and the National Park Service," Center for Studies in Higher Education, University of California, Berkeley, https://perma.cc/SQ9C-5A4Z..

University of California faculty members were heavily involved in the start of the Sierra Club, the noted conservation organization that started as a protector of the Sierra Nevada Mountains. Joseph N. LeConte, J. Henry Senger (professor of philology), and Cornelius B. Bradley (professor of English) were all among the small group of founders of the Sierra Club in 1892, joining with John Muir and others from the San Francisco Bay Area.[168] The university also had strong ties to the launching of the National Park Service as a branch of the federal government, as described succinctly by Martin,[169] more fully by Merritt,[170] and in a video documentary series by Ken Burns.[171] The first two directors of the National Park Service—Stephen Mather and Horace Albright—were both graduates of the University of California and closely tied to it. By virtue of its rich and varied terrain, California is home to nine wilderness national parks—Yosemite, Kings Canyon, Sequoia, Lessen Volcanic, Redwood, Joshua Tree, Death Valley, Channel Islands, and Pinnacles—and a national seashore (Point Reyes).

The distinguished Berkeley field biologist and zoologist, Joseph Grinnell, was the founding director of the Museum of Vertebrate Zoology at Berkeley with the financial support of Annie Alexander, who had also supported James Meriam in starting the Museum of Paleontology at Berkeley (see chapter 9). Grinnell participated with the National Park Service in establishing a program of public instruction in the parks, which went on for a number of years. As well, he used the parks as a laboratory, establishing a scientific mission for them.

For many others, including this author, the Sierra Nevada mountain range has provided a strong recreational attraction binding them to California.

Many University of California faculty members have been drawn to conservation efforts, in part as the colleges of agriculture have

---

[168] Michael P. Cohen, *The History of the Sierra Club, 1892–1970* (Sierra Club Books, 1988), https://perma.cc/9M47-5ZVG.

[169] Glen Martin, "Love National Parks? Thank UC Berkeley, and What Transpired Here 100 Years Ago," *California Magazine*, Cal Alumni Association, March 19, 2015, https://perma.cc/7K9T-MENU..

[170] Merritt, 2017, *loc. cit.*

[171] Ken Burns, producer, *The National Parks: America's Best Idea*, PBS, https://perma.cc/7SSE-EYAD.

expanded mission to include natural resources, with there now being an almost complete switch in that direction at Berkeley. The interests have been contagious. Highly successful efforts to save San Francisco Bay from encroachments and landfill were launched and led for decades by Sylvia McLaughlin, Kay Kerr, and Esther Gulick—spouses of a regent, a president, and a Berkeley faculty member, respectively[172]

The Sierra Nevada Research Institute has been a valuable founding organized research unit for the Merced campus (chapter 10).

THE PACIFIC RIM

One major trend of the 150 years that the University of California has been in existence has been the development of the economy and global influence of the Pacific Rim. The opening of the Panama Canal in 1914 greatly facilitated commerce between a Eurocentric world and Pacific Asian nations, as well as the West Coast of the United States, which had been reached earlier by the US transcontinental railroad. It was natural for California to develop close ties with Asian countries.

Within the University of California, the Pacific Rim has proven to be a rich area for intellectual development. As examples, the following organized research units and formal research centers on the Berkeley campus deal specifically with the Pacific Rim nations.

>Asia Business Center
>Center for Buddhist Studies
>Center for Chinese Studies
>Center for Japanese Studies
>Center for Korean Studies
>Center for Southeast Asia Studies
>Institute for South Asia Studies
>Institute of East Asian Studies
>Pacific Earthquake Engineering Research Center
>Richard B. Gump South Pacific Research

---

[172] Jill Leovy, "Sylvia McLaughlin Dies at 99; Longtime San Francisco Bay Environmental Activist," *Los Angeles Times*, January 21, https://perma.cc/B4HW-LAY2..

UC San Diego has a very well respected School of Global Policy and Strategy[173] that focuses upon the Pacific Rim.

Recognizing the importance of the Pacific Rim for the University of California and for California itself, UC president David Gardner in 1986–87 established the Pacific Rim Program "with the goal of fostering and enhancing research on the economic, political, social, trade, finance, cultural, security, and related issues pertaining to this region and its interactions with the world."[174] This program thrived for over two decades before falling victim to the UC state budget reductions and the decision to focus university-wide research funding on new initiatives.

Another measure of the importance of the Pacific Rim to the University of California is the large student enrollment from the region. In fall 2016, 86.5 percent of enrolled undergraduate international students came from Pacific Rim countries, with 65 percent of total international undergraduates from China alone.[175]

MEXICO

Among the individual states, California has had one of the most positive relationships with Mexico, and thus the geographic location of California adjacent to Mexico has been important to the University of California. Since 2003, the university has maintained Casa de la Universidad de California en México,[176] located in Mexico City a short distance away from the National Autonomous University of Mexico, UNAM. This building complex houses the UC Education Abroad Program in Mexico, is a headquarters for UC researchers doing research in Mexico, and provides a meeting space available for various purposes. The facility is designed to be catalytic to UC-Mexico

---

[173] School of Global Policy and Strategy, University of California, San Diego, https://web.archive.org/web/20171107162538/http://gps.ucsd.edu/.
[174] David P. Gardner, *Earning My Degree: Memoirs of an American University President* (University of California Press, 2005), p. 224, http://escholarship.org/uc/item/1r0625vt.
[175] "Fall Enrollment at a Glance," InfoCenter, University of California, accessed May 16, 2017, https://www.universityofcalifornia.edu/infocenter/fall-enrollment-glance.
[176] "University of California, Mexico City," University of California, https://perma.cc/4HAJ-6TEP.

interactions in research and teaching. A multicampus research unit, UC-MEXUS is headquartered at the Riverside campus and serves to foster and financially support University of California research on Mexico, including research collaborative with investigators from Mexico.[177]

EARTHQUAKE COUNTRY

California is earthquake country, being on the Pacific Ring of Fire. Superficially, this fact would probably be viewed as a liability rather than an attraction, except that the location has made the university a principal home of research on seismic matters and earthquake-resistant structures. The University of California has thereby drawn a number of noted researchers in these areas and has several research institutes devoted to the subjects, most notably the Pacific Earthquake Engineering Research Center, consisting of ten core partner universities, of which five are University of California campuses, with the Berkeley campus as lead institution.[178]

VARIED CLIMATE AND TOPOGRAPHY

California has extremely varied topography. The lowest (Badwater in Death Valley, 279 feet below sea level) and highest (Mount Whitney, 14,505 feet) points in the contiguous United States are 156 miles apart from one another within California. Rainfall varies from that of the coastal redwood forests of the northwestern part of the state to that of the Mojave and other deserts of southeastern California. Given the very different distributions of population and rainfall, California moves an immense volume of water from the north to the south. The California Aqueduct alone, flowing from the Sacramento River to the

---

[177] UC-MEXUS, University of California Institute for Mexico and the United States, University of California, Riverside, https://perma.cc/994K-8KMY.
[178] "PEER Core Institution," Pacific Earthquake Engineering Research Center, https://perma.cc/CX35-WUVP.

Los Angeles area, has a capacity of 13,000 cubic feet (370 cubic meters) of water per *second*.[179]

The diverse terrains and climates have created marvelous outdoor laboratories, which draw many researchers of different types. The Natural Reserve System of the University of California maintains 760,000 acres in thirty-nine such sites. A few examples are

- Hans Jenny Pygmy Forest on the ecological staircase of the Mendocino Coast;
- White Mountain Research Station with locations at altitudes of 4,108 feet, 10,151 feet, 12,470 feet, and 14,242 feet (1252, 3094, 3,801, and 4341 meters);
- Boyd Deep Canyon Desert Research Center, a major drainage system descending from the high peaks of the Santa Rosa Mountains down to the Colorado Desert; and
- Merced Vernal Pools and Grassland Reserve, associated with the newest campus and with preserving unique San Joaquin Valley terrain (chapter 10).

The coastal locations in California attracted and enabled the Scripps Institute of Oceanography, which preceded the UC San Diego campus, and the strong marine biology programs which initially built research on the Santa Barbara campus.

---

[179] "California Aqueduct," *Wikipedia*, https://perma.cc/9W2A-MJYZ.

20.

Retrospective

The purpose of this chapter is to draw on the contents of the foregoing chapters so as to look at research universities from three standpoints:
- Why are well-respected research universities important? What are the essential features? What are world trends?
- What general features are most conducive to the development of outstanding research universities?
- What have been the most important specific factors in the development of the University of California, and how do they contrast with what has occurred in other potentially similar states in the United States?

THE IMPORTANCE OF RESEARCH UNIVERSITIES

The Rush toward Research Universities for Economic Development
A strong research university brings a core of intellectual activity and potential innovation to the surrounding area. If the university has research that is important for sparking and/or supporting innovations in the business world, it can draw research-based businesses. When coupled with venture capital and the other support services needed for start-ups, a research university can become a key catalyst for new business development and societal improvements. It provides an attractive source of higher education, which can draw outstanding indigenous students, countering the possibilities of a brain drain to other countries or, in the United States, to other states. It should also produce a more enlightened, thoughtful, satisfied, and broadly capable population.

University-associated research parks and government-organized development laboratories can also become key players in industrial start-ups. Some well-known successes in California are Silicon Valley, which sprang in large measure from Stanford Industrial Park, and the

San Diego/La Jolla area, both described and analyzed in chapter 18. Some of the other examples in the United States are the MIT/Route 128 combination in Massachusetts, the Research Triangle in North Carolina, and the Austin, Texas, area. In other countries, success stories have included the Industrial Technology Research Institute (ITRI) and the surrounding Hsinchu Science and Industrial Park in Taiwan,[1,2] Cambridge University and the adjoining "Silicon Fen" development in the United Kingdom, and the many developments in Bangalore, India.

The reputations of very positive economic and developmental impacts from these endeavors have spawned a rash of new developments around the world. Typically, these involve a central, and often new, research-university campus with a business or research park in the close environs. Some examples are

- King Abdullah University of Science and Technology (KAUST) and the King Abdullah Economic City (KAEC) in Saudi Arabia,
- KAIST (an acronym for what was formerly Korea Advanced Institute of Science and Technology) and the surrounding Daedeok Science Town in South Korea,
- Skolkovo Institute of Science and Technology and Skolkovo Innovation Center near Moscow in Russia,
- the new Mission Bay campus of the University of California, San Francisco, and its industrial-research environs,
- the development of high-tech industry around UNICAMP Brazil,
- Nazarbayev University in Kazakhstan and its associated Nazarbayev University Research and Innovation System, and
- the recently (2016) approved Sparrow Hills research center in Moscow, involving Moscow State University and the Russian Academy of Sciences.

Other very large and extensive initiatives are in China. Project 985 promotes the development of what are now forty world-class research universities, many with surrounding industrial parks and/or

---

[1] Otto C. Lin, *Innovation and Entrepreneurship: Choice and Challenge*, World Scientific Publishing, Singapore, 2018.

[2] Otto C. Lin, interview by Robin Li and Emily Hamilton, "Promoting Education, Innovation, and Chinese Culture in the Era of Globalization," vol. 1, oral history, pp. 158–272, Regional Oral History Office, University of California, Berkeley, 2007-2009, https://perma.cc/C5KN-XV9V.

development centers. A companion effort, Project 211, aims to strengthen about one hundred research universities. There are also developments in China that are being driven by the establishment of industrial or research parks (e.g., the Shanghai Zhangjiang Hi-Tech Park). The list goes on.

But can all these ventures succeed? Do they involve a sufficient amount of all the necessary and helpful features? And what are the necessary features? One approach to answering the latter question is that of this book—to infer and generalize important factors from an examination of the University of California.

ACADEMIC EXCELLENCE AND RANKINGS

For better or for worse, the projects identified above and the associated ambitions are pointed toward what is essentially a single definition of world-class universities ("WCUs") and role models, with a spate of quantitative rating and ranking systems having strong influence as a means of setting goals and measuring success. These systems are considered in the appendix. New ratings continually crop up. These approaches tend to combine different selections among, and weightings of, the same or similar factors, most of which are subject to relatively simplistic measurement. Some systems focus in addition or instead upon reputational surveys.

In a World Bank report[3] Salmi presents the general features that he concludes are needed for the development of WCUs, placing the needs in three broad categories, as follows:
1. a high concentration of talent (faculty and students),
2. abundant resources to offer a rich learning environment and to conduct advanced research, and
3. favorable governance features that encourage strategic vision, innovation, and flexibility and that enable institutions to make decisions and to manage resources without being encumbered by bureaucracy.

---

[3] J. Salmi, "The Challenge of Establishing World Class Universities," World Bank, Washington, DC, 2009a, https://perma.cc/UWX4-YRWF..

The World Bank has important roles for financing projects in developing countries; hence Salmi's analysis has been influential for planning in many nations.

Paradeise and Thoenig[4,5] have examined the internal sociological dynamics in universities relating to matters of academic excellence and reputation. Using the Berkeley campus of the University of California and MIT as prime examples, they paint the picture of a total focus on, and commitment to, academic and research quality as being a prime characteristic of top-rated research universities.

Douglass[6], and Douglass and Hawkins[7] have also recently analyzed the drive toward WCUs. Douglass stresses that needs differ for different countries and has suggested approaches and measures that may be more suitable for leading universities to be most effective for their own countries. Douglass and Hawkins consider these issues for Asian universities expressly.

As noted by these and other authors, attention to the various rating and ranking systems tends to drive competing universities and countries toward a large degree of sameness—a single conforming model. That fact is unfortunate for several reasons. First, a mix of diverse approaches is much needed in both universities and research. That diversity has long been considered a valuable hallmark of higher education in the United States, and the same should be true in the rest of the world, especially with such great differences in the levels of development, cultures, traditions, resources, and goals of different countries. Different students fit better with different forms of education, and research-university education is not for everyone. In research, differences in organizational structures and approaches help to foster innovation of different sorts. Secondly, by the very nature of rankings, only a few universities can be at the top, and to have a

---

[4] Catherine Paradeise and Jean-Claude Thoenig, *In Search of Academic Quality* (London: Palgrave Macmillan, 2015).
[5] Jean-Claude Thoenig and Catherine Paradeise, "Organizational Governance and the Production of Academic Quality," *Minerva* 4 (2014): pp. 381–417.
[6] John A. Douglass, ed., *The New Flagship University: Changing the Paradigm from Global Ranking to National Relevancy* (London: Palgrave Macmillan, 2016).
[7] John A. Douglass and John N. Hawkins, eds., *Envisioning the Asian New Flagship University: Its Past and Vital Future* (Berkeley: Berkeley Public Policy Press, 2017).

hundred or more universities vying for those top positions is a recipe for frustration for most of them.

This situation is accentuated by the fact that there is very little turnover, even from decade to decade, at the top. Top-rated universities are attractive to faculty members because of the inspiration and collaboration that can be gained from outstanding colleagues, the prestige associated with the institution, and the ability to have outstanding student and postdoc coworkers. Graduate students and postdocs are drawn to top universities because of the perception that experiences there will be more intellectually stimulating and valuable and because it adds to one's résumé. As well, granting agencies or corporations may find value in associating with top-ranked universities. All these factors discourage turnover in rankings across the years.

THE RATIONALE FOR RESEARCH UNIVERSITIES: SYNERGY

A research university combines three missions—education, research, and service. Those missions can be described succinctly as follows:
- **Education** instills new concepts, knowledge, creativity, working methodology, and habits in students.
- **Research** discovers and codifies new knowledge.
- **Service** involves using knowledge and understanding to address issues and problems of society, both outside and inside the university.

Each of those broad functions has multiple components. Graduate education is different and more intense and specialized than undergraduate education. Professional education and continuing education are different yet. The nature of research differs among fields, particularly among the professions and among the social sciences. The service mission is relatively new in many parts of the world, but it is long established for public research universities in the United States, having typically started with support of agricultural practice and allowance and encouragement of government service by faculty members. It now includes service in university governance, consulting services to industry and government, participation[8] in studies made by the National Academies, community service, and service to disciplinary or professional societies.

For several reasons, it is advantageous to combine these three seemingly separate missions into a single institution. The processes of discovering and codifying new knowledge create a thorough mastery of existing knowledge en route, and they keep faculty members both current and at the forefronts of their fields. One of the best ways of developing creative abilities is by doing research, especially formulating new research questions and avenues toward answering them. Guided tutorial participation in research and the joint student-faculty research done in the sciences and a growing number of other fields are time-tested intensive methods of developing creativity and research abilities in individuals. Service requires and utilizes a mastery of knowledge and keeps faculty members up to date on current issues and realities of the world, thereby informing teaching and research. Having one type of institution serve these multiple purposes is efficient, and it creates synergy, since fulfilling each of the missions provides important wherewithal for the other missions. The synergies and the complexities and multidimensionalities of research universities were classically analyzed by Clark Kerr in his 1963 Godkin Lectures at Harvard which became his book *The Uses of the University*.[9]

There are, of course, institutions that serve one or two, but not all three of these purposes. A liberal arts college will emphasize teaching, but without much research, and can supply much greater attentiveness to individual students. However, it cannot instill research awareness and creativity in the same ways. Institutions such as the national laboratories of the United States or the Max Planck Institutes in Germany are focused on research without the teaching component. They cannot as effectively provide the next generation of researchers and leaders of industry and society, and they for the most part miss intellectually valuable student coworkers. Colocation of a national laboratory and a leading university, as at Berkeley, is therefore a valuable synergy. A company like the Rand Corporation or

---

[8] Participation in these studies is not limited to actual members of the National Academies.
[9] Clark Kerr, *The Uses of the University* (Cambridge, MA: Harvard University Press). The book went through five editions: 1963, 1972, 1982, 1995, and 2001.

organizations such as agricultural extensions can emphasize service. But in terms of gaining synergies and efficient use of resources by grouping these three functions together, there seems to be general recognition that the research university is the most effective mechanism that has been devised so far.

FEATURES OF SUCCESSFUL, HIGH-IMPACT RESEARCH UNIVERSITIES

An outstanding high-impact public research university will carry out highly respected and influential research as viewed by peers, have the essential characteristics to educate and nurture the full capabilities of succeeding generations of excellent researchers and leaders of society and industry, be perceived as highly useful by industry and entrepreneurs, and have good means of interacting with industry and entrepreneurs to help in the development of new technology and new companies.

Accomplishing Research of the Highest Quality

The sine qua non for an outstanding research university is having faculty members with high research ability and accomplishment. That ability takes the form of the insights and creativity needed to define promising research that can lead to new discoveries, new understanding, and/or new and powerful codifications of knowledge. Those abilities are best identified, cultivated, and evaluated in other people by leading researchers themselves. Measures of that ability include candid opinions of peers and various national and international recognitions such as awards from professional societies, national academy memberships, and Nobel and other major worldwide prizes. These measures are represented in many of the rating and ranking systems.

Excellent faculty members must be sought, identified, recruited, supported, and sustained. They should be continually incentivized, reviewed, and rewarded. Efforts should be made to interest people of all sorts to go on in higher education and to consider academic careers. Native creative talent is everywhere. Searches for potential faculty members must be widespread and should be coupled with a sound means of recognizing and assessing talents and abilities by leading researchers themselves. In the development of first-tier research in the physical sciences at Berkeley, critical assessments by people such as Gilbert Lewis, Raymnd Birge, Joel Hildebrand, and Griffith Evans were essential (chapter 9). The University of California system of continual, career-long advancement reviews involving Academic Senate Committees on Academic Personnel (chapter 11) has been particularly effective for providing independent, evidence-based assessment, incentive, and reward.

A culture of excellence and respect for accomplishment should pervade the institution, and continual steps should be taken to enable and reinforce that culture. The involvement of a large fraction of the faculty in shared governance through the Academic Senate and in the academic advancement system has been effective for that purpose within the University of California, since it gives faculty members continual reminders of the shared values of excellence. It is very important for the institution to have an intellectual meritocracy rather than a civil-service-like system of nearly automatic advancement that limits opportunities for exceptional advancement. Continual objective program reviews (chapter 12) serve a similar purpose of involving many faculty members and reinforcing high standards.

There should be policies and support services in a research university that best enable faculty members to do research limited only by their own creativity and not by other extraneous constraints. Faculty members themselves should select their areas of research and conceive their own new lines of research, rather than being assigned areas of research or research topics. It is the faculty member who understands her or his field best and can most effectively recognize new opportunities. That goal is not meant to suggest that faculty members should work in isolation. They need continual interaction with peers to assure a good flow of new thoughts and ideas. Particularly in the social sciences, faculty researchers need insulation against political interference.

Outstanding researchers draw outstanding coworkers—faculty colleagues, graduate students, and postdoctoral researchers. That fact was well demonstrated in the initial development of the San Diego campus of the University of California. In turn, outstanding colleagues, graduate students, and postdocs draw outstanding faculty members. It is a chicken-and-egg situation, and, as already noted, has been one of the key reasons why there is surprisingly little turnover in the lists of outstanding research universities from year to year.

Part of enabling faculty members to pursue the leads that they, themselves, identify and choose is ample and diverse availability of financial support for research. The US approach of support from a wide array of government agencies, private foundations, and industrial companies has proven to be effective in enabling support of a wide range of research, with other sources to try if one source fails. Competitive and selective allocation of research funding based upon strong peer-review assessment gives faculty members much incentive to think their proposals out fully and choose striking, high-impact research. It is also important that provisions be made in peer review processes to enable sufficient grant support for entry-level faculty members.

As knowledge has grown, disciplines, subdisciplines, and areas of research have tended to become narrower and more compartmentalized. Yet many of the most critically needed areas of research are highly multidisciplinary. It is therefore important for a research university to have organizational structures, facilities, and review mechanisms for promoting multidisciplinary research. For the University of California, those include organized research units with reporting lines that differ from those of academic departments, national laboratories, and large research institutes.

Among the draws for top-notch researchers can be unique user facilities, such as the Advanced Light Source at the Lawrence Berkeley National Laboratory and the UC-Caltech Keck telescopes. The King Abdullah University of Science and Technology (KAUST) recognized the value of this approach as it started up de novo with the aim of rapidly becoming a first-tier research university. Cutting-edge facilities and major instrumentation were provided at the start and served as lures for recruitment of highly regarded faculty members.[10]

---

[10] "Core Labs and Major Facilities," King Abdullah University of Science and Technology (KAUST), https://web.archive.org/web/20140626051208/http://www.kaust.edu.sa:80/core-lab-major-facilities.html.

Finally, it is valuable to establish a Silicon Valley–like culture where failures are recognized as essential components of the route to success—that is, where risk taking in the selection of research is rewarded rather than viewed as a stigma when things don't work out. High impact often comes from high risk.

Educating and Attracting Capable Researchers, Potential Entrepreneurs, and Inquiry-Aware Citizens

A research university should have several educational missions that relate closely to its research mission. The most basic is to educate all its students to value intellectual curiosity, research inquiry, and healthy skepticism. A second is to interest, identify, and cultivate the researchers of tomorrow. And a third is to supplement an education and a research understanding with the personal knowledge and skills that can make successful innovators, entrepreneurs, and citizens.

Ways of accomplishing these goals at the undergraduate level are well spelled out in the Boyer Commission Report of 1998.[11] To accomplish these goals, research universities should stress the incorporation of inquiry and research concepts and examples into courses, seminars, and student projects. As one example, for almost a hundred years, it has proven particularly effective at Berkeley to follow a policy of matching faculty members who are both outstanding researchers and outstanding teachers with the freshman chemistry course, a tradition that started with Joel Hildebrand and the forty thousand students that he taught in freshman chemistry over many years.

Research experiences for undergraduates can come about in many ways, ranging from small research projects within courses to longer-term experiences with a faculty research group. Participants in research groups can either have an independent project or take part in a larger research project with a pedagogically capable graduate student or postdoc. Effective ways of providing undergraduate research

---

[11] Boyer Commission on Educating Undergraduates in the Research University, *Reinventing Undergraduate Education: A Blueprint for America's Research Universities* (Stanford, CA: Carnegie Foundation for the Advancement of Teaching, 1998), https://perma.cc/TD4W-BMQ8.

experience are considered in a recent National Academies report.[12] Douglass and Zhao[13] utilized data from the Student Experience in the Research University survey (SERU)[14] to measure the degree of involvement in research of undergraduates at the nine undergraduate University of California campuses and six other leading research universities. They found that 81 percent of undergraduates had carried out at least one project or written a research paper as part of a course, 39 percent had taken at least one student research course, and 40 percent had assisted faculty in research with or without course credit and with or without pay.

Research and the development of research and creative abilities are of course the main goals of doctoral education. There and in postdoctoral education, it is vital to involve students as full intellectual partners in research, both for their own education and for what they can and will bring to the research themselves. If the student is not a full partner in defining and guiding the research, a vital pedagogical opportunity is lost.

High Economic Impact and Regional Development

There are avenues that a research university can and should pursue internally to promote economic and societal impact of its research. Active ways should be sought to promote the use of the fruits of university research for economic development and societal improvement. This requires marketing efforts and knowledgeable staff members who can help university researchers achieve technological liaisons with companies. University relations with industry need to be wider than just licensing of patents and processing of research grants and contracts. As noted in chapter 18, technology-transfer and patent-

---

[12] Undergraduate Research Experiences for STEM Students: Successes, Challenges, and Opportunities (Washington DC: National Academies Press, 2017), https://perma.cc/R6DM-NLFM.
[13] John A, Douglass and Chun-Mei Zhao, "Undergraduate Research Engagement at Major US Research Universities," Research & Occasional Papers Series, no. 14.13, Center for Studies in Higher Education, University of California, Berkeley, November 2013, https://perma.cc/J8HM-W6DZ.
[14] "Student Experience in the Research University (SERU)," Center for Studies in Higher Education (CSHE), https://perma.cc/RT6T-BB33.

licensing offices have become much more sophisticated over the years and can doubtless improve further.

Other activities in the region near a university greatly influence whether or not that region can be fertile for technological innovation and entrepreneurism. Multidimensional resources and services must be available to support corporate start-ups, including venture capital, specialized legal and financial services, flexible laboratory facilities, a skilled workforce, leaders experienced in start-up ventures, and a culture that is supportive of technological ventures and risk taking. There must be ways in which the large middle ground between discovery and commercialization can be bridged. One possibility is for industrial corporations in the area to have strong in-house capabilities for development of research discoveries and innovations toward commercialization. Alternatively, as was well demonstrated by the Industrial Technology Research Institute (ITRI) in Taiwan,[15] inclusion of an "intermediary" technological laboratory and/or demonstration facility along with a university and a surrounding corporate park can be effective. Yet another approach is large-scale multidisciplinary university research institutes like the four Governor Gray Davis Institutes for Science and Innovation at the University of California.

A research university can take steps to work synergistically with its region to develop regional innovation and entrepreneurism. The UC CONNECT operation (chapter 18) started by the San Diego campus of the University of California was highly effective for that purpose and helped turn San Diego from a military, wartime economy into the multidimensional, high-tech economy that exists there today. Campus-located or campus-affiliated incubators can help faculty members and students turn ideas into successful corporate ventures. A university can also seek faculty members who will develop areas of research that fit the attributes and resources of the region.

Government Roles

In California, the role of government with regard to higher education itself and economic and societal benefits stemming from university research is largely one of enablement rather than any more

---

[15] Lin, 2018, 2007–09, *locs. cit.*

hands-on or limiting approach. Constitutional autonomy and the fact that it was the higher education community itself that developed the 1960 Master Plan for Higher Education have both been important, as have been the relatively long appointment terms of the regents (twelve years, formerly sixteen years).

For public research universities, involvement from the political processes of government invariably gets in the way of development and maintenance of academic quality, because it turns attention to other issues and affects the academic reputation of the university adversely.

THE ATTRIBUTES MOST IMPORTANT FOR THE UNIVERSITY OF CALIFORNIA

What I believe are the most essential factors for the success of the University of California were listed at the start of this book in table 1-1. This section summarizes these factors and compares them with situations for public research universities elsewhere in the United States, working serially through the factors.

The Best and the Brightest. Attention to hiring the best and the brightest faculty members is hardly unique to the University of California; it is a goal expressed by essentially all leading research universities. But the University of California—through resources, policies, and practices—has paid particular attention to *enablement* of its faculty to have the resources, facilities, and time to do outstanding research and teaching, with the goal of having their own capabilities be the only limitation. That is one important reason for the overall general success of UC faculty members.

Single University with Multiple Campuses. The structure of the University of California as a single university of ten campuses, all with the same mission and aspirations, is unique. Most multicampus state-university systems in the United States are composed of separate universities or multicampus universities (e.g., New York, Illinois, Texas, Texas A&M) with missions that differ, either through specification or de facto. The University of Illinois and the University of Nevada, as examples, have each succeeded in developing two campuses that are recognized and accomplished research institutions. The State University of New York has three such campuses (Buffalo, Stony Brook, and Albany) among its sixty-four components. The University of North Carolina has two major research campuses (UNC Chapel Hill and North Carolina State University at Raleigh), originally separate universities. The State University System of Florida, formed through amalgamation in 2003, contains multiple research universities with varying degrees of distinction. But no state even approaches the ten substantial research-university campuses of the University of California or the number of campuses ranked near the top.

The structure as a single university with multiple campuses all having the same mission has advantages in several ways. It allows new campuses to be formed from within (see below). It enables a focus on the research-university mission without the distraction of additional missions. It enables a single budget with internal methods of distributing that budget, thereby minimizing extramural pressures. It provides single voices to the state and federal governments. On the other hand, systems of campuses and universities with a variety of missions can potentially do a better job of articulation for transfer education within the system.

Shared Governance. Shared governance exists in name in nearly all major universities and is generally stronger in public universities than in private ones. But I have found no other university in the United States where it is as organized and as comprehensive as at the University of California. The UC structure serves many beneficial and stabilizing purposes. It enables the faculty themselves to have responsibility for overseeing the academic quality of the institution and results in the involvement of more good minds in governance. It promotes faculty allegiance to the university. It continually involves faculty members in considerations where the common purpose is assessing and sustaining the academic quality of the institution, thereby sustaining that purpose. It has in many instances enabled faculty members from different disciplines to find common interests and participate together in multidisciplinary research, teaching, or both. The clearly recognizable importance of shared governance within the University of California brings intellectual leaders from the campuses into it. Indeed, it was the intellectually most respected faculty members, largely in the physical sciences, who met with the Board of Regents in 1919 to establish the modern structure of shared governance for the university.

Career-Long Peer Review of Faculty Members. One of the key aspects of shared governance at the University of California is the continual career-long academic-performance review of faculty members by peers, an elaborate process that is described in chapter 11. That structure provides strong incentives for faculty members to excel, serves as a constant monitor and reminder of the academic quality of the institution, and provides a thorough and fair process where the views of no one individual can carry untoward weight. It also provides post-tenure review, something that is often recognized as needed but is contentious and difficult to implement in the rest of the academic world. This system of continual reviews throughout one's entire career is at least unusual among major research universities and may be unique.

Building from Within. The University of California has been almost completely built from within, whereas many other public-university systems or multicampus universities have usually been built by bringing together preexisting institutions. Some examples of the latter approach include the State University of New York, the University of Texas, the University of North Carolina, and the University System of Florida. The differences between the two approaches may seem subtle, but they are not. It is very difficult to change the culture of an existing institution or to upgrade it academically. By contrast, the formation of new University of California campuses occurred with a set of standards and policies for personnel evaluation and other academic needs being present from the start and being brought into play through the Academic Senate structure by faculty members from existing campuses. Initial faculty members for the new campus were hired with reviews from Academic Senate committees composed of faculty members from existing campuses, with the high standards of those existing campuses being applied. The rapid rises of many of the UC campuses to high stature and reputation reflect this fact.

Historically High Levels of Support from the State of California. The state of California has, over the years and until recently, given strong support to the University of California. That support stems from the original 1868 goal of rivaling the best (private) eastern universities and the establishment of constitutional autonomy in 1879, on through the interest of the Progressives of the early twentieth century in public higher education. Three factors fortuitously coexisted after World War II – a large state budgetary surplus, two governors (Earl Warren and Pat Brown) who gave the University of California very high priority, and a surge of returning veterans and immigrants from other states, which necessitated and enabled a large expansion of the university.

In many of the eastern states of the United States, strong private universities were already in existence when the Morrill Act of 1862 facilitated the creation of public land-grant universities. The existences of these strong private universities provided a rationale for allowing a lesser degree of distinction for the public universities when they were formed. Because of its newness as a state and the rough-and-ready way in which it came to be, California had no strong private universities at the time of the Morrill Act, and resources and attention were devoted instead to the public university, the University of California. The strong private universities—Stanford University, Caltech, the University of Southern California, and others—came later, after the role, mission, and desire for distinction of UC had been established.

Constitutional Autonomy. The incorporation of constitutional autonomy for the University of California into the state constitution of 1879 served to assure self-governance under the Board of Regents without a way for the state legislative process to impose requirements or limitations on the university. There is of course still an annual budgeting process for the university as part of the state budget proposed by the governor, considered and enacted by the legislature, and subject to line-item veto by the governor. But the prohibitions against the legislature getting into other areas and the governor acting independently of his or her role as one member of the UC Regents provide a considerable amount of self-determination to the university. The level of constitutional autonomy for the University of California is rivaled in the US only by the constitutional situations for the University of Minnesota and all public universities in Michigan.

Master Plan for Higher Education. The 1960 California Master Plan for Higher Education formally differentiated the missions of the three sectors of public higher education, creating economic efficiency and wide access to public higher education independent of ability to pay. It also confirmed a wide reach of higher education by virtue of the transfer route and a role for the University of California that solidified its position as a preeminent research university. Important factors for UC were (1) the preservation of the research role and nearly all of doctoral education to UC, such that UC could determine how best to organize and manage it; (2) lessening of what would otherwise have been huge enrollment pressure for UC through of the roles of the California State University and transfer education; and (3) the concepts of eligibility and guaranteed access, which defined high school college-going curricula and established a clear rationale regarding which students could take part in UC (and CSU) education. The California Master Plan has no parallel in other states of the United States.

Location. Several aspects of the location of the University of California have been important to the university. The fact that California has been regarded as a land of opportunity and has had continual, stunning population growth has created an ever-increasing enrollment and ever-increasing resources for higher education until the stringencies of recent years. The sanguine climate of coastal California has been a strong attraction for recruiting faculty, as have the many recreational opportunities of the state. The Silicon Valley phenomenon and areas of economic growth such as biotechnology and the wine industry have created a strong synergy among the university, industry, and the economy within the state.

Multidisciplinary Opportunities. Due to the ever-increasing depth of knowledge in the various disciplines and the fact that many of the most pressing societal needs involve multiple disciplines, progress is often most effectively achieved by bringing the full power of several disciplines together in a well-integrated fashion. Thus universities must facilitate faculty members from different disciplines working together in both research and teaching. The University of California has had a good start down this road in several ways. The cyclotron work of Lawrence led to a large multidisciplinary laboratory on the hill east of the Berkeley campus, which became a national laboratory and moved into many other multidisciplinary fields such as energy, environment, and biotechnology. The university was one of the first to establish organized research units (ORUs), most of which are multidisciplinary, as government support of research grew after World War II. The four

Governor Gray Davis Institutes for Science and Innovation, established in 2000, moved the university further along these lines and positioned it well for subsequent competitions, such as the worldwide competition for BP's Energy Biosciences Institute.

Integration of Professional Fields with the Academic Disciplines. One way in which the University of California did not model the great eastern universities, notably the Ivy League universities, was by providing professional schools with the same status as academic departments. Faculty members from professional schools participate fully in shared governance with the faculty from the rest of the campus. Review committees for appointment, promotion, and advancement of faculty members contain both professional-school and academic-discipline faculty members. Faculty members from throughout the campus participate in organized research units together. This situation contrasts with universities such as Harvard where professional schools are much more independent in governance and are "tubs on their own bottoms" financially. In the University of California, the professional schools and academic disciplines reinforce one another fully intellectually.

21.
The Future for the University of California and Public Research Universities

Higher education is the engine driving America to a better future for all its citizens—not a consumer good but a public investment—and a public good. It is the single most important driver of opportunity and prosperity at home, and for American influence and idealism abroad.
  —Robert M. Gates[1]

These days students pay more of the cost of attending public universities than state governments ...The money public colleges collect in tuition surpassed the money they receive from state funding in 2012. Tuition accounted for 25 percent of school revenue, up from 17 percent in 2003. State funding, meanwhile, plummeted from 32 percent to 23 percent during the same period.
  —Washington Post, 2015[2]

As the story goes, if you put a frog into a pot of boiling water, he will jump out immediately. But if you put the frog into the pot of water and then turn on the heat, he won't realize it is boiling until too late...That slow simmering to a boil is the essential challenge in public higher education.
  —Matthew Lambert[3]

---

[1] Robert M. Gates, Charter Day Remarks, College of William and Mary, Williamsburg, VA, February 8, 2013, https://perma.cc/RZC3-ZZ7M. Also cited by Matthew T. Lambert, *Privatization and the Public Good: Public Universities in the Balance* (Cambridge, MA: Harvard Education Press, 2014), p. 221.
[2] Danielle Douglas-Gabriel, *Washington Post*, January 5, 2015, https://perma.cc/P47Z-5C87. referencing "Higher Education: State Funding Trends and Policies on Affordability," US Government Accountability Office, December 2014, https://perma.cc/VX76-2REL.
[3] Lambert, 2014, *op. cit.*, p. 7.

If...public institutions are no longer state supported, who owns them? Who should govern them? Who[m] should they serve?...The defunding of public higher education by the states inevitably inaugurates a new conversation about who controls them and whose interests are to be served.
—*Thomas Mortenson*[4]

There are cogent reasons for concern about the future of public research universities and public higher education in the United States. The University of California is not immune from these concerns. This chapter explores those issues and what they may mean for the future.

CHALLENGES

The most obvious cause for alarm is the decline in state funding to public colleges and universities that has occurred during the early years of the twenty-first century. It has presented serious financial challenges to all of public higher education and shows little likelihood of improvement. Between the years 2000 and 2014, there was a cumulative decrease of 30 percent in state funding for all public universities and colleges in the United States.[5] There are other fundamental forces as well, some of which derive from the fall in public funding. For example, governments, reflecting ever-tighter state budgets, increasingly seek accountability and performance-based funding. Even though they may themselves have participated in reducing state funding, some politicians take strong public stances

---

[4] Thomas G. Mortenson, "State Funding: A Race to the Bottom," *The Presidency*, American Council on Education, Winter 2012, https://perma.cc/K9LL-NHUP.
[5] "Public Research Universities: Changes in State Funding," The Lincoln Project, American Academy of Arts and Sciences, Figure 4, p. 7, 2015, https://perma.cc/7DAC-VJ37.

objecting to the resultant increases in tuition. Yet desires for partaking of public higher education remain strong.

Declines in state funding have brought about increased tuition for public institutions. Higher tuitions for both public and private universities have increased student debt, to an extent where the amount of that debt is now a major national issue. As well, the spread in the distribution of wealth in the United States steadily becomes greater, having now reached an all-time high, increasing the financial needs associated with assuring access for those with lower incomes.

There are also forces in the US that can lead to a reduction in government research funding. These include growing suspicions of science and of universities themselves, as well as a severe tightening of the federal budget, both of which may or may not be short-term effects associated with the unusual national administration and power structure of the federal government in 2017 as this book is completed.

Beyond the drop in public funding, there are broader ills. Mettler[6] has traced the development of two other factors that have interacted with decreased state funding in the United States and student-debt issues to reduce the access of low-income students to higher education and thereby accentuate class differences, despite favorable access policies of public universities and the large Pell Grant program of the federal government. One of these factors is the lack of policy updating at the congressional level that has resulted from polarized national politics and that has badly delayed needed modernization of the Pell Grant program, the main vehicle for financial aid to low-income students. The second trend is the huge subsidization by the federal government of for-profit institutions of higher education, many of which have business plans based upon the widespread availability of government loans to students. Many for-profit institutions avidly seek and enroll students, many of them low-income and minority, who obtain federal student loans to pay high tuitions. Then many of those students do not graduate and/or cannot find employment of a sort that gives them the wherewithal to repay the loans. They are then saddled with debt that cannot be waived or reduced. The federal government

---

[6] Suzanne Mettler, *Degrees of Inequality: How the Politics of Higher Education Sabotaged the American Dream* (New York: Basic Books, 2014).

thereby enables an industry that could not sustain itself on its own. The issue is enmeshed in the politics of Congress, since there are large contributions by for-profit institutions to political campaigns.

Another bothersome trend is the tendency for governments (and other institutions such as the stock market) to look at matters from an immediate, short-term viewpoint rather than dealing effectively with the longer term. California and other states have adopted term limits for legislators, which serve to exacerbate this tendency.[7] Term-limited legislators tend to want demonstrable results now and are less concerned with what may happen after their terms end. So, while they may recognize that reducing public funding for a university and/or urging it to take additional, unfunded enrollment will cause a loss of quality, it seems that the decline will not be precipitous and probably will not harm constituents greatly while the legislator is in office.

Similarly, shifting facilities costs from up-front payment to bonding saves immediate capital costs but creates a continuing operating-cost burden for repayment on the bonds that is over and above costs of instruction and day-to-day operation. The use of long-term bonds makes repayment of principal less of an issue but leaves a university with the interest as a component of the operating budget for the entire term of the bonds. Issuance of more such bonds then compounds the burden on the operating budget. On a statewide scale, increases in retirement benefits as an alternative to increases in current wages in contracts negotiated with public-employee unions reduce the immediate cost for wages at the expense of future retirement obligations. Ever-larger future obligations are being created and pushed along in time in these ways.

These issues raise the question of whether public research universities in the US can continue to compete in academic quality with private research universities over the long term and can continue to perform their essential access function.

---

[7] The effects of term limits (Proposition 140, passed in 1990) upon the California Legislature have been analyzed by Bruce E. Cain and Thad Kousser in *Adapting to Term Limits: Recent Experiences and New Directions* (San Francisco: Public Policy Institute of California, 2004). See also Public Policy Institute of California, "How Have Term Limits Affected the California Legislature?," Research Note, no. 94, November 2004, https://perma.cc/AVJ9-DPD7.

PROSPECTS FOR IMPROVEMENT

State Funding

State budgets in the United States are under considerable pressure because of many competing demands, growing costs, debt loads, longer lives bringing mounting costs of health care and retirement benefits, growing commitments far into the future, and political reluctance to raise taxes. In California the initiative-referendum system has increased unfunded obligations and has taken most of the budget away from direct legislative control. As described in chapter 2, higher education further suffers by being part of what is now in California the very small discretionary portion of the budget, which is also subject to high year-to-year volatility in revenues. The tax issue is further complicated by a well-organized bloc of older voters resisting taxes, insufficiently offset by the younger, more heavily minority and immigrant, voters who could benefit from government services. There does not appear to be much prospect for marked improvement of state funding of the university.

Federal Government Policies

There is more hope over the longer haul for ultimate change in federal government policies and politics that have led to the perverse situation for low-income and minority students described by Mettler[8] and considered above. Zumeta et al.[9] have discussed both the need and potential paths for gaining policies that will enhance access to higher education and provide more balance in income level and ethnicity among those partaking of higher education. What is required is a greater spirit of cooperation between the political parties on policy development, something that should be attainable if voters recognize that the antidote to polarized politics is to elect more solution-oriented people as their government representatives.

During the Obama administration (2009–16), the federal government moved against the practices of for-profit universities, but as of 2017 there has been a reversal of those actions, resulting from

---

[8] Mettler, 2014, *loc. cit.*
[9] William Zumeta et al., *Financing American Higher Education in the Era of Globalization* (Cambridge, MA: Harvard Education Press, 2012).

the composition of Congress and a president who himself created a for-profit university. Hopefully future administrations and congresses will recognize that situation for what it is and deal with it.

Paying More Attention to the Future

The principal issues impeding more attention to the future are the problems posed by term limits and the need for government leaders who will look more responsibly further down the road. The two issues are strongly linked, and both relate to the need for the general public to give more priority to the future. It remains to be seen whether and how much the liabilities associated with term limits and mortgaging the future will be recognized and acted upon by the public.

PREDICTIONS AND ADVICE FROM MANY QUARTERS

Given the stresses imposed by sharply reduced state funding and the rapid changes brought about by advances in information technology and globalization of all sorts, analyses and forecasts on the future of higher education abound. As a sampling, Christensen and Eyring[10] take Christensen's concepts of disruptive innovation and apply them to universities with dire predictions that the universities will lose both market and primacy. Selingo[11] predicts major change brought about through decoupling higher education by means such as massive online open courses (MOOCs), adaptive learning, project-based learning, and unbundling of degree credits, including competency-based certification. Brady has made a more balanced consideration of the likelihood and consequences of unbundling the various aspects of higher education,[12] and has compared and contrasted the situation of

---

[10] Clayton M. Christensen and Henry J. Eyring, *The Innovative University: Changing the DNA of Higher Education from the Inside Out* (San Francisco: Jossey-Bass, 2011).

[11] Jeffrey J. Selingo, *College Unbound: The Future of Higher Education and What It Means for Students* (New York: New Harvest, 2013); "Rebuilding the Bachelor's Degree," *Chronicle of Higher Education*, April 13, 2016.

[12] Henry Brady, "Rebundling Higher Education: A Critical Move to Avoid the Fate of the Newspaper", *The EvoLLLution*, April 4, 2013, https://perma.cc/N92E-LEMV.

universities with changes undergone by the railroads, newspapers, and health care.[13] Fethke and Policano[14] believe that public universities will have to transition toward a private-university model, with high tuition coupled with high student financial aid, greater use of adjunct and temporary faculty, reduced program scope that is differentiated among universities, tuition differentiated by program within universities, more and better student services, increased accountability, and governance that is less shared and much more top-down. Earlier, Garland had made similar recommendations and added changing the form of state funding to portable voucher scholarships belonging to the student and usable at any university, presumably public or private, within that state.[15] In return, Garland proposed that universities would set tuition, determine salaries, establish enrollment and admissions guidelines, and assume greater autonomy over capital expenditures.[16] Zemsky et al.[17] explore many of the ways in which market forces affect universities and how they may be used to advantage. On the other hand, Newfield[18] argues that it is the introduction of business methodology, attention to markets, and close interactions with the private sector that have degraded US higher education. Bowen and McPherson[19] identify a number of national needs—including overall higher levels of educational attainment, increased college completion rates, reduced time to degree, equality among races, affordability and student debt, and leadership capacity—and then go on to discuss desirable approaches, including greater use of instructional technology and altered governance. The fully online Western Governors

---

[13] Henry Brady, "Let's Not Railroad Higher Education", PS: Political Science and Politics, v. 46, no. 1, pp. 94-101, 2013, https://perma.cc/XH9P-EW9W.
[14] Gary C. Fethke and Andrew J. Policano, *Public No More: A New Path to Excellence for America's Public Universities* (Stanford, CA: Stanford Business Books, Stanford University Press, 2012)
[15] A voucher approach for partial coverage of tuition was instituted in the state of Colorado in 2004 for resident undergraduate students attending the state's public institutions, as well as resident Pell Grant recipients enrolled at eligible private nonprofit institutions. See, e.g., Brian T. Prescott, "Is Colorado's Voucher System Worth Vouching For?," *Change*, July-August, 2010.
[16] James C. Garland, *Saving Alma Mater: A Rescue Plan for America's Public Universities* (Chicago: University of Chicago Press, 2009), pp. 189–215.
[17] Robert Zemsky, Gregory R. Wegner, and William F. Massy, *Remaking the American University: Market-Smart and Mission-Centered* (New Brunswick, NJ: Rutgers University Press, 2005).
[18] Christopher Newfield, *The Great Mistake: How We Wrecked Public Universities and How We Can Fix Them* (Baltimore, MD: Johns Hopkins University Press, 2016).
[19] Bowen and McPherson, 2016, *loc. cit.*

University[20] has been in operation for almost twenty years, and it thereby affords another model. In the extreme, Thiel Fellowships[21] pay highly capable people $100,000 *not* to go to college and instead proceed directly into a world of commercial innovation.

Much of the debate centers, tacitly or more explicitly, around the extent to which college or university education should now be viewed more as preparation for a career as opposed to enlightening the mind for all elements of a lifetime and honing abilities for critical thinking. Delbanco[22] gives a strong and well-reasoned defense of the latter need, couched in the United States tradition of liberal education. Cole[23] explores that subject as well, citing the thoughts of Hannah Holborn Gray expressed in her Clark Kerr Lectures at Berkeley, as follows:

> The modern view sees the liberal arts as, literally, liberating, as freeing the mind from unexamined opinions and assumptions to think independently and exercise critical judgment, to question conventional doctrines and inherited claims to truth, to gain some skill in analysis and some capacity to deal with complexity, to embrace a certain skepticism in the face of dogma, and to be open to many points of view.[24]

Careerism has served to increase enrollments in fields such as computer science and engineering, while decreasing student interests in humanities. Yet the humanities are a vital component of liberal education. Decreasing enrollments in humanities majors at the undergraduate and graduate levels raise the question of whether those fields will be able to continue production of both good scholarship and succeeding generations of faculty members.[25]

---

[20] "Western Governors University, WGU," https://web.archive.org/web/20170823063248/https://www.wgu.edu/.
[21] "The Thiel Fellowship," https://perma.cc/XJ3A-TWN5.
[22] Anthony Delbanco, *College: What It Was, Is, and Should Be* (Princeton, NJ: Princeton University Press, 2012).
[23] Jonathan R. Cole, *Toward a More Perfect University* (New York: Public Affairs, 2016).
[24] Hannah Holborn Gray, *Searching for Utopia: Universities and Their Histories* (Berkeley: Center for Studies in Higher Education and University of California Press, 2012), p. 43.
[25] MLA Task Force on Doctoral Study in Modern Language and Literature, *Report of the MLA Task Force on Doctoral Study in Modern Language and Literature*, Modern Language Association, May 2014, https://perma.cc/3YDW-7326.

Current trends are toward career preparation. However, as is argued in chapter 13, liberal education is of great value not only for illuminating the mind for all aspects of a lifetime but also for the broad understanding that enables a graduate to work effectively in a multidisciplinary setting and to change roles and even careers during a lifetime. The ever-more-rapid changes attributable to technological advances, globalization, and other factors, as well as to the interactions among them,[26] make a strong case for education that equips university graduates to adjust to new employment situations and opportunities as these changes occur throughout their working lifetimes.

Using developments at Arizona State University during the presidency (2002–) of Michael Crow as the model, Crow and Dabars[27] promote the concept of very large public research universities, where the scale promotes both access and efficiency of operation, while giving the benefit of the research atmosphere to all students and faculty. In a sense, those authors endorse combining what in California are the University of California and California State University, which would provide the attributes of a research university to CSU students as well. This proposal logically leads to the question of whether there is a desirable benefit from keeping UC and CSU separate with distinctly different missions. It also raises the issue of whether the advantages of education on a campus of, for example, twenty-five to thirty-five thousand students outweigh the impersonal aspects of a very large campus with, say, seventy-five thousand enrolled. The California Master Plan did indeed achieve a substantial cost efficiency through mission differentiation and also enabled the high research stature that the University of California has achieved. For these reasons the California approach should be preferable.

TWO FUNDAMENTAL UNCERTAINTIES

Two large issues with yet-to-be-known ultimate outcomes strongly affect both the nature of universities and future prospects for public

---

[26] Thomas L. Friedman, *Thank You for Being Late* (New York: Farrar, Straus & Giroux, 2016).
[27] Michael M. Crow and William B. Dabars, *Designing the New American University* (Baltimore, MD: Johns Hopkins University Press, 2015).

funding of higher education. Both are currently very much in play, but the answers are not yet clear.

Perceptions of Public versus Private Benefits

The question of the relative extents to which higher education provides private (i.e., personal) and public benefits underlies views on public funding for it. Higher education is a private or personal benefit to the extent that it enhances a person's career, earning power, and richness of life experience. It is a public benefit to the extent that it benefits society and the economy in general. Both sorts of benefits do of course accrue. The public benefit was the rationale through which public higher education came into being in the United States and was fostered through the Morrill Act of 1862. It is as well the main reason why higher education in most of the rest of the world is publicly funded, either entirely or in large part. Public funding extends opportunities for higher education to the most capable and deserving people in the entire population, without regard to their ability to pay. Public higher education has had much to do with the development of the United States and the opportunities and assimilation that it has provided for immigrant people. The United States has historically been a land of upward social and economic mobility, with public-university higher education being used to achieve that mobility. In that regard the United States has been a model for the rest of the world.

Attention to careerism and personal benefits has increased in recent years as pressures on state budgets have grown and costs to individuals for higher education have risen through resultant tuition increases. Government-sponsored loans have become more prevalent through the rationale that they can be repaid through the increased earning power that is engendered by a college degree (i.e., the private benefit). Unfortunately, the ready availability of government loans has also launched an industry of for-profit higher-education with the attendant problems already noted.

An extensive economic study of the benefits of higher education was carried out by McMahon,[28] who found that the public benefits are

---

[28] Walter W. McMahon, *Higher Learning, Greater Good: The Private and Social Benefits of Higher Education* (Baltimore, MD: Johns Hopkins University Press, 2009).

much higher than are ordinarily recognized and that over half the benefit is public rather than private. The societal benefits of bachelor's degrees on an individual basis were calculated as about $28,000 per year in 2007 dollars, including such things as lower crime, improved environment, political stability, reduced inequalities among people, promotion of human rights, and greater civic participation. Allowance for the effects of higher education and research from research universities on growth of the economy, as ascertained through the studies described in chapter 16, would make the amount of public benefit still greater. McMahon's work is summarized by Lambert,[29] who further explores the public-versus-private benefit question. The subject is also discussed by Bowen and McPherson,[30] who bring out the work of Moretti[31] which also shows a substantial societal benefit attributable to higher education. Cole[32] also considers the point.

The United States must come to grips with the issue of private versus public benefits of higher education, and the balance between public funding and tuition can and should be set accordingly. This will probably be accomplished indirectly through many piecemeal decisions and contentions on numerous more specific issues, but the process must occur.

Uses of Instructional Technology in Higher Education

Remarkably rapid advances in the capabilities of information technology (IT) have strongly affected almost everything in the world and certainly higher education. In contrast with the striking continual advances in computing hardware that have occurred through transistor packing reflecting Moore's "Law," it has been much more difficult to predict the developments of approaches and software that will most effectively deploy IT in various fields of endeavor. Higher education is a case in point.

---

[29] Matthew T. Lambert, *Privatization and the Public Good: Public Universities in the Balance* (Cambridge, MA: Harvard Education Press, 2014).
[30] Bowen and McPherson, 2016, *op. cit.*, pp. 75–77.
[31] Enrico Moretti, "Estimating the Social Return to Higher Education: Evidence from Longitudinal and Repeated Cross-Sectional Data," *Journal of Econometrics* 121, nos. 1–2 (2004): pp. 175–212, https://perma.cc/9LUN-DHWH.
[32] Cole, 2016, *op. cit.* pp. 129–133.

Fully online courses have come into large-scale use. As of 2013, eleven percent of all US students seeking undergraduate degrees were in online-only programs, and 27 percent took at least some of their classes online.[33] There is even greater use of online courses for continuing education and career-oriented master's degrees. University extension, the continuing-education arm of the University of California, provided thirty-two hundred online courses with total enrollments of eighty-four thousand as of 2013, counting all ten campuses.[34] Saxenian prepared a thoughtful analysis[35] of the status and potential of online education technology for the Berkeley campus in 2012. Online education is here and much in use, but the extents and rates of further growth, the roles assumed by it, and especially the financial implications for the future remain unclear.

Initial efforts to share online instructional material among institutions and individuals included the OpenCourseWare (OCW)[36] initiative started by MIT in 2001. Following that, massive open online courses (MOOCs) have been given much attention, and companies such as Coursera, Udacity (both venture backed and for-profit), and edX (not for profit, open-access and -source) have been founded on the concept. MOOCs can be taken as is by individuals alone or imported to a remote location, where discussion, amplification, and further interpretation can be provided by a resident instructor in what has become known as a flipped-classroom approach. MOOCs have been hailed by some as the low-cost panacea for undergraduate education, but they are not yet that and are unlikely to become so. They are one useful potential component of the educational model. Some of the issues relating to the use and further development of MOOCs are

---

[33] Data from the Integrated Postsecondary Education Data System (IPEDS) of the US Department of Education as cited by David Figlio, "A Silver Lining for Online Higher Education?," Brookings Institution, November 10, 2016, https://perma.cc/KM6Q-4W3L.
[34] "Online Education at the University of California," Office of the President, University of California, Oakland, CA, August 20, 2013, https://perma.cc/89CQ-LZJ4.
[35] AnnaLee Saxenian, "Can Online Education Technology Improve Excellence and Access at Berkeley?", March 2, 2012, https://perma.cc/STK3-JW72.
[36] MIT OpenCourseWare, Massachusetts Institute of Technology, https://perma.cc/QC4T-3YN5.

discussed by Cole under the heading "Will Clicks Eliminate Bricks?,"[37] and are considered in greater detail by Rhoads.[38]

Present-day conclusions about MOOCs cited by Richard Levin,[39] ex-president of Yale and until recently president of Coursera, are that they work well for developing mastery and retention of knowledge but are less effective than traditional education for developing critical thinking skills. Thille et al. conclude that "although they can provide much richer learning experiences than a printed book alone, current MOOCs pale in comparison with face-to-face instruction by a thoughtfully invested human instructor."[40] For mature, goal-oriented students taking career-oriented or "how-to" courses, online delivery has been found to work well, particularly if the course material has substantial interactive, connective, and exploratory components (cMMOCs) as opposed to being more simply web-cast versions of traditional classroom courses (xMOOCs).[41]

For undergraduate students, fully online courses have worked less well. Undergraduates in traditional higher education benefit from, and have their attention held by, classroom, seminar, and office-hours contact with faculty members; by contact with one another outside the classroom; and by other aspects of structure. Yet with more lectures and supplemental material migrating online, there is a growing tendency for undergraduate students in traditional universities to skip classes and work instead from the online material, probably with the same problem of not sticking to the structure of the coursework sufficiently and thereby with less educational value. On the other hand, in parts of the world where traditional undergraduate education of sufficient quality is simply not available, online instruction at the undergraduate level can be the best alternative available. These

---

[37] Cole, 2016, *op. cit.*, pp. 148–162.
[38] Robert A. Rhoads, *MOOCS, High Technology, and Higher Learning* (Baltimore, MD: Johns Hopkins Press, 2015).
[39] Richard Levin, "MOOCs and the Future of Higher Education," seminar given at Center for Studies in Higher Education, University of California, Berkeley, April 26, 2017, video accessed June 5, 2017, https://www.youtube.com/watch?v=TABDIb6eEQw.
[40] Candace Thille, John Mitchell, and Mitchell Stevens, "What We've Learned from MOOCs," *Inside Higher Education*, September 22, 2015, https://perma.cc/VTC7-YT32.
[41] Rhoads, 2015, *loc. cit.*

conclusions are supported by the fact that for Coursera two-thirds of MOOC takers are between ages twenty-two and forty-five, 77 percent are from countries other than the United States, and a full 46 percent are from developing countries.[42]

Creators of MOOCs are presently concentrated in elite universities, and such courses may not be suitable for all types and levels of students.[43] In any event, prolific use of the same course and instructional methodology for all students and in many different settings is not in line with the US tradition of an institutionally diverse system of higher education.

Financial Aspects. Online courses have a financial structure that is very different from that of traditional classroom instruction. Both require that the instructor first organize and extend her or his knowledge into a logical form that is effective for conveying it to students. For online instruction the instructor must go much further before the course can be given. The presentation and arguments must be tested and refined since discussion will be much less possible in an online offering. Media-creation expertise is needed to devise and implement the online format. Although online courses can be continually improved through trials and subsequent adjustment, it is more difficult and expensive to change them than it is for traditional classroom instruction. On the other hand, the marginal cost of instructing an additional student is much less for online courses than it is for conventional classroom courses. There is also a question whether the economic advantages of even large-capacity online courses outweigh those of conventional approaches on a cost-benefit basis, taking into account the current trends toward more use of lecturers and adjunct and part-time faculty members within colleges and universities.[44]

The most attractive financial model for MOOCs delivered to individuals or interinstitutionally remains unclear. OCW and edX are free, so participating in them provides no direct financial incentive to

---

[42] Levin, 2017, *loc. cit.*
[43] Rhoads, 2015, *loc. cit.*
[44] Rita Kirshstein and Jane Wellman, "Technology and the Broken Higher Education Cost Model: Insights from the Delta Cost Project, *Educause Review* (September/October 2012): pp. 12–22, https://perma.cc/7UCM-76JM.

the providing institutions. While individuals taking courses from Coursera do pay for enrolling, they can also apply for a waiver of fee. The large portion of current Coursera enrollments coming from developing countries does not, in itself, suggest a large source of income. Levin[45] has expressed the view that supplying in-house courses to corporations, government, and the military is likely to become a more reliable and effective source of revenue.

Hybrid Courses. Online courses have benefits of scale and can afford a digital enrichment of content beyond what has been typical for conventional courses, whereas conventional courses have benefits of much greater and more flexible and personalized interactions between instructor and student and more ways of instilling critical-thinking skills. Thus, the two modes of instruction are presently complementary, and hybrid courses can be more effective than either type alone. Many hybrid courses do exist, stemming from original efforts such as the digital enhancements of chemistry courses described by Whitnell et al.[46] and Harley et al.[47] But hybrid courses are also more expensive than are courses in either mode alone.

Research Universities. Information technology provides effective ways of bringing research into the classroom or for research to be given as assignments for individual study. Faculty members in research universities, being creative souls with strong mastery of their subject matter, will have their own ideas as to how instruction is best done and will be less attracted toward using a "canned" online instructional product.

---

[45] Levin, 2017, *loc. cit.*
[46] Robert M. Whitnell et al., "Multimedia Chemistry Lectures," *Journal of Chemical Educ*ation 71 (1994): pp. 721–725.
[47] Diane Harley et al., "Costs, Culture, and Complexity: An Analysis of Technology Enhancements in a Large Lecture Course at UC Berkeley," Center for Studies in Higher Education, University of California, Berkeley, March 2003, https://escholarship.org/uc/item/68d9t1rm.

PATHS FORWARD

There are two basic approaches for dealing with the fundamental issue of reduced public funding. Reduce expenses, possibly with sacrifice in ability to meet the mission, and/or derive revenue from other sources. We will consider them serially.

Expenditure Reduction

Cost Control. Cost control is a vital issue for universities for many reasons. In addition to the efficiencies and synergies that can be gained by good cost management, there is a major issue of image. Public universities are now in the vulnerable situation where tuitions are rising percentagewise much faster from year to year than are the actual costs of operation, which may actually decrease. The underlying reason has been the continual reduction in state support, which casts more burden on tuition and other sources of revenue just to keep expenditures even. The causes and effects at play are not well understood by the public,[48] and hence there is a tendency for people to conclude that expenditures are rising, out of control, at the same percentage rate as tuition. Universities cannot expect better public financial support if they do not demonstrate convincingly that they are attentive to costs and are managing them well.

In a classic work[49] extended from an earlier study of the performing arts,[50] Bowen concluded that the labor-intensive aspect of higher education and the lack of productivity increases attainable with the traditional methods of instruction serve to assure that costs of higher

---

[48] There is even a postulate known as the Bennett hypothesis, put forward originally by William Bennett, which postulates that increases in federal financial aid availability drive tuition upward more demonstrably than reductions in public funding. See Jason Delisle, "The Disinvestment Hypothesis: Don't Blame State Budget Cuts for Rising tuition at Public Universities," Brookings Institution, June 1, 2017, https://perma.cc/3W6T-VRUQ. However, there is a demonstrable cause-and-effect relationship when state funding is reduced, and in response part of the loss is covered by an increase in tuition with no increase (and probably a reduction) in expenditures. The Bennett hypothesis seems to apply more to for-profit institutions of higher education than to public or non-profit private universities.

[49] William J. Bowen, *The Economics of Major Private Universities* (Berkeley: Carnegie Commission on Higher Education, 1968).

[50] William J. Baumol and William G. Bowen, "On the Performing Arts: The Anatomy of Their Economic Problems," *The American Economic Review* 55, no. 1/2 (1965): pp. 495–502.

education rise faster than the rate of inflation. The infrastructure of this issue is more complex and subtle, however, since universities' staffing patterns can and do change[51] and information technology is becoming used more and more in various ways in instruction.

Ehrenberg,[52] looking primarily at elite private not-for-profit universities, identified and analyzed several other cost drivers. Among these are (1) the race toward the top in academic rankings, (2) shared governance, (3) federal government policies (especially for private universities), (4) budgetary control being placed at the decanal level, where local sub-optimizations can occur, (5) excessive deferral of maintenance, (6) defined-benefit retirement plans and longer lives, (7) the nature of scientific research and the factors surrounding it, (8) inter-university recruitment of faculty, and (9) practices for appointing and evaluating deans. Several of these factors are also very positive contributors to institutional academic quality and hence to impacts of the university and its graduates on the economy and society. Consequently, answers regarding them must lie in cost-benefit analyses.

Massy[53] considers cost control in universities in a way that does seek to balance considerations of cost with those of academic quality. He urges that universities dig into their cost structure and obtain deeper understanding by using modern capabilities and concepts of data science and the availability and further creation of large databases. He observes that most research and analysis on costs in universities has been focused upon teaching, whereas research and service are also major components of research-university activities. Research excellence in particular relates to academic quality and stature. For analyzing teaching, he promotes a concept that he names

---

[51] Donna M. Desrochers and Rita Kirshstein, "Labor Intensive or Labor Extensive? Changing Staffing and Compensation Patterns in Higher Education," issue brief, Delta Cost Project, American Institutes for Research, February 2014, https://perma.cc/DP39-BRY9.

[52] Ronald G. Ehrenberg, *Tuition Rising: Why College Costs So Much* (Cambridge, MA: Harvard University Press, 2000). See also a summary by the same title as chapter 5 in Maureen Devlin and Joel Meyerson, eds., *Forum Futures: Exploring the Future of Higher Education; 2000 Papers* (San Francisco: Jossey-Bass, 2001).

[53] William F. Massy, *Reengineering the University: How to be Mission Centered, Market Smart, and Margin Conscious* (Baltimore, MD: Johns Hopkins University Press, 2016).

Chapter 21

activity-based costing (ABC). Massy also has substantial previous work on this subject, including a sequence of proposed initiatives.[54]

Another effort to analyze university costs has been the Delta Cost Project, from which several reports and analyses are available.[55] Some of the earlier findings from this project are summarized by Kirshstein and Wellman.[56] Here and elsewhere,[57] Wellman points out that cost per degree is a more appropriate objective function than is cost per student enrolled. By this logic, inefficiencies in moving students from initial enrollment to ultimate degrees are real costs, and greater attention should be paid to increasing graduation rates, rates of course completion by students, and successful transfer of would-be transfer students from community colleges to four-year institutions.

In many situations gains in efficiency are where there will be the best payoff per amount of effort exerted. Impressive examples are the large gains in graduation rate and the evening out of graduation rates among ethnic groups achieved by Georgia State University through relatively inexpensive means such as data analysis and targeted counseling.[58] A similar effort made in California could have a big payout in student success, especially for transfer.

Berkeley. The University of California campuses have taken various steps toward cost reduction in recent years as the financial crisis has worn onward. One of the most systematic approaches has been at Berkeley, where, to launch an initiative denoted Operational Excellence, the campus commissioned the Bain Corporation to support and coordinate a major study of costs in all areas except core academics and course delivery. The report from the diagnostic phase of

---

[54] William F. Massy, "Stretching the Higher Education Dollar," Special Report 1, *Initiatives for Containing the Cost of Higher Education* (Washington, DC: American Enterprise Institute, 2013), https://perma.cc/HX44-QVYZ.
[55] Delta Cost Project, accessed June 4, 2017, https://web.archive.org/web/20171028055952/https://deltacostproject.org/delta-products..
[56] Kirshstein and Wellman, 2012, *loc. cit.*
[57] Jane Wellman, "Historic Dynamics Shaping the Higher Education Budget in California," commissioned background research for "Securing the Public Trust: Practical Steps toward Higher Education Finance Reform in California," College Futures Foundation, 2016, https://perma.cc/MX7N-GADF.
[58] "Complete College Georgia: 2015 Status Report," Georgia State University, Atlanta, GA, https://perma.cc/V25N-HUNH.

that study is available in the form of a large PowerPoint presentation.[59] Five specific areas were identified for particular attention—procurement, organizational simplification (including human resources and finance), information technology, energy management, and student services. Efforts were pursued in all of these areas.

As part of addressing organizational simplification, the Berkeley campus undertook the campus-wide Shared Services initiative, described in chapter 6, which as of 2017 is being pulled back to a level where the sharing is within groups of kindred units. Another move has been to include funding of projected maintenance costs in the costs for construction and, where possible, renovation projects.

Program Pruning and Consolidation. Universities should continually review and modify academic programs using procedures such as those described in chapter 12. Among the many reasons for regular reviews is that, left alone, academic program elements will almost surely multiply, a phenomenon that Smelser explored in some depth and labeled "accretion."[60] Furthermore, programs not subjected to review are much less likely to stay current and on the forefront of knowledge. Program-review processes are very valuable academically, but are usually not a good route toward major budgetary savings achieved over a relatively short period of time. Recommendations are at least as likely to cost more rather than less in the short run, and major program reduction is a sensitive process which, if done, usually needs to be carried out over time. Consolidation of smaller academic departments into larger ones is perhaps the route that is most achievable for short-term budget reduction, but the savings are likely to be relatively small.

One of the larger program reductions in the United States came when, as a result of severe budgetary difficulties, New York University (NYU) sold off its Washington Heights campus in the Bronx in 1973 and concomitantly eliminated its School of Engineering and Science. That school then merged into Polytechnic Institute of Brooklyn, which

---

[59] University of California, Berkeley, and the Bain Corporation, "Achieving Operational Excellence at University of California, Berkeley," April 2010, https://perma.cc/M7JN-L2XK..
[60] Neil J. Smelser, *Dynamics of the Contemporary University: Growth, Accretion, and Conflict* (Berkeley: University of California Press, 2013).

Chapter 21

thereby became Polytechnic Institute of New York. That dynamic came full circle when Polytechnic University, as Polytechnic Institute of New York had been renamed, was acquired by and merged into NYU in 2008.[61, 62]

A prominent instance of attempted program reduction that did not succeed was Yale University's attempt in the early 1990s to reduce the size of the faculty of Arts and Sciences selectively by 11 percent for budgetary reasons, largely to release funds for use in renovating aging university buildings. A select committee chaired by Yale's provost heard much input from around the campus, but did not engage in any substantial two-way consultation before formulating and releasing its plan. That plan was to close the departments of linguistics and operations research, reduce the sociology faculty by 40 percent, reduce and merge three separate engineering departments into one, and scale back and merge the departments of physics and applied physics.[63] The plan led to great faculty contention and controversy, ultimately resulting in the successive resignations of the dean of Yale College, the provost, and the president.[64] It is interesting to conjecture whether this effort could have been more successful if based upon the traditions and consulting mechanisms that are associated with the Academic Senate of the University of California. At the very least, the degrees of impact and unhappiness would have been found out earlier, giving an opportunity for modifications to be made.[65]

---

[61] "History of New York University," *Wikipedia*, https://perma.cc/A64H-K34N.
[62] Eileen Reynolds, "A Rich History of Engineering at New York University," *Cable*, New York University, Fall 2013,
https://web.archive.org/web/20170504011136/http://engineering.nyu.edu/cable/issue/fall-2013/news/alumni/rich-history-engineering-nyu.
[63] Anthony DePalma, "Yale Panel Proposes Deep Cuts in Faculty and in Departments," *New York Times*, January 17, 1992.
[64] Richard Bernstein, "The Yale Schmidt Leaves Behind," *New York Times Magazine*, June 14, 1992.
[65] At the time that this contention developed at Yale, the author was chair of a high-level external committee finishing an in-depth, five-year study of physical sciences and engineering for Yale through Yale's University Council. That study laid out a path for rebuilding engineering through faculty appointments and reinstitution of the dean of engineering position, following the large shrinkage that had occurred in the years starting in 1960. There was some faculty concern at Yale that the committee had concluded that growth in engineering beyond the budgetary desires or capabilities of Yale was needed, thereby causing of the recommendation of the Select Committee to consolidate and reduce engineering further. However, the new Yale president, Richard Levin, followed the advice of the University Council review, and, enabled in part by extremely successful investment of the university's endowment, rebuilt engineering essentially as recommended.

Outsourcing. In some situations it is more economical to outsource an activity to the private sector rather than for a university to perform it in-house. This can be a sensitive issue for a public university, however, because of concerns by labor unions—and in California, hence the state government—about job losses. The University of California has guidelines[66] on outsourcing and submits annual reports[67] to the legislature.

A particularly large example of outsourcing is the Merced 2020 project to build additional facilities to enable continued growth of enrollment at the Merced campus. That project, described in chapter 10, is contracted to a single development team that designs, builds, and partially finances the entire project and then operates and maintains the resultant buildings through a thirty-nine-year, performance-based project agreement. Since it is an add-on, the outsourced project does not eliminate internal jobs.

Coordination and Mutual Support among Universities. There are various ways in which efficiencies and hence cost reductions can be achieved by cooperation among universities in the areas of academic program and support services.

As has been pointed out by Fethke and Policano,[68] a logical route for budgetary control within universities is to focus upon program areas that fit the institution particularly well while leaving coverage of other areas to other colleges and universities. Most states have statewide planning and coordination mechanisms for public universities that provide an avenue through which program differentiation of this sort among public institutions can occur. Programmatic offerings and access to them can also be coordinated among neighboring states, utilizing mechanisms such as that afforded

---

[66] "University Guidelines on Contracting for Services," Office of the President, University of California, revised May 31, 2018, https://perma.cc/9Q69-LAUR.
[67] See, e.g., "Contracting Out for Services," legislative report, January 2017, https://perma.cc/2U57-2XFM.
[68] Fethke and Policano, 2012, *loc. cit.*

by the Western Interstate Commission for Higher Education[69] whereby students participating across state lines do not have to pay full nonresident tuition.

Cole[70] has urged the formation of leagues or associations to share and mutually reinforce intellectual activities among cooperating universities. Such associations could enable member institutions to share, consolidate, and differentiate programs and enhance library access. An association of this sort that already exists is the Big Ten Academic Alliance (BTAA),[71] formerly known as the Committee on Institutional Cooperation (CIC), which consists of fourteen major midwestern state universities. CIC was initiated in 1958 by the member universities of the Big Ten athletic conference to share expertise, libraries, and specialized courses. The alliance also gives common access to the education-abroad programs of the member universities. The academic support services for the campuses of the University of California provided by the Office of the President, such as the digital library, interlibrary sharing of materials, Education Abroad Program, Washington Center, and Sacramento Center, have similar functions and characteristics to those of the BTAA.

There are also a number of instances where cross-registration has been established among universities, allowing students to take courses at the other member institutions as well as their own. As examples, MIT has long had a program of cross-registration with Wellesley, and a similar program exists for the BOW Collaboration (Babson, Olin, Wellesley) in the Boston area. The Lincoln Project of the American Academy of Arts and Sciences has urged more similar collaborations for public universities as an avenue for cost reduction.[72] There is also a longstanding cross-registration program for the Claremont Colleges in Southern California.

---

[69] "Western Undergraduate Exchange (WUE)," Western Interstate Commission for Higher Education (WICHE), https://web.archive.org/web/20160723051240/https://www.wiche.edu/wue.
[70] Cole, 2016, *op. cit.*, pp. 172–183.
[71] "Big Ten Academic Alliance, https://perma.cc/4K87-A324.
[72] "Public Research Universities Recommitting to Lincoln's Vision: An Educational Compact for the 21st Century," pp. 12–13, Lincoln Project, American Academy of Arts and Sciences, 2016, https://perma.cc/D56J-W6AJ.

It can make good economic sense for colleges and universities to share support services of various kinds if they are located close enough to one another. For more than ninety years, the Claremont Colleges Consortium[73] has provided shared support services to the seven separate private institutions that make up the Claremont Colleges complex. There are now over thirty such services, including the library, information technology, student-support services, safety, and financial and administrative services. The Atlanta University Center[74] has provided similar services to Clark Atlanta, Morehouse College, Spelman College, and the Morehouse School of Medicine in Atlanta, Georgia. Several other such arrangements are described by Gose.[75]

Consolidation, Mergers, and Dissolutions. A book edited by Martin and Samels[76] gives a variety of perspectives on consolidation, synergy through partnerships, mergers, and even termination of colleges and universities. In view of the increasing financial pressures on both public and private institutions, these events can be expected to occur more frequently than they have so far. Some of the most noteworthy such actions over the past seventy years have been the 1948 formation of the State University of New York (SUNY) from twenty-nine previously unaffiliated institutions, the 1967 merger of Carnegie Institute of Technology and the Mellon Institute to form Carnegie-Mellon University, and the convoluted sequence of events involving New York University and Polytechnic Institute/University of Brooklyn/New York, described above. There have also been a number of instances where an existing university has acquired a formerly freestanding medical school (e.g., UC Irvine, chapter 10) or law school (e.g., the acquisition of McGeorge School of Law by the University of the Pacific in 1966).

More recently the University System of Georgia has taken a systematic approach toward consolidation of a large number of individual state institutions of higher education. The process and recommendations are described in a combined presentation to the

---

[73] Claremont Colleges Consortium, https://web.archive.org/web/20180119113900/https://services.claremont.edu/.
[74] Atlanta University Center Consortium, https://perma.cc/2XVF-2TLW.
[75] Ben Gose, "How Colleges Cut Costs by Embracing Collaboration," *Chronicle of Higher Education*, March 26, 2017.
[76] James Martin and James E. Samels, eds., *Consolidating Colleges and Merging Universities* (Baltimore, MD: Johns Hopkins University Press, 2016).

Regents of the University System of Georgia.[77] The largest such consolidation so far is the integration of Georgia Perimeter College into Georgia State University.[78] Some of the cultural issues involved in these mergers are recounted by Gardner,[79] who also notes that the cost savings were not large.

As noted throughout this book, mergers or incorporations of existing colleges or universities into another university encounter the problem of merging existing cultures, which can be difficult and take a long time.

Altering the Distribution of Expenses and Revenue

Management of Cross Subsidies. Universities' budgets are typically structured so that academic programs are cross subsidized, meaning that their expenses are not matched to the income that the programs themselves generate through enrollments and in other ways. Instead, revenues from the state, tuition, and some other sources are usually mingled and allocated as budgets to academic units by the central administration on the basis of assessments of programmatic need. An exception is institutions, notably Harvard, that follow an "every tub on its own bottom" (ETOB) approach.[80] Another semiexception is the concept of responsibility-center management (RCM)[81] that is being used at some universities to give everything, including space, a cost and to formalize the amounts of subsidies to those units that have them.

---

[77] "Recommended Consolidations," Regents of the University System of Georgia, January 2012 and November 12, 2013, https://perma.cc/XC7B-BYMG.
[78] "Overview," Georgia State University/Georgia Perimeter College, https://perma.cc/Z7SG-PTRB.
[79] Lee Gardner, "Georgia's Mergers Offer Lessons, and Cautions, to Other States," *Chronicle of Higher Education*, June 19, 2017.
[80] ETOB as a system for financial management is explained in "ETOB, Harvard A to Z," *Harvard Magazine*, May-June 2004, http://perma.cc/A226-P8XP.
[81] John R. Curry, Andrew L. Laws, and Jon C. Strauss, *Responsibility Center Management: A Guide to Balancing Academic Entrepreneurship with Fiscal Responsibility,* 2nd ed. (National Association of College and University Business Officers, 2013).

Fethke and Policano[82] predict that, as public universities in the United States adapt to their new financial world, subsidized academic programs will be more vulnerable and subject to elimination. Strictly matching budgets for academic units to the revenue they generate favors disciplines matched with high-income fields and thereby impedes the concept of a broad or liberal education. It also discourages multidisciplinary and interdepartmental efforts unless there are specific economic incentives for them. Hence, cross subsidies should be regarded as normal and needed, but it can still be useful for administrative leaders to be aware of them and monitor them for possible inefficiencies through means such as RCM.

Differential Program Fees. As part of the initial response to declining state funding in the early 1990s, the University of California instituted higher tuition for some professional-degree programs.[83] Higher fees were originally set for degrees in high-paying professional areas such as law, medicine, and business. The rationale was that graduates could readily repay loans taken to cover the higher fees through the high wages generally associated with the profession. The concept has now been widened beyond those initial programs, and as of 2015-16 there were higher fees for sixty-four programs on the various campuses, including some lower-salaried fields such as public policy and social welfare.[84]

The Faculty Budget. The traditional University of California model has been that members of the tenure-track faculty are expected to do both teaching and research, in approximately equal amounts (chapter 11), with the recognition that the two functions inform and reinforce one another. Adherence to this model means that teaching and research remain in effectively constant proportions to one another, independent of faculty size. There are, of course, ways in which the proportion can be altered by using other types of faculty positions. For example, lecturers and adjunct faculty do teaching without research,

---

[82] Fethke and Policano, 2012, *loc. cit.*
[83] "Regents Policy 3103: Policy on Professional Degree Supplemental Tuition," Board of Regents, University of California, http://perma.cc/GN9P-UHJP.
[84] "University of California 2015–16 Tuition and Fee Levels," http://perma.cc/D3JT-9HT3,

and research professors or members of the University of California Professional Research series[85] do research without teaching.

Because of budget stringencies and the desire to reduce long-term commitments, there has been a trend in the United States toward proportionately greater use of non-tenure-track and part-time faculty members for teaching.[86] There are conflicting reported results as to whether this trend is helpful or damaging to teaching quality.[87, 88, 89]

Present University of California policy for placing faculty academic-year salaries on nonstate funds is relatively conservative. Beyond state funding and tuition revenue, the only other allowable sources for regular faculty positions are endowment income, fee income from high-fee graduate professional programs, and income from fully self-supporting degree programs (see below). There is a limit of 7 percent of the total faculty positions on a campus that may be funded from these other sources and a limit of 15 percent within any one college or school. In addition, at least 10 percent of the faculty funding base must be used for temporary appointments, thereby providing a safeguard against effects of funding fluctuations on the ability to fund the regular faculty positions.[90]

The 2007 Hewlett Foundation gift of $113 million to the Berkeley campus, described in chapter 2, is a prime example of using private money for sustained coverage of faculty salaries. That gift provided half the costs of each of one hundred endowed chairs, with much of the proceeds going into the faculty salary pool to relieve what would otherwise be state funds. The Hewlett Foundation made this gift

---

[85] "Professional Research Series," Section 310-4, *Academic Personnel Manual*, University of California, http://perma.cc/GFX8-WWUS.
[86] Ronald G. Ehrenberg, "American Higher Education in Transition," *Journal of Economic Perspectives* 26, no. 2 (Winter 2012), table 1, p. 196; pp. 193–216.
[87] Ehrenberg, 2012, *loc. cit.*
[88] Ronald G. Ehrenberg, "What's the Future of Public Higher Education? A Review Essay on Gary C. Fethke and Andrew J. Policano's *Public No More: A New Path to Excellence for America's Public Universities,*" *Journal of Economic Literature* 52, no. 4 (2014): pp. 1142–1150.
[89] David M. Figlio, Morton O. Schapiro, and Kevin B. Soter, "Are Tenure Track Professors Better Teachers?," *National Bureau of Economic Research*, working paper no. 19406 (September 2013).
[90] "Policy on the Use of Non-19900 Fund Sources to Support Ladder-Rank Faculty," appendix F to section APM-190, *Academic Personnel Manual*, University of California, adopted June 1, 1999, http://perma.cc/7EBW-YSB2.

expressly for the purpose of helping to preserve high-quality public higher education in California.

Other universities, most of them private, have at times required or strongly urged that members of their regular faculty who are capable of securing government grants defray substantial amounts of their academic-year salaries through recharges to government grants. That is common practice everywhere in the United States for summer salaries of the faculty, but requiring it for academic-year salaries is both riskier and more controversial for tenured faculty members, since government grants do end and the process for getting new grants is highly competitive. However, using grant funds toward academic-year salaries is allowed under policies of the National Science Foundation[91] and some other federal government agencies. The practice is most prevalent in health-sciences disciplines. Moving more to "soft" research-grant money to support faculty positions raises questions of faculty allegiance and equity.[92]

While not all campuses have the same access to private money, the University of California policy does have substantial room for additional funding of faculty positions from the three sources considered by the UC policy statement cited above. Consideration should also be given to increasing the 7 percent limitation and/or allowing some other sources such as guaranteed support for the duration of a faculty member's career from foundations, individual donors, or other sufficiently secure extramural sources.

"Privatization"

The most obvious way for public universities to replace public funding is to move in various ways toward the financial model of the leading private universities, although that model is itself also under stress.[93] Moves in this direction are typically called "privatization," without much attention being given to the various meanings of the

---

[91] "NSF 07-140_V. Allowability of Costs," http://perma.cc/SUP6-4KPQ.
[92] See, e.g., Donald G. Stein, "Hard Money/Soft Money," *The Academic Exchange* 9, no. 6 (May 2007), Emory University, May 2007, http://perma.cc/JQ4F-BV3S.
[93] Ronald G. Ehrenberg, "Is the Golden Age of the Private Research University Over?," *Change* 45, no. 3 (2013): pp. 16–23.

word or the differences among forms of privatization. In that the alternative to public resources is, by definition, private resources, nearly all steps to gain resources from other sources can be called privatization. But it is also important to distinguish financial resources from mission. To whatever extent public universities "privatize" resources, their goal should be to retain as much of the public mission as possible, notably facile access without regard to ability to pay.

The word "privatization" can also be taken to imply running universities more like a corporate business, although that is not the meaning adopted here. Newfield[94] argues that acceptance of business models and practices from the corporate world, along with associated corporate thinking and priorities, is the fundamental reason for the decline in the situations of public universities in the United States.

The two principal sources in the revenue portfolios of private universities that public universities have to substantially lesser extents are tuition and yields from endowment. Fethke and Policano[95] contend that higher tuition is the only viable replacement for state funding and that it is feasible only to the extent that demand for admission is sufficiently inelastic with respect to cost of attendance. As state support has dwindled, public universities have raised tuition to make up for some of the loss. The limits to raising tuition are considered in the following section.

Endowment is a different matter. Comparison of the sizes of endowments of leading private universities with those of leading public universities is striking, particular if placed on a basis of endowment per enrolled student.[96] Leading private universities have built up large amounts of endowment over many years. It will not be possible for public universities to do this over a few years or even a few decades. But they should get started and make development of endowment a high priority. Many are making intensive efforts to do just that and have been doing so since the 1980s and before. This objective requires the same staffing and intensity of fund-raising activities that have been

---

[94] Newfield, 2016, *loc. cit.*
[95] Fethke and Policano, 2014, *op. cit.*, p. 63.
[96] "List of Colleges and Universities in the United States by Endowment," *Wikipedia*, http://perma.cc/KX6G-YH7S.

characteristic of major private universities. In that sense, building fundraising capacity is an investment and may not pay off all that well in the early years while institutional capability and cultivation of donors are developed. Offsetting the fact that public-university graduates may be less prosperous on the average is the fact that there are individual donors and foundations who are attracted by the public mission itself.

The ins and outs of privatization in the sense of maintaining the public mission have been considered by Matthew Lambert,[97] vice president for institutional advancement at the College of William and Mary, who carried out in-depth studies of the states of Virginia, North Carolina, and California, including talking with about 150 legislators in those states to obtain their views. His book contains a chapter specific to California.[98]

Increasing Tuition Revenue

The Need to Build Financial Aid Simultaneously. If access is to be maintained in public universities, increases in tuition must be accompanied by increases in need-based financial aid. The approach used by the University of California is to devote one-third of revenue from tuition increases to need-based aid. Universities should also recognize that the upper level of family incomes that qualify a student as needy should also rise as tuitions rise.

The Limits on Tuition for Public Universities. There are four plausible upper limits on the amount of tuition that can be charged by public universities following the model in which very substantial portions of increases in tuition are devoted to need-based financial aid. These are the *market limit* (the point at which enrollment cannot be sustained in view of higher tuition), the ability to *maintain the public mission* (access independent of ability to pay), the size of accumulated *student debt*, and *political* limits in various forms, some of them relating to access and debt.

Fethke and Policano[99] discuss various aspects of market response to higher tuition. More specifically for the University of California, as of

---

[97] Lambert, 2014, *loc. cit.*
[98] Lambert, 2014, *op. cit.*, chapter 7, pp. 185–219.
[99] Fethke and Policano, 2012, *op. cit.*, chapter 4, pp. 49–66.

2016 eight of the nine undergraduate campuses (all except Merced) cannot admit all eligible applicants who apply and are therefore selective among eligible applicants. Therefore, by market analysis alone, they could raise tuition while sustaining enrollment. Some of the UC campuses are much more selective than others. The most selective campuses could, in principle, raise tuition much more than the others and still maintain enrollment. However, doing that would result in tuitions that differ among campuses, something that the university has not been willing to have.

Raising tuition also brings extra costs beyond the need to devote a substantial amount of the tuition increase to financial aid. In order to avoid excessive elasticity of demand, another large expense area incurred with higher tuition should be for upgrading student services, moving toward the level provided by the leading private universities. The purposes are both to draw students and to cultivate satisfied alumni who will be supportive donors after graduation.

Even when a substantial fraction of revenue from tuition increases is dedicated to need-based financial aid, higher tuitions will engender increased student borrowing and hence greater accumulated student debt. Student debt loads have now become high enough that they are a major national concern, financially and politically. That issue and how it might be overcome are described in the following two sections.

Opponents of the higher-tuition, higher-aid approach argue that "sticker shock" from higher tuition will drive away low-income students and their families, who will not persist to discover the availability of the aid. They also note that, once a higher-tuition, higher-aid policy is established in a state, the aid component can be cut or withdrawn by the state government in times of economic stringency, leaving only the high tuition.

Many people who are more affluent believe that low-cost public education is an obligation of the state, even for wealthier residents. Their votes may offset the votes of the low-income residents who would benefit from the high-aid portion of the policy. Thus the tuition-aid structure is inherently a political matter. The political nature is underscored by the fact that Lambert[100] found in his interviews with

---

[100] Lambert, 2014, *loc. cit.*

state legislators that a number of them recognize and expect that higher tuition is needed to offset, in part, the loss of public funding for universities. However, they will still vocally oppose higher tuition because of the political benefits that they derive from so doing. Fethke and Policano[101] report similar findings. To the extent that the state legislature has control over tuition, either directly or through the budget, politics can limit or severely impede higher tuitions even with a large portion of the tuition increase returned to aid.

Political opposition to higher tuition should wax and wane depending upon legislators' perceptions of public attitudes. It thus behooves public universities to find ways of spreading awareness of true costs to students and their families when tuition and living expenses are discounted by the available financial aid and to find ways of lessening student debt or making it more manageable. One approach, not without political danger itself, is tuition pricing that is differential by income level.

In 2014 tuition for undergraduate, in-state students at the University of California was about 20 percent higher than for the average of the other twenty-eight public universities that are members of the Association of American Universities (AAU). However, UC tuition is still only about 28 percent as high as the tuitions of the twenty-six AAU members that are private universities.[102]

A 2011 recommendation from a meeting of twenty-two former chancellors of campuses of the University of California considered new funding models for the university and went so far as to recommend a doubling of the tuition. This increase would be coupled with a rearrangement of state funding whereby all state support would be devoted to need-based financial aid.[103] In support of this recommendation, the former chancellors argued:

---

[101] Fethke and Policano, 2014, *loc. cit.*
[102] University of California, *Accountability Report 2015*, fig. 2.1.1, http://perma.cc/DAJ3-9AHM.
[103] "Former University of California Chancellors Urge New Funding Models for UC," Research and Occasional Papers Series, no. 15-11, Center for Studies in Higher Education, University of California, Berkeley, October, 2011, https://perma.cc/A2AB-LVMB.

Under the model we are suggesting, the State's current contribution of approximately $12,000 per student, traditionally used by UC as general institutional support for its education programs, would henceforth be used solely for financial aid. In effect, these State funds would become a subsidy to students who are California residents. This would enable the University to reallocate much, if not all, of the tuition income it has perforce returned to financial aid to preserve the quality of the education we provide for residents and nonresidents alike.

By this rationale, state support would be directly tied to financial-aid support for needy California-resident students, without the political opportunity to try to separate the two matters in the minds of legislators and voters. As already noted, a similar suggestion was made by Garland, with the state financial aid being in the form of portable vouchers that could be taken to the student's institution of choice. As described by Hyatt [104] and in more detail by Garland, [105] Miami University of Ohio instituted a system whereby it charges the same tuition for residents and nonresidents of the state, but it has two forms of scholarships that are available only to residents: one the same for all residents and the other need-based. It should be noted, however, that this approach too runs the risk that the state-supported financial aid could be lost in a time of state financial crisis.

Student Debt. Both the recent increases in tuitions and the marketing and financial practices of for-profit universities have increased student borrowing sharply. The situation has now gotten to the point where it is a major national issue in the United States, even reflected in political campaign stances for the 2016 presidential election. An October 2015 report[106] based on a detailed annual study by The Institute for College Access and Success cites 1.3 trillion dollars

---

[104] James A, Hyatt, "Redefining State Support," *Business Officer*, National Association of College and University Business Officers (NACUBO), November 2005.
[105] Garland, 2009, *op. cit.*, appendix A, pp. 221–230.
[106] The Institute for College Access and Success (TICAS), "Student Debt and the Class of 2014," October 2015, https://perma.cc/GA54-3XT6.

in accumulated student loans for the college class of 2014 that graduated from public and private not-for-profit colleges and universities. Sixty-nine percent of graduating seniors had accumulated student-loan debt, owing an average of $28,950 per borrower. Inclusion of private, for-profit institutions, from which it is much harder to obtain data, would have made the figures substantially higher. Strikingly, although women constitute about 56 percent of those enrolled in higher education, they account for 65 percent of accumulated debt.[107] Among the states California has comparatively less debt per student, but the issue is still present in California.

Most of the borrowing has been from government-sponsored or government-guaranteed loan programs. Much has been made in the media about the burden of repayment created by these programs and the fact that even bankruptcy does not relieve the obligation. The debt burden is not evenly distributed among students from different types of institution. A recent University of California accountability report[108] indicated that the 2011–12 cumulative debt level for UC undergraduates was $20,200 per student for those students graduating with debt, compared to $25,700 for other public four-year, $30,740 for private nonprofit four-year, and $37,840 for private for-profit institutions. The same source indicated that about 55 percent of the UC class of 2013–14 graduated with debt.

It has been reported that nearly seven million Americans, or about 17 percent of borrowers, have gone at least a year without making a payment on their federal student loans.[109] Defaults are concentrated toward borrowers at for-profit schools and, to a lesser extent, two-year institutions and other nonselective institutions.[110]

---

[107] Kevin Miller, "Deeper in Debt: Women and Student Loans," American Assn. of University Women, May 2017, https://perma.cc/9VL7-KJ3G.
[108] "Undergraduate Students—Affordability," chapter 2 in *Accountability Report 2015*, University of California, http://perma.cc/DAJ3-9AHM.
[109] Josh Mitchell, "School-Loan Reckoning: 7 Million Are in Default," *Wall Street Journal*, August 21, 2016.
[110] Adam Looney and Constantine Yannelis, "A Crisis in Student Loans? How Changes in the Characteristics of Borrowers and in the Institutions They Attended Contributed to Rising Loan Defaults," Brookings Papers on Economic Activity, Brookings Institution, Fall 2015, https://perma.cc/C43L-SNLK.

Dynarski[111] analyzed reasons for student debt and the difficulties that graduates in the United States have in repayment. The problem areas include a relatively short ten-year repayment period, which occurs while incomes are still low, as well as the fact that for the original program the required repayment amounts are constant over time and cannot be waived. As already noted, even bankruptcy does not relieve debt obligations for student loans.

These blanket statements mask a more subtle and differentiated infrastructure of student debt, which is analyzed by Baum[112] and by Akers and Chingos[113] in work that is also briefly summarized by Supiano.[114] They make arguments that the crisis is not as severe as the aggregate figures make it appear and that the debt is concentrated toward those who have taken loans to obtain advanced degrees and those who should not have sought college education in the first place, typified by students recruited avidly by the for-profit institutions.

Income-Contingent Loans. Income-contingent student loans came into use on a widespread basis in Australia in 1989, during a time of financial difficulty in the national budget. Those loans are issued by the government and are repayable through income tax filings once the earnings of the former student have risen to a certain level after graduation. They thereby provide a clear and manageable path of repayment. The Australian system has been discussed by Harman,[115] and Chapman[116, 117] has examined the approach in more general form.

---

[111] Susan Dynarski, "America Can Fix Its Student Loan Crisis; Just Ask Australia," *New York Times*, July 9, 2016.

[112] Sandy Baum, *Student Debt: Rhetoric and Realities of Higher Education Financing* (London: Palgrave Macmillan, 2016).

[113] Beth Akers and Matthew M. Chingos, *Game of Loans: The Rhetoric and Reality of Student Debt* (Princeton, NJ: Princeton University Press, 2016).

[114] Beckie Supiano, "Economists Offer Unconventional Wisdom of Student-Loan 'Crisis,'" *Chronicle of Higher Education*, September 27, 2016.

[115] Grant Harman, "Australia's Experiment: Tuition Fees, Student Loans, and University Income Generation," chapter 5 in John A. Douglass, C. Judson King, and Irwin Feller, eds., *Globalization's Muse: Universities and Higher Education Systems in a Changing World* (Berkeley: Berkeley Public Policy Press, Institute of Governmental Studies, University of California, 2009), pp. 93–110.

[116] Bruce Chapman, "Income Contingent Loans for Higher Education: International Reform," discussion paper no. 491, Centre for Economic Policy Research, Research School of Social Sciences, The Australian National University, Australia, June 2005, https://perma.cc/M9XH-BPV5.

[117] Bruce Chapman, "Income Contingent Loans in Higher Education Financing," *IZA World of Labor*, February 2016, https://perma.cc/M27F-K88P.

The use of income-contingent loans for public higher education had as of 2016 spread to at least nine other countries, including New Zealand, South Korea, the Netherlands, and Great Britain.[118] An approach with some similar characteristics was launched in the US by the Obama administration through PAYE (Pay As You Earn) loans (2012) and REPAYE loans (2015). These loans have less favorable eligibility and repayment conditions than the Australian model and, as of 2017, are also in jeopardy of not being continued by the Trump administration. Income–contingent loans were also adopted in the state of Oregon in 2013 on a trial basis.[119]

Income-contingent loans in Australia tie repayment to the career earnings of the student, with formulae that keep the payments manageable and with the amount due remaining at zero if the graduate's income never reaches the threshold level. Such a program requires that the government generate a sufficient amount of money up front to create the loan pool, such as through issuance of bonds. In the United States there needs to be a mechanism to sustain repayments even when graduates move among states.

Widespread use of government income-contingent loans for student higher-education costs makes good sense for the United States, California, and the University of California. As things stand, the political limit is probably most restrictive with regard to UC tuition increases. Institution of a widely used, well-understood income-contingent loan system would probably create enough sense of security among the public so that political stances against higher tuition would be mitigated significantly.

It should also be recognized that income-contingent loans move the cost of higher education from resources available at the time of enrollment, which are probably parental resources, to the earning power of the graduate that has been engendered by higher education.

---

[118] Chapman, 2016, *loc. cit.*
[119] Rebecca Nathanson, "Paying It Forward, One State at a Time," *The Nation*, August 16, 2013, https://perma.cc/LV4B-YZ5G.

Out-of-State and International Students. One of the steps taken by the University of California and other major public research universities in response to diminished state funding has been to increase substantially enrollments of full-fee-paying out-of-state and international students. Enrollment of those students provides sufficient net funds to subsidize the enrollment of additional state-resident students beyond those covered by state funding. The University of Virginia and the University of Michigan experienced difficulties in state funding earlier and successfully went down this road sooner. Public universities in some smaller states with less public funding have historically had very high out-of-state enrollment. The Universities of Vermont and Delaware have only about 25 percent[120] and 38 percent[121] in-state enrollment, respectively.

From an overall national viewpoint, enrollment of out-of-state US students is a zero-sum game. There are students who will pay more for public higher education in another state for personal or family reasons or because they perceive it to be a better education for them.

From another standpoint, many students who come to California from other states and countries have stayed and are important contributors to California's economy. Many have themselves started California-based companies. Since the rise of Silicon Valley in the 1960s and 1970s, the California economy has had many very important contributions from immigrants.

Because of political concerns that nonresident students take up enrollment spots that could have been used for eligible California students, and as already noted in chapters 2 and 15, the Regents of the University of California in 2017 adopted a policy limiting the percentage of nonresidents among undergraduate students to current values in the 19 to 24 percent range at Berkeley, San Diego, UCLA, and Irvine, and to 18 percent at the remaining general campuses. This was a political response to public and legislative concerns at the time.

---

[120] Zach Despart, "UVM's Incoming Class Has Fewer Vermonters," *Burlington Free Press*, November 17, 2015.
[121] "UD Facts and Figures, 2015–16," University of Delaware, https://perma.cc/C8TD-6M6G.

But what are academically optimum levels of international and US nonresident students? And what levels are politically defensible? Figure 21-1 shows the percentage of state-resident, US-non-resident, and international students among undergraduates for Fall 2016 enrollment for comparison public universities in the United States, along with the University of California as a whole and the average for AAU public universities other than UC.

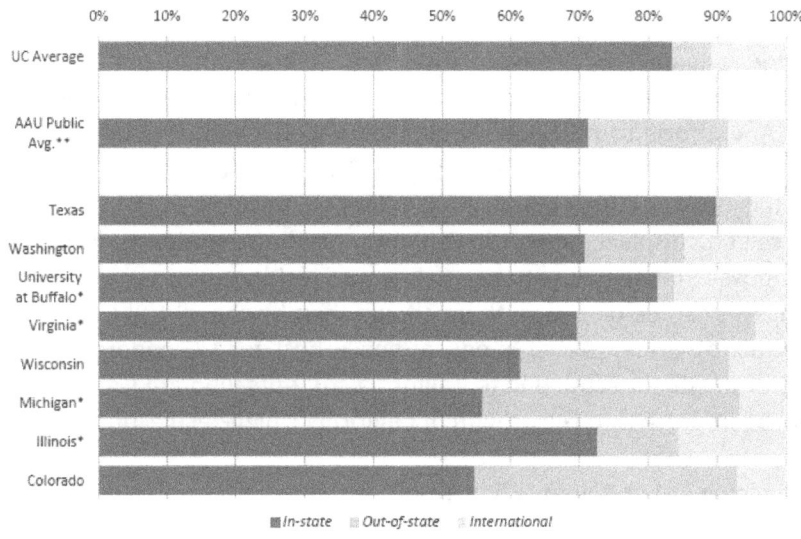

Figure 21-1. Resident, US Nonresident, and International Undergraduate Enrollments at UC and Comparison US Public Universities, Fall 2016.[122]

A survey [123] of 2015–16 international [124] enrollments at US universities shows several private universities, including Illinois

---

[122] Accountability Report 2017, Univerrsity of California, Figure 1.4.1, https://perma.cc/JTF4-VVML.

Institute of Technology and Carnegie-Mellon University, in the range of 20–33 percent, with UC San Diego as the highest public institution at 23 percent, followed among University of California campuses by Irvine at 16 percent.

In comparison with the values for other states shown in figure 21-1, the figures for the University of California suggest that the percentages of nonresident students could logically be increased. But the population and political situation are different in California, the state is large, and the geographical location is more isolated. Those facts probably necessitate a limit for the out-of-state and international undergraduate student population that is lower than the 30 to 40 percent range that is prevalent in the midwestern state universities.

Any efforts to raise the enrollment of international and/or out-of-state US students at the University of California beyond the levels set by the Board of Regents in 2017 will need to address the matter of perceived displacement of California-resident students from the campuses most sought by California residents. If displacement concerns can be dispelled, there should then be thoughtful analyses of the mix of students that is educationally best for UC undergraduates and of needs for attracting to California students who are likely to stay and be important to the growth of California's high-tech economy.

Enhancing Other Revenue Sources

Broader Federal Government Support. The public universities in the United States belong to the states. The federal government funds universities (both public and private) by two primary means—research support and student financial aid. The financial aid largely takes the form of loans but also includes Pell Grants in direct support of students from low-income families. An obvious path to explore is whether the federal government could assume a wider role in supporting the nation's public universities. The political process of the federal government would make it virtually impossible to create programs benefitting a few states at the expense of the rest. Broad-brush,

---

[123] "Most International Students," *U.S. News and World Report*, https://web.archive.org/web/20170506101833/https://www.usnews.com/best-colleges/rankings/national-universities/most-international.

[124] Not including out-of-state US students.

flexible support would probably be spread so widely that the net influence would likely be small, and as well there would properly be issues of accountability. The best approaches are probably new competitive, peer-reviewed programs targeted for specific purposes. Another useful approach could be cost matching with states, which would provide an incentive for state funding. A program for university facilities that matches state funding subject to a peer-review process is one possibility. This would address the reduction of spending for university facilities that has occurred in many states, including California. Tax policy could also be used advantageously. Tax preferences are already in place for private donations to qualified not-for-profit universities and for industrial funding of research. Ways could be devised to increase these benefits further for individuals and companies.

Foundation Funding. The foundations classically dealing with higher education, such as the Carnegie Corporation and the Mellon, Ford, and Hewlett Foundations, traditionally welcomed projects dealing with a variety of needs and opportunities, leaving the selection and development of the project area largely up to the proposing institution. This situation has changed significantly in recent years, with many foundations and a growing number of other philanthropic vehicles now working in an activist, agenda-driven way that prescribes not only the need but also the desired means of addressing it. Approaches of this sort have come to dominate the world of foundation philanthropy for higher education. The issue is not specific to higher education; it applies broadly within the charitable world.[125]

As part of this trend, several major foundations dealing with higher education—most notably the Gates and Lumina Foundations and to lesser extents the Hewlett and Kresge Foundations—have taken strong interests in promoting access and greater participation in higher education. Their efforts should be beneficial toward those particular ends, which are important.

The agenda-driven emphasis and the similaritiy of the agendas of different foundations reduce the possibilities for support of broader-

---

[125] See, e.g., David Callahan, *The Givers: Wealth, Power, and Philanthropy in a New Gilded Age* (New York: Knopf, 2017).

based innovations in higher education that do not fit the methodology predefined by the foundation.[126] Would-be grant recipients of course try to fit their proposals to the objectives and preferred methodology of the foundation to which they are applying, thereby reducing the overall diversity of projects.

Foundation support should be regarded as valuable for carrying out research and launching innovations. Most foundations have policies of not providing on-going support or endowments. They also usually have policies that favor distributing their largesse widely rather than focusing in on a few beneficiaries. Despite growth in charitable giving and in the number of foundations, the amount of funding potentially available to universities from foundations remains only a small fraction of what comes through state support (for public universities), tuition, federal research grants, and collected, targeted private giving by individuals.

Private Support from Individuals. Major gifts from individuals will continue as vital components of university funding portfolios and will grow for public universities as they devote more energy to the area. But gifts from individuals can rarely be used for general support of a university. Donors are more motivated by specific subjects and projects that are of particular interest to them.

Employer Support. The people, discoveries, and innovations that come out of US research universities have been of great value to industry. The contributions of universities to society and the economy, including industry, have been documented in many ways, including the comprehensive book by Jonathan Cole,[127] a study by the National Research Council,[128] and the Lincoln Project of the American Academy

---

[126] *The Chronicle of Higher Education* devoted most of its issue of July 14, 2013, to this issue. See, e.g., Ben Gose, "Strategic Philanthropy Comes to Higher Education," *The Chronicle of Higher Education*, July 14, 2013.

[127] Jonathan Cole, *The Great American University: Its Rise to Preeminence, Its Indispensable National Role, Why It Must Be Protected* (New York: Public Affairs, 2012), pp. 45–87.

[128] Committee on Research Universities, Board on Higher Education and Workforce, Policy and Global Affairs, National Research Council, *Research Universities and the Future of America: Ten Breakthrough Actions Vital to Our Nation's Prosperity and Security* (Washington, DC: National Academies Press, 2012), https://perma.cc/ZZM3-P8D8..

of Arts and Sciences (AAAS),[129] It was the growth of university research in scientific areas that enabled many major companies to make the decisions that they did in the 1970s and 1980s to wind back and/or reorient in-house research. Yet research universities are funded much more by state and federal governments and by students and their families than by the ultimate users of the talent that comes from them. Of course, companies do pay taxes, and companies and industrial organizations do sometimes supply help to public universities in the state political process. But the general lack of direct financial assistance from industrial employers to higher education other than through sponsored research is still striking. It could make sense to tie a set portion of state corporate taxes directly to university funding, in the same way that California dedicates state gasoline taxes to road and transportation projects. This coupling might engender less resistance from industry to tax increases. The above-mentioned Lincoln Project of the AAAS has recommended creating state incentives for corporations to support scholarships at public research universities, or even following the model of agreements by corporations with employee and executive search firms, giving one-third of the first year's salary to the university from which a new hire graduated.[130]

Entrepreneurial Activities

The area of greatest recent growth in generation of revenue by universities has been in what can be called entrepreneurial activities. These occur at both institutional and subinstitutional levels and generally take the form of efforts to market or otherwise utilize an

---

[129] The Lincoln Project, American Academy of Arts and Sciences, "Public Research Universities: Serving the Public Good," 2016, https://perma.cc/89ER-LGBF.

[130] The Lincoln Project, American Academy of Arts and Sciences, "Public Research Universities: Recommitting to Lincoln's Vision—An Educational Compact for the 21st Century," p. 22, 2016, http://perma.cc/UCD6-ES56. See also Robert Birgeneau and Henry Brady, "Public Research Universities: Recommitting to Lincoln's Vision: An Educational Compact for the 21st Century," video and slides of seminar, September 8, 2016, Center for Studies in Higher Education, University of California, Berkeley, https://www.youtube.com/watch?v=onYh5n3GdOo&t=0s&list=PLBCSDvIH2ZdX3fZp-Ov2f5e-ch2K2HNSU&index=4 , 46:38 and 56:00 minutes.

intellectual asset of the university, such as specific knowledge, educational know-how, or useful research discoveries.

International Partnerships and Branch Campuses. Many international partnerships involving US universities have been initiated in recent decades. There are also a number of instances where US universities have launched branch campuses overseas. Most of these efforts relate to marketing US higher education and exporting the US model, and most provide substantial net income for the partner university in the United States. They can also serve the very useful purpose of providing international experience for US students in a period of increasing globalization. A few of the leading examples portray the varied nature and scope.

- **Carnegie-Mellon University**, with its home base in Pittsburgh, Pennsylvania, had by 2016 developed operations in twenty-two other locations around the world, ranging from satellite campuses with free-standing degree programs to partnerships with universities in other countries.[131]
- **Education City**[132] **in Doha, Qatar,** is largely financed by the Qatar Foundation and is a cluster of complementary satellite operations of eight universities—Virginia Commonwealth University (fine arts), Weill Cornell Medical College, Texas A&M (engineering), Carnegie Mellon (business, computer science), Georgetown (foreign service), Northwestern (journalism, communication), École des Hautes Études Commerciales de Paris (business), and University College, London (archaeology, curation)—coupled with research parks and other activities. Education City fits the model of an "education hub," which has been considered more generally by Knight and coauthors[133] for the cases of Qatar, the United Arab Emirates, Hong Kong, Singapore, Malaysia, and Botswana.

---

[131] "Carnegie Mellon University's Global Presence," https://web.archive.org/web/20161222051303/https://www.cmu.edu/global/presence/.
[132] "Education City," *Wikipedia*, http://perma.cc/3QF4-5CQ8.
[133] Jane Knight, ed., *International Education Hubs: Student, Talent, Knowledge-Innovation Models* (London: Springer, 2014).

- **New York University** has satellite campuses in Abu Dhabi[134] and Shanghai,[135] along with eleven other global academic centers around the world. The design is that students and faculty should move interchangeably among the three campuses.
- **Yale-NUS College**[136] is a liberal arts college formed as a partnership between Yale University and the National University of Singapore, designed to bring that form of education to Asia. Degrees are from Yale-NUS, not from Yale or NUS themselves.
- **Duke Kunshan University**[137] is a joint effort of Duke University, Wuhan University, and the city of Kunshan, China, to create a new liberal-arts-based research university.
- **KAUST** (the King Abdullah University of Science and Technology)[138] is designed to be a graduate-level-only version of Caltech. While not a partnership effort institutionally, the university was started (2009) with partnerships in various disciplines and research areas with universities around the world, each receiving substantial funding from KAUST to help with definition of programs and recruitment and screening of faculty in a particular academic area.

Interestingly, most of these partnerships and branch campuses have so far been conducted by private, rather than public, universities, in the United States. This probably reflects the greater agility and acceptance of risk by private universities, as well as the obligation felt by public universities to pay first attention to their state. In all cases, there is substantial revenue to the US university partner.

Data on international branch campuses are maintained by the Cross-Border Education Research Team at the University at Albany, State University of New York, who in 2017 recorded 247 international

---

[134] "NYU Abu Dhabi," New York University Abu Dhabi, https://perma.cc/J7YF-KRSX .
[135] "NYU Shanghai," https://perma.cc/U2NQ-SEBZ.
[136] "Yale-NUS College," Yale-NUS College, https://perma.cc/RRC4-KGZC.
[137] "Duke Kunshan University: A Truly International University in China," https://perma.cc/4NPR-QTXV.
[138] "King Abdullah University of Science & Technology," https://perma.cc/RKP8-TSMU.

branch campuses in operation, with the US (77) and UK (38) being the largest exporters and China (32) and the United Arab Emirates (32) being the largest importers.[139] As of 2015 about 30 branches (12%) that had been created had been closed.[140]

A quite different approach is a University of California university-wide effort that supplies academic advice and oversight to the American University of Armenia,[141] That university, started in Yerevan, Armenia, in 1991, is a partnership effort of the Armenian General Benevolent Union (a worldwide Armenian-diaspora charitable organization), the Regents of the University of California, and the government of Armenia. In contrast to the other examples, the University of California relationship is budget neutral (i.e., no money changes hands). The incentive to UC for its participation can be regarded as more political than financial; there is a substantial Armenian American population in California, and the governor at the time of the founding was an Armenian American.[142]

Yet another approach is that of "microcampuses" overseas, currently being undertaken by the University of Arizona.[143] The idea is to enable students from other countries to obtain a University of Arizona degree while living primarily or even exclusively in their home countries, thereby saving the considerable extra expense associated with relocating and enrolling at the home campus in the United States. As of 2017 the university had thirteen agreements with overseas universities in place, two of them already in operation, with plans to increase to more than twenty-five by 2020. The micro-campuses use online instruction from faculty members at the home campus,

---

[139] "Quick Facts", Cross-Border Education Reseaerch Team, University at Albany, State University of New York, https://web.archive.org/web/20171105140240/http://cbert.org/.

[140] Geoff Maslen, "Why a Branch Campus Failed", *Chronicle of Higher Education, International*, February 25, 2015.

[141] "American University of Armenia," https://perma.cc/5T8F-DKH2.

[142] The author has been a member of the board of the American University of Armenia Corporation since 1995 and chaired it for fourteen years.

[143] Elizabeth Redden, "Arizona Embarks on Plan to Develop 25 Global Microcampuses," *Inside Higher Education*, May 23, 2017, https://perma.cc/Q57Y-PFUH..

augmented by use of the flipped-classroom approach conducted by faculty members from the partner university. Currently three undergraduate majors—business, civil engineering, and law—are offered in a format wherein degrees can be obtained simultaneously from both universities. The plan is to increase the number of available majors over time.

One of the ultimate intended features is for students from the home campus in Tucson, Arizona, to "study at any microcampus, and take courses with partner university students, while advancing seamlessly in their degree programs."[144] This micro-campus approach has the potential of enabling US students in very structured majors such as engineering to participate in study abroad, something that is difficult otherwise. The micro-campus approach, combining instructional and education-aboard aspects, could be attractive for the University of California, which as of 2017 had 402 Education Abroad programs in forty-two countries.[145]

Self-Sustaining Specialized Academic Programs. Another new class of high-revenue programs offered by the University of California, akin to the previously mentioned high-fee professional degree programs, is self-supporting graduate professional degree programs. These programs focus on special needs, often advanced education for working professionals. They utilize no state support, and are therefore purely entrepreneurial academic efforts. There were sixty-two of these among the campuses as of 2016,[146] a number that is continually growing. Fees for these programs are specific to the program and are set by campuses with approval by the president.[147] Both these programs and the high-fee professional programs provide revenue that is retained by the academic unit. They thereby contribute to a growing sense of different standards of living among academic departments.

---

[144] "Global Micro-Campus Network," University of Arizona, https://perma.cc/X7W4-V4FN.
[145] "Build Your Study Abroad," Education Abroad Program, University of California, https://perma.cc/SVT8-ABCC.
[146] "2015–16 Self-Supporting Graduate Professional Degree Programs," University of California, https://perma.cc/J3FX-XPE8.
[147] "Policy on Self-Supporting Graduate Degree Programs," University of California, September 23, 2011, https://perma.cc/DRE3-GKK7.

Building on Research Discoveries. The existence of some well-known blockbuster discoveries[148] that have, or could have, reaped considerable value for the universities involved has inspired many research universities to seek to generate income from technology-transfer patent-licensing activities. But the financial results of these ventures have been very chancy. Many university technology-transfer offices do not make sufficient money to cover their expenses, and studies have shown that only rarely do university inventions hit it big financially. There is no good way to predict winners in advance. It is better to let general relations with industry be the driver for the establishment of technology-transfer efforts and then to let adventitious serendipity take its course. Net income from technology transfer and licensing should not be incorporated into budgetary planning until it is actually realized.

Some universities, including the University of California since 2014,[149] have gone still further by investing directly in companies commercializing technology based on university research. For UC this enables taking equity in return for use of university facilities and services, such as incubators, during the initial development phases.

There are of course other, less direct ways in which universities derive revenue from the impact of their research. Land-rich universities, such as Stanford and the Irvine campus of the University of California, have received rents and land-usage fees from companies that choose to locate on university-owned land near the campus because of the attractiveness of being near university researchers. That

---

[148] Three early examples are (1) the Wisconsin Alumni Research Foundation (WARF), which managed and licensed patents for the use of ultraviolet radiation to add vitamin D to milk and then for warfarin, a blood anticoagulant named for WARF and originally used as a rat poison but now widely used for treatment of vascular and heart disease in humans ("WARF Decade by Decade, Wisconsin Alumni Research Foundation, https://perma.cc/8AL9-ZSPF); (2) Gatorade, originally developed at the University of Florida as a means of electrolyte-replacement for athletes (Joe Kays and Arline Phillips-Han, "Gatorade: The Idea That Launched an Industry," University of Florida, https://perma.cc/XA7T-4UYR]; and, later, (3) the Boyer-Cohen patent of Stanford and the University of California on recombinant DNA (chapter 18), which was a backbone for the development of the biotechnology industry.

[149] Janet Napolitano, "My June Newsletter," Office of the President, University of California, June 27, 2014, https://perma.cc/54JA-QKSN.

desire was the genesis for Stanford Industrial Park (chapter 18). The impact and attractiveness of a university's research can also be credited as much of the reason that various large research arrangements have been made between industrial companies and universities, ranging from Monsanto's early involvement with Harvard forward to the BP Energy Biosciences Institute at Berkeley (chapter 18).

Expanding Horizons and Acquisitions. Another route for deriving new revenue and/or creating the wherewithal to generate it is to expand the activities of a college or university into new activities. A striking example has been Southern New Hampshire University,[150] a relatively new public university that has now devoted considerable attention to building and expanding online education and now has over eighty thousand online students along with three thousand plus on-campus students. Its activities are primarily professional education with only limited research. There are currently schools of business, education, and arts and sciences.

A very different venture to build online education has recently been taken by Purdue University, which in 2017 acquired Kaplan University from Kaplan, Inc.[151] Kaplan was a for-profit university and is one that has been subject to accusations and lawsuits claiming overly aggressive marketing and profiteering so as to derive income through government loans to students for tuition payment. It has fifteen in-house locations in the United States, largely in the Midwest, and a large online program.

Upon acquisition by Purdue, Kaplan University (KU) became a nonprofit public benefit corporation, with academic design and oversight by Purdue and support services and some budgetary control by Kaplan, Inc. By act of the Indiana State Legislature at the time of acquisition, KU became exempt from public records laws and several other public accountability measures. This is a striking, but allowable, status for a unit of a public university. Through this action KU will not have to file financial information with the Securities and Exchange

---

[150] "About Us," University of Southern New Hampshire, https://perma.cc/6ARX-U8F6.
[151] Other business activities of Kaplan, Inc., have been test preparation, licensing, and additional aspects of continuing education and professional development.

Commission (SEC) as it did in its former status.[152] There is to be no state funding for KU, but Indiana residents will receive discounted tuition.

Uncertainties include whether, when, and to what extent Purdue can derive net revenue from the arrangement; how much the Purdue brand will help the bottom line for KU, which presently loses money; and what will come from approval processes such as accreditation.[153]

Positive aspects of the arrangement cited by Purdue are positioning Purdue for growth in online education, serving those who cannot now get on-campus degrees, and in effect moving toward a new, more comprehensive public-university mission suited to the information age.[154] Levine[155] cites upgrading the overall quality of online education, a useful learning experience for Purdue, and recognition of the transition to a digital society. Among the concerns raised have been the unusual latitude and secrecy afforded to KU, the potential for sullying Purdue's name through continuation of KU's marketing practices, too much control remaining with Kaplan, Inc., and the risk of substantial long-term financial losses for Purdue.[156]

From a governance standpoint, the Purdue administration did not consult with their (faculty) university senate before the acquisition and did not inform the senate leaders until very shortly before the deal was finalized and announced. There have been resultant tensions.

---

[152] Goldie Blumenstyk, "In Purdue's New Vision, How 'Public' Will Kaplan Be?" *Chronicle of Higher Education*, May 5, 2017.

[153] Paul Fain, "Regulators and Accreditor Begin Review of Purdue's Boundary-Testing Deal with Kaplan," *Inside Higher Education*, May 30, 2017, https://perma.cc/5HL9-S8CB.

[154] "Purdue to Acquire Kaplan University, increase Access for Millions," Purdue University, April 27, 2017, https://perma.cc/CH28-QBSU.

[155] Arthur Levine, "3 Reasons to Applaud Purdue's Kaplan Deal," *Chronicle of Higher Education*, May 19, 2017.

[156] Robert Shireman, "There's a Reason the Purdue-Kaplan Deal Sounds Too Good to Be True," *Chronicle of Higher Education*, April 30, 2017; "Can Purdue Create a 'Public' University Controlled by Investors?," The Century Foundation, May 31, 2017, https://web.archive.org/web/20180331221643/https://tcf.org/content/commentary/can-purdue-create-public-university-controlled-investors/.

Pitfalls for Entrepreneurial Presidents. Experience so far on institutional-partnership entrepreneurial activities has identified some of the principal impediments to success. These include (1) the institutional leadership getting too far out in front of the faculty and not being able to deliver what has been promised, (2) reluctance of faculty members to travel or relocate, (3) proposed intellectual partnerships that do not blossom, (4) the president being too far out in front of (or behind!) the trustees, and above all, (5) issues of risk management. Presidents will do well to seek true, attractive benefits for all parties and not just revenue, to work in synergy with their faculty, and to enable rather than prescribe.

Activities at the Level of Academic Units. Except for the KAUST partnerships, the entrepreneurial activities described so far all involve entire educational institutions. Of at least comparable importance are the myriad entrepreneurial efforts that are stemming from academic departments or organized research units and even individual faculty members. Many of these are responses to reductions in state funding, as units look to "stay alive."

There are several good reasons why partnerships initiated by faculty members or groups of faculty members may ultimately be the most successful ones. The creativity of a research university lies with the faculty members. Within research universities it is easier to build in a bottom-up rather than in a top-down mode. And by starting small and then building up, one can evaluate and adjust while growing rather than trying to define fully out in front. Consequently, it should be possible to preclude large mistakes.

One primary mechanism for entrepreneurship at the level of individual academic units is the provision of specialized courses. An example underlies the original development of this book. While the author was director of Berkeley's Center for Studies in Higher Education, the center received budget cuts, and we developed week-long courses on university structure, governance, and building and maintenance of quality for university and ministry officials from around the world as a means of generating offsetting revenue.

Another common form of entrepreneurism among faculty members is the development of external partnerships, primarily in research. These may be revenue-bearing, but in most cases enrichment of the research is the driver. In a recent study[157] of scholarly communication in seven academic disciplines (economics, molecular biology, astrophysics, political science, music, history, and archaeology), one question was about partnerships among faculty members at different institutions and the factors that make them most successful. Four factors stood out—complementary expertise, specialized facilities and/or instrumentation, the need to deal well with multidisciplinary grand-challenge issues, and facilitation of fieldwork and the locations of objects of study.

When partnerships with other institutions are created by individual faculty members, groups of faculty members, or academic departments, the role of the campus administration becomes one of enablement—identifying which partnerships to foster in what ways and wisely monitoring partnerships through appropriate policies.

Policy Needs. Entrepreneurial activities within universities are rapidly growing and do afford viable paths for revenue enhancement. However, they raise several issues for which policies need to be developed, similar to what was done during the 1980s and 1990s to govern interactions with industry. Policies, coordinating mechanisms, or both will be needed in areas such as these:

- the use of the institutional "brand name,"
- pricing structures,
- avoidance or management of situations where the activities of one unit cause problems for other units within the university,
- the proportion of a faculty member's time devoted to entrepreneurial activities as opposed to usual university duties,
- determination of what content is appropriate for entrepreneurial programs rather than falling within a university's core public mission,
- the appropriateness of additional salary from university entrepreneurial activities, and
- payment for institutional services supporting such activities.

---

[157] Diane Harley et al., "Assessing the Future Landscape of Scholarly Communication: An Exploration of Faculty Values and Needs in Seven Disciplines," Center for Studies in Higher Education, University of California, Berkeley, January 2010, accessed July 26, 2016, http://escholarship.org/uc/cshe_fsc.

It should help for a university campus to create what is effectively a minister of entrepreneurism—someone who will maintain awareness of what is going on; look for linkages, interactions, conflicts, and so on, within the university; encourage integration of efforts across the campus; look for policy needs; and initiate policy development where needed.

Less State Control

As public research universities have had to supplement state funding with ever larger amounts of revenue from other sources, some of them have sought to reduce the amount of state control, so as to give them needed flexibility for achieving efficiencies and funding from nonstate sources. A notable example took place in Virginia, where what was originally a charter university initiative for the University of Virginia, Virginia Tech, and William and Mary morphed during the process of political give-and-take into the Restructured Higher Education Financial and Administrative Operations Act of 2005.[158, 159, 160] Through it, public universities achieved one of three levels of flexibility in return for an acknowledgement of substantially lesser levels of state support and a general agreement as to deliverables. Leslie and Berdahl[161] describe the political sausage making that occurred through the process and question whether there was net positive benefit for the three public universities that undertook the initiative.

An examination of the terms and delegations[162] of the Virginia arrangement shows that essentially all of the flexibility that was given already exists for the University of California by virtue of constitutional

---

[158] Hyatt, 2005, *loc. cit.*
[159] Lambert, 2015, *op. cit.*, pp. 136–138.
[160] Sarah Turner, "Higher Tuition, Higher Aid, and the Quest to Improve Opportunities for Low-Income Students: The Case of Virginia," chapter 12 in Ronald G. Ehrenberg, ed., *What's Happening to Public Higher Education*, Praeger Series on Higher Education (Westport, CT: Praeger Publishers, 2006).
[161] David W. Leslie and Robert O. Berdahl, "The Politics of Restructuring Higher Education in Virginia: A Case Study," *Review of Higher Education* 31, no. 3 (2008): 309–328, https://perma.cc/2KEG-9XXB.
[162] Hyatt, 2005, *loc. cit.*

autonomy. For the University of California, greater flexibility is probably better achieved through changes in internal governance (see below), rather than seeking greater flexibility in the relationship with the state. One exception would be renegotiation of the student capacity to be maintained under the Master Plan.

Another effort of a similar sort to that in Virginia was undertaken in 2010–11 by Chancellor Biddy Martin of the Madison campus of the University of Wisconsin system.[163] In an unlikely partnership with Wisconsin governor Scott Walker, who was generally regarded as unsupportive of public higher education, Martin endeavored to separate the Madison campus from the rest of the University of Wisconsin system and thereby obtain greater autonomy and flexibility for the Madison campus. This effort was predictably opposed by the other campuses of the UW system and was eventually abandoned.

The data on such efforts so far are relatively slim but do indicate that the necessary political process to achieve increased flexibility may be too much of a damper for truly helpful arrangements to be achieved. A long-time University of California assistant vice president for state government relations has observed that the more the state budget for the university is cut, the more controversial the university's coping actions become, and the more aggressive the state government becomes in seeking to block those actions.[164]

Two Additional Issues for the University of California

Several other issues bearing on the University of California relate closely to the changing bases of support. Two of them are the different situations of the different UC campuses for raising other sources of funding and the question of maintaining the Master Plan capacity. There are also some who push for dissolution of the single university, letting different campuses or groups of campuses go their own way, either as a confederation, as separate public universities, or somehow converted to private status. That proposal does not stand up well to analysis, because of the governmental and state-funding chaos that would be created as well as the loss of the many advantages of the

---

[163] Fethke and Policano, 2012, *op. cit.*, pp. 188–189.
[164] Steven A. Arditti, personal communication, January 18, 2017.

single-university structure noted in chapter 5 and the multifaceted services to the state that the university has provided.

Differences among Campuses. The UC campuses have differing circumstances, brought about through different founding dates and hence different numbers and ages of alumni, different emphases, and different geographical locations. Berkeley and Los Angeles—the oldest campuses—have a full spectrum of ages of alumni; many of the younger campuses do not. That fact affects potentials for private fundraising. Berkeley, UCLA, and Davis have the most professional schools, many of which are productive for fund-raising. The programmatic dimensions of Davis and Riverside give them particular access to the agricultural community. The six campuses with medical schools—San Francisco, Los Angeles, San Diego, Davis, Irvine, and now Riverside—have resultant opportunities for fund-raising, but they are also subject to the ups and downs of federal Medicare and state Medicaid funding.

An ultimate question for UC as one university is whether state- and/or fee-generated resources will be distributed among campuses in a way that somehow recognizes these differences in access to other funds, rather than simply on a weighted-enrollment basis, as is the case now (chapter 6). Another issue, addressed later in this chapter, is whether the governance of the university should change to recognize these differences among the campuses.

Yet another question is whether undergraduate tuitions should differ among the UC general campuses. As noted above, enrollment pressures from eligible students at UCLA, Berkeley, and San Diego in particular are high enough that these universities could raise tuition without losing enrollment. There are two counteracting forces. One is the desire of the elected officials in the state government to keep tuition from increasing. The other is that the public might infer that campuses with higher tuition have different education quality as opposed to just different application pressure. Adoption of different tuitions for different campuses is a complicated arena that is best avoided until there are no better alternatives left.

Capacity for Students. Another major set of questions is whether UC can continue to meet capacity obligations under the Master Plan and whether the percentage of high school graduates to be accommodated should be either increased above that level, as would be desirable for enabling UC education to serve a greater portion of the populace, or decreased, as may be necessary in view of funding limitations. The political pressures will be to take more students, and indeed taking smaller portions of students would serve to feed apprehensions that UC is elitist and not serving ordinary Californians.

Growth means more campuses, larger campuses, and/or alternative ways of educating students. It is a particularly challenging issue because of the general reluctance of the term-limited state government to think ahead, reinforced by the 2011 defunding of the California Postsecondary Education Commission.

Starting more campuses does not seem to be an option in the present fiscal climate.[165] Even allowing for growth at Merced and Riverside, growth at other campuses will at some point require negotiation of long-range development plans with the communities, which has been a difficult process in the past. With 2016 UCLA and Berkeley enrollments at forty-five thousand and forty thousand students, respectively, there is also the matter of how large is too large—that is, to what extent the quality of the academic experience decreases with further growth.

A better and more achievable approach is probably to foster transfer education, through more students choosing, or being required, to use the transfer route, coupled with a major upgrading of counseling and other ways of encouraging and supporting transfer. Another related alternative would be the use of lower division satellite campuses located in different but nearby communities.[166]

GOVERNANCE CHANGES FOR CHANGING TIMES

The increasingly varied and complex mix of revenues and the diminished proportion of state funds create a very different set of dynamics for public research universities in general and the University

---

[165] This conclusion reinforces the wisdom and foresight of Clark Kerr and the Board of Regents in launching so many new general campuses in the late 1950s and 1960s.

[166] Saul Geiser, "Expanding Off-Campus Enrollment Capacity at Berkeley: A Concept Paper," Research & Occasional Papers Series no. 2.17, February 2017, https://perma.cc/YK5J-2MXU..

of California in particular. Management and oversight of UC have become more multidimensional and specific to the natures and needs of the individual campuses. Some observers have suggested that internal university governance structures are too cumbersome and slow for the changes that have to be made and that a more corporate, top-down approach is needed for the issues that must be faced. The targets that they recommend for change typically include shared governance and what is sometimes described as an "hourglass" governance structure[167] with powerful boards at the top, faculty-dominated academic departments and senates at the bottom, and relatively weak central administrations in between.

Shared Governance

If it is well structured and well used, shared governance is a considerable asset rather than a liability. As is discussed through examples in chapter 7, the Academic Senate can be a valuable asset when change is needed because the senate provides process and an effective consultation mechanism, and its role can be structured so that it need not slow things down excessively.

Sufficiency of the Central Administrative Role

The Fethke-Policano hourglass model, mentioned above, may exist at some universities, but it does not have to be. Much depends upon the nature and skill sets of the top leadership of the university or campuses. When the leadership relates well with both the board and the faculty and effectively calls either or both of them into play at the right times on matters of importance, governance runs smoothly and can accomplish many things. But, as the central players in governance, university leaders must recognize when and in what ways they should best bring the other players in. The analogy is sometimes made to a skilled conductor of a symphony orchestra.

Board-Level Governance

The public universities of the United States were established by the individual states. Usually funding and governance came largely or

---

[167] Fethke and Policano, 2012, *op. cit.*, pp. 172–181.

completely through the state.[168] As the years went on, and particularly since World War II, funding sources have become much more varied and diverse. The percentage of public-university revenues that is received from the states has decreased considerably. This situation has come about both because states have been allocating lessening proportions of their state budgets to higher education and because universities have been successful in raising other revenue—notably private gift funds, federal and industrial support of research projects, and income from auxiliary enterprises—as well as increasing tuition and fees. Of the $26.7 billion of income received by the University of California in 2014–15, only 14.1 percent came from the state with another 11.7 percent coming from student tuition and fees.[169] The remainder—7.5 percent from private support, 15.2 percent from the government (mostly federal and for research in various forms), 28.8 percent income to medical centers, 20.8 percent from other sales and services, and 1.8 percent from other sources—was received at the campus level rather than university-wide. Revenue now comes substantially more directly to the campuses than university-wide.

The Board of Regents operates at the university-wide level and has members primarily appointed by the governor and confirmed by the California State Senate. The university is so large and multidimensional and has so many critical issues within it that the regents cannot become familiar with all of them. Yet many issues of the individual campuses do require board-level attention and can benefit from board-level attention. As has been noted, the campuses differ substantially in academic emphases, local situations, and needs. Board-level governance structure should recognize this fact. In accord with the principle of subsidiarity (chapter 6), both board and administrative decisions should be delegated to appropriate levels, where those making the decisions can be equipped with sufficient understanding.[170]

---

[168] Clemson University and the Universities of Delaware and Vermont were exceptions, as were Cornell and MIT, which are private land-grant universities.

[169] *Budget for Current Operations, 2015–16*, p. 51, University of California, updated December 2014, https://perma.cc/P88J-KVZ2.

[170] C. Judson King, "Board Governance of Public University Systems: Balancing Institutional Independence and System Coordination," in J. E. Lane and D. B. Johnstone, eds., *Higher Education Systems 3.0: Harnessing Systemness, Delivering Performance* (Albany, NY: SUNY Press, 2013). Also "Board Governance of Public University Systems: Stresses and Needs," Center for Studies in

Public Research Universities in General. Nearly all public universities continue to have boards of the sort exemplified by the Regents of the University of California—appointed through processes of the state government or the electorate and responsible for representing the people of the state in the oversight of the university. In contrast with boards of private universities, the members of these public boards are not chosen particularly for their individual expertise or allegiance to the university. There are drawbacks of this governance structure for seeking, gaining, and responsibly overseeing the uses of the very large and varied amount of nongovernmental funds that come to the university. The fact that a public board will oversee funds is sometimes a discouragement to private donors who would prefer custodians of the donated funds to have less political susceptibility, greater business acumen, and/or other values.

These issues can be addressed by two sorts of changes in the board structure of public research universities. The first is to gain varied and specific expertise on boards. Several ways of doing this were reviewed in chapter 4. The second useful change is a tiered board structure, of the sort used in North Carolina and Florida, and in a different way for the State University of New York, as was also described in chapter 4. Overall governance and responsibility would remain with the state-appointed or elected main board, but items more specific to individual campuses would be delegated to sub-boards for the individual campuses that would be created, appointed, and overseen by the main board. As well, some matters of governance that would now be handled internally by the campus (e.g., development policy, fiscal planning) could be matters for the campus boards. Doing so would yield more direct and specific knowledge of the individual campuses than the parent board would otherwise have. This approach has been discussed in more detail in chapter 4 and by the author elsewhere.[171] It would be best for campus boards to have many of the characteristics of private-university boards in terms of appointment (by the main board)

Higher Education, University of California, Berkeley, Research and Occasional Papers Series no. 16-12, November 2012, https://perma.cc/8X7K-7BFB..
[171] King, 2013, *loc. cit.*

—expertise, allegiance, and ability to help secure new sources of income and partnerships. The public responsibility would still be fulfilled by the oversight of the main board.

Possibilities for the University of California

In a book[172] exploring new financial and governance models for public universities in the United States, James Garland, who was president of Miami University (Ohio) from 1996 to 2006, proposes formation of campus boards under the Board of Regents of the University of California. The author and four then-leaders of the Berkeley campus proposed a model[173] of tiered-board governance for the University of California in which the regents would create sub-boards on each of the individual campuses under the aegis of the Board of Regents. This option is available to the regents under the existing structure of the university, and no new legislation would be needed. The aim would be to gain the depth and individuality of attention to individual campuses and their needs described above, to delegate some of the more specific responsibilities of the regents to these boards so as to free time for the regents to deal with major university-wide matters, and to gain for the campus boards some of the individual allegiance and support characteristic of private-university boards. Possibilities for the delegation of duties are suggested in the referenced paper but would of course be subject to further deliberation. In that paper it is suggested that regents be rotated as members among the individual campus boards. However, upon further reflection, I now believe that it would better preserve the role of the president to have no regents as campus board members; otherwise, a regent member of a campus board could bring a matter to the main Board of Regents without it having passed through the president. This tiered-board arrangement should fully preserve the structure of the University of California as a single university, with one budget, one set

---

[172] James C. Garland, *Saving Alma Mater: A Rescue Plan for Public Universities* (Chicago: University of Chicago Press, 2009), p. 200.
[173] Robert Birgeneau, George Breslauer, Judson King, et al., "Modernizing Governance at the University of California: A Proposal that the Regents Create and Delegate Some Responsibilities to Campus Boards," Research and Occasional Papers Series, no. 4-12, April 2012, https://perma.cc/Y4PK-DLZK.

of dealings with the state government, one set of policies and policy envelopes, and so on, while enabling the provision of more individualized attention and help to campuses.

Planning. Planning, particularly academic planning, within the University of California has now been almost entirely delegated to the individual campuses. That is helpful to the campuses but is probably not the most effective approach for academic efficiency or on an overall economic basis. Economic efficiency is particularly important in times of fiscal stringency and/or rapid change. As urged already in chapter 12, it would behoove the university to reinstitute a more effective university-wide planning mechanism with the usual involvement of the Academic Council so as to develop issues for consideration with the campuses.

SUMMARY AND CONCLUSIONS

Financing Public Research Universities

Even with all the alternatives explored in this chapter, for public universities there is no real substitute for government funding. Revenue from any other source brings with it obligations and constraints. The discussion should focus on how to return to needed levels of state support, how to reduce services and functions with the least injury, and what other sources of revenue can be built compatibly with the public-university mission and academic quality.

There seems to be little likelihood of a return any time soon to the levels of state financial support for public higher education that existed in the past for the United States; however, this should not be taken to mean that public universities should not present their cases to the state and press for funding using the most cogent arguments that they can make. The challenge is to find means and revenue sources that maintain academic quality and access to the greatest extents possible. The result otherwise will be a two-tier system of higher education in the United States, where the academic quality and research accomplishments of the top tiers of private universities will substantially outstrip those of the major public universities. Yet the public research universities have been one of the most identifiable reasons for the success that the United States has had in economic and social development, technological innovation, and upward mobility of its people.

Research universities should continue to seek instructional enhancement and efficiency. The most obvious path is through uses of instructional technology, but progress there is still a matter of creating and trying different approaches to find what will work best for various purposes. Another factor is that, for undergraduates, present uses of information technology work best for enriching and enhancing traditional methods of instruction rather than for providing lower-cost instruction of the same quality.

The move of public research universities toward the financial structure of the major private universities must continue through private fund-raising (development) with resultant building of endowment. Endowment provides steady revenue that is a secure economic flywheel, available through good economic times and bad. Most of it will be restricted to particular uses, however.

Diminishing state support necessitates higher tuition, another move toward the financial structure of private universities. In order to maintain the access component of the public mission, it is necessary that large portions of increased tuition revenue be devoted to need-based financial aid, leading to a *higher-tuition/higher-aid* model. It can be made clearer to the public and state government that state support provides access for those with less or no ability to pay by tying state support to need-based aid for state residents in the minds of the public, the legislature, and the governor. Two models for accomplishing this are the state of Ohio plan for Miami University and the recommendation made in 2011 by twenty-two ex-chancellors of University of California campuses.

The political feasibility of the higher-tuition/higher-aid model can be enhanced by overcoming the very negative public image associated with current levels of student debt. Two avenues for accomplishing that are better control of for-profit higher education and income-contingent loans that couple tuition repayment with the future earning power of graduates in ways that are manageable for graduates.

Financial necessity creates entrepreneurship, especially among research-university faculty members who have been selected for their creativity. Innovative, revenue-generating activities will continue to grow both at the grassroots and institutional levels, and policies will be needed to control them for academic nature, cost recovery, and political defensibility. Among these activities will be high-fee degree and certificate programs and highly specialized education.

The budget for faculty salaries is a sufficiently large component of research-university expenditures that there will be substantial pressure on it. Resultant changes will include greater proportions of nonresearch faculty (e.g., lecturers and adjuncts) and more charging of faculty salaries to nonstate sources, such as endowment (through endowed chairs) and other sources that are secure during a faculty member's career.

Two sources that could potentially be increased are funding from the federal government, probably through specific programs such as competitive grants for facilities, and from employers of graduates, perhaps through direct linkage of corporate taxation to public-university funding.

Some aspects of research universities can be pooled among universities to gain economies of scale. This is already done with research telescopes, sharing among libraries, and consortia such as the Claremont colleges. Candidates for sharing include digital libraries, education-abroad programs, and specialized majors. Beyond that, mergers of universities themselves will probably also increase as ways of gaining more consolidation along with some economic efficiency.

University Governance

Shared governance remains a useful component of university governance and will remain effective as long as attention is given to its ability to move with the issues and sustaining positive approaches on both sides. Effective administrators can still maintain the central administrative role, staying in close contact with trustees, the faculty, and students as needed.

State revenues for public universities are now outweighed by other revenue sources. Most newer sources of revenue come into multi-campus universities at the campus level rather than centrally, and most come from private rather than public sources. These changes call for board-level governance that can be sufficiently attentive to, and supportive of, individual campus situations, needs, and opportunities. It also calls for specific expertise on boards. For the University of California, it would make sense for the Board of Regents to create sub-boards for each campus, control and approve membership on the sub-boards, and delegate appropriate responsibilities to them in line with the principle of subsidiarity in governance.

APPENDIX
National and International Reputations, Ratings, and Rankings of Universities

MEASURES AND SURROGATES OF STANDING AND ACCOMPLISHMENT

The Qualitative

The stature of a research university is essentially determined by the collective reputations of the individual faculty members, integrated with the reputations of individual departments and institutes composing the university. The accomplishments of graduates of the university are also important. Three interacting factors—the desires of students at all levels to gain admission to the university, the resultant selectivity in admissions, and the attractiveness of graduates to potential employers—are other measures.

The two foremost missions of research universities are education and research, two topics that are closely intertwined because one of the prime objectives of research universities is to produce creative graduates—whether to be employed in higher education, industry, government, or independent research institutions, or to become individual proprietors or consultants. It is, however, specific research accomplishments that most readily capture attention and respect within the academy and outside the university. Because it is inwardly directed, teaching is much harder to assess in a way that can be compared among institutions. The importance of research accomplishments can be evaluated through awards, prizes, academy memberships, and other forms of peer recognition. These measures, and hence the reputations and standings of research universities, are determined by perceptions as to whether outputs of researchers at the institution generate important discoveries, new knowledge, or new codifications of knowledge that make it much more powerful. In general, a good measure would be how often the research evokes these responses: "That's really important," "That truly opens up new fields and vistas," and "Why didn't I think of that myself?"

The fruits of university research enhance the economy and create other societal improvements. Other measures of success are therefore the extent to which research-based industries have chosen to locate near the university so as to foster and build upon the research and expertise resident there, and what founders of successful start-up corporations have come from the university. Classic examples are MIT, Harvard, and Route 128 in Massachusetts; Stanford University and Silicon Valley; and the biotechnology industry that has formed around the San Francisco and San Diego campuses of the University of California. As is discussed in chapter 18, there have also been studies to trace the threads of research, development, and commercialization that have led to major innovations.

The Quantitative

With the arrival of the twenty-first century, efforts to use objective and quantitative methods to rate and rank universities have mushroomed, both worldwide and within the United States. There have been varied motivations for these endeavors, including providing standards against which countries with developing university systems can measure themselves and gauge upward progress, furnishing information for students and families choosing colleges, and, in the case of the media, creating engaging stories.

This plethora of rankings has been at best a mixed blessing. The ratings do provide guidance for those who are trying to build the stature of universities and for those who seek certain characteristics within universities. But they also tend to define academic quality through a small number of specific measures, and universities can distort themselves toward those measures to the detriment of other valuable things that they should be doing. The ratings become obsessive, in that institutions can devote great effort to improving their standings in the rankings, while paying less attention to more qualitative educational and research values. Having a single set of criteria also serves to promote a single model for universities rather than encouraging differences in mission, goals, and the very nature of universities. People and nations differ from one another, and they have different needs and goals. Society has a variety of different needs from institutions of higher education. Hence, diversity among universities is important and should be nurtured.

Nonetheless, it is useful to look at the various rating schemes to see what factors have been identified as reflective of the qualities of universities and university education for various purposes. After a discussion of general issues involved in ratings, I tally the factors that are incorporated in various combinations into current quantitative university rating and ranking schemes. The list is necessarily incomplete because of the large number of ranking efforts, varying degrees of prominence, and the fact that new rating and ranking systems currently appear virtually every month.

Other summaries and comparisons of rating systems have been made by Salmi[1] and by Paradeise and Thoenig,[2] both of them with an eye to international rankings and a focus on Europe.

GENERAL ISSUES

Many broad issues pertain to the ratings systems, when viewed as a whole. Some of them are the following.

Balance of Teaching and Research

The ranking systems differ greatly as to how much attention they give to teaching and education, as opposed to research output. Research reinforces teaching and vice versa, but each deserves its own measures.[3]

---

[1] Jamil Salmi, *The Challenge of Establishing World-Class Universities* (Washington, DC: World Bank, 2009), https://perma.cc/9K8N-LL59.
[2] Catherine Paradeise and Jean-Claude Thoenig, *In Search of Academic Quality* (London: Palgrave Macmillan, 2016), pp. 38–39.
[3] Lest we conclude that research standing and educational effectiveness are two entirely different things not much related, it is important to recognize the essential feature of research universities, which is that research and research abilities bear heavily on education, especially the education of researchers and other creative people. There are many examples of that connection in this book. Three of them are (1) the roles of G. N. Lewis in chemistry and Ernest Lawrence in physics at Berkeley in spawning students and coworkers who themselves achieved Nobel Prizes and other major recognitions; (2) the roles of the star researchers hired early on by the UC San Diego campus in generating an excellent undergraduate program, including an effective residential-college system; and (3) the abilities of research faculty to devise important changes in education

Reputation versus Factual Data

Early approaches to comparing universities through rankings dealt heavily with reputations of universities, as reflected by surveys of peers at other institutions. More recently there has been a movement toward quantitative data that can be measured independently rather than reliance upon opinions. That movement has been facilitated by continued development of large databases of information on colleges and universities, for example, the Integrated Postsecondary Education Data System (IPEDS) of the US Department of Education[4], and the international data bases of Thomson-Reuters and now Clarivate Analytics such as Web of Science[5] and InCites.[6] Reputations are more comprehensive and multidimensional, are based upon different factors for different observers, and do tend to lag, since individual perceptions accrue over a lifetime. However, hard data measure rather few specific benchmarks, which can then be addressed by institutions to the neglect of other criteria that may be important. As the nascent field of data science develops and massive data bases become more common, the quantitatative methods will probably grow in both number and complexity.

Extensive versus Intensive Measures

Some measures are dependent upon the size of an institution (extensive) and others are independent of size (intensive). Through intensive measures a small institution such as Caltech can be ranked on a more comparative basis with, for example, Stanford or Berkeley.

Balance among Academic Fields

Some rating systems are devoted almost exclusively to the sciences, or to sciences and engineering. Others cover all fields broadly.

---

to move with changing times, for example, the reorganization of biology in the 1980s and the creation of the School of Information in the early 1990s at Berkeley (see chapter 12 for both).
[4] IPEDS Integrated Postsecondary Education Data System, US Department of Education, https://perma.cc/LG49-LB8B.
[5] *Web of Science*, Clarivate Analytics, https://perma.cc/W3W3-BVVF.
[6] InCites, Clarivate Analytics, https://perma.cc/G4DR-FB3M.

Inputs versus Outputs

Measures such as research funding and alumni giving are inputs that show what the institution and the faculty have to work with. (Of course, they are also measures of what funding agencies and alumni think of the institution.) Measures such as awards won by the faculty are outputs in that they are actual academic accomplishments.

How to Measure Instructional Effectiveness

There are several well-accepted measures of research stature and accomplishments (e.g., awards, academy memberships, citations, and reputations among peers), but measurement of instructional effectiveness is more vague and controversial. Measures such as ratings by students, alumni, and faculty peers are all useful within institutions, but it is much more difficult to compare one institution with another on instructional effectiveness. In addition, different people learn in different ways, and what is effective instruction for one person may not be as useful for another. Surveys tend to look at input measures, such as the faculty/student ratio or institutional budget per student, without regard to how effectively these resources are used.

Value Added

There is always an issue as to what value has been added to graduates by an institution as opposed to the institution simply enrolling strong students. This may not matter to employers seeking to hire graduates, but it should be important to prospective students and families who are deciding among universities and colleges.

Accomplishments of the Few versus the Many

Measures such as the number of Nobel Prizes received by faculty members or alumni reflect singular accomplishments, but they do not say much about faculty or alumni in general. Measures such as citations of published papers reflect the faculty in more widespread fashion, although again they can be distorted by the accomplishments of very few faculty members, since landmark papers tend to be highly cited. Citations can also reflect characteristics other than the perceived quality of the research.

Private versus Public Universities

There are large differences between public and private universities. Private universities tend to stand higher on measures such as alumni giving, since they do not have direct support from the public treasury and have been doing private fund-raising much longer than have public universities. Public universities have the mission of creating access for all, whereas private universities can self-determine the population groups from which they most want to cultivate students, perhaps so as to increase graduation rates. There is also the issue of value received for money paid, i.e., cost-efficiency.

Margin of Error

Rankings are usually reported by the media in terms of the rank orders, not the actual numerical rating scores. The margin of error in measurement or in ranking methodology in any large survey nearly always exceeds the differences between adjacent institutions. This is more and more of an issue as one goes further down on a ranked list.

RANKINGS OF RESEARCH UNIVERSITIES

Ranking Entities

Different types of organizations carry out ranking efforts, with a variety of different motivations and varying announced objectives, such as measuring quality of the undergraduate expeience, the quality of research and/or the impact of that research, and value to the student for the money spent as net tuition. Because new rankings continually appear, any list of them is necessarily incomplete. Some of the entities producing rankings as of 2017 were the following:

Organizations of Universities. The National Research Council and formerly the American Council on Education have for many years carried out reputational surveys in the United States. Another such effort is U-Multirank, funded by the European Commission and located at the Center for Higher Education Policy Studies at the University of Twente in the Netherlands.

Individual Universities or Components of Universities. Among these are the CWTS rankings of the Centre for Science and Technology Studies (Centrum voor Wetenschap en Technologische Studies) at the University of Leiden in the Netherlands, the Shanghai Jiao Tong Ranking of World Universities in China, the National Taiwan University Ranking of Scientific Papers, the Center for Measuring Performance at Arizona State University, and the Ranking Web of Universities of the Cybermetrics Laboratory of the National Research Council of Spain, which ranks universities by Internet presence and traffic.

The Media. Since 1983 *U. S. News and World* Report has carried out a Best Colleges ranking for US universities and college with attention to educational benefit. As of 2015, *U. S. News and World* Report has also reported rankings of worldwide universities with research the major factor. *Times Higher Education* ranks universities worldwide on research and education through both a World University ranking (WUR) and a World Reputational Rankings (WRR). *Times Higher Education* also partners with the *Wall Street Journal* to produce rankings of 500 US universities in perceived quality of education. Reuters has rated and ranked worldwide universities in terms of innovations and contributions to the world economy. *USA Today*, *Forbes*, *Washington Monthly*, *Niche.com* and *Money* carry out rankings of US Universities. Columnist David Leonhardt of the *New York Times* analyzes and rates universities on the basis of public access.

Individual Researchers. An example is the book by Graham and Diamond.[7]

Independent Organizations and Corporations. The Center for World University Rankings, headquartered in the United Arab Emirates, carries our rankings of what it regards as the top 1000 universities. Quacquarelli Symonds (QS) Ltd. partnered with *Times Higher Education* from 2004 to 2009 to generate rankings of world research universities, following which the two organizations went their separate ways, with QS continuing the original methodology. Scimago Lab maintains the Scimago Institutions Ranking as to assess what as of 2017 are 741 worldwide universities and research-focused institutions.

---

[7] Hugh Davis Graham and Nancy Diamond, *The Rise of American Research Universities: Elites and Challengers in the Postwar Era* (Baltimore, MD: Johns Hopkins Press, 1997).

Appendix

Measures Utilized

The different ranking systems draw in various combinations from the following sorts of measures. Rather than link the individual measures with specific surveys, I categorize them by the qualities that they purport to measure. Some are inverse measures, in that lower is better. No judgements of the worth of individual measures are implied. Some do seem misleading.

Reputation
- Surveys of faculty, employers, and/or high school counselors
- Global and regional research reputations

Research Quality
- Faculty, other academic staff, and/or alumni receiving Nobel Prizes and Fields Medals (Mathematics)
- Memberships in National Academies
- Researchers in the Thomson-Reuters list of Highly Cited Researchers
- Numbers of papers published in *Nature* and *Science*
- Papers indexed in Science Citation Index, and/or the Expanded and Social Science Citation Index
- Papers in journals included in the Thomson Reuters *Web of Science*.
- Total numbers of journal publications, books, and papers in conference proceedings
- H-indices[8] for individual researchers combined somehow, such as being weighted appropriately for length of career to date
- Extramural research funding, total or scaled by staff numbers and/or normalized for purchasing-power parity
- Ratio of doctoral to bachelor's degrees

---

[8] The h-index is that number of an author's papers that individually have at least that number of citations in the literature. For example, an h factor of 44 means that the author has forty-four papers, each of which has been cited at least forty-four times in the literature. Like all attempts to quantify measures of academic quality, this too can be misleading and is probably overused. For example, one's h-index is helped by working in a field where there are many other researchers to cite papers, by writing review articles, by measuring physical or chemical properties of matter that would be cited just for the values of those properties, by coauthoring papers, and by dividing one's research up into smaller packets for publication. A text or reference book will also get many citations, while not usually being original research as such. On the other hand, a text or reference book typically takes much longer to prepare and write than does a research paper. But h-indices are at least qualitatively useful measures for obtaining first approximations of the research accomplishments of individuals.

- Number of PhD degrees awarded (total or per academic staff member)
- The number and proportion of a university's publications that, compared with other publications in the same field and in the same year, belong to the top 1 (or 10, or 50) percent most frequently cited
- Number of grants and fellowships received in arts and humanities
- Faculty awards
- Postdoctoral fellows
- Thematic concentration of publication output
- Number of different authors represented in publications from the institution

Educational Inputs[9]
- Student/faculty ratio
- Ratio of institutional income to number of academic staff members
- SAT scores of incoming students
- Proportion of faculty with the highest degrees in their fields
- Average faculty salary, possibly counting benefits and adjusted for regional cost of living
- Percentage of faculty who are full-time
- Student admissions selectivity
- Percent of accepted students who enroll
- Reading and mathematics SAT or ACT scores
- Portion of incoming students who graduated in the top 10 percent of their high school classes
- Percentage of faculty members who are full-time
- Degree of interaction between teachers and students as measured by student surveys
- Number of accredited programs
- Student ratings of faculty
- Proportion of classes with fewer than twenty students
- Proportion of classes with fewer than fifty students

Educational Attainments
- Six-year and/or four-year graduation rates

---

[9] The methodologies in this and the following section favor private institutions over public institution in a number of ways.

- Graduation rates in comparison with other institutions that receive students with similar precollege records
- Graduation rate versus graduation rate predicted by a variety of input factors
- Percentage of first-year students returning for a second year
- Percentage of alumni who have gone on to receive a PhD
- Percentage of graduates becoming Rhodes Scholars or National Science Foundation or Fulbright Fellows

Student Engagement
- Size of ROTC programs relative to the size of the university
- Number of alumni serving in the Peace Corps relative to the size of the university
- Percentage of federal government work-study money that was spent on community-service projects
- Number of students participating in community service and total service hours performed
- Percentage of staff supporting community service
- Percentage of courses that incorporate service
- Whether the institution provides scholarships for community service

Economic Betterment of Graduates
- Starting salary "boost" in comparison with graduates in the same field from other colleges and universities
- Midcareer salary "boost" by the same sort of comparison
- Value added to graduate salary
- Value added to student loan repayment rate
- Earnings of graduates during the first five years after graduation and midcareer earnings
- The same two factors adjusted for the mix of majors at the university
- The same two factors adjusted for the economic and academic profiles of students
- Career-services staffing per student
- Having a program connecting job-seeking students with alumni
- Brookings Institution's calculation of the market value of the twenty-five skills that graduates most often list on their LinkedIn profiles
- Alumni appearing on America's Leaders list
- Student debt upon graduation
- The odds that a student will not be able to pay back a student loan

Access
- Percentage of students who hold Pell Grants and graduate within six years
- Percentage of students receiving Pell Grants normalized by the predicted percentage based upon SAT/ACT scores and percentage of applicants admitted.
- Net price (tuition minus financial aid) of institution for recipients of Title IV aid
- Student-loan default rate
- Student diversity
- Staff diversity

Involvement of the Institution with Industry; Effect on the Economy[10]
- Research income from industry per academic staff member
- Patent applications filed
- Portion of patent applications resulting in actual patents
- Percentage of patent filings made with the US, European, or Japanese patent offices
- Total citations of patents by examiners in the cases of other patents
- Patent citation impact as determined from the Patents Citation Index and the proportion of patents that have been cited by other patents
- Average number of times journal articles from an institution have been mentioned in patents
- Citations of journal articles in articles written by authors in industry
- Percentage of articles from a university that have industrial coauthors

International
- Percentages of international faculty, students, and/or papers with an international author
- Portion of research output produced with international collaborators

---

[10] This methodology is problematic in several ways. It takes no account of start-up ventures, which are a principal way in which innovation spreads from universities in the United States. It assumes that granted patents are the primary measure of innovation, yet most granted patents are worthless. Further, there are industries such as computing hardware and software, consumer electronics, and so on, where patents play only a small role in innovation. Most university research is fundamental and yet often provides the necessary first basis of understanding for eventual important innovations. Those initial inroads are most often not reflected in citations in patent applications or by patent examiners. Consulting by faculty with industry is not considered, and yet it too is a primary route of innovation from universities to industry.

Institutional Financing
- Value of endowment assets
- Annual private giving
- University financing per student.

Internet Presence and Traffic
- Volume of web contents for an institution
- Number of external linkages or "hits" that an institution's site receives

GENERAL COMMENT

Reviewing all the factors considered in these various ranking schemes reinforces the conclusion that the methods are arbitrary and lack precision. Although concerns can be raised about the factors in all categories, those relating to quality of education and innovation and economic impact are most problematic. The quality-of-education factors are nearly all input measurementss rather than reflections of actual accomplishments and they largely do not take into account the mission of publc universities. The innovation and economic-impact factors focus on patents and industrial collaborations, whereas most patents go unused. Measures of the involvement of faculty members and graduates in start-ups and participation of faculty in consulting are missing.

INDEX

A

AAAS. *See* American Academy of Arts and Sciences
AAU (Association of American Universities), 2–3, 251, 325, 368, 415–16, 721, 727
  Membership, 2–3, 368, 415–16
AAUP (American Association of University Professors), 251, 422
ABC (activity-based costing), 708
Academic Council, x, 43, 90, 111, 177, 183, 213–15, 232, 237–38, 401, 409, 438, 448, 493, 499–500, 749
academic freedom, 37, 216, 422, 642–43, 647
Academic Personnel Manual (APM), 19, 169, 185, 217, 417, 421, 427–28, 438, 440–41, 564, 652–53, 655, 716
Academic Personnel Office, 199, 424–26
academic planning, 92, 183, 186, 203, 206, 216–17, 236, 321, 401–2, 447, 449–50, 469, 481, 749
Academic Planning and Program Review Board. *See* APPRB
Academic Planning Board, 469
Academic Planning Council, 203, 206, 236–37, 451
Academic Senate, 29–31, 60–62, 92–95, 169–70, 176–77, 207–14, 216–23, 227–32, 239, 264–65, 318–20, 364–65, 384, 422–23, 446–48, 453–55, 462–68, 471–72, 499, 545–46
  committees, 29, 215, 290, 409, 455, 478, 520, 687
  structure, 205, 307, 687
  Task Force on University-Industry Partnerships, 647
  university-wide, 236, 320, 548
accountability, 96, 114–18, 121–22, 692, 729
  measures, 96, 117–18
  UC annual report, 3, 6, 74, 119–21, 149–50, 152, 554, 721, 723, 727
activity-based costing (ABC), 708
admissions, 5, 57–58, 117, 120, 131, 140–41, 150–51, 153–55, 198, 215, 217–18, 242, 451, 533–35, 537–51, 553, 555–62, 571, 573–74, 577
  Bakke decision, 50, 312, 561
  cascading, 557, 562
  conditions for, 30, 58, 212–13, 227, 233, 533, 537, 546
  criteria, 50, 154, 534, 537, 547, 553
  by exception, 538, 542
  guarantee of, 154, 555–56
  policies, 185, 198, 537–38, 543, 553–54
AEC (Atomic Energy Commission), 7, 175, 259, 298, 303, 490–96
Affiliated Colleges, San Francisco, 339–40
affirmative action, 49–50, 57–58, 215, 229, 312, 475, 534, 541, 543–46, 555, 573
Agricultural Experiment Station (AES), 181, 337, 465

agriculture, 6, 15–18, 35, 78, 99, 137, 215, 254, 307–9, 311, 313, 332, 356, 461, 465, 565–67, 601, 608, 650, 667–68
  research, 41, 193, 308, 311, 329, 413, 567, 583, 600, 608
Aldrich, Daniel G., Jr., 370, 372–74, 379
alumni associations, 100, 110–11, 176, 197
American Academy of Arts and Sciences (AAAS), 4, 516, 584, 606, 692, 712, 731
American Association of University Professors (AAUP), 251, 422
American Chemical Society, 254, 257, 262, 613
American University of Armenia, 734
APM. See Academic Personnel Manual
Applied Physics Laborator, Johns Hopkins University, 505
APPRB (Academic Planning and Program Review Board), 183–84, 203, 206, 449, 456
Argonne National Laboratory, 488, 493, 505, 509
Arizona, 75, 598, 734–35
  Board of Regents, 190
Ashburner, William, 287–88
Asian American Task Force (AATF), 544
Association of American Universities. See AAU
astronomy, 20, 52, 210, 247, 249–51, 394
Atkinson, Richard C., 12, 57–58, 138, 160, 178–79, 185, 187–88, 232, 357–58, 360, 364–68, 387, 511, 548–49, 551, 553, 584, 618, 629, 662
atomic bomb, 6, 32–33, 484, 490, 494
Atomic Energy Commission. See AEC
AVLIS (atomic-vapor laser isotope separation), 487

B

Bain Corporation, 204, 708–9
Barrows, Davd P., 30, 210, 252
Bay Area Council Economic Institute, 138–39, 156, 580–81
Bayh-Dole Act, 256, 475, 606, 609, 612–14
BCDC (Buildings and Campus Development Committee), 90–91
Bell Labratories (AT&T), 281, 515, 613, 622, 627
Bennett hypothesis, 706
Berkeley, Bishop George, 11, 13
Berkeley and UCLA, 33, 35, 131, 155, 175, 304, 311, 363, 369, 558, 590–91, 598, 616
Berkeley campus, xi–xii, 1–6, 186–88, 202–4, 276–78, 287–90, 422–26, 430–33, 446–47, 449–54, 459–63, 469–71, 504–6, 518–20, 581–82, 623–25, 628, 637–42, 644–49, 657–59
  Nobel Prizes, 281, 506
  Richmond Field Station, 192
  School of Education, 184, 456

Berkeley Division, Academic Senate, x, 214, 216–18, 423, 642
Berkeley-Haas Entrepreneurship Program, 657
Berkeley-Novartis Agreement, 640
Berkeley Revolution, 29, 78, 84, 90, 174, 209, 211, 233, 264, 284, 289, 422
Berkeley's name, 13
Berkeley UNIX Software Distribution, 626
Big Ideas@Berkeley, 528, 658
Big Ten Academic Alliance (BTAA), 712
biological sciences, 202, 261, 293, 311, 319, 330, 349, 353, 356–58, 375–77, 391, 432, 461–64, 467, 473, 481, 492, 497, 520, 637
biophysics, 298, 343, 346–48, 350
biotechnology, 349–50, 514, 581, 607, 618, 634, 638–40, 648, 650, 658, 689
  industry, 3, 353, 413, 581, 604, 613, 629, 634–35, 638–39, 665, 736, 754
Birge, Raymond T., 253, 269–74, 279–80, 284–85, 291–92, 412, 663, 680
Bishop, J. Michael, 342, 347, 353
board governance, 112, 241, 746–47
Board of Admissions and Relations with Schools (see BOARS)
Board of Patents, 611–12
Board of Regents, University of California, 71, 73, 105–6, 121, 190, 207, 209, 212, 241–42, 328, 331, 357, 359, 545–46, 574, 613–14, 687–88, 744, 746, 748
Board of Research, 24, 246, 251–53, 297
Board on Admissions and Relations with Schools. *See* BOARS
Boards of Study (UCSC), 384, 388, 412, 530
BOARS (Board on Admissions and Relations with Schools), 217, 549, 551, 553, 555
Boelter, Llewellyn M. K., 301, 356
Boren, David L., 76, 202
Bowen, William G., 152, 225, 230, 376, 477, 697, 701, 706
Boyer, Herbert, 342–43, 345, 348, 350, 413, 612, 634, 636
BP (corporation), 65, 221, 640, 644–48, 659
Brewer, William H., 287–88
Brown, Edmond G., Jr.(Jerry), CA Governor, 75, 113, 155, 222, 477
BTAA (Big Ten Academic Alliance), 712
budget, 28–29, 46–47, 55, 57–58, 63–64, 102, 104, 118–19, 168, 180–81, 215, 217–18, 284–85, 333, 335, 417, 422–24, 505–6, 601, 695
  decentralization, 178, 194, 205
Budget Committee (Berkeley), 92, 285, 290, 378, 417, 422–24, 426, 432–34, 436, 438, 463–64
Budgeting of UC, 165, 167, 169, 171, 173, 175, 177, 179, 181, 183, 185, 187, 189, 191, 193, 195, 197, 199, 201, 203

Budget Manual, University of California, 180
Buildings and Campus Development Committee (BCDC), 90–91
Busch, Lawrence, 643
Bush, Vannevar, 35, 485, 620

C

CACB (Chancellor's Advisory Council on Biology), 463–66
Cal Grants, 75, 133, 162
California Air Resources Board, 335–36
California Aqueduct, 671–72
California College of Medicine, 379
California Community Colleges (see community colleges)
California Constitution, 19, 58, 99–100, 109
  Article IX, language of, 99–100
California Coordinating Council for Higher Education (CCHE), 387, 539, 593
California Council on Science and Technology. See CCST
California Digital Library, 12, 38, 60–61, 186, 206, 563, 565, 568–70
California economy, 3, 40, 65, 136, 523–24, 664–65, 726
California Geological Survey, 287–88
California Institute for Regenerative Medicine (CIRM), 600
California Institute for Telecommunications and Information Technology (CalIT2), 511, 524–25, 644
California Institute of Technology (Caltech), 28, 52–53, 178, 252, 258, 260, 268, 280, 322, 327, 335, 355, 391, 395, 505, 530, 578, 634, 647, 688
California Master Plan for Higher Education, 40–41, 81–82, 85–87, 112–13, 123–25, 127–29, 131–37, 145–51, 153–59, 161–63, 396–97, 404–5, 456, 539, 556, 558–59, 561–62, 597, 688–89, 742–43
California NanoSystems Institute (CNSI), 525, 644
California Postsecondary Education Commission. See CPEC
California State University. See CSU
calutrons, 32–33, 486–88, 490, 492
Calvert, Seymour, 338
Calvin, Melvin E., 39, 260, 263–64, 491
Campbell, William Wallace, 249, 252, 272, 292
CARA (California Research Alliance), 649
careerism, 698, 700
Carr, Ezra S., 15–17, 97, 254, 609
catastrophic risk management, 520
CCHE, 593–95
CCR (Council for Chemical Research), 607, 613
CCST (California Council on Science and Technology), 565, 578–80, 599, 603

CE-CERT (College of Engineering - Center for Environmental Research and Technology), 336
Centers & Institutes, 519
Cerro Grande Fire, 501
Chancellor's Advisory Council on Biology. See CACB
Charter Hill, 278–79, 486
Cheadle, Vernon, 93, 316, 318–22, 326
chemical engineering, 257, 265–68, 302, 432
childbearing, 439–40
China, 53, 252, 407, 500, 511, 535, 558, 582, 621, 670, 674–75, 733–34, 759
Chiron Corporation, 637–38
CIC (Committee on Institutional Cooperation), 712
CIRM (California Institute for Regenerative Medicine), 600
Citrus Experiment Station, Riverside, 24, 33, 85, 171, 327–30, 332–33
Civil Engineering Test Laboratory, 277
Civil War, US, 14, 17
Claremont Colleges, 381, 712–13, 751
Clarivate Analytics, 756
classified materials, 500
Clemson University, 107, 746
CNSI (California NanoSystems Institute), 525, 644
Cohen, Stanley, 350, 634, 636
College of Agriculture, 99, 309, 311, 461, 668
College of California (predecessor of UC), 13–14, 533, 535, 592, 663

College of Chemistry, Berkeley, 174, 247, 254, 256, 258, 265–69, 349, 491, 606, 609–10, 649, 657
College of Letters and Science, 85, 268–69, 290, 317, 321, 327, 330, 332, 375, 431, 455, 460–62, 465–67, 471, 528
College of Natural Resources, Berkeley, 461, 465–66, 641–42
Columbia University, 39, 76, 81, 263, 266, 281, 303, 324, 358, 364, 513, 593
Committee on Academic Personnel, 169–71, 217, 378, 409, 417, 423, 438
Committee on Budget and Interdepartmental Relations, Berkeley, 217, 284, 417, 422–23, 433, 450
Committee on Institutional Cooperation (CIC), 712
Communist Party, 36–37
community colleges, 23, 40, 47, 70, 86, 101–2, 113, 117, 125, 127–32, 135–42, 150, 157–60, 162–64, 172, 217, 224, 456, 573, 578
community college system, 159, 316
comparison universities, 593–95
comprehensive review, x, 169, 543, 550–51, 553, 556, 562
Conant, James B., 278
confederation, 91, 742
Connerly, Ward (Regent), 545, 561
Conrad, Albert G., 317
constitutional autonomy, 8–9, 17, 19, 54, 77, 97–99, 101–5,

121, 135, 201, 471, 539, 553, 587, 592, 685, 688
constitutional convention, 17, 48, 97–98
consultation, 89, 176–77, 183–84, 209, 213, 217, 221, 226, 229, 231–32, 234–36, 364, 378, 425, 427, 444, 447, 468, 479, 574
contract renewals, national laboratory management, 66, 498, 502, 509
Coons, Arthur, 128–29
Cooperative Research and Development Agreement. *See* CRADAs
coordination, statewide, 75, 107, 121, 131, 133–34, 146–47, 157, 162–63, 388, 556, 595
Corley, James M., 172–73, 356
Cornell University, 21, 61, 108, 208, 256, 337, 593, 609, 746
Cottrell, Frederick G., 255–56, 262, 266, 276, 609
Council for Chemical Research (CCR), 607, 613
Council of Chancellors, 185, 237, 239
Coursera Corporation, 480, 702–5
Cowell College, UCSC, 383–85
Cowell Foundation, 382, 385
CPEC (California Postsecondary Education Commission), 49, 75, 113, 133, 146–47, 154–55, 157, 539, 549, 577, 593–95, 744
CRADAs (Cooperative Research and Development Agreement), 497, 608
Creative Studies, College of, UCSB, 320, 528

Criminology, School of, Berkeley, 202, 452–54, 456, 472–74, 481
CSU (California State University), 66–67, 70, 101, 113, 124, 128–33, 136–48, 150–55, 158–59, 162–64, 217, 222, 456, 458, 538–39, 561, 571–72, 594, 597, 699
CTVC (California Technology Ventures Corporation), 615
culture of excellence, 365, 369, 418, 434, 436, 680
cyclotrons, 274–81, 484, 486, 490, 520, 610

D

DARPA (Defense Advanced Research Projects Agency), 626–27
data science, 471–72, 707, 756
Davis, Angela, 415
Davis, Gray, CA Governor, 46, 65, 105, 119, 551, 592, 599–600, 603, 644
Davis campus, 17, 19, 33, 35, 41–42, 151–52, 167, 198, 308–13, 316, 318, 329–30, 337, 406–7, 413, 415, 448–49, 597, 616, 743
  Medical School, 50, 312
Davisville, 308
Death Valley, 668, 671
decentralization, 89, 172–73, 196, 199–200, 203, 265, 659
  optimal degree of, 199
Delaware, 108, 112, 726, 746
dentistry, 18, 130, 144, 198, 339, 342, 429

Department of Defense, US, 45, 184, 360, 622
Department of Energy (DOE), US, 35, 65, 493, 495, 498–99, 501–5, 508, 510
departments, 92, 239–40, 243–44, 269, 271–72, 284–85, 287, 317, 348–49, 412, 425–26, 435–36, 447–50, 460–62, 464–66, 471, 514, 521–22, 528–30, 641–43
Deukmejian, Governor George, 51
Deutsch, Provost Monroe, 173, 285
DNA, recombinant, 342, 461, 634–36, 736
doctorates, joint, x, 128, 143–44
DOE. *See* Department of Energy
Donner Laboratory, 276–77
Douglass, Aubrey, 590
drip irrigation, 568
Duke Kunshan University, 733
Durant, Henry, 13–14

E

EAOP (Early Academic Outreach Program), 573
EAP (Education Abroad Program), 185, 191, 317–18, 712, 735
Early Academic Outreach Program (EAOP), 573
EBI. *See* Energy Biosciences Institute
EdD (Doctor of Education), 125, 130, 143–44, 458–59
education
  graduate, 42, 86, 130, 259–60, 267, 317, 330, 377, 410, 677
  state board of, 40, 125, 146, 590
  teacher, 314, 317, 458, 538
Education Abroad Program. *See* EAP
educational disadvantage, 575
Educational Partnerships, 181, 573, 576–77
Education City, Qatar, 732
edX, 477, 480, 702, 704
EECS (Electrical Engineering and Computer Science), 625–26
Eisenhower, President Dwight D., 76
ELC (Eligibility in the Local Context), 118, 549–50, 553, 556
Electrical Engineering and Computer Science (EECS), 625–26
electrostatic precipitator, 256, 276, 609
eligibility and admission, 154, 186, 217, 533, 535, 537, 539, 541, 543, 545, 547, 549, 551, 553, 555, 557, 559–61
Eligibility in the Local Context. *See* ELC
eligibility rates, 49, 58, 131, 137–39, 150, 152, 539, 545, 549, 556, 572, 574, 586, 597
endowment, 26, 99–100, 115, 195, 255, 386, 398, 588, 620, 718, 730, 750–51
Energy Biosciences Institute (EBI), Berkeley, 65, 221, 644–45, 648–49, 659
Energy Research and Development Agency. *See* ERDA
engineering, 4, 10, 125–27, 266–69, 300–302, 306, 313, 317–18, 323–27, 338, 355, 357, 359–60, 366–67, 529–30,

578, 583, 631, 657–58, 709–11
engineering education, 125–26, 301–2, 387, 408, 530
enrollment cap, 86, 597
enrollment capacity, 94, 194, 406, 558, 560
entrepreneurism, 81, 161, 402, 535, 581, 617, 619, 624, 645, 657–59, 674, 679, 682, 684, 739, 741, 750
Equal Opportunity Program (EOP), 541
ERDA (Energy Research and Development Agency), 495, 497, 502
eScholarship, 61–62, 96, 186, 569–70
ESPM (Environmental Science, Policy, and Management), 466
ETR (Eligible to Review) category for eligibility, 131, 136, 555–56
Evans, Griffith C., 282, 284–87, 291–92, 412, 680
exaction, 196
Executive Budget Committee, 236
executive compensation, 70–72
Experimental College Program, Berkeley, 528
extension, cooperative, 6, 565, 567–68, 653

F

faculty recruitment, 26, 266, 273, 307, 321, 347, 365, 392, 451, 588
faculty salaries, x, 31, 51, 69, 586, 593–95, 716, 751
Fairchild Semiconductor Corporation, 630
fairy shrimp, 63, 399
Federal Bureau of Investigation (FBI), 500
Federal Government Relations, office, 192, 196
finance, 31, 63, 119, 130, 143, 148, 163, 175, 193, 239, 299, 379, 490, 502, 507, 509, 569, 594, 605, 650
financial aid, 6, 74, 96, 133, 136, 149–50, 153, 180, 198, 216, 562, 573, 693, 697, 720, 722, 728, 763
  need-based, 68, 114, 148, 560, 562, 719–21, 750
Florida, 106, 166, 188, 329, 475, 686–87, 736, 747
Food Technology, 310
for-profit institutions, 145, 150, 628, 693–94, 706, 723–24
foundations, 11, 168, 195, 276, 288, 383, 398, 401, 524, 527–29, 535, 588, 605, 610, 615, 627, 629, 717, 719, 729–30
Free Speech Movement, Berkeley, 43, 177, 214, 305, 320, 457
Funding Streams Initiative, 179–80, 182
Fung Institute for Engineering Leadership, 657

G

Galbraith, John S., 363

Gardner, David Pierpont, 8–9, 12, 36, 51–55, 57, 71, 184–85, 188, 194, 235, 265, 459, 499, 534, 670, 714
Garland, James C., 207, 225–26, 697, 722, 748
Gates, Robert M., 76, 691
Gatorade, 736
Genentech, Inc., 342, 345, 350, 636–38
General Advisory Committee (GAC), Atomic Energy Commission, 491, 493–94
General Atomics (corporation), 630–32
general campus, x, 1, 3, 33, 42, 82, 85, 87–88, 94, 167, 310–12, 316–18, 321, 329, 406–7, 413, 415–16, 586, 595, 597–98
General Dynamics (corporation), 356–57, 630
general education, 140, 167, 513, 529
geology, 14, 210, 263, 287, 289–90, 306
geophysics, 263, 287, 289, 304, 306
Georgia, 14, 166, 598, 713–14
Georgia State University, 708, 714
Germany, 250, 292, 326, 678
Giauque, William F., 39, 263
GI Bill, 34, 302, 475, 518, 590–92
Gifford, Bernard R., 460
Gilman, Daniel Coit, 15–16, 18, 20–21, 44, 97, 247–48, 254, 257, 268, 282, 307, 445, 533, 535, 592
Gilman Hall, 257, 260, 485
globalization, 475, 674, 695–96, 699

gold rush, California, 287, 663–64
Goodpaster, Andrew J., 502
Gould, Samuel B., 317–18
governance, tiered-board, 748
Governor Gray Davis Institutes, 65, 78, 193, 199, 524, 526, 601, 648, 658, 684, 690
graduate students, 3, 183, 243, 246, 259–60, 297, 301, 303, 319, 337, 359, 361, 377, 394, 404, 411, 457, 664, 677, 680–82
graduation rates, 6, 114, 117, 152, 708, 758, 762
Grange, CA State, 15, 97–98
Gray, Hannah Holborn, 698
Groves, Lt. Gn. Leslie R., 488–90

H

Harvard University, 15, 39, 42, 83, 93, 248, 278–79, 283, 285, 306, 362, 381, 394–95, 412, 434, 476–77, 488, 593–94, 620, 714
Hastings College of Law, 19, 339
Hawaii, 52–53, 178, 194, 252, 394
Hearst, Phoebe Apperson, 24–25, 27, 339
Hennessy, John L., 626
Hershman, Lawrence C., 119
Hewlett Foundation, 69, 156, 478, 716, 729
Heyman, Ira Michael, 357, 459–60, 462
higher education, sectors of, 40–41, 134, 147, 161
higher-tuition, higher-aid model, 720

Hildebrand, Joel H., 29, 31, 38, 174, 210, 245, 249–50, 253, 256, 260–62, 264–65, 268, 271, 284–87, 291–92, 356, 412, 423, 680, 682
Hilgard, Eugene W., 17–18, 78, 308, 566
Hinderaker, Ivan, 331–33, 335–38, 356, 373–78, 451
h-index, 760
Hitch, Charles J., 45, 49, 183–84, 203, 206, 376, 387, 449, 648
Holden, Edward S., 20–21, 248–50, 292, 484
Home Economics, 171, 310, 314
honorary degrees, 212
Hullar, Theodore, 337
Hurricane Katrina, 520
Huttenback, Robert A., 322, 324
Hybritech, 629, 632, 639
hydrogen bomb, 494–95, 509

I

Illinois, 8, 188, 190, 202, 235, 325, 348, 374, 493, 593–94, 598, 644–46, 685, 727
income-contingent loans, 724–25
incubators, 526, 608, 657–59, 736
Indiana, 115
Indiana University, 107
indirect costs, 179, 192–93, 601–2, 618, 641, 646
industrial funding, 605, 624, 729
Industrial Innovation, 256, 582–83, 609–10
industrial park, 608, 621, 628, 674
Industrial Technology Research Institute (ITRI), Taiwan, 674, 684

Industry-University Cooperative Research Program. *See* IUCRP
innovation, disruptive, 445–46, 479–80, 696
Institute for Theoretical Physics (ITP), UCSB, 322–23, 327
Institute of Medicine, 4, 367, 380
Institutes for Science and innovation, 119, 199, 524, 526, 531, 592, 600, 603, 644, 684, 690
Integrated Postsecondary Education Data System (IPEDS), 702, 756
Integrative Biology, 466
intellectual property, 611, 617–18, 646, 653, 656
Intercampus Recruitment, 199
Interdepartmental Relations, 217, 284–85, 417, 422–23, 433, 447, 450
Intersegmental Committees (CA higher education), 215, 217
Intersegmental General Education Transfer Curriculum (IGETC), 140
IPAs (institutional patent agreements), 612
IPEDS (Integrated Postsecondary Education Data System), 702, 756
IPIRA (Intellectual Property and Industrial Research Alliances), Berkeley campus, 617
Irvine, 89, 93–94, 167, 169, 179, 182, 198, 369–74, 377, 380, 401, 406, 408, 410–12, 415, 559, 597, 608, 726, 728

Irvine campus, ix, 3, 57, 194, 202, 331, 335, 368, 370–74, 378–80, 410, 647, 713, 736
Irvine Ranch, 42, 370, 372
Irvine Research Park, 608
Ishi, 20
Isla Vista, adjoining UCSB, 321, 414
ITRI (Industrial Technology Research Institute), Taiwan, 674, 684
IUCRP (Industry-University Cooperative Research Program), 65, 618, 624, 659

J

Jacobs, Irwin, 630–32
Jacobs, Paul, 631
Jacoby, Neil H., 297–99, 301–2, 307, 412, 661
Jendresen Report, 499, 502, 507
Jet Propulsion Laboratory (JPL), 505
Johns Hopkins University, 248, 277, 283, 387, 505
JPL (Jet Propulsion Laboratory), 505

K

KAEC (King Abdullah Economic City), 674
Kaiser Center, 189
Kaplan University, 737–38
KAUST (King Abdullah University of Science and Technology), 530, 674, 681, 733
Kavli Foundation, 322
Kavli institute for Theoretical Physics, UCSB, 322–23

Keck Foundation, 53
Keck Telescopes, 52–53
Kennedy, John F., 585
Kerr, Clark, 8–9, 11–12, 38–45, 81–86, 88–95, 123–24, 165–66, 173–79, 296–97, 304–6, 316, 318–19, 328–31, 335, 340–42, 359–63, 372–76, 380–81, 383–84, 394–96
Kerr, Kay, 669
King, Clarence, 287–88
King Abdullah Economic City (KAEC), 674
King Abdullah University, 530, 674, 681, 733
King Abdullah University of Science and Technology. *See* KAUST
Knudsen, Vern O., 297, 306–7
Kohn, Walter, 322, 325–26, 368
Koshland, Daniel E., 462–63
Krevans, Julius, 348, 412

L

labor unions, 104, 222, 711
La Brea Tar Pits (Los Angeles), 290
Langmuir, Irving, 272, 610
Latimer, Wendell M., 263, 265–66
Lawrence, Ernest O., ix, 6, 32–33, 39, 50, 65, 78, 246, 253, 269, 273–81, 291–92, 401, 403, 483–94, 497, 504, 506, 508, 517
Lawrence, John H., 276–77
Lawrence Berkeley National Laboratory (LBNL), 9, 32–33, 268–69, 274, 280, 282, 498, 504–5, 509–10, 519–20, 531, 644–46, 649, 654, 681

Lawrence Hall of Science, 564–65
Lawrence Livermore National
  Laboratory (LLNL), 65–66,
  313, 359, 487, 494, 497–98,
  500–501, 503, 507, 509, 651
Lawrence Livermore National
  Security, LLC, 503
Lawrence Radiation Laboratory
  (LRL), 490, 498
LBL, LBNL. *See* Lawrence Berkeley
  National Laboratory
LeConte, John, 15, 269, 283
LeConte, Joseph, 14, 288–89, 667
LeConte, Joseph N., 667–68
Legislative Analyst's Office (State
  of CA), 46–47, 130, 143, 156
Leonhardt, David, 2, 5–6, 68, 149
Leuschner, Armin O., 78, 210,
  245–47, 249–53, 256, 272,
  278, 284–85, 291–92, 297,
  663
Levin, Richard, 703–5, 711
Lewis, Gilbert Newton, 26, 210,
  245, 253–54, 256–66, 270–
  72, 275, 278, 281, 284–85,
  291–92, 308, 346, 348, 412,
  588, 610, 663, 680, 755
Lewis, Warren K., 610
Liaison Committee (CA Higher
  Education), 40, 125–27
Libby, Willard F., 39, 263–64, 303–
  4, 306–7, 358, 375
liberal arts colleges, 147–48, 224,
  315, 327–30, 396, 678, 733
liberal education, 10, 117, 408,
  476, 527, 532, 606, 698–99,
  715
libraries, 59–61, 102, 192, 202,
  212, 216, 233, 235, 294, 319,
  462, 467–68, 470–71, 473,
  481, 568–70, 712–13, 751

digital, 60, 186, 191–92, 203,
  568, 571, 712, 751
Library and Information Studies,
  School of, Berkeley, 431,
  452, 472–74
licensing, 192, 605, 609, 617, 623,
  650, 656, 659, 736–37
Lick, James, 15, 20, 27, 247
Lick Observatory, 20–21, 30, 33,
  78, 193, 247–51, 292, 394
Lilly, Eli (corporation), 636, 639
Linkabit (corporation), 630–31
Livermore Laboratory (see
  Lawrence Livermore National
  Laboratory (LLNL))
LLL (Lawrence Livermore
  Laboratory), 359, 498
LLNL. *See* Lawrence Livermore
  National Laboratory
loans, 478, 487, 693, 724–25, 728
  income-contingent, 724–25, 750
Loeb, Leonard, 253, 270, 272–74
Lohman, Joseph D., 453–54
Long-range development plans.
  See LRDPs
Loomis, Alfred L., 277, 485
Los Alamos National Laboratory,
  33, 61, 66, 280, 378, 483,
  487–88, 490, 494, 497–501,
  506–9
Los Alamos National Security, LLC,
  503
Los Angeles, 1–2, 5, 28, 167–68,
  172–75, 179, 182, 198, 294–
  99, 301, 304–7, 309–10,
  379–80, 406–7, 448, 564–65,
  624, 626, 661, 743
Los Angeles campus (see UCLA)
Los Angeles Normal School, 295
Louderback, George D., 210, 289–
  90

776

LRDPs (Long-range development plans), 194, 399, 449, 481, 559, 744
LRL (Lawrence Radiation Laboratory), 490, 498

M

Management Fee, 504
Manhattan Engineer District, 488, 490–91
Manhattan Project, ix, 6, 32, 280, 358, 484–85, 487–88, 490–92, 494, 509
Mansfield, Edwin, 582–83
massive open online courses. *See* MOOCs
Master Plan (see California Master Plan for Higher Education)
Master Plan Survey Team, 127, 129
materials-testing accelerator (MTA), 494
mathematics, 250, 254, 277, 282–85, 287, 291, 293, 296, 367, 375, 460, 572–73, 640, 760–61
Mathematics, Engineering, Science Achievement (MESA), 572–73, 575
Mauna Kea, 52–53, 178, 194, 252, 394
MCAP (Middle Class Access Plan), Berkeley, 74–75
McCarthy, Joseph R. (US Senator), 36
McElroy, William D., 364
McGill, William J., 43, 364, 414–15
McHenry, Dean E., 93, 129, 374, 381–84, 390, 395–96

McMillan, Edwin M., 278, 281–82, 506
medical education, 25–26, 340
medical physics, 277–79
medical schools, 11, 177, 192, 298, 312, 340, 344, 363, 379–80, 408, 603, 629, 634, 662, 743
medicine, 4, 198, 201, 306–7, 311, 313, 341, 349–50, 352, 367–68, 379–80, 517, 520, 542, 561, 578, 638–39, 650, 713, 715
Merced campus, ix, 62–64, 93, 118, 151–52, 170, 378, 398, 401–6, 410, 412–13, 473, 530, 540, 557, 560, 597, 669, 711
  project, 63, 399, 401, 408
Merced Vernal Pools and Grassland Reserve, ix, 400–401, 672
MESA (Mathematics, Engineering, Science Achievement), 572–73, 575
Messinger, Sheldon L., 454–55
Metallurgical Laboratory, University of Chicago, 491, 493
Mexico, 13, 377, 520, 535, 582, 648, 670–71
Miami University, Ohio, 208, 226, 722, 748, 750
Michigan, 2, 17, 39, 97–98, 101, 106, 112, 208, 228, 235, 250, 281, 475–76, 479, 530, 587, 592–94, 688, 726
micro-campus approach, U. of Arizona, 735
MICRO Program, 618, 624, 627, 659

Middle Class Access Plan (MCAP), Berkeley, 74–75
Minnesota, 73, 86, 97, 101, 264, 273, 375, 587, 688
Mission Bay (UCSF), ix, 352–53
mission differentiation, 125, 157–58, 163, 586, 699
MOOCs (massive open online courses), 476, 696, 702–4
Moore, Gordon E., 622
Moores, John J., 242, 523
Morehouse College, 713
Morehouse School of Medicine in Atlanta, 713
Morrill Act, 7, 13–14, 16, 96, 100, 107–8, 535, 688, 700
Moscow, 674
Mrak, Emil M., 310–13
MRUs (multicampus research units), 193–94, 518
multicampus universities, 42, 172, 187, 199–200, 235, 237, 239–41, 243, 374, 597–98, 685, 687
multidisciplinary, 355, 469, 514, 516–17, 519–22, 527–29, 531, 681, 689, 715, 740
  approaches, 346, 363, 520, 524, 530
  research, 9, 78, 194, 220, 276, 437, 506, 516–18, 522, 531, 681, 686
  units, 521–22
Murphy, Franklin D., 294, 298, 305

N

narrative evaluation system (NES), UCSC, 384
NASA (National Aeronautics and Space Administration), 52, 252, 338
National Academies, US, 4, 306, 313, 326, 338, 367, 380, 394, 529, 578–79, 583, 624, 678, 760
National Academy of Engineering, US, 4, 306, 313, 326, 338, 367, 380, 529, 624
National Academy of Medicine, US, 4, 306, 313, 352, 380
National Academy of Sciences, US, 4, 14, 35, 249, 270, 285–87, 292, 303, 306, 313, 326, 335, 338, 352, 354, 358, 365, 367, 379–80, 462
National Aeronautics and Space Administration (NASA), 52, 252, 338
national laboratories, 32, 65, 192, 221, 278, 483, 485, 487, 489, 491, 493, 495–97, 499–505, 507, 509–10, 608, 617, 678, 681, 689
National Park Service, 667–68
National Research Council, US, 251, 267, 273, 276, 641, 730, 758–59
National Science Foundation, 35, 298, 322, 338, 364, 505, 578, 612, 618, 626–27, 717
New Jersey, 269, 622
New Mexico, 32, 49, 483–84, 488, 490, 508
New York University (NYU), 647, 709–10, 733
Nierenberg, William A., 353
Nobel Laureates, 3, 39, 260, 272, 278, 280–81, 304, 325, 367–68, 412

Nobel Prizes, 3, 39, 93, 263–64, 281, 293, 303–4, 322, 339, 342, 352, 357–58, 367, 377, 582, 635, 757
North Carolina, 106, 166, 188, 190, 674, 686–87, 719, 747
Novartis (corporation), 350, 637, 640–43, 648, 650, 656, 659
Novartis-UCB agreements, 642, 647
Noyes, Arthur A., 256–58, 610
nuclear weapons, 488, 495, 497, 500, 502
NYU. *See* New York University

O

OAC. *See* Online Archive of California
Oak Ridge, 32–33, 486–88, 492, 509
Oak Ridge National Laboratories, 492, 505
O'Brien, Morrough P., 127, 171, 266–67, 301, 356
OECD (Organisation for Economic Co-operation and Development), 123–24, 134, 139
Office of Science and Technology Policy (OSTP), 578
Office of Technology Transfer, UC, 614–15, 659
Ohio, 43, 106–7, 115, 208, 226, 487, 722, 748
O'Neill, Edmond, 254, 256
Online Archive of California (OAC), 12, 38, 255, 569
online courses, 702–5

online education, 242, 476–79, 702–4, 737–38
OpenCourseWare, 702
Oppenheimer, J. Robert, ix, 6, 32, 278–80, 483–84, 488–89, 491, 493–94, 508
Orbach, Raymond L., 337–38
organic chemistry, 257, 263, 265, 513, 622
Organisation for Economic Co-operation and Development. *See* OECD
ORUs (organized research units), 193, 446, 454, 517–22, 529, 531, 669, 681, 689–90, 739
OSTP (Office of Science and Technology Policy), 578
outreach, academic, 50, 58, 103, 153, 545, 563, 565, 571–72, 574–77
Outreach Task Force, UC, 58, 153, 574–75

P

Pacific Earthquake Engineering Research Center, 669, 671
Pacific Rim Program, 669–70
Palo Alto, 36, 73, 341, 563, 621–22
Parnassus Heights, San Francisco, 19, 339–41, 345, 351
participation rate, 54, 151, 557, 559, 562
partnerships
  international, 732
  school-centered, 575–76
Patent, Trademark and Copyright Office. *See* PTCO

patents, 256, 276, 606, 609, 611–14, 617, 635, 650, 683, 763–64
Patterson, David A., 626–27
Pauley, Edwin W., 307, 360
peer review, 62, 524, 599, 624
Pell Grants, 5, 75, 96, 149–50, 560, 763
Peltason, Jack W., 185, 202, 331, 374–76, 378, 380–81, 410
Penhoet, Edward E., 348–50
Penn (University of Pennsylvania), 262
Pennsylvania, 112, 156, 262, 322, 325, 582, 732
Pereira, William L., 378–79
pharmacy, 18, 20, 198, 339–40
physical chemistry, 256–57, 260, 263, 347, 513
physical sciences, 245, 247, 249, 251, 253, 255, 257, 259, 261, 263, 265, 267, 269, 271, 273, 275, 283–85, 287, 289–91, 374–75
physical therapy programs, 130, 143, 145
physics, 39, 45, 269–71, 273–74, 276–77, 279–81, 291, 293, 297, 306, 313, 319, 322, 325–26, 358–59, 375, 377, 380, 508, 513
physics department, 253, 270–72, 378, 504, 710
physiology, 26, 272, 307, 340, 352, 368, 461
Pister, Karl S., 394
Pitzer, Kenneth S., 259–61, 263, 265–69, 348, 360, 363, 412, 493–94
planning, 86, 154, 178, 180, 183–85, 193–94, 215, 217–18, 443, 445, 447, 449, 451, 453, 455, 457, 459, 461, 477–79, 749
Plant and Microbial Biology (PMB), 641
policy envelopes, 167–69, 205, 652, 749
postdocs, 243, 260, 677, 681–82
practice, nursing, 130, 145
President's Council on the National Laboratories, 502–3, 507
President's Scientific Advisory Council (PSAC), US, 361
Preuss School, UCSD, 565
Princeton, 85, 152, 225, 258, 326, 362, 376, 378, 381, 477, 512, 593, 604, 622, 698, 724
private support, 26–27, 119, 642, 730, 746
privatization, 147, 691, 701, 717–19
process engineering, UC Berkeley, 267
Product Development Program (PDP), Berkeley, 657
Professional Degree Supplemental Tuition, 715
professional doctorates, 144–46
professional schools, 181, 311, 339–40, 372–73, 384, 387, 424, 430–31, 434, 452, 455, 459–60, 467, 474, 481, 519, 522, 559–60, 565, 690
professional schools and colleges, xii, 91, 429, 431, 447, 452, 455, 468
Professional Schools Restructuring Initiative, UCLA, 202, 451
program reductions, 709–10

Program Review, 194, 213, 233, 443, 445–47, 449, 451, 453, 455, 457, 459, 461, 463, 465, 467–69, 471–73, 475, 477, 479, 481
Progressive Era, California, 586, 588
Progressives, in California, 22, 588–89, 688
Proposition 209, California, 57–58, 150, 534, 544–51, 553, 555
provost for professional schools and colleges, 91, 431, 452
PSAC (President's Scientific Advisory Council), 361
PTCO (Patent, Trademark and Copyright Office), 611–12, 614–15
public service, 118, 121, 427–28, 430, 498, 506, 509, 564, 569, 654
Puente Project, 573, 575
Purdue University, 76, 126, 338, 737–38

Q

Qatar, 732
QB3, 525–26, 644, 648, 658
QB3 Garages, 658
QS (Quacquarelli Symonds), 759
Qualcomm (corporation), 630–31

R

Radiation Laboratory, 278–79, 281, 484–88, 490, 493, 495
Randall, Merle, 245, 260
RCM (responsibility-center management), 714–15

rebenching, UC initiative, x, 179, 181–82, 394
Regenerative Medicine, 600
Regents General Counsel, 197, 201
regents meeting, 89–90, 212, 405–6, 478, 524, 550
Regents' Opportunity Fund, 518, 602
Regents' Resolution SP-1, 551
Reimers, Niels J., 612
Reines, Frederick, 376–77, 380
Reinhardt, William, 341, 343–44
RES (Research Enterprise Services), 519
Research Corporation, 256, 276, 609
Research Enterprise Services (RES), 519
Research Laboratory of Applied Chemistry, MIT, 257
Research Laboratory of Physical Chemistry, MIT, 256–57, 260
responsibility-center management (RCM), 714–15
retirement system, 55–57, 69–70, 195
Revelle, Roger R. D., ix, 293, 299, 303, 353–55, 357–62, 367, 369, 410–12, 517, 630, 661
Revelle plan for UCSD, 356, 359, 367, 369, 372, 377, 411, 632, 638
review committees, 417, 427–28, 434, 442, 455, 463, 652
external, 447–48
reviews, post-tenure, 435, 687
Riverside, 33–35, 41–42, 82, 85, 167, 178–79, 182, 198, 320–21, 327, 329–38, 403, 406, 411, 413, 416, 450–51, 558–59, 597–98, 743–44

Riverside campus, 171, 327, 329, 335, 338, 373, 407, 671
Riverside smog, 334
Rockefeller Foundation, 276–77, 279, 484
Romer, Paul M., 582
Rothblatt, Sheldon, 84, 124
Rowland, F. Sherwood, 368, 375, 377, 380
Ruben, Samuel, 260, 264
Rutter, William J., 343–50, 412, 517, 635–38

S

Sacramento County Hospital, 312
SAIC (Science Applications International Corporation), 630
Salary Scale, 102, 420, 438, 593–94
Salk Institute for Biological Studies, x, 363, 369, 413, 631–32
San Diego, 27–28, 93–94, 167, 179, 198, 353–56, 358–61, 364–65, 367, 372, 377, 401, 406–8, 410–14, 558, 564–65, 629–35, 638–39, 661, 684
  business community, 367
San Diego campus, ix, 3, 143, 187, 299, 303, 325, 329, 353–54, 357–58, 361–69, 372, 375, 377, 380, 401, 559, 565, 629–33, 638–39
  colleges, 528
San Diego City Council, 631
San Diego History, 357
San Diego/La Jolla area, 619, 674

San Diego State University, 143, 360
San Francisco, 18–20, 33, 35, 171, 181, 198, 339–41, 349–53, 380–82, 413, 525, 527, 533, 634–35, 637, 658–59, 661–62, 666, 694, 696
San Francisco Art Institute, 20, 34
San Jose State University, 477
Santa Barbara, 34–35, 41–42, 87, 89, 93, 96, 139, 141, 148, 167–68, 314–17, 320, 323, 325, 329–30, 406–7, 409–10, 413, 597–98, 624–25
Santa Barbara campus, 3, 96, 182, 314, 316–20, 324–27, 338, 413–14
Santa Barbara City College, 316
Santa Barbara State College, 33, 85, 171, 314
Santa Barbara State Normal School, 171, 314
Santa Cruz, 87, 89, 93–94, 167, 178–79, 221–22, 369–70, 381–84, 387, 389–98, 401, 408, 412–13, 416, 448, 450–51, 525, 558–59, 591, 597–98
Santa Cruz campus, ix, 148, 381, 386–87, 391–96, 398, 411–12, 415, 528, 530
SAT (tests), 551, 553
Saxon, David S., 45, 48, 52, 184, 206, 364, 449, 662
School of Criminology, Berkeley, 452–54, 473, 481
School of Education, Berkeley, Los Angeles, 317, 456–57, 459, 468, 472, 474, 481

School of Information, Berkeley, ix, 103, 221, 467, 469–70, 481, 521, 756
School of Library and Information Studies, Berkeley, 202, 467, 470–71, 481
School of Veterinary Medicine, San Francisci, Davis, 19, 310, 312–13
schools, single-department, 426
Schraer, Rosemary S. J., 337
Schrieffer, J. Robert, 322, 326
Schudson, Michael, 513, 527, 529
Science Applications International Corporation (SAIC), 630
Scripps Institution for Oceanography. *See* SIO
Seaborg, Glenn T., 35, 39, 175, 257, 260, 263, 269, 280–82, 360, 485, 491–93, 506
search committees, multidepartmental, 522
security, 99–100, 486, 501–2, 670, 725, 730
selective campuses, 153, 547, 550–51, 555, 557–58, 720
separation, electromagnetic, 486–88
services, shared, 204–5
shared governance, 31, 77, 95, 169, 207–9, 211, 213, 215, 217, 219–31, 233–34, 243, 266, 300, 333, 680, 686–87, 690, 745, 751
Sierra Club, 261, 289, 667–68
Sierra Nevada Mountains, 248, 261, 343, 403, 413, 666–68
Sierra Nevada Research Institute, Merced, 403, 413, 669
Silicon Valley, 3, 126, 365, 383, 387, 390, 477, 604, 619–20,
622–28, 630, 636, 659, 665, 673, 682, 726, 754
Silliman, Benjamin, 14
Singapore, 674, 732–33
Sinsheimer, Robert L., 87, 383–84, 386–93, 395–96
SIO (Scripps Institution for Oceanography), 353, 357, 407, 631
SLAC (Stanford Linear Accelerator Center), 505
Smelser, Neil J., 43, 81, 85, 124–25, 230, 445, 457–59, 474–75, 527, 591, 709
Smith, Lloyd H. "Holly", 341–45, 348
smog, photochemical, 333–36, 413, 667
social sciences, 24, 220, 325, 332, 375–76, 402–3, 517, 520, 606, 677, 680, 724
Solow, Robert M., 582
sommelier's taste, 348, 411–12
Southern Branch, UC, 28, 167, 172, 295, 310, 316
Southern New Hampshire, University of, 737
Spieth, Herman, 330
Sproul, Robert Gordon, 31–32, 34, 36–37, 39, 84, 89, 172–76, 183, 246, 278–79, 285, 299, 304–5, 330, 356, 483, 489–91, 509
SRI (Stanford Research Institute), 622
SRI International, 252, 622
Stanford, A. Leland., 110, 621
Stanford Industrial Park, 608, 622, 673, 737
Stanford Linear Accelerator Center (SLAC), 505

Stanford Office of Technology Licensing, 612
Stanford Research Institute (SRI), 622
Stanford Research Park, 621, 623
Stanford's land, 621
Stanford University, 110, 127, 129, 340–41, 350, 363, 365, 367, 387, 476–77, 533–34, 593–94, 611–12, 614, 619–24, 626, 628–30, 634–37, 639, 736
Starr, Kevin, 308, 563, 585, 588
state colleges, 40, 124–28, 167, 314–16, 387, 456, 538, 590
state funding, 22, 46, 48–49, 64–67, 117–18, 523, 525, 557, 559–60, 562, 577, 596, 600, 691–93, 695, 697, 716, 718, 726, 738–39
state government relations, 168, 175, 196, 742
state support, 26, 592, 618, 706, 718, 721–22, 730, 735, 741, 749–50
State University of New York (SUNY), 97, 106, 108, 166, 171, 188, 190, 318, 325, 593–94, 686–87, 713, 733–34, 747
Statewide Air Pollution Research Center, 335–36
Stevens, Robert B., 393
Stevenson College, UCSC, 385–86
strawberries, 566, 665
Strayer, George D., 589–90
Stringham, Irving, 254, 283–84, 292
student activism, 43, 45, 87, 311–12, 320–21, 414

student debt, 114, 149, 697, 719–22, 724, 750, 762
Student Loans, 723–24, 763
student regent, 111
students
 international, 558, 670, 726–27
 nonresident, 68, 557, 726, 728
subsidiarity, 200, 206, 746, 752
SUNY. *See* State University of New York

T

Taylor, Louise, 462
technological innovation, 161, 367, 619, 625, 645, 684, 750
technology, instructional, 698, 701, 750
technology transfer, 578, 580, 603–5, 607, 609, 611, 613–17, 619, 621, 623, 625, 627, 629, 631, 633, 635, 637, 639, 641, 659
telescopes, 20, 52–53, 248–49, 252, 292
Teller, Edward, ix, 280, 313, 494, 509
Tennessee, 32–33, 115, 486–87
Tenney, Jack (CA Senator), 36
tenure, 31, 74, 92, 165, 170, 215–16, 218, 225, 332, 347, 390, 421–22, 426–27, 433–36, 440, 450–51, 454, 591
 decisions, 177, 192, 303, 321, 389, 426–27, 433
 reviews, 389, 422
Terman, Frederick E., 126, 365, 387, 620–22, 628

Texas, 73, 76, 112, 135, 165–66, 188, 190, 242, 279, 475, 479, 549, 674, 685, 687
Theoretical Physics, 322, 326–27, 413, 488
Throop Polytechnic Institute, 28
Times Higher Education, 759
Tompkins, Gordon, 343–44, 346, 348–49
Torrey Pines Mesa, 363, 630–31, 633
transfer, 6, 17, 28, 33, 91, 125, 132, 136, 139–42, 157, 159–60, 162, 316, 345, 356, 379, 392, 538, 551, 558
  admission, 141, 151, 162, 551
  articulation for, 136, 140, 205
  education, 23, 41, 135, 140, 157–59, 163, 686, 689, 744
  students, 6, 118, 139–42, 159, 163, 172, 362, 561, 708
Transfer Admission Guarantee, 141
tuition, 68, 74–75, 114, 132–33, 145, 148–49, 162, 180, 557, 560, 562, 691, 693, 697, 700–701, 706, 714, 718–22, 730, 743

U

UARC (University-Affiliated Research Center), 387
UC (Campus) (See campus name)
UCLA (UC Los Angeles), 5, 32–35, 41–42, 45, 69, 151–52, 293–99, 301–7, 329, 374–75, 411–12, 415–16, 423, 451, 558–59, 565, 590–91, 597–98, 661–62, 743
UCLA School of Medicine, 298
UCO (University of California Observatories), 193–94
UCORP (University Committee on Research Policy), AScademic Senate, 499
UC San Francisco. See UCSF
UCSF (UC San Francisco), 15, 18, 42, 48, 93, 339, 341–47, 349–53, 363, 408, 412–13, 517, 612, 634–38, 662
Udacity (corporation), 477, 702
UIUC (University of Illinois at Urbana-Champaign), 268, 325, 644, 646
ultracentrifugation, 486–87
undergraduate education, 42, 130, 137, 147, 295, 299, 330, 361, 377, 382, 410, 526, 532, 559, 677, 702
Underhill, Robert M., 483, 489–90
United Arab Emirates, 732, 734, 759
university, for-profit, 145, 695–96, 722, 737
University-Affiliated Research Center (UARC), 387
University Committee on Research Policy (UCORP), 499
University Extension, 194, 374, 462, 564, 702
University Farm, 24, 33, 41, 308–9, 407
university governance, 93, 219, 233, 240, 244, 246, 545, 677, 751
University Hall, 186, 188
University of California Observatories (UCO), 193–94

University of Chicago, 92, 263, 272–73, 299, 303, 306, 491–92, 496, 505–6, 513, 661
University of Illinois at Urbana-Champaign. *See* UIUC
University System of Georgia, 166, 713–14
university systems, 73, 106, 134–35, 165–66, 168, 187, 199–200, 240, 382, 406, 409
uranium isotopes, 303, 486
Urey, Harold C., 263, 303, 357–58, 360, 368, 411

V

Varmus, Harold E., 343, 345, 413
venture capitalists, 603, 633, 637
VERIPs (Voluntary Early Retirement Incentive Program), 54–57, 70
vernal pools, ix, 63, 399–401
veterans, returning World War II, 34, 539, 589–90, 688
veterinary medicine, 19, 108, 130, 144, 310–13
Vietnam War, 43, 320, 361, 364, 414
Virginia, 115, 146, 187, 242, 487, 512, 585, 594, 719, 726, 741–42
Vollmer, August, 452
Voluntary Early Retirement Incentive Program. *See* VERIPs

W

Walker, William H., 257–58, 269, 610

Walshok, Mary Lindenheim, 367, 630–31, 633
WARF (Wisconsin Alumni Research Foundation), 736
Warren, Earl, CA Governor, 37, 78, 105, 298, 362, 585, 588–90, 598, 600, 666, 688
Warren, Stafford, 298
Washington DC Center, UC, 185, 191–92
Watkins, Gordon, 328–29
Webster, Daniel, 95, 191
Wellesley College, 282, 712
Wellman, Harry R., 44, 177, 311, 328, 331, 341, 356
Western Interstate Commission for Higher Education (WICHE), 712
Wheeler, Benjamin Ide, 21–22, 24, 29–30, 73, 78, 84, 100, 209, 249–50, 256–57, 340, 538, 588, 663
Whitney, Josiah D., 287–88
WICHE (Western Interstate Commission for Higher Education), 712
Wilke, Charles R., 265–66, 269, 320, 431–32
Wilson, Peter B. (Pete), CA Governor, 548, 561
Wilson, Woodrow, 378
Winans, Joseph, 98–99, 121
Wisconsin Alumni Research Foundation (WARF), 736
Wootten, Carl B., 614–16
Workingmen's Party, 98
World Bank, 675–76, 755
"World Class Universities" (WCU), 675–76
World Cultures Institute, 403

World War II, 6–7, 32–34, 36, 297–98, 302–3, 315, 484, 490–91, 495, 505, 508–9, 514–15, 517–18, 586–89, 591–92, 596–97, 605, 620, 629–30, 688–89

X

Xerox PARC (Palo Alto Research Center), 623, 626

Y

Y-12 Plant, 32–33, 486
Yale-Gilman model, 84
Yale-NUS College, 733
Yale University, 13–15, 273–74, 279, 285, 317, 353, 358, 362, 375, 381, 394, 476, 479, 487, 592–94, 634, 638, 703, 710, 733
  University Council, 710
York, Herbert F., ix, 360–61, 363–64, 370, 375, 411, 494–95, 710
Yudof, Mark G., 73–74, 96

www.ingramcontent.com/pod-product-compliance
Lightning Source LLC
Chambersburg PA
CBHW070902300426
44113CB00008B/919